01-28-22

sixth edition

computer | science

an overview

j. glenn brookshear
Marquette University

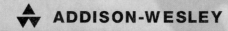
ADDISON-WESLEY

An imprint of Addison Wesley Longman, Inc.

Reading, Massachusetts · Menlo Park, California · New York · Harlow, England
Don Mills, Ontario · Sydney · Mexico City · Madrid · Amsterdam

Senior Acquisitions Editor: Susan Hartman
Senior Production Editor: Amy Rose
Editorial Assistant: Lisa Kalner
Composition: Northeast Compositors, Inc.
Text design: Melinda Grosser for *silk*
Copyeditor: Stephanie Magean
Proofreader: Trillium Project Management
Art source: George Nichols
Design Editor: Lynne Reed
Cover Design: Dede Cummings

Access the latest information about Addison-Wesley books from our World Wide Web site: http://www.awlonline.com

Many of the designations used by manufacturers and sellers to distinguish their products are claimed as trademarks. Where those designations appear in this book, and Addison-Wesley was aware of a trademark claim, the designations have been printed in initial caps or all caps.

The programs and applications presented in this book have been included for their instructional value. They have been tested with care, but are not guaranteed for any particular purpose. The publisher does not offer any warranties or representations, nor does it accept any liabilities with respect to the programs or applications.

Library of Congress Cataloging-in-Publication Data
Brookshear, J. Glenn.
    Computer science : an overview / J. Glenn Brookshear. – 6th ed.
      p.   cm.
    Includes bibliographical references and index.
    ISBN 0-201-35747-X
    1. Computer science.   I. Title.
  QA76.B743   2000
  004—dc21   99-29326
                                                  CIP

Reprinted with corrections, January 2000

4 5 6 7 8 9 10   0201

To my parents
Garland and Reba Brookshear

PREFACE

This book presents an introduction to the science of computing. It reveals the breadth of the subject while including enough depth to convey an honest appreciation for the topics involved. I wrote the text with two audiences in mind.

Computer Science Majors

The first audience consists of computer science majors in the early stages of their academic careers. Students at this stage tend to equate computer science with programming and Web browsing because that is essentially all they have seen. Yet computer science is much more than this. In turn, beginning computer science students need exposure to the breadth of the subject in which they are planning to major. Providing this exposure is the purpose of this book. It gives students an overview of computer science—a foundation from which they can appreciate the relevance and interrelationships of future courses in the field.

Students of Other Disciplines

I also designed this book for majors of other disciplines. A computer science course for nonmajors should provide a fundamental understanding of the entire field. Such a background gives students the ability to relate to the technical society in which they live and to continue to learn independently—a capability that is mandatory in today's rapidly changing environment. This is the model used for survey courses in the natural sciences, and this is the model on which this book is designed. After taking a course based on this text, students will have an understanding of computer science that will continue to pay dividends well into the future.

Organization

The text follows a bottom-up approach that progresses from the concrete to the abstract—an order that results in a sound pedagogical presentation in which each topic leads to the next. Part 1 presents issues associated with hardware. It begins by explaining how information is represented and recorded in machines and how these techniques affect the machine's characteristics (Chapter 1). It then describes how machines manipulate data by means of machine language programs (Chapter 2).

In Part 2 the text advances to topics associated with software, beginning with how the activities of a machine are coordinated by an operating system and how this coordination of activities is expanding to incorporate entire networks and internetworks (Chapter 3). At this point students will have obtained a useful understanding of a typical computer system. In fact, Chapters 1 through 3 could be used as a text for a short course titled "What Every Savvy Computer User Should Know."

Part 2 continues by addressing issues of software development, including the topics of algorithm development and analysis (Chapter 4), programming languages and programming paradigms (Chapter 5), and software engineering (Chapter 6).

Part 3 expands on the ideas in Part 2 by considering the relationship between algorithms and data storage organizations. In particular, this part includes an introduction to data structures (Chapter 7), the rudiments of file storage (Chapter 8), and an overview of database systems (Chapter 9).

The plot culminates in Part 4 by investigating the ultimate capabilities of machines. This part begins with a chapter on artificial intelligence, which explores techniques used to produce computers that exhibit the ability to perceive and reason (Chapter 10). It closes by examining the constraints inherent in algorithmic systems and the boundaries that these constraints place on the capabilities of machines (Chapter 11).

In addition to this overall plot, there are several themes woven throughout the text. One is that computer science is dynamic. The text repeatedly presents topics in a historical perspective, discusses the state of the art, and indicates directions of current research. Another theme is the role of abstraction and the way in which abstract tools are used to control complexity. Indeed, even the book's organization reinforces this theme by presenting topics in an order of progressing abstraction—hardware provides abstract tools used by system software, and system software provides abstract tools used by application software.

To the Student

I was introduced to the field of computing during my tour in the US Navy back in the late 1960s and early 1970s. (Yes, that makes me old—but it will happen to you also.) I spent most of these Navy days maintaining the system software at the Navy's computer installation in London, England. After my tour was completed, I returned to school and finished my PhD in 1975. I've been teaching computer science and mathematics ever since.

A lot has changed in computer science over the years, but a lot has remained the same. In particular, computer science was, and still is, fascinating. There are a lot of awesome things going on out there. The development of the Internet, progress in artificial intelligence, and the ability to collect and disseminate information in unheard of proportions are only some of the things that will affect your life. You live in an exciting, changing world, and you have the opportunity to be a part of the action. Take it! The more you learn, the better prepared you will be. This book will provide a foundation, but it is not the end. Read it, and then read more. One of the most rewarding skills you can develop is the ability to learn on your own.

To the Instructor

There is more material in this text than can normally be covered in a single semester so do not hesitate to skip topics that do not fit your course objectives. I wrote the book to be used as a course resource—not as a course definition. You will find that, although the entire text follows a plot, the topics are covered in an independent manner that allows you to pick and choose as you desire. I have used asterisks in the table of contents at the beginning of each chapter to indicate those sections that I suggest as optional, but these are certainly not cast in stone. I also suggest that you consider covering some topics as reading assignments. I think we underrate students when we assume that we have to explain everything in class. I often assign an entire chapter as a reading assignment and then use class time to explain certain points or to expand portions of the text from my own experiences.

I have already explained that the text follows a bottom-up, concrete-to-abstract organization, but I want to expand on this a bit. As academics we too often assume that students will appreciate our perspective of a subject—often one that we have developed over years of working in a field. As teachers we do better by presenting material from the student's perspective. This is why the text starts with data representation/storage and builds from there. Today's students are familiar with magnetic disks, modems, and CDs, and I find that they respond to learning how these devices work. I see them discovering answers to many of their "why" questions and learning to view the course as practical rather than theoretical. From this beginning it is natural to investigate the software that controls these devices and then to consider how they can develop their own software. This leads into such abstract issues as algorithm development, representation, and complexity, which is the heart of most traditional introductory computer science courses.

We are all aware that students learn a lot more than we teach them directly, and the lessons they learn indirectly are often better absorbed than those that are studied explicitly. This is significant when it comes to "teaching" problem solving. Students do not learn to solve problems by studying problem-solving methodologies as an isolated subject. They learn to solve problems by solving problems. So I have included numerous problems throughout the text. I encourage you to use them and to expand on them.

Another topic that I place in this same category is that of professionalism, ethics, and social responsibility. I do not believe that this material should be presented as an isolated subject. Instead, it should surface when it is relevant, which is the approach I have taken in this text. In particular, you will find that Sections 0.5, 3.7, 6.1, 6.7, 9.6, 10.1, and 10.7 present such topics as security, privacy, liability, and social awareness in the context of networking, database systems, software engineering, and artificial intelligence. You will also find that each chapter includes a collection of questions called *Social Issues* that challenge students to think about the relationship between the material in the text and the society in which they live.

Pedagogical Features

This text is the product of many years of teaching. As a result, it is rich in pedagogical aids. Paramount is the abundance of problems to enhance the student's participation. Each section within a chapter closes with *Questions/Exercises* to challenge students to think independently. This feature reviews the material just discussed, extends the previous discussion, or hints at related topics to be covered later. These questions are answered in Appendix F.

Moreover, each chapter (except for the introductory chapter) closes with two sets of problems. The first of these is a set of *Chapter Review Problems* that are designed to serve as "homework" problems in that they cover the material from the entire chapter and are not answered in the text. Following these problems is a set of questions called *Social Issues* that are designed for thought and discussion. Many of them can be used to launch research assignments culminating in short written or oral reports.

Each chapter also ends with a list called *Additional Reading* that contains references to other materials relating to the subject of the chapter. The Web site, described later in this preface, is also a good place to look for related material.

Web Site

This text is supported by a Web site at `http://www.awlonline.com/brookshear`. At this site you will find materials for both students and teachers—including supporting software, laboratory manuals in a variety of programming languages, links to additional topics of interest, and links to materials developed by other users of the text.

The Sixth Edition

Although this sixth edition maintains the same chapter-by-chapter structure as previous editions, topics have been added, some have been deleted, and much of the remaining material has been rewritten to provide an up-to-date and relevant picture of the science of computing. The following is a summary of the major changes reflected in this edition.

The subject of data compression has moved from Chapter 2 to the new Section 1.8. This new section also contains material on LZ77 and image representation including GIF and JPEG. The material on analysis of algorithms that used to be in Chapter 11 has been expanded and moved to Chapter 4 (Algorithms). Chapter 4 has been made more accessible by removing the quick sort. Section 5.5 on object-oriented programming has been added to Chapter 5 (Programming Languages). Some of this material used to appear in Chapter 7. Most of Chapter 6 (Software Engineering) has been rewritten. It now includes an introduction to design patterns and a new section on testing. Chapter 7 (Data Structures) has a new Section 7.7 that introduces indirect addressing at the machine language level. Chapter 8 (File Structures) has been rewritten to be more accessible by avoiding an overload of examples in specific languages. Section 9.4 on object-oriented database systems has been rewritten and Section 9.6 on the social impact of database technology is new. Chapter 10 (Artificial Intelligence) has two new sections—Section 10.5 (Genetic algorithms) and Section 10.7 (Considering the Consequences). Moreover, the old sections 10.3, 10.4, and 10.5 have been streamlined and combined into one. Section 11.6 (Public Key Encryption) has been added to Chapter 11 (Theory of Computation).

In addition to these changes to chapter contents, I have added a bit of spice to the entire text by means of side boxes that help link the material in the text to the real world. Many of these include references to Web sites where additional information is available.

Acknowledgments

I first thank those of you who have supported this book by reading and using it in previous editions. I am honored.

With each new edition, the list of those who have contributed to the book grows. Today this list includes J. M. Adams, C. M. Allen, D. C. S. Allison, B. Auernheimer, P. Bankston, M. Barnard, K. Bowyer, P. W. Brashear, C. M. Brown, B. Calloni, M. Clancy, R. T. Close, D. H. Cooley, F. Deek, M. J. Duncan, S. Fox, N. E. Gibbs, J. D. Harris, D. Hascom, L. Heath, P. Henderson, L. Hunt, L. A. Jehn, K. Korb, G. Krenz, J. Liu, T. J. Long, C. May,

S. J. Merrill, J. C. Moyer, M. Murphy, J. P. Myers, Jr., D. S. Noonan, S. Olariu, G. Rice, N. Rickert, C. Riedesel, J. B. Rogers, G. Saito, W. Savitch, R. Schlafly, J. C. Schlimmer, S. Sells, J. C. Simms, M. C. Slattery, J. Slimick, J. A. Slomka, D. Smith, J. Solderitsch, R. Steigerwald, L. Steinberg, W. J. Taffe, J. Talburt, P. Tromovitch, E. Wright, and M. Ziegler. To these individuals I give my sincere thanks.

I also thank my friends at Addison-Wesley whose efforts are reflected within these pages. They do a great job of turning a raw manuscript into a superb book. In particular, Lisa Kalner and Amy Rose were the two who had to put up with me on a daily basis. They have lots of stories they could tell.

And, I thank my wife Earlene for all the support she has given me over the years. I survived a heart attack on the morning of December 11, 1998 because she got me to the hospital in time.

J. G. B.

CONTENTS

Chapter 0   Introduction   1

0.1   The Study of Algorithms   2
0.2   The Origins of Computing Machines   6
0.3   The Evolution of Computer Science   10
0.4   The Role of Abstraction   11
0.5   Ethical/Social/Legal Repercussions   12
        Social Issues   13
        Additional Reading   14

PART ONE: MACHINE ARCHITECTURE   15

Chapter 1   Data Storage   17

1.1   Storage of Bits 18
1.2   Main Memory 26
1.3   Mass Storage 29
1.4   Representing Information as Bit Patterns 35
1.5   The Binary System 44
1.6   Storing Integers 47
1.7   Storing Fractions 55
1.8   Data Compression 60
1.9   Communication Errors 65
        Chapter Review Problems 70
        Social Issues 76
        Additional Reading 77

Chapter 2   Data Manipulation   79

2.1   The Central Processing Unit   80
2.2   The Stored-Program Concept   85
2.3   Program Execution   89
2.4   Arithmetic/Logic Instructions   95
2.5   Communicating with Other Devices   99
2.6   Other Architectures   104
       Chapter Review Problems   108
       Social Issues   114
       Additional Reading   115

PART TWO: SOFTWARE   117

Chapter 3   Operating Systems and Networks   119

3.1   The Evolution of Operating Systems   120
3.2   Operating System Architecture   124
3.3   Coordinating the Machine's Activities   130
3.4   Handling Competition Among Processes   136
3.5   Networks   141
3.6   Network Protocols   149
3.7   Security   158
       Chapter Review Problems   162
       Social Issues   165
       Additional Reading   166

Chapter 4   Algorithms   167

4.1   The Concept of an Algorithm   168
4.2   Algorithm Representation   170
4.3   Algorithm Discovery   178
4.4   Iterative Structures   184
4.5   Recursive Structures   196
4.6   Efficiency and Correctness   206
       Chapter Review Problems   218
       Social Issues   223
       Additional Reading   224

Chapter 5   Programming Languages   225

5.1   Historical Perspective   226
5.2   Traditional Programming Concepts   236
5.3   Procedural Units   248
5.4   Language Implementation   255
5.5   Object-Oriented Programming   265
5.6   Programming Concurrent Activities   268
5.7   Declarative Programming   271
       Chapter Review Problems   278

Social Issues   281
Additional Reading   283

Chapter 6   Software Engineering   285

6.1   The Software Engineering Discipline   286
6.2   The Software Life Cycle   288
6.3   Modularity   294
6.4   Design Methodologies   300
6.5   Testing   308
6.6   Documentation   310
6.7   Software Ownership and Liability   312
        Chapter Review Problems   314
        Social Issues   316
        Additional Reading   317

PART THREE: DATA ORGANIZATION   319

Chapter 7   Data Structures   321

7.1   Arrays   322
7.2   Lists   325
7.3   Stacks   332
7.4   Queues   337
7.5   Trees   341
7.6   Customized Data Types   353
7.7   Pointers in Machine Language   360
        Chapter Review Problems   361
        Social Issues   366
        Additional Reading   367

Chapter 8   File Structures   369

8.1   The Role of the Operating System   370
8.2   Sequential Files   371
8.3   Text Files   377
8.4   Indexing   381
8.5   Hashing   385
        Chapter Review Problems   391
        Social Issues   394
        Additional Reading   395

Chapter 9   Database Structures   397

9.1   General Issues   398
9.2   The Layered Approach to Database
        Implementation   401
9.3   The Relational Model   404
9.4   Object-Oriented Databases   418

9.5   Maintaining Database Integrity   421

9.6   Social Impact of Database Technology   425

Chapter Review Problems   428

Social Issues   432

Additional Reading   433

PART FOUR: THE POTENTIAL OF ALGORITHMIC MACHINES   435

Chapter 10   Artificial Intelligence   437

10.1   Intelligence and Machines   438

10.2   Understanding Images   442

10.3   Reasoning   445

10.4   Artificial Neural Networks   459

10.5   Genetic Algorithms   468

10.6   Applications of Artificial Intelligence   473

10.7   Considering the Consequences   481

Chapter Review Problems   484

Social Issues   488

Additional Reading   489

Chapter 11   Theory of Computation   491

11.1   A Bare Bones Programming Language   492

11.2   Turing Machines   497

11.3   Computable Functions   503

11.4   A Noncomputable Function   507

11.5   Complexity of Problems   513

11.6   Public Key Cryptography   523

Chapter Review Problems   532

Social Issues   535

Additional Reading   536

Appendixes   537

A   ASCII   539

B   Circuits to Manipulate Two's Complement Representations   541

C   A Typical Machine Language   545

D   Program Examples   547

E   The Equivalence of Iterative and Recursive Structures   557

F   Answers to Questions/Exercises   559

Index   599

0.1 The Study of Algorithms

0.2 The Origins of Computing Machines

0.3 The Evolution of Computer Science

0.4 The Role of Abstraction

0.5 Ethical/Social/Legal Repercussions

chapter

INTRODUCTION

zero

Computer science is the discipline that seeks to build a scientific foundation for such topics as computer design, computer programming, information processing, algorithmic solutions of problems, and the algorithmic process itself. Consequently, it provides the underpinnings for today's computer applications as well as the foundations for tomorrow's applications. It follows that we cannot become knowledgeable in computer science by studying only a few topics as isolated subjects or by merely learning how to use the computing tools of today. Rather, to understand the science of computing, we must grasp the scope and dynamics of a wide range of topics.

This book is designed to provide such a background. It presents computer science through an integrated introduction to the subjects that constitute a typical university computer science curriculum. The book can therefore serve as a foundation for beginning computer science students or as a source for other students seeking an introduction to the science behind today's computer-oriented society.

0.1 The Study of Algorithms

We begin with the most fundamental concept of computer science—that of an algorithm. Informally, an **algorithm** is a set of steps that defines how a task is performed.[1] For example, there are algorithms for constructing model airplanes (expressed in the form of instruction sheets), for operating washing machines (usually displayed on the inside of the washer's lid), for playing music (expressed in the form of sheet music), and for performing magic tricks (Figure 0.1).

Before a machine can perform a task, an algorithm for performing that task must be discovered and represented in a form that is compatible with the machine. A machine-compatible representation of an algorithm is called a **program.** Programs, and the algorithms they represent, are collectively referred to as **software,** in contrast to the machinery itself, which is known as **hardware.**

The study of algorithms began as a subject in mathematics. The search for algorithms was a significant activity of mathematicians long before the development of today's computers. The major goal of that search was to find a single set of directions that described how any problem of a particular type could be solved. One of the best known consequences of this early search for algorithms is the long division algorithm for finding the quotient of two multiple-digit numbers. Another example is the Euclidean algorithm, discovered by the ancient Greek mathematician Euclid, for finding the greatest common divisor of two positive integers (Figure 0.2).

Once an algorithm for performing a task has been found, the performance of that task no longer requires an understanding of the principles on which the algorithm is based. Instead, the performance of the task is reduced to the process of merely following directions. We can follow the long division algorithm to find a quotient or the Euclidean algorithm to find a greatest common divisor without understanding why the algorithm works. In a sense, the intelligence required to perform the task is encoded in the algorithm.

It is through this ability to capture and convey intelligence by means of algorithms that we are able to build machines that display intelligent behavior. Consequently, the level of intelligence displayed by machines is limited by the intelligence that can be conveyed through algorithms. Only if we find an algorithm that directs the performance of a task can we construct a machine to perform that task. In turn, if no algorithm exists for performing a task, then the performance of that task lies beyond the capabilities of machines.

A major undertaking throughout the computing field, then, is the development of algorithms, and consequently a significant part of computer science is concerned with issues relating to that task. We can thus gain an understanding of the breadth of computer science by considering some of these issues. One

---

[1]More precisely, an algorithm is an ordered set of unambiguous, executable steps that define a terminating activity. These details are discussed in Chapter 4.

FIGURE 0.1

Effect: the performer places some cards from a normal deck of playing cards face down on a table and mixes them thoroughly while spreading them out on the table. Then, as the audience requests either red or black cards, the performer turns over cards of the requested color.

Secret and Patter:

Step 1. From a normal deck of cards, select ten red cards and ten black cards. Deal these cards face up in two piles on the table according to color.

Step 2. Announce that you have selected some red cards and some black cards.

Step 3. Pick up the red cards. Under the pretense of aligning them into a small deck, hold them face down in your left hand and, with the thumb and first finger of your right hand, pull back on each end of the deck so that each card is given a slightly backward curve. Then place the deck of red cards face down on the table as you say, "Here are the red cards in this stack."

Step 4. Pick up the black cards. In a manner similar to that in step 3, give these cards a slight forward curve. Then return these cards to the table in a face-down deck as you say, "And here are the black cards in this stack."

Step 5. Immediately after returning the black cards to the table, use both hands to mix the red and black cards (still face down) as you spread them out on the tabletop. Explain that you are thoroughly mixing the cards.

Step 6. As long as there are face-down cards on the table, repeatedly execute the following steps:

   6.1. Ask the audience to request either a red card or a black card.

   6.2. If the color requested is red and there is a face-down card with a concave appearance, turn over such a card while saying, "Here is a red card."

   6.3. If the color requested is black and there is a face-down card with a convex appearance, turn over such a card while saying, "Here is a black card."

   6.4. Otherwise, state that there are no more cards of the requested color and turn over the remaining cards to prove your claim.

An algorithm for a magic trick

such issue deals with the question of how algorithms are discovered in the first place—a question that is closely related to that of problem solving in general. To discover an algorithm for solving a problem is essentially to discover a solution for the problem. It follows that studies in this branch of computer science draw heavily from such areas as the psychology of human problem solving and theories of education. We consider some of these ideas in Chapter 4.

FIGURE 0.2

Description: This algorithm assumes that its input consists of two positive integers and proceeds to compute the greatest common divisor of these two values.

Procedure:

Step 1. Assign M and N the value of the larger and smaller of the two input values, respectively.

Step 2. Divide M by N, and call the remainder R.

Step 3. If R is not 0, then assign M the value of N, assign N the value of R, and return to step 2; otherwise, the greatest common divisor is the value currently assigned to N.

The Euclidean algorithm for finding the greatest common divisor of two positive integers

Once an algorithm for solving a problem has been discovered, the next step is to represent the algorithm so it can be communicated to a machine or to other humans. This means that we must transform the conceptual algorithm into a clear set of instructions and represent these instructions in an unambiguous manner. Studies emerging from these concerns draw from our knowledge of language and grammar and have led to an abundance of algorithm representation schemes, known as programming languages, which are based on a variety of approaches to the programming process, known as programming paradigms. We consider some of these languages and the paradigms on which they are based in Chapter 5.

The design of large software systems involves more than the development of the individual algorithms for performing the required activities. It entails designing the interaction among these components as well. Thus, the difficulties encountered when developing large software systems are significantly greater than those encountered when developing short programs, and computer science has turned to the well-established field of engineering in hopes of finding tools for handling such problems. The result is the branch of computer science known as software engineering, which today draws from such diverse fields as engineering, project management, personnel management, and programming language design. As our society grows increasingly dependent on large software systems, the need for improved software development tools and principles will continue to increase. In turn, software engineering is an important topic of current research. We study software engineering in Chapter 6.

Still another important branch of computer science deals with the design and construction of machines. We consider these topics in Chapters 1 and 2. Although our study of computer architecture incorporates some discussions of technological issues, our goal is not to master the details of how today's architecture is implemented in electronic circuitry. That would lead us too far into the subject of electrical engineering. Moreover, just as yesterday's gear-driven calculators gave way to electronic devices, today's electronics may soon be replaced by other technologies, a prime candidate being optics. Our goal is to understand enough of today's technology so that we can appreciate its ramifications in today's machines as well as its influence on the development of computer science.

Ideally, we would like the architecture of computers to be a consequence solely of our knowledge of algorithmic processes and not be limited by the capabilities of technology. That is, rather than allowing the dictates of technology to determine machine design and thus the way we represent algorithms, we would like our knowledge of algorithms to be the driving force behind modern machine architecture. As technology advances, this dream is becoming more of a reality. Today, it is possible to construct machines that allow algorithms to be represented as multiple sequences of instructions that are executed simultaneously or as patterns of connections between numerous processing units, in much the same way that our minds represent information as links between neurons (Chapter 10).

Another context in which we study computer architecture relates to data storage and retrieval. Here the internal features of a machine are often reflected in the machine's external characteristics. We consider these features and ways of avoiding their undesirable effects in Chapters 1, 7, 8, and 9.

Closely related to the design of computing machinery is the design of a machine's interface with the outside world. How, for example, will algorithms be inserted into a machine, and how will the machine be told which algorithm to execute? Resolving such problems in an environment in which the machine is expected to provide a variety of services requires the solution to many problems involving coordination of activities and resource allocation. We investigate some of these solutions in our discussion of operating systems in Chapter 3.

As machines have been asked to perform more and more intelligent tasks, computer science has turned to the study of human intelligence for leadership. The hope is that by understanding how our own minds reason and perceive, we will be able to design algorithms that mimic these processes and thus transfer these capabilities to machines. The result is the area of computer science known as artificial intelligence, which leans heavily on research in such areas as psychology, biology, and linguistics. We discuss some of these topics in artificial intelligence in Chapter 10.

The search for algorithms to direct increasingly complex tasks also leads to questions regarding the ultimate limitations of algorithmic processes. If no algorithm exists for performing a task, then that task cannot be performed by a machine. We say that a task that can be described by an algorithm is algorithmic. In short, then, machines are only capable of performing algorithmic tasks.

The realization that there are nonalgorithmic tasks surfaced as a subject in mathematics in the early 1900s with the publication of Kurt Gödel's incompleteness theorem. This theorem essentially states that in any mathematical theory encompassing our traditional arithmetic system, there are statements that can be neither proved nor disproved. In short, any complete study of our arithmetic system lies beyond the capabilities of algorithmic activities.

The desire to study the limitations of algorithmic methods that followed Gödel's discovery led mathematicians to design abstract machines for executing algorithms (this was before technology was able to provide actual machines for investigation) and to study the theoretical powers of such hypothetical machines. Today, this study of algorithms and machines forms the theoretical backbone of computer science. We discuss some of the topics in this area in Chapter 11.

0.2 The Origins of Computing Machines

The abstract machines hypothesized by mathematicians in the early 1900s form an important part of the family tree for today's computers. Other branches of that tree extend much further back in time. Indeed, the quest for machines that perform algorithmic tasks has had a long history.

One of the first computing devices was the abacus. Its history has been traced as far back as the ancient Greek and Roman civilizations. The machine is quite simple, consisting of beads strung on rods that are in turn mounted in a rectangular frame. As the beads are moved back and forth on the rods, their positions represent stored values. It is in the positions of the beads that this "computer" represents and stores data. For control of an algorithm's execution, the machine relies on the human operator. Thus the abacus alone is merely a data storage system; it must be combined with a human to create a complete computational machine.

In more recent years, the design of computing machines was based on the technology of gears. Among the inventors were Blaise Pascal (1623–1662) of France, Gottfried Wilhelm Leibniz (1646–1716) of Germany, and Charles Babbage (1792–1871) of England. These machines represented data through gear positioning, with data being input mechanically to establish gear positions. Output from Pascal's and Leibniz's machines was achieved by observing the final gear positions in much the same way that we read the numbers on a car's odometer. Babbage, on the other hand, envisioned a machine that would print output values on paper so that the possibility of transcription errors would be eliminated.

As for the ability to follow an algorithm, we can see a progression of flexibility in these machines. Pascal's machine was built to follow only the addition algorithm. Consequently, the appropriate sequence of steps was embedded into the structure of the machine itself. In a similar manner, Leibniz's machine had its algorithms firmly embedded in its architecture, although it offered a variety of arithmetic operations from which the operator could select. Babbage's machine, in contrast, was designed so that the sequence of steps the machine was to perform could be communicated to the machine in the form of holes in paper cards. Thus, Babbage's machine was programmable. Indeed, his assistant Augusta Ada Byron is often identified today as the world's first programmer.

The idea of communicating an algorithm via holes in paper was not originated by Babbage. In 1801, Joseph Jacquard had applied a similar technique to control weaving looms in France (Figure 0.3). In particular, he developed a loom in which the steps to be performed during the weaving process were determined by patterns of holes in paper cards. In this manner, the algorithm followed by the machine could be easily changed to produce different woven designs.

Later, Herman Hollerith (1860–1929) applied the ideal of representing information as holes in paper cards to speed up the tabulation process in the 1890 U.S. census. It was, in fact, this work by Hollerith that led to the creation of IBM.

The technology of the time lacked the precision required to popularize the complex gear-driven calculators of Pascal, Leibniz, and Babbage. Not until electronics began to supplement mechanical devices could technology support the theoretical developments taking place in the embryonic science of computing. Examples of this advance include the electromechanical machine of George Stibitz, completed in 1940 at Bell Laboratories, and the Mark I, completed in 1944 at Harvard University by Howard Aiken and a group of IBM engineers (Figure 0.4). These machines made heavy use of electronically controlled mechanical relays. In this sense they were obsolete almost as soon as they were built, because other researchers were applying the technology of vacuum tubes to construct totally electronic digital computers. The first of these machines was apparently the Atanasoff–Berry machine, constructed during the period from 1937 to 1941 at Iowa State College (now Iowa State University) by John Atanasoff and his assistant, Clifford Berry. Another was a machine called COLOSSUS, built in England to decode German messages during the latter part of World War II. Other, more flexible machines such as the ENIAC (electronic numerical integrator and calculator) developed by John Mauchly and J. Presper Eckert at the Moore School of Electrical Engineering, University of Pennsylvania, soon followed.

From that point on, the history of computing machines is largely that of advancing technology, including the invention of transistors and the subsequent

FIGURE 0.3

Jacquard's loom (Courtesy of International Business Machines Corporation. Unauthorized use not permitted.)

development of integrated circuits, the establishment of communication satellites, and advances in optic technology. Today, desktop-size machines (as well as their smaller, portable cousins known as laptops) have more computing power than the room-size machines of the 1940s and can exchange information quickly via global communication systems.

The origins of these small machines can be traced to the computer hobbyists who began to experiment with homemade computers shortly after the development of the large research machines of the 1940s. It was within this "underground" of hobby activity that Steve Jobs and Stephen Wozniak built a

FIGURE 0.4

The Mark I computer

commercially viable home computer and, in 1976, established Apple Computer, Inc., to manufacture and market their products. Although Apple products were popular, they were not widely accepted by the business community, which continued to look to the well-established IBM for the majority of its computing needs.

In 1981, IBM introduced its first desktop computer, called the personal computer or PC for short, whose underlying software was developed by a struggling young company known as Microsoft. The PC was an instant success and legitimized the desktop computer as an established commodity in the minds of the business community. Today, the term *PC* is widely used to refer to all those machines (from various manufacturers) whose design has evolved from IBM's initial desktop computer, most of which continue to be marketed with software from Microsoft. At times, however, the term *PC* is used interchangeably with the generic term *desktop*.

The availability of desktop computers has brought computer technology to the forefront of today's society. Indeed, computer technology is so prevalent now that knowing how to use it is fundamental to being a member of modern society. It is by means of this technology that millions of individuals gain access to the global connection system known as the Internet, which promises to have a major influence in both the private and commercial sectors. But, knowing how to use today's products is not the same as understanding the science behind their operation. Our goal here will be to explore the scope of this relatively new field of science.

0.3 The Evolution of Computer Science

Such conditions as limited data storage capabilities and detailed, time-consuming programming procedures restricted the complexity of the algorithms to which early machines were applied. However, as these limitations began to disappear, machines were applied to increasingly larger and more complex tasks. As attempts to express the composition of these tasks in algorithmic form began to tax the abilities of the human mind, more and more research efforts were directed toward the study of algorithms and the programming process.

It was in this context that the theoretical work of mathematicians began to pay dividends. Indeed, as a consequence of Gödel's incompleteness theorem, mathematicians had already been investigating those questions regarding algorithmic processes that advancing technology began to raise. With that, the stage was set for the emergence of a new discipline known as computer science.

Today, this new discipline has established itself as the science of algorithms. As we have seen, the scope of this science is broad, drawing from such diverse subjects as mathematics, engineering, psychology, biology, business administration, and linguistics. In the chapters that follow, we will discuss many of the topics of this science. In each case our goal will be to introduce the central ideas in the subject, the current topics of research, and some of the techniques being applied to advance knowledge in the area. For example, our discussion of programming is not geared toward developing programming skills but concentrates on the principles behind the programming tools of today, how these tools have evolved, and the problems current research is trying to overcome.

As we progress through this study of topics, it is easy to lose track of the overall picture. We therefore collect our thoughts by identifying some questions that define the science of computing and provide the focus for its study.

- Which problems can be solved by algorithmic processes?
- How can the discovery of algorithms be made easier?

- How can the techniques of representing and communicating algorithms be improved?
- How can our knowledge of algorithms and technology be applied to provide better machines?
- How can the characteristics of different algorithms be analyzed and compared?

Note that the theme common to all of these questions is the study of algorithms (Figure 0.5).

0.4 The Role of Abstraction

Today's computer systems are extremely complex and can be overwhelming when viewed in all their detail. It is common therefore to approach such systems at various levels of detail. At each level we envision the system in terms of components whose internal characteristics we ignore. This allows us to concentrate on how components interact with other components at the same level and how they are used to construct higher-level components.

The distinction between the external properties of a component and the internal details of the component's construction is known as **abstraction.** Abstraction is an important simplification technique with which our society has created a lifestyle that would otherwise be impossible. For example, few of us understand how the various conveniences of daily life are actually implemented.

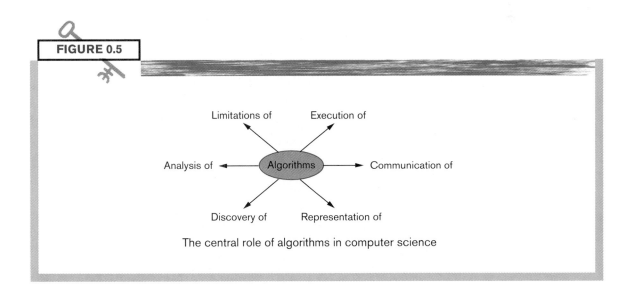

FIGURE 0.5

The central role of algorithms in computer science

We eat food and wear clothes that we alone cannot produce. We use electrical devices without understanding the underlying technology. We use the services of others without knowing the details of their activities. With each new advancement, a small part of society chooses to specialize in its implementation while the rest of us learn to use the results as **abstract tools,** that is, as tools whose interior implementation we need not understand. In this manner, society's warehouse of abstract tools expands and society's ability to advance further increases.

Abstraction is a recurring theme throughout computer science. It is by means of abstraction that today's large, complex hardware and software systems are designed, constructed, and managed, and it is by means of abstraction that the science is able to advance. In fact, our study itself will progress through a hierarchy of abstractions, beginning in Chapters 1 and 2 with issues relating to how individual steps of an algorithm are executed within a machine and progressing up to the topics in Chapter 11 that involve properties of entire classes of algorithms.

0.5 Ethical/Social/Legal Repercussions

Advances in science and technology are blurring many distinctions on which our society has based decisions in the past and is even challenging many of society's principles. What is the difference between the presence of intelligent behavior and the presence of intelligence itself? When does life begin? When does it end? What is the difference between a plant and an animal? Such questions are forcing individuals to reassess their beliefs and often to reconstruct the very foundation of those beliefs.

Computer science is generating such questions in a variety of contexts. In law, questions arise regarding the degree to which software can be owned and the rights and liabilities that accompany that ownership. In ethics, individuals are faced with numerous options that challenge the traditional principles on which their behavior is based. In government, questions arise regarding the extent to which computer technology and its applications should be regulated.

Resolving such dilemmas in a rational manner requires a basic knowledge in the relevant science or technology. For example, if a society is to make sound decisions regarding the storage and disposal of nuclear waste, its members must comprehend the effects of radiation, understand what is required to protect against its dangers, and calculate a realistic estimate about the time span over which the radiation risk will persist. Likewise, to judge whether governments or companies should be allowed to develop large, integrated databases containing information about its citizens or customers, members of that society must have a basic understanding of the capabilities, limitations, and ramifications of database technology.

This text provides a fundamental background from which you can approach such issues in an informed manner. Some sections, in fact, are devoted to social, ethical, and legal issues themselves. For example, we discuss matters of privacy in relation to the Internet and database technology and issues of software ownership and ownership rights in relation to software development. Although not a part of computer science itself, these topics are important for lay audiences as well as for those contemplating careers in computer related fields.

Of course, factual knowledge alone does not necessarily provide solutions to many of the questions generated by today's advances in computer science. There is often no single correct answer, and many valid solutions are compromises between opposing views. Thus, finding solutions often requires the ability to listen, to recognize other points of view, to carry on a rational debate, and to expand one's own opinions as new insights are gained. With this in mind, each chapter of this text ends with a segment called Social Issues. These are not necessarily questions to be answered. Instead, they are questions to be considered. In many cases, an answer that may appear obvious at first will cease to satisfy you as you explore alternatives. We close this introduction with a collection of such questions that relate to computing issues in general.

SOCIAL ISSUES

The following questions are provided to help you understand some of the ethical/social/legal issues associated with the field of computing as well as investigate your own beliefs and their foundations. The goal is not merely to answer these questions. You should also consider why you answered as you did and whether your justifications are consistent from one question to the next.

1. The premise that our society is different from what it would have been without the computer revolution is generally accepted. Is our society better than it would have been without the revolution? Is our society worse? Would your answer differ if your position within society were different?

2. Is it acceptable to participate in today's technical society without making an effort to understand the basics of that technology? For instance, do members of a democracy, whose votes often determine how technology will be supported and used, have an obligation to try to understand that technology? Does your answer depend on what technology is being considered? For example, is your answer the same when considering nuclear technology as when considering computer technology?

3. By using cash in financial transactions, individuals have traditionally had the option to manage their financial affairs without service charges. However, as more and more of our economy is becoming automated, financial institutions are implementing service charges for access to these automated systems. Is there a point at which these charges unfairly restrict an individual's access to the economy? For example, suppose an employer pays employees only by check, and all financial institutions place a service charge on check cashing and depositing. Are the employees unfairly treated? What if an employer insists on paying only via direct deposit?

4. When interactive television or an equivalent phenomenon becomes a household reality, to what extent should a company be allowed to retrieve information from children (perhaps via an interactive game format) regarding the household? For example, should a company be allowed to obtain a child's report on his or her parents buying patterns? What about information about the child?

5. To what extent should a government regulate computer technology and its applications? Consider, for example, the issues mentioned in Questions 3 and 4. What justifies governmental regulation?

6. To what extent will our decisions regarding technology in general, and computer technology in particular, affect our grandchildren?

7. As technology advances, our educational system is constantly challenged to reconsider the level of abstraction at which topics are presented. Many questions take the form of whether a skill is still necessary or whether students should be allowed to rely on an abstract tool. Students of trigonometry are no longer taught how to find the values of trigonometric functions using tables. Instead, they use calculators as abstract tools to find these values. Some argue that long division should also give way to abstraction. What other subjects are involved with similar controversies? Will the use of video technology someday remove the need to read? Do automated spelling checkers eliminate the need for spelling skills?

8. Assume that the concept of public libraries is largely based on the premise that all citizens in a democracy must have access to information. As more and more information is stored and disseminated via computer technology, does access to this technology become a right of every individual? If so, should public libraries be the channel by which this access is provided?

9. What ethical concerns arise in a society that relies on the use of abstract tools? Are there cases in which it is unethical to use a product or service without knowing how it is produced?

ADDITIONAL READING

Dejoie, D., G. Fowler, and D. Paradice. *Ethical Issues in Information Systems.* Boston: Boyd and Fraser, 1991.

Edgar, S. L. *Morality and Machines.* Sudbury, MA: Jones and Bartlett, 1997.

Forester, T., and P. Forrison. *Computer Ethics: Cautionary Tales and Ethical Dilemmas.* Cambridge, MA: MIT Press, 1990.

Goldstine, J. J. *The Computer from Pascal to von Neumann.* Princeton: Princeton University Press, 1972.

Johnson, D. G. *Computer Ethics*, 2nd ed. Englewood Cliffs, NJ: Prentice-Hall, 1994.

Johnson, D. G. *Ethical Issues in Engineering.* Englewood Cliffs, NJ: Prentice-Hall, 1991.

Mollenhoff, C. R. *Atanasoff: Forgotten Father of the Computer.* Ames: Iowa State University Press, 1988.

Neumann, P. G. *Computer Related Risks.* Reading, MA: Addison-Wesley, 1995.

Randell, B. *The Origins of Digital Computers.* New York: Springer-Verlag, 1973.

Shurkin, J. *Engines of the Mind.* New York: Norton, 1984.

part
o n e

MACHINE ARCHITECTURE

A major process in the development of a science is the construction of theories that are confirmed or rejected by experimentation. In some cases these theories lie dormant for extended periods, waiting for technology to develop to the point that they can be tested. In other cases the capabilities of current technology influence the concerns of the science.

The development of computer science possesses both of these characteristics. We have already seen that the science grew from theories that originated well before technology could produce the machines envisioned by early researchers. Even today, our advancing knowledge of algorithmic processes is leading to new machine designs that challenge the limits of technology. In contrast, other subjects in the science are rooted in the application of today's technology. In sum, computer science is a blend of theoretical research and advancing technology, each influencing the other in a mutually beneficial relationship.

It follows that to appreciate the role of various subjects within computer science, one should understand the basics of today's technology and how it influences the design and implementation of today's computers. Providing this foundation is the purpose of the following two chapters. In Chapter 1 we will discuss techniques by which information is represented and stored inside computers, and in Chapter 2 the ways in which today's machines manipulate data.

chapter

DATA STORAGE

o n e

In this chapter we will consider issues associated with data representation and storage within a computer. At times we will address issues of technology, since these matters are often reflected in the external characteristics of today's machines. However, much of our discussion will deal with topics that will be germane to computer design well after today's technologies have been replaced with those of tomorrow.

1.1 Storage of Bits
Gates and Flip-Flops
Other Storage Techniques
Hexadecimal Notation

1.2 Main Memory

1.3 Mass Storage
Magnetic Disks
Compact Disks
Magnetic Tape
File Storage and Retrieval

1.4 Representing Information as Bit Patterns
Representing Text
Representing Numeric Values
Representing Images

*1.5 The Binary System
Binary Addition
Fractions in Binary

*1.6 Storing Integers
Two's Complement Notation
Excess Notation

*1.7 Storing Fractions
Floating-Point Notation
Truncation Errors

*1.8 Data Compression
Generic Data Compression Techniques
Compressing Images

*1.9 Communication Errors
Parity Bits
Error-Correcting Codes

*Asterisks indicate suggestions for optional sections.

1.1 Storage of Bits

Today's computers represent information as patterns of bits. A **bit** (binary digit) is either one of two digits—0 and 1—which for now we will consider merely as symbols with no numeric meaning. Indeed, we will see that the meaning of a bit varies from one application to another. Storing a bit within a machine requires a device that can be in one of two states, such as a switch (on or off), a relay (open or closed), or a flag on a flag pole (raised or lowered). One state is used to represent 0, the other to represent 1. Our immediate goal is to consider ways in which bits are stored within today's machines.

Gates and Flip-Flops

We begin by introducing the operations AND, OR, and XOR (exclusive or) as summarized in Figure 1.1. These operations are similar to the arithmetic operations TIMES and PLUS in that they combine a pair of values, the operation's input, to produce a third value, the operation's output. In contrast to arithmetic operations, however, the only digits manipulated by the AND, OR, and

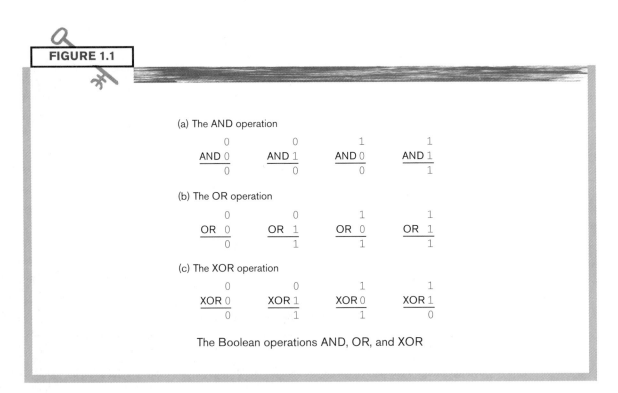

FIGURE 1.1

(a) The AND operation

0	0	1	1
AND 0	AND 1	AND 0	AND 1
0	0	0	1

(b) The OR operation

0	0	1	1
OR 0	OR 1	OR 0	OR 1
0	1	1	1

(c) The XOR operation

0	0	1	1
XOR 0	XOR 1	XOR 0	XOR 1
0	1	1	0

The Boolean operations AND, OR, and XOR

XOR operations are 0 and 1. In this context we think of the digit 0 as representing the value *false* and the digit 1 representing the value *true*. Operations that manipulate true/false values are called **Boolean operations,** in honor of the mathematician George Boole (1815–1864).

The Boolean operation AND is designed to reflect the truth or falseness of a statement formed by combining two smaller statements with the conjunction *and*. Such statements have the generic form

> *P* AND *Q*

where *P* represents one statement and *Q* represents another—for example,

> Kermit is a frog AND Miss Piggy is an actress.

The inputs to the AND operation represent the truth or falseness of the compound statement's components; the output represents the truth or falseness of the compound statement itself. Since a statement of the form P AND Q is true only when both of its components are true, we conclude that 1 AND 1 should be 1, whereas all other cases should produce an output of 0, in agreement with Figure 1.1.

In a similar manner, the OR operation is based on compound statements of the form

> *P* OR *Q*

where, again, *P* represents one statement and *Q* represents another. Such statements are true when at least one of their components is true, which agrees with the OR operation depicted in Figure 1.1.

There is not a single conjunction in the English language that captures the meaning of the XOR operation. XOR produces an output of 1 (true) when one of its inputs is 1 (true) and the other is 0 (false). For example, a statement of the form *P* XOR *Q* means "either *P* or *Q* but not both."

The operation NOT is another Boolean operation. It differs from AND, OR, and XOR in that it has only one input. Its output is the opposite of that input; if the input of the operation NOT is true, the output is false, and vice versa. Thus, if the input of the NOT operation is the truth or falseness of the statement

> Fozzie is a bear

then the output would represent the truth or falseness of the statement

> Fozzie is not a bear.

A device that produces the output of a Boolean operation when given the operation's input values is called a **gate.** Gates can be constructed from a variety of technologies such as gears, relays, and optic devices. Today's computers usually implement gates as small electronic circuits in which the digits 0 and 1 are represented as voltage levels. We need not concern ourselves with such details, however. For our purposes, it suffices to represent gates in their symbolic form,

FIGURE 1.2

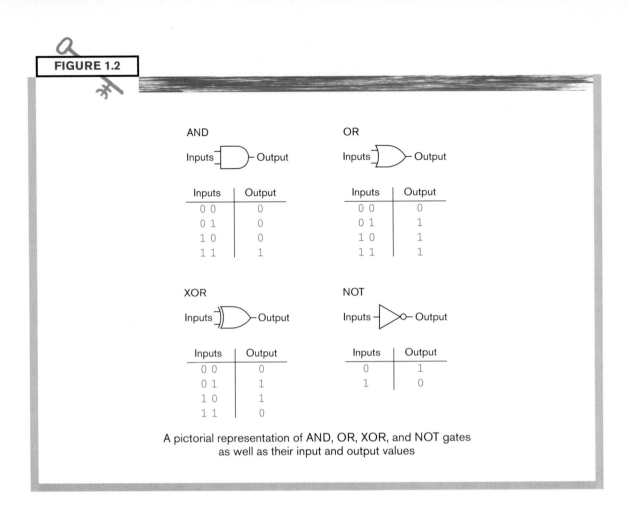

A pictorial representation of AND, OR, XOR, and NOT gates
as well as their input and output values

as shown in Figure 1.2. Note that the AND, OR, XOR, and NOT gates are represented by distinctively shaped diagrams, with the input values entering on one side and the output exiting on the other.

Gates such as these provide the building blocks from which computers are constructed. One important step in this direction is depicted in the circuit in Figure 1.3. This is a particular example from a collection of circuits known as flip-flops. A **flip-flop** is a circuit that produces an output value of 0 or 1 that remains constant until a temporary pulse from another circuit causes it to shift to the other value. In other words, the output will flip or flop between two values under control of external stimuli. As long as both inputs in the circuit in Figure 1.3 remain 0, the output (whether 0 or 1) will not change. However, temporarily placing a 1 on the upper input will force the output to be 1, whereas temporarily placing a 1 on the lower input will force the output to be 0.

FIGURE 1.3

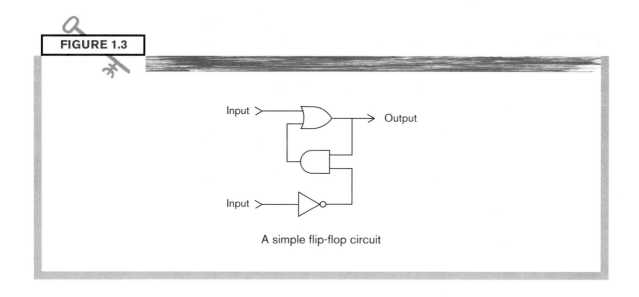

A simple flip-flop circuit

Let us consider this claim in more detail. Without knowing the current output of the circuit in Figure 1.3, suppose that the upper input is changed to 1 while the lower input remains 0 (Figure 1.4a). This will cause the output of the OR gate to be 1, regardless of the other input to this gate. In turn, both inputs to the AND gate will now be 1, since the other input to this gate is already 1 (obtained by passing the lower input of the flip-flop through the NOT gate). The output of the AND gate will then become 1, which means that the second input to the OR gate will now be 1 (Figure 1.4b). This guarantees that the output of the OR gate will remain 1, even when the upper input to the flip-flop is changed back to 0 (Figure 1.4c). In summary, the flip-flop's output has become 1, and this output value will remain after the upper input returns to 0.

In a similar manner, temporarily placing the value 1 on the lower input will force the flip-flop's output to be 0, and this output will persist after the input value returns to 0.

The significance of a flip-flop from our perspective is that it is ideal for the storage of a bit within a computer. The value stored in it is the output value of the flip-flop. Other circuits can easily adjust this value by sending pulses to the flip-flop's inputs, and still other circuits can respond to the stored value by using the flip-flop's output as their inputs.

There are, of course, other ways to build a flip-flop. One alternative is shown in Figure 1.5. If you experiment with this circuit, you will find that, although it has a different internal structure, its external properties are the same as those of Figure 1.3. This leads us to our first example of the role of abstract tools. When designing a flip-flop, an engineer considers the alternative ways in which a flip-flop can be constructed using gates as building blocks. Then, once

FIGURE 1.4

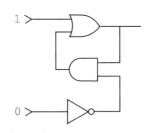

(a) 1 is placed on the upper input.

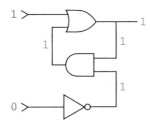

(b) This causes the output of the OR gate to be 1 and, in turn, the output of the AND gate to be 1.

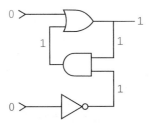

(c) The 1 from the AND gate keeps the OR gate from changing after the upper input returns to 0.

Setting the output of a flip-flop to 1

FIGURE 1.5

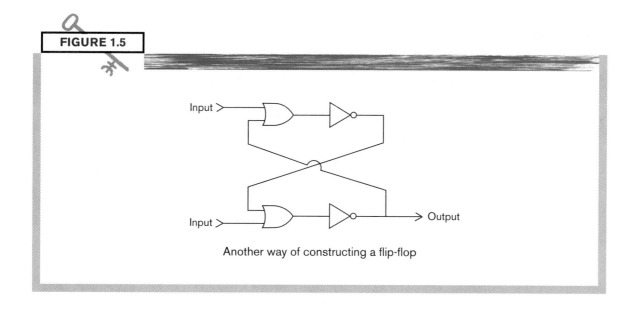

Input

Input

Output

Another way of constructing a flip-flop

flip-flops and other basic circuits have been designed, the engineer can use them as building blocks to construct more complex circuitry. In turn, the design of computer circuitry takes on a hierarchical structure, each level of which uses the lower level components as abstract tools.

Other Storage Techniques

In the 1960s, bits were stored in computers using small donut-shaped rings of magnetic material, called **cores,** threaded on wires. By passing electric current through the wires, each core could be magnetized in one of two directions. Later, the direction of the magnetic field could be detected by observing its effect on an electric current passing through the center of the core. Thus, a core provided a means of storing a bit—a 1 was represented by a magnetic field in one direction, a 0 was represented by a magnetic field in the other. Such systems are obsolete today due to their size and power requirements.

A more recent method of storing a bit is the capacitor, which consists of two small metallic plates positioned parallel to each other with a small distance between them. If a voltage source is connected to the plates—positive to one plate and negative to the other—the charges from the voltage source will distribute themselves on the plates. Then, when the voltage source is removed, these charges will be left on the plates. If the plates are later connected, current will flow through the connection and the charge will be neutralized. Thus, a capacitor can be in one of two states, charged or discharged, one of which can be used to represent a 0, the other to represent a 1. Today's technology is capable of constructing millions of tiny capacitors along with their related circuitry on a single wafer (called a **chip**). In turn, the capacitor has become a popular technology for bit storage within machines.

Flip-flops, cores, and capacitors provide examples of storage systems with different degrees of volatility. A core will retain its magnetic field after the machine is turned off. A flip-flop looses the data entrusted to it when its power source is turned off. In addition, the charges on tiny capacitors are so fragile that they tend to dissipate on their own, even while the machine is running. Thus, the charge on a capacitor has to be replenished regularly by a circuit known as a refresh circuit. In recognition of this volatility, computer memory (Section 1.2) constructed from such technology is often called **dynamic memory.**

Hexadecimal Notation

When considering the internal activities of a computer, we must deal with strings of bits, some of which can be quite long. Unfortunately, the human mind has difficulty handling such detail. Merely transcribing the pattern 101101010011 is tedious and error-prone. To simplify the representation of bit patterns, therefore, we usually use a shorthand notation called **hexadecimal notation.** This notation takes advantage of the fact that bit patterns within a machine tend to have lengths in multiples of four. In particular, hexadecimal notation uses a single symbol to represent four bits, meaning that a string of twelve bits can be represented by only three symbols.

Figure 1.6 presents the hexadecimal coding system. The left column displays all possible bit patterns of length four; the right column shows the symbol used in hexadecimal notation to represent the pattern to its left. Using this system, the bit pattern 10110101 is represented as B5. This is obtained by dividing the bit pattern into substrings of length four and then representing each substring by its hexadecimal equivalent—1011 is represented by B and 0101 is represented by 5. In this manner, the 16-bit pattern 1010010011001000 can be reduced to the more palatable form A4C8.

We will use hexadecimal notation extensively in the next chapter. There you will come to appreciate its efficiency.

QUESTIONS/EXERCISES

1. What input bit patterns will cause the following circuit to produce an output of 1?

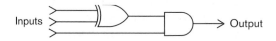

FIGURE 1.6

Bit pattern	Hexadecimal representation
0000	0
0001	1
0010	2
0011	3
0100	4
0101	5
0110	6
0111	7
1000	8
1001	9
1010	A
1011	B
1100	C
1101	D
1110	E
1111	F

The hexadecimal coding system

2. In the text, we claimed that placing a 1 on the lower input of the flip-flop in Figure 1.3 (while holding the upper input at 0) will force the flip-flop's output to be 0. Describe the sequence of events that occurs within the flip-flop in this case.

3. Assuming that both inputs to the flip-flop in Figure 1.5 are 0, describe the sequence of events that occurs when the upper input is temporarily set to 1.

4. It is often necessary to coordinate the activities of various parts of a circuit. This is accomplished by connecting a pulsating signal (called a *clock*) to those parts of the circuit that require coordination. As the clock alternates between the values 0 and 1, it activates the various circuit components. Below is an example of one part of such a circuit that involves the flip-flop shown in Figure 1.3. For what clock values will the flip-flop be shielded from the effects of the circuit's input values? For what clock values will the flip-flop respond to the circuit's input values?

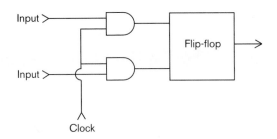

5. Use hexadecimal notation to represent the following bit patterns:
   a. 0110101011110010   b. 1110100001010100010111
   c. 01001000
6. What bit patterns are represented by the following hexadecimal patterns?
   a. 5FD97   b. 610A   c. ABCD   d. 0100

1.2 Main Memory

For the purpose of storing data, a computer contains a large collection of circuits, each capable of storing a bit. This bit reservoir is known as the machine's **main memory.** The storage circuits in a machine's main memory are arranged in manageable units called **cells** (or *words*), with a typical cell size being eight bits. In fact, bit collections of size eight have become so popular that the term **byte** is now widely used in reference to bit collections of that size.

Small computers used in such household devices as microwave ovens may have main memory sizes measured in only a few hundred cells, whereas large computers used to store and manipulate extensive amounts of data can have billions of cells in their main memories. The size of a machine's main memory is often measured in terms of 1,048,576-cell units. (The value 1,048,576 is a power of two, namely 2^{20}, so it is more natural as a unit of measure within a computer than an even 1,000,000.). The term *mega* is used to indicate this unit of measure. The abbreviation MB is often used for the term *megabyte*. Thus a memory of 4 MB contains 4,194,304 (4 × 1,048,576) cells, each of which is one byte in size. Other units of measuring memory size are *kilobyte* (abbreviated as KB), which is equal to 1024 bytes (2^{10} bytes), and *gigabyte* (abbreviated as GB), which is equal to 1024 MB, or 2^{30} bytes.

To identify individual cells in a machine's main memory, each cell is assigned a unique name, called its **address.** The system is analogous to, and uses the same terminology as, the technique of identifying houses in a city by addresses. In the case of memory cells, however, the addresses used are entirely numeric. To be more precise, we can envision all the cells being placed in a single row and numbered in this order starting with the value zero. The cells in a

FIGURE 1.7

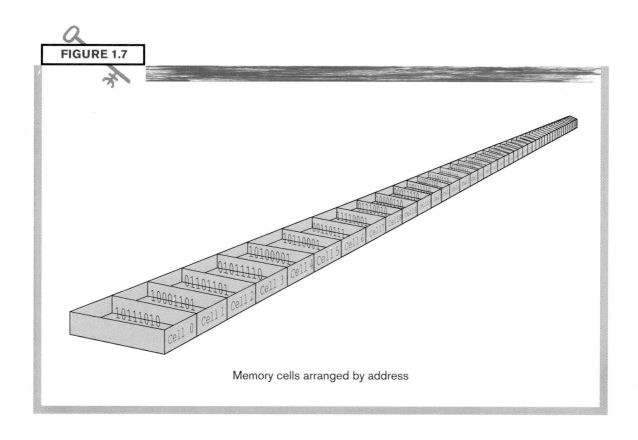

Memory cells arranged by address

machine with a 4 MB memory would be therefore addressed as 0, 1, 2, ..., 4194304. Note that such an addressing system not only gives us a way of uniquely identifying each cell but also associates an order to the cells (Figure 1.7), giving us phrases such as "the next cell" or "the previous cell."

To complete the main memory of a machine, the circuitry that actually holds the bits is combined with the circuitry required to allow other circuits to store and retrieve data from the memory cells. In this way, other circuits can get data from the memory by electronically asking for the contents of a certain address (called a *read* operation), or they can record information in the memory by requesting that a certain bit pattern be placed in the cell at a particular address (called a *write* operation).

An important consequence of organizing a machine's main memory as small, addressable cells is that each cell can be accessed individually. That is, data stored in a machine's main memory can be processed in random order—which explains why a machine's main memory is often referred to as **random access memory (RAM).** This random accessibility of small data units is in stark contrast to the mass storage systems that we will discuss in the next section, in

FIGURE 1.8

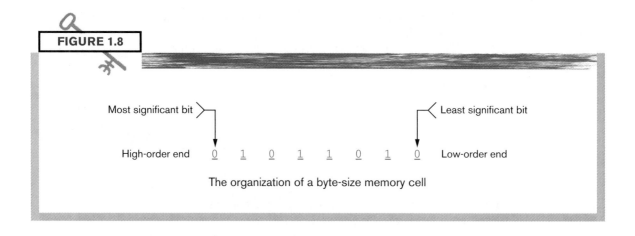

Most significant bit

Least significant bit

High-order end   0 1 0 1 1 0 1 0   Low-order end

The organization of a byte-size memory cell

which long strings of bits must be manipulated as a block. When RAM is constructed from dynamic memory technology, it is often referred to as DRAM (Dynamic RAM).

We envision the bits within a memory cell as being arranged in a row. We call one end of this row the **high-order end** and the other the **low-order end.** Although there is no left or right within a machine, we imagine the bits arranged in a row from left to right with the high-order end on the left. The bit at this end is often called either the high-order bit or the **most significant bit;** similarly, the bit at the other end is referred to as the low-order bit or the **least significant bit.** Thus we may represent the contents of a byte-size cell as shown in Figure 1.8.

An important consequence of the ordering of both the cells in main memory and the bits within each cell is that the entire collection of bits within a machine's main memory is essentially ordered in one long row. Pieces of this long row can therefore be used to store bit patterns that may be longer than the length of a single cell. In particular, if the memory is divided into byte-size cells, we can still store a string of 16 bits merely by using two consecutive memory cells.

QUESTIONS/EXERCISES

1. If the memory cell whose address is 5 contains the value 8, what is the difference between writing the value 5 into cell number 6 and moving the contents of cell number 5 into cell number 6?
2. Suppose you want to interchange the values stored in memory cells 2 and 3. What is wrong with the following sequence of steps:

   Step 1. Move the contents of cell number 2 to cell number 3.
   Step 2. Move the contents of cell number 3 to cell number 2.

Design a sequence of steps that correctly interchanges the contents of these cells.

3. How many bits would be in the memory of a computer with 4KB memory?

1.3 Mass Storage

Due to the volatility and limited size of a computer's main memory, most machines are provided with additional memory devices called **mass storage systems**—which include magnetic disks, CDs, and magnetic tapes. The advantages of mass storage systems over main memory include less volatility, large storage capacities, and in many cases, the ability to remove the storage medium from the machine for archival purposes.

The terms *on-line* and *off-line* are often used to describe devices that can be either attached to or detached from a machine. **On-line** means that the device or information is connected and readily available to the machine without human intervention. In contrast, **off-line** means that human intervention is required before the device or information can be accessed by the machine—perhaps because the device must be turned on or the medium holding the information must be inserted into some mechanism.

A major disadvantage of mass storage systems is that they typically require mechanical motion and therefore have much greater response times when compared to a machine's main memory, which performs all activities electronically.

Magnetic Disks

One of the most common forms of mass storage in use today is the magnetic disk, in which a thin spinning disk with magnetic coating is used to hold data. Read/write heads are placed above and/or below the disk so that as the disk spins, each head traverses a circle, called a **track,** around the disk's upper or lower surface. By repositioning the read/write heads, different concentric tracks can be accessed. In many cases, a disk storage system consists of several disks mounted on a common spindle, one on top of the other, with enough space for the read/write heads to slip between the platters. In such cases, the read/write heads move in unison. Each time the read/write heads are repositioned, a new set of tracks—which is called a **cylinder**—becomes accessible.

Since a track can contain more information than we would normally want to manipulate at any one time, each track is divided into arcs called **sectors** on which information is recorded as a continuous string of bits (Figure 1.9). Each track within a disk system contains the same number of sectors and each sector

FIGURE 1.9

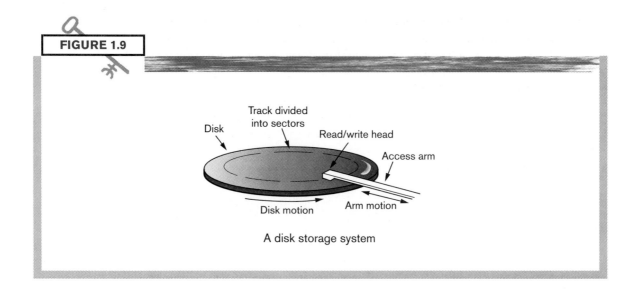

Track divided
into sectors

Disk

Read/write head

Access arm

Disk motion

Arm motion

A disk storage system

contains the same number of bits. (This means that the bits within a sector are more compactly stored on the tracks nearer the center of the disk than those on the tracks near the outer edge.)

Thus, a disk storage system consists of many individual sectors, each of which can be accessed as an independent string of bits. The number of tracks per surface and the number of sectors per track vary greatly from one disk system to another. Sector sizes tend to be no more than a few KB; sectors of 512 bytes or 1024 bytes are common.

The location of tracks and sectors is not a permanent part of a disk's physical structure. Instead, they are marked magnetically through a process called **formatting** (or initializing) the disk. This process is usually performed by the disk's manufacturer, resulting in what are known as formatted disks. Most computer systems can also perform this task. Thus, if the format information on a disk is damaged, the disk can be reformatted, although this process destroys all the information that was previously recorded on the disk.

The capacity of a disk storage system depends on the number of disks used and the density in which the tracks and sectors are placed. Lower-capacity systems consist of a single plastic disk known as a diskette or, in those cases in which the disk is flexible, by the less prestigious title of floppy disk. (Today's 3½-inch diameter floppy disks are housed in rigid plastic cases, which do not constitute as flexible a package as their older 5¼-inch diameter cousins that were housed in paper sleeves.) Diskettes are easily inserted and removed from their corresponding read/write units and are easily stored. As a consequence, diskettes are often used for off-line storage of information. The generic 3½-inch diskette is capable of holding 1.44 MB of data, but nongeneric diskettes are available with much higher capacities. An example is the Zip disk system from Iomega Corporation, which provides storage capacities up to several hundred MB on a single rigid diskette.

High-capacity disk systems, capable of holding several gigabytes, consist of perhaps five to ten rigid disks mounted on a common spindle. The fact that the disks used in these systems are rigid leads them to be known as hard-disk systems, in contrast to their floppy counterparts. To allow for faster rotation speeds, the read/write heads in these systems do not touch the disk but instead "float" just above the surface. The spacing is so close that even a single particle of dust could become jammed between the head and disk surface, destroying both (a phenomenon known as a *head crash*). Thus hard-disk systems are housed in cases sealed at the factory.

Several measurements are used to evaluate a disk system's performance: (1) **seek time** (the time required to move the read/write heads from one track to another); (2) **rotation delay** or **latency time** (half the time required for the disk to make a complete rotation, which is the average amount of time required for the desired data to rotate around to the read/write head once the head has been positioned over the desired track); (3) **access time** (the sum of seek time and rotation delay); and (4) **transfer rate** (the rate at which data can be transferred to or from the disk).

Hard-disk systems generally have significantly better characteristics than floppy systems. Since the read/write heads do not touch the disk surface in a hard-disk system, one finds rotation speeds on the order of 3000 to 4000 revolutions per minute, whereas disks in floppy-disk systems rotate in the 300 revolutions-per-minute range. Consequently, transfer rates for hard-disk systems, usually measured in megabytes per second, are much greater than those associated with floppy-disk systems, which tend to be measured in kilobytes per second.

Since disk systems require physical motion for their operation, both hard and floppy systems suffer when compared to speeds within electronic circuitry. Indeed, delay times within an electronic circuit are measured in units of nanoseconds (billionths of a second) or less, whereas seek times, latency times, and access times of disk systems are measured in milliseconds (thousandths of a second). Thus the time required to retrieve information from a disk system can seem like an eternity to an electronic circuit awaiting a result.

Compact Disks

Another popular data storage technology is the compact disk (CD). These disks are 12 centimeters (approximately 5 inches) in diameter and consist of reflective material covered with a clear protective coating. Information is recorded on them by creating variations in their reflective surfaces. This information can then be retrieved by means of a laser beam that monitors irregularities on the reflective surface of the CD as it spins.

CD technology was originally applied to audio recordings using a recording format known as CD-DA (compact disk-digital audio). The CDs used today for computer data storage are similar to their audio predecessors, except that they employ a format known as CD-ROM (compact disk–read-only memory). The difference between CD-DA and CD-ROM is the interpretation of the data fields. For example, CD-DA reserves certain fields for storage of timing information, whereas CD-ROM utilizes that space for arbitrary data.

In contrast to magnetic disk storage in which information is recorded on separate, concentric tracks, information on a CD is stored on a single track that spirals around the CD like a groove in an old-fashioned record. (Unlike old-fashioned records, however, the track on a CD spirals from the inside out.) This track is divided into units called sectors. All sectors contain the same amount of data and each has its own identifying markings. A sector in CD-ROM format contains 2KB of data. The same space in CD-DA format contains $^1/_{75}$ of a second of music.

Note that the distance around the spiral track is greater toward the outer edge of the disk than at the inner portion. To maximize the capacity of a CD, information is stored at a uniform linear density over the entire spiraled track, which means that more information is stored in a loop around the outer portion of the spiral than in a loop around the inner portion. In turn, more sectors will be read in a single revolution of the disk when the laser beam is scanning the outer portion of the spiraled track than when the beam is scanning the inner portion of the track. Thus, to obtain a uniform rate of data transfer, CD players are designed to vary the CD's rotation speed depending on the location of the laser beam.

As a consequence of such design decisions, CD storage systems perform best when dealing with long, continuous strings of data, as is the case when reproducing music. In contrast, when an application requires access to data in a random manner (as in a reservation system) the approach used in magnetic disk storage (individual, concentric tracks, each containing the same number of sectors) outperforms the spiral approach used in CDs.

CDs using CD-ROM format have capacities slightly over 600 MB. However, still newer formats such as DVD (Digital Versatile Disk) provide storage capacities on the order of 10 GB. Such CDs are capable of storing multimedia presentations in which audio and video data are combined to present information in a more interesting and more informative manner than would be possible by means of traditional text. Indeed, a major application of the DVD standards is to provide a means of recording entire movies on a single CD.

Another variation of CD technology is CD-WORM (compact disk–write once, read many) that allows data to be recorded on a CD after it is manufactured rather than during the manufacturing process. These devices are convenient for archival purposes and for producing CD products in small quantities.

FIGURE 1.10

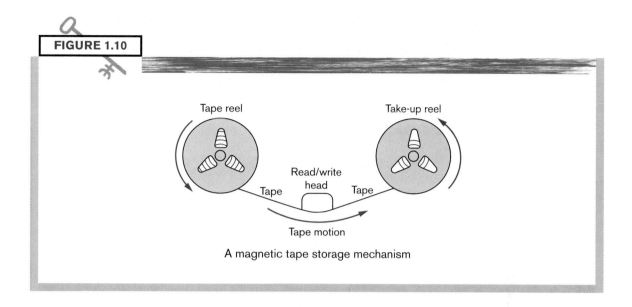

A magnetic tape storage mechanism

Magnetic Tape

An older form of mass storage device uses magnetic tape (Figure 1.10). Here, information is recorded on the magnetic coating of a thin plastic tape that is, in turn, wound on a reel for storage. To access the data, this tape is mounted in a device called a tape drive that typically can read, write, and rewind the tape under control of the computer. Tape drives range in size from small cartridge units, called streaming tape units, that use tape similar in appearance to that in stereo systems to older, large reel-to-reel units. Although the capacity of these devices depends on the format used, most can hold several gigabytes.

Modern streaming tape systems divide a tape into segments, each of which is magnetically marked by a formatting process similar to that of disk storage devices. Each of these segments contains several tracks that run parallel to one another lengthwise on the tape. These tracks can be accessed independently, meaning that the tape ultimately consists of numerous individual strings of bits in a manner similar to the sectors on a disk.

A major disadvantage of streaming tape systems is that moving between different positions on a tape can be very time-consuming owing to the significant amount of tape that must be moved between the reels. Thus tape systems have much longer data access times than magnetic disk systems in which different sectors can be accessed by short movements of the read/write head. In turn, tape systems are not popular for on-line data storage. But when the goal is offline data storage for archival purposes, the high capacity, reliability, and cost efficiency of tape make this technology the best choice among today's data storage systems.

File Storage and Retrieval

Information is stored on mass storage systems in large units called **files.** A typical file may consist of a complete text document, a photograph, a program, or a collection of data about the employees in a company. The physical properties of mass storage devices dictate that these files be stored and retrieved in multiple byte units. For example, each sector on a magnetic disk must be manipulated as one continuous string of bits. A block of data conforming to the physical characteristics of a storage device is called a **physical record.** Thus, a file stored in mass storage will typically consist of many physical records.

In contrast to this division into physical records, a file usually has natural divisions determined by the information represented. For example, a file containing information regarding a company's employees would consist of multiple units, each consisting of the information about one employee. Such naturally occurring blocks of data are called **logical records.**

Logical record sizes rarely match the physical record size dictated by a mass storage device. In turn, one may find several logical records residing within a single physical record or perhaps a logical record split between two or more physical records (Figure 1.11). The result is that a certain amount of unscrambling is often associated with retrieving data from mass storage systems. A common solution to this problem is to set aside an area of main memory that is large enough to hold several physical records and to use this memory space as a regrouping area. That is, blocks of data compatible with physical records can be transferred between this main memory area and the mass storage system, while

FIGURE 1.11

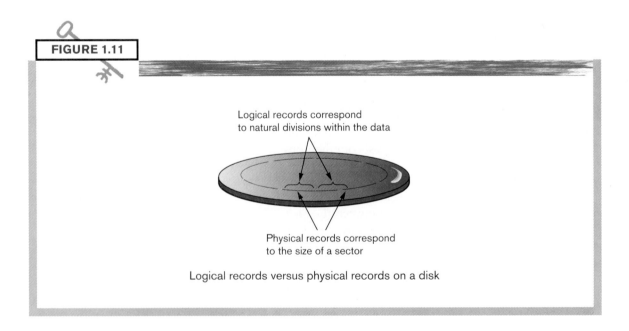

Logical records correspond
to natural divisions within the data

Physical records correspond
to the size of a sector

Logical records versus physical records on a disk

the data residing in main memory can be referenced in terms of logical records. An area of memory used in this manner is called a **buffer.**

The use of a buffer exemplifies the relative roles of main memory and mass storage. Main memory is used to hold data for processing purposes, whereas mass storage is used as a permanent depository for data. Thus, updating data stored in mass storage involves transferring the data to main memory, updating the data, and then transferring the updated data back to mass storage.

We conclude that main memory, magnetic disks, compact disks, and magnetic tape exhibit decreasing degrees of random access to data. The addressing system used in main memory allows rapid random access to individual bytes of data. Magnetic disks provide random access only to entire sectors of data. Moreover, retrieving a sector involves seek and rotation delays. Compact disks also provide random access to individual sectors, but the delays encountered are greater than those for magnetic disks due to the additional time required to locate the spiraling track and to adjust the rotation speed of the disk. Finally, magnetic tape offers little in the way of random access. Modern tape systems mark positions on the tape so that different segments of the tape can be referenced individually, but the physical structure of the tape dictates that the retrieval time for segments far down the tape will be significant.

QUESTIONS/EXERCISES

1. What advantage does a hard-disk system gain from the fact that its disks spin faster than those in a floppy-disk system?
2. When recording data on a multiple-disk storage system, should we fill a complete disk surface before starting on another surface or should we first fill an entire cylinder before starting on another cylinder?
3. Why should the data in a reservation system that is constantly being updated be stored on a magnetic disk instead of on tape?
4. Suppose that logical records of 450 bytes each are to be stored on a disk whose sectors consist of 512 bytes each. Give an argument to the effect that only one logical record should be stored per physical record even though this means that 62 bytes of each sector will be wasted.

1.4 Representing Information as Bit Patterns

We will now consider how information is represented within machines in the form of bit patterns, focusing in particular on popular methods for coding text, numerical data, and images. Each of these systems has repercussions that are often visible to a typical computer user. Our goal is to understand enough about these techniques so that we can recognize their consequences for what they are.

Representing Text

Information in the form of text is normally represented by means of a code in which each of the different symbols in the text (such as the letters of the alphabet or punctuation marks) is assigned a unique bit pattern. The text is then represented as a long string of bits in which the successive patterns represent the successive symbols in the original text.

In the early years of computers, many such codes were designed and used in connection with different pieces of equipment, producing a corresponding proliferation of communication problems. To alleviate this situation, the **American National Standards Institute (ANSI)** adopted the **American Standard Code for Information Interchange (ASCII,** pronounced "as'–kee"), which has become extremely popular. This code uses bit patterns of length seven to represent the upper- and lowercase letters of the English alphabet, punctuation symbols, the digits 0 through 9, and certain control information such as line feeds, carriage returns, and tabs. Today, ASCII is often extended to an eight-bit-per-symbol format by adding a 0 at the most significant end of each of the seven-bit patterns. This technique not only produces a code in which each pattern fits conveniently into a typical byte-size memory cell but also provides 128 additional bit patterns (those obtained by assigning the extra bit the value 1) that can represent symbols excluded in the original ASCII. Unfortunately, because vendors tend to use their own interpretations for these extra patterns, data in which these patterns appear are often not easily transported from one vendor's application to another.

THE AMERICAN NATIONAL STANDARDS INSTITUTE

The American National Standards Institute (ANSI) was founded in 1918 by a small consortium of engineering societies and government agencies as a nonprofit federation to coordinate the development of voluntary standards in the private sector. Today, ANSI membership includes more than 1300 businesses, professional organizations, trade associations, and government agencies. ANSI is headquartered in New York and represents the United States as a member body in the ISO. The Web site for the American National Standards Institute is at http://www.ansi.org

Similar organizations in other countries include Standards Australia (Australia), Standards Council of Canada (Canada), China State Bureau of Quality and Technical Supervision (China), Deutsches Institur für Normung (Germany), Japanese Industrial Standards Committee (Japan), Dirección General de Normas (Mexico), State Committee of the Russian Federation for Standardization and Metrology (Russia), Swiss Association for Standardization (Switzerland), and British Standards Institution (United Kingdom).

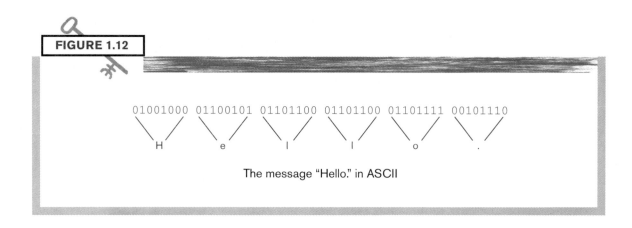

01001000 01100101 01101100 01101100 01101111 00101110

H   e   l   l   o   .

The message "Hello." in ASCII

Appendix A shows a portion of ASCII in an eight-bit-per-symbol format, and Figure 1.12 demonstrates that, in this system, the bit pattern

```
01001000 01100101 01101100
01101100 01101111 00101110
```

represents "Hello."

Although ACSII is the most common code used today, other more extensive codes, capable of representing documents in a variety of languages, are gaining in popularity. One of these, **Unicode,** was developed through the cooperation of several of the leading manufacturers of hardware and software. This code uses a unique pattern of 16 bits to represent each symbol. As a result, Unicode consists of 65,536 different bit patterns—enough to allow the most common Chinese and Japanese symbols to be repre-

THE INTERNATIONAL ORGANIZATION FOR STANDARDIZATION

The International Organization for Standardization (ISO) was established in 1947 as a worldwide federation of standardization bodies, one from each country. Today, it is headquartered in Geneva, Switzerland and has more than 100 member bodies as well as numerous correspondent members. (A correspondent member is usually a standardization body from a country that does not have a nationally recognized standardization body. Such members cannot participate directly in the development of standards but are kept informed of ISO activities.) ISO maintains a Web site at http://www.iso.ch

sented. A code that will probably compete with Unicode is being developed by the **International Organization for Standardization** (also known as **ISO,** in reference to the Greek word *isos,* meaning equal). Using patterns of 32 bits to represent symbols, this code has the potential of representing more than 17 million symbols. Which of these codes will ultimately win the vote of popularity remains to be seen.

Representing Numeric Values

Although the method of storing information as coded characters is quite useful, it is inefficient when the information being recorded is purely numeric. To see why, suppose we want to store the number 25. If we insist on storing it as coded symbols in ASCII using one byte per symbol, we need a total of 16 bits. Moreover, the largest number we can store using 16 bits is 99. A more efficient approach is to store the value in its base two, or binary, representation.

Binary notation is a way of representing numeric values using only the digits 0 and 1 rather than the digits 0, 1, 2, 3, 4, 5, 6, 7, 8, and 9 as in the traditional decimal, or base ten, system. Recall that in the base ten system, each position in a representation is associated with a quantity. In the representation 375, the 5 is in the position associated with the quantity one, the 7 is in the position associated with ten, and the 3 is in the position associated with the quantity one hundred (Figure 1.13). Each quantity is ten times that of the quantity to its right. The value represented by the entire expression is obtained by multiplying the value of each digit by the quantity associated with that digit's position and then adding those products. To illustrate, the pattern 375 represents (3 × hundred) + (7 × ten) + (5 × one).

The position of each digit in binary notation is also associated with a quantity, except that the quantity associated with each position is twice the quantity associated with the position to its right. More precisely, the rightmost digit in a binary representation is associated with the quantity one (2^0), the next position to the left is associated with two (2^1), the next is associated with four (2^2), the next with eight (2^3), and so on. For example, in the binary representation 1011, the rightmost 1 is in the position associated with the quantity one, the 1 next to

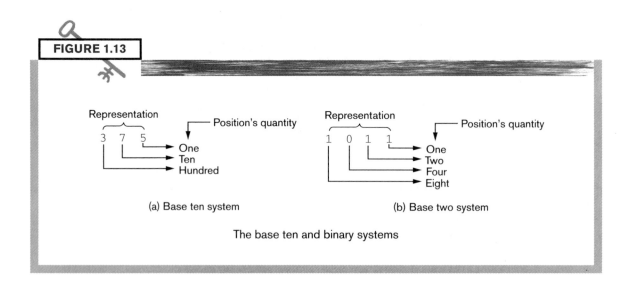

FIGURE 1.13

Representation   Position's quantity
3   7   5
          → One
          → Ten
          → Hundred

(a) Base ten system

Representation   Position's quantity
1   0   1   1
              → One
              → Two
              → Four
              → Eight

(b) Base two system

The base ten and binary systems

it is in the position associated with two, the 0 is in the position associated with four, and the leftmost 1 is in the position associated with eight (Figure 1.13b).

To extract the value represented by a binary representation, we follow the same procedure as in base ten—we multiply the value of each digit by the quantity associated with its position and add the results. For example, the value represented by 100101 is 37, as shown in Figure 1.14. Note that since binary notation uses only the digits 0 and 1, this multiply-and-add process reduces merely to adding the quantities associated with the positions occupied by 1s. Thus the binary pattern 1011 represents the value eleven, because the 1s are found in the positions associated with the quantities one, two, and eight.

Note that the sequence of binary representations obtained by counting from zero to eight is the following:

0

1

10

11

100

101

110

111

1000

FIGURE 1.14

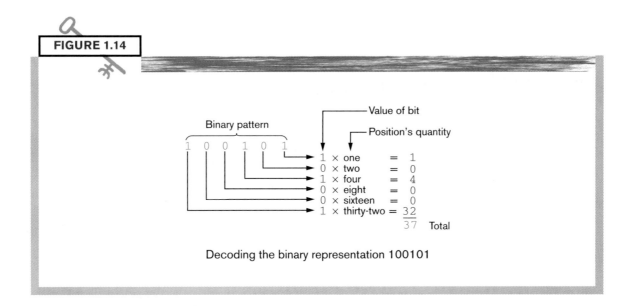

Decoding the binary representation 100101

ALTERNATIVES TO THE BINARY SYSTEM

Early computers did not take advantage of the binary notational system. In fact, the manner in which numeric values should be represented in computing machines was a subject of active debate in the late 1930s and throughout the 1940s. One candidate was the bi-quinary system in which each digit in the base ten representation of a number was replaced by two digits—one having the value of 0, 1, 2, 3, or 4, the other being either 0 or 5—so that the sum equaled the associated base ten digit. This was the system used in the ENIAC. Another candidate was base eight notation. In the paper "Binary Calculation" that appeared in the *Journal of the Institute of Actuaries* in 1936, E. W. Phillips wrote, "The ultimate aim is to persuade the whole civilized world to abandon decimal numeration and to use octonal numeration in its place; to discontinue counting in tens and to count in eights instead."

There are numerous approaches to generating this sequence, and although not elegant in theoretical content, they do provide a quick way of obtaining the binary representation for small values. One approach is to imagine a car's odometer whose display wheels contain only the digits 0 and 1. The odometer starts at 0 and rotates to a 1 as the car is driven. Then, as that 1 rotates back to a 0, it causes a 1 to appear to its left, producing the pattern 10. The 0 on the right then rotates to a 1, producing 11. Now the rightmost 1 rotates back to 0, causing the 1 to its left to rotate to a 0 as well. This in turn causes another 1 to appear in the third column, producing the pattern 100.

For finding binary representations of large values, you may prefer the more systematic approach described by the algorithm in Figure 1.15. Let us apply this algorithm to the value thirteen (Figure 1.16). We first divide thirteen by two, obtaining a quotient of six and a remainder of one. Since the quotient was not zero, Step 2 tells us to divide the

FIGURE 1.15

Step 1. Divide the value by two and record the remainder.

Step 2. As long as the quotient obtained is not zero, continue to divide the newest quotient by two and record the remainder.

Step 3. Now that a quotient of zero has been obtained, the binary representation of the original value consists of the remainders listed from right to left in the order they were recorded.

An algorithm for finding the binary representation of a positive integer

FIGURE 1.16

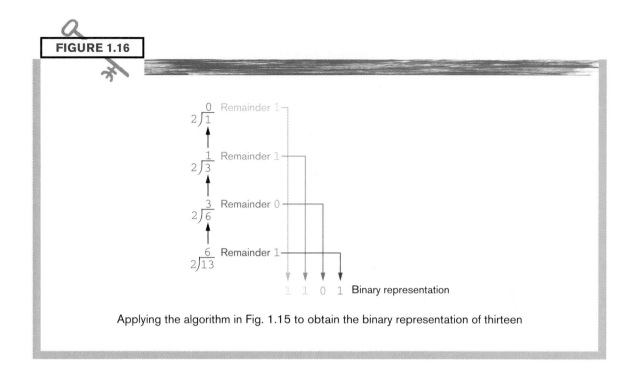

Applying the algorithm in Fig. 1.15 to obtain the binary representation of thirteen

quotient (six) by two, obtaining a new quotient of three and a remainder of zero. The newest quotient is still not zero, so we divide it by two, obtaining a quotient of one and a remainder of one. Once again, we divide the newest quotient (one) by two, this time obtaining a quotient of zero and a remainder of one. Since we have now acquired a quotient of zero, we move on to Step 3, where we learn that the binary representation of the original value (thirteen) is 1101.

Now recall our original problem of storing numeric data. Using binary notation, in one byte we can store any integer between 0 and 255 (00000000 to 11111111), and given two bytes, we can store the integers from 0 to 65535. This is a drastic improvement over the ability to store only the integers from 0 to 99 when coding characters using one ASCII pattern per byte.

For this and other reasons, it is common to store numeric information in a form of binary notation rather than in coded symbols. We say "a form of binary notation" because, the straightforward binary system just described is only the basis for several numeric storage techniques used within machines. Some of these variations of the binary system are discussed later in this chapter. For now, we merely note that a system called two's complement notation is common for storing whole numbers because it provides a convenient method for representing negative numbers as well as positive. For representing numbers with fractional parts such as 4 ½ or ¾, another technique, called floating-point notation, is used. Thus, a particular value (such as 25) may be represented by several different bit patterns (coded characters, two's complement notation, or in floating-point notation as 25 ½); conversely, a particular bit pattern may be given several interpretations.

At this point, we should mention a significant problem with numeric storage systems that we deal with in more depth later. Regardless of the pattern size that a machine might allocate for the storage of numeric values, there will still be values too large or fractions too small to be stored in the space allotted. The result is the constant potential for errors such as overflow (values too large) and truncation (fractions too small) that must be dealt with, or an unsuspecting computer user can soon be faced with a multitude of erroneous data.

Representing Images

Today's computer applications involve more than just text and numeric data. They include pictures, audio, and video. In comparison to character and numeric storage systems, the techniques for representing data of these additional forms are in their infancy and consequently are not as standardized across the data processing community.

Popular techniques for representing images can be classified into two categories: **bit map techniques** and **vector techniques.** In the case of bit map techniques, an image is considered to be a collection of dots, each of which is called a **pixel,** short for "picture element." In its simplest form, an image is represented as a long string of bits representing the rows of pixels in the image, where each bit is either 1 or 0 depending on whether the corresponding pixel is black or white. Color images are only slightly more complicated, since each pixel can be represented by a combination of bits indicating the color of that pixel. When bit map techniques are used, the resulting bit pattern is often called a bit map, meaning that the bit pattern is little more than a map of the image being represented.

Many of today's computer peripherals, such as facsimile machines, video cameras, and scanners, convert color images into bit map form. These devices generally record the color of each pixel as three components—a red component, a green component, and a blue component—corresponding to the three primary colors. One byte is typically used to represent the intensity of each color component. In turn, three bytes of storage are required to represent a single pixel in the original image.

This three-component-per-pixel approach also corresponds to the way in which today's computer screens display images. These devices display a myriad of pixels, each consisting of three components—one red, one green, and one blue—as is readily apparent via close inspection of the screen. (You might prefer to use a magnifying glass.)

The three-byte-per-pixel format means that an image consisting of 1280 rows of 1024 pixels (a typical photograph) requires several megabytes of storage, which exceeds the capacity of a typical floppy disk. In Section 1.8, we will consider two popular techniques (GIF and JPEG) that are used to compress such images into more manageable sizes.

One disadvantage of bit map techniques is that an image cannot be easily rescaled to any arbitrary size. Essentially, the only way to enlarge the image is to make the pixels bigger, which leads to a grainy appearance—a phenomenon that also occurs in film-based photography. Vector techniques provide a means of overcoming this scaling problem of bit map images. In such systems, an image is represented as a collection of lines and curves. Such a description leaves the details of how the lines and curves are drawn to the device that ultimately produces the image rather than insisting that the device reproduce a particular pixel pattern. The various fonts available on today's printers and monitors are usually represented in this manner to provide flexibility in character size, resulting in **scalable fonts.** For example, TrueType (developed by Microsoft and Apple Computer) is a system for describing how symbols in text are to be drawn. Likewise, PostScript (developed by Adobe Systems) provides a means of describing characters as well as more general pictorial data. Vector representations are also popular in computer-aided design (CAD) systems in which line drawings of three-dimensional objects are displayed and manipulated on computer screens. However, vector techniques are not able to provide the photographic quality images that are available via bit maps. This is why bit map techniques are used in today's digital cameras.

QUESTIONS/EXERCISES

1. Here is a message coded in ASCII using eight bits per symbol. What does it say?

   01000011 01101111 01101101 01110000 01110101 01110100
   01100101 01110010 00100000 01010011 01100011 01101001
   01100101 01101110 01100011 01100101

2. In the ASCII code, what is the relationship between the codes for an uppercase letter and the same letter in lowercase?
3. Code these sentences in ASCII:
   a. Where are you?
   b. "How?" Cheryl asked.
   c. 2 + 3 = 5.
4. Describe a device from everyday life that can be in either of two states, such as a flag on a flagpole that is either up or down. Assign the symbol 1 to one of the states and 0 to the other, and show how the ASCII representation for the letter b would appear when stored with such bits.

5. Convert each of the following binary representations to its equivalent base ten form:

a. 0101　　b. 1001　　c. 1011　　d. 0110

e. 10000　　f. 10010

6. Convert each of the following base ten representations to its equivalent binary form:

a. 6　　b. 13　　c. 11　　d. 18

e. 27　　f. 4

7. What is the largest numeric value that could be represented with three bytes if each digit were coded using one ASCII pattern per byte? What if binary notation were used?

8. An alternative to hexadecimal notation for representing bit patterns is *dotted decimal notation* in which each byte in the pattern is represented by its base ten equivalent. In turn, these byte representations are separated by periods. For example, 12.5 represents the pattern 0000110000000101 (the byte 00001100 is represented by 12, and 00000101 is represented by 5), and the pattern 1000100000100000000111 is represented by 136.16.7. Represent each of the following bit patterns in dotted decimal notation.

a. 0000111100001111　　　　b. 0011001100000000010000000

c. 0000101010100000

1.5 The Binary System

Before pursuing the numeric storage techniques used in today's machines, we need a few more details about the binary representation system.

Binary Addition

To add two values represented in binary notation, we begin, just as we did with base ten in elementary school, by memorizing the addition facts (Figure 1.17). These facts are used to add two strings of decimal digits. That is, add the digits in the right-hand column, write the least significant digit of this sum under the column, carry the more significant digit of the sum (if there is one) to the next column to the left, and proceed by adding that column. To solve the problem

```
 00111010
+00011011
```

we begin by adding the rightmost 0 and 1; we obtain 1, which we write below the column. Now we add the 1 and 1 from the next column, obtaining 10. We

FIGURE 1.17

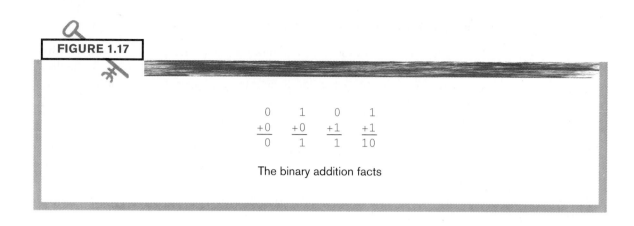

$$
\begin{array}{cccc}
0 & 1 & 0 & 1 \\
\underline{+0} & \underline{+0} & \underline{+1} & \underline{+1} \\
0 & 1 & 1 & 10
\end{array}
$$

The binary addition facts

write the 0 from this 10 under the column and carry the 1 to the top of the next column. At this point, our solution looks like this:

```
        1
  00111010
+ 00011011
        01
```

We add the 1, 0, and 0 in the next column, obtain 1, and write the 1 under this column. The 1 and 1 from the next column total 10; we write the 0 under the column and carry the 1 to the next column. Now our solution looks like this:

```
       1
  00111010
+ 00011011
      0101
```

The 1, 1, and 1 in the next column total 11; we write the low-order 1 under the column and carry the other 1 to the top of the next column. We add that 1 to the 1 and 0 already in that column to obtain 10. Again, we record the low-order 0 and carry the 1 to the next column. We now have

```
      1
  00111010
+ 00011011
    010101
```

Now we add the 1, 0, and 0 from the next to the last column, obtaining 1, which we record below the column with nothing to carry. Finally, we add the last column, which yields 0, and record this under the column. Our final solution is this:

```
  00111010
+ 00011011
  01010101
```

Fractions in Binary

To extend binary notation to accommodate fractional values, we use a **radix point** in the same role as the decimal point in decimal notation. That is, the digits to the left of the point represent the integer part of the value and are interpreted as in the binary system discussed previously. The digits to its right represent the fractional part of the value and are interpreted in a manner similar to the other bits, except their positions are assigned fractional quantities. That is, the first position to the right of the radix is assigned the quantity $\frac{1}{2}$, the next position the quantity $\frac{1}{4}$, the next $\frac{1}{8}$, and so on. Note that this is merely a continuation of the rule stated previously: Each position is assigned a quantity twice the size of the one to its right. With these quantities assigned to the bit positions, decoding a binary representation containing a radix point requires the same procedure as used without a radix point. In particular, we multiply each bit value by the quantity assigned to that bit's position in the representation. To illustrate, the binary representation 101.101 decodes to $5\frac{5}{8}$, as shown in Figure 1.18.

For addition, the techniques applied in the base ten system are also applicable in binary. That is, to add two binary representations having radix points, we merely align the radix points and apply the same addition process as before. For example, 10.011 added to 100.11 produces 111.001, as shown here:

```
  10.011
+100.11
 111.001
```

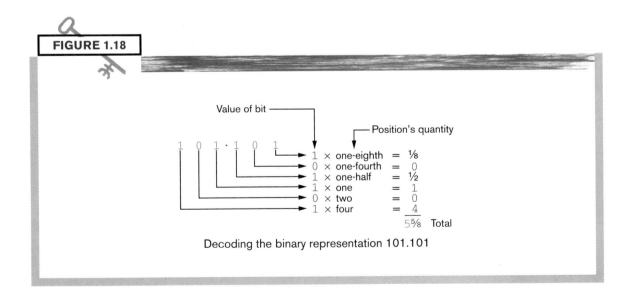

FIGURE 1.18

Decoding the binary representation 101.101

QUESTIONS/EXERCISES

1. Convert each of the following binary representations to its equivalent base ten form:
   a. 101010   b. 100001   c. 10111   d. 0110
   e. 11111

2. Convert each of the following base ten representations to its equivalent binary form:
   a. 32   b. 64   c. 96   d. 15   e. 27

3. Convert each of the following binary representations to its equivalent base ten form:
   a. 11.01   b. 101.111   c. 10.1   d. 110.011
   e. 0.101

4. Express the following values in binary notation:
   a. $4\frac{1}{2}$ b. $2\frac{3}{4}$ c. $1\frac{1}{8}$ d. $\frac{5}{16}$ e. $5\frac{5}{8}$

5. Perform the following additions in binary notation:

   a. 11011
      +1100

   b. 1010.001
      +1.101

   c. 11111
      +   1

   d. 111.11
      +   .01

1.6 Storing Integers

Mathematicians have long been interested in numeric notational systems, and many of their ideas have turned out to be very compatible with the design of digital circuitry. In this section we consider two of these notational systems, two's complement notation and excess notation, that are used for representing integer values in computing equipment. These systems are based on the binary system presented in Section 1.5 but have additional properties that make them more compatible with computer design. With these advantages, however, come disadvantages as well. Our goal is to understand these properties and how they affect computer usage.

Two's Complement Notation

The most popular system for representing integers within today's computers is **two's complement notation.** This system uses a fixed number of bits to represent each of the values in the system. In today's equipment, it is common to use a two's complement system in which each value is represented by a pattern of 32 bits. Such a large system allows a wide range of numbers to be represented but is awkward for demonstration purposes. Thus, to study the properties of two's complement systems, we will concentrate on smaller systems.

FIGURE 1.19

(a) Using patterns of length three		(b) Using patterns of length four	
Bit pattern	Value represented	Bit pattern	Value represented
011	3	0111	7
010	2	0110	6
001	1	0101	5
000	0	0100	4
111	−1	0011	3
110	−2	0010	2
101	−3	0001	1
100	−4	0000	0
		1111	−1
		1110	−2
		1101	−3
		1100	−4
		1011	−5
		1010	−6
		1001	−7
		1000	−8

Two's complement notation systems

Figure 1.19 shows two complete two's complement systems—one based on bit patterns of length three, the other based on bit patterns of length four. Such a system is constructed by starting with a string of 0s of the appropriate length and then counting in binary until the pattern consisting of a 0 followed by 1s is reached. These patterns represent the values 0, 1, 2, 3, …. The patterns representing negative values are obtained by starting with a string of 1s of the appropriate length and then counting backward in binary until the pattern consisting of a 1 followed by 0s is reached. These patterns represent the values −1, −2, −3, …. (If counting backward in binary is difficult for you, merely start at the very bottom of the table with the pattern consisting of a 1 followed by 0s, and count up to the pattern consisting of all 1s.)

Note that in a two's complement system, the leftmost bit of a bit pattern indicates the sign of the value represented. Thus, the leftmost bit is often called the **sign bit.** In a two's complement system, negative values are represented by the patterns whose sign bits are 1; nonnegative values are represented by patterns whose sign bits are 0.

In a two's complement system, there is a convenient relationship between the patterns representing positive and negative values of the same magnitude. They are identical when read from right to left, up to and including the first 1. From there on, the patterns are complements of one another. (The **complement** of a pattern is the pattern obtained by changing all the 0s to 1s and all the 1s to 0s; 0110 and 1001 are complements.) For example, in the four-bit system in Figure 1.19 the patterns representing 2 and −2 both end with 10, but the pattern representing 2 begins with 00, whereas the representing −2 begins with 11. This observation leads to an algorithm for converting back and forth between bit patterns representing positive and negative values of the same magnitude. We merely copy the original pattern from right to left until a 1 has been copied, then we complement the remaining bits as they are copied (Figure 1.20).

Understanding these basic properties of two's complement systems also leads to an algorithm for decoding two's complement representations. If the pattern to be decoded has a sign bit of 0, we need merely read the value as though the pattern were a binary representation. For example, 0110 represents the value 6, because 110 is binary for 6. If the pattern to be decoded has a sign bit of 1, we know the value represented is negative and all that remains is to find the magnitude of the value. We do this by copying the original pattern from

FIGURE 1.20

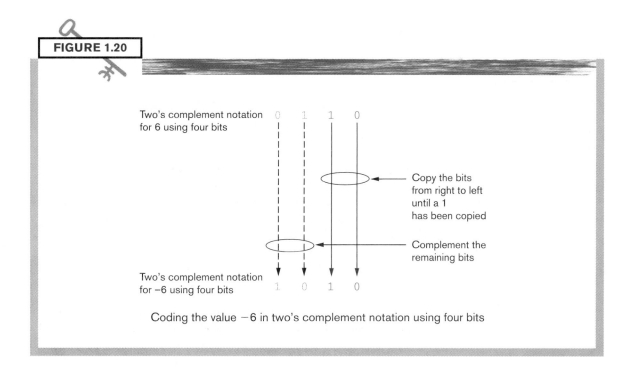

Two's complement notation for 6 using four bits   0   1   1   0

Copy the bits from right to left until a 1 has been copied

Complement the remaining bits

Two's complement notation for −6 using four bits   1   0   1   0

Coding the value −6 in two's complement notation using four bits

right to left until a 1 has been copied, then complementing the remaining bits as they are copied, and finally decoding the pattern obtained as though it were a binary representation.

For example, to decode the pattern 1010, we first recognize that since the sign bit is 1, the value represented is negative. Hence, we convert the pattern to 0110, recognize that this represents 6, and conclude that the original pattern represents −6.

Addition in Two's Complement Notation   To add values represented in two's complement notation, we apply the same algorithm that we used for binary addition, except that all bit patterns, including the answer, are the same length. This means that when adding in a two's complement system, any extra bit generated on the left of the answer by a final carry must be truncated. Thus "adding" 0101 and 0010 produces 0111, and "adding" 0111 and 1011 results in 0010 (0111 + 1011 = 10010, which is truncated to 0010).

With this understanding, consider the three addition problems in Figure 1.21. In each case, we have translated the problem into two's complement notation (using bit patterns of length four), performed the addition process previously described, and decoded the result back into our usual base ten notation.

Observe that if we were to use the traditional techniques taught in elementary school, the third problem would require an entirely different process (subtraction) than the previous problems. On the other hand, by translating the problems into two's complement notation, we can compute the answer in all

FIGURE 1.21

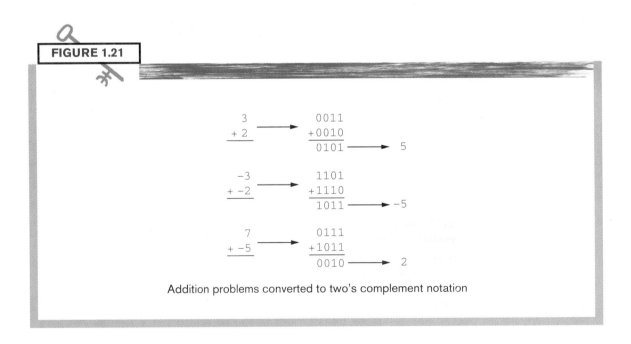

Addition problems converted to two's complement notation

cases by applying the same addition algorithm. This is a major benefit of two's complement notation: Addition of any combination of signed numbers can be accomplished using the same algorithm.

In contrast to elementary schoolchildren, who must first learn to add and later to subtract, a machine using two's complement notation needs to know only how to add and negate. For example, the subtraction problem $7 - 5$ is the same as the addition problem $7 + (-5)$. Consequently, if a machine were asked to subtract 5 (stored as 0101) from 7 (stored as 0111), it would first change the 5 to -5 (represented as 1011) and then perform the addition process of 0111 + 1011 to obtain 0010, which represents 2, as follows:

$$
\begin{array}{c}
7 \\
\underline{-5}
\end{array}
\rightarrow
\begin{array}{c}
0111 \\
\underline{-0101}
\end{array}
\rightarrow
\begin{array}{c}
0111 \\
\underline{+1011} \\
0010 \rightarrow 2
\end{array}
$$

We see, then, that when two's complement notation is used to represent numeric values, a circuit for addition combined with a circuit for negating a value is sufficient for solving both addition and subtraction problems. (Such circuits are shown and explained in Appendix B.)

The Problem of Overflow   One problem we have avoided in the preceding examples is that in any of the numeric systems we have introduced, there is a limit to the size of the values that can be represented. When using two's complement with patterns of four bits, the value 9 has no pattern associated with it—which means that we cannot hope to obtain the correct answer to the problem 5 + 4. In fact, the result would appear as -7. Such an error is called **overflow,** the problem that occurs when the value to be represented falls outside the range of values that can be represented. When using two's complement notation, this might occur when adding two positive values or when adding two negative values. In either case, the condition can be detected by checking the sign bit of the answer. That is, an overflow is indicated if the addition of two positive values results in the pattern for a negative value or if the sum of two negative values appears to be positive.

Of course, because most machines manipulate longer bit patterns than we have used in our examples, larger values can be manipulated without causing an overflow. Today, it is common to use patterns of 32 bits for storing values in two's complement notation, allowing for positive values as large as 2,147,483,647 to accumulate before overflow occurs. If still larger values are needed, longer bit patterns can be used or perhaps the units of measure can be changed. For instance, finding a solution in terms of miles instead of inches results in smaller numbers being used and may still provide the accuracy required.

The point is that computers can make mistakes. So, the person using the machine must be aware of the dangers involved. One problem is that computer programmers and users become complacent and ignore the fact that small values can accumulate to produce large numbers. For example, in the past it was common to use patterns of 16 bits for representing values in two's complement notation, which meant that overflow would not occur until the value 2^{15} = 32,768 was reached. On September 19, 1989 a hospital computer system malfunctioned after years of reliable service. Close inspection revealed that this date was 32,768 days after January 1, 1900. What do you think the problem turned out to be?

Excess Notation

Another method of representing integer values is **excess notation.** Each of the values in an excess notation system is represented by a bit pattern of the same length. To establish an excess system, we first select the pattern length to be used, then write down all the different bit patterns of that length in the order they would appear if we were counting in binary. Next, we observe that the first pattern with a 1 as its most significant bit appears approximately halfway through the list. We pick this pattern to represent zero; the patterns following this are used to represent 1, 2, 3, ...; and the patterns preceding it are used for −1, −2, −3, ...The resulting code, when using patterns of length four, is shown in Figure 1.22. There we see that the value 5 is represented by the pat-

FIGURE 1.22

Bit pattern	Value represented
1111	7
1110	6
1101	5
1100	4
1011	3
1010	2
1001	1
1000	0
0111	−1
0110	−2
0101	−3
0100	−4
0011	−5
0010	−6
0001	−7
0000	−8

An excess eight conversion table

FIGURE 1.23

Bit pattern	Value represented
111	3
110	2
101	1
100	0
011	−1
010	−2
001	−3
000	−4

An excess notation system using bit patterns of length three

tern 1101 and −5 is represented by 0011. (Note that the difference between an excess system and a two's complement system is that the sign bits are reversed.)

The system represented in Figure 1.22 is known as excess eight notation. To understand why, first interpret each of the patterns in the code using the traditional binary system and then compare these results to the values represented in the excess notation. In each case, you will find that the binary interpretation exceeds the excess notation interpretation by the value 8. For example, the pattern 1100 normally represents the value 12, but in our excess system it represents 4; 0000 normally represents 0, but in the excess system it represents −8. In a similar manner, an excess system based on patterns of length five would be called excess 16 notation, because the pattern 10000, for instance, would be used to represent 0 rather than representing its usual value of 16. Likewise, you may want to confirm that the three-bit excess system would be known as excess four notation (Figure 1.23).

QUESTIONS/EXERCISES

1. Convert each of the following two's complement representations to its equivalent base ten form:
   - a. 00011
   - b. 01111
   - c. 11100
   - d. 11010
   - e. 00000
   - f. 10000

2. Convert each of the following base ten representations to its equivalent two's complement form using patterns of eight bits:

   a. 6   b. 26   c. 217   d. 13   e. 21   f. 0

3. Suppose the following bit patterns represent values stored in two's complement notation. Find the two's complement representation of the negative of each value:

   a.   00000001   b.   01010101   c.   11111100
   d.   11111110   e.   00000000   f.   01111111

4. Suppose a machine stores numbers in two's complement notation. What are the largest and smallest numbers that could be stored if the machine uses bit patterns of the following lengths?

   a.   four   b. six   c. eight

5. In the following problems, each bit pattern represents a value stored in two's complement notation. Find the answer to each problem in two's complement notation by performing the addition process described in the text. Then check your work by translating the problem and your answer into base ten notation.

   a.   0101   b.   0011   c.   0101   d.   1110   e.   1010
       +0010   +0001   +1010   +0011   +1110

6. Solve each of the following problems in two's complement notation, but this time watch for overflow and indicate which answers are incorrect because of this phenomenon.

   a.   0100   b.   0101   c.   1010   d.   1010   e.   0111
       +0011   +0110   +1010   +0111   +0001

7. Translate each of the following problems from base ten notation into two's complement notation using bit patterns of length four, then convert each problem to an equivalent addition problem (as a machine might do), and perform the addition. Check your answers by converting them back to base ten notation.

   a.   6   b.   3   c.   4   d. 2   e.   1
       +1   -2   -6   +4   -5

8. Can overflow ever occur when adding values in two's complement notation when one value is positive and the other is negative? Explain your answer.

9. Convert each of the following excess eight representations to its equivalent base ten form without referring to the table in the text:

   a.   1110   b.   0111   c.   1000
   d.   0010   e.   0000   f.   1001

10. Convert each of the following base ten representations to its equivalent excess eight form without referring to the table in the text:

    a. 5   b. −5   c. 3   d. 0   e. 7   f. −8

11. Can the value 9 be represented in excess eight notation? What about representing 6 in excess four notation? Explain your answer.

1.7 Storing Fractions

In contrast to the storage of integers, the storage of a value with a fractional part requires that we store not only the pattern of 0s and 1s representing its binary representation but also the position of the radix point. A popular way of doing this is based on scientific notation and is called **floating-point notation.**

Floating-Point Notation

Let us explain floating-point notation with an example using only one byte of storage. Although machines normally use much longer patterns, this eight-bit format is representative of actual systems and serves to demonstrate the important concepts without the clutter of long bit patterns.

We first designate the high-order bit of the byte as the sign bit. Once again, a 0 in the sign bit will mean that the value stored is nonnegative, and a 1 will mean that the value is negative. Next, we divide the remaining seven bits of the byte into two groups, or fields, the **exponent field** and the **mantissa field.** Let us designate the three bits following the sign bit as the exponent field and the remaining four bits as the mantissa field. Figure 1.24 illustrates how the byte is divided.

We can explain the meaning of the fields by considering the following example. Suppose a byte contains the bit pattern 01101011. Analyzing this pattern with the preceding format, we see that the sign bit is 0, the exponent is 110, and the mantissa is 1011. To decode the byte, we first extract the mantissa and place a radix point on its left side, obtaining

```
.1011
```

Next, we extract the contents of the exponent field (110) and interpret it as an integer stored using the three-bit excess method (see again Figure 1.20). Thus

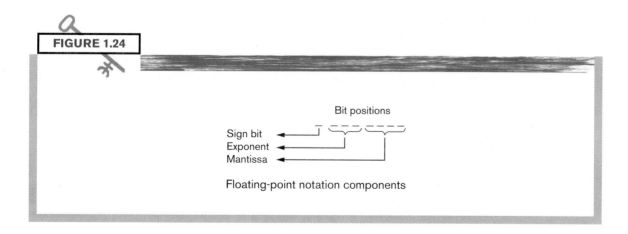

FIGURE 1.24

Bit positions

Sign bit

Exponent

Mantissa

Floating-point notation components

the pattern in the exponent field in our example represents a positive 2. This tells us to move the radix in our solution to the right by two bits. (A negative exponent would mean to move the radix to the left.) Consequently, we obtain

```
10.11
```

which is the binary representation for $2\frac{3}{4}$. Next, we note that the sign bit in our example is 0; the value represented is thus nonnegative. We conclude that the byte 01101011 represents $2\frac{3}{4}$.

As another example, consider the byte 10111100. We extract the mantissa to obtain

```
.1100
```

and move the radix one bit to the left, since the exponent field (011) represents the value -1. We therefore have

```
.01100
```

which represents $\frac{3}{8}$. Since the sign bit in the original pattern is 1, the value stored is negative. We conclude that the pattern 10111100 represents $-\frac{3}{8}$.

To store a value using floating-point notation, we reverse the preceding process. For example, to code $1\frac{1}{8}$, first we express it in binary notation and obtain 1.001. Next, we copy the bit pattern into the mantissa field from left to right, starting with the leftmost 1 in the binary representation. At this point, the byte looks like this:

```
_ _ _ _ 1 0 0 1
```

We must now fill in the exponent field. To this end, we imagine the contents of the mantissa field with a radix point at its left and determine the number of bits and the direction the radix must be moved to obtain the original binary number. In our example, we see that the radix in .1001 must be moved one bit to the right to obtain 1.001. The exponent should therefore be a positive 1 so we place 101 (which is positive 1 in excess four notation) in the exponent field. Finally, we fill the sign bit with 0 because the value being stored is nonnegative. The finished byte looks like this:

```
0 1 0 1 1 0 0 1
```

There is a subtle point you may have missed when filling in the mantissa field. The rule is to copy the bit pattern appearing in the binary representation from left to right, starting with the leftmost 1. To clarify, consider the process of storing the value $\frac{3}{8}$, which is .011 in binary notation. In this case the mantissa will be

```
_ _ _ _ 1 1 0 0
```

It will not be

```
_ _ _ _ 0 1 1 0
```

This is because we fill in the mantissa field *starting with the leftmost 1* that appears in the binary representation. This rule eliminates the possibility of multiple representations for the same value. It also means that the representation for all nonzero values will have a mantissa that starts with 1. This representation is said to be in **normalized form.** Note that the value zero must be a special case; its floating-point representation is a bit pattern of all 0s.

Truncation Errors

Let us consider the annoying problem that occurs if we try to store the value $2\frac{5}{8}$ with our one-byte floating-point system. We first write $2\frac{5}{8}$ in binary, which gives us 10.101. But when we copy this into the mantissa field, we run out of room, and the rightmost 1 (which represents the last $\frac{1}{8}$) is lost (Figure 1.25). If we ignore this problem for now and continue by filling in the exponent field and the sign bit, we end up with the bit pattern 01101010, which represents $2\frac{1}{2}$ instead of $2\frac{5}{8}$. What has occurred is called a **truncation error,** or **round-off error**—meaning that part of the value being stored is lost because the mantissa field is not large enough.

The significance of such errors can be reduced by using a longer mantissa field. As with integer storage, it is common to use at least 32 bits for storing values in floating-point notation instead of the eight we have used here. This approach also allows for a longer exponent field at the same time. Even with these longer formats, however, there are still times when more accuracy is required.

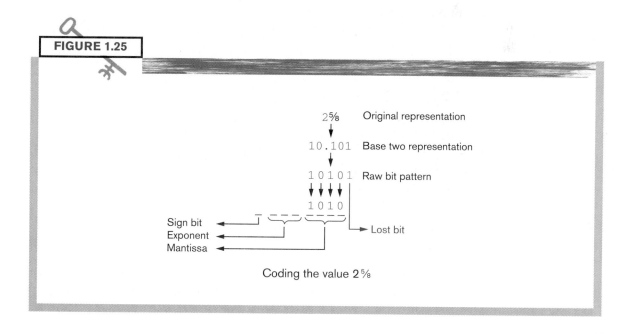

FIGURE 1.25

$2\frac{5}{8}$ Original representation

10.101   Base two representation

1 0 1 0 1   Raw bit pattern

1 0 1 0

Sign bit
Exponent
Mantissa

Lost bit

Coding the value $2\frac{5}{8}$

ANALOG VERSUS DIGITAL

A debate in the early days of computers was whether computing devices should be based on digital or analog technology. In a digital system, values are represented in terms of a limited number of distinct digits (such as 0 and 1). In an analog system, each value is represented by a single device that can hold any value within a continuous range.

Let us compare the two approaches in terms of buckets of water. To simulate a digital system, we could agree to let an empty bucket represent the digit 0 and a full bucket represent the digit 1. Then we could store a numeric value in a row of buckets using floating-point notation. In contrast, we could simulate an analog system by partially filling a single bucket to the point at which the water level agreed with the numeric value being represented. At first glance, the analog system may appear to be more accurate since it would not suffer from the truncation errors inherent in the digital system. However, any movement of the bucket in the analog system could cause errors in detecting the water level, whereas a significant amount of sloshing would have to occur in the digital system before the distinction between a full bucket and an empty bucket would be blurred. Thus, the digital system would be less sensitive to error than the analog system. This robustness is a major reason that many applications that were originally based on analog technology (such as telephone communication, audio recordings, and television) are shifting to digital technology.

Another source of truncation errors is a phenomenon that you are already accustomed to in base ten notation: the problem of nonterminating expansions, such as those found when trying to express $\frac{1}{3}$ in decimal form. Some values cannot be accurately expressed regardless of how many digits we use.

The difference between our normal base ten notation and binary notation is that more values have nonterminating representations in binary than in decimal notation. For example, the value one-tenth is nonterminating when expressed in binary. Imagine the problems this might cause the unwary person using floating-point notation to store and manipulate dollars and cents. In particular, if the dollar is used as the unit of measure, the value of a dime could not be stored accurately. A solution in this case is to manipulate the data in units of pennies so that all values are integers that can be accurately stored using a method such as two's complement.

Truncation errors and their related problems are an everyday concern for people working in the area of numerical analysis. This branch of mathematics deals with the problems involved when doing actual computations that are often massive and require significant accuracy.

The following is an example that would warm the heart of any numerical analyst. Suppose we are asked to add the following three values using our one-byte floating-point notation defined previously:

$$2\tfrac{1}{2} + \tfrac{1}{8} + \tfrac{1}{8}$$

If we add the values in the order listed, we first add $2\tfrac{1}{2}$ to $\tfrac{1}{8}$ and obtain $2\tfrac{5}{8}$, which in binary is 10.101. Unfortunately, because this value cannot be stored accurately (as seen previously), the result of our first step ends up being stored as $2\tfrac{1}{2}$ (which is the same as one of the values we were adding). The next step is to add this result to the last $\tfrac{1}{8}$. Here again a truncation error occurs, and our final result turns out to be the incorrect answer $2\tfrac{1}{2}$.

Now let us add the values in the opposite order. We first add $\frac{1}{8}$ to $\frac{1}{8}$ to obtain $\frac{1}{4}$. In binary this is .01; so the result of our first step is stored in a byte as 00111000, which is accurate. We now add this $\frac{1}{4}$ to the next value in the list, $2\frac{1}{2}$, and obtain $2\frac{3}{4}$, which we can accurately store in a byte as 01101011. The result this time is the correct answer.

In summary, when adding values, the order in which they are added can be important. The problem is that if a very large number is added to a very small number, the small number may be truncated. Thus, the general rule for adding multiple values is to add the smaller values together first, in hopes that they will accumulate to a value that is significant when added to the larger values. This was the phenomenon experienced in the preceding example.

Designers of today's commercial software packages do a good job of shielding the uneducated user from problems such as this. In a typical spreadsheet system, correct answers will be obtained unless the values being added differ in size by a factor of 10^{16} or more. Thus, if you found it necessary to add one to the value

        10,000,000,000,000,000

you may get the answer

        10,000,000,000,000,000

rather than

        10,000,000,000,000,001

Such problems are much more significant in applications such as navigational systems in which minor errors can be compounded in additional computations and ultimately produce significant consequences.

QUESTIONS/EXERCISES

1. Decode the following bit patterns using the floating-point format discussed in the text:
   a. 01001010   b. 01101101   c. 00111001   d. 11011100
   e. 10101011
2. Code the following values into the floating-point format discussed in the text. Indicate the occurrence of truncation errors.
   a. $2\frac{3}{4}$ b. $5\frac{1}{4}$ c. $\frac{3}{4}$ d. $-3\frac{1}{2}$ e. $-4\frac{3}{8}$
3. In terms of the floating-point format discussed in the text, which of the patterns 01001001 and 00111101 represents the larger value? Describe a simple procedure for determining which of two patterns represents the larger value.
4. When using the floating-point format discussed in the text, what is the largest value that can be represented? What is the smallest positive value that can be represented?

1.8 Data Compression

For the purpose of storing or transferring data, it is often helpful (and some-times mandatory) to reduce the size of the data involved. The technique for accomplishing this is called **data compression.** We begin this section by consid-ering some generic data compression methods and then look at some approaches designed specifically for compressing images.

Generic Data Compression Techniques

Numerous data compression techniques have been developed, each with its own best-case and worst-case scenarios. The method called **run-length encod-ing** produces its best results when the data being compressed consist of long sequences of the same value. Indeed, run-length encoding is the process of replacing such sequences with a code indicating the value that is repeated and the number of times it occurs in the sequence. For example, less space is required to indicate that a bit pattern consists of 253 ones, followed by 118 zeros, followed by 87 ones than to actually list all 458 bits.

In some cases, the information involved consists of blocks of data, each of which differs slightly from the preceding one. An example would be consecu-tive frames of a motion picture. In these cases, techniques using **relative encod-ing** are helpful. Their approach is to record the differences between consecutive data blocks rather than entire blocks; that is, each block is coded in terms of its relationship to the previous block.

Another approach to reducing the size of data is to use **frequency-depen-dent encoding,** a system in which the length of the bit pattern used to repre-sent a data item is inversely related to the frequency of the item's use. Such codes are examples of variable length codes, meaning that items are represented by patterns of different lengths. In a frequency-dependent code for text in the English language, the more frequently used characters (*e, t, a,* and *i*) would be represented by short bit patterns, while the less frequently used letters (*z, q,* and *x*) would be represented by longer patterns. The result would be a shorter rep-resentation of the entire text than would be obtained by the use of a uniform length code such as ASCII or Unicode. David Huffman is credited with discov-ering an algorithm that is commonly used for developing frequency-dependent codes, and it is common practice to refer to codes developed in this manner as **Huffman codes.** In turn, most frequency-dependent codes in use today are Huffman codes.

Although we have introduced run-length encoding, relative encoding, and frequency-dependent encoding as generic compression techniques, each tends to have its own application realm. In contrast, systems based on **Lempel-Ziv encoding** (named after their creators, Abraham Lempel and Jacob Ziv) are more truly general-purpose compression systems. Indeed, users of the Internet (Chapter 3) have most likely seen, and perhaps used, programs such as zip and unzip, which use Lempel-Ziv techniques, to compress and decompress a variety of data.

Lempel-Ziv encoding systems are examples of **adaptive dictionary encoding.** Here the term *dictionary* refers to the collection of building blocks from which the message being compressed is constructed. If we wanted to compress text in the English language, the building blocks might be the alphabetic characters. If we wanted to compress data stored in a computer, the building blocks might be the digits 0 and 1. In an adaptive dictionary encoding system, the dictionary is allowed to change during the encoding process. For example, in the case of English text, after coding part of a message, we might decide to add *ing* and *the* to the dictionary. Then the space required by future copies of *ing* and *the* could be reduced by coding these patterns as single references to the dictionary rather than three references. Lempel-Ziv encoding systems apply clever and efficient ways to adapt the dictionary during the encoding (or compression) process. In particular, the dictionary at any point in the process consists of those patterns that have already been encoded (compressed).

As an example, let us consider how we could compress a message using the particular Lempel-Ziv system known as LZ77. We could start by actually quoting the initial part of the message, but at some point we would shift to representing future segments by triples, each consisting of two integers followed by a symbol from the message. Each triple would describe how to construct the next part of the message. For example, we were decompressing a message of the form

$$\alpha\beta\alpha\alpha\beta\rho\beta \; (5, 4, \alpha)$$

where we have represented the symbols in the message by Greek letters to avoid implying a particular context. The string $\alpha\beta\alpha\alpha\beta\rho\beta$ is the part of the message that is already decompressed. The first step in decompressing the rest of the message is to extend this string by appending a segment that already appears in the string (Figure 1.26). The first number of the triple tells us how far to count backward in the string to locate the segment to be appended. In our case, we count backward 5 symbols, which leads us to the second α from the left in the decompressed string. The second number in the triple tells us how many consecutive symbols to the right of this position make up the segment to be appended. In our case this number is 4, so the segment to be appended is $\alpha\alpha\beta\rho$. Thus, we copy this pattern at the end of the decompressed string to obtain

$$\alpha\beta\alpha\alpha\beta\rho\beta\alpha\alpha\beta\rho$$

Finally, the last entry in the triple should be placed at the end of the extended string. In our example, this symbol is α, so we complete the decompression process by adding this symbol to the end of the extended string. This produces

$$\alpha\beta\alpha\alpha\beta\rho\beta\alpha\alpha\beta\rho\alpha$$

FIGURE 1.26

α β α α β ρ β

(a) Count backward 5 symbols.

α β α α β ρ β

(b) Identify the 4-bit segment to be appended to
the end of the string.

α β α α β ρ β α α β ρ

(c) Copy the 4-bit segment onto the end of the message.

α β α α β ρ β α α β ρ α

(d) Add the symbol identified in the triple to the
end of the message.

Decompressing αβααβρβ (5, 4, α)

which is the decompressed message.

Now suppose the compressed version of the message was

αβααβρβ (5, 4, α) (0, 0, δ) (8, 6, β)

We would begin by decompressing the first triple as before to obtain

αβααβρβααβρα (0, 0, δ) (8, 6, β)

We would then decompress the second triple to obtain

αβααβρβααβραδ (8, 6, β)

Note that the triple (0, 0, δ) was used because the symbol δ had not yet appeared in the message. Finally, decompressing the third triple would produce the decompressed message

αβααβρβααβραδρβααβρβ

To compress a message using LZ77, we could first quote a beginning segment of the message and then search through the pattern quoted to find the longest segment that agrees with the remaining message to be compressed. This would be the pattern referenced in the first triple. Future triples would be formed by a similar process.

Finally, you may have noted that our examples do not reflect very much compression since the triples involved have represented only short segments. When applied to long bit patterns, however, it is reasonable that long segments will be represented by single triples—resulting in significant data compression.

Compressing Images

In Section 1.4, we saw that the bit map images produced by today's image digitizers tend to represent images in a three-byte-per-pixel format, which leads to large, unmanageable bit maps. Many compression schemes have been developed specifically to reduce these storage requirements. One system known a GIF (Graphic Interchange Format) was developed by CompuServe. It approaches the problem by reducing the number of colors that can be assigned to a pixel to only 256, which means that the value of each pixel can be represented in a single byte rather than requiring three. Each of the 256 potential pixel values is associated with a red-green-blue combination by means of a table known as the palette. By changing the palette associated with an image, we can change the colors appearing in the image.

One of the colors in a GIF image palette is normally assigned the value "transparent," which means that the background is allowed to show through any region assigned this "color." This option, combined with the relative simplicity of the GIF system, makes GIF a logical choice in computer action games in which multiple images move around on the screen.

Another compression system for color images is JPEG. It is a standard developed by the Joint Photographic Experts Group (hence the standard's name) within ISO. JPEG has proved to be an effective standard for representing color photographs. Indeed, it is the standard adopted by manufacturers of today's digital cameras and promises to have a major impact in the realm of digital imagery for years to come.

The JPEG standard actually encompasses several methods of image representation, each with its own goals. For example, in those situations that require the utmost in precision, JPEG provides a "lossless" mode whose name implies that no information is lost in the process of encoding the picture. In JPEG's lossless mode, space is saved by storing the difference between consecutive pixels rather than the pixel intensities themselves—the theory being that, in most cases, the amount by which adjacent pixels differ can be represented by shorter bit patterns than the values of the pixels. These differences are then coded using a variable-length code to further conserve storage space.

Unfortunately, the use of JPEG's lossless mode does not lead to bit maps with sizes that are manageable with today's technology and thus it is seldom used. Instead, most applications use JPEG's baseline standard. Here each pixel is again represented by three components, but these consist of a brightness component and two color components. Roughly speaking, if we were to look at only the brightness components, we would see a gray version of the original image since these components represent only the pixels' luminance.

The purpose for distinguishing between luminance and color is that the human eye is more sensitive to changes in brightness than to changes in color.

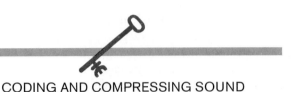

CODING AND COMPRESSING SOUND

The most generic method of coding audio information for computer storage and manipulation is to sample the amplitude of the sound wave at regular intervals and record the series of values obtained. For instance, the series 0, 1, 2, 1, 2, 3, 4, 2, 0 would represent a sound wave that rises in amplitude, falls briefly, rises to a higher level, and then drops back to 0. To achieve acceptable sound quality, music on today's CDs is recorded with a sample rate of 44,100 samples per second. The data collected from each sample is represented in 16 bits (32 bits for stereo recordings). Consequently, one second of music recorded in stereo requires more than a million bits of storage space.

Such space requirements are acceptable for musical recordings distributed on CDs, but they challenge the abilities of technology when combined with video to produce motion picture recordings. Thus, the Motion Picture Experts Group within ISO has developed compression techniques that significantly reduce audio storage space requirements. One of these is known as MP3 (MPEG-1 Audio Layer-3), which can obtain compression ratios of 12 to 1. Using MP3, musical recordings can be reduced to a size that can be economically transferred across the Internet—a possibility that could revolutionize the music recording industry.

Consider, for example, two blue backgrounds that are identical except that one contains a very small bright dot whereas the other contains a very small green dot of the same brightness as the blue background. Your eye would more readily find the bright dot than the green dot. JPEG's baseline standard takes advantage of this phenomenon by encoding each brightness component but averaging the values of the color components over four pixel blocks and recording only these four block averages. Thus, the final representation preserves sudden changes in brightness but tends to blur sudden changes in color. The benefit is that each four-pixel block is represented by only six values (four brightness values and two color values) rather than the 12 values that would be required in a three-value-per-pixel system.

Additional space is saved by recording data that indicate how the various brightness and color components change rather than their actual values. Here, as in JPEG's lossless mode, the motivation is that as an image is scanned, the degree to which nearby pixel values differ can be recorded using fewer bits than would be required if the actual values were recorded. (Actually, these changes are encoded by applying a mathematical technique known as the discrete cosine transform to eight-by-eight blocks of pixels.) The final bit pattern is further compressed by applying variable-length techniques. The result is that JPEG's baseline standard can represent reasonable quality color images using bit patterns that are in the range of one-twentieth the size required by the three-byte-per-pixel format produced by most scanners.

The fact that JPEG's baseline standard leads to significant savings in storage space while producing little, if any, noticeable loss in image quality is why JPEG is growing in popularity. Other techniques, however, have advantages in certain applications. GIF, for example, does a better job of representing images consisting of blocks of uniform colors with sharp edges (such as color cartoons) than does JPEG.

In closing, we should note that research in data compression represents a wide and active field. We have discussed only two of many techniques for compressing images. Moreover, there are many strategies for compressing audio and video. For example, techniques similar to those used in JPEG's baseline standard have been adopted by the Motion Picture Experts Group (MPEG) within ISO to establish standards for coding (compressing) motion video. The underlying theme is to start a picture sequence with an image similar to JPEG's baseline and then to represent the rest of the sequence using relative encoding techniques.

QUESTIONS/EXERCISES

1. Below is a message that was compressed using LZ77. What is the decompressed string?

   101101011 (7, 5, 0) (12, 10, 1) (18, 13, 0)

2. Even though we did not concentrate on the algorithm for compressing data based on LZ77, try compressing the message

   ββαββΒααΒαΒααΒαΒααΒαΒααα

3. In this section we claimed that GIF is better than JPEG when representing color cartoons. Explain why.

4. At most, how many bytes would be required to represent a 1024 by 1024 pixel image using GIF? What if JPEG's baseline standard were used?

5. What characteristic of the human eye does JPEG's baseline standard exploit?

1.9 Communication Errors

When information is transferred back and forth among the various parts of a computer, or transmitted from the earth to the moon and back, or, for that matter, merely left in storage, a chance exists that the bit pattern finally retrieved may not be identical to the original one. Particles of dirt or grease on a magnetic recording surface or a malfunctioning circuit may cause data to be incorrectly recorded or read. Moreover, in the case of some technologies, background radiation can alter patterns stored in a machine's main memory.

To resolve such problems, a variety of coding techniques have been developed to allow the detection and even the correction of errors. Today, because these techniques are largely built into the internal components of a computer system, they are not apparent to the personnel using the machine. Nonetheless, their presence is important and represents a significant contribution to scientific research. In fact, many of these techniques are prime examples of the contributions made by theoretical mathematics. It is fitting therefore that we investigate some of these techniques that lie behind the reliability of today's equipment.

Parity Bits

A simple method of detecting errors is based on the principle that if each bit pattern being manipulated has an odd number of 1s and a pattern is found with an even number of 1s, an error must have occurred.

To use this principle, we need a system in which each pattern contains an odd number of 1s. This is easily obtained by first adding an additional bit, the **parity bit,** to each pattern in a system already available (usually at the high-order end). (Thus the eight-bit ASCII code becomes a nine-bit code, or a sixteen-bit pattern representing a value in two's complement notation becomes a seventeen-bit pattern.) In each case, we assign the value 1 or 0 to this new bit so that the resulting pattern has an odd number of 1s. As Figure 1.27 shows, the ASCII code for A becomes 101000001 (parity bit 1), and the ASCII for F becomes 001000110 (parity bit 0). Although the eight-bit pattern for A has an even number of 1s and the eight-bit pattern for F has an odd number of 1s, both the nine-bit patterns have an odd number of 1s. Once our coding system has been modified in this way, a pattern with an even number of 1s indicates that an error has occurred and that the pattern being manipulated is incorrect.

The particular parity system just described is called **odd parity,** because we designed our system so that each pattern would contain an odd number of 1s. Another technique used is **even parity.** In such a system, each pattern is designed to contain an even number of 1s, and thus an error is signaled by the occurrence of a pattern with an odd number of 1s.

Today, it is not unusual to find parity bits being used in a computer's main memory. Although we envision these machines as having memory cells of eight bits, in reality they may have nine-bit cells, one bit of which is used as a parity bit. Each time an eight-bit pattern is given to the memory circuitry for storage, the circuitry adds a parity bit and stores the resulting nine-bit pattern. When the pattern is later retrieved, the circuitry checks the parity of the nine-bit pattern. If this does not indicate an error, the memory removes the parity bit and confidently returns the remaining eight-bit pattern. Otherwise, the memory returns the eight data bits with a warning that the pattern being returned may not be the same pattern that was originally entrusted to memory.

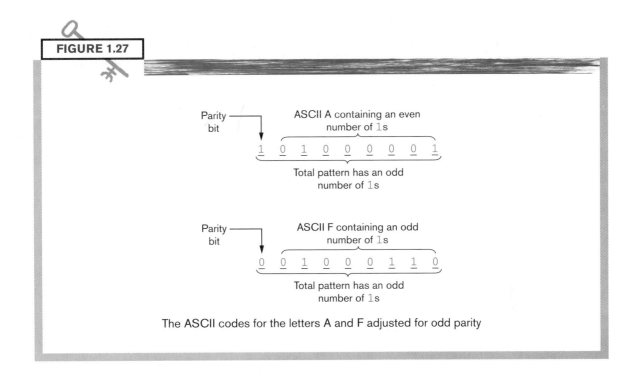

FIGURE 1.27

Parity bit

ASCII A containing an even number of 1s

1 0 1 0 0 0 0 0 1

Total pattern has an odd number of 1s

Parity bit

ASCII F containing an odd number of 1s

0 0 1 0 0 0 1 1 0

Total pattern has an odd number of 1s

The ASCII codes for the letters A and F adjusted for odd parity

Long bit patterns are often accompanied by a collection of parity bits making up a **checkbyte.** Each bit within the checkbyte is a parity bit associated with a particular collection of bits scattered throughout the pattern. For instance, one parity bit may be associated with every eighth bit in the pattern starting with the first bit, while another may be associated with every eighth bit starting with the second bit. In this manner, a collection of errors concentrated in one area of the original pattern is more likely to be detected, since it will be in the scope of several parity bits. Variations of this checkbyte concept lead to error detection schemes known as checksums and cyclic redundancy codes (CRC).

Error-Correcting Codes

Although the use of a parity bit allows the detection of an error, it does not provide the information needed to correct the error. Many people are surprised that **error-correcting codes** can be designed so that errors can be not only detected but also corrected. After all, intuition says that we cannot correct errors in a received message unless we already know the information in the message. However, a simple code with such a corrective property is presented in Figure 1.28.

To understand how this code works, we first define the **Hamming distance** (named after R. W. Hamming, who pioneered the search for error-correcting

FIGURE 1.28

Symbol	Code
A	000000
B	001111
C	010011
D	011100
E	100110
F	101001
G	110101
H	111010

An error-correcting code

codes after becoming frustrated with the lack of reliability of the early relay machines of the 1940s) between two patterns to be the number of bits in which the two differ. For example, the Hamming distance between A and B in the code in Figure 1.28 is four, and the Hamming distance between B and C is three. The important feature of this code is that any two patterns are separated by a Hamming distance of at least three. If a single bit is modified by a malfunctioning device, the error can be detected since the result will not be a legal pattern. (We must change at least three bits in any pattern before it will look like another legal pattern.)

If a single error has occurred in a pattern from Figure 1.28, we can also figure out what the original pattern was. Indeed, the modified pattern will be a Hamming distance of only one from its original form but at least two from any of the other legal patterns. To decode a message, we simply compare each received pattern with the patterns in the code until we find one that is within a distance of one from the received pattern. We consider this to be the correct symbol for decoding. For example, suppose we receive the bit pattern 010100. If we compare this pattern to the patterns in the code, we obtain the table in Figure 1.29. Thus, we can conclude that the character transmitted must be a D because this is the closest match.

You will observe that using this technique with the code in Figure 1.28 actually allows us to detect up to two errors per pattern and to correct one error. If we designed the code so that each pattern was a Hamming distance of at least five from each of the others, we would be able to detect up to four errors per pattern and correct up to two. Of course, the design of efficient codes

FIGURE 1.29

Character	Distance between the received pattern and the character being considered
A	2
B	4
C	3
D	1 (Smallest distance)
E	3
F	5
G	2
H	4

Decoding the pattern 010100 using the code in Figure 1.28

associated with large Hamming distances is not a straightforward task. In fact, it constitutes a part of the branch of mathematics called algebraic coding theory, which is a subarea of linear algebra and matrix theory.

Error-correcting techniques are used extensively to increase the reliability of computing equipment. For example, they are often used in high-capacity magnetic disk drives to reduce the possibility that flaws in the magnetic surface will corrupt data. Moreover, a major distinction between the original CD format used for audio disks and the later CD-ROM format used for computer data storage is in the degree of error correction involved. CD-DA format incorporates error-correcting features that reduce the error rate to only one error for two CDs. This is quite adequate for audio recordings, but a company using CDs to supply software to customers would find that flaws in 50 percent of the disks would be intolerable. Thus, additional error-correcting features are employed in CD-ROM format, which reduce the probability of error to one in 20,000 disks.

QUESTIONS/EXERCISES

1. The following bytes were originally coded using odd parity. In which of them do you know that an error has occurred?
   a. 10101101   b. 10000001   c. 00000000   d. 11100000
   e. 11111111

2. Could errors have occurred in a byte from Question 1 without your knowing it? Explain your answer.
3. How would your answers to Questions 1 and 2 change if you were told that even parity had been used instead of odd?
4. Code these sentences in ASCII using odd parity by adding a parity bit at the high-order end of each character code:
   a.   Where are you?
   b.   "How?" Cheryl asked.
   c.   2 + 3 = 5.
5. Using the error-correcting code presented in Figure 1.28, decode the following messages:
   a.   001111 100100 001100
   b.   010001 000000 001011
   c.   011010 110110 100000 011100
6. Construct a code for the characters A, B, C, and D using bit patterns of length five so that the Hamming distance between any two patterns is at least three.

CHAPTER REVIEW PROBLEMS

(Asterisked problems are associated with optional sections.)

1. Determine the output of each of the following circuits, assuming that the upper input is 1 and the lower input is 0.

   a.
   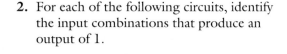

   b.
   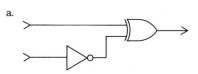

   c.
   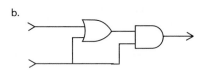

2. For each of the following circuits, identify the input combinations that produce an output of 1.

   a.
   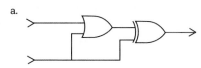

   b.
   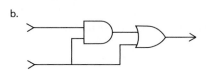

   c.
   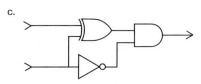

3. In each circuit below, the rectangles represent the same type of gate. Based on the input and output information given, identify whether the gate involved is an AND, OR, or XOR.

a.

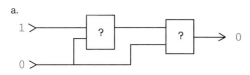

b.

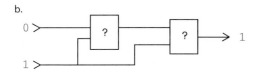

c.

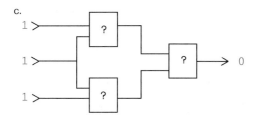

4. Assume that both of the inputs in the circuit below are 1. Describe what would happen if the upper input were temporarily changed to 0. Describe what would happen if the lower input were temporarily changed to 0.

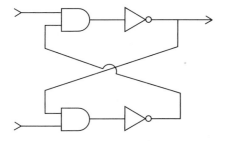

5. The following table represents the addresses and contents (using hexadecimal notation) of some cells in a machine's main memory. Starting with this memory arrangement, follow the sequence of instructions and record the final contents of each of these memory cells:

Address	Contents
00	AB
01	53
02	D6
03	02

Step 1. Move the contents of the cell whose address is 03 to the cell at address 00.

Step 2. Move the value 01 into the cell at address 02.

Step 3. Move the value stored at address 01 into the cell at address 03.

6. How many cells can be in a computer's main memory if each cell's address can be represented by three hexadecimal digits?

7. What bit patterns are represented by the following hexadecimal notations?

   a. BC   b. 67   c. 9A   d. 10   e. 3F

8. What is the value of the most significant bit in the bit patterns represented by the following hexadecimal notations?

   a. FF   b. 7F   c. 8F   d. 1F

9. Express the following bit patterns in hexadecimal notation:

   a. 101010101010

   b. 110010110111

   c. 000011101011

10. Suppose a monitor screen displays 24 rows containing 80 text characters each. If the contents of the screen were stored in memory by representing each character by its ASCII code (one character per byte), how many bytes of the machine's memory would be required to hold the entire screen image?

11. Suppose a picture is represented on a monitor screen by a rectangular array containing 1024 columns and 768 rows of pixels. If eight bits are required to code the color and intensity of each pixel, how many byte-size memory cells are required to hold the entire picture?

12. a. Identify two advantages that a machine's main memory has over disk storage.

    b. Identify two advantages that disk storage has over a machine's main memory.

13. Suppose you are about to use your personal computer to write a term paper that you estimate will be 40 typed pages. Your machine has a disk drive for 3½-inch floppy disks with a capacity of 1.44MB per disk. Will your completed term paper fit on one of these disks? If so, how many such papers can be stored on one disk? If not, how many disks are required to hold your 40-page paper?

14. Suppose that only 100MB of your personal computer's 5GB hard-disk drive is empty and you are about to replace that drive with a 10GB drive. You want to save all the information stored on the hard drive on 3½-inch floppy disks while the conversion is made. Is this practical? Explain your answer.

15. If each sector on a disk contains 512 bytes, how many sectors are required to store a single typed page if each character requires one byte?

16. A typical 3½-inch floppy disk has a capacity of 1.44MB. How does this compare to the size of a 400-page novel in which each page contains 3500 characters?

17. If a floppy disk with 16 sectors per track and 512 bytes per sector spins at the rate of 300 revolutions per minute, at approximately what rate, measured in bytes per second, does data pass by the read/write head?

18. If a desktop computer using the floppy disk in Problem 17 executed ten instructions every microsecond (millionth of a second), how many instructions could it execute in the time between consecutive bytes passing the read/write head?

19. If a floppy disk is rotating at 300 revolutions per minute and the machine can execute one hundred instructions in a microsecond (millionth of a second), how many instructions can the machine perform during the disk's latency time?

20. Compare the latency time of the typical floppy disk in Problem 19 with that of a typical hard-disk drive spinning at 60 revolutions per second.

21. What is the average access time for a hard disk spinning at 60 revolutions per second with a seek time of 10 milliseconds?

22. Suppose a typist could type 60 words per minute continuously day after day. How long would it take the typist to fill a CD whose capacity is 640MB? Assume one word is five characters and each character requires one byte of storage.

23. Here is a message in ASCII. What does it say?

```
01010111  01101000  01100001
01110100  00100000  01100100
01101111  01100101  01110011
00100000  01101001  01110100
00100000  01110011  00110001
01111001  00111111
```

24. The following is a message coded in ASCII using one byte per character and then represented in hexadecimal notation. What is the message?

68657861646563696D616C

25. Code the following sentences in ASCII using one byte per character.

a. $100/5 = 20$

b. To be or not to be?

c. The total cost is $7.25.

26. Express your answers to Problem 25 in hexadecimal notation.

27. List the binary representations of the integers from 6 to 16.

28. a. Write the number 13 by representing the 1 and 3 in ASCII.

b. Write the number 13 in binary representation.

29. What values have binary representations in which only one of the bits is 1? List the binary representations for the smallest six values with this property.

*30. Code the following sentences in ASCII using one byte per character. Use the most significant bit of each byte as an (odd) parity bit.

a. $100/5 = 20$

b. To be or not to be?

c. The total cost is $7.25.

*31. The following message was originally transmitted with odd parity in each short bit string. In which strings have errors definitely occurred?

```
11011 01011 10110 00000 11111
10101 10001 00100 01110
```

*32. Suppose a 24-bit code is generated by representing each symbol by three consecutive copies of its ASCII representation (for example, the symbol A is represented by the bit string 010000010100000101000001). What error-correcting properties does this new code have?

*33. Using the error-correcting code described in Figure 1.28, decode the following words:

a. 111010 110110

b. 101000 100110 001100

c. 011101 000110 000000 010100

d. 010010 001000 001110 101111
   000000 110111 100110

e. 010011 000000 101001 100110

*34. Convert each of the following binary representations to its equivalent base ten representation:

a. 111   b. 0001   c. 11101

d. 10001   e. 10111   f. 000000

g. 100   h. 1000   i. 10000

j. 11001   k. 11010   l. 11011

*35. Convert each of the following base ten representations to its equivalent binary representation:

a. 7   b. 12   c. 16

d. 15   e. 33

*36. Convert each of the following excess 16 representations to its equivalent base ten representation:

a. 10000   b. 10011   c. 01101

d. 01111   e. 10111

*37. Convert each of the following base ten representations to its equivalent excess four representation:

a. 0   b. 3   c. −3

d. −1   e. 1

*38. Convert each of the following two's complement representations to its equivalent base ten representation:

a. 10000   b. 10011   c. 01101

d. 01111   e. 10111

*39. Convert each of the following base ten representations to its equivalent two's complement representation in which each value is represented in seven bits:

a. 12   b. −12   c. −1

d. 0   e. 8

*40. Perform each of the following additions assuming the bit strings represent values in two's complement notation. Identify each case in which the answer is incorrect because of overflow.

a. 00101
   +01000

b. 01111
   +00001

c. 11111
   +00001

d. 10111
   +11010

e. 00111
   +00111

f. 00111
   +01100

g. 11111
   +11111

h. 01010
   +10101

i. 01000
   +01000

j. 01010
   +00011

*41. Solve each of the following problems by translating the values into two's complement notation (using patterns of 5 bits), converting any subtraction problem to an equivalent addition problem, and performing that addition. Check your work by converting your answer to base ten notation. (Watch out for overflow.)

a. 7
   +1

b. 7
   −1

c. 12
   −4

d. 8
   −7

e. 12
   +4

f. 4
   +11

*42. Convert each of the following binary representations into its equivalent base ten representation:

a. 11.001   b. 100.1101   c. .0101

d. 1.0   e. 10.01

*43. Express each of the following values in binary notation:

a. 5 ¾   b. ¹⁄₁₆   c. 7 ⅞

d. 1 ¼   e. 6 ⅝

*44. Decode the following bit patterns using the floating-point format described in Section 1.7:

a. 01011100   b. 11001000

c. 00101010   d. 10111001

*45. Code the following values using the eight-bit floating-point format described in Section 1.7. Indicate each case in which a truncation error occurs.

a. ½   b. 7 ½   c. −3 ¾

d. ³⁄₃₂   e. ³¹⁄₃₂

*46. What is the best approximation to the square root of 2 that can be expressed in the eight-bit floating-point format described in Section 1.7? What value is actually obtained if this approximation is squared by a machine using this floating-point format?

*47. What is the best approximation to the value one-tenth that can be represented using the eight-bit floating-point format described in Section 1.7?

*48. Explain how errors can occur when measurements using the metric system are recorded in floating-point notation. For example, what if 110 cm was recorded in units of meters?

*49. Using the eight-bit floating-point format described in Section 1.7, what would be the result of computing the sum ⅛ + ⅛ + ⅛ + 2 ½ from left to right? How about from right to left?

*50. What answer would be given to each of the following problems by a machine using the eight-bit floating-point format described in Section 1.7?

a. 1 ½ + ³⁄₁₆ =

b. 3 ¼ + 1 ⅛ =

c. 2 ¼ + 1 ⅛ =

*51. In each of the following addition problems, interpret the bit patterns using the eight-bit floating-point format presented in Section 1.7, add the values represented, and code the answer in the same floating-point format. Identify those cases in which truncation errors occur.

a.   01011100   b.   01101010
    +01101000   +00111000

c.   01111000   d.   01011000
    +00011000   +01011000

*52. One of the bit patterns 01011 and 11011 represents a value stored in excess 16 notation and the other represents the same value stored in two's complement notation.

   a. What can be determined about this common value?

   b. What is the relationship between a pattern representing a value stored in two's complement notation and the pattern representing the same value stored in excess notation when both systems use the same bit pattern length?

*53. The three bit patterns 01101000, 10000010, and 00000010 are representations of the same value in two's complement, excess, and the eight-bit floating-point format presented in Section 1.7, but not necessarily in that order. What is the common value, and which pattern is in which notation?

*54. In each of the following cases, the different bit strings represent the same value but in different numeric coding systems that we have discussed. Identify each value and the coding systems used to represent it.

   a. 11111010   0011   1011

   b. 11111101   01111101   11101100

   c. 1010   0010   01101000

*55. Which of the following bit patterns are not valid representations in an excess 16 notation system?

   a. 01001   b. 101   c. 010101

d. 00000   e. 1000   f. 000000

g. 1111

*56. Which of the following values cannot be represented accurately in the floating-point format introduced in Section 1.7?

   a. $6\frac{1}{2}$ b. 9   c. $1\frac{3}{16}$

   d. $\frac{17}{32}$ e. $\frac{15}{16}$

*57. If you doubled the length of the bit strings being used to represent integers in binary from four bits to eight bits, what change would be made in the value of the largest integer you could represent? What if you were using two's complement notation?

*58. What would be the hexadecimal representation of the largest memory address in a memory consisting of 4MB if each cell had a one-byte capacity?

*59. Using gates, design a circuit with four inputs and one output such that the output is 1 or 0 depending on whether the four-bit input pattern has odd or even parity, respectively.

*60. The following message was compressed using LZ77. Decompress the message.

0100101 $(4, 3, 0)\,(8, 7, 1)\,(17, 9, 1)\,(8, 6, 1)$

*61. Here is a part of a message that was compressed using LZ77. Based on the information given, how long was the original message?

αβγ $(\_, 3, β)\,(\_, 6, γ)$

*62. Write a set of directions explaining how to compress a string using LZ77.

*63. Write a set of directions explaining how to decompress a string using LZ77.

SOCIAL ISSUES

The following questions are provided to help you understand some of the ethical/social/legal issues associated with the field of computing as well as investigate your own beliefs and their foundations. The goal is not merely to answer these questions. You should also consider why you answered as you did and whether your justifications are consistent from one question to the next.

1. A truncation error has occurred in a critical situation, causing extensive damage and loss of life. Who is liable, if anyone? The designer of the hardware? The designer of the software? The programmer who actually wrote that part of the program? The person who decided to use the software in that particular application? What if the software had been corrected by the company that originally developed it, but that update had not been purchased and applied in the critical application? What if the software had been pirated?

2. Is it acceptable for an individual to ignore the possibility of truncation errors and their consequences when developing his or her own applications?

3. Was it ethical to develop software in the 1970s using only two digits to represent the year (such as using 76 to represent the year 1976), ignoring the fact that the software would be flawed as the turn of the century approached? Is it ethical today to use only three digits to represent the year (such as 982 for 1982 and 015 for 2015)? What about only four digits?

4. Many argue that coding information often dilutes or otherwise distorts the information, since it essentially forces the information to be quantified. They argue that a questionnaire in which subjects are required to record their opinions by responding within a scale from one to five is inherently flawed. To what extent is information quantifiable? Can the pros and cons of different locations for a waste disposal plant be quantified? Is the debate over nuclear power and nuclear waste quantifiable? Is it dangerous to base decisions on averages and other statistical analysis? Is it ethical for news agencies to report polling results without including the exact wording of the questions? Is it possible to quantify the value of a human life? Is it acceptable for a company to stop investing in the improvement of a product, even though additional investment could lower the possibility of a fatality relating to the product's use?

5. With the development of digital cameras, the ability to alter or fabricate photographs is being placed within the abilities of the general public. What changes will this bring to society? What ethical and legal issues could arise?

6. Should there be a distinction in the rights to collect and disseminate data depending on the form of the data? That is, should the right to collect and disseminate photographs, audio, or video be the same as the right to collect and disseminate text?

7. Whether intentional or not, a report submitted by a journalist usually reflects that journalist's bias. Often by changing only a few words, a story can be given either a positive or negative connotation.

(Compare "The majority of those surveyed did not believe that..." to "A significant portion of those surveyed agreed that...") Is there a difference between altering a story (by leaving out certain points or carefully selecting words) and altering a photograph?

8. Suppose that the use of a data compression system results in the loss of subtle but significant items of information. What liability issues might be raised? How should they be resolved?

ADDITIONAL READING

Gibbs, S. J., and D. C. Tsichritzis. *Multimedia Programming*. Reading, MA: Addison-Wesley, 1995.

Hamacher, V. C., Z. G. Vranesic, and S. G. Zaky. *Computer Organization*, 4th ed. New York: McGraw-Hill, 1996.

Kay, D. C. and J. R. Levine. *Graphics File Formats*, 2nd ed. New York: McGraw-Hill, 1995.

Knuth, D. E. *The Art of Computer Programming*, vol. 2, 3rd ed. Reading, MA: Addison Wesley Longman, 1998.

Patterson, D. A., and J. L. Hennessy. *Computer Organization and Design*. San Francisco: Morgan Kaufmann, 1994.

Sayood, K. *Introduction to Data Compression*. San Francisco: Morgan Kaufmann, 1996.

2.1 The Central Processing Unit
Registers
CPU/Memory Interface
Machine Instructions

2.2 The Stored-Program Concept
Instructions as Bit Patterns
A Typical Machine Language

2.3 Program Execution
An Example of Program Execution
Programs Versus Data

*2.4 Arithmetic/Logic Instructions
Logic Operations
Rotation and Shift Operations
Arithmetic Operations

*2.5 Communicating with Other Devices
Communication via Controllers
Data Communication Rates

*2.6 Other Architectures
CISC Versus RISC Architectures
Pipelining
Multiprocessor Machines

chapter

DATA MANIPULATION

t w o

In Chapter 1 we studied the concepts relating to the storage of data and a computer's memory. In addition to being able to store data, an algorithmic machine must be able to manipulate the data as directed by an algorithm. Data manipulation requires that the machine have the mechanism for performing operations on data and coordinating the sequence of these operations. In the typical computer, this mechanism is called the central processing unit. It is the study of this unit and related topics on which this chapter concentrates.

*Asterisks indicate suggestions for optional sections.

2.1 The Central Processing Unit

The circuitry in a typical computer that performs operations (such as addition and subtraction) on data is not directly connected to the storage cells in the machine's main memory. Instead, this circuitry is isolated in a part of the computer called the **central processing unit,** or **CPU.** This unit consists of two parts: the **arithmetic/logic unit,** which contains the circuitry that performs data manipulation, and the **control unit,** which contains the circuitry for coordinating the machine's activities.

Registers

For temporary storage of information, the CPU contains cells, or **registers,** that are similar to main memory cells. These registers can be classified as either **general-purpose registers** or **special-purpose registers.** We will meet some of the special-purpose registers in Section 2.3. For now, our concern is the role of the general-purpose registers.

General-purpose registers serve as temporary holding places for data being manipulated by the CPU. These registers hold the inputs to the arithmetic/logic unit's circuitry and provide storage space for results produced by that unit. To perform an operation on data stored in main memory, it is the control unit's responsibility to transfer the data from memory into the general-purpose registers, to inform the arithmetic/logic unit which registers hold the data, to activate the appropriate circuitry within the arithmetic/logic unit, and to tell the arithmetic/logic unit which register should receive the result.

It is instructive to consider registers in the context of a machine's overall memory facilities. Registers are used to hold the data immediately applicable to the operation at hand; main memory is used to hold the data that will be needed in the near future; and mass storage is used to hold data that will likely not be needed in the near future.

In many machines, an additional level, called cache memory, is added to

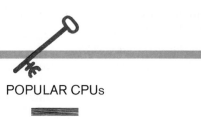

POPULAR CPUs

Perhaps the best known CPUs on the market today are those belonging to the Pentium series developed by Intel and the PowerPC series produced by Motorola and IBM. The Pentium series is popular in the "PC" desktop line of machines, whereas the PowerPC is the choice of Apple Computer Corporation. These CPUs are packaged as small flat squares with pin connections compatible with today's circuit board construction. To increase performance, these CPUs are capable of retrieving multiple bytes from memory in a single step. In particular, they routinely fetch more than one instruction at a time and, in many cases, can execute more than one instruction simultaneously.

As we shall see in Section 2.6, the Pentium and PowerPC CPUs represent two different design philosophies—the Pentium CPUs are examples of CISC architecture, the PowerPC CPUs are examples of RISC architecture.

this hierarchy. **Cache memory** is a section of high-speed memory with response times similar to that of the CPU's registers, often located within the CPU itself. In this special memory area, the machine attempts to keep a copy of that portion of main memory that is of current interest. In this setting, data transfers that normally would be made between registers and main memory are made between registers and cache memory. These changes are then transferred collectively to main memory at a more opportune time.

CPU/Memory Interface

For the purpose of transferring bit patterns between a machine's CPU and main memory, these units are connected by a collection of wires called a **bus** (Figure 2.1). Through this bus, the CPU is able to extract, or read, data from main memory by supplying the address of the pertinent memory cell along with a read signal. In a similar manner, the CPU can place, or write, data in memory by providing the address of the destination cell and the data to be stored together with a write signal.

With this mechanism in mind, we see that performing an operation such as addition on data stored in main memory involves more than the mere execution of the addition operation itself. The process involves the combined efforts of both the control unit, which coordinates the transfer of information between the registers and main memory, and the arithmetic/logic unit, which performs the operation of addition when instructed to do so by the control unit. The

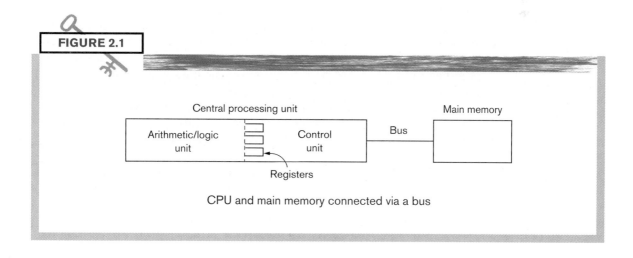

FIGURE 2.1

Central processing unit

Main memory

Arithmetic/logic unit

Control unit

Bus

Registers

CPU and main memory connected via a bus

FIGURE 2.2

Step 1. Get one of the values to be added from memory and place it in a register.

Step 2. Get the other value to be added from memory and place it in another register.

Step 3. Activate the addition circuitry with the registers used in Steps 1 and 2 as inputs and another register designated to hold the result.

Step 4. Store the result in memory.

Step 5. Stop.

Adding values stored in memory

complete process of adding two values stored in memory might be broken down into the five steps listed in Figure 2.2.

Machine Instructions

The steps in Figure 2.2 provide examples of the types of instructions a typical CPU must be able to follow. Such instructions are called **machine instructions.** You may be surprised to learn that the list of machine instructions is quite short. One of the fascinating aspects of computer science is that once a machine can perform certain elementary but well-chosen tasks, adding more features does not increase the machine's theoretical capabilities. In other words, beyond a certain point, additional features may increase such things as convenience and speed but add nothing to the machine's basic abilities. We discuss these ideas further in Chapter 11.

When discussing the instructions in a machine's repertoire, it is helpful to recognize that they can be classified into three categories: (1) the data transfer group, (2) the arithmetic/logic group, and (3) the control group.

Data Transfer The first group consists of instructions that request the movement of data from one location to another. Steps 1, 2, and 4 in Figure 2.2 fall into this category. As in the case of main memory, it is unusual for the data being transferred from any location in a machine to be erased from its original location. The process involved in a transfer instruction is more like copying the data into another location rather than moving it. In this sense, the popular *transfer* or *move* terminology is actually a misnomer, with more descriptive terms being *copy* or *clone*. While on the subject of terminology, we should mention that special terms are used when referring to the transfer of data between the CPU and main memory. A request to fill a general-purpose register with the contents of a memory cell is commonly referred to as a LOAD instruction; conversely, a request to transfer the contents of a register to a memory cell is called a STORE instruction. In Figure 2.2, Steps 1 and 2 are LOAD instructions and Step 4 is a STORE instruction.

An important group of instructions within the data transfer category consists of the commands for communicating with devices outside the CPU-main memory context. Since these instructions handle the input/output (I/O) activities of the machine, they are classified as the I/O instructions and are sometimes considered as a category in their own right. On the other hand, Section 2.6 describes how these I/O activities are often handled by the same instructions that request data transfers between the CPU and main memory, which means that placing them in a separate category would be somewhat misleading.

Arithmetic/Logic The arithmetic/logic group consists of the instructions that tell the control unit to request an activity within the arithmetic/logic unit. Step 3 in Figure 2.2 falls into this group. As its name suggests, the arithmetic/logic unit is capable of performing operations other than the basic arithmetic operations. Some of these additional operations are the common logic operations AND, OR, and XOR, which we introduced in Chapter 1 and will discuss more deeply later in this chapter. These operations are often used for manipulating individual bits within a general-purpose register without disturbing the rest of the register. Another collection of operations available within most arithmetic/logic units allows the contents of registers to be moved to the right or the left within the register. These operations are known as either SHIFT or ROTATE operations, depending on whether the bits that "fall off the end" of the register when its contents are moved are merely discarded (SHIFT) or are used to fill the holes left at the other end (ROTATE).

Control The control group consists of those instructions that direct the execution of the program rather than the manipulation of data. Step 5 in Figure 2.2 falls into this category, although it is an extremely elementary example. This group contains many of the more interesting instructions in a machine's repertoire, such as the family of JUMP (or BRANCH) instructions used to direct the control unit to execute an instruction other than the next one in the list. These JUMP instructions appear in two varieties: unconditional jumps and conditional jumps. An example of the former would be the instruction "Skip to Step 5"; an example of the latter would be "If the value obtained is 0, then skip to Step 5." The distinction is that a conditional jump results in a "change of venue" only if

FIGURE 2.3

Step 1. LOAD a register with a value from memory.

Step 2. LOAD another register with another value from memory.

Step 3. If this second value is zero, JUMP to Step 6.

Step 4. Divide the contents of the first register by the second register and leave the result in a third register.

Step 5. STORE the contents of the third register in memory.

Step 6. Stop.

Dividing values stored in memory

a certain condition is satisfied. As an example, the sequence of instructions in Figure 2.3 represents an algorithm for dividing two values where Step 3 is a conditional jump that protects against the possibility of division by zero.

QUESTIONS/EXERCISES

1. What sequence of events do you think would be required in a machine to move the contents of one memory cell to another?
2. What information must the CPU supply to the main memory circuitry to write a value into a memory cell?
3. Why might the term *move* be considered an incorrect name for the operation of moving data from one location in a machine to another?
4. In the text, JUMP instructions were expressed by identifying the destination explicitly by stating the name (or step number) of the destination within the JUMP instruction (for example, "Jump to Step 6"). A drawback of this technique is that if an instruction name (number) is later changed, we must be sure to find all jumps to that instruction and change that name also. Describe another way of expressing a JUMP instruction so that the name of the destination is not explicitly stated.
5. Is the instruction "If 0 equals 0, then jump to Step 7" a conditional or unconditional jump? Explain your answer.

2.2 The Stored-Program Concept

Early computing devices were not known for their flexibility, as the program that each device executed tended to be built into the control unit as a part of the machine. Such a system is analogous to a music box that always plays the same tune when what is needed is the flexibility of a CD changer. One approach used to gain this flexibility in early electronic computers was to design the control units so they could be conveniently rewired. This flexibility was accomplished by means of a pegboard arrangement similar to old telephone switchboards in which the ends of jumper wires were plugged into holes.

Instructions as Bit Patterns

A breakthrough (credited, perhaps incorrectly, to John von Neumann[1]) came with the realization that a program, just like data, can be coded and stored in main memory. If the control unit is designed to extract the program from memory, decode the instructions, and execute them, a computer's program can be changed merely by changing the contents of the computer's memory instead of rewiring the control unit. This **stored-program concept** has become the standard approach used today. To apply it, a machine is designed to recognize certain bit patterns as representing certain instructions. This collection of instructions along with the coding system is called the **machine-language** because it defines the means by which we communicate algorithms to the machine.

The coded version of a machine instruction typically consists of two parts: the **op-code** (short for operation code) **field** and the **operand field.** The bit pattern appearing in the op-code field indicates which of the elementary operations, such as STORE, SHIFT, XOR, and JUMP, is requested by the instruction. The bit patterns found in the operand field provide more detailed information about the operation specified by the op-code. For example, in the case of a STORE operation, the information in the operand field indicates which register contains the data to be stored and which memory cell is to receive the data.

The concept of storing a program in memory is not difficult at all. What made it difficult to think of originally was that everyone thought of programs and data as different entities: Data were stored in memory; programs were part of the control unit. The result was a prime example of not being able to see the forest for the trees. It is easy to be caught in such ruts, and the development of computer science might well remain in many of them today without our know-

---

[1]Many claim that the stored-program concept was actually the idea of J. P. Eckert, Jr. at the Moore School, and that John von Neumann learned of it during his visits there.

ing it. Indeed, part of the excitement of the science is that new insights are constantly opening doors to new theories and applications.

A Typical Machine Language

Let us see how the instructions of a typical machine might be coded. The machine that we will use for our discussion is described in Appendix C and summarized in Figure 2.4. It has 16 general-purpose registers and 256 main memory cells, each with a capacity of eight bits. For referencing purposes we label the registers with the values 0 through 15 and address the memory cell with the values 0 through 255, except that we think of these values in base two and represent the resulting bit patterns in hexadecimal notation. Thus, the registers are labeled 0 through F and the memory cells are addressed 00 through FF.

Op-Codes   Referring again to the machine language in Appendix C, we find that each instruction is coded with a total of 16 bits, represented in the listing

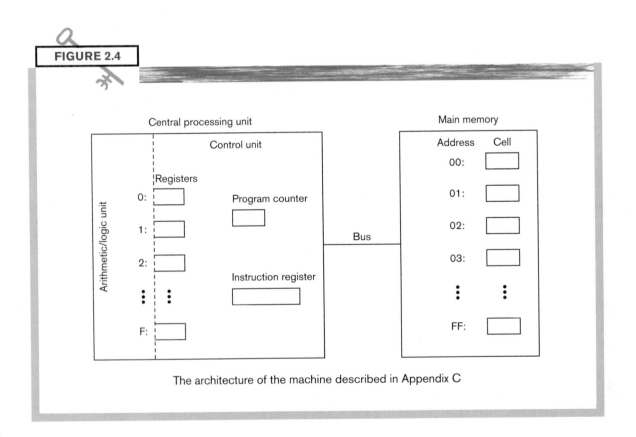

FIGURE 2.4

The architecture of the machine described in Appendix C

FIGURE 2.5

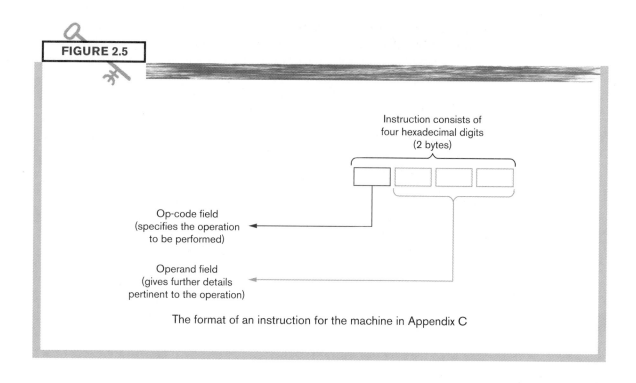

Instruction consists of
four hexadecimal digits
(2 bytes)

Op-code field
(specifies the operation
to be performed)

Operand field
(gives further details
pertinent to the operation)

The format of an instruction for the machine in Appendix C

by four hexadecimal digits (Figure 2.5). The op-code for each instruction con-sists of the first four bits or, equivalently, the first hexadecimal digit. The entire instruction list consists of only 12 basic instructions whose op-codes are repre-sented by the hexadecimal digits 1 through C. Thus any instruction code start-ing with the hexadecimal digit 3 (bit pattern 0011) refers to a STORE instruction, and any instruction code starting with hexadecimal A refers to a ROTATE instruction.

The machine has two ADD instructions: one for adding two's complement representations and one for adding floating-point representations. This distinc-tion results from the fact that adding bit patterns that represent values coded in binary notation requires different activities within the arithmetic/logic unit than when adding floating-point notation.

Operands Now we take a look at the operand field. It consists of three hexa-decimal digits (12 bits) and in each case (except for the HALT instruction, which needs no further refinement) clarifies the general instruction given by the op-code. For example, if the first hexadecimal digit of an instruction were 1 (the op-code for loading from memory), the next hexadecimal digit of the instruction would indicate which register is to be loaded, and the last two hexa-decimal digits would indicate which memory cell is to provide the data. Thus the instruction 1347 (hexadecimal) translates to the statement "LOAD register

3 with the contents of the memory cell at address 47." In the case of the op-code hexadecimal 7, which requests that the contents of two registers be ORed, the next hexadecimal digit indicates where the result should be placed, while the last two hexadecimal digits of the operand field are used to indicate which two registers are to be ORed. Thus the instruction 70C5 translates to the statement "OR the contents of register C with the contents of register 5 and leave the result in register 0."

A subtle distinction exists between our machine's two LOAD instructions. Here we see that the op-code 1 (hexadecimal) refers to the instruction that loads a register with the contents of a memory cell, whereas the op-code 2 (hexadecimal) refers to the instruction that loads a register with a particular value. The difference is that the operand field in an instruction of the first type contains an address, whereas in the second type it contains the bit pattern to be loaded.

An interesting situation occurs in the case of the JUMP instruction (op-code hexadecimal B). The first hexadecimal digit of the operand field indicates which register is to be compared with register 0. If this register contains the same pattern as register 0, the machine jumps to the instruction at the address indicated by the last two hexadecimal digits of the operand. Otherwise, the execution of the program continues as usual. In general, this provides a conditional jump. However, if the first hexadecimal digit of the operand field is 0, the instruction requests that register 0 be compared with register 0. Since a register is always equal to itself, the jump is always taken. Consequently, any instruction whose code starts with the hexadecimal digits B0 translates to an unconditional jump.

A Program Example   We close this section with the following coded version of the instructions in Figure 2.2. We have assumed that the values to be added are stored in two's complement notation at memory addresses 6C and 6D and the sum is to be placed in memory at address 6E.

Step 1. 156C
Step 2. 166D
Step 3. 5056
Step 4. 306E
Step 5. C000

QUESTIONS/EXERCISES

1. Write the example program appearing at the end of this section in actual bit patterns.
2. The following are instructions written in the machine language described in Appendix C. Rewrite them in English.
   a. 368A   b. BADE   c. 803C   d. 40F4

3. What is the difference between the instructions 15AB and 25AB in the machine language of Appendix C?
4. Here are some instructions in English. Translate each of them into the machine language of Appendix C.
   a. LOAD register number 3 with the hexadecimal value 56.
   b. ROTATE register number 5 three bits to the right.
   c. JUMP to the instruction at location F3 if the contents of register number 7 are equal to the contents of register 0.
   d. AND the contents of register A with the contents of register 5 and leave the result in register 0.

2.3 Program Execution

A computer follows a program stored in its memory by copying the instructions from memory into the control unit as needed. Once in the control unit, each instruction is decoded and obeyed. The order in which the instructions are fetched from memory corresponds to the order in which the instructions are stored in memory unless otherwise specified by a JUMP instruction. To understand how the overall execution process takes place, it is necessary to take a closer look at the control unit inside the CPU. Within this unit are two special-purpose registers: the **program counter** and the **instruction register** (see again Figure 2.4). The program counter contains the address of the next instruction to be executed, thereby serving as the machine's way of keeping track of where it is in the program. The instruction register is used to hold the instruction being executed.

The control unit performs its job by continually repeating an algorithm, the **machine cycle,** which consists of three steps: fetch, decode, and execute (Figure 2.6). During the fetch step, the control unit requests that main memory provide it with the next instruction to be executed. The unit knows where the next instruction is in memory because its address is kept in the program counter. The control unit places the instruction received from memory in its instruction register and then increments the program counter so that the counter contains the address of the next instruction.

With the instruction now in the instruction register, the control unit decodes the instruction, which involves breaking the operand field into its proper components based on the instruction's op-code.

The control unit then executes the instruction by activating the appropriate circuitry to perform the requested task. For example, if the instruction is a load from memory, the control unit causes the load to occur; if the instruction is for an arithmetic operation, the control unit activates the appropriate circuitry in the arithmetic/logic unit with the correct registers as inputs.

FIGURE 2.6

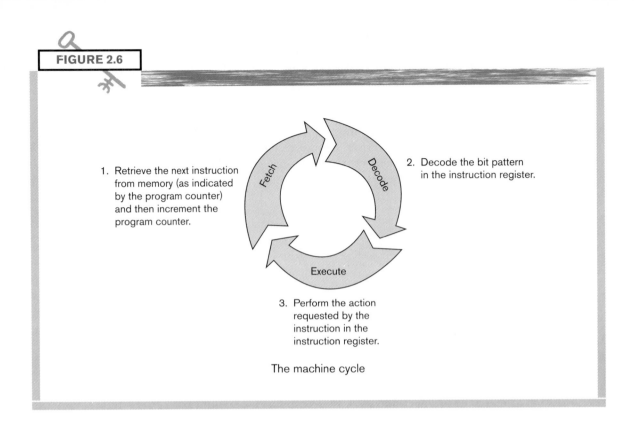

1. Retrieve the next instruction from memory (as indicated by the program counter) and then increment the program counter.

2. Decode the bit pattern in the instruction register.

3. Perform the action requested by the instruction in the instruction register.

The machine cycle

When the instruction has been executed, the control unit again begins the machine cycle with the fetch step. Observe that since the program counter was incremented at the end of the previous fetch phase, it again provides the control unit with the correct instruction address.

A somewhat special case is the execution of a JUMP instruction. Consider, for example, the instruction B258, which translates into "JUMP to the instruction at address 58 if the contents of register 2 is the same as that of register 0." In this case, the execute step of the machine cycle begins with the comparison of registers 2 and 0. If they are different, the execute step terminates and the next machine cycle begins. If, however, the contents of these registers are equal, the machine places the value 58 in its program counter during the execute step. In this case, then, the next fetch step finds 58 in the program counter, so the instruction at that address is the next instruction executed.

To coordinate the activities in the machine cycle, the activities of various circuits must be synchronized. For this purpose a pulsating signal called the clock is connected to the circuits involved. This clock oscillates back and forth between the values 0 and 1, and the various circuits are designed so that their activities are triggered by the various phases of the clock cycle. In turn, the speed of the clock determines the speed at which the CPU performs its machine cycle.

An Example of Program Execution

Let us follow the machine cycle applied to the program we coded at the end of Section 2.2. We first need to put the program somewhere in memory. For our example, suppose the program is stored in consecutive addresses, starting at address A0 hexadecimal. A table representing the contents of this area of memory appears in Figure 2.7. With the program stored in this manner, we can cause the machine to execute it by placing the address (A0) of the first instruction in the program counter and starting the machine.

The control unit begins the fetch step of the machine cycle by extracting the instruction at location A0 and plac-

COMPARING COMPUTER POWER

When shopping for a personal computer, you will find that clock speeds are often used to compare machines. A computer's clock is an oscillating circuit whose pulses are used to coordinate the machine's activities—the faster this oscillating circuit generates pulses, the faster the machine performs its tasks. Clock speeds are measured in hertz (abbreviated as Hz)—with one Hz equal to one cycle (or pulse) per second. Typical clock speeds in desktop computers are in the range of a few hundred megahertz (MHz)—with one MHz equal to 1 million Hz.

Unfortunately, different CPU designs often do different amounts of work in one clock cycle, and thus clock speeds fail to be relevant when comparing machines with different CPU designs. If comparing a machine based on a PowerPC to one based on a Pentium, it would be more meaningful to compare performance by means of **benchmarking**, which is the process of comparing the performance of different machines when executing the same program, known as a benchmark. By selecting a benchmark that is representative of a type of application, a comparison can be obtained that is meaningful for a particular market segment. It is often true that the best machine for one application is not the best for another.

ing this instruction (156C) in its instruction register. Notice that, in our machine, instructions are 16 bits (two bytes) long. Thus, the instruction to be fetched occupies the memory cells at both address A0 and A1. The control unit is designed to take this into account so it retrieves the contents of both cells and places these data in the instruction register, which is 16 bits long. The control unit then adds 2 to the program counter so that this register contains the address of the next instruction. At the end of the fetch phase of the first machine cycle, the program counter and instruction register contain the following data:

Program Counter: A2

Instruction Register: 156C

Next, the control unit analyzes the instruction in its instruction register and concludes that it is to load register 5 with the contents of the memory cell at

FIGURE 2.7

Address	Contents
A0	15
A1	6C
A2	16
A3	6D
A4	50
A5	56
A6	30
A7	6E
A8	C0
A9	00

Our "add" program stored in memory starting at address A0

address 6C. This load activity is performed during the execution step of the machine cycle, and the control unit then begins the next cycle.

This cycle begins by fetching the instruction 166D from the two memory cells starting at address A2. The control unit places this instruction in the instruction register, and increments the program counter to A4. The values in the program counter and instruction register therefore become the following:

Program Counter: A4

Instruction Register: 166D

Now the control unit decodes the instruction 166D and determines that it is to load register 6 with the contents of memory address 6D. It then executes the instruction, at which time register 6 is actually loaded.

Since the program counter now contains A4, the control unit extracts the next instruction starting at this address. The result is that 5056 is placed in the instruction register, and the program counter is incremented to A6. The control unit now decodes the contents of its instruction register and executes it by activating the two's complement addition circuitry with inputs being registers 5 and 6.

During this execution step, the arithmetic/logic unit performs the requested addition, leaves the result in register 0 (as requested by the control unit), and reports to the control unit that it has finished. The control unit then begins another machine cycle. Once again, with the aid of the program counter, it fetches the next instruction (306E) from the two memory cells starting at memory location A6 and increments the program counter to A8. This instruction is then decoded and executed. At this point, the sum is placed in memory location 6E.

The next instruction is fetched starting from memory location A8, and the program counter is incremented to AA. The contents of the instruction register (C000) are now decoded as the halt instruction. Consequently, the machine stops during the execute step of the machine cycle, and the program is completed.

In summary, we see that the execution of a program stored in memory involves the same process you and I might use if we needed to follow a detailed list of instructions. Whereas we might keep our place by checking the instructions off as we do them, the computer keeps its place by using the program counter. After determining which instruction to execute next, we would read the instruction and extract its meaning. Finally, we would perform the task requested and return to the list for the next instruction in the same manner that the machine executes the instruction in its instruction register and then continues with another fetch.

Programs Versus Data

Many programs can be stored simultaneously in a computer's main memory, as long as they occupy different locations. Which program will be run when the machine is started can then be determined merely by setting the program counter appropriately.

One must keep in mind, however, that because data are also contained in memory and coded in terms of 0s and 1s, the machine alone has no way of knowing what is data and what is program. If the program counter is assigned the address of data instead of the address of the desired program, the computer, not knowing any better, extracts the data bit patterns as though they were instructions and executes them. The final result depends on the data involved.

We should not conclude that providing programs and data with a common appearance in a machine's memory is bad. In fact, it has proved a useful attribute because it allows one program to manipulate other programs (or even itself) as it would data. Imagine, for example, a program that modifies itself in response to its interaction with its environment and thus exhibits the ability to learn. Or perhaps a program that writes and executes other programs in order to solve problems presented to it.

QUESTIONS/EXERCISES

1. Suppose the memory cells from addresses 00 to 05 in the machine described in Appendix C contain the (hexadecimal) bit patterns given in the following table:

Address	Contents
00	14
01	02
02	34
03	17
04	C0
05	00

If we start the machine with its program counter containing 00, what bit pattern is in the memory cell whose address is hexadecimal 17 when the machine halts?

2. Suppose the memory cells at addresses B0 to B8 in the machine described in Appendix C contain the (hexadecimal) bit patterns given in the following table:

Address	Contents
B0	13
B1	B8
B2	A3
B3	02
B4	33
B5	B8
B6	C0
B7	00
B8	0F

a. If the program counter starts at B0, what bit pattern is in register number 3 after the first instruction has been executed?

b. What bit pattern is in memory cell B8 when the halt instruction is executed?

3. Suppose the memory cells at addresses A4 to B1 in the machine described in Appendix C contain the (hexadecimal) bit patterns given in the following table:

Address	Contents
A4	20
A5	00
A6	21
A7	03
A8	22
A9	01
AA	B1
AB	B0
AC	50
AD	02

AE	B0
AF	AA
B0	C0
B1	00

When answering the following questions, assume that the machine is started with its program counter containing A4.

a. What is in register 0 the first time the instruction at address AA is executed?

b. What is in register 0 the second time the instruction at address AA is executed?

c. How many times is the instruction at address AA executed before the machine halts?

4. Suppose the memory cells at addresses F0 to F9 in the machine described in Appendix C contain the (hexadecimal) bit patterns described in the following table:

Address	Contents
F0	20
F1	C0
F2	30
F3	F8
F4	20
F5	00
F6	30
F7	F9
F8	FF
F9	FF

If we start the machine with its program counter containing F0, what does the machine do when it reaches the instruction at address F8?

2.4 Arithmetic/Logic Instructions

As indicated earlier, the arithmetic/logic group of instructions consists of instructions requesting arithmetic, logic, and shift operations. In this section, we look at these operations more closely.

Logic Operations

We introduced the logic operations AND, OR, and XOR (exclusive or) in Chapter 1 as operations that combine two input bits to produce a single output bit. These operations can be extended to operations that combine two strings of bits to produce a single output string by applying the basic operation to individual columns. For example, the result of ANDing the patterns 10011010 and 11001001 results in

```
     10011010
AND  11001001
     10001000
```

where we have merely written the result of ANDing the two bits in each column at the bottom of the column. Likewise, ORing and XORing these patterns would produce

```
    10011010          10011010
OR  11001001      XOR  11001001
    11011011          01010011
```

One of the major uses of the AND operation is for placing 0s in one part of a bit pattern while not disturbing the other part. Consider, for example, what happens if the byte 00001111 is the first operand of an AND operation. Without knowing the contents of the second operand, we still can conclude that the four most significant bits of the result are 0s. Moreover, the four least significant bits of the result are a copy of that part of the second operand, as shown in the following example:

```
     00001111
AND  10101010
     00001010
```

This use of the AND operation is an example of the process called **masking.** Here one operand, called the **mask,** determines which part of the other operand will affect the result. In the case of the AND operation, masking produces a result that is a partial replica of one of the operands, with 0s occupying the nonduplicated positions.

Such an operation is useful when manipulating a **bit map,** a string of bits in which each bit represents the presence or absence of a particular object. We have already encountered bit maps in the context of representing images, where each bit is associated with a pixel. As another example, a string of 52 bits, in which each bit is associated with a particular playing card, can be used to represent a poker hand by assigning 1s to those 5 bits associated with the cards in the hand and 0s to all the others. Likewise, a bit map of 52 bits, of which 13 are 1s, can be used to represent a hand of bridge, or a bit map of 32 bits can be used to represent which of 32 ice cream flavors are available.

Suppose, then, that an eight-bit memory cell is being used as a bit map, and we want to find out whether the object associated with the third bit from the high-order end is present. We merely need to AND the entire byte with the mask 00100000, which produces a byte of all 0s if and only if the third bit from the high-order end of the bit map is itself 0. A program can then act accordingly by following the AND operation with a condition branch instruction. Moreover, if the third bit from the high-order end of the bit map is a 1, and we want to change it to a 0 without disturbing the other bits, we can AND the bit map with the mask 11011111 and then store the result in place of the original bit map.

Where the AND operation can be used to duplicate a part of a string while placing 0s in the nonduplicated part, the OR operation can be used to duplicate a part of a bit string while putting 1s in the nonduplicated part. For this we again use a mask, but this time we indicate the bit positions to be duplicated with 0s and use 1s to indicate the nonduplicated positions. For example, ORing any byte with 11110000 produces a result with 1s in its most significant four bits while its remaining bits contain a copy of the least significant four bits of the other operand, as demonstrated by the following example:

```
      11110000
OR  10101010
      11111010
```

Consequently, whereas the mask 11011111 can be used with the AND operation to force a 0 in the third bit from the high-order end of an eight-bit bit map, the mask 00100000 can be used with the OR operation to force a 1 in that position.

A major use of the XOR operation is in forming the complement of a bit string. For example, note the relationship between the second operand and the result in the following example:

```
       11111111
XOR  10101010
       01010101
```

XORing any byte with a byte of 1s produces the complement of the first byte.

Rotation and Shift Operations

The operations in the class of rotation and shift operations provide a means for moving of bits within a register and are often used in solving alignment problems, such as preparing a byte for future use in masking operations or manipulating the mantissa of floating-point representations. These operations are classified as to the direction of motion (right or left) and as to whether the process is circular. Within these classification guidelines are numerous variations with mixed terminology. Let us take a quick look at the ideas involved.

If we consider starting with a byte of bits and shifting its contents one bit to the right or the left, we might imagine the bit on one end falling off the edge and a hole appearing at the other end. What happens with this extra bit and the hole is the distinguishing feature among the various shift operations. One technique is to place the extra bit in the hole at the other end. The result is a circular shift, also called a rotation. Thus, if we perform a right circular shift on a byte eight times, we obtain the same bit pattern we started with, and seven right circular shifts are equivalent to a single left circular shift.

Another technique is to discard the bit that falls off the edge and always fill the hole with a 0. The term **logical shift** is often used to refer to these operations. Such shifts to the left can be used for multiplying two's complement representations by 2. After all, shifting binary digits to the left corresponds to multiplication by 2, just as a similar shift of decimal digits corresponds to multiplication by ten. Moreover, division by 2 can be accomplished by shifting the binary string to the right. In either shift, care must be taken to preserve the sign bit when using certain notational systems. Thus, we often find right shifts that always fill the hole (which occurs at the sign bit position) with its original value. Shifts that leave the sign bit unchanged are sometimes called **arithmetic shifts.**

Arithmetic Operations

Although we have already mentioned the arithmetic operations of add, subtract, multiply, and divide, a few loose ends must still be connected. First, as we have mentioned, this collection of operations can often be generated from the single add operation and a negation process. For this reason, some small computers are designed with only the add or perhaps only the add and subtract instructions.

We should also mention that for each arithmetic operation, numerous variations exist. We have already alluded to this in relation to the add operations available on our machine in Appendix C. In the case of addition, for example, if the values to be added are stored in two's complement notation, the addition process must be performed as a straightforward binary add. However, if the operands are stored as floating-point values, the addition process must extract the mantissa of each, shift them right or left according to the exponent fields, check the sign bits, perform the addition, and translate the result into floating-point notation. We see then that although both operations are considered addition, the action of the machine is not the same. As far as the machine is concerned, the two operations may have no relationship at all.

QUESTIONS/EXERCISES

1. Perform the indicated operations.

a.
```
    01001011
AND 10101011
```
b.
```
    10000011
AND 11101100
```
c.
```
    11111111
AND 00101101
```
d.
```
    01001011
OR 10101011
```
e.
```
    10000011
OR 11101100
```
f.
```
    11111111
OR 00101101
```
g.
```
    01001011
XOR 10101011
```
h.
```
    10000011
XOR 11101100
```
i.
```
    11111111
XOR 00101101
```

2. Suppose you want to isolate the middle three bits of a seven-bit string by placing 0s in the other four bits without disturbing the middle three bits. What mask must you use together with what operation?

3. Suppose you want to complement the three middle bits of a seven-bit string while leaving the other four bits undisturbed. What mask must you use together with what operation?

4. a. Suppose you XOR the first two bits of a string of bits and then continue down the string by successively XORing each result with the next bit in the string. How is your result related to the number of 1s appearing in the string?

   b. How does this problem relate to determining what the appropriate parity bit should be when coding a message?

5. It is often convenient to use a logical operation in place of a numeric one. For example, the logical operation AND combines two bits in the same manner as multiplication. Which logical operation is almost the same as adding two bits, and what goes wrong in this case?

6. What logical operation together with what mask can you use to change ASCII codes of lowercase letters to uppercase? What about uppercase to lowercase?

7. What is the result of performing a three-bit right circular shift on the following bit strings:

   a. 01101010   b. 00001111   c. 01111111

8. What is the result of performing a one-bit left circular shift on the following bytes represented in hexadecimal notation? Give your answer in hexadecimal form.

   a. AB   b. 5C   c. B7   d. 35

9. A right circular shift of three bits on a string of eight bits is equivalent to a left circular shift of how many bits?

10. What bit pattern represents the sum of 01101010 and 11001100 if the patterns represent values stored in two's complement notation? What if the patterns represent values stored in the floating-point format discussed in Chapter 1?

11. Using the machine language of Appendix C, write a program that places a 1 in the most significant bit of the memory cell whose address is A7 without modifying the remaining bits in the cell.

12. Using the machine language of Appendix C, write a program that copies the middle four bits from memory cell E0 into the least significant four bits of memory cell E1, while placing 0s in the most significant four bits of the cell at location E1.

2.5 Communicating with Other Devices

The main memory and CPU form the core of a computer. In this section, we investigate how this core communicates with peripheral devices, such as disk storage systems, printers, and other computers.

Communication via Controllers

Communication between a machine and other devices is normally handled through an intermediary device known as a **controller.** In the case of a personal computer, a controller has the physical form of a circuit board that plugs into a slot on the computer's main circuit board (the motherboard). From there the controller connects via cables to peripheral devices within the machine or perhaps to a connector on the back of the machine where external devices can be attached.

Each controller handles communication for a particular type of device. Some are designed to handle communication with a monitor, others handle communication with disk drives, and others handle communication with CD devices. For this reason a new controller is sometimes purchased along with a new peripheral device. The controller converts messages and data back and forth between forms compatible with the internal characteristics of the machine and those of the peripheral device to which it is attached. These controllers are often small computers within themselves, each with its own memory circuitry and CPU that performs a program directing the activities of the controller.

When a controller is plugged into one of the slots on the computer's motherboard, it is electronically connected to the same bus that connects the machine's CPU and main memory (Figure 2.8). From this position each controller monitors the signals sent out from the machine's CPU and responds

FIGURE 2.8

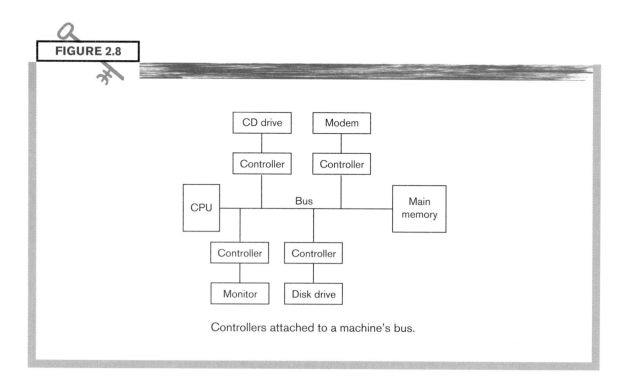

Controllers attached to a machine's bus.

when it detects that the signal is directed to itself. Moreover, by being connected to the machine's bus, the controller can send read and write signals directly to the machine's main memory during those microseconds in which the CPU is not using the bus.

This ability of a controller to access main memory is known as **direct memory access (DMA),** and it is a significant asset to a machine's performance. If the controller for a machine's disk drive has direct memory access, the CPU can send requests coded as bit patterns to the controller asking the controller to read a particular sector from the disk and place the data in a specified block of memory cells. (Such a block of memory is called a **buffer.** More generally, a buffer is any location where one system leaves data to be picked up later by another.) The CPU can then continue with other tasks while the controller performs the read operation. Thus two activities will be performed at the same time. The CPU will be executing a program and the controller will be overseeing the transfer of data between the disk and main memory. In this manner, the computing resources of the CPU are not wasted during the relatively slow data transfer.

The use of DMA also has the detrimental effect of increasing the amount of communication being handled by a computer's bus. Bit patterns must move between the CPU and main memory, between the CPU and each controller, and between each controller and main memory. Coordination of all this activity on the bus is a major design issue. Even with excellent designs, the central bus can become an impediment, known as the **von Neumann bottleneck,** as the CPU and the controllers compete for bus access.

Communication between a machine's CPU and a controller is handled in much the same way as communication between the CPU and main memory. To send a bit pattern to a controller, the bit pattern is first constructed in one of the CPU's general-purpose registers. Then an instruction similar to a STORE instruction is executed by the CPU to "store" the bit pattern in the controller. Thus the only difference between storing a pattern in main memory and sending a pattern to a controller is in the pattern's destination. In fact, in many machines the same machine language op-code is used for both situations. In these cases, the main memory circuitry is designed to ignore references to particular memory locations while the controller is designed to respond to references to those locations. Thus, when the CPU sends the message on the bus to store data at that memory location, the data is received by the controller rather than main memory. Likewise, if the CPU tries to read data from that memory location, as in a LOAD instruction, it will receive a bit pattern from the controller rather than from memory. Such a communication system is called **memory-mapped I/O** because the machine's input/output devices appear to be in various memory locations, and the "memory" addresses assigned to a controller in this manner are collectively called a **port** in that they represent a "location" through which information enters and leaves the machine (Figure 2.9).

The transfer of data between two computer components is rarely a one-way affair. Even though we may think of a printer as a device that receives data, the truth is that a printer also sends data back to the computer. Indeed, a computer

FIGURE 2.9

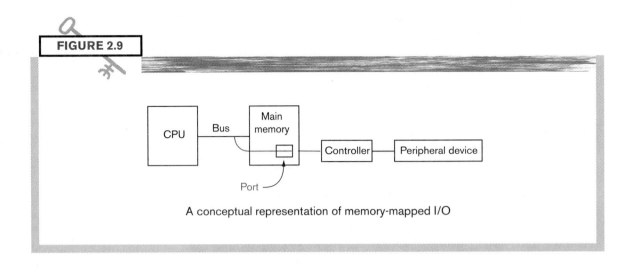

A conceptual representation of memory-mapped I/O

can produce and send characters to a printer much faster than the printer can print them. If a computer blindly sent data to a printer, the printer could quickly fall behind, resulting in lost data. Thus a process such as printing a document involves a constant two-way dialogue in which the computer and the peripheral device exchange information about the device's status.

Such a dialogue often involves a **status word,** a bit pattern that is generated by the peripheral device and sent to the controller. The bits in the status word reflect the conditions of the device. For example, in the case of a printer, the value of the least significant bit of the status word may indicate whether the printer is out of paper, while the next bit may indicate whether the printer is ready for additional data. Depending on the system, the controller may respond to this status information itself or make it available to the CPU. In either case either the program within the controller or the program being executed by the CPU can be designed to delay sending data to the printer until the appropriate status information is received.

Data Communication Rates

The rate in which bits are transferred from one computing component to another is measured in **bits per second (bps).** Common units include **Kbps** (kilo-bps, equal to 1000 bps), **Mbps** (mega-bps, equal to 1 million bps), and **Gbps** (giga-bps, equal to 1 billion bps). The maximum rate available in a particular case depends on the type of the communication path and the technology used in its implementation.

There are two basic types of communication paths: parallel and serial. These terms refer to the manner in which the bit patterns are transferred with respect to each other. In the case of **parallel communication,** several bits are transferred at the same time, each on a separate line. Such a technique is capable of transferring data rapidly but requires a relatively complex communication path. Examples include a computer's internal bus and much of the communication between the computer and its peripheral devices, such as mass storage systems and printers. In these cases rates measured in Mbps and higher are common.

In contrast, **serial communication** is based on transferring only one bit at a time. This technique tends to be slower but requires a simpler data path because all the bits are transferred over the same line, one after the other. Serial communication is typically used for communication between different computers, where the simpler data path proves to be economical.

For example, existing telephone lines have been and still are a staple for intercomputer communication. These are inherently serial communication

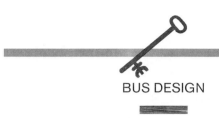

BUS DESIGN

The design of a computer's bus has long been a delicate matter. For example, the wires in a poorly designed bus can act as small antennas—picking up transmission signals (radio, television, etc.) and disrupting communication between the machine's CPU, memory, and peripheral devices. Moreover, the length of the bus (perhaps six inches in a desktop computer) is significantly longer than the length of the "wires" within the CPU itself (measured in microns). Thus the time required for signals to travel over the bus is much greater than that required for signals to be transferred within the CPU. The result is that bus technology is in a constant race to keep up with CPU technology. Today's personal computers reflect a variety of bus designs that differ in such features as the amount of data that can be transferred simultaneously, the rate in which the signals on the bus can be changed, and the physical properties of the connections between the bus and controller cards. These designs include ISA (Industrial Standard Architecture), EISA (Extended Industrial Standard Architecture), and PCI (Peripheral Component Interconnect).

systems in that they transfer tones one after the other. Communication between computers over these lines is accomplished by first converting bit patterns into audible tones by means of a **modem** (short for *modulator-demodulator*), transferring these tones serially over the telephone system, and then converting the tones back into bits by another modem at the destination.

In reality, simply representing bit patterns by tones of different frequencies (known as frequency-shift keying) is used only for low-speed communication of no more than 1200 bps. To achieve transfer rates of 2400 bps, 9600 bps, and higher, modems combine changes in a tone's frequency, amplitude (volume), and phase (the degree to which the transmission of the tone is delayed). To achieve still higher rates, data compression techniques are often applied, producing apparent transfer rates of up to 57.6 Kbps.

These transfer rates appear to be the limit to what can be achieved over traditional telephone lines, yet they fall far short of the rates required by today's communication needs. At the rate of 57.6 Kbps, the time required to transfer a typical photograph (consisting of at least a megabyte) is measured in minutes, and the task of transferring video at the same time that it is being viewed is impossible. Thus new technologies are continually being developed for inter-computer communication. These include optic fibers with transfer rates measured in hundreds of Mbps and potential rates measured in Gbps.

QUESTIONS/EXERCISES

1. Assume that the machine described in Appendix C uses memory mapped I/O and the address B5 is the location within the printer port to which data to be printed should be sent.
   a. If register 7 contains the ASCII code for the letter A, what machine language instruction should be used to cause that letter to be printed at the printer?
   b. If the machine executes a million instructions per second, how many times can this character be sent to the printer in one second?
   c. If the printer is capable of printing five traditional pages of text per minute, will it be able to keep up with the characters being sent to it in (b)?
2. Suppose that the hard disk on your personal computer rotates at 3000 revolutions a minute and that each track contains 16 sectors, and each sector contains 1024 bytes. Approximately what communication rate is required between the disk drive and the disk controller if the controller is going to receive bits from the disk drive as they are read from the spinning disk?
3. How long would it take to transfer a 300-page novel coded in ASCII at a transfer rate of 57,600 bps?

2.6 Other Architectures

To broaden our perspective, let us consider some alternatives to the machine architecture of the previous sections.

CISC Versus RISC Architectures

The design of a machine's language involves numerous decisions, one of which is whether to build a complex machine that can decode and execute a wide variety of instructions or a simpler machine that has a limited instruction set. The former results in what is called a **complex instruction set computer (CISC)**; the latter produces a **reduced instruction set computer (RISC)**. The more complex machine is easier to program because a single instruction can be used to accomplish a task that requires a multi-instruction sequence in the simpler machine. However, the complex machine is harder and more costly to build and perhaps more costly to operate. Moreover, many of the complex instructions can find limited applications and thus tend merely to increase overhead.

To minimize the amount of circuitry required, CISC processors are often constructed in a two-tiered fashion in which each machine instruction is actually executed as a sequence of simpler instructions. In such designs, the CPU contains a block of special memory cells, known as **micromemory,** where a program, called the **microprogram,** is stored. It is this microprogram that directs the execution of the complex machine language instruction. In particular, the meaning of the machine language instructions can be altered by changing the microprogram. Thus, in addition to providing a CISC architecture without the complex circuitry that would otherwise be required to support an elaborate instruction repertoire, the microprogram approach allows a single CPU design to be customized to include special machine-language instructions by merely changing its microprogram.

However, proponents of RISC architecture argue that these benefits do not outweigh the overhead associated with the microprogram. They argue that a better approach is to design a simple machine with a small, well-designed instruction set. This approach removes the complexity involved with a micromemory and results in a simpler CPU design. On the other hand, it means that programs represented in the machine's language must be longer than those in a CISC architecture, because several instructions are required to perform the complex operations represented by single instructions in a CISC architecture.

Both CISC and RISC processors are commercially available. The Pentium series of processors, developed by Intel, are examples of CISC architecture; the PowerPC series of processors, developed by Apple Computer, IBM, and Motorola, are examples of RISC architecture.

Pipelining

Electric pulses travel through a wire no faster than the speed of light. Since light travels approximately 1 foot in a nanosecond (one billionth of a second), it requires at least 2 nanoseconds for the control unit in the CPU to fetch an instruction from a memory cell that is 1 foot away. (The read request must be sent to memory, requiring at least 1 nanosecond, and the instruction must be sent back to the control unit, requiring at least another nanosecond.) Consequently, to fetch and execute an instruction in such a machine requires several nanoseconds—which means that increasing the execution speed of a machine ultimately becomes a miniaturization problem. Although fantastic advances have been made in this area, there appears to be a limit.

In an effort to solve this dilemma, computer engineers replaced the concept of execution speed with **throughput**—the total amount of work the machine can accomplish in a given amount of time rather than how long it takes to do one task.

One example of how a machine's throughput can be increased without requiring an increase in execution speed involves **pipelining,** which is the technique of allowing the steps in the machine cycle to overlap. In particular, while one instruction is being executed, the next instruction can be fetched, which means that more than one instruction can be in "the pipe" at any one time, each at a different stage of being processed. In turn, the total throughput of the machine is increased even though the time required to fetch and execute each individual instruction remains the same. Of course, when a jump instruction is reached, any gain that would have been obtained by pre-fetching is not realized because the instructions in "the pipe" are not the ones needed after all.

Modern machine designs push the pipelining concept beyond our simple example. They are often capable of fetching several instructions at the same time, and actually executing more than one instruction at a time when those instructions do not rely on each other.

Multiprocessor Machines

Pipelining can be viewed as a first step toward **parallel processing,** which is the performance of several activities at the same time. However, true parallel processing requires more than one processing unit, resulting in machines known as multiprocessor machines.

One argument in favor of multiprocessor machines looks to the human mind as a model. Today's technology is approaching the ability to construct electronic circuitry with roughly as many switching circuits as there are neurons in the human brain (neurons are believed to be nature's switching circuits), yet the capabilities of today's machines still fall far short of those of the human mind. This, so it is claimed, is a result of the inefficient use of a machine's components as dictated by its architecture. After all, if a machine is constructed with a lot of memory circuits but only a single CPU, then most of its circuitry is destined to be idle most of the time. In contrast, much of the human mind can be active at any given moment. For this reason, the proponents of parallel processing argue in favor of a machine with many processing units. This, they argue, results in a configuration with the potential of a much higher utilization factor.

A variety of machines today are designed with this idea in mind. One strategy is to attach several processing units, each resembling the CPU in a single processor machine, to the same main memory. In this configuration, the processors can proceed independently yet coordinate their efforts by leaving messages to one another in their common memory cells. For instance, when one processor is faced with a large task, it can store a program for part of that task in the common memory and then request another processor to execute it. The result is a machine in which different instruction sequences are performed on different sets of data, which is called a **MIMD** (multiple-instruction stream, multiple-data stream) architecture, as opposed to the more traditional **SISD** (single-instruction stream, single-data stream) architecture.

A variation of multiple-processor architecture is to link the processors together such that they execute the same sequence of instructions in unison, each with its own set of data. The result is an example of **SIMD** (single-instruction stream, multiple-data stream) architecture. Such machines are useful in applications in which the same task must be applied to each set of similar items within a large block of data.

Another approach to parallel processing is to construct large machines as conglomerates of smaller machines, each with its own memory and CPU. Within such an architecture, each of the small machines is coupled to its neighbors so that tasks assigned to the whole system can be divided among the individual machines. Thus, if a task assigned to one of the internal machines can be broken into independent subtasks, that machine can ask its neighbors to perform these subtasks concurrently. The original task can then be completed in much less time than would be required by a single processor machine.

Current problems in the development and use of multiprocessor machines involve issues of **load balancing**—that is, dynamically allocating tasks to the various processes so that all processors are used efficiently. Closely associated with this problem is that of **scaling,** or dividing the present task into a number of subtasks compatible with the number of processors available. Another problem entails handling the complexity of distributed task allocation. Indeed, as the number of tasks increases, the work required to allocate the assignments and to coordinate the interaction between the various tasks grows exponentially. If there are four tasks, then there are six potential pairs of tasks that may need to communicate with one another. If there are five tasks, this number of potential communication paths grows to ten; in the case of six tasks, the number jumps to fifteen.

In Chapter 10 we will study artificial neural networks, whose design is based on our understanding of the human brain. These machines represent another form of multiprocessor architecture in that they consist of many elementary processors, or processing units, each of whose output is merely a simple reaction to its combined inputs. These simple processors are linked to form a network in which the outputs of some processors are used as inputs to others. Such a machine is programmed by adjusting the extent to which each processor's output is allowed to influence the reaction of those processors to which it is connected. This simulates the way in which we believe our brains learn. Apparently, biological neural networks learn to produce a particular reaction to a given stimulus by adjusting the chemical composition of the junctions (synapses) between neurons, which in turn adjusts the ability of one neuron to affect the actions of others.

QUESTIONS/EXERCISES

1. Why does the CPU in a microprogrammed machine require two program counters and two instruction registers?

2. Referring back to Question 3 of Section 2.3, if the machine used the pipeline technique discussed in the text, what will be in "the pipe" when the instruction at address AA is executed? Under what conditions would the pipelining technique not be beneficial at this point in the program?

3. What conflicts must be resolved when running the program in Question 4 of Section 2.3 on a pipeline machine?

4. Suppose there were two "central" processing units attached to the same memory and executing different programs. Furthermore, suppose that one of these processors needs to add one to the contents of a memory cell at roughly the same time that the other needs to subtract one from the same cell. (The net effect should be that the cell ends up with the same value with which it started.)
   a. Describe a sequence in which these activities would result in the cell's ending up with a value one less than its starting value.
   b. Describe a sequence in which these activities would result in the cell's ending up with a value one greater than its starting value.

CHAPTER REVIEW PROBLEMS

(Asterisked problems are associated with optional sections.)

1. Give a brief definition of each of the following:
   a. Register   b. Cache memory
   c. Main memory   d. Mass storage

2. Suppose a block of data is stored in the memory cells of the machine described in Appendix C from address B9 to C1, inclusive. How many memory cells are in this block? List their addresses.

3. What is the value of the program counter in the machine described in Appendix C immediately after executing the instruction B0BA?

4. Suppose the memory cells at addresses 00 through 05 in the machine described in Appendix C contain the following bit patterns:

Address	Contents
00	21
01	04
02	31
03	00
04	C0
05	00

Assuming that the program counter initially contained 00, record the contents of the program counter, instruction register, and memory cell at address 00 at the end of each fetch phase of the machine cycle until the machine halts.

5. Suppose three values (x, y, and z) are stored in a machine's memory. Describe the sequence of events (loading registers

from memory, saving values in memory, and so on) that lead to the computation of $x + y + z$. How about $(2x) + y$?

6. The following are instructions written in the machine language described in Appendix C. Translate them into English.
   a. 407E   b. 9028   c. A302
   d. B3AD   e. 2835

7. Suppose a machine language is designed with an op-code field of four bits. How many different instruction types can the language contain? What if the op-code field is increased to eight bits?

8. Translate the following instructions from English into the machine language described in Appendix C.
   a. LOAD register 8 with the contents of memory cell 55.
   b. LOAD register 8 with the hexadecimal value 55.
   c. ROTATE register 4 three bits to the right.
   d. AND the contents of registers F and 2 leaving the result in register 0.
   e. Jump to the instruction at memory location 31 if the contents of register 0 equals the value in register B.

9. Classify each of the following instructions (in the machine language of Appendix C) in terms of whether its execution changes the contents of the memory cell at location 3B, retrieves the contents of the memory cell at location 3B, or is independent of the contents of the memory cell at location 3B.
   a. 153B   b. 253B   c. 353B
   d. 3B3B   e. 403B

10. Suppose the memory cells at addresses 00 through 03 in the machine described in Appendix C contain the following bit patterns:

Address	Contents
00	23
01	02
02	C0
03	00

   a. Translate the first instruction into English.
   b. If the machine is started with its program counter containing 00, what bit pattern is in register 3 when the machine halts?

11. Suppose the memory cells at addresses 00 through 05 in the machine described in Appendix C contain the following bit patterns:

Address	Contents
00	10
01	04
02	30
03	45
04	C0
05	00

   When answering the following questions, assume that the machine starts with its program counter equal to 00.

   a. Translate the instructions that are executed into English.
   b. What bit pattern is in the memory cell at address 45 when the machine halts?
   c. What bit pattern is in the program counter when the machine halts?

12. Suppose the memory cells at addresses 00 through 09 in the machine described in Appendix C contain the following bit patterns:

Address	Contents
00	1A
01	02

02	2B
03	02
04	9C
05	AB
06	3C
07	00
08	C0
09	00

Assume that the machine starts with its program counter equal to 00.

a. What will be in the memory cell at address 00 when the machine halts?
b. What bit pattern will be in the program counter when the machine halts?

13. Suppose the memory cells at addresses 00 through 0D in the machine described in Appendix C contain the following bit patterns:

Address	Contents
00	20
01	03
02	21
03	01
04	40
05	12
06	51
07	12
08	B1
09	0C
0A	B0
0B	06
0C	C0
0D	00

Assume that the machine starts with its program counter equal to 00.

a. What bit pattern will be in register 1 when the machine halts?
b. What bit pattern will be in register 0 when the machine halts?
c. What bit pattern is in the program counter when the machine halts?

14. Suppose the memory cells at addresses F0 through FD in the machine described in Appendix C contain the following (hexadecimal) bit patterns:

Address	Contents
F0	20
F1	00
F2	21
F3	01
F4	23
F5	05
F6	B3
F7	FC
F8	50
F9	01
FA	B0
FB	F6
FC	C0
FD	00

If we start the machine with its program counter equal to F0, what is the value in register 0 when the machine finally executes the halt instruction at location FC?

15. If the machine in Appendix C executes an instruction every microsecond (a millionth of a second), how long does it take to complete the program in Problem 14?

16. Suppose the memory cells at addresses 00 through 05 in the machine described in Appendix C contain the following (hexadecimal) bit patterns:

Address	Contents
00	25
01	B0
02	35
03	04
04	C0
05	00

If we start the machine with its program counter equal to 00, when does the machine halt?

17. In each of the following cases, write a short program in the machine language described in Appendix C to perform the requested activities. Assume that each of your programs is placed in memory starting at address 00.

   a. Move the value at memory location 8D to memory location B3.

   b. Interchange the values stored at memory locations 8D and B3.

   c. If the value stored in memory location 45 is 00, then place the value CC in memory location 88; otherwise, put the value DD in memory location 88.

18. A popular game among computer hobbyists is core wars—a variation of battleship. (The term *core* originates from an early memory technology in which 0s and 1s were represented as magnetic fields in little rings of magnetic material.) The game is played between two opposing programs, each stored in different locations of the same computer's memory. The computer is assumed to alternate between the two programs, executing an instruction from one followed by an instruction from the other. The goal of each program is to destroy the other by writing extraneous data on top of it; however, neither program knows the location of the other.

   a. Write a program in the machine language of Appendix C that approaches the game in a defensive manner by being as small as possible.

   b. Write a program in the language of Appendix C that tries to avoid any attacks from the opposing program by moving to different locations. More precisely, write your program to start at location 00, copy itself to location 70, and then jump to this new copy.

   c. Extend the program in (b) to continue relocating to new memory loca-

tions. In particular, make your program move to location 70, then to E0 (=70 + 70), then to 60 (=70 + 70 + 70), etc.

19. Write a program in the machine language of Appendix C to compute the sum of the two's complement values stored at memory locations A1, A2, A3, and A4. Your program should store the total at memory location A5.

20. Suppose the memory cells at addresses 00 through 05 in the machine described in Appendix C contain the following (hexadecimal) bit patterns:

Address	Contents
00	20
01	C0
02	30
03	04
04	00
05	00

What happens if we start the machine with its program counter equal to 00?

21. What happens if the memory cells at addresses 06 and 07 of the machine described in Appendix C contain the bit patterns B0 and 06, respectively, and the machine is started with its program counter containing the value 06?

22. Suppose the following program, written in the machine language of Appendix C, is stored in main memory beginning at address 30 (hexadecimal). What task will the program perform when executed?

```
2003
2101
2200
2310
1400
3410
5221
5331
```

```
3239
333B
B248
B038
C000
```

23. Summarize the steps involved when the machine described in Appendix C performs an instruction with op-code B. Express your answer as a set of directions as though you were telling the CPU what to do.

*24. Summarize the steps involved when the machine described in Appendix C performs an instruction with op-code 5. Express your answer as a set of directions as though you were telling the CPU what to do.

*25. Summarize the steps involved when the machine described in Appendix C performs an instruction with op-code 6. Express your answer as a set of directions as though you were telling the CPU what to do.

*26. Suppose the registers 4 and 5 in the machine described in Appendix C contain the bit patterns 3C and C8, respectively. What bit pattern is left in register 0 after executing each of the following instructions:

a. 5045 b. 6045 c. 7045
d. 8045 e. 9045

*27. Using the machine language described in Appendix C, write programs to perform each of the following tasks: A6 while leaving the other bits at location A6 undisturbed.

  a. Copy the bit pattern stored in memory location 66 into memory location BB.

  b. Change the least significant four bits in the memory cell at location 34 to 0s while leaving the other bits undisturbed.

  c. Copy the least significant four bits from memory location A5 into the least significant four bits of location A6 while leaving the other bits at location A6 undisturbed.

  d. Copy the least significant four bits from memory location A5 into the most significant four bits of A5. (Thus, the first four bits in A5 will be the same as the last four bits.)

*28. Perform the indicated operations:

a.
```
    111000
AND 101001
```
b.
```
    000100
AND 101010
```

c.
```
    000100
AND 010101
```
d.
```
    111011
AND 110101
```

e.
```
    111000
OR 101001
```
f.
```
    000100
OR 101010
```

g.
```
    000100
OR 010101
```
h.
```
    111011
OR 110101
```

i.
```
    111000
XOR 101001
```
j.
```
    000100
XOR 101010
```

k.
```
    000100
XOR 010101
```
l.
```
    111011
XOR 110101
```

*29. Identify both the mask and the logical operation needed to accomplish each of the following objectives:

  a. Put 0s in the middle four bits of an eight-bit pattern without disturbing the other bits.

  b. Complement a pattern of eight bits.

  c. Complement the most significant bit of an eight-bit pattern without changing the other bits.

  d. Put a 1 in the most significant bit of an eight-bit pattern without disturbing the other bits.

  e. Put 1s in all but the most significant bit of an eight-bit pattern without disturbing the most significant bit.

*30. Identify a logical operation (along with a corresponding mask) that, when applied to an input string of eight bits, produces an output string of all 0s if and only if the input string is 10000001.

*31. Describe a sequence of logical operations (along with their corresponding masks) that, when applied to an input string of eight bits, produces an output byte of all 0s if the input string both begins and ends with 1s. Otherwise, the output should contain at least one 1.

*32. What would be the result of performing a four-bit left circular shift on the following bit patterns?
a. `10101` b. `11110000` c. `001`
d. `101000` e. `00001`

*33. What would be the result of performing a one-bit right circular shift on the following bytes represented in hexadecimal notation (give your answers in hexadecimal notation)?
a. 3F b. 0D c. FF d. 77

*34. Write a program in the machine language of Appendix C that reverses the contents of the memory cell at address 8C.

*35. Can a printer, printing 40 characters per second, keep up with a string of ASCII characters (each with a parity bit) arriving serially at the rate of 300 bps? What about 1200 bps?

*36. Suppose a person is typing 30 words per minute at a keyboard. (A word is considered to be five characters.) If a machine executes one instruction every microsecond (millionth of a second), how many instructions does the machine execute during the time between the typing of two consecutive characters?

*37. How many bits per second must a keyboard transmit to keep up with a typist typing 30 words per minute? (Assume each character is coded in ASCII along with a parity bit and each word consists of five characters.)

*38. A communication system capable of transmitting any sequence of eight different states at the rate of at most 300 states per second could be used to transfer information at what rate in bits per second?

*39. Suppose the machine described in Appendix C communicates with a printer using the technique of memory mapped I/O. Suppose also that address FF is used to send characters to the printer, and address FE is used to receive information about the printer's status. In particular, suppose the least significant bit at the address FE indicates whether the printer is ready to receive another character (with a 0 indicating "not ready" and a 1 indicating "ready"). Starting at address 00, write a machine language routine that waits until the printer is ready for another character and then send the character represented by the bit pattern in register 5 to the printer.

*40. Write a program in the machine language described in Appendix C that places 0s in all the memory cells from address A0 through C0 but is small enough to fit in the memory cells from address 00 through 13 (hexadecimal).

*41. Suppose a machine has 500MB of storage space available on a hard disk and receives data over a telephone connection at the rate of 14,400 bps. At this rate, how long would it take to fill the available storage space?

*42. Suppose a communication line is being used to transmit data serially at 14,400 bps. If a burst of interference lasts .01 second, how many data bits would be affected?

*43. Suppose you are given 32 processors, each capable of finding the sum of two multi-digit numbers in a millionth of a second. Describe how parallel processing techniques can be applied to find the sum of 64 numbers in only six-millionths of a second. How much time does a single processor require to find this same sum?

*44. Summarize the difference between a CISC architecture and a RISC architecture.

*45. Summarize the distinction between main memory and micromemory.

*46. Identify two approaches to increasing throughput.

*47. Describe how the average of a collection of numbers can be computed more rapidly with a multiprocessor machine than a single processor machine.

SOCIAL ISSUES

The following questions are provided to help you understand some of the ethical/social/legal issues associated with the field of computing as well as investigate your own beliefs and their foundations. The goal is not merely to answer these questions. You should also consider why you answered as you did and whether your justifications are consistent from one question to the next.

1. Suppose a computer manufacturer develops a new machine architecture. To what extent should the company be allowed to own that architecture? What policy would be best for society?

2. In a sense, the year 1923 marks the birth of what many now call *planned obsolescence*. This was the year that General Motors, led by Alfred Sloan, introduced the automobile industry to the concept of model years. The idea was to increase sales by changing styling rather than necessarily introducing a better automobile. Sloan is quoted as saying, "We want to make you dissatisfied with your current car so you will buy a new one." To what extent is this marketing ploy used today in the computer industry? Is the machine that was the top-of-the-line six months ago really old-fashioned today?

3. We often think in terms of how computer technology has changed our society. Many argue, however, that this technology has often kept changes from occurring by allowing old systems to survive and, in some cases, become more entrenched. For example, would the dominance of the New York Stock Exchange or the U.S. government's role in society have survived without computer technology? To what extent would centralized authority be present today had computer technology not been available? To what extent would we be better off or worse off without computer technology?

4. Is it ethical for an individual to take the attitude that he or she need not know anything about the internal details of a machine because someone else will build it, maintain it, and fix any problems that

arise? Does your answer depend on whether the machine is a computer, automobile, nuclear power plant, or toaster?

5. Suppose a manufacturer produces a computer chip and later discovers a flaw in its design. Suppose further that the manufacturer decides not to recall the chips already shipped but to keep the flaw a secret, reasoning that none of the chips already in use are being used in an application in which the flaw will have consequences. Is anyone hurt by the manufacturer's decision?

6. Is advancing technology a cure for heart disease or the source of a sedentary life style that leads to heart disease?

7. In *Walden,* Henry David Thoreau argues that we have become tools of our tools, that is, instead of benefiting from the tools that we have, we spend our time obtaining and maintaining our tools. To what extent is this true in regards to computing? For example, if you own a personal computer, how much time do you spend earning the money to pay for it, learning how to use it, maintaining it, upgrading it, and worrying about it in comparison to the amount of time you spend benefiting from it? When you use it, is your time well spent? Are you more socially active with or without a personal computer?

8. It is easy to imagine financial or navigational disasters that may occur as the result of arithmetic errors due to overflow and truncation problems. What consequences could result from mistakes caused by errors in image storage systems (perhaps in reconnaissance or medical diagnosis)?

ADDITIONAL READING

Hamacher, V. C., Z. G. Vranesic, and S. G. Zaky. *Computer Organization,* 4th ed. New York: McGraw-Hill, 1996.

Knuth, D. E. *The Art of Computer Programming,* vol. 1, 3rd ed. Reading, MA: Addison Wesley Longman, 1998.

Patterson, D. A., and J. L. Hennessy. *Computer Organization and Design.* San Francisco: Morgan Kaufmann, 1994.

SOFTWARE

In Part 1 we discussed the major components of a computer—the tangible parts that are classified as hardware. In contrast, the programs that this hardware executes are intangible and are classified as software. In Part 2, we turn our attention to topics associated with software, which leads us to the core of computer science—the study of algorithms. In particular, we will investigate the discovery, representation, and communication of algorithms.

We begin by discussing operating systems in Chapter 3. These systems are large, complex software packages that control the overall activities of a machine or group of machines connected as a network. Thus, our study of operating systems will naturally lead us to the study of networks. Chapter 4 focuses on algorithms, with an emphasis on how algorithms are discovered and represented. In Chapter 5, we turn to the topic of how algorithms are communicated to machines through the programming process and investigate properties of popular programming languages. Chapter 6 considers the entire software development process in the context of software engineering.

c h a p t e r

OPERATING SYSTEMS AND NETWORKS

t h r e e

Today's computer applications often require a single machine to perform activities that may compete with one another for the machine's resources. For example, a machine may be connected to several terminals or workstations from which different users can simultaneously request machine services. Even in a single-user installation, the user may require several intertwined activities such as printing a document, modifying another document, and creating a graphical display to be inserted into a document. These demands require a high degree of coordination to ensure that unrelated activities do not interfere with one another and that communication between related activities is efficient and reliable. This coordination is handled by a software system known as an operating system.

Similar coordination and communication problems arise when different machines are connected to form a computer network. Solving these problems is a natural extension of the subject of operating systems. In this chapter we discuss fundamental concepts relating to operating systems and networking.

3.1 The Evolution of Operating Systems
Single-Processor Systems
Multiprocessor Systems

3.2 Operating System Architecture
A Software Survey
Components of an Operating System
Getting It Started

3.3 Coordinating the Machine's Activities
The Concept of a Process
Process Administration
The Client/Server Model

*3.4 Handling Competition Among Processes
Semaphores
Deadlock

3.5 Networks
Network Classification
The Internet

*3.6 Network Protocols
Controlling Transmission Privileges
The Layered Approach to Network Software
The TCP/IP Protocol Suite

3.7 Security

*Asterisks indicate suggestions for optional sections.

3.1 The Evolution of Operating Systems

We approach our study of operating systems and networking with a historical perspective, from the early single-processor systems to the more recent multi-processor systems.

Single-Processor Systems

The single-processor machines of the 1940s and 1950s were not very flexible or efficient. Program execution required significant preparation of equipment in terms of mounting tapes, placing punched cards in the card reader, setting switches, and so on. The execution of each program, called a *job,* was handled as an isolated activity. When several users needed to share a machine, sign-up sheets were provided so that users could reserve the machine for blocks of time. During the time period allocated to a user, the machine was totally under that user's control. The session usually began with program setup, followed by short periods of program execution. It was often completed in a hurried effort to do just one more thing ("It will only take a minute") while the next user was impatiently starting to set up.

In such an environment, operating systems began as systems for simplifying program setup and for streamlining the transition between jobs. One early development was the separation of users and equipment, which eliminated the physical transition of people in and out of the computer room. For this purpose a computer operator was hired to perform the actual operation of the machine. Anyone wanting a program run was required to submit it, along with any required data and special directions about the program's requirements, to the operator and return later for the results. The operator, in turn, loaded these materials into the machine's mass storage where the operating system could access them for execution. This was the beginning of **batch processing**—the execution of jobs by collecting them in a single batch, then executing them without further interaction with the user. The jobs residing in mass storage waited for execution in a **job queue** (Figure 3.1).

A **queue** is a storage organization in which objects (in our case, jobs) are ordered in **first-in, first-out (FIFO)** fashion. That is, the objects are removed from the queue in the order in which they arrived. In reality, most job queues do not rigorously follow the FIFO structure, since most operating systems provide for consideration of job priorities. As a result, a job waiting in the job queue can be bumped by a higher-priority job.

In early batch processing systems, each job was accompanied by a set of instructions explaining the steps required to prepare the machine for that particular job. These instructions were coded in a job control language (JCL) and stored with the job in the job queue. When the job was selected for execution, the operating system printed these instructions at a printer where they could be

FIGURE 3.1

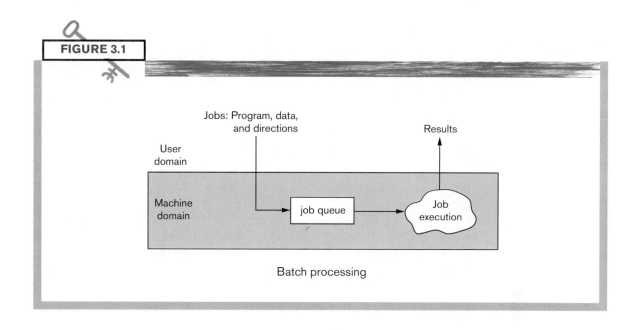

Batch processing

read and followed by the operator. The instructions that required action by the operator dealt mainly with issues of off-line equipment, and since these activities are minimal today, job control languages have become a conduit for communication with the operating system rather than a computer operator. Indeed, the position of computer operator is becoming obsolete. Today, institutions hire system administrators to manage the computer system—obtaining and overseeing the installation of new equipment and software, enforcing local regulations such as the issuing of new accounts and establishing the disk space limits for the various users, and coordinating efforts to resolve problems that arise in the system—rather than operating machines in a hands-on manner.

The major drawback to traditional batch processing is that the user has no interaction with the program once it is submitted to the job queue. This approach is acceptable for some applications, such as payroll processing, in which the data and all processing decisions are established in advance. However, it is not acceptable when the user must interact with the program during its execution. Examples include reservation systems in which reservations and cancellations must be reported as they occur, word processing systems in which documents are developed in a dynamic write and rewrite manner, and computer games in which interaction with the machine is the central feature of the game.

To accommodate these needs, new operating systems were developed that allowed the execution of programs that carried on a dialogue with the user through remote terminals or workstations—a feature known as **interactive processing** (Figure 3.2). These interactive systems required that the activities taking place in a machine be coordinated with the activities in the machine's

FIGURE 3.2

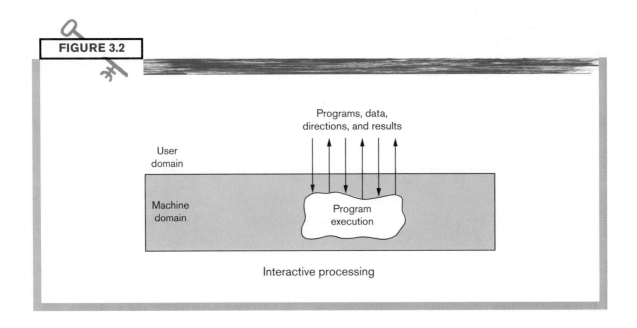

Interactive processing

environment. This coordination between the machine and its environment is called **real-time processing.**

If interactive systems had been required to serve only one user at a time, real-time processing would have been no problem. But machines were expensive, and so each machine had to serve more than one user. In turn, it was common for several users to seek interactive service of a machine at the same time, and real-time considerations presented obstacles. If the operating system for such a multiuser environment insisted on executing only one job at a time, only one user would receive satisfactory real-time service.

A solution to this problem was to design the operating system so that it rotated the various jobs in and out of execution by a process called **time-sharing,** which is the technique of dividing time into intervals, or time slices, and then restricting the execution of a job to only one time slice at a time. At the end of each time slice, the current job is set aside and another is allowed to execute during the next time slice. By rapidly shuffling the jobs in this manner, the illusion of several jobs executing simultaneously is created. Depending on the types of jobs being executed, early time-sharing systems were able to provide acceptable real-time processing to as many as 30 users at the same time.

Today, time-sharing is used in single-user as well as multiuser systems, although in the former it is usually called **multitasking,** in reference to the illusion of more than one task being performed simultaneously. Regardless of whether the environment is single-user or multiuser, the use of time-sharing has been found to increase the overall efficiency of a machine. This finding may be surprising when one considers that the shuffling process required by time-sharing introduces a significant overhead. Indeed, the time spent switching between jobs is nonproductive. However, without time-sharing a computer system spends much of its time waiting for peripheral devices to complete tasks or for a user to make the next request. Time-sharing allows this lost time to be given to another task. Hence, progress on one task can be made while another task is waiting. In turn, a collection of tasks will often be completed in less time when executed in a time-sharing environment than when executed in a sequential manner.

Multiprocessor Systems

In recent years the need to share information and resources among different machines has spawned the desire to link the machines for the exchange of information. To fill that need, coupled computer systems called **networks** have become popular. Today, the concept of a large central machine serving many users has largely given way to the concept of many small machines connected via a network in which users share resources—such as printing capabilities, software packages, data storage facilities, and information—that are scattered throughout the system. A prime example is the **Internet,** a network of networks that today links millions of machines worldwide. We will study the Internet more closely in Sections 3.5 and 3.6.

Many of the coordination problems that occur in network designs are the same or very similar to those faced by operating systems. In fact, software for controlling a network can be viewed as a network-wide operating system. In this light, network software development is a natural extension of the field of operating systems. Whereas early networks were constructed as loosely coupled individual machines, each under the control of its own operating system, network research is moving toward network-wide systems in which the resources in a network are shared equally among the tasks assigned to the network. These resources are in turn

BENEFICIAL UNIFORMITY OR DETRIMENTAL MONOPOLY?

Since a computer's operating system establishes the basis on which communication with the machine is performed, it seems reasonable that the use of a standard operating system across a wide range of machines would be a good thing. Such a standard would mean that operating skills learned on one machine could easily be transferred to other machines. Moreover, developers of application software would not have to produce products that were compatible with multiple operating system designs. However, these arguments overlook many of the realities of today's society. In particular, the producer of a universal operating system would have tremendous power in the marketplace. If misused, this power could potentially be more harmful than beneficial to the users of computers. Many of these issues have been documented by the parties involved in the U.S. Government's antitrust lawsuit against Microsoft that began in 1998. To learn about this and similar lawsuits, your local librarian may be able to give you free access to some of the excellent news archival services on the Web. If you don't have library assistance, you might want to check out the Web sites at http://newsweek.com, http://www.npr.org http://www.nytimes.com, and http://washingtonpost.com

assigned tasks according to the needs of the network, regardless of their physical locations. An example is the name server system used in the Internet, which we will study in Section 3.5. This system allows a variety of machines scattered around the world to work together to translate an Internet address from its human compatible mnemonic form into its network compatible numeric form.

Networks represent only one example of the multiprocessor designs that are inspiring the development of today's operating systems. Whereas a network produces a multiprocessor system by combining machines, each of which may contain only one CPU, other multiprocessor systems are designed as single machines containing more than one processor. An operating system for such a machine must not only coordinate the competition between the various activities that are actually executing simultaneously but also control the assignment of activities to the processors in the machine. This process involves problems of **load balancing** (making sure that the processors are used efficiently) as well as **scaling** (breaking tasks into a number of subtasks compatible with the number of processors in the machine).

We see then that the development of multiprocessor systems has added new dimensions to the subject of operating systems, and the field promises to remain active for years to come.

QUESTIONS/EXERCISES

1. Identify examples of queues. In each case, indicate any situations that violate the FIFO structure.
2. Which of the following would require real-time processing?
   a. Printing mailing labels
   b. Playing a computer game
   c. Displaying letters on a monitor screen as they are typed at the keyboard
   d. Executing a program that predicts the state of next year's economy
3. What is the difference between real-time processing and interactive processing?
4. What is the difference between time-sharing and multitasking?

3.2 Operating System Architecture

To understand the architecture of a typical operating system, it is helpful to grasp the complete spectrum of software found within a typical computer system. We begin this task with a software survey in which we present a scheme for classifying software. Such classifications invariably place similar software units in different classes in the same manner as the assignment of time zones dictates that nearby communities must set their clocks an hour apart even though there is no significant difference between the occurrence of sunrise and sunset. Moreover, in the case of software classification, the dynamics of the subject and the lack of a definitive authority lead to contradictory terminology. For example, users of Microsoft's Windows 98 will find a program group known as accessories that includes software from our application class as well as our utility class. The following classification should therefore be viewed as a means of gaining a foothold in a complex subject rather than as a statement of universally accepted fact.

A Software Survey

Let us first divide a machine's software into two broad categories: **application software** and **system software** (Figure 3.3). Application software consists of the programs for performing tasks particular to the machine's utilization. A machine used to maintain the inventory for a manufacturing company will contain different application software from that found on a machine used by an electrical engineer. Examples of application software include spreadsheets, database systems, desktop publishing systems, program development software, and games.

In contrast to application software, system software performs those tasks that are common to computer systems in general. In a sense, the system software provides the environment in which the application software resides, in much the same manner as a nation's infrastructure provides the foundation on which its citizens rely for their individual lifestyles.

Within the class of system software are two categories, one being the operating system itself and the other consisting of software units collectively known

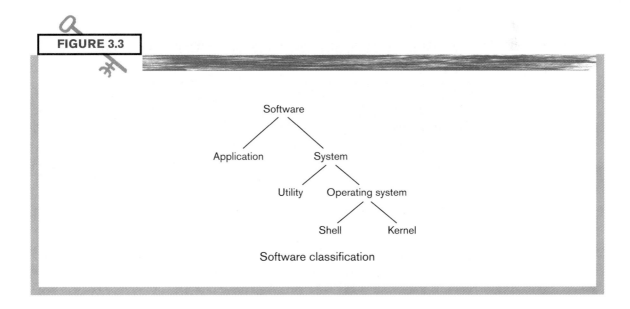

FIGURE 3.3

Software classification

as **utility software.** The majority of an installation's utility software consists of programs for performing activities that are fundamental to computer installations yet not included in the operating system. In a sense, utility software consists of software units that extend the capabilities of the operating system. For example, the ability to format a disk or to copy a file is often not implemented within the operating system itself but instead is provided by means of a utility program. Other instances of utility software include software for communicating through a modem over telephone lines, software to compress and decompress data, and software for handling network communication.

By implementing certain activities as utility software, the design of an operating system can be less complex than it would be otherwise. Moreover, the routines implemented as utility software can be customized more readily to the needs of a particular installation. Indeed, it is not uncommon to find companies or individuals who have modified, or added to, the utility software that was originally provided with their machine's operating system.

The distinction between application software and utility software is often vague. From our point of view, the distinction is whether the package is part of the software infrastructure. Thus a new application may evolve into a utility if it becomes a fundamental tool. The distinction between utility software and the operating system is equally vague. Some systems implement the software for providing such basic services as listing files in mass storage as utility software; others include it within the operating system.

Components of an Operating System

The portion of an operating system that defines the interface between the operating system and its users is often called the **shell.** The job of the shell is to communicate with the user, or users, of the machine. Modern shells perform this task by means of a **graphical user interface (GUI)** in which objects to be manipulated, such as files and programs, are represented pictorially on the monitor screen as icons. These systems allow users to issue commands by pointing to and pushing these icons on the screen by means of a hand-held device called a mouse. Older shells communicate via users through textual messages using a keyboard and monitor screen.

Although an operating system's shell plays an important role in establishing a machine's functionality, this shell is merely an interface between a user and the real heart of the operating system (Figure 3.4). This distinction between the shell and the internal parts of the operating system is emphasized by the fact that some operating systems allow a user to select among different shells to obtain the most compatible interface for that particular user. Users of the UNIX operating system, for example, can select among a variety of shells including the Borne shell, the C shell, and the Korn shell. Early versions of Microsoft Windows were essentially replacement shells for MS-DOS. In these cases the operating system remains the same except for the way it communicates with the machine's users.

FIGURE 3.4

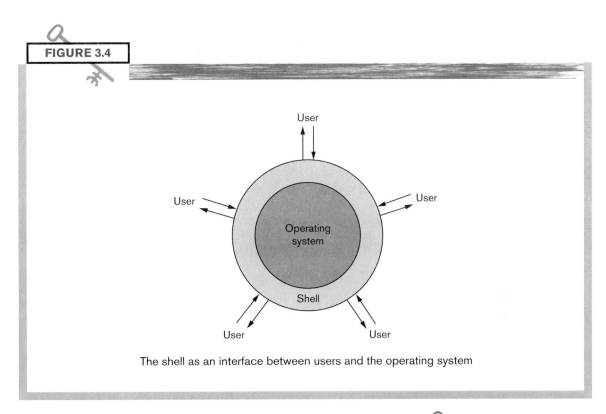

The shell as an interface between users and the operating system

A major component within today's GUI shells is the **window manager,** which allocates blocks of space on the screen, called windows, and keeps track of which application is associated with each window. When an application wants to display something on the screen, it notifies the window manager, and the window manager places the desired pattern in the window assigned to the application. In turn, when a mouse button is pressed, it is the window manager that computes the mouse's location on the screen and notifies the appropriate application of the mouse action.

In contrast to an operating system's shell, the internal part of an

LINUX

For the computer enthusiast who wants to experiment with the internal components of an operating system, there is Linux. Linux is an operating system originally designed by Linus Torvalds while a student at the University of Helsinki. It is a nonproprietary product and thus available, along with its source code (see Chapter 5) and documentation, without charge. Because it is freely available in source code form, it has become popular among computer hobbyists, students of operating systems, and programmers in general. It has also become popular as a substitute for the commercial operating systems on the market. However, installing Linux usually involves a higher level of expertise than that of the commercial products such as Microsoft's Windows, which is usually preinstalled on personal computers. You can learn more about Linux from the Web site at http://www.linux.org

operating system is often called its **kernel.** An operating system's kernel contains those software components that perform the very basic functions required by the computer installation. One such unit is the **file manager,** whose job is to coordinate the use of the machine's mass storage facilities. More precisely, the file manager keeps records of all the files stored in mass storage, including where each file is located, which users are allowed to access the various files, and what portions of mass storage are available for new or extending files.

For the convenience of the machine's users, most file managers allow files to be grouped into a bundle called a **directory** or **folder.** This approach allows a user to organize his or her files according to their purposes by placing related files in the same directory. Moreover, by allowing directories to contain other directories, called subdirectories, a hierarchical organization can be constructed. For example, a user may create a directory called Records that contains subdirectories called FinancialRecords, MedicalRecords, and HouseholdRecords. Within each of these subdirectories could be files that fall within that particular category. A chain of directories within directories is called a directory **path.**

Any access to a file by other software units is obtained at the discretion of the file manager. The procedure begins by requesting that the file manager grant access to the file through a procedure known as opening the file. If the file manager approves of the requested access, it provides the information needed to find and manipulate the file. This information is stored in an area of main memory called a **file descriptor.** It is by referencing the information in this file descriptor that individual operations are performed on the file.

Another component of the kernel consists of a collection of **device drivers,** which are the software units that communicate with the controllers (or at times, directly with the devices) to carry out operations on the machine's peripheral devices. Each device driver, uniquely designed for its particular type of device (such as a printer, disk drive, magnetic tape unit, or monitor), translates general requests into the more technical steps required by the device assigned to that driver. In this manner, the design of other software units can be independent of the unique details of particular devices. The result is a generic operating system that can be customized for particular peripheral devices by merely installing the appropriate device drivers.

Still another component of an operating system's kernel is the **memory manager,** charged with the task of coordinating the machine's use of main memory. Such duties are minimal in an environment in which the machine is asked to perform only one task at a time. In these cases, the program for performing the current task is placed in main memory, executed, and then replaced by the program for performing the next task. However, in multiuser or multitasking environments in which the machine is asked to address many needs at the same time, the duties of the memory manager are extensive. In these cases, many programs and blocks of data must reside in main memory concurrently, each in an area of memory set aside for it by the memory manager. As the needs of different activities come and go, the memory manager must find places to fulfill their memory requirements and keep track of those memory areas no longer occupied.

The task of the memory manager is complicated further when the total main memory space required exceeds the space actually available in the machine. In this case the memory manager may create the illusion of additional memory space by rotating programs and data back and forth between main memory and mass storage. This illusionary memory space is called **virtual memory.** Suppose, for example, that a main memory of 64 megabytes is required but only 32 megabytes is actually available. To create the illusion of the larger memory space, the memory manager would divide the required space into units called **pages** and store the contents of these pages in mass storage. A typical page size is no more than four kilobytes. As different pages are actually required in main memory, the memory manager would exchange them for pages that are no longer required, and thus the other software units could execute as though there were actually 64 megabytes of main memory in the machine.

Also within the kernel of an operating system are the **scheduler** and **dispatcher,** which we study in the next section. For now we merely note that in a time-sharing system the scheduler determines which activities are to be considered for execution and the dispatcher controls the allocation of time slices to these activities.

Getting It Started

We have seen how an operating system communicates with the machine's users and how the components of the operating system work together to coordinate the execution of activities within the machine, but we have not considered how the operating system itself gets started. This is accomplished through a procedure known as **boot strapping** (often shortened to **booting**) that is performed by the machine each time it is turned on. The first step to understanding this procedure is to understand why it is necessary in the first place.

A CPU is designed so that its program counter starts with a particular predetermined address each time the CPU is turned on. It is at this location, then, that the CPU expects to find the first instruction to be executed. To ensure that the desired program is present, this portion of memory is normally constructed in such a way that its content is permanent. Such memory is known as **read-only memory (ROM).** Once bit patterns are placed in ROM by a special process analogous to blowing fuses on a chip, it remains there whether the machine is on or off.

In the case of small computers used as control devices in microwave ovens, automobile ignition systems, and stereo receivers, it is feasible to devote significant portions of main memory to ROM since flexibility is not an issue. The program to be executed by such devices is the same each time the device is turned on. But this is not the case in general-purpose computers, so it is not practical to devote large portions of the main memory in these machines to fixed, predetermined programs. Instead, the contents of the memory in these machines must be changeable. In fact, most of the memory in a general-purpose computer today is constructed so that its content is not only changeable but is lost when the machine is turned off. Such memory is said to be volatile.

For the purpose of booting a general-purpose machine, then, only a small part of its main memory is constructed from ROM. This area of ROM constitutes the memory cells at which the CPU expects to find instructions when it is first turned on. The small program that is permanently stored at this location is called the **bootstrap.** This is the program that is executed automatically when the machine is turned on. It directs the CPU to transfer material from a predetermined location in mass storage into the volatile area of main memory (Figure 3.5). In most cases this material is the operating system. Once the operating system has been placed in main memory, the bootstrap directs the CPU to execute a jump instruction to that area of memory. At this point, the operating system takes over and begins controlling the machine's activities.

In most personal computers today, the bootstrap is designed to try to extract the operating system from a floppy disk first. If no such disks are found to be inserted in the machine, the bootstrap will automatically try to extract the operating system from the machine's hard disk. If, however, a floppy disk is inserted in a drive and that disk does not contain a copy of the operating system, the bootstrap will pause with an error message to the machine's operator. You have probably experienced this phenomenon if you have turned on a personal computer with data disks inserted in the machine's floppy disk drives.

QUESTIONS/EXERCISES

1. List the components of a typical operating system and summarize the role of each in a single phrase.
2. What is the difference between application software and utility software?
3. What is virtual memory?
4. Summarize the booting procedure.

3.3 Coordinating the Machine's Activities

In this section we consider how an operating system coordinates the execution of application software, utility software, and units within the operating system itself. We begin with the concept of a process.

FIGURE 3.5

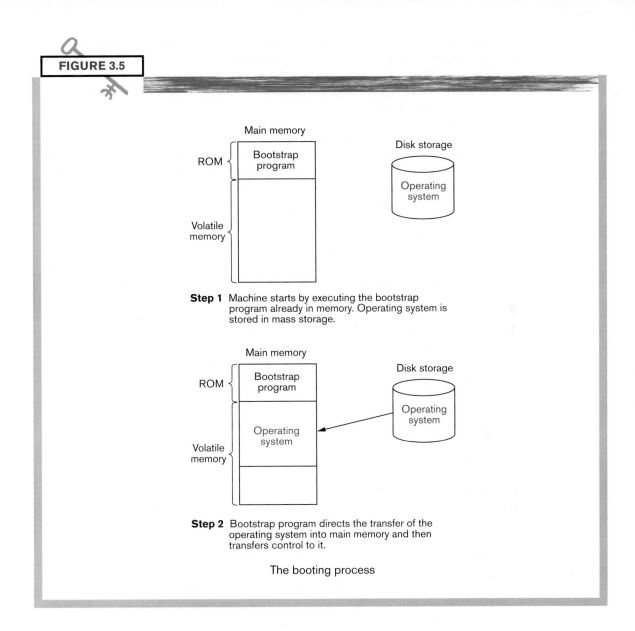

Step 1 Machine starts by executing the bootstrap program already in memory. Operating system is stored in mass storage.

Step 2 Bootstrap program directs the transfer of the operating system into main memory and then transfers control to it.

The booting process

The Concept of a Process

One of the most fundamental concepts of modern operating systems is the distinction between a program and the activity of executing a program. The former is merely a static set of directions, the latter is a dynamic activity whose properties change as time progresses. This activity is known as a **process.** A process encompasses the current status of the activity, called the **process state.** This state includes the current position in the program being executed (the value of the program counter) as well as the values in the other CPU registers and the associated memory cells. Roughly speaking, the process state is a snapshot of the machine at that time. At different times during the execution of a program (at different times in a process) different snapshots (different process states) will be observed.

To emphasize the distinction between a program and a process, note that a single program can be associated with more than one process at the same time. For example, in a multiuser, time-sharing system two users may wish to edit separate documents at the same time. Both activities may use the same editing program, but each would be a separate process with its own set of data and its own rate of progress. In this situation an operating system may keep only one copy of the editor program in main memory and allow each process to use it during its time slice.

In a typical time-sharing computer installation, many processes are normally competing for time slices. These processes include the execution of application and utility programs as well as portions of the operating system. It is the task of the operating system to coordinate these processes. Coordination involves ensuring that each process has the resources (peripheral devices, space in main memory, access to data, and access to a CPU) that it needs, that independent processes do not interfere with one another, and that processes that need to exchange information are able to do so. Communication between processes is called **interprocess communication.**

Process Administration

The tasks associated with process coordination are handled by the scheduler and dispatcher within the operating system's kernel. As such, the scheduler maintains a record of the processes present in the computer system, introduces new processes to this pool, and removes processes that are complete. To keep track of all the processes, the scheduler maintains a block of information in main memory called the **process table.** Each time a new task is assigned to the machine, the scheduler creates a process for that task by placing a new entry in the process table. This entry contains such information as the memory area assigned to the process (obtained from the memory manager), the priority of the process, and whether the process is ready or waiting. A process is **ready** if it is in a state in which its progress can continue; it is **waiting** if its progress is currently delayed until some external event occurs, such as the completion of a disk access or the arrival of a message from another process.

The dispatcher is the component of the kernel that ensures that the scheduled processes are actually executed. In a time-sharing system this task is accomplished by dividing time into short segments, each called a **time slice** or **quantum** (typically about 50 milliseconds), and then switching the CPU's attention among the processes as each is allowed to execute for no longer than one time slice (Figure 3.6). The procedure of changing from one process to another is called a **process switch.**

FIGURE 3.6

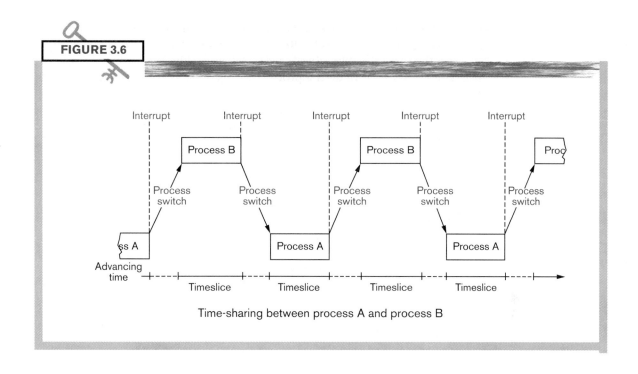

Time-sharing between process A and process B

Each time a process begins its time slice, the dispatcher initiates a timer circuit that will measure the next quantum. At the end of the quantum the timer circuit generates a signal called an **interrupt.** The CPU reacts to this signal in much the same way that you react when interrupted from a task. You stop what you are doing, record where you are in the task, and take care of the interrupting entity. When the CPU receives an interrupt signal, it completes its current machine cycle, saves its position in the current process (we will return to this step in a moment), and begins executing a program, called the **interrupt handler,** that is stored at a predetermined location in main memory.

In our time-sharing scenario, the interrupt handler is a part of the dispatcher. Thus the effect of the interrupt signal is to preempt the current process and transfer control back to the dispatcher. At this point, the dispatcher allows the scheduler to update the process table (for instance, the priority of the process that has just completed its time slice may need to be lowered and the priorities of other processes may need to be raised). The dispatcher then selects the process from the process table that has the highest priority among the ready processes, restarts the timer circuit, and allows the selected process to begin its time slice.

Paramount to the success of a time-sharing system is the ability to stop, and later restart, a process. If you are interrupted while reading a book, your ability to continue reading at a later time depends on your ability to remember your location in the book as well as the information that you had accumulated to that point. In short, you must be able to re-create the environment that was present immediately prior to the interruption. Such an environment in the case of a process is the process's state. Recall that this state includes the value of the program counter as well as the contents of the registers and pertinent memory cells. Machines designed for time-sharing systems incorporate the task of saving this information as part of the CPU's reaction to the interrupt signal. These machines also tend to have machine-language instructions for reloading a previously saved state. Such machine features simplify the task of the dispatcher when performing a process switch and exemplify how the design of modern machines is influenced by the needs of today's operating systems.

At times a process's time slice is terminated before the timer has expired. For example, if a process executes an I/O request, such as a request to retrieve data from a disk, the time slice of that process will be terminated since the process would merely waste the remaining time waiting for the controller to perform the request. In this case, the scheduler will update the process table to reflect the process's waiting status and the dispatcher will assign a new quantum to a process that is ready. Later (perhaps several hundred milliseconds), when the controller indicates that the I/O request has been completed, the scheduler will reclassify the process as ready, and thus that process will again compete for a time slice.

The Client/Server Model

The various units within an operating system normally execute as individual processes that, in a time-sharing system, compete for time slices under control of the dispatcher. To coordinate their activities, these processes must communicate with one another. For example, to schedule a new process, the scheduler must obtain memory space from the memory manager for that process, and to access a file in mass storage, any process must first obtain information from the file manager.

To simplify this interprocess communication, the components of an operating system are often designed to conform to the **client/server model** (Figure 3.7). This model defines the basic roles played by the components as being that of either a **client,** which makes requests of other units, or a **server,** which satisfies the requests made by clients. For example, the file manager would take the form of a server that provides access to files as requested by its clients. Based on this model, interprocess communication within an operating system consists of requests from processes playing the client role and replies from processes playing the server role.

Compliance to the client/server model in the design of software leads to software units with well-defined roles. A client merely sends requests to servers and waits for replies; a server merely performs the services requested and sends replies back to the clients. The role of a server is the same whether the client being served resides on the same machine or on a distant machine within a network. The distinction is in the software handling the communication—not in

FIGURE 3.7

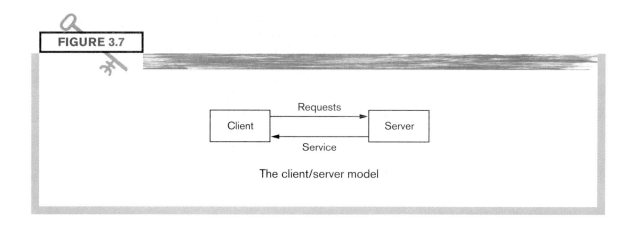

The client/server model

the clients and servers. In turn, if the components of a software system are designed as clients and servers, then these components can perform their tasks when residing on the same machine or when residing on different machines separated by great distances (Figure 3.8). Thus, as long as the underlying software provides a means of sending requests and replies, a collection of clients and servers can be distributed among the machines in any configuration that is convenient for the network.

FIGURE 3.8

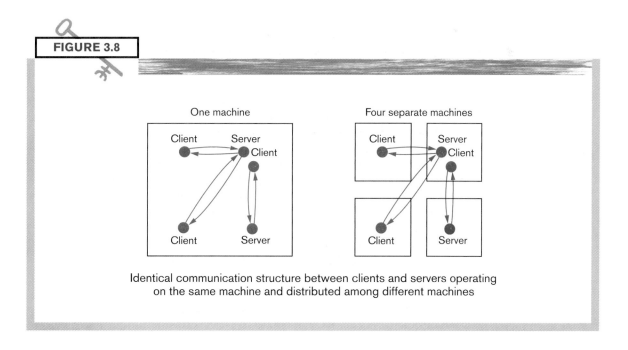

Identical communication structure between clients and servers operating on the same machine and distributed among different machines

The desire to establish a uniform message-passing system that can support such a distributed system in computer networks is the underlying goal of the set of standards and specifications known as CORBA (Common Object Request Broker Architecture). In short, CORBA provides a standard for network-wide communication between software units known as objects (such as clients and servers). It was developed by the Object Management Group, which is a consortium of hardware and software manufacturers as well as users who are interested in promoting and expanding the scope of object-oriented technology—a subject that we will introduce in Chapter 5 and repeatedly discuss in future chapters.

QUESTIONS/EXERCISES

1. Summarize the difference between a program and a process.
2. Summarize the steps performed by the CPU when an interrupt occurs.
3. In a time-sharing system, how can high-priority processes be allowed to run faster than others?
4. If each quantum in a time-sharing system is 50 milliseconds and each process switch requires 5 milliseconds, how many processes can the machine service in a single second?
5. If each process uses its complete quantum in the machine in Exercise 4, what fraction of the machine's time is spent actually performing processes? What would this fraction be if each process executes an I/O request after only 5 milliseconds of its quantum?
6. Identify some relationships in society that conform to the client/server model.

3.4 Handling Competition Among Processes

A universal task among the components of an operating system's kernel is the allocation of the machine's resources to the processes in the system. Here we are using the term *resource* in a broad sense, including the machine's peripheral devices as well as features within the machine itself. The file manager allocates both access to current files and disk space for the construction of new files; the memory manager allocates memory space; the scheduler allocates space in the process table; and the dispatcher allocates time slices. As with many problems in computer systems, this allocation task may appear simple on the surface. Below the surface, however, lie several problems that can lead to malfunctions in a poorly designed system. Remember, a machine does not think for itself; it merely follows directions. Thus to construct reliable operating systems, we must develop algorithms that cover every possible issue, regardless of how minuscule it may appear.

Semaphores

Consider a time-sharing operating system controlling the activities of a machine with a single printer. If a process needs to print its results, it must request that the operating system give it access to the printer's device driver. At this point, the operating system must decide whether to grant this request, depending upon whether the printer is already being used by another process. If it is not, the operating system should grant the request and allow the process to continue; otherwise, the operating system should deny the request and perhaps classify the process as a waiting process until the printer becomes available. Indeed, if two processes were given simultaneous access to the machine's printer, the results would be worthless to both.

To control access to the printer, the operating system must keep track of whether the printer has been allocated. One approach to this task would be to use a flag, which in this context refers to a bit in memory whose states are often referred to as *set* and *clear*, rather than 1 and 0. A clear flag indicates that the printer is available and a set flag indicates that the printer is currently allocated. On the surface this approach seems to hold no unforeseen problems. The operating system merely checks the flag each time a request for printer access is made. If it is clear, the request is granted and the operating system sets the flag. If the flag is set, the operating system makes the requesting process wait. Each time a process finishes with the printer, the operating system either allocates the printer to a waiting process or, if no process is waiting, merely clears the flag.

Although this solution looks good at first glance, it has a problem. The task of testing and possibly setting the flag requires several machine steps. It is therefore possible for the task to be interrupted after a clear flag has been detected but before the flag has been set. The following scenario could therefore take place.

Suppose the printer is currently available and a process requests use of it. The corresponding flag is checked and found to be clear, indicating that the printer is available. However, at this point, the process is interrupted and another process begins its time slice. It too requests the use of the printer. Again, the flag is checked and found still clear because the previous process was interrupted before the operating system had time to set the flag. Consequently, the operating system allows the second process to begin using the printer. Later, the original process resumes execution where it left off, which is immediately after the operating system found the flag to be clear. Thus the operating system continues by granting the original process access to the printer. Two processes are now using the same printer.

The problem here is that the task of testing and possibly setting the flag must be completed without interruption. One solution is to use the interrupt disable and interrupt enable instructions provided in most machine languages.

If the operating system starts the flag-testing routine with a disable interrupt instruction and ends it with an enable interrupt instruction, no other activity can interrupt the routine once it starts.

Another approach is to use the **test-and-set** instruction that is available in many machine languages. This instruction directs the CPU to retrieve the value of a flag, note the value received, and then set the flag all within a single machine instruction. The advantage here is that since the CPU always completes an instruction before recognizing an interrupt, the task of testing and setting the flag cannot be interrupted when it is implemented as a single instruction.

A properly implemented flag, as just described, is called a **semaphore,** in reference to the railroad signals used to control access to sections of track. In fact, semaphores are used in software systems in much the same way as they are in railway systems. Corresponding to the section of track that can contain only one train at a time is a sequence of instructions that can be executed by only one process at a time. Such a sequence of instructions is called a **critical region.** The requirement that only one process at a time be allowed to execute a critical region is known as **mutual exclusion.** In summary, a common way of obtaining mutual exclusion to a critical region is to guard the critical region with a semaphore. To enter the critical region, a process must find the semaphore clear and then set the semaphore before entering the critical region; then upon exiting the critical region, the process must clear the semaphore.

Deadlock

Another problem that can arise during resource allocation is **deadlock,** the condition in which two or more processes are blocked from progressing because each is waiting for access to resources allocated to another. For example, one process may have access to the machine's printer but be waiting for the tape drive, while another process has access to the tape drive but is waiting for the printer. Another example occurs when processes create new processes to perform subtasks. If the scheduler has no space left in the process table and each process in the system must create an additional process before it can complete its task, then no process can continue. Such conditions, as in other settings (Figure 3.9), can severely degrade a system's performance.

Analysis of deadlock has revealed that it cannot occur unless all three of the following conditions are satisfied:

1. There is competition for nonshareable resources.
2. The resources are requested on a partial basis; that is, having received some resources, a process will return later to request more.
3. Once a resource has been allocated, it cannot be forcibly retrieved.

The point of isolating these conditions is that the deadlock problem can be removed by attacking any one of the three. In general, techniques that attack

FIGURE 3.9

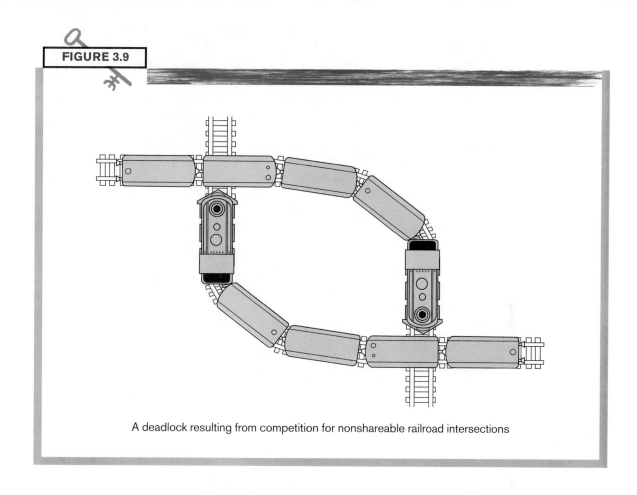

A deadlock resulting from competition for nonshareable railroad intersections

the third condition tend to fall in the category known as deadlock detection and correction schemes. In these cases, the occurrence of deadlock is considered so remote that no effort is made to avoid the problem. Instead, the approach is to detect it should it occur and then correct it by forcibly retrieving some of the allocated resources. Our example of a full process table falls in this class. A system administrator will usually establish a process table that is large enough for that particular installation. If, however, deadlock should occur due to a full table, the administrator merely uses his or her powers as "super user" to remove (the technical term is *kill*) some of the processes, which releases space in the process table so that the remaining processes can continue their tasks.

Techniques that attack the first two conditions tend to be known as deadlock avoidance schemes. One, for example, attacks the second condition by requiring each process to request all its resources at one time. Another perhaps more imaginative technique attacks the first condition, not by removing the competition directly but by converting nonshareable resources into shareable ones. For example, suppose the resource in question is a printer and a variety of processes require its use. Each time a process requests the printer, the operating system grants the request. However, instead of connecting the process to the printer's device driver, the operating system connects it to a device driver that stores the information to be printed on a disk rather than sending it to the printer. Thus each process, thinking it has access to the printer, executes in its normal way. Later, when the printer is available, the operating system can transfer the data from the disk to the printer. In this manner, the operating system has made the nonshareable resource appear shareable by creating the illusion of more than one printer. This technique of holding data for output at a later but more convenient time is called **spooling** and is quite popular on systems of all sizes.

Of course, when processes compete for a machine's resources, other problems arise. For example, a file manager should normally grant several processes access to the same file if the processes are merely reading data from the file, but conflicts can occur if more than one process tries to alter a file at the same time. Thus a file manager may allocate file access according to the needs of the processes, allowing several processes to have read access but only one having write access at any given time. Other systems may divide the file into pieces so that different processes can alter different parts of the file concurrently. Additional problems must still be resolved, however. How, for example, should those processes with only read access to a file be notified when a process with write access alters the file?

QUESTIONS/EXERCISES

1. Suppose process A and process B are sharing time on the same machine, and each needs the same nonshareable resource for short periods of time. (For example, each process may be printing a series of independent, short reports.) Each process may then repeatedly acquire the resource, release it, and later request it again. What is a drawback to controlling access to the resource in the following manner:

    Begin by assigning a flag the value 0. If process A requests the resource and the flag is 0, grant the request. Otherwise, make process A wait. If process B requests the resource and the flag is 1, grant the request. Otherwise, make process B wait. Each time process A finishes with the resource, change the flag to 1. Each time process B finishes with the resource, change the flag to 0.

2. Suppose a two-lane road converges to one lane to pass through a tunnel. To coordinate the use of the tunnel, the following signal system has been installed:

    A car entering either end of the tunnel causes red lights above the tunnel entrances to be turned on. As the car exits the tunnel, the

lights are turned off. If an approaching car finds a red light on, it waits until the light is turned off before entering the tunnel.
What is the flaw in this system?
3. Suppose the following solutions have been proposed for removing the deadlock that occurs on a single-lane bridge when two cars meet. Identify which condition for deadlock given in the text is removed by each solution.
   a. Do not let a car onto the bridge until the bridge is empty.
   b. If cars meet, make one of them back up.
   c. Add a second lane to the bridge.
4. Suppose we represent each process in a time-sharing system with a dot and draw an arrow from one dot to another if the process represented by the first dot is waiting for a resource being used by the second. Mathematicians call the resulting picture a *directed graph*. What property of the directed graph is equivalent to deadlock in the system?

3.5 Networks

A typical early computer network consisted of isolated machines that could do little more than transfer files over temporary telephone connections using software that was added to the machines' operating systems in the form of utility software. Today, the interaction of machines via networking is much more extensive, and modern operating systems, being designed with networking in mind, are beginning to incorporate many of these features. For instance, software implementing the TCP/IP protocol suite (which we will learn about shortly) is supplied as a part of many of today's operating systems. In this section and the next, we address some of the topics associated with this expanded realm of operating systems.

Network Classification

Every computer network falls into one of two broad categories: **local area networks (LANs)** and **wide area networks (WANs).** A LAN normally consists of a collection of computers in a single building or building complex. For example, the computers used on a university campus or those used in a manufacturing plant might be connected by a LAN. A WAN links machines that may be on opposite sides of a city or the world. A major distinction between LANs and WANs is found in the technologies used to establish communication paths. (Satellite links, for example, are appropriate for WANs, but not for LANs.) Today, the software that deals with these distinctions is usually isolated in a small part of the overall network software package—which means that from a software perspective, the distinction between LANs and WANs is becoming less and less important.

Another dichotomy of networks is based on whether the ownership of the network's internal design is in the public domain or held by an individual corporation. A network of the former type is called an *open network;* a network of the latter type is called a *closed,* or a *proprietary, network.* The Internet is an open system. Indeed, communication throughout the Internet is governed by an open collection of standards known as the TCP/IP protocol suite, which we discuss in the next section. In contrast, Novell Inc. is a major provider of network software that it has developed and owns. Thus, network systems installed and maintained by Novell are closed systems.

Still another way of classifying networks is based on the configuration of the network, which refers to the pattern in which the machines are connected. Figure 3.10 represents four popular configurations: (1) the ring, in which the machines are connected in a circular fashion; (2) the bus, in which the machines are all connected to a common communication line called a bus; (3) the star, in which one machine serves as a hub to which all the others are connected; and (4) the irregular configuration, in which the machines are connected in what appears to be a haphazard manner. The irregular configuration is common in WANs, whereas the ring and bus configurations are usually found in local environments where the network's construction is more likely to fall under a single authority.

The Internet

If we connect more than one existing network we get a network of networks, which is known as an **internet.** The most notable example is the Internet (note the uppercase *I*), which originated from a research program initiated in 1973 by the Defense Advanced Research Projects Agency (DARPA). The goal of this program was to develop the ability to connect a variety of computer networks so that they could function as a single, reliable network. Today, the Internet is a worldwide combination of WANs and LANs involving millions of machines. Each network in the Internet is connected to another network by a machine called a **router.** That is, a router is a machine belonging to two networks that allows messages in one network to be transferred into the other network.[1]

Internet Addressing Conceptually, the Internet can be viewed as a collection of network clusters known as **domains** (Figure 3.11), each of which normally consists of those networks operated by a single organization such as a university,

---

[1]Some people use the term *gateway* instead of *router.* However, a gateway usually refers to a more elaborate link than provided by a router. For example, the term gateway is often used to refer to a machine that connects two internets using different internet protocols. Thus, a machine linking the Internet with a proprietary internet would be called a gateway.

FIGURE 3.10

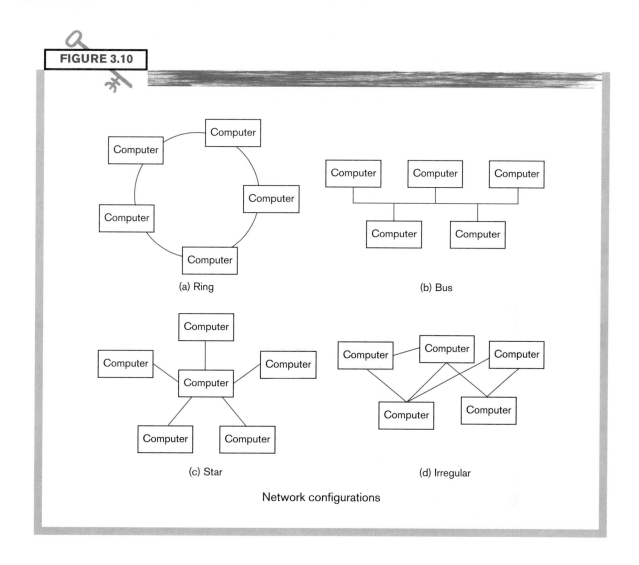

(a) Ring

(b) Bus

(c) Star

(d) Irregular

Network configurations

company, or government institution. Each domain is an autonomous system that can be configured as the local authority desires, perhaps even as a global collection of WANs.

The address of each machine in the Internet is a pattern of 32 bits consisting of two parts: a pattern identifying the domain in which the machine resides and a pattern identifying the particular machine within the domain. The part of the address identifying the domain, the **network identifier,** is assigned by the InterNIC (Internet Network Information Center) at the time the domain is established and registered with the InterNIC. It is this registration process that ensures that each domain in the Internet has a unique network identifier. The

FIGURE 3.11

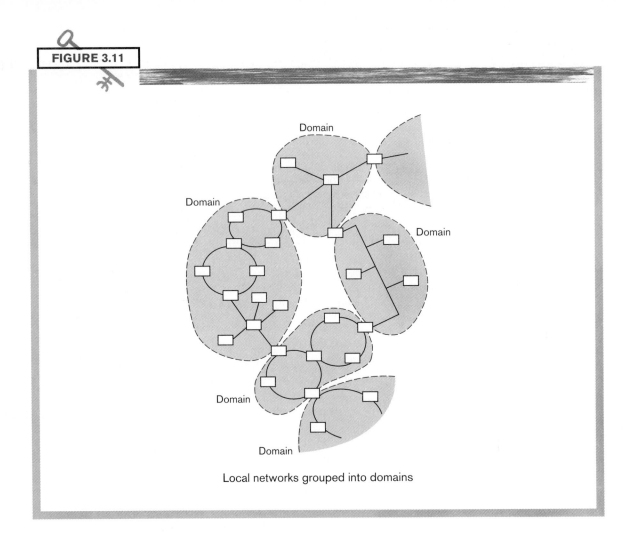

Local networks grouped into domains

portion of the address that identifies a particular machine within a domain is called the **host address.** (The term **host** is often used in reference to a machine in a network in recognition of its role in hosting the requests of other machines.) The host address is assigned by the domain's local authority—usually a person with a job title such as network administrator or system administrator. For example, the network identifier of the Addison Wesley Longman publishing company is 192.207.177 (network identifiers are traditionally written in dotted decimal notation; see Exercise 8 at the end of Section 1.4). In turn, a machine within this domain would have an address such as 192.207.177.133, the last byte of which is the host address.

Addresses in bit-pattern form are rarely conducive to human consumption. For this reason the InterNIC also assigns each domain a unique mnemonic address known as a **domain name.** Each local authority is then free to extend this domain name to obtain mnemonic names for the machines within its domain. For example, the domain name of Addison Wesley Longman, is `awl.com`. An individual machine within that domain may be identified as `ssenterprise.awl.com`.

The dotted notation used in mnemonic addresses is not related to the dotted decimal notation used to represent addresses in bit pattern form. Instead, the sections in a mnemonic address identify the machine's location within a hierarchical classification system. In particular, the address ssenterprise.awl.com indicates a machine known as ssenterprise within the institution awl within the class of commercial institutions com. (In addition to com there are numerous domain classifications including edu for educational institutions, gov for government institutions, and org for more generally classified organizations.) In the case of large domains, a local authority may break its domain into subdomains, in which case the mnemonic addresses of the machines within the domain may be longer. For example, suppose Nowhere University was assigned the domain name nu.edu and chose to divide its domain into subdomains. Then, a machine at Nowhere University could have an address such as `r2d2.compsc.nu.edu`, meaning that the machine *r2d2* is in the subdomain *compsc* within the domain *nu* within the class of educational domains *edu*.

For the purpose of transferring messages among individual users of the Internet (a system known as **e-mail,** short for electronic mail), each local authority assigns an e-mail address to each authorized user within its domain. This address consists of a character string identifying the user, followed by the symbol @, and finally the domain name for the machine assigned the task of hadling the domain's e-mail activities. Thus the e-mail address of an individual at Addison Wesley Longman, Inc. might appear as `wshakespeare@mailroom.awl.com`. In other words, the machine known as `mailroom` within the domain `awl.com` handles e-mail for the user `wshakespeare`.

Each domain's local authority is responsible for maintaining a directory containing the mnemonic address and the corresponding numeric Internet address of those machines within its domain. This directory is implemented on a designated machine within the domain in the form of a server, called a **name server,** that

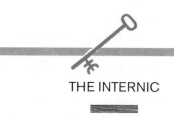

THE INTERNIC

The InterNIC was established in 1993 when the National Science Foundation contracted with three companies (AT&T, General Atomics, and Network Solutions) to assume the responsibilities of the Internet's operation, such as handling the registration of domains and the maintenance of the databases required to identify the domain name servers throughout the Internet. Prior to this, domain registration was handled by the Defense Information Systems Agency Network Information Center (DISA NIC). These original contracts have now expired and the future structure of the Internet's "governing body" is being debated. The argument is that the Internet has ceased to be a scientific research activity and therefore should no longer fall under the auspices of the National Science Foundation. In fact, the National Science Foundation is currently supporting the development of Internet 2–a new system devoted to the scientific research community. Currently, Network Solutions still handles the registration of Internet domains. To learn more about this registration process, check out the Web site at http://internic.net

responds to requests regarding address information. Together, all of the name servers throughout the Internet constitute an Internet-wide directory system that is used to convert addresses in mnemonic form into their equivalent numeric forms. In particular, when a human requests that a message be sent to a destination given in mnemonic form, this system of name servers is used to convert that mnemonic address into its equivalent bit-pattern form that is compatible with the Internet software. Normally, such a task is completed in a fraction of a second.

When an organization decides to join the Internet, it can either become a part of an existing domain or find a point in the Internet at which it can place a router and establish its own domain. The advantage of establishing a new domain is that the organization has local authority over its facilities rather than being subject to the authority of another organization. To establish a new domain, the organization must register with the InterNIC to obtain a network identifier and a domain name.

An individual normally obtains access to the Internet through membership in an organization with a domain. Several companies, called **Internet access providers,** offer Internet access to individuals on a commercial basis. These companies, which normally have established their own domain in the Internet, provide software on their machines that allows their customers to establish telephone connections. Through such a connection a customer can access the Internet services to which he or she has subscribed. Many Internet access providers also offer links to the Internet to organizations wanting to establish their own domains.

The World Wide Web In addition to being a means of communicating via e-mail, the Internet has become a means of propagating multimedia documents consisting of **hypertext,** which is text containing words, phrases, or images that are linked to other documents. A reader of a hypertext document can access these related documents as desired, usually by pointing and clicking with the mouse or using the arrow keys on the keyboard. For example, suppose the sentence "The orchestra's performance of 'Bolero' by Maurice Ravel was outstanding" appeared in a hypertext document and the name *Maurice Ravel* was linked to another document—perhaps giving information about the composer. A reader might choose to view that associated material by pointing to the name *Maurice Ravel* with the mouse and pressing the mouse button. Moreover, if the proper links are installed, the reader might listen to an audio recording by selecting the name *Bolero*.

In this manner, a reader of hypertext documents can explore related documents or follow a train of thought from document to document. As portions of various documents are linked to other documents, an intertwined web of related information is formed. When implemented on a computer network, the documents within such a web can reside on different machines, forming a network-wide web. Similarly, the web that has evolved on the Internet spans the entire globe and is known as the **World Wide Web.**

Software packages that assist readers of hypertext with the task of traversing hypertext links tend to fall into one of two categories: programs that play the role of clients and programs that play the role of servers. A client resides on the reader's machine and is charged with the tasks of obtaining materials requested by the user and presenting these materials to the user in an organized manner. It is the client that provides the user interface that allows a user to browse within the Web. In turn, a client is often referred to as a **browser,** or sometimes as a Web browser. A hypertext server resides on a machine containing documents to be accessed. Its task is to provide access to the documents on its machine as requested by a client. In summary, a user gains access to hypertext documents by communicating with a browser residing on the user's machine, and this browser fulfills the reader's requests by soliciting the services of the hypertext servers scattered throughout the Internet.

SEARCH ENGINES

To assist in the task of finding information on the World Wide Web, several organizations have established Web sites known as "search engines," where Internet users can search through large databases containing links to Web pages throughout the Internet. These databases classify documents on the Web by keywords. Thus, to find information about Ford's model T cars, an Internet user could ask a search engine to search its database for the key words such as "Ford," "model T," "antique cars," "collector cars," etc.

Information in a search engine's database is collected in two ways. One is by means of programs (sometimes called *spiders*) that simply crawl through the Web, following links from one Web page to another and reporting the pages discovered. The other is by direct notification; that is, the developer of a Web page can notify the manager of a search engine and request to be included in the database. Popular search engines include (but are not limited to) AltaVista at http://www.altavista.com, Infoseek at http://infoseek.go.com and Webcrawler at http://www.webcrawler.com

The collection of browsers available today include a variety of products from competing companies that are capable of handling documents consisting of sound, photographs, and video. Such documents are sometimes referred to as **hypermedia** to distinguish them from traditional hypertext.

Creating hypertext requires the ability to establish links between documents. For this purpose, each document is identified by a unique address, a **uniform resource locator (URL).** The information within a URL allows a browser to contact the proper server and request the desired document. A typical URL is illustrated in Figure 3.12. Sometimes a URL may not explicitly identify a document but instead consist of only a protocol and the mnemonic name of a machine. In these cases, the server at that machine will return a predetermined document, often called a home page, that probably describes the information available at the machine. Such shortened URLs provide a means of contacting organizations. For example, the URL http://www.awl.com will lead one to the home page of Addison Wesley Longman, Inc., which contains links to numerous other documents relating to the company and its products.

FIGURE 3.12

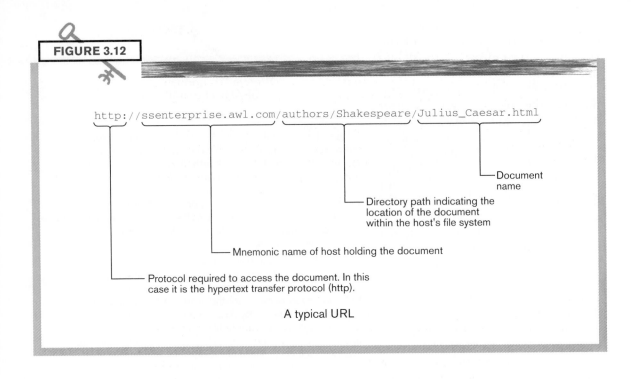

```
http://ssenterprise.awl.com/authors/Shakespeare/Julius_Caesar.html
```

Document
name

Directory path indicating the
location of the document
within the host's file system

Mnemonic name of host holding the document

Protocol required to access the document. In this
case it is the hypertext transfer protocol (http).

A typical URL

A hypertext document is similar to a traditional text document in that its text is coded character by character using a system such as ASCII or Unicode. The distinction is that a hypertext document also contains special markers that describe how the document should appear on the computer screen and which items within the document are to be linked to other documents. This system of markers is known as **Hypertext Markup Language (HTML).** Thus it is in terms of HTML that an author of a Web page describes the information that a browser needs to perform its task.

QUESTIONS/EXERCISES

1. What is an open network?
2. What is a router?
3. What are the components of the complete Internet address of a machine?
4. What is a URL? A browser?
5. In a LAN based on the ring configuration, what is a disadvantage of restricting the transfer of messages to a single direction?

3.6 Network Protocols

The rules that govern the communication between different components within a computer system are called **protocols,** a term derived from the protocols used in society to govern the interactions among people. Within a computer network, protocols define the details of each activity, including how messages are addressed, how the right to transmit messages is delegated among the machines, and how the duties of packaging messages for transmission and unpacking received messages are to be handled. Let us begin by considering protocols for controlling the right of a machine to transmit its own messages over the network.

Controlling Transmission Privileges

One approach to coordinating the right to transmit messages is the token ring protocol for networks configured as a ring. In this protocol, each machine transmits messages only to its "right" and receives messages only from its "left," as shown in Figure 3.13. A message from one machine to another must therefore be forwarded counterclockwise around the network until it reaches its destination. When the message reaches its destination, the destination machine keeps a copy of it and forwards a copy around the ring. When the forwarded copy reaches the originating machine, that machine knows that the message must have reached its destination and removes the message from the ring. Of course, this system depends on intermachine cooperation. If each machine insists on constantly transmitting messages of its own rather than forwarding those of the other machines, nothing will be accomplished.

To solve this problem, a unique bit pattern, called a *token,* is passed around the ring. Possession of this token gives a machine the authority to transmit its own message; without the token, a machine is only allowed to forward messages. Normally, each machine merely relays the token from left to right in the same manner in which it relays messages. If, however, the machine receiving the token has messages of its own to introduce to the network, it transmits one message while holding the token. When this message has completed its cycle around the ring, the machine forwards the token to the next machine in the ring. Likewise, when the next machine receives the token, it can either forward the token immediately or transmit its own new message before sending the token on to the next machine. In this manner, each machine in the network has equal opportunity to introduce messages of its own as the token circles around the ring.

Another protocol for coordinating the right to transmit is found in an Ethernet, which is a popular version of a bus network. In an Ethernet, the right

FIGURE 3.13

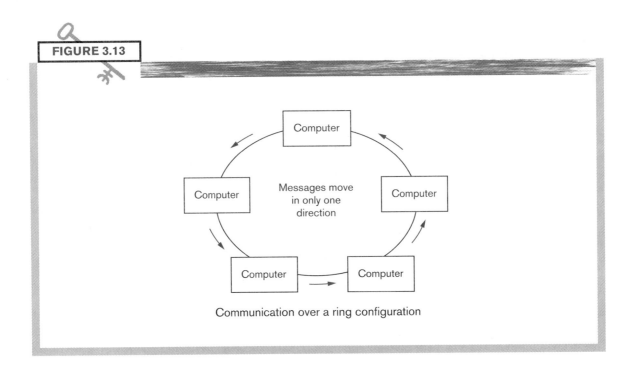

Communication over a ring configuration

to transmit messages is controlled by a protocol known as CSMA/CD (Carrier Sense, Multiple Access with Collision Detection). This protocol dictates that each message transmitted by any machine be broadcast to all the machines on the bus (Figure 3.14). Each machine monitors all the messages but keeps only those addressed to itself. To transmit a message, a machine waits until the bus is silent, at which time it begins transmitting while continuing to monitor the bus. If another machine also begins transmitting, both machines detect the clash and pause for a brief random period of time before trying to transmit again. The result is a system similar to that used by a small group of people in a conversation. If two people start to talk at once, they both stop. The difference is that people may go through a series such as, "I'm sorry, what were you going to say," "No, no. You go first," whereas under the CSMA/CD protocol each machine merely tries again.

The Layered Approach to Internet Software

A major task of network software is to provide the abstract tools required for transferring messages across the network. In the case of the Internet, this task also involves transferring messages between networks. The process involved is

FIGURE 3.14

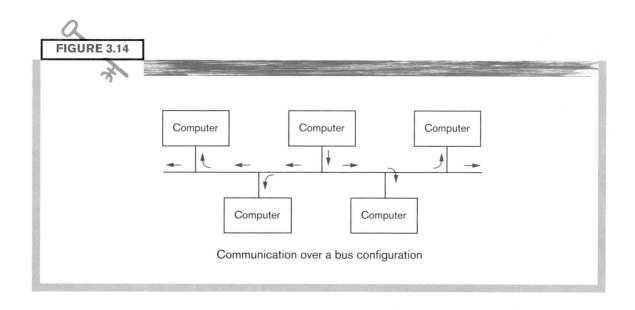

Communication over a bus configuration

analogous to that which you may use if you had to send replacement parts to a customer in a distant city. In particular, you would wrap the parts and address the package. Then you would deliver the package to a shipping company. The shipping company would place the package along with others in a large container and deliver the container to an airline. The airline would place the container in an airplane and transfer it to the destination city, perhaps with intermediate stops along the way. At the final destination, the airline would remove the container from the aircraft and give it to the shipping company's office at the destination. In turn, the shipping company would take the package out of the container and deliver it to the addressee.

In short, the transportation of the parts is carried out by a three-level hierarchy (Figure 3.15): (1) the user level (consisting of you and your customer), (2) the shipping company, and (3) the airline. Each level uses the next lower level as an abstract tool. (You are not concerned with the details of the shipping company, and the shipping company is not concerned with the internal operations of the airline.) Each level in the hierarchy has representatives at both the origin and the destination, with the representatives at the destination tending to do the reverse of their counterparts at the origin. Such is the case with software for controlling communication over the Internet, except that there are four layers rather than three, each consisting of a collection of software routines rather than people and businesses.

The four layers (application, transport, network, and link) of the Internet software are summarized in Figure 3.16. The column on the left represents the software layers used by the machine at a message's origin; the column on the right

FIGURE 3.15

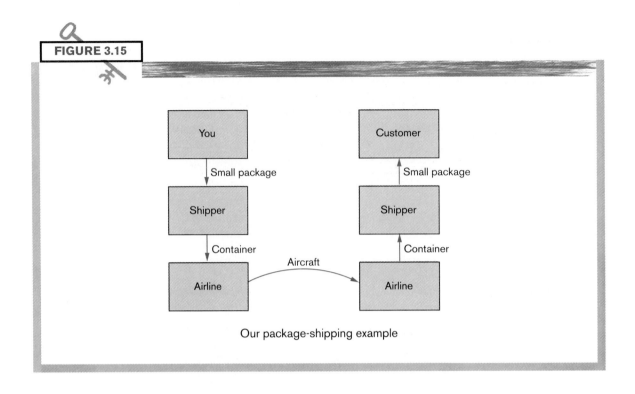

Our package-shipping example

represents the layers used by the machine at the message's destination. As in our shipping analogy, the software layers at the origin and destination are the same.

The arrows in Figure 3.16 represent the path traversed by a message. A typical message originates in the application layer. From there it is passed down the left column of the figure as it is prepared for transmission. Finally, it is transmitted by the link layer at the origin machine and received by the link layer at the destination machine. There the message is passed up the hierarchy until it reaches the application layer at the message's destination.

The uppermost layer in the Internet software hierarchy is the application layer, which although their names are similar, should not be confused with application software as classified in Section 3.2. (Indeed, we will soon see that much of the software in the application layer of the Internet software hierarchy falls within the category of utility software.) This layer of the Internet hierarchy consists of software units that must communicate with each other across the Internet. A traditional example is a collection of routines for transferring files across the Internet using a protocol known as the *file transfer protocol* (FTP). These routines are often implemented as a complete application program

FIGURE 3.16

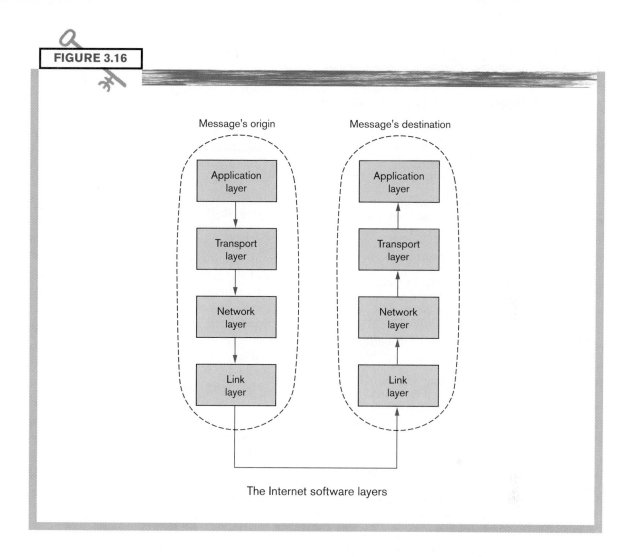

Message's origin   Message's destination

The Internet software layers

known as FTP, in recognition of the underlying protocol. Another example is the package known as *telnet* that was developed as a means of allowing users to access a machine across the Internet as though they were a local user of that machine. Both FTP and telnet were originally envisioned as application software in the sense of Section 3.2, but today they have become a part of the infrastructure found in most personal computers. Indeed, these software units are now used as abstract tools in the construction of larger applications such as Web browsers. In this sense, then, they have become utility software.

TRADITIONAL INTERNET APPLICATIONS

Here are some brief introductions to some of the traditional Internet application software.

telnet: In contrast to a personal computer in which a single user accesses the machine by means of a monitor, keyboard, and mouse directly connected to the machine, many computer users access machines from remote sites. Telnet was designed as a means of obtaining such remote access via the Internet. Using telnet, a person in one part of the world can sign on to a machine in another part of the world with the same convenience as being in the next room. In most cases the user needs merely to tell the telnet software the mnemonic name of the machine to be contacted and then to proceed as if he or she had direct access to the machine—usually by providing name and password information.

FTP: FTP was developed as a means of transferring files across the Internet. To use FTP, a user normally tells the FTP software on his or her machine the mnemonic name of a distant machine. This initiates contact with the FTP software at the distant machine. The user then signs on to the distant machine using an approved name and password. At this point files can be transferred between the machines using *get* (to receive a file) and *put* (to send a file) commands. It is by means of the name and password system that access to files via FTP is controlled. If it is desired to make a file accessible to everyone on the Internet, the machine's administrator can make the file accessible to anyone signing on with the name *anonymous*. Such files are said to be accessible via "anonymous FTP." When transferring files via FTP, it is important to specify whether the file is a binary file or a text file. The reason is that different systems indicate the end of a line of text in different ways (see the first few paragraphs of Section 8.2), and therefore certain conversions may be required when moving a text file from one machine to another.

The transport layer in the Internet software hierarchy views the application layer as the source of messages. That is, the application layer hands messages to be transmitted to the transport layer in much the same way that you hand packages to a shipping company. Just as it is your responsibility to provide an address compatible with the specifications of the shipping company, it is the application layer's responsibility to provide an address that is compatible with the transport layer. It is to fulfill this need that the application layer requires the services of the name servers within the Internet to translate mnemonic addresses used by humans into network-compatible addresses.

It is the task of the transport layer at a message's origin to see that the message is sent to the transport layer at the destination, where it will be turned over to the appropriate application software. Thus it is the duty of the transport layer to carry out those tasks that must be handled at the message's origin and final destination without concern for intermediate stops along the way. In particular, the transport layer divides long messages into segments of a size compatible with the underlying network layer. It then adds sequence numbers to these segments so that the original message can be reconstructed at the message's destination. Then the transport layer attaches the destination address to each segment and hands the resulting units, known as **packets,** to the network layer.

We see then that messages find their way across the Internet in the form of small packets, each of which consists of message data plus additional "wrapping" that consists of information that is added for the sake of transferring the message. It is not unusual for the size of a packet's wrapping to exceed the size of the message unit found within. Message units consisting of single bytes are common, whereas each packet contains more than 50 bytes of wrapping. Although this appears to be inefficient, the system works quite well.

The network layer is responsible for seeing that the packets it receives are properly forwarded from one network within the Internet to another until they reach their final destinations. Thus, in contrast to the transport layer that deals with a message's origin and final destination, the network layer oversees the intermediate steps made by packets as they find their way across the Internet. It does this by appending an intermediate destination address to each packet. This intermediate address is determined as follows: If the final destination of the packet is within the current network, the appended address will be a duplicate of the ultimate destination address; otherwise, the appended address will be that of a router in the current network. In this way, a packet destined for a machine within the current network will be sent to that machine, whereas a packet destined for a machine outside the current network will be sent to a router where it will be transferred into an adjacent network. The network layer, then, wraps the packets it receives from the transport layer with additional wrapping that reflects the intermediate address rather than the original address. These extended packets are then handed to the link layer.

The link layer's responsibility is to deal with the communication details particular to the individual network in which the machine resides. If that network is a token ring, the link layer must wait for possession of the token before transmitting. If the network uses CSMA/CD, the link layer must listen for a silent bus before transmitting. Moreover, each individual network within the Internet has its own addressing system that is independent from the addressing system used by the Internet. After all, many of these networks functioned on their own long before their owners decided to attach them to the Internet. Thus the link layer must translate the Internet addresses appearing on the outside of the packets into the appropriate local addressing system and add these translated addresses to the packet in the form of an additional layer of wrapping.

Each layer in the Internet software hierarchy also plays a role in the process of receiving messages, which is roughly that of reversing the task performed by its counterpart at the message's origin. Thus, the link layer receives packets from the network communication lines, strips off the outer wrapping (the address in local network compatible form) that was placed there by the link layer at the message's origin, and hands the underlying packets to its network layer.

Each time the network layer receives a packet from its link layer, it strips off the intermediate Internet address that was previously appended by its counterpart and considers the ultimate destination address that it finds underneath. If this is its own address, the network layer hands the underlying packet to its transport layer; otherwise, the network layer knows that the underlying packet should be forwarded on through the Internet. In this case, it must rewrap the underlying packet by appending a new intermediate address to the segment and send the rewrapped packet back down to the link layer for transmission. In this manner, packets hop from one machine to another until they reach their final destinations. At each intermediate step, it is the network layer that is charged with determining the destination of the next hop.

To assist with this readdressing process, the network layer maintains a routing table that contains the final destination addresses that it has dealt with recently and the intermediate addresses to which it forwarded each of those packets. The various network layers within the Internet routinely exchange the data in their routing tables so that information about forwarding addresses tends to propagate through the Internet. Each network layer keeps only that information that it thinks it may need and also deletes stale entries from its routing table on a routine basis so that the table does not grow too large. The contents of the routing tables throughout the Internet are therefore dynamic, and it is possible for packets representing different parts of the same message to find their way through the Internet along different paths.

Note that the network layer hands its transport layer only those packets that are addressed to the local machine. Thus only the link and network layers are involved in the forwarding of packets destined to other machines. The transport and application layers are shielded from this distraction and see only those packets addressed to their machine (Figure 3.17). As the transport layer receives packets from the network layer, it extracts the underlying message segments and reconstructs the original message according to the sequence numbers supplied by the transport layer at the message's origin. Once the message is complete, the transport layer hands it to its application layer—thus completing the message transmission process.

In conclusion, communication over the Internet involves the interaction of several layers of software residing on many machines throughout the system. In this context, it is amazing that the response time of the Internet is measured in milliseconds. Indeed, most transactions appear to take place instantaneously.

The TCP/IP Protocol Suite The demand for open networks has generated a need for published standards by which manufacturers can supply equipment and software that function properly with products from other vendors. One standard that has resulted is the Open System Interconnection (OSI) reference model, produced by the International Organization for Standardization. This standard is based on a seven-level hierarchy as opposed to the four-level system used by the Internet. It has become an often-quoted model because it carries the authority of an international organization, but it has not been readily implemented, mainly because it was established after the TCP/IP protocol suite had already been developed, implemented, widely publicized, and proved reliable as the protocol system for the Internet.

The **TCP/IP protocol suite** is a collection of protocols defining the four-level hierarchy used by the Internet. Actually, TCP (Transmission Control Protocol) and IP (Internet Protocol) are the names of only two of the protocols in this collection—so the fact that the entire collection is referred to as the TCP/IP protocol suite is rather misleading. More precisely, TCP defines a version of the transport layer. We say a *version* because the TCP/IP protocol suite

FIGURE 3.17

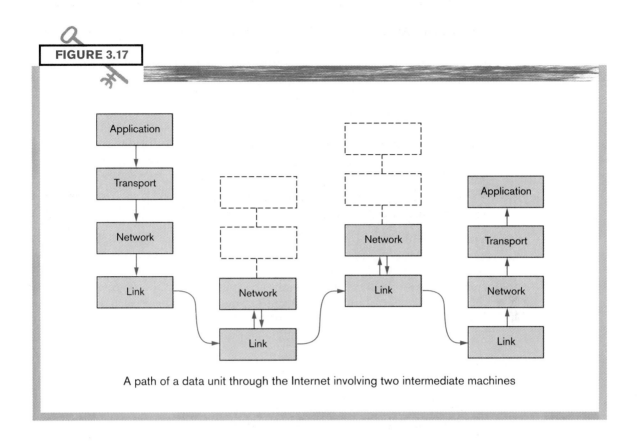

A path of a data unit through the Internet involving two intermediate machines

provides for two ways of implementing the transport layer, the second being defined by UDP (User Datagram Protocol). This is analogous to the fact that when shipping the replacement parts to your customer, you have a choice of different shipping companies, each of which offers the same basic service but with its own unique characteristics. Thus, depending on the particular quality of service required, the application layer software may choose to send data via a TCP or UDP version of the transport layer.

There are two basic differences between TCP and UDP. The first is that before sending data, a transport layer based on TCP sends a message to the transport layer at the destination telling it that data are about to be sent and which application layer software is to receive the data. It then waits for this message to be acknowledged before starting to send message segments. In this manner, a TCP transport layer is said to establish a connection before sending data. A transport layer based on UDP does not establish such a connection prior to sending data. It merely sends the data to the address it was given and forgets about it. For all it knows, the destination machine may not even be operational. For this reason, UDP is called a connectionless protocol.

The second basic difference between TCP and UDP is that TCP transport layers at the origin and destination work together by means of acknowledgments and segment retransmissions to confirm that all segments of a message are successfully transferred to the destination. In turn, TCP is called a reliable protocol, whereas UDP, which does not offer such retransmission services, is said to be an unreliable protocol. This does not mean that UDP is a poor choice. Indeed, a transport layer based on UDP is more streamlined than a layer based on TCP, and thus if an application is prepared to handle the potential consequences of UDP, that option is the better choice.

IP is the Internet's standard for the network layer. Among its features is that each time an IP network layer prepares a packet to be handed to the link layer, it appends a value called a *hop count*, or time to live, to that packet. This value is the limit to the number of times the packet should be forwarded as it tries to find its way through the Internet. Each time an IP network layer forwards a packet, it decrements that packet's hop count by one. With this information, the network layer can protect the Internet from packets circling endlessly within the system. Although the Internet continues to grow on a daily basis, an initial hop count of 64 remains more than sufficient to allow a packet to find its way through the maze of LANs, WANs, and routers.

QUESTIONS/EXERCISES

1. What layers of the Internet software hierarchy are used to forward an incoming message to another machine?
2. What are some differences between a transport layer based on the TCP protocol and another based on the UDP protocol?
3. How does the Internet software ensure that messages are not relayed within the Internet forever?
4. What keeps a machine on the Internet from recording copies of all the messages passing through it?

3.7 Security

When a machine is connected to a network, it becomes accessible to many potential users. The problems encountered fall into two general categories: unauthorized access to information and vandalism. One approach to solving the problem of unauthorized access is to use passwords, either to control access to the machine itself or to control access to particular items of data. Unfortunately, passwords can be obtained by various means. Some computer users simply share their passwords with friends—a practice with questionable ethics. In other cases passwords are stolen. One approach to this is to exploit flaws within a machine's operating system to obtain its password records. Another is to design a program that simulates the local system's login process so that users, thinking they are communicating with the operating system, type their passwords, which are then recorded by the program. Still another way of obtaining passwords is to try the most obvious passwords and see if they work. For example, users who fear forgetting their passwords may use their own names as passwords. Dates such as birthdays are also popular password choices.

In an effort to thwart those playing the guess-the-password game, operating systems can be designed to report any avalanche of incorrect passwords. Many operating systems are also designed to report the time that an account was last used each time a new session under that account is started. This allows users to detect any unauthorized use of their accounts. A more sophisticated defense against password guessers is to create the illusion of success (called a *trapdoor*) when false passwords are given and to proceed to give the intruder misinformation while trying to record the intruder's origin.

THE COMPUTER EMERGENCY RESPONSE TEAM

In November 1988 a worm released into the Internet caused significant disruption of service. Consequently, the Defense Advanced Research Projects Agency (DARPA) formed the Computer Emergency Response Team (CERT), located at the CERT Coordination Center at Carnegie-Mellon University. The CERT is the Internet's security "watchdog." Among its duties are the investigation of security problems, the issuance of security alerts, and the implementation of public awareness campaigns to improve Internet security. The CERT Coordination Center maintains a Web site at http://www.cert.org where it posts notices of its activities.

Another approach to protecting data from unauthorized access is to encrypt the data, the idea being that even if the data are obtained by an intruder, the information remains safe. For this purpose, a variety of encryption techniques have been developed. One popular approach to encryption of messages sent over the Internet is called **public-key encryption.** It allows many people to send secure messages to a central receiver. Public-key encryption involves the use of two values called keys. One key, known as the public key, is used to encode messages and is known by all people authorized to generate messages; the other, known as the private key, is required to decode messages and is known by only the person who is to receive messages. Knowledge of the public key does not allow messages to be decoded. Thus, little damage is done if it falls into unauthorized hands. It gives the unauthorized person the ability to generate messages but not the ability to decode intercepted messages. Knowledge of the private key is, of course, more sensitive, but it is inherently more secure than the public key because it is held by only one person. We will investigate a particular public-key encryption system in Chapter 11.

There are also many legal issues regarding unauthorized access to information, some of which deal with distinguishing between authorized and unauthorized parties. For example, is an employer authorized to monitor the communication of employees? To what extent does an Internet access provider have authorized access to the information being communicated by its clients? To what extent is an Internet access provider responsible for the content of its client's communication? Such questions are challenging today's legal community.

In the United States, many of these questions are addressed by the Electronic Communication Privacy Act (ECPA) of 1986, which has its origins in legislation to control wire-tapping. Although the act is lengthy, its scope is captured in a few short excerpts. In particular, it states that

> Except as otherwise specifically provided in this chapter any person who intentionally intercepts, endeavors to intercept, or procures any other person to intercept or endeavor to intercept, any wire, oral, or electronic communication ... shall be punished as provided in subsection (4) or shall be subject to suit as provided in subsection (5).

and

> ...any person or entity providing an electronic communication service to the public shall not intentionally divulge the contents of any communication ... on that service to any person or entity other than an addressee or intended recipient of such communication or an agent of such addressee or intended recipient.

In brief, the ECPA confirms an individual's right to private communication—it is illegal for unauthorized personnel to eavesdrop on another's communication, and it is illegal for a network provider to release information about the communication of its clients. However, the act also states the following:

> It shall not be unlawful ... for an officer, employee, or agent of the Federal Communications Commission, in the normal course of his employment and in discharge of the monitoring responsibilities exercised by the Commission in the enforcement of chapter 5 of title 47 of the United States Code, to intercept a wire or electronic communication, or oral communication transmitted by radio, or to disclose or use the information thereby obtained.

Thus the ECPA explicitly gives the Federal Communications Commission (FCC) the right to monitor electronic communication under some restrictions. This leads to some rather complicated issues. First, in order for the FCC to exercise its rights under the ECPA, the target communication systems must be constructed and programmed so that communications can be monitored. To establish these capabilities was the goal of the Communications Assistance for Law Enforcement Act (CALEA). It requires telecommunication carriers to modify their equipment to accommodate law enforcement taps. However, implementation of this act has proved to be complex and expensive, resulting in extensions to the deadline for compliance.

A more controversial issue involves the clash between the FCC's right to monitor communications and the public's right to use encryption. After all, if the messages being monitored are well encrypted, then merely tapping the communication is worthless to law enforcement agencies. Thus the U.S. government is moving toward a registration system that would require the registration of encryption keys (or perhaps keys to the keys). But we live in a world in which corporate espionage has become as significant as military espionage. Thus it is understandable that requiring the registration of encryption keys would make many law-abiding citizens uncomfortable. How secure can the registration system be? Such questions are not unique to the United States. Similar registration systems are being considered in Canada and Europe.

The problem of vandalism is exemplified by the occurrence of such afflictions as computer viruses and network worms. In general, a **virus** is a program segment that attaches itself to other programs in the computer system. For example, a virus may insert itself at the beginning of a program already in the system, so each time the host program is executed, the virus is performed first. When executed, the virus may perform malicious acts that are readily noticeable or merely search for other programs to which it can attach copies of itself. If an infected program is transferred to a new machine, either via a network or via a floppy disk, the virus will begin to infect programs on the new machine as soon as the transferred program is executed. In this manner, the virus moves from machine to machine. In some cases, viruses are designed to spread themselves to other programs until a predetermined condition, such as the arrival of a particular date, is met and then perform more malicious vandalism. This increases the likelihood that the virus will be spread to numerous machines before it is detected.

The term **worm** normally refers to an autonomous program that transfers itself through a network, taking up residence in machines and forwarding copies of itself through the network. As in the case of viruses, these programs can be designed merely to replicate themselves or to perform additional vandalism.

As the popularity of networks increases, the potential for damage from unauthorized access to information and vandalism also grows. This leads to a multitude of questions regarding the wisdom of placing sensitive information on a networked machine, the liability for the release of inadequately protected information, and the liability for vandalism. In turn, the ethical and legal questions associated with these issues promise to lead to extensive debate in the future.

QUESTIONS/EXERCISES

1. Technically, the term *data* refers to representations of information, whereas *information* refers to the underlying meaning. Does the use of passwords protect data or information? Does the use of encryption protect data or information?
2. What are the basic points in the ECPA?
3. Explain how the CALEA demonstrates that passing a law requiring an action may not actually get the job done.

CHAPTER REVIEW PROBLEMS
(Asterisked problems are associated with optional sections.)

1. List four activities of a typical operating system.

2. Summarize the distinction between batch processing and interactive processing.

3. What is the difference between interactive processing and real-time processing?

4. What is a multitasking operating system?

5. What information is contained in a process table within an operating system?

6. What is the difference between a process that is ready and a process that is waiting?

7. What is the difference between virtual memory and main memory?

8. What complications could arise in a time-sharing system if two processes require access to the same file at the same time? Are there cases in which the file manager should grant such requests? Are there cases in which the file manager should deny such requests?

9. Define load balancing and scaling in the context of multiprocessor architectures.

10. Summarize the booting process.

11. Suppose a time-sharing operating system is allotting time slices of 50 milliseconds. If it normally takes 8 milliseconds to position a disk's read/write head over the desired track and another 17 milliseconds for the desired data to rotate around to the read/write head, how much of a program's time slice can be spent waiting for a read operation from a disk to take place? If the machine is capable of executing one instruction each microsecond, how many instructions can be executed during this waiting period? (This is why a time-sharing system normally allows another process to run while the first process is waiting for the services of a peripheral device.)

12. List five resources to which a multitasking operating system might have to coordinate access.

13. A process is said to be I/O-bound if it requires a lot of I/O operations, whereas a process that consists of mostly computations within the CPU/memory system is said to be compute-bound. If both a compute-bound process and an I/O-bound process are waiting for a time slice, which should be given priority? Why?

14. Would greater throughput be achieved by a system running two processes in a time-sharing environment if both processes were I/O-bound (refer to Problem 13) or if one was I/O-bound and the other was compute-bound? Why?

15. Design a set of instructions that tells an operating system's dispatcher what to do when a process's time slice is over.

16. Identify the components of the state of a process.

17. Identify a situation in a time-sharing system in which a process does not consume the entire time slice allocated to it.

18. List in chronological order the major events that take place when a process is interrupted.

19. Describe the client/server model.

20. What is CORBA?

21. Identify two ways of classifying computer networks.

22. Explain the components of the e-mail address

```
kermit@frogs.animals.com
```

23. Define each of the following:
a. Name server
b. Domain
c. Router
d. Host

24. Suppose the address of a host on the Internet is quoted as 134.48.4.123. What is the 32-bit address in hexadecimal notation?

25. What is the difference between an open network and a closed network?

26. Define each of the following:
a. Hypertext
b. HTML
c. Browser

27. What is the World Wide Web?

28. Identify the components of the following URL and describe the meaning of each.

```
http://frogs.animals.com/
animals/moviestars/kermit.html
```

29. In the context of computer networks, what is the difference between a worm and a virus?

30. What are some concerns dealing with internet security and privacy?

31. What is the ECPA and the CALEA?

*32. Explain an important use for the test-and-set instruction found in many machine languages. Why is it important for the entire test-and-set process to be implemented as a single instruction?

*33. A banker with only $100,000 loans $50,000 to each of two customers. Later, both customers return with the story that before they can repay their loans they must each borrow another $10,000 to complete the business deals in which their previous loans are involved. The banker resolves this deadlock by borrowing the additional funds from another source and passing on this loan (with an increase in the interest rate) to the two customers. Which of the three conditions for deadlock has the banker removed?

*34. Students who want to enroll in Model Railroading II at the local university are required to obtain permission from the instructor and pay a laboratory fee. The two requirements are fulfilled independently in either order and at different locations on campus. Enrollment is limited to 20 students; this limit is maintained by both the instructor, who will grant permission to only 20 students, and the financial office, which will allow only 20 students to pay the laboratory fee. Suppose that this registration system has resulted in 19 students having successfully registered for the course, but with the final space being claimed by two students—one who has only obtained permission from the instructor and another who has only paid the fee. Which requirement for deadlock is removed by each of the following solutions to the problem:
a. Both students are allowed in the course.
b. The class size is reduced to 19, so neither of the two students is allowed to register for the course.
c. The competing students are both denied entry to the class and a third student is given the twentieth space.
d. It is decided that the only requirement for entry into the course is the payment of the fee. Thus the student who has paid the fee gets into the course, and entry is denied to the other student.

*35. Explain how deadlock can occur as two pawns approach each other in a chess game. What nonshareable resources are involved? How is such deadlock normally broken?

*36. Suppose each nonshareable resource in a computer system is classified as a level 1, level 2, or level 3 resource. Moreover, suppose each process in the system is required to request the resources it needs according to this classification. That is, it must request all the required level 1 resources at once before requesting any level 2 resources. Once it receives the level 1 resources, it can request all the required level 2 resources, and so on. Can deadlock occur in such a system? Why or why not?

*37. Each of two robot arms is programmed to lift assemblies from a conveyor belt, test them for tolerances, and place them in one of two bins depending on the results of the test. The assemblies arrive one at a time with a sufficient interval between them. To keep both arms from trying to grab the same assembly, the computers controlling the arms share a common memory cell. If an arm is available as an assembly approaches, its controlling computer reads the value of the common cell. If the value is nonzero, the arm lets the assembly pass. Otherwise, the controlling computer places a nonzero value in the memory cell, directs the arm to pick up the assembly, and places the value 0 back into the memory cell after the action is complete. What sequence of events could lead to a tug-of-war between the two arms?

*38. Suppose each computer in a ring network is programmed to transmit simultaneously in both directions those messages that originate at that station and are addressed to all the other stations belonging to the network.

Moreover, suppose this is done by first acquiring access to the communication path to the machine's left, retaining this access until access to the path to the right is acquired, and then transmitting the message. Identify the deadlock that occurs if all the machines in the network tried to originate such a message at the same time.

*39. Identify the use of a queue in the process of spooling output to a printer.

*40. The pavement in the middle of an intersection can be considered as a nonshareable resource for which cars approaching the intersection compete. A traffic light rather than an operating system is used to control the allocation of the resource. If the light is able to sense the amount of traffic arriving from each direction and is programmed to give the green light to the heavier traffic, the lighter traffic might suffer from what is called starvation. What is meant by starvation? What could happen in a multiuser computer system where routines are assigned priorities and competition for resources is always resolved strictly by priority?

*41. In what sense can a process starve if the dispatcher always assigns time slices according to a priority system in which the priority of each process remains fixed? (*Hint:* What is the priority of the process that just completed its time slice in comparison to the processes that are waiting, and consequently which routine gets the next time slice?)

*42. What is the similarity between deadlock and starvation? (Refer to Problem 41.) What is the difference between deadlock and starvation?

*43. What problem arises as the length of the time slices in a time-sharing system are made smaller and smaller? What about as they become longer and longer?

*44. What is the OSI reference model?

*45. In a network based on the bus configuration, the bus is a nonshareable resource for which the machines must compete in order to transmit messages. How is deadlock controlled in this context?

*46. Token-based protocols can be used to control the right to transmit in networks that do not have a ring configuration. Design a token-based protocol to control the right to transmit in a LAN with a bus configuration.

*47. Describe the steps followed by a machine that wants to transmit a message in a network using the CSMA/CD protocol.

*48. List the four layers in the Internet software hierarchy and identify a task performed by each layer.

*49. In what way could TCP be considered a better protocol for implementing the transport layer than UDP? In what way could UDP be considered better than TCP?

*50. What does it mean to say that UDP is a connectionless protocol?

SOCIAL ISSUES

The following questions are provided to help you understand some of the ethical/social/legal issues associated with the field of computing as well as investigate your own beliefs and their foundations. The goal is not merely to answer these questions. You should also consider why you answered as you did and whether your justifications are consistent from one question to the next.

1. Suppose you are using a multiuser operating system that allows you to view the names of the files belonging to other users as well as to view the contents of those files that are not otherwise protected. Would viewing such information without permission be similar to wandering through someone's unlocked home without permission, or would it be more like reading materials placed in a common lounge such as a physician's waiting room?

2. When you have access to a multiuser computer system, what responsibilities do you have when selecting your password?

3. The ability to connect computers via networks has popularized the concept of working at home. What are some pros and cons of this movement? Will it effect the consumption of natural resources? Will it strengthen families? Will it reduce "office politics"? Will those who work at home have the same career advancement opportunities as those who work on site? Will community ties be weakened? Will reduced personal contact with peers have a positive or negative effect?

4. The Internet stands on the brink of becoming an alternative to "hands on" shopping. What effect will such a shift in shopping habits have on communities? What about shopping malls? What about small shops, such as bookstores and cloth-

ing stores, in which you like to browse without buying? To what extent is buying at the lowest possible price good or bad? Is there any moral obligation to pay more for an item in order to support a local business? Is it ethical to compare products at a local store and then order your selection at a lower price via the Internet? What are the long-term consequences of such behavior?

5. To what extent should a government control its citizen's access to the Internet (or any international network) in the name of national security? What are some security issues that may occur?

6. Electronic bulletin boards allow users of networks to post messages (often anonymously) and read messages posted by others. Should the manager of such a bulletin board be held responsible for its contents? Should a telephone company be held responsible for the contents of telephone conversations? Should the manager of a grocery store be held responsible for the contents of a community bulletin board located in the store?

7. Should the use of the Internet be monitored? Should it be regulated? If so, by whom?

8. How much time do you spend accessing the Internet? Is that time well spent? Has Internet access altered your social activities? Do you find it easier to talk to people via the Internet than in person?

9. When you buy a software package for a desktop computer, the developer usually asks you to register with the developer so that you can be notified of future upgrades. This registration process is increasingly being handled via the Internet. You are usually asked to give such things as your name, address, and perhaps how you learned of the product, and then the developer's software automatically transfers this data to the developer. What ethical issues would be raised if the developer designed the registration software so that it sent additional information to the developer during the registration process? For example, the software might scan the contents of your system and report the other software packages found.

ADDITIONAL READING

Denning, D. E., and P. J. Denning. *Internet Besieged*. Reading, MA: Addison Wesley Longman, 1998.

Dietel, H. M. *An Introduction to Operating Systems,* 3rd ed. Reading, MA: Addison-Wesley, 1994.

Shay, W. A. *Understanding Data Communications and Networks*. Boston: PWS, 1994.

Silberschatz, A. and P. B. Galvin. *Operating System Concepts,* 5th ed. Reading, MA: Addison-Wesley, 1998.

Stein, L. D. *How to Set Up and Maintain a Web Site*. Reading, MA: Addison-Wesley, 1997.

Stevens, W. R. *TCP/IP Illustrated,* vol. 1. Reading, MA: Addison-Wesley, 1994.

c h a p t e r

ALGORITHMS

f o u r

We have seen that before a computer can perform a task, it must be given an algorithm telling it precisely what to do; consequently, the study of algorithms is the cornerstone of computer science. In this chapter we introduce many of the fundamental concepts of this study, including the issues of algorithm discovery and representation as well as the major control concepts of iteration and recursion. In so doing we also present a few well-known algorithms for searching and sorting.

4.1 The Concept of an Algorithm

4.2 Algorithm Representation
Primitives
Pseudocode

4.3 Algorithm Discovery
The Theory of Problem Solving
Getting a Foot in the Door

4.4 Iterative Structures
The Sequential Search Algorithm
Loop Control
The Insertion Sort Algorithm

4.5 Recursive Structures
The Binary Search Algorithm
Recursive Control

4.6 Efficiency and Correctness
Algorithm Efficiency
Software Verification

4.1 The Concept of an Algorithm

In the introductory chapter we informally defined an algorithm as a set of steps that define how a task is performed. In this section we look more closely at this fundamental concept. We begin by emphasizing the distinction between an algorithm and its representation—a distinction that is analogous to that between a story and a book. A story is abstract, or conceptual, in nature; a book is a physical representation of a story. If a book is translated into another language or republished in a different format, it is merely the representation of the story that changes—the story itself remains the same.

In the same manner, an algorithm is abstract and distinct from its representation. A single algorithm can be represented in many ways. As an example, the algorithm for converting temperature readings from Celsius to Fahrenheit is traditionally represented as the algebraic formula

$$F = (9/5)C + 32$$

But it could be represented by the instruction

Multiply the temperature reading in Celsius by 9/5 and then add 32 to the product

or even in the form of an electronic circuit. In each case the underlying algorithm is the same; only the representations differ.

In the context of distinguishing between algorithms and their representations, we should also clarify the distinction between two other related concepts—programs and processes. A program is a representation of an algorithm. In fact, computer scientists use the term *program* to refer to a formal representation of an algorithm designed for computer application. We defined a process in Chapter 3 to be the activity of executing a program. Note, however, that to execute a program is to execute the algorithm represented by the program, so a process could equivalently be defined as the activity of executing an algorithm. We conclude that processes, algorithms, and programs are distinct, yet related, entities.

Consider now the formal definition of an algorithm given in Figure 4.1, beginning with the requirement that the set of steps in an algorithm be ordered. This means that the steps in an algorithm must have a well-established structure in terms of the order in which its steps are executed. This does not mean that the steps must be executed in a sequence consisting of a first step, followed by a second, and so on. Some algorithms, known as **parallel algorithms,** for example, contain more than one sequence of steps, each designed to be executed by different processors in a multiprocessor machine. In such cases the overall algorithm does not possess a single thread of steps that conforms to the first-step, second-step scenario. Instead, the algorithm's structure is that of multiple threads that branch and reconnect as different processors perform different parts of the overall task. Other examples include algorithms executed by circuits such as the flip-flop in Section 1.1, in which each gate performs a single step of

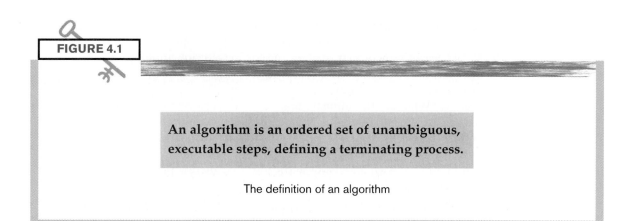

FIGURE 4.1

An algorithm is an ordered set of unambiguous, executable steps, defining a terminating process.

The definition of an algorithm

the overall algorithm. Here the steps are ordered by cause and effect, as the action of each gate propagates throughout the circuit.

Next, consider the requirement that an algorithm must consist of executable steps. To appreciate this condition, consider the instructions

Step 1. Make a list of all positive integers.
Step 2. Arrange this list in descending order (from largest to smallest).
Step 3. Extract the first integer from the resulting list.

These instructions do not describe an algorithm, because Steps 1 and 2 are impossible to perform. One cannot make a list of all the positive integers, and the positive integers cannot be arranged in descending order starting with the "largest." Computer scientists use the term *effective* to capture the concept of being executable. That is, to say that a step is effective means that it is doable.

Another requirement imposed by the definition in Figure 4.1 is that the steps in an algorithm be unambiguous. This means that during execution of an algorithm, the information in the state of the process must be sufficient to determine uniquely and completely the actions required by each step. In other words, the execution of each step in an algorithm does not require creative skills. Rather, it requires only the ability to follow directions.

In our discussion of ambiguity the distinction between an algorithm and its representation is significant. Ambiguities in an algorithm's representation are often misinterpreted as ambiguities within the underlying algorithm. A common example involves the level of detail at which an algorithm must be described. Among meteorologists, the instruction "Convert the Celsius reading to its Fahrenheit equivalent" may suffice, but a layperson, requiring a more detailed description, would argue that the instruction is ambiguous. Note that the problem is not that the underlying algorithm is ambiguous but that the algorithm is not represented in enough detail for the layperson. Thus the ambiguity is in the algorithm's representation rather than in the algorithm. In the next section we will see how the concept of primitives can be used to eliminate such ambiguity problems in an algorithm's representation.

The requirement that an algorithm define a terminating process means that the execution of an algorithm must lead to an end. The origin of this requirement is in theoretical computer science, where the goal is to answer such questions as "What are the ultimate limitations of algorithms and machines?" Here computer science seeks to distinguish between problems whose answers can be obtained algorithmically and problems whose answers lie beyond the capabilities of algorithmic systems. In this context, a line is drawn between processes that culminate with an answer and those that merely proceed forever without producing a result.

In more applied settings, the requirement that an algorithm define a terminating process is useful in that it rules out endless processes that never produce meaningful results. For example, following the instruction "Do this step again" is of little value. There are, however, meaningful applications for nonterminating processes, including monitoring the vital signs of a hospital patient and maintaining an aircraft's attitude in flight. Some would argue that these applications involve merely the repetition of algorithms, each of which reaches an end and then automatically repeats. Others would counter that such arguments are simply attempts to cling to an overly restrictive formal definition.

Regardless of which side is correct, the fact is that the term *algorithm* is often used in applied, informal settings in reference to sets of steps that do not necessarily define terminating processes. An example is the long-division algorithm, which does not define a terminating process when dividing 1 by 3.

QUESTIONS/EXERCISES

1. Summarize the distinctions between a process, an algorithm, and a program.
2. Give some examples of algorithms with which you are familiar. Are they really algorithms in the precise sense?
3. Identify some points of vagueness in our informal definition of an algorithm introduced in Section 0.1.
4. In what sense do the steps described by the following list of instructions fail to constitute an algorithm?
   Step 1. Take a coin out of your pocket and put it on the table.
   Step 2. Return to Step 1.

4.2 Algorithm Representation

In this section we consider issues relating to an algorithm's representation. Our goal is to introduce the basic concepts of primitives and pseudocode as well as to establish a representation system for our own use.

Primitives

The representation of an algorithm requires some form of language. In the case of humans this may be a traditional natural language (English, Russian, Japanese) or perhaps the language of pictures, as demonstrated in Figure 4.2, which describes an algorithm for folding a bird from a square piece of paper. Often, however, such natural channels of communication lead to misunderstandings, sometimes because the terminology used may have more than one meaning. The sentence, "Visiting grandchildren can be nerve-racking," could mean either that the grandchildren cause problems when they come to visit or that going to see them is problematic. Problems also arise over misunderstandings regarding the level of detail required. Few readers could successfully fold a bird from the directions given in Figure 4.2, yet a student of origami would probably have little difficulty. In short, communication problems arise when the language used for an algorithm's representation is not precisely defined or when information is not given in adequate detail.

Computer science approaches these problems by establishing a well-defined set of building blocks from which algorithm representations can be constructed. Such a building block is called a **primitive.** Assigning precise definitions to these primitives removes many problems of ambiguity, and requiring algorithms to be described in terms of these primitives establishes a uniform level of detail. A collection of primitives along with a collection of rules stating how the primitives can be combined to represent more complex ideas constitutes a **programming language.**

Each primitive consists of two parts: its syntax and its semantics. **Syntax** refers to the primitive's symbolic representation, and **semantics** refers to the concept represented, or the meaning of the primitive. The syntax of *air* consists of three symbols, whereas the semantics is a gaseous substance surrounding the world. As an example, Figure 4.3 presents some of the primitives used in origami.

To obtain a collection of primitives to use in representing algorithms for computer execution, we could turn to the individual instructions that the machine is designed to execute. If an algorithm is expressed at this level of detail, we will certainly have a program suitable for machine execution. However, expressing algorithms at this level is tedious, and so one normally uses a collection of "higher-level" primitives, each being an abstract tool constructed from the lower-level primitives provided in the machine's language. The result is a formal programming language in which algorithms can be expressed in a conceptually higher form than in the actual machine language. We discuss such programming languages in the next chapter.

Pseudocode

For now, we forgo the introduction of a formal programming language in favor of a less formal, more intuitive notational system known as pseudocode. In general, a **pseudocode** is a notational system in which ideas can be expressed informally during the algorithm development process.

FIGURE 4.2

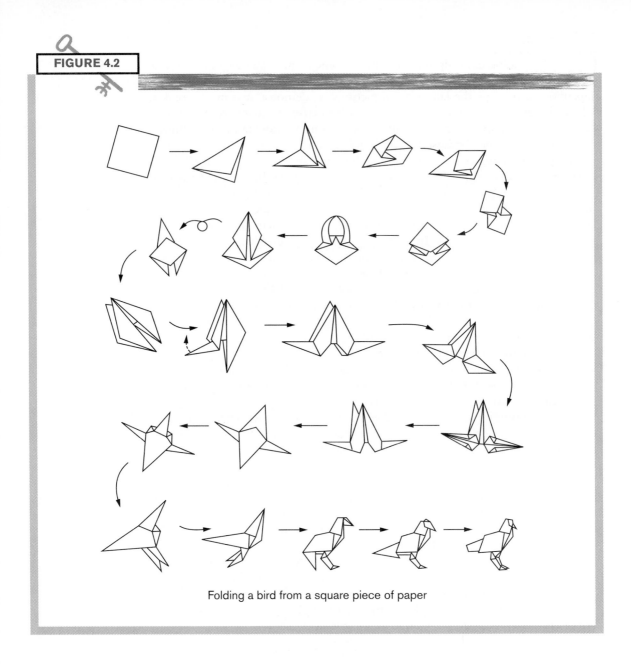

Folding a bird from a square piece of paper

One way to obtain a pseudocode is simply to loosen the rules of the formal language in which the final version of the algorithm is to be expressed. This approach is commonly used when the target programming language is known in advance. There the pseudocode used during the early stages of program development consists of syntax-semantic structures similar to, but less formal than, those used in the target programming language.

FIGURE 4.3

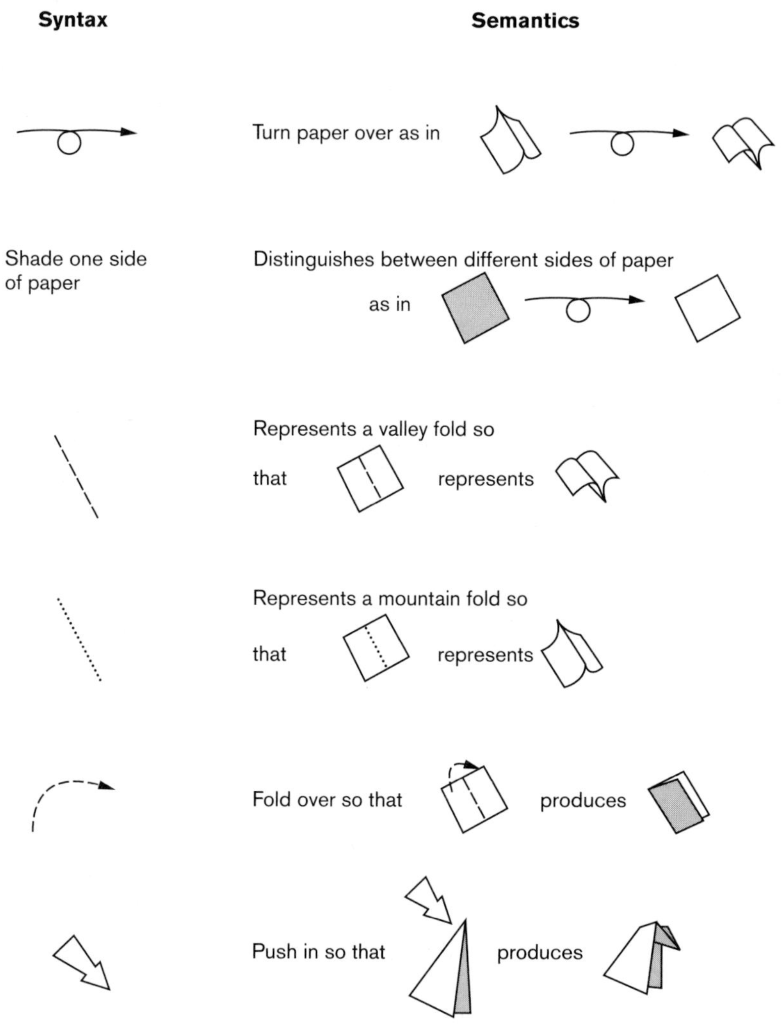

Syntax

Semantics

Turn paper over as in

Shade one side of paper

Distinguishes between different sides of paper

as in

Represents a valley fold so

that   represents

Represents a mountain fold so

that   represents

Fold over so that   produces

Push in so that   produces

Origami primitives

ALGORITHM REPRESENTATION DURING ALGORITHM DESIGN

The task of designing an algorithm requires that the designer keep track of numerous interrelated concepts—a requirement that can exceed the capabilities of the human mind. (In an article in the *Psychological Review* in 1956, George A. Miller reported research indicating that the human mind is capable of manipulating only about seven details at any one time.) Thus the designer of complex algorithms needs a way to record and recall portions of an evolving algorithm as his or her concentration requires.

During the 1950s and 1960s, flowcharts (by which algorithms are represented by geometric shapes connected by arrows) represented the state-of-the-art design tool. However, flowcharts often became tangled webs of crisscrossing arrows that made understanding the structure of the underlying algorithm difficult at best. Thus, the use of flowcharts as design tools has given way to other representation techniques. An example is the pseudocode used in this text, by which algorithms are represented with precisely defined textual structures. On the other hand, flowcharts are still beneficial when the goal is presentation rather than design. For example, Figures 4.8 and 4.9 apply flowchart notation to demonstrate the algorithmic structure represented by popular control statements.

The search for better design notations is a continuing process. In Chapter 6 we will see that the trend is to use graphical techniques to assist in the global design of large software systems, while pseudocode remains popular for designing the smaller procedural components within a system.

Our goal, however, is to consider the issues of algorithm development and representation without confining our discussion to a particular programming language. Thus our approach to pseudocode is to develop a consistent, concise notation for representing recurring semantic structures. In turn, these structures will become the primitives in which we attempt to express future ideas.

For example, the need to select one of two possible activities depending on the truth or falseness of some condition is a common algorithmic structure. Examples include:

If the gross domestic product has increased, buy common stock; otherwise, sell common stock.

Buy common stock if the gross domestic product has increased and sell it otherwise.

Buy or sell common stock depending on whether the gross domestic product has increased or decreased, respectively.

Each of these statements could be rewritten to conform to the structure

if (*condition*) **then** (*activity*)
      else (*activity*)

where we have used the key words if, then, and else to announce the different substructures within the main structure and parentheses to delimit the boundaries of these substructures. By adopting this syntactic structure for our pseudocode, we acquire a uniform way in which to express this common semantic structure. This, then, is what we do.

Whereas the statement

Depending on whether or not the year is a leap year, divide the total by 366 or 365, respectively.

may possess a more creative literary style, we will consistently opt for the straightforward

```
if (year is leap year)
    then (divide total by 366)
    else (divide total by 365)
```

We also adopt the shorter syntax

if (*condition*) **then** (*activity*)

for those cases not involving an else activity. Using this notation, the statement

> Should it be the case that sales have decreased, lower the price by 5%.

will be reduced to

if (sales have decreased) **then** (lower the price by 5%)

Another common algorithmic structure involves the need to continue executing a statement or sequence of statements as long as some condition remains true. Informal examples include

> As long as there are tickets to sell, continue selling tickets.

and

> While there are tickets to sell, keep selling tickets.

For such cases, we adopt the uniform pattern

while (*condition*) **do** (*activity*)

for our pseudocode. In short, such a statement means to check the *condition* and, if it is true, perform the *activity* and return to check the *condition* again. If the *condition* is ever found to be false, move on to the next instruction following the while structure. Thus both of the preceding statements are reduced to

while (tickets remain to be sold) **do** (sell a ticket)

We will often want to refer to values by descriptive names. To make such associations, we will use the form

assign *name* **the value** *expression*

where *name* is the descriptive name and *expression* describes the value to be associated with the name. For example, the statement

assign Total **the value** Price + Tax

associates the result of adding the values of Price and Tax with the name Total.

Indentation often enhances the readability of a program. For example, the statement

```
if (item is taxable)
    then (if (price > limit)
            then (pay x)
            else (pay y)
        )
    else (pay z)
```

is easier to comprehend than the otherwise equivalent

> **if** (item is taxable) **then** (**if** (price $>$ limit) **then** (pay x)
> **else** (pay y)) **else** (pay z)

Thus we will adopt the use of indentation in our pseudocode. (Note that we have even aligned the parentheses associated with the outer then clause to clarify the beginning and ending of that structure.)

We want to use our pseudocode to describe activities that can be used as abstract tools in other applications. Computer science has a variety of terms for such program units, including subprogram, subroutine, procedure, module, and function, each with its own variation of meaning. We will adopt the term *procedure* for our pseudocode and use this term to announce the title by which the pseudocode unit will be known. More precisely, we will begin a pseudocode unit with a statement of the form

> **procedure** *name*

where *name* is the particular name of the unit. We will then follow this introductory statement with the statements that define the unit's action. For example, Figure 4.4 is a pseudocode representation of a procedure called Greetings that prints the message "Hello" three times.

When the task performed by a procedure is required elsewhere in our pseudocode, we will merely request it by name. For example, if two procedures were named ProcessLoan and RejectApplication, then we could request their services within an if-then-else structure by writing

> **if** (...) **then** (Execute the procedure ProcessLoan)
> **else** (Execute the procedure RejectApplication)

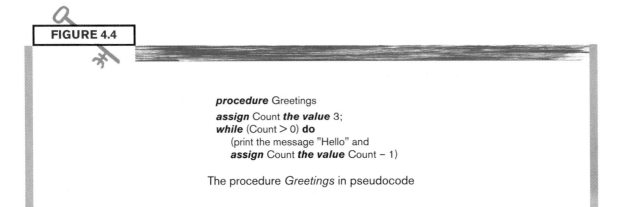

FIGURE 4.4

> *procedure* Greetings
> *assign* Count *the value* 3;
> *while* (Count $>$ 0) **do**
>   (print the message "Hello" and
>   *assign* Count *the value* Count − 1)

The procedure *Greetings* in pseudocode

which would result in the execution of the procedure ProcessLoan if the tested condition were true or in the execution of RejectApplication if the condition were false.

Procedures should be designed to be as generic as possible. A procedure for sorting lists of names should be designed to sort any list—not a particular one—so it should be written in such a way that the list to be sorted is not specified in the procedure itself. Instead, the list should be referred to by a generic name within the procedure's representation.

In our pseudocode, we will adopt the convention of listing these generic names in parentheses on the same line on which we identify the procedure's name. In particular, a procedure named Sort, which is designed to sort any list of names, would begin with the statement

procedure Sort (List)

Later in the representation where a reference to the list being sorted is required, the generic name List would be used. In turn, when the services of Sort are required, we will identify which list is to be substituted for List in the procedure Sort. Thus we will write something such as

Apply the procedure Sort to the organization's membership list

and

Apply the procedure Sort to the wedding guest list

depending on our needs.

Keep in mind that the purpose of our pseudocode is to provide a means of jotting down rough outlines of algorithms—not the writing of finished, formal programs. Thus we will feel free to insert informal phrases that request activities whose details are not rigorously specified. (How these details are resolved is not so much a feature of the algorithm being expressed as it is a property of the language in which the formal program is ultimately written.) If, however, we find a particular idea recurring in our outlines, we will adopt a consistent syntax for representing it and thus extend our pseudocode.

QUESTIONS/EXERCISES

1. A primitive in one context may turn out to be a composite of primitives in another. For instance, our *while* statement is a primitive in our pseudocode, yet it is implemented as a composite of machine-language instructions. Give two examples of this phenomenon in a noncomputer setting.

2. In what sense is the construction of procedures the construction of primitives?

3. The Euclidean algorithm finds the greatest common divisor of two positive integers X and Y by the following process:

As long as the value of neither X nor Y is zero, continue dividing the larger of the values by the smaller and assigning X and Y the values of the divisor and remainder, respectively. (The final value of X is the greatest common divisor.)

Express this algorithm in our pseudocode.

4. Describe a collection of primitives that are used in a subject other than computer programming.

4.3 Algorithm Discovery

The development of a program consists of two activities—discovering the underlying algorithm and representing that algorithm as a program. Up to this point we have been concerned with the issues of algorithm representation without considering the question of how algorithms are found in the first place. Yet algorithm discovery is usually the more challenging step in the software development process. After all, to discover an algorithm is to find a method of solving that problem whose solution the algorithm is to compute. Thus, to understand how algorithms are discovered is to understand the problem-solving process.

The Theory of Problem Solving

The techniques of problem solving and the need to learn more about them are not unique to computer science, but rather they are topics pertinent to almost any field. The close association between the process of algorithm discovery and that of general problem solving has caused computer scientists to join with those of other disciplines in the search for better problem-solving techniques. Ultimately, one would like to reduce the process of problem solving to an algorithm in itself, but this has been shown to be impossible. (This is a result of the material in Chapter 11, where we show that there are problems that do not have algorithmic solutions.) Thus the ability to solve problems remains more of an artistic skill to be developed than a precise science to be learned.

As evidence of the illusive, artistic nature of problem solving, the following loosely defined problem-solving phases presented by the mathematician G. Polya in 1945 remain the basic principles on which attempts to teach problem-solving skills are based today.

Phase 1. Understand the problem.
Phase 2. Devise a plan for solving the problem.
Phase 3. Carry out the plan.
Phase 4. Evaluate the solution for accuracy and for its potential as a tool for solving other problems.

Translated into the context of program development, these phases become

Phase 1. Understand the problem.

Phase 2. Get an idea as to how an algorithmic procedure might solve the problem.

Phase 3. Formulate the algorithm and represent it as a program.

Phase 4. Evaluate the program for accuracy and for its potential as a tool for solving other problems.

Having presented Polya's list, we should emphasize that these phases are not steps to be followed when trying to solve a problem but rather phases that will be completed sometime during the solution process. The key word here is *followed*. You do not solve problems by following. Rather, to solve a problem, you must take the initiative and lead. If you approach the task of solving a problem in the frame of mind depicted by "Now I've finished Phase 1, it's time to move on to Phase 2," you are not likely to be successful. However, if you become involved with the problem and ultimately solve it, you most likely can look back at what you did and realize that Polya's four phases had been completed.

Another important observation is that Polya's four phases are not necessarily completed in sequence. Contrary to the claim made by many authors, successful problem solvers often start formulating strategies for solving a problem (Phase 2) before the problem itself is entirely understood (Phase 1). Then, if these strategies fail (during Phases 3 or 4), the potential problem solver gains a deeper understanding of the intricacies of the problem and, based on this deeper understanding, can return to form other and hopefully more successful strategies.

Keep in mind that we are discussing how problems are solved—not how we would like them to be solved. Ideally, we would like to eliminate the waste inherent in the trial-and-error process just described. In the case of developing large software systems, discovering a misunderstanding as late as Phase 4 can represent a tremendous loss in resources. Avoiding such catastrophes is a major goal of software engineers (Chapter 6), who have traditionally insisted on a thorough understanding of a problem before proceeding with a solution. One could argue, however, that a true understanding of a problem is not obtained until a solution has been found, that the mere fact that a problem is unsolved implies a lack of understanding. To insist on a complete understanding of the problem before proposing any solutions is therefore somewhat idealistic.

As an example, consider the following problem:

> Person A is charged with the task of determining the ages of person B's three children. B tells A that the product of the children's ages is 36. After considering this clue, A replies that another clue is required, so B tells A the sum of the children's ages. Again, A replies that another clue is needed, so B tells A that the oldest child plays the piano. After hearing this clue, A tells B the ages of the three children.
> How old are the three children?

At first glance the last clue seems to be totally unrelated to the problem, yet it is this clue that allows A to finally determine the ages of the children. How can this be? Let us proceed by formulating a plan of attack and following this plan, even though we still have many questions about the problem. Our plan will be to trace the steps described by the problem statement while keeping track of the information available to person A as the story progresses.

The first clue given A is that the product of the children's ages is 36. This means that the triple representing the three ages is one of those listed in Figure 4.5(a). The next clue is the sum of the desired triple. We are not told what this sum is, but we are told that this information is not enough for A to isolate the correct triple; therefore the desired triple must be one whose sum appears at least twice in the table of Figure 4.5(b). But the only triples appearing in (b) with identical sums are (1,6,6) and (2,2,9), both of which produce the sum 13. This is the information available to A at the time the last clue is given. It is at this point that we finally understand the significance of the last clue. It has nothing to do with playing the piano; rather it is the fact that there is an oldest child. This rules out the triple (1,6,6) and thus allows us to conclude that the children's ages are 2, 2, and 9.

In this case, then, it is not until we attempt to implement our plan for solving the problem (Phase 3) that we gain a complete understanding of the problem (Phase 1). Had we insisted on completing phase 1 before proceeding, we would probably never have found the children's ages. Such irregularities in the problem-solving process are fundamental to the difficulties in developing systematic approaches to problem solving.

Another irregularity is the mysterious inspiration that may come to a potential problem solver who, having worked on a problem without apparent success, may at a later time suddenly see the solution while doing another task. This phenomenon was identified by H. von Helmholtz as early as 1896 and was discussed by the mathematician Henri Poincaré in a lecture before the Psychological Society in Paris. There, Poincaré described his experiences of real-

FIGURE 4.5

(1,1,36)	(1,6,6)		1 + 1 + 36 = 38	1 + 6 + 6 = 13
(1,2,18)	(2,2,9)		1 + 2 + 18 = 21	2 + 2 + 9 = 13
(1,3,12)	(2,3,6)		1 + 3 + 12 = 16	2 + 3 + 6 = 11
(1,4,9)	(3,3,4)		1 + 4 + 9 = 14	3 + 3 + 4 = 10

(a) Triples whose product is 36   (b) Sums of triples from part (a)

izing the solution to a problem he had worked on after he had set it aside and begun other projects. The phenomenon reflects a process in which a subconscious part of the mind appears to continue working and, if successful, forces the solution into the conscious mind. Today, the period between conscious work on a problem and the sudden inspiration is known as an incubation period, and its understanding remains a goal of current research.

Getting a Foot in the Door

We have been discussing problem solving from a somewhat philosophical point of view while avoiding a direct confrontation with the question of how we should go about trying to solve a problem. There are, of course, numerous problem-solving approaches, each of which can be successful in certain settings. We will identify some of them shortly. For now, we note that there seems to be a common thread running through these techniques, which simply stated is "get your foot in the door." As an example, let us consider the following simple problem:

> Before A, B, C, and D ran a race they made the following predictions:
>
> A predicted that B would win.
> B predicted that D would be last.
> C predicted that A would be third.
> D predicted that A's prediction would be correct.
>
> Only one of these predictions was true, and this was the prediction made by the winner. In what order did A, B, C, and D finish the race?

After reading the problem and analyzing the data, it should not take long to realize that since the predictions of A and D were equivalent and only one prediction was true, the predictions of both A and D must be false. Thus neither A nor D were winners. At this point we have our foot in the door, and obtaining the complete solution to our problem is merely a matter of extending our knowledge from here. If A's prediction was false, then B did not win either. The only remaining choice for the winner is C. Thus, C won the race, and C's prediction was true. Consequently, we know that A came in third. That means that the finishing order was either CBAD or CDAB. But the former is ruled out because B's prediction must be false. Therefore the finishing order was CDAB.

Of course, being told to get our foot in the door is not the same as being told how to do it. Obtaining this toehold, as well as realizing how to expand this initial thrust into a complete solution to the problem, requires creative input from the would-be problem solver. There are, however, several general approaches that have been proposed by Polya and others for how one might go about getting a foot in the door. One is to try working the problem backward. For instance, if the problem is to find a way of producing a particular output from a given input, one might start with that output and attempt to back up to the given input. This approach is typical of someone trying to discover the bird-folding algorithm in the previous section. They tend to unfold a completed bird in an attempt to see how it is constructed.

Another general problem-solving approach is to look for a related problem that is either easier to solve or has been solved before and then try to apply its solution to the current problem. This technique is of particular value in the context of program development. Often the major difficulty in program development is not that of solving a particular instance of a problem but rather of finding a general algorithm that can be used to solve all instances of the problem. More precisely, if we were faced with the task of developing a program for alphabetizing lists of names, our task would not be to sort a particular list but to find a general algorithm that could be used to sort any list of names. Thus, although the instructions

Interchange the names David and Alice.
Move the name Carol to the position between Alice and David.
Move the name Bob to the position between Alice and Carol.

correctly sort the list David, Alice, Carol, and Bob, they do not constitute the general-purpose algorithm we desire. What we need is an algorithm that can sort this list as well as other lists we may encounter. This is not to say that our solution for sorting a particular list is totally worthless in our search for a general-purpose algorithm. We might, for instance, get our foot in the door by considering such special cases in an attempt to find general principles that can in turn be used to develop the desired general-purpose algorithm. In this case, then, our solution is obtained by the technique of solving a collection of related problems.

Still another approach to getting a foot in the door is to apply **stepwise refinement,** which is essentially the technique of not trying to conquer an entire task (in all its gory detail) at once. Rather, stepwise refinement proposes that one first view the problem at hand in terms of several subproblems. The idea is that by breaking the original problem into subproblems, one is able to approach the overall solution in terms of steps, each of which is easier to solve than the entire original problem. In turn, stepwise refinement proposes that these steps be decomposed into smaller steps and these smaller steps be broken into still smaller ones until the entire problem has been reduced to a collection of easily solved subproblems.

In this light, stepwise refinement is a top-down methodology in that it progresses from the general to the specific. In contrast, bottom-up methodologies progress from the specific to the general. Although contrasting in theory, the two approaches actually complement each other in practice. For instance, the decomposition of a problem proposed by the top-down methodology of stepwise refinement is often guided by the problem solver's intuition, which is working in a bottom-up mode.

Solutions produced by stepwise refinement possess a natural modular structure, and herein lies a major reason for the popularity of stepwise refinement in algorithm design. If an algorithm has a natural modular structure, then it is easily adapted to a modular representation, which is conducive to the development of a manageable program. Furthermore, the modules produced by stepwise refinement are compatible with the concept of team programming, in which several people are assigned the task of developing a software product as a team. After all, once the task of the software has been broken into subproblems (or potential modules), the personnel on the team can work independently on these subtasks without getting in each other's way.

These advantages of stepwise refinement in the context of software development have produced many followers of the technique. However, with all its good points, stepwise refinement is not the final word in algorithm discovery. Rather, it is essentially an organizational tool whose problem-solving attributes are consequences of this organization. Stepwise refinement is a natural methodology to use when organizing a nationwide political campaign, writing a term paper, or planning a sales convention. Similarly, most software development projects in the data processing community have a large organizational component. The task is not so much that of discovering a startling new algorithm as it is a problem of organizing the tasks to be performed into a coherent package. For these reasons, stepwise refinement has correctly become a major design methodology in data processing.

But stepwise refinement remains only one of many design methodologies of interest to computer scientists, and thus one should not be misled into believing that all algorithm discoveries can be achieved by means of stepwise refinement. In fact, bringing preconceived notions and preselected tools to the problem-solving task can sometimes mask a problem's simplicity. Consider the following problem:

As you step from a pier into a boat, your hat falls into the water, unbeknownst to you. The river is flowing at 2.5 miles per hour so your hat begins to float downstream. In the meantime, you begin traveling upstream in the boat at a speed of 4.75 miles per hour relative to the water. After 10 minutes you realize that your hat is missing, turn the boat around, and begin to chase your hat down the river. How long will it take to catch up with your hat?

Most students of high school algebra as well as pocket calculator enthusiasts approach this problem by first determining how far upstream the boat will have traveled in 10 minutes as well as how far downstream the hat will have traveled during that same time. Then, they try to determine how long it will take for the boat to travel downstream to this position. But, when the boat reaches this position, the hat will have floated farther downstream! Thus, the would-be problem solver becomes trapped in a cycle of computing where the hat will be each time the boat goes to where the hat was.

The problem is much simpler than this, however. The trick is to resist the urge to begin writing formulas and making calculations. Instead, we need to put these skills aside and adjust our perspective. The entire problem takes place in the river. The fact that the water is moving in relation to the shore is irrelevant. Think of the same problem posed on a large conveyer belt instead of a river. First, solve the problem with the conveyer belt stopped. If you place your hat at your feet while standing on the belt and then walk away from your hat for 10 minutes, it will take 10 minutes to return to your hat. Now turn on the conveyer belt. This means that the scenery will begin to move past the belt, but, because you are on the belt, this does not change your relationship to the belt or your hat. It will still take 10 minutes to return to your hat.

We conclude that algorithm discovery remains a challenging art that must be developed over a period of time rather than taught as a subject consisting of well-defined methodologies. Indeed, to train a potential problem solver to follow certain methodologies is to quash those creative skills that should instead be nurtured.

QUESTIONS/EXERCISES

1. a. Find an algorithm for solving the following program: Given a positive integer n, find the list of positive integers whose product is the largest among all the lists of positive integers whose sum is n. For example, if n is 4, the desired list is 2, 2 because $2 + 2$ is larger than $1 + 1 + 1 + 1$, $2 + 1 + 1$, and $3 + 1$. If n is 5, the desired list is 2, 3.
   b. What is the desired list if $n = 2001$?
   c. Explain how you got your foot in the door.
2. a. Suppose we are given a checkerboard consisting of 2^n rows and 2^n columns of squares, for some positive integer n, and a box of L-shaped tiles, each of which can cover exactly three squares on the board. If any single square is cut out of the board, can we cover the remaining board with tiles such that tiles do not overlap or hang off the edge of the board?
   b. Explain how your solution to (a) can be used to show that $2^{2^n} - 1$ is divisible by 3 for all positive integers n.
   c. How are (a) and (b) related to Polya's phases of problem solving?
3. Decode the following message, then explain how you got your foot in the door.

   Pdeo eo pda yknnayp wjosan.

4.4 Iterative Structures

Our goal now is to study some of the repetitive structures used in describing algorithmic processes. In this section we discuss **iterative structures** in which a collection of instructions is repeated in a looping manner. In the next section we introduce the technique of recursion. As a side effect, we will introduce some popular algorithms—the sequential search, the binary search, and the insertion sort. We begin by introducing the sequential search algorithm.

The Sequential Search Algorithm

Consider the problem of searching a list for the occurrence of a particular target value. We want to develop an algorithm that determines whether that value is in the list. If the value is in the list, we consider the search a success; otherwise, we consider it a failure. We assume that the list is sorted according to some rule for ordering its entries. For example, if the list is a list of names, we assume the names appear in alphabetical order, or if the list consists of numeric values, we assume its entries appear in order of increasing magnitude.

To get our foot in the door, we imagine how we might search a guest list of perhaps 20 entries for a particular name. In this setting we might scan the list from its beginning, comparing each entry with the target name. If we find the target name, the search terminates as a success. However, if we reach the end of the list or reach a name greater than (alphabetically) the target name, our search terminates as a failure. (Remember, the list is arranged in alphabetical order, so reaching a name greater than the target name indicates that the target does not appear in the list.) In summary, our rough idea is to continue searching down the list as long as there are more names to be investigated and the target name is less than the name currently being considered.

In our pseudocode this process can be represented as

Select the first entry in the list as the test entry.
while (target value > test entry and
        there remain entries to be considered)
   do (Select the next entry in the list as the test entry)

Upon terminating the while structure, one of two conditions will be true: either the target value has been found or the target value is not in the list. In either case we can detect a successful search by comparing the test entry to the target value. If they are equal, the search has been successful. Thus we add the statement

if (target value = test entry)
  then (Declare the search a success.)
  else (Declare the search a failure.)

to the end of our pseudocode routine.

Finally, we observe that the first statement in our routine, which selects the first entry in the list to play the role of the test entry, is based on the assumption that the list in question contains at least one entry. We might reason that this is a safe guess, but just to be sure, we can position our routine as the else option of the statement

```
if (List empty)
    then (Declare search a failure.)
    else ( … )
```

This produces the procedure shown in Figure 4.6. Note that this procedure can be used to perform searches in other procedures by using statements such as

Apply the procedure Search to the passenger list to look for the name Darrel Baker.

to find out if Darrel Baker is a passenger and

Apply the procedure Search to the list of ingredients using nutmeg as the target value.

to find out if nutmeg appears in the list of ingredients.

In summary, the algorithm represented by Figure 4.6 sequentially considers the entries in the order in which they occur in the list. For this reason, the algorithm is called the **sequential search** algorithm. Because of its simplicity, it is often used for short lists or when other concerns dictate its use. However, in the case of long lists, sequential searches are not as efficient as other techniques (as we shall soon see).

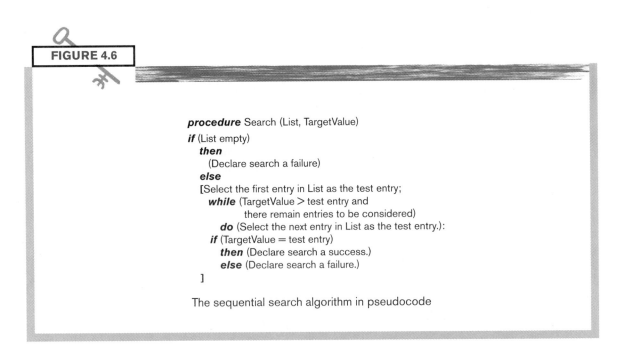

FIGURE 4.6

```
procedure Search (List, TargetValue)
if (List empty)
    then
        (Declare search a failure)
    else
    [Select the first entry in List as the test entry;
        while (TargetValue > test entry and
                there remain entries to be considered)
            do (Select the next entry in List as the test entry.):
        if (TargetValue = test entry)
            then (Declare search a success.)
            else (Declare search a failure.)
    ]
```

The sequential search algorithm in pseudocode

Loop Control

The repetitive use of an instruction or sequence of instructions is an important algorithmic concept. One method of implementing such repetition is the iterative structure known as the **loop,** in which a collection of instructions, called the body of the loop, is executed in a repetitive fashion under the direction of some control process. A typical example is found in the sequential search algorithm represented in Figure 4.6. Here we use a while statement to control the repetition of the single statement Select the next entry in List as the TestEntry. Indeed, the while statement

> **while** (*condition*) **do** (*body*)

exemplifies the concept of a loop structure in that its execution traces the cyclic pattern

> check the *condition*
> execute the *body*
> check the *condition*
> execute the *body*
> .
> .
> .
> check the *condition*

until the condition fails.

As a general rule, the use of a loop structure produces a higher degree of flexibility than would be obtained merely by explicitly writing the body several times. For example, although the loop structure

> Execute the statement "Add a drop of sulfuric acid" three times.

is equivalent to the sequence

> Add a drop of sulfuric acid.
> Add a drop of sulfuric acid.
> Add a drop of sulfuric acid.

we cannot produce a similar sequence that is equivalent to the loop described by

> **while** (the pH level is greater than 4) **do**
> (add a drop of sulfuric acid)

because we do not know in advance how many drops of acid will be required.

ITERATIVE STRUCTURES IN MUSIC

Musicians were using and programming iterative structures centuries before computer scientists. Indeed, the structure of a song (being composed of multiple verses, each followed by the chorus) is exemplified by the **while** statement

> **while** (there is a verse remaining) **do**
> (sing the next verse;
> sing the chorus)

Moreover, the notation

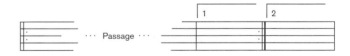

is merely a composer's way of expressing the structure

> **assign** N **the value** 1;
> **while** (N < 3) **do**
> (play the passage;
> play the Nth ending;
> **assign** N **the value** N + 1)

Let us now take a closer look at the composition of loop control. You may be tempted to view this part of a loop structure as having minor importance. After all, it is typically the body of the loop that actually performs the task at hand (for example, adding drops of acid)—the control activities appear merely as the overhead involved because we chose to execute the body in a repetitive fashion. However, experience has shown that the control of a loop is the more error-prone part of the structure and therefore deserves our attention.

The control of a loop consists of the three activities initialize, test, and modify (Figure 4.7), with the presence of each being required for successful loop control. The test activity has the obligation of causing the termination of the looping process by watching for a condition that indicates termination should take place. This condition is known as the termination condition. It is for the purpose of this test activity that we provide a condition within each while statement of our pseudocode. In the case of the while statement, however, the condition stated is the condition under which the body of the loop should be executed—the termination condition is the negation of the condition appearing in the while structure. Thus, in the while statement of Figure 4.6, the termination condition is

(target value ≤ test entry) or (there are no more entries to be considered)

The other two activities in the loop control ensure that the termination condition will ultimately occur. The initialization step establishes a starting condition, and the modification step moves this condition toward the termination condition. For instance, in Figure 4.6, initialization takes place in the statement preceding the while statement, where the current test entry is established as the first list entry. The modification step in this case is actually accomplished within

FIGURE 4.7

Initialize: Establish an initial state that will be modified toward the termination condition

Test: Compare the current state to the termination condition and terminate the repetition if equal

Modify: Change the state in such a way that it moves toward the termination condition

Components of repetitive control

the loop body, where our position of interest (identified by the test entry) is moved toward the end of the list. Thus, having executed the initialization step, repeated application of the modification step results in the termination condition being reached. (Either we will reach a test entry that is less than or equal to the target value or we ultimately reach the end of the list.)

We should emphasize that the initialization and modification steps must lead to the appropriate termination condition. This characteristic is critical for proper loop control, and thus one should always double-check for its presence when designing a loop structure. Failure to make such an evaluation can lead to errors even in the simplest cases. A typical example is found in the statements

> **assign** Number **the value** 1
> **while** (Number ≠ 6) **do**
>   (**assign** Number **the value** Number + 2)

Here the termination condition is *Number* = 6. But the value of Number is initialized at 1 and then incremented by 2 in the modification step. Thus, as the loop cycles, the values assigned to Number will be 1, 3, 5, 7, 9, and so on, but never the value 6. In turn, the loop will never terminate.

There are two popular loop structures that differ merely in the order in which the loop control components are executed. The first is exemplified by our pseudocode statement

> **while** (*condition*) **do** (*activity*)

whose semantics is represented in Figure 4.8 in the form of a **flowchart.** Such charts use various shapes to represent individual steps and arrows to indicate the order of the steps. The distinction between the shapes indicates the type of action involved in the associated step. A diamond indicates a decision and a rectangle indicates an arbitrary statement or sequence of statements. Note that the test for termination in the while structure occurs before the loop's body is executed.

In contrast, the structure in Figure 4.9 requests that the body of the loop be executed before the test for termination is performed. In this case, the loop's body is always performed at least once, whereas in the while structure, the body is never executed if the termination condition is satisfied the first time it is tested.

We use the syntactic form

> **repeat** (*activity*) **until** (*condition*)

in our pseudocode to represent the structure shown in Figure 4.9. The statement

> **repeat** (take a coin from your pocket)
> **until** (there are no coins in your pocket)

FIGURE 4.8

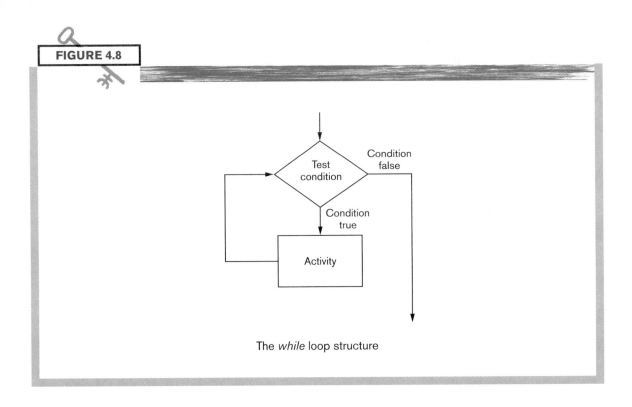

The *while* loop structure

FIGURE 4.9

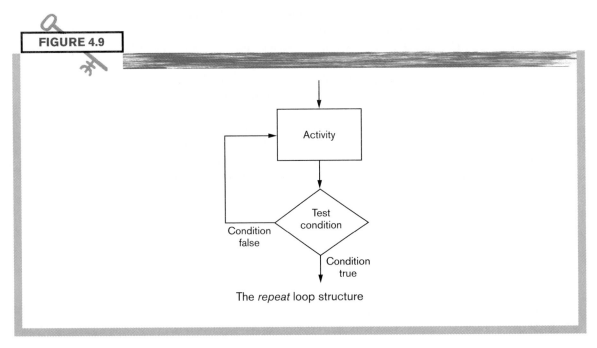

The *repeat* loop structure

assumes there is a coin in your pocket at the beginning, but

> **while** (there is a coin in your pocket) **do**
>   (take a coin from your pocket)

does not.

The Insertion Sort Algorithm

As an additional example of iterative structures, let us consider the problem of sorting a list of names into alphabetical order. But before proceeding, we should identify the constraints under which we will work. Simply stated, our goal is to sort the list "within itself." In other words, we want to sort the list by shuffling its entries as opposed to moving the list to another location. Our situation is analogous to the problem of sorting a list whose entries are recorded on separate index cards spread out on a crowded desktop. We have cleared off enough space for the cards but are not allowed to push additional materials back to make more room. This restriction is typical in computer applications, not because the workspace within the machine is necessarily crowded like our desktop, but simply because we want to use the storage space available in an efficient manner.

Let us get a foot in the door by considering how we might sort the names on the desktop. Consider the list of names

> Fred
> Alice
> David
> Bill
> Carol

One approach to sorting this list is to note that the sublist consisting of only the top name, Fred, is sorted but the sublist consisting of the top two names, Fred and Alice, is not. Thus we might pick up the card containing the name Alice, slide the name Fred down into the space where Alice was, and then place the name Alice in the hole at the top of the list, as represented by the first row in Figure 4.10. At this point our list would be

> Alice
> Fred
> David
> Bill
> Carol

Now the top two names form a sorted sublist, but the top three do not. Thus we might pick up the third name, David, slide the name Fred down into

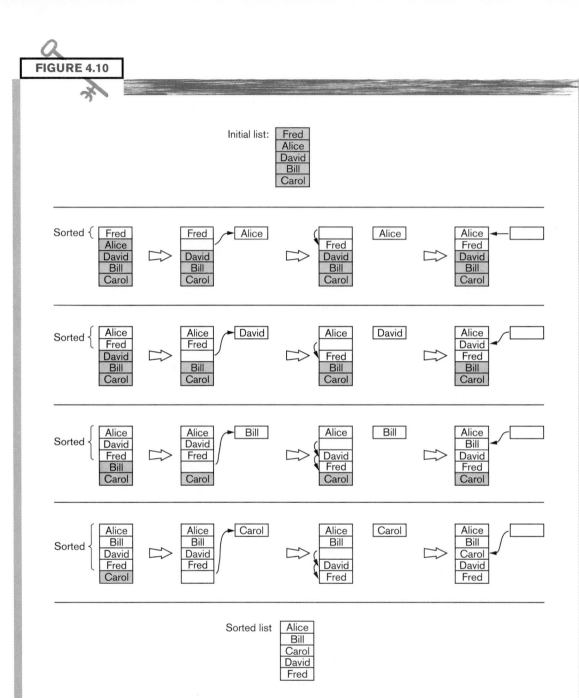

FIGURE 4.10

Sorting the list Fred, Alice, David, Bill, and Carol alphabetically

the hole where David was, and then insert David in the hole left by Fred, as summarized in the second row of Figure 4.10. The top three entries in the list would now be sorted. Continuing in this fashion, we could obtain a list in which the top four entries are sorted by picking up the fourth name, Bill, sliding the names Fred and David down, and then inserting Bill in the hole (see the third row of Figure 4.10). Finally, we can complete the sorting process by picking up Carol, sliding Fred and David down, and then inserting Carol in the remaining hole (see the fourth row of Figure 4.10).

Having analyzed the process of sorting a particular list, our task now is to generalize this process to obtain an algorithm for sorting general lists. To this end, we observe that each row of Figure 4.10 represents the same general process: Pick up the first name in the unsorted portion of the list, slide the names greater than the extracted name down, and insert the extracted name back in the list where the hole appears. If we identify the extracted name as the pivot entry, this process can be expressed in our pseudocode as

Move the pivot entry to a temporary location leaving a hole in List;
while (there is a name above the hole and that name is greater than the pivot) **do**
   (move the name above the hole down into the hole leaving a hole above the name)
Move the pivot entry into the hole in List

Next, we observe that this process should be executed repeatedly. To begin the sorting process, the pivot should be the second entry in the list and then, before each additional execution, the pivot selection should be one more entry down the list until the last entry has been positioned. That is, as the preceding routine is repeated, the initial position of the pivot entry should advance from the second entry to the third, then to the fourth, etc., until the routine has positioned the last entry in the list. Following this lead we can control the required repetition with the statements

assign N **the value** 2;
while (the value of N does not exceed the length of List) **do**
(Select the Nth entry in List as the pivot entry;
   .
   .
   .
  assign N **the value** N + 1)

where N represents the counter, the length of List refers to the number of entries in the list, and the dots indicate the location where the previous routine should be placed.

Our complete pseudocode program is shown in Figure 4.11. In short, the program sorts a list by repeatedly removing an entry and inserting it into its proper place. It is because of this repeated insertion process that the underlying algorithm is called the **insertion sort.**

FIGURE 4.11

procedure Sort (List)

assign N **the value** 2;

while (the value of N does not exceed the length of List) **do**
  (Select the Nth entry in List as the pivot entry;
  Move the pivot entry to a temporary location leaving a hole in List;
  while (there is a name above the hole and that name is greater than the pivot) **do**
    (move the name above the hole down into the hole leaving a hole above the name)
  Move the pivot entry into the hole in List;
  assign N **the value** N + 1
)

The insertion sort algorithm expressed in pseudocode

Note that the structure of Figure 4.11 is that of a loop within a loop, the outer loop being expressed by the first while statement and the inner loop represented by the second while statement. Each execution of the body of the outer loop results in the inner loop being initialized and executed until its termination condition is obtained. Thus a single execution of the outer loop's body will result in several executions of the inner loop's body.

The initialization component of the outer loop's control consists of establishing the initial value of the counter N with the statement

assign N **the value** 2;

The modification component is handled by incrementing the counter N at the end of the loop's body with the statement

assign N **the value** N + 1

The termination condition occurs when the value of the counter N exceeds the length of the list.

The inner loop's control is initialized by removing the pivot entry from the list that creates a hole. The loop's modification step is accomplished by moving entries above the hole down, thus moving the hole up. The termination condition consists of the hole being immediately below a name that is not greater than the pivot or of the hole reaching the top of the list.

QUESTIONS/EXERCISES

1. Modify the sequential search procedure in Figure 4.6 to allow for lists that are not sorted.
2. Convert the pseudocode routine

   assign Z **the value** 0;
   assign X **the value** 1;
   while (X < 6) **do**
   (**assign** Z **the value** Z + X;
    assign X **the value** X + 1)

   to an equivalent routine using a repeat statement.
3. Suppose the insertion sort as presented in Figure 4.11 was applied to the list George, Cheryl, Alice, and Bob. Describe the organization of the list at the end of each execution of the body of the outer while structure.
4. Why would we not want to change the phrase greater than in the while statement in Figure 4.11 to greater than or equal to?
5. A variation of the insertion sort algorithm is the **selection sort.** It begins by selecting the smallest entry in the list and moving it to the front. It then selects the smallest entry from the remaining entries in the list and moves it to the second position in the list. By repeatedly selecting the smallest entry from the remaining portion of the list and moving that entry forward, the sorted version of the list grows from the front of the list, while the back portion of the list consisting of the remaining unsorted entries shrinks. Use our pseudocode to express a procedure similar to that in Figure 4.11 for sorting a list using the selection sort algorithm.
6. Another well-known sorting algorithm is the **bubble sort.** It is based on the process of repeatedly comparing two adjacent names and interchanging them if they are not in the correct order relative to each other. Let us suppose that the list in question has n entries. The bubble sort would begin by comparing (and possibly interchanging) the entries in positions n and $n - 1$. Then, it would consider the entries in positions $n - 1$ and $n - 2$, and continue moving forward in the list until the first and second entries in the list had been compared (and possibly interchanged). Observe that this pass through the list will pull the smallest entry to the front of the list. Likewise, another such pass will ensure that the next to the smallest entry will be pulled to the second position in the list. Thus, by making a total of n − 1 passes through the list, the entire list will be sorted. (If one watches the algorithm at work, one sees the small entries bubble to the top of the list—an observation from which the algorithm gets its name.) Use our pseudocode to express a procedure similar to that in Figure 4.11 for sorting a list using the bubble sort algorithm.

4.5 Recursive Structures

Recursive structures provide an alternative to the loop paradigm for repetitive structures. As a way of introducing recursion, we consider the **binary search** algorithm, which applies a divide-and-conquer methodology to the search process.

The Binary Search Algorithm

Let us again tackle the problem of searching a sorted list to see whether it contains a particular entry, but this time we get our foot in the door by considering the procedure we follow when searching a telephone directory. We do not search such a directory by performing a sequential entry-by-entry or even a page-by-page procedure. Rather, we begin by opening the directory to a page in the area where we believe the target entry is located. If we are lucky, we will find the target entry there; otherwise, we must continue searching. But at this point we will have narrowed our search either to that portion of the directory preceding our current position or to that portion following our current position.

Figure 4.12 is a pseudocode representation of this approach applied to a generic sorted list. In this general setting we do not have the advantage of knowing approximate locations of entries, so the directions in the figure tell us to begin by opening the list to the "middle" entry. We have placed the word *middle* in quotation marks to indicate the possibility that the list may have an even number of entries and thus no middle entry in the exact sense. In this case, let us agree that the *middle* entry refers to the first entry in the second half of the list.

If the selected entry is not the target of the search, the routine in Figure

SEARCHING AND SORTING

The sequential and binary search algorithms are only two of many algorithms for performing the search process. (We will discuss the use of indexes and hashing in Chapter 8.) Likewise, the insertion sort is only one of many sorting algorithms. Other classic algorithms for sorting include the merge sort (discussed in Chapter 11), the selection sort (Question/Exercise 5 in Section 4.4), the bubble sort (Question/Exercise 6 in Section 4.4), the quick sort (which applies a divide-and-conquer approach to the sorting process), and the heap sort (which uses a clever technique for finding the entries that should be moved forward in the list).

You will find discussions of these algorithms in the books listed under Additional Reading at the end of this chapter. Although rather advanced for beginning students, the third volume of Donald E. Knuth's *The Art of Computer Programming* is generally accepted as the definitive word on searching and sorting techniques. In this multivolume set (which may some day grow to seven volumes), Knuth has collected a wealth of information regarding the fundamental algorithms of computing and has thus produced a classic found in the libraries of computer scientists and data processors as well.

FIGURE 4.12

Select the "middle" entry in List as the test entry;
Execute one of the following blocks of instructions
   depending on whether TargetValue is equal to, less
   than, or greater than the test entry
   Case 1: TargetValue = test entry
     (Declare the search a success.)
   Case 2: TargetValue < test entry
    [Apply the procedure Search to see whether TargetValue is
      in the portion of List preceding the test entry, and
     if (that search is successful)
      then (Declare this search a success.)
      else (Declare this search a failure.)
    ]
   Case 3: TargetValue > test entry
    [Apply the procedure Search to see whether TargetValue is
      in the portion of List following the test entry, and
     if (that search is successful)
      then (Declare this search a success.)
      else (Declare this search a failure.)
    ]

The core of the binary search

4.12 provides two options (search either the front half or the back half of the list), both of which require a secondary search performed by a procedure named Search. To complete our program, therefore, we must provide such a procedure, describing how this secondary search is to be performed. Note that this procedure must be robust enough to handle a request to search an empty list. For instance, if the routine in Figure 4.12 is given a list containing only one entry that is not the target value, then the procedure is requested to search either the sublist above or below the single entry, both of which are empty.

We could use the sequential search developed in the previous section as the required procedure, but this is not the technique we probably would use when searching a telephone directory. Rather, we probably would repeat the same process on the restricted portion of the directory that we used for the whole directory. That is, we would select an entry toward the middle of that portion of the directory and use it to narrow our search further.

FIGURE 4.13

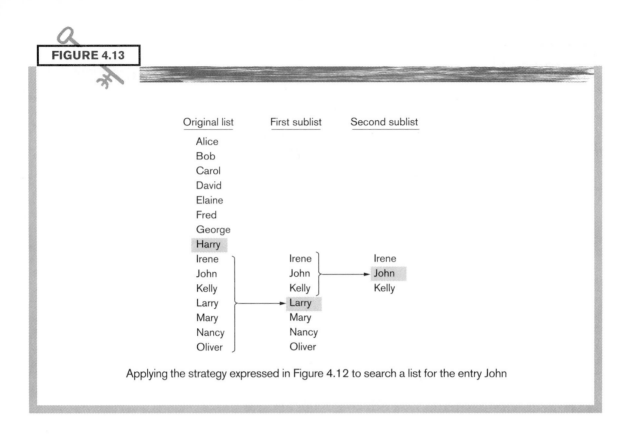

Applying the strategy expressed in Figure 4.12 to search a list for the entry John

This approach to the searching process is summarized in Figure 4.13, where we consider the task of searching the list on the left of the figure for the entry John. We first consider the middle entry Harry. Since our target belongs after this entry, the search continues by considering the lower half of the original list. The middle of this sublist is found to be Larry. Since our target should precede Larry, we turn our attention to the first half of the current sublist. When we interrogate the middle of that secondary sublist, we find our target John and declare the search a success. In short, our strategy is to successively divide the list in question into smaller segments until the target is found or the search is narrowed to an empty segment.

We can implement this strategy in our pseudocode by modifying the routine in Figure 4.12 to handle the case of an empty list and then giving the resulting procedure the name Search to obtain the pseudocode program shown in Figure 4.14. If we were following this procedure and came to the instruction Apply the module Search ..., we would apply the same search technique to the

FIGURE 4.14

procedure Search (List TargetValue)

if (List empty)
    then
      (Declare the search a failure.)
    else
      Select the "middle" entry in List as the test entry;
      Execute one of the following blocks of instructions
        depending on whether TargetValue is equal to, less
        than, or greater than the test entry
        Case 1: TargetValue = test entry
          (Declare the search a success.)
        Case 2: TargetValue < test entry
         [Apply the procedure Search to see whether TargetValue is
           in the portion of List preceding the test entry, and
          if (that search is successful)
           then (Declare this search a success.)
           else (Declare this search a failure.)
         ]
        Case 3: TargetValue > test entry
         [Apply the procedure Search to see whether TargetValue is
           in the portion of List following the test entry, and
          if (that search is successful)
            then (Declare this search a success.)
           else (Declare this search a failure.)
         ]

The binary search algorithm in pseudocode

smaller list that we were applying to the original one. If that search succeeded, we would return to declare our original search successful; if this secondary search failed, we would declare our original search a failure.

To see how the procedure in Figure 4.14 performs its task, let us follow it as it searches the list Alice, Bill, Carol, David, Evelyn, Fred, and George, for the target value Bill. Our search begins by selecting David (the middle entry) as the test entry under consideration. Since the target value (Bill) must precede this test entry, we are instructed to apply the procedure Search to the list of entries preceding David—that is, the list Alice, Bill, and Carol. In so doing, we create a second copy of the search procedure and assign it to this secondary task.

For a while, we have two copies of our search procedure being executed, as summarized in Figure 4.15. Progress in the original copy is temporarily suspended at the instruction

Apply the procedure Search to see whether TargetValue is
in the portion of List preceding the test entry

while we apply the second copy to the task of searching the list Alice, Bill, and Carol. When we complete this secondary search, we will discard the second copy of the procedure, report its findings to the original copy, and continue progress in the original. In this way, the second copy of the procedure executes as a subordinate to the original, performing the task requested by the original module and then disappearing.

The secondary search selects Bill as its test entry because that is the middle entry in the list Alice, Bill, and Carol. Since this is the same as the target value, it declares its search to be a success and terminates.

At this point, we have completed the secondary search as requested by the original copy of the procedure, so we are able to continue the execution of that original copy. Here we are told that if the secondary search was successful, we should declare the original search a success. Our process has correctly determined that Bill is a member of the list Alice, Bill, Carol, David, Evelyn, Fred, and George.

Let us now consider what happens if we ask the procedure in Figure 4.14 to search the list Alice, Carol, Evelyn, Fred, and George for the entry David. This time the original copy of the procedure selects Evelyn as its test entry and concludes that the target value must reside in the preceding portion of the list. It therefore requests another copy of the procedure to search the list of entries appearing in front of Evelyn—that is, the two-entry list consisting of Alice and Carol. At this stage our situation is as represented in Figure 4.16.

The second copy of the procedure selects Carol as its current entry and concludes that the target value must lie in the latter portion of its list. It then requests a third copy of the procedure to search the list of names following Carol in the list Alice and Carol. This sublist is empty, so the third copy of the procedure has the task of searching the empty list for the target value David. Our situation at this point is represented by Figure 4.17. The original copy of the procedure is charged with the task of searching the list Alice, Carol, Evelyn, Fred, and George, with the test entry being Evelyn; the second copy charged with searching the list Alice and Carol, with its test entry being Carol; and the third copy is about to begin searching the empty list.

Of course, the third copy of the procedure quickly declares its search to be a failure and terminates. The completion of the third copy's task allows the second copy to continue its task. It notes that the search it requested was unsuccessful, declares its own task to be a failure, and terminates. This report is what the original copy of the procedure has been waiting for, so it can now proceed. Since the search it requested failed, it declares its own search to have failed and

FIGURE 4.15

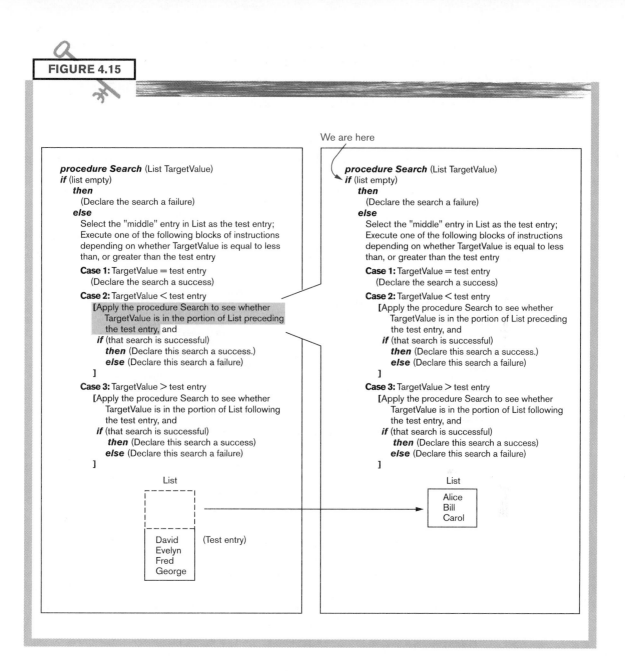

We are here

procedure Search (List TargetValue)
if (list empty)
  then
    (Declare the search a failure)
  else
    Select the "middle" entry in List as the test entry;
    Execute one of the following blocks of instructions
    depending on whether TargetValue is equal to less
    than, or greater than the test entry
    Case 1: TargetValue = test entry
      (Declare the search a success)
    Case 2: TargetValue < test entry
      [Apply the procedure Search to see whether
      TargetValue is in the portion of List preceding
      the test entry, and
      if (that search is successful)
        then (Declare this search a success.)
        else (Declare this search a failure)
      ]
    Case 3: TargetValue > test entry
      [Apply the procedure Search to see whether
      TargetValue is in the portion of List following
      the test entry, and
      if (that search is successful)
        then (Declare this search a success)
        else (Declare this search a failure)
      ]

        List

        David   (Test entry)
        Evelyn
        Fred
        George

procedure Search (List TargetValue)
if (list empty)
  then
    (Declare the search a failure)
  else
    Select the "middle" entry in List as the test entry;
    Execute one of the following blocks of instructions
    depending on whether TargetValue is equal to less
    than, or greater than the test entry
    Case 1: TargetValue = test entry
      (Declare the search a success)
    Case 2: TargetValue < test entry
      [Apply the procedure Search to see whether
      TargetValue is in the portion of List preceding
      the test entry, and
      if (that search is successful)
        then (Declare this search a success.)
        else (Declare this search a failure)
      ]
    Case 3: TargetValue > test entry
      [Apply the procedure Search to see whether
      TargetValue is in the portion of List following
      the test entry, and
      if (that search is successful)
        then (Declare this search a success)
        else (Declare this search a failure)
      ]

        List

        Alice
        Bill
        Carol

terminates. Our routine has correctly concluded that David is not contained in the list Alice, Carol, Evelyn, Fred, and George.

In summary, if we were to look back at the previous examples, we could see that the process employed by the algorithm represented in Figure 4.14 is to

FIGURE 4.16

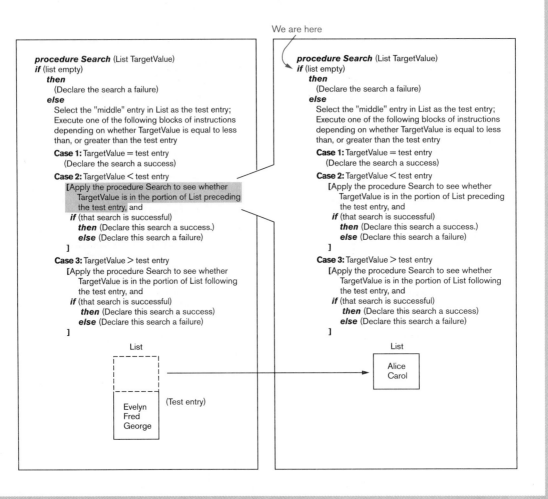

We are here

procedure Search (List TargetValue)
if (list empty)
    then
        (Declare the search a failure)
    else
        Select the "middle" entry in List as the test entry;
        Execute one of the following blocks of instructions
        depending on whether TargetValue is equal to less
        than, or greater than the test entry

    Case 1: TargetValue = test entry
        (Declare the search a success)

    Case 2: TargetValue < test entry
        [Apply the procedure Search to see whether
        TargetValue is in the portion of List preceding
        the test entry, and
            if (that search is successful)
                then (Declare this search a success.)
                else (Declare this search a failure)
        ]

    Case 3: TargetValue > test entry
        [Apply the procedure Search to see whether
        TargetValue is in the portion of List following
        the test entry, and
            if (that search is successful)
                then (Declare this search a success)
                else (Declare this search a failure)
        ]

                    List
                                (Test entry)
                    Evelyn
                    Fred
                    George

procedure Search (List TargetValue)
if (list empty)
    then
        (Declare the search a failure)
    else
        Select the "middle" entry in List as the test entry;
        Execute one of the following blocks of instructions
        depending on whether TargetValue is equal to less
        than, or greater than the test entry

    Case 1: TargetValue = test entry
        (Declare the search a success)

    Case 2: TargetValue < test entry
        [Apply the procedure Search to see whether
        TargetValue is in the portion of List preceding
        the test entry, and
            if (that search is successful)
                then (Declare this search a success.)
                else (Declare this search a failure)
        ]

    Case 3: TargetValue > test entry
        [Apply the procedure Search to see whether
        TargetValue is in the portion of List following
        the test entry, and
            if (that search is successful)
                then (Declare this search a success)
                else (Declare this search a failure)
        ]

                    List
                    Alice
                    Carol

FIGURE 4.17

We are here →

procedure Search (List TargetValue)
if (list empty)
   then
      (Declare the search a failure)
   else
      Select the "middle" entry in List as the test entry;
      Execute one of the following blocks of instructions
      depending on whether TargetValue is equal to less
      than, or greater than the test entry
      Case 1: TargetValue = test entry
        (Declare the search a success)
      Case 2: TargetValue < test entry
        [Apply the procedure Search to see whether
        TargetValue is in the portion of List preceding
        the test entry, and
        if (that search is successful)
        then (Declare this search a success.)
        else (Declare this search a failure)
        ]
      Case 3: TargetValue > test entry
        [Apply the procedure Search to see whether
        TargetValue is in the portion of List following
        the test entry, and
        if (that search is successful)
        then (Declare this search a success)
        else (Declare this search a failure)
        ]

procedure Search (List TargetValue)
if (list empty)
   then
      (Declare the search a failure)
   else
      Select the "middle" entry in List as the test entry;
      Execute one of the following blocks of instructions
      depending on whether TargetValue is equal to less
      than, or greater than the test entry
      Case 1: TargetValue = test entry
        (Declare the search a success)
      Case 2: TargetValue < test entry
        [Apply the procedure Search to see whether
        TargetValue is in the portion of List preceding
        the test entry, and
        if (that search is successful)
        then (Declare this search a success.)
        else (Declare this search a failure)
        ]
      Case 3: TargetValue > test entry
        [Apply the procedure Search to see whether
        TargetValue is in the portion of List following
        the test entry, and
        if (that search is successful)
        then (Declare this search a success)
        else (Declare this search a failure)
        ]

procedure Search (List TargetValue)
if (list empty)
   then
      (Declare the search a failure)
   else
      Select the "middle" entry in List as the test entry;
      Execute one of the following blocks of instructions
      depending on whether TargetValue is equal to less
      than, or greater than the test entry
      Case 1: TargetValue = test entry
        (Declare the search a success)
      Case 2: TargetValue < test entry
        [Apply the procedure Search to see whether
        TargetValue is in the portion of List preceding
        the test entry, and
        if (that search is successful)
        then (Declare this search a success.)
        else (Declare this search a failure)
        ]
      Case 3: TargetValue > test entry
        [Apply the procedure Search to see whether
        TargetValue is in the portion of List following
        the test entry, and
        if (that search is successful)
        then (Declare this search a success)
        else (Declare this search a failure)
        ]

List
Evelyn
Fred
George
(Test entry)

List
Alice
Carol

List

repeatedly divide the list in question into two smaller pieces in such a way that the remaining search can be restricted to only one of these pieces. This divide-by-two approach is the reason why the algorithm is known as the binary search.

Recursive Control

The binary search algorithm is similar to the sequential search in that each algorithm requests the execution of a repetitive process. However, the implementation of this repetition is significantly different. Whereas the sequential search involves a circular form of repetition, the binary search executes each stage of the repetition as a subtask of the previous stage. This technique is known as **recursion.**

As we have seen, the illusion created by the execution of a recursive algorithm is the existence of multiple copies of itself, called *activations,* that appear and disappear as the algorithm advances. Of those activations existing at any given time, only one is actively progressing. The others are effectively in limbo, each waiting for another activation to terminate before it can continue.

Being a repetitive process, recursive systems are just as dependent on proper control as are loop structures. Just as in loop control, recursive systems are dependent on testing for a termination condition and on a design that ensures

RECURSIVE STRUCTURES IN ART

The following recursive procedure can be applied to a rectangular canvas to produce drawings of the style of the Dutch painter Piet Mondrian (1872–1944) who produced paintings in which the rectangular canvas was divided into successively smaller rectangles. Try following the procedure yourself to produce drawings similar to the one shown. Begin by applying the procedure to a rectangle representing the canvas on which you are working.

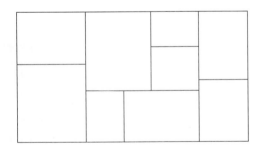

procedure Mondrian (Rectangle)
if (the size of Rectangle is too large for your artistic taste)
    then (divide Rectangle into two smaller rectangles;
        apply the procedure Mondrian to one of the smaller rectangles;
        apply the procedure Mondrian to the other smaller rectangle)

this condition will be reached. In fact, proper recursive control involves the same three ingredients—initialization, modification, and test for termination—that are required in loop control.

In general, a recursive routine is designed to test for the termination condition (often called the *base* or *degenerative case*) before requesting further activations. If the termination condition is not met, the routine assigns another activation of the routine to the task of solving a revised problem that is closer to the termination condition than that assigned to the current activation. However, if the termination condition is met, a path is taken that causes the current activation to terminate without creating additional activations. This means that one of the activations in limbo is allowed to continue execution,

DESIGNING RECURSIVE PROCEDURES

The secret to developing recursive procedures is to consider how the problem at hand can be reduced to smaller problems of the same type and how the solutions to these smaller problems can be used as abstract tools to construct a solution for the original one. Let us apply this approach to the task of finding an exit in a maze such as the one shown. We begin by moving forward until we come to the first branch. At this point we envision each option as representing an entrance into a smaller maze. If we could find an exit in any one of these smaller mazes, our task would be complete. This line of thought leads to the procedure below.

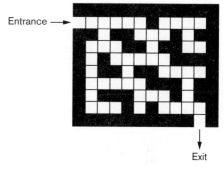

Entrance →

↓
Exit

procedure FindExit (Maze)
Move through Maze until a branch, a dead end, or an exit is reached;
Perform the instructions associated with the appropriate case:
   case 1: the exit is reached: (report "exit found")
   case 2: a dead end is reached: (report "failure")
   case 3: a branch is reached:
     (**while** (there is a branch at this point that starts with unexplored territory
           and an exit has not been found) **do**
       (apply FindExit to the maze represented by one of the unexplored branches;
        if (that application reports an exit found)
          then (report "exit found.")
)
    if (all options at this branch fail) **then** (report "failure")
)

complete its task, and in turn, allow yet another dormant activation to resume its activities. In this fashion, all the activations that are generated ultimately terminate, leaving the original task completed.

Let us see how the initialization and modification phases of repetitive control are implemented in our recursive binary search routine of Figure 4.14. In this case, the creation of additional activations is terminated once the target value is found or the task is reduced to that of searching an empty list. The process is initialized implicitly by being given an initial list and a target value. From this initial configuration the routine modifies the task it is assigned to that of searching a smaller list. Since the original list is of finite length and each modification step reduces the length of the list in question, we are assured that the target value ultimately is found or the task is reduced to that of searching the empty list. We can therefore conclude that the repetitive process is guaranteed to cease.

Having seen both iterative and recursive control structures, we may wonder whether the two are equivalent in power. That is, if an algorithm were designed using a loop structure, could another algorithm using only recursive techniques be designed that would solve the same problem and vice versa? Such questions are important in computer science because their answers tell us what features should be provided in a programming language in order to obtain the most powerful programming system possible. We return to these ideas in Chapter 11 where we consider some of the more theoretical aspects of computer science and its mathematical foundations. With this background, we then can prove the equivalence of iterative and recursive structures in Appendix E.

QUESTIONS/EXERCISES

1. What names are interrogated by the binary search (Figure 4.14) when searching for the name Joe in the list Alice, Bob, Carol, David, Evelyn, Fred, George, Henry, Irene, Joe, Karl, Larry, Mary, Nancy, and Oliver?
2. What is the maximum number of entries that must be interrogated when applying the binary search to a list of 200 entries? What about a list of 100,000 entries?

4.6 Efficiency and Correctness

Of the remaining topics we could discuss as a part of our formal introduction to algorithms, this section discusses two that should linger in your mind as you develop algorithms on your own. The first of these is efficiency, and the second is correctness.

Algorithm Efficiency

Even though today's machines are capable of executing millions of instructions each second, efficiency remains a major concern in algorithm design. Often the choice between efficient and inefficient algorithms can make the difference between a practical solution to a problem and an impractical one.

Let us consider the problem of a university registrar faced with the task of retrieving and updating student records. Although the university has an actual enrollment of approximately 10,000 students during any one semester, its "current student file" contains the records of more than 30,000 students who are considered current students in the sense that they have registered for at least one course in the past few years but have not completed a degree. For now, let us assume that these records are stored in the registrar's computer as a list ordered by student identification numbers. To find any student record, the registrar would therefore search this list for a particular identification number.

We have presented two algorithms for searching such a list: the sequential search and the binary search. Our question now is whether the choice between these two algorithms makes any difference in the case of the registrar. We consider the sequential search first.

Given a student identification number, the sequential search algorithm starts at the beginning of the list and compares the entries it finds to the number desired. Not knowing anything about the source of the target value, we cannot conclude how far into the list this search must go. We can say, though, that after many searches we expect the average depth of the searches to be halfway through the list; some will be shorter, but others will be longer. We conclude that over a period of time, the sequential search will investigate roughly 15,000 records per search. If retrieving and checking each record for its identification number requires ten milliseconds (ten one-thousandths of a second), such a search would require an average of 150 seconds or 2 ½ minutes—an unbearably long time for the registrar to wait for a student's record to appear on the screen. Even if the time required to retrieve and check each record were reduced to only 1 millisecond, the search would still require an average of 15 seconds, which is still a long time to wait.

In contrast, the binary search proceeds by comparing the target value to the middle entry in the list. If this is not the desired entry, then at least the remaining search is restricted to only half of the original list. Thus, after interrogating the middle entry in the list of 30,000 student records, the binary search has at most 15,000 records still to consider. After the second inquiry, at most 7500 remain, and after the third retrieval, the list in question has dropped to no more than 3750 entries. Continuing in this fashion, we see that the target record will be found after retrieving at most 15 entries from the list of 30,000 records. Thus, if each of these retrievals can be performed in 10 milliseconds, the process of searching for a particular record requires only 0.15 of a second—meaning that access to any particular student record will appear to be instantaneous from the registrar's point of view. We conclude that the choice between the sequential search algorithm and the binary search algorithm would have a significant impact in this application.[1]

This example indicates the importance of the area of computer science known as algorithm analysis that encompasses the study of the resources, such as time or storage space, that algorithms require. A major application of such studies is the evaluation of the relative merits of alternative algorithms. In our case, we analyzed the time required by the sequential and binary search algorithms in order to determine which was the better solution in a particular application. In general such analysis is performed in a more generic context. That is, when considering algorithms for searching lists, we do not focus on a list of a particular length, but instead try to identify a formula that would indicate the algorithm's performance for lists of arbitrary lengths. Such analyses usually involve a best-case analysis, a worst-case analysis, and an average-case analysis.

Our previous analysis focused on the average case performance of the sequential search algorithm and the worst case performance of the binary search algorithm. Although we concentrated on a list of a particular length, it is not difficult to generalize our reasoning to lists of arbitrary lengths. In particular, when applied to a list with n entries, the sequential search algorithm will interrogate an average of $n/2$ entries, whereas the binary search algorithm will interrogate at most lg n entries in its worst-case scenario. (lg n represents the base two logarithm of n, which is the number of times n can be divided by two.)

Let us analyze the insertion sort algorithm (summarized in Figure 4.11) in a similar manner. Since the activity of comparing two names dominates the algorithm, our approach will be to count the number of such comparisons that are performed when sorting a list whose length is n.

Recall that the insertion sort involves selecting a list entry, called the pivot entry, comparing this entry to those preceding it until the proper place for the pivot is found, and then inserting the pivot entry in this place. The algorithm begins by selecting the second list entry to be the pivot. It then progresses by picking successive entries as the pivot until it has reached the end of the list. In the best possible case, each pivot is already in its proper place, and thus it needs to be compared to only a single name before this is discovered. Thus, in the best case, applying the insertion sort to a list with n entries requires $n - 1$ comparisons. (The second entry is compared to one name, the third entry to one name, and so on.)

In contrast, the worst scenario is that each pivot must be compared to all the preceding entries before its proper location can be found. This occurs if the original list is in reverse order. In this case the first pivot (the second list entry) is compared to one name, the second pivot (the third list entry) is compared to two

---

[1]To reap the benefits of the binary search algorithm, the student records must be stored in a manner that allows the middle entries of successively smaller sublists to be retrieved without undue hardship. This can be accomplished by storing the records in an indexed file—a structure that we will study in Chapter 8. In reality, such an application would probably be handled by a hashed file structure—again a topic that is discussed in Chapter 8.

FIGURE 4.18

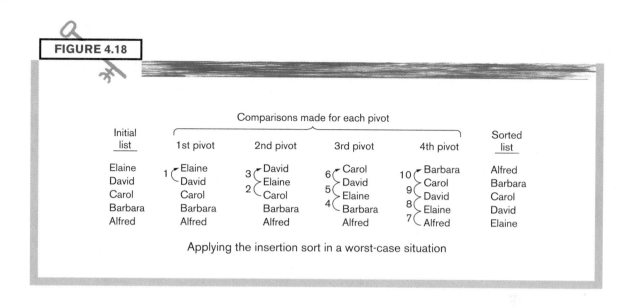

Comparisons made for each pivot

Applying the insertion sort in a worst-case situation

names, and so on (Figure 4.18). Thus the total number of comparisons when sorting a list of n entries is $1 + 2 + 3 + \ldots + (n - 1)$, which is equivalent to $n(n - 1)/2$ or $(1/2)(n^2 - n)$. In particular, if the list contained 10 entries, the worst-case scenario of the insertion sort algorithm would require 45 comparisons.

In the average case of the insertion sort, we would expect each pivot to be compared to half of the entries preceding it. This results in half as many comparisons as were performed in the worst case, or a total of $(1/4)(n^2 + n)$ comparisons to sort a list of n names. If, for example, we use the insertion sort to sort a variety of lists of length 10, we expect the average number of comparisons per sort to be 22.5.

The significance of these results is that the number of comparisons made during the execution of the insertion sort algorithm gives an approximation of the amount of time required to execute the algorithm. Using this approximation, Figure 4.19 shows a graph indicating how the time required to execute the insertion sort algorithm increases as the length of the list increases. This graph is based on our worst-case analysis of the algorithm, where we concluded that sorting a list of length n would require at most $(1/2)(n^2 - n)$ comparisons between list entries. On the graph, we have marked several list lengths and indicated the time required in each case. Notice that as the list lengths increase by uniform increments, the time required to sort the list increases by increasingly greater amounts. Thus the algorithm becomes less efficient as the size of the list increases.

Let us apply a similar analysis to the worst-case scenario of the binary search algorithm. Recall that we concluded that searching a list with n entries using this algorithm would require interrogating at most lg n entries, which again gives an approximation to the amount of time required to execute the algo-

FIGURE 4.19

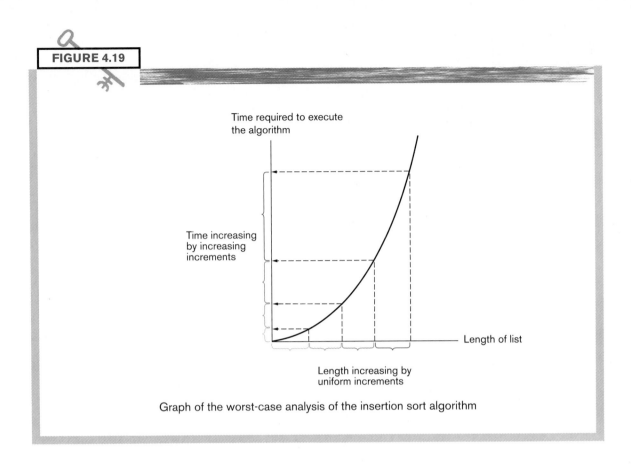

Graph of the worst-case analysis of the insertion sort algorithm

rithm for various list sizes. Figure 4.20 shows a graph based on this analysis on which we have again marked several list lengths of uniformly increasing size and identified the time required by the algorithm in each case. Note that the time required by the algorithm increases by decreasing increments. That is, the binary search algorithm becomes more efficient as the size of the list increases.

The distinguishing factor between Figures 4.19 and 4.20 is, of course, the general shape of the graphs involved. It is the general shape of the graph, not its specifics, that indicates how well an algorithm performs for larger and larger inputs. Note that the general shape of a graph is determined by the type of the expression being graphed rather than the specifics of the expression—all linear expressions produce a straight line; all quadratic expressions produce a parabolic curve; all logarithmic expressions produce the logarithmic shape shown in Fig. 4.20. It is customary to identify a shape with the simplest expression that produces that shape. In particular, we identify the parabolic shape with the expression n^2 and the logarithmic shape with the expression $\lg n$.

We have seen that the shape of the graph obtained by comparing the time required for an algorithm to perform its task to the size of the input data reflects

FIGURE 4.20

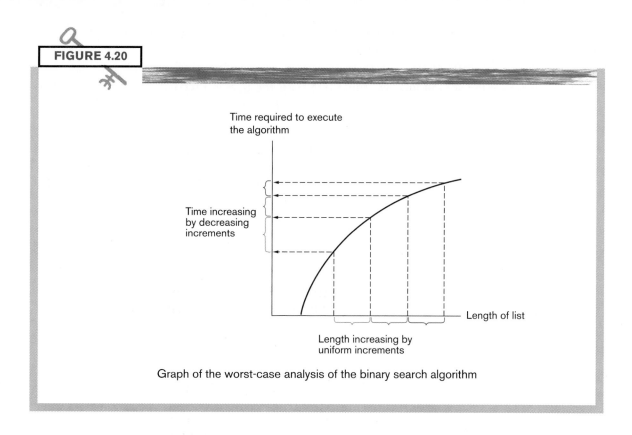

Graph of the worst-case analysis of the binary search algorithm

the efficiency characteristics of the algorithm. Thus it is common to classify algorithms according to the shapes of these graphs—normally based on the algorithm's worst-case analysis. The notation used to identify these classes is sometimes called "big-theta notation." All algorithms whose graphs have the shape of a parabola, such as the insertion sort, are classified in the class represented by $\Theta(n^2)$; all algorithms whose graphs have the shape of a logarithmic expression, such as the binary search, fall in the class represented by $\Theta(\lg n)$. An algorithm in $\Theta(\lg n)$ is inherently more efficient than an algorithm in $\Theta(n^2)$.

Software Verification

Recall that the fourth phase in Polya's analysis of problem solving (Section 4.3) is to evaluate the solution for accuracy and for its potential as a tool for solving other problems. The significance of the first part of this phase is exemplified by the following example:

> A traveler with a gold chain of seven links must stay in an isolated hotel for seven nights. The rent each night consists of one link from the chain. What is the fewest number of links that must be cut so that the traveler

can pay the hotel one link of the chain each morning without paying for lodging in advance?

We first realize that not every link in the chain must be cut. If we cut only the second link, we could free both the first and second links from the other five. Following this insight, we are led to the solution of cutting only the second, fourth, and sixth links in the chain, a process that releases each link while cutting only three (Figure 4.21). Furthermore, any fewer cuts leaves two links connected, so we conclude that the correct answer to our problem is three.

Upon reconsidering the problem, however, we might make the observation that when only the third link in the chain is cut, we obtain three pieces of chain of lengths one, two, and four (Figure 4.22). With these pieces we can proceed as follows:

First morning: Give the hotel the single link.
Second morning: Retrieve the single link and give the hotel the two-link piece.
Third morning: Give the hotel the single link.
Fourth morning: Retrieve the three links held by the hotel and give the hotel the four-link piece.
Fifth morning: Give the hotel the single link.

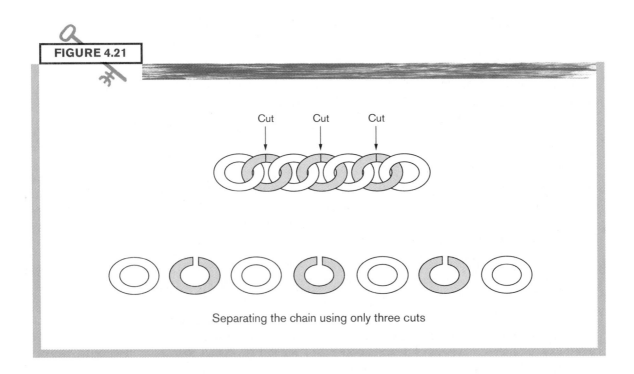

FIGURE 4.21

Cut   Cut   Cut

Separating the chain using only three cuts

FIGURE 4.22

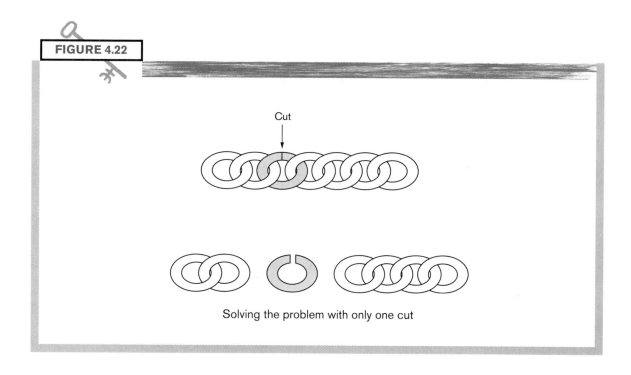

Cut

Solving the problem with only one cut

Sixth morning: Retrieve the single link and give the hotel the double-link piece.

Seventh morning: Give the hotel the single link.

Consequently, our first answer, which we were sure was correct, is incorrect. How, then, can we be sure that our new solution is correct? We might argue as follows: Since a single link must be given to the hotel on the first morning, at least one link of the chain must be cut, and since our new solution requires only one cut, it must be optimal.

Translated into the programming environment, this example emphasizes the distinction between a program that is believed to be correct and a program that is correct. The two are not necessarily the same. The data processing community is rich in horror stories involving software that although "known" to be correct still failed at a critical moment because of some unforeseen situation. Verification of software is therefore an important undertaking, and the search for efficient verification techniques constitutes an active field of research in computer science.

One current line of research in this area attempts to apply the techniques of formal logic to prove the correctness of a program. That is, the goal is to apply formal logic to prove that the algorithm represented by a program does what it is intended to do. The underlying thesis is that by reducing the verification process to a formal procedure, one is protected from the inaccurate conclusions that may be associated with intuitive arguments, as was the case in the gold chain problem. Let us consider this approach to program verification in more detail.

Just as a formal mathematical proof is based on axioms (geometric proofs are often founded on the axioms of Euclidean geometry, whereas other proofs may be based on the axioms of set theory), a formal proof of a program's correctness is based on the specifications under which the program was designed. To prove that a program correctly sorts lists of names, we are allowed to begin with the assumption that the program's input is a list of names, or if the program is designed to compute the average of one or more positive numbers, we can assume that the input does, in fact, consist of one or more positive numbers. In short, a proof of correctness begins with the assumption that certain conditions, called **preconditions,** are satisfied at the beginning of the program's execution.

The next step in a proof of correctness is to consider how the consequences of these preconditions propagate through the program. For this purpose, researchers have analyzed various program structures to determine how a statement, known to be true before the structure is executed, is affected by executing the structure. As a simple example, if a certain statement about the value of Y is known to hold prior to executing the instruction

assign X **the value** of Y

then that same statement can be made about X after the instruction has been executed. More precisely, if the value of Y is not 0 before the instruction is executed, then we can conclude that the value of X will not be 0 after the instruction is executed.

A slightly more involved example occurs in the case of an if-then-else structure such as

if (*condition*) **then** (*instruction 1*)
       else (*instruction 2*)

Here, if some statement is known to hold before execution of the structure, then immediately before executing *instruction 1,* we know that both that statement and the condition tested are true, whereas if *instruction 2* is to be executed, we know the statement and the negation of the condition must hold.

Following rules such as these, a proof of correctness proceeds by identifying statements, called **assertions,**

BEYOND VERIFICATION OF SOFTWARE

Verification problems, as discussed in the text, are not unique to software. Equally important is the problem of confirming that the hardware that executes a program is free of flaws. This involves the verification of circuit designs as well as machine construction. Again, the state of the art relies heavily on testing, which, as in the case of software, means that subtle errors can find their way into finished products. Records indicate that the Mark I, constructed at Harvard University in the 1940s, contained wiring errors that were not detected for many years. A more recent example is a flaw in the floating-point portion of the early Pentium microprocessors. In both of these cases, the error was detected before serious consequences developed.

that can be established at various points in the program. The result is a collection of assertions, each being a consequence of the program's preconditions and the sequence of instructions that lead to the point in the program at which the assertion is established. If the assertion so established at the end of the program corresponds to the desired output specifications, we can conclude that the program is correct.

As an example, consider the typical while loop structure represented in Figure 4.23. Suppose, as a consequence of the preconditions given at point A, we can establish that a particular assertion is true each time the test for termination is performed (point B) during the repetitive process. (Such an assertion within a loop is known as a **loop invariant.**) Then, if the repetition ever terminates, execution moves to point C, where we can conclude that both the loop invariant and the termination condition hold. (The loop invariant still holds

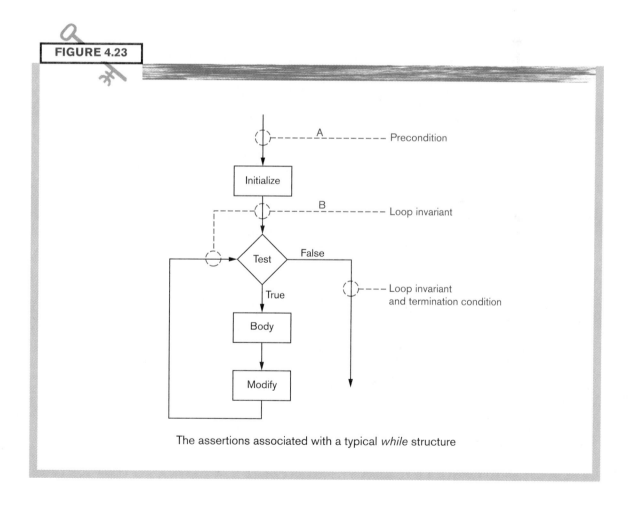

FIGURE 4.23

The assertions associated with a typical *while* structure

because the test for termination does not alter any values in the program, and the termination condition holds because otherwise the loop does not terminate.) If these combined statements imply the desired output, our proof of correctness can be completed merely by showing that the initialization and modification components of the loop ultimately lead to the termination condition.

You should compare this analysis to our example of the insertion sort shown in Figure 4.11. The outer loop in that program is based on the loop invariant

> Each time the test for termination is performed, the names preceding the Nth entry form a sorted list

and the termination condition is

> The value of N is greater than the length of the list.

Thus, if the loop ever terminates, we know that both conditions must be satisfied, which implies that the entire list would be sorted.

Unfortunately, formal program verification techniques have not been refined to the point that they can be easily applied in general applications. The result is that in most cases today, software is "verified" by testing it under various conditions—a process that is shaky at best. After all, verification by testing proves nothing more than that the program runs correctly for the cases under which it was tested. Any additional conclusions are merely projections. The errors contained in a program are often consequences of subtle oversights that are easily overlooked during testing as well. Consequently errors in a program, just as our error in the gold chain problem, can, and often do, go undetected, even though significant effort may be exerted to avoid it. A dramatic example occurred at AT&T: An error in the software controlling 114 switching stations went undetected from its installation in December 1989 until January 15, 1990, at which time a unique set of circumstances caused approximately five million calls to be unnecessarily blocked over a nine-hour period.

QUESTIONS/EXERCISES

1. Suppose we find that a machine programmed with our insertion sort algorithm requires an average of one second to sort a list of 100 names. How long do you estimate it takes to sort a list of 1000 names? How about 10,000 names?
2. Give an example of an algorithm in each of the following classes: $\Theta(\lg n)$, $\Theta(n)$, and $\Theta(n^2)$.
3. List the classes $\Theta(n^2)$, $\Theta(\lg n)$, $\Theta(n)$, and $\Theta(n^3)$ in decreasing order of efficiency.

4. Consider the following problem and a proposed answer. Is the proposed answer correct? Why or why not?

Problem: Suppose a box contains three cards. One of three cards is painted black on both sides, one is painted red on both sides, and the third is painted red on one side and black on the other. One of the cards is drawn from the box, and you are allowed to see one side of it. What is the probability that the other side of the card is the same color as the side you see?

Proposed answer: One-half. Suppose the side of the card you can see is red. (The argument would be symmetric with this one if the side were black.) Only two cards among the three have a red side. Thus the card you see must be one of these two. One of these two cards is red on the other side, while the other is black. Thus the card you can see is just as likely to be red on the other side as it is to be black.

5. The following program segment is an attempt to compute the quotient (forgetting any remainder) of two positive integers (a dividend and a divisor) by counting the number of times the divisor can be subtracted from the dividend before what is left becomes less than the divisor. For instance, 7/3 should produce 2 because 3 can be subtracted from 7 twice. Is the program correct? Justify your answer.

```
assign Count the value 0;
assign Remainder the value of Dividend;
repeat (assign Remainder the value of Remainder – Divisor;
        assign Count the value of Count + 1)
until (Remainder < Divisor)
assign Quotient the value of Count
```

6. The following program segment is designed to compute the product of two nonnegative integers X and Y by accumulating the sum of X copies of Y—that is, 3 times 4 is computed by accumulating the sum of three 4s. Is the program correct? Justify your answer.

```
assign Product the value of Y;
assign Count the value 1;
while (Count < X) do
   (assign Product the value Product + Y;
    assign Count the value Count + 1)
```

7. Assuming the precondition that the value associated with N is a positive integer, establish a loop invariant that leads to the conclusion that if the following routine terminates, then Sum is assigned the value $0 + 1 + \ldots + N$.

```
assign Sum the value 0;
assign I the value 0;
while (I < N) do
```

(**assign** I **the value** I + 1;
    assign Sum **the value** Sum + I)

Provide an argument to the effect that the routine does in fact terminate.

8. Suppose that both a program and the hardware that executes it have been formally verified to be accurate. Does this ensure accuracy?

CHAPTER REVIEW PROBLEMS

1. Give an example of a set of steps that conforms to the informal definition of an algorithm given in the opening paragraph of Section 4.1 but does not conform to the definition given in Figure 4.1.

2. Explain the distinction between an ambiguity in a proposed algorithm and an ambiguity in the representation of an algorithm.

3. Describe how the use of primitives helps remove ambiguities in an algorithm's representation.

4. Does the following program represent an algorithm in the strict sense? Why or why not?

    assign Count **the value** 0;
    while (Count not 5) **do**
        (**assign** Count **the value** Count + 2)

5. In what sense do the following steps not constitute an algorithm?

    Step 1: Draw a straight line segment between the points with rectangular coordinates (2,5) and (6,11).
    Step 2: Draw a straight line segment between the points with rectangular coordinates (1,3) and (3,6).
    Step 3: Draw a circle with radius two and center at the intersection of the previous line segments.

6. Rewrite the following program segment using a repeat structure rather than a while structure. Be sure the new version prints the same values as the original.

    assign Count **the value** 2;
    while (Count < 7) **do**
        (print the value assigned to Count and
            assign Count **the value** Count + 1)

7. Rewrite the following program segment using a while structure rather than a repeat structure. Be sure the new version prints the same values as the original.

    assign Count **the value** 1;
    repeat (print the value assigned to Count and
              assign Count **the value** Count + 1)
    until (Count = 5)

8. Design an algorithm that, when given an arrangement of the digits 0, 1, 2, 3, 4, 5, 6, 7, 8, 9, rearranges the digits so that the new arrangement represents the next larger value that can be represented by these digits (or reports that no such rearrangement exists if no rearrangement produces a larger value). Thus 5647382901 would produce 5647382910.

9. What is the difference between a formal programming language and a pseudocode?

10. What is the difference between syntax and semantics?

11. Four prospectors with only one lantern must walk through a mineshaft. At most, two prospectors can travel together and

any prospector in the shaft must be with the lantern. The prospectors, named Andrews, Blake, Johnson, and Kelly, can walk through the shaft in one minute, two minutes, four minutes, and eight minutes, respectively. When two walk together they travel at the speed of the slower prospector. How can the prospectors get through the mineshaft in only 15 minutes? After you have solved this problem, explain how you got your foot in the door.

12. Starting with a large wine glass and a small wine glass, fill the small glass with wine and then pour that wine into the large glass. Next, fill the small glass with water and pour some of that water into the large glass and mix it with the wine. Now, pour the mixture back into the small glass until the small glass is full. Will there be more water in the wine or more wine in the water? After you have solved this problem, explain how you got your foot in the door.

13. Two bees, named Romeo and Juliet, live in different hives but have met and fallen in love. On a windless spring morning, they simultaneously leave their respective hives to visit each other. Their routes meet at a point 50 meters from the closest hive, but they fail to see each other and continue on to their destinations. At their destinations, they spend the same amount of time to discover that the other is not home and begin their return trips. On their return trips, they meet at a point that is 20 meters from the closest hive. This time they see each other and have a picnic lunch before returning home. How far apart are the two hives? After you have solved this problem, explain how you got your foot in the door.

14. Design an algorithm that, given two strings of characters, tests whether the first string appears as a substring somewhere in the second.

15. The following algorithm is designed to print the beginning of what is known as the Fibonacci sequence. Identify the body of the loop. Where is the initialization step for the loop control? The modification step? The test step? What list of numbers is produced?

> **assign** Last **the value** 0;
> **assign** Current **the value** 1;
> **while** (Current < 100) **do**
>   (print the value assigned to Current;
>   **assign** Temp **the value** of Last;
>   **assign** Last **the value** of Current; and
>   **assign** Current **the value** Last + Temp)

16. What sequence of numbers is printed by the following algorithm if it is started with input values 0 and 1?

> **procedure** MysteryWrite (Last, Current)
> **if** (Current < 100) **then**
>   (print the value assigned to Current;
>   **assign** Temp **the value** of Current + Last;
>   apply MysteryWrite to the values
>   Current and Temp)

17. Modify the procedure MysteryWrite in the preceding problem so that the values are printed in reverse order.

18. What letters are interrogated by the binary search (Figure 4.14) if it is applied to the list A, B, C, D, E, F, G, H, I, J, K, L, M, N, O when searching for the value J? What about the value Z?

19. On the average, how many times must two names be compared when searching a list of 6000 entries using the sequential search? What can be said about the binary search?

20. Identify the body of the following loop structure and count the number of times it

will be executed. What happens if the test is changed to read while (Count not 6)?

```
assign Count the value 1;
while (Count not 7) do
    (print the value assigned to Count and
        assign Count the value Count + 3)
```

21. What problems do you expect to arise if the following program is implemented on a computer? (*Hint:* Remember the problem of round-off errors associated with floating-point arithmetic.)

```
assign Count the value one-tenth;
repeat
    (print the value assigned to Count and
        assign Count the value Count +
        one-tenth)
until (Count equals 1)
```

22. Design a recursive version of the Euclidean algorithm (Question 3 of Section 4.2).

23. Suppose we apply both Test1 and Test2 (defined below) to the input value 1. What is the difference in the printed output of the two routines?

```
procedure Test1 (Count)
    if (Count not 5)
    then (print the value assigned to Count
        and apply Test1 to the value Count + 1)

procedure Test2 (Count)
    if (Count not 5)
    then (apply Test2 to the value Count + 1
        and print the value assigned to Count)
```

24. Identify the important constituents of the control mechanism in the routines of the previous problem. In particular, what condition causes the process to terminate? Where is the state of the process modified toward this termination condition? Where is the state of the control process initialized?

25. Design an algorithm to generate the sequence of positive integers (in increasing order) whose only prime divisors are 2 and 3; that is, your program should produce the sequence 2, 3, 4, 6, 9, 12, 16, 18, 24, 27, ... Does your program represent an algorithm in the strict sense?

26. Answer the following questions in terms of the list: Alice, Byron, Carol, Duane, Elaine, Floyd, Gene, Henry, Iris.
   a. Which search algorithm (sequential or binary) will find the name Gene more quickly?
   b. Which search algorithm (sequential or binary) will find the name Alice more quickly?
   c. Which search algorithm (sequential or binary) will detect the absence of the name Bruce more quickly?
   d. Which search algorithm (sequential or binary) will detect the absence of the name Sue more quickly?
   e. How many entries will be interrogated when searching for the name Elaine when using the sequential search? How many will be interrogated when using the binary search?

27. The factorial of 0 is defined to be 1. The factorial of a positive integer is defined to be the product of that integer times the factorial of the next smaller nonnegative integer. We use the notation $n!$ to express the factorial of the integer n. Thus the factorial of 3 (written 3!) is $3 \times (2!) = 3 \times (2 \times (1!)) = 3 \times (2 \times (1 \times (0!))) = 3 \times (2 \times (1 \times (1))) = 6$. Design a recursive algorithm that computes the factorial of a given value.

28. a. Suppose you must sort a list of five names, and you have already designed an algorithm that sorts a list of four names. Design an algorithm to sort the list of five names by taking advantage of the previously designed algorithm.

b. Design a recursive algorithm to sort arbitrary lists of names based on the technique used in (a).

29. The puzzle called the Tower of Hanoi consists of three pegs, one of which contains several rings stacked in order of descending diameter from bottom to top. The problem is to move the stack of rings to another peg. You are allowed to move only one ring at a time, and at no time is a ring to be placed on top of a smaller one. Observe that if the puzzle involved only one ring, it would be extremely easy. Moreover, when faced with the problem of moving several rings, if you could move all but the largest ring to another peg, the largest ring could then be placed on the third peg, and then the problem would be to move the remaining rings on top of it. Using this observation, develop a recursive algorithm for solving the Tower of Hanoi puzzle for an arbitrary number of rings.

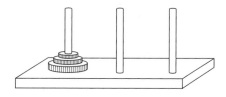

30. Another approach to solving the Tower of Hanoi puzzle (Problem 29) is to imagine the pegs arranged on a circular stand with a peg mounted at each of the positions of 4, 8, and 12 o'clock. The rings, which begin on one of the pegs, are numbered 1, 2, 3, and so on, starting with the smallest ring being 1. Odd-numbered rings, when on top of a stack, are allowed to move clockwise to the next peg; likewise, even-numbered rings are allowed to move counterclockwise (as long as that move does not place a ring on a smaller one). Under this restriction, always move the largest numbered ring that can be moved. Based on this observation, develop a non-recursive algorithm for solving the Tower of Hanoi puzzle.

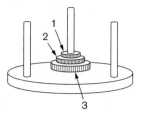

31. Develop two algorithms, one based on a loop structure and the other on a recursive structure, to print the daily salary of a worker who each day is paid twice the previous day's salary (starting with one penny for the first day's work) for a 30-day period. What problems relating to number storage are you likely to encounter if you implement your solutions on an actual machine?

32. Design an algorithm to find the square root of a positive number by starting with the number itself as the first guess and repeatedly producing a new guess from the previous one by averaging the previous guess with the result of dividing the original number by the previous guess. Analyze the control of this repetitive process. In particular, what condition should terminate the repetition?

33. Design an algorithm that lists all possible rearrangements of the symbols in a string of five distinct characters.

34. Design an algorithm that, given a list of names, finds the longest name in the list. Determine what your solution does if there are several "longest" names in the list. In particular, what would your algorithm do if all the names had the same length?

35. Design an algorithm that, given a list of five or more numbers, finds the five smallest and five largest numbers in the list without sorting the entire list.

36. Arrange the names Brenda, Doris, Raymond, Steve, Timothy, and William in an order that requires the least number of comparisons when sorted by the insertion sort algorithm (Figure 4.11).

37. What is the largest number of entries that are interrogated if the binary search algorithm (Figure 4.14) is applied to a list of 4000 names? How does this compare to the sequential search (Figure 4.6)?

38. Use big-theta notation to classify the traditional grade school algorithms for addition and multiplication. That is, if asked to add two numbers each having n digits, how many individual additions must be performed. If requested to multiply two n-digit numbers, how many individual multiplications are required?

39. Sometimes a slight change in a problem can significantly alter the form of its solution. For example, find a simple algorithm for solving the following problem and classify it using big-theta notation:

> Divide a group of people into two disjoint subgroups (of arbitrary size) such that the difference in the total ages of the members of the two subgroups is as large as possible.

Now change the problem so that the desired difference is as small as possible and classify your approach to the problem.

40. From the following list, extract a collection of numbers whose sum is 3165. How efficient is your approach to the problem?

26, 39, 104, 195, 403, 504, 793, 995, 1156, 1673

41. Does the loop in the following routine terminate? Explain your answer. Explain what might happen if this routine is actually executed by a computer (refer to Section 1.7)

assign X **the value** 0;
assign Y **the value** 1/2;
while (X not equal 1) **do**
  (**assign** X **the value** X + Y;
   assign Y **the value** Y ÷ 2)

42. The following program segment is designed to compute the product of two nonnegative integers X and Y by accumulating the sum of X copies of Y; that is, 3 times 4 is computed by accumulating the sum of three 4s. Is the program segment correct? Explain your answer.

assign Product **the value** 0;
assign Count **the value** 0;
repeat (**assign** Product **the value** Product + Y,
        assign Count **the value** Count + 1)
until (Count = X)

43. The following program segment is designed to report which of the positive integers X and Y is larger. Is the program segment correct? Explain your answer.

assign Difference **the value** of X − Y;
if (Difference is positive)
  then (print "X is bigger than Y")
  else (print "Y is bigger than X")

44. The following program segment is designed to find the largest entry in a nonempty list of integers. Is it correct? Explain your answer.

assign TestValue **the value** of the first list entry;
assign CurrentEntry **the value** of the first list
        entry;
while (CurrentEntry is not the last entry) **do**
  (**if** (CurrentEntry > TestValue)
    then (**assign** TestValue **the value**
            CurrentEntry)
    assign CurrentEntry **the value** of the next
            list entry)

45. a. Identify the preconditions for the sequential search as represented in

Figure 4.6. Establish a loop invariant for the while structure in that program that, when combined with the termination condition, implies that upon termination of the loop, the algorithm will report success or failure correctly.

b. Give an argument showing that the while loop in Figure 4.6 does in fact terminate.

46. Based on the preconditions that X and Y are assigned nonnegative integers, identify a loop invariant for the following while structure that, when combined with the termination condition, implies that the value associated with Z upon loop termination must be $X - Y$.

assign Z **the value** of X;
assign J **the value** 0;
while (J < Y) **do**
   (**assign** Z **the value** Z − 1;
    assign J **the value** J + 1)

SOCIAL ISSUES

The following questions are provided to help you understand some of the ethical/social/legal issues associated with the field of computing as well as investigate your own beliefs and their foundations. The goal is not merely to answer these questions. You should also consider why you answered as you did and whether your justifications are consistent from one question to the next.

1. Since it is currently impossible to verify completely the accuracy of complex programs, under what circumstances, if any, should the creator of a program be liable for errors?

2. Suppose you have an idea and develop it into a product that many people can use. Moreover, it has required a year of work and an investment of $50,000 to develop your idea into a form that is useful to the general public. In its final form, however, the product can be used by most people without buying anything from you. What right do you have for compensation? Is it ethical to pirate computer software?

3. Suppose a software package is so expensive that it is totally out of your price range. Is it ethical to copy it for your own use? (After all, you are not cheating the supplier out of a sale because you would not have bought the package anyway.)

4. Ownership of "things" has always been an issue. Ownership of rivers, forests, oceans, etc. has been well debated. In what sense should someone or some institution be given ownership of an algorithm?

5. Suppose someone discovers an algorithm for breaking the security features in a multiuser operating system. Should that person be entitled to ownership rights to that algorithm? If so, what rights should the person have? Should algorithm ownership rights be dependent on the subject of the algorithm? Is it ethical to advertise and circulate techniques for breaking security? Does it matter what is being broken into?

6. Some people feel that new algorithms are discovered, whereas others feel that new

algorithms are created. To which philosophy do you subscribe? Would the different points of view lead to different conclusions regarding ownership of algorithms and ownership rights?

7. Is it ethical to design an algorithm for performing an illegal act? Does it matter whether the algorithm is ever executed?

8. An author is paid for the motion picture rights to a novel even though the story is often altered in the film version. How much of a story has to change before it becomes a different story? What alterations must be made to an algorithm for it to become a different algorithm?

9. Educational software is now being marketed for children in the 18 months or younger age group. Proponents argue that such software provides sights and sounds that would otherwise not be available to many children. Opponents argue that it is a poor substitute for personal parent/child interaction. What is your opinion? Should you form an opinion without knowing more about the software?

ADDITIONAL READING

Brassard, G., and P. Bratley. *Fundamentals of Algorithmics.* Englewood Cliffs, NJ: Prentice-Hall, 1996.

Cormen, T. H., C. E. Leiserson, and R. L. Rivest. *Introduction to Algorithms.* New York: McGraw-Hill, 1990.

Gries, D. *The Science of Programming.* New York: Springer-Verlag, 1981.

Harbin, R. *Origami—the Art of Paper Folding.* London: Hodder Paperbacks, 1973.

Knuth, D. E. *The Art of Computer Programming,* vol. 3, 3rd ed. Reading, MA: Addison Wesley Longman, 1998.

Kruse, R. L., and A. J. Ryba. *Data Structures and Program Design in C++.* Upper Saddle River, NJ: Prentice Hall, 1999.

Polya, G. *How to Solve It.* Princeton, NJ: Princeton University Press, 1973.

Rawlins, G. J. E. *Compared to What? An Introduction to the Analysis of Algorithms.* New York: Computer Science Press, 1992.

Roberts, E. S. *Thinking Recursively.* New York: Wiley, 1986.

Sedgewick, R., and P. Flajolet. *An Introduction to the Analysis of Algorithms.* Reading, MA: Addison-Wesley, 1996.

5.1 Historical Perspective
Early Generations
**Machine Independence
and Beyond**
Programming Paradigms

**5.2 Traditional
Programming Concepts**
**Variables, Constants, and
Literals**
Data Type
Data Structure
Assignment Statements
Control Statements
Comments

5.3 Procedural Units
Procedures
Parameters
Functions
Input/Output Statements

**5.4 Language
Implementation**
The Translation Process
Linking and Loading
**Software Development
Packages**

***5.5 Object-Oriented
Programming**

***5.6 Programming
Concurrent Activities**

***5.7 Declarative
Programming**
Logical Deduction
Prolog

*Asterisks indicate suggestions for
optional sections.

chapter
PROGRAMMING
LANGUAGES
f i v e

The development of complex software systems such as
operating systems and network software would likely be
impossible if humans were forced to express the algorithms
involved directly in machine language. Dealing with the
massive amount of intricate detail would be a taxing experience, to say the least. Consequently, programming languages similar to our pseudocode have been developed
that allow algorithms to be expressed in a form that is both
palatable to humans and easily convertible into machine
language instructions. These languages allow humans to
avoid the intricacies of registers, memory addresses, and
machine cycles during the program development process
and, instead, to concentrate on the properties of the problem being solved. In this chapter we investigate the subject
of programming languages.

5.1 Historical Perspective

We begin our study by tracing the historical development of programming languages.

Early Generations

Originally the programming process was accomplished by requiring the programmer to express all algorithms in the machine's language. This approach added significantly to the already exacting task of an algorithm's design and more often than not led to errors that had to be located and corrected (a process known as debugging) before the job was finished.

The first step toward removing these complexities from the programming process was to do away with the use of numeric digits for representing the op-codes and operands found in a machine's language. To this end, it became popular to assign mnemonics to the various op-codes and to use them in place of hexadecimal representation during the design process. In place of the op-code for loading a register, for example, a programmer might write LD, or to store the contents of a register, ST might be used. In the case of operands, rules were designed by which the programmer could assign descriptive names (often called *identifiers*) to locations in memory and use these names in place of the memory cell addresses in an instruction. A special case of this idea was the assignment of names such as R0, R1, R2,... to the registers in the CPU.

By choosing descriptive names for the memory cells and using mnemonics for representing op-codes, programmers could greatly increase the readability of a sequence of machine instructions. As an example, let us return to the machine-language routine at the end of Section 2.2 that added the contents of memory cells 6C and 6D and placed the result in location 6E. Recall that the instructions in hexadecimal notation appeared as follows:

```
156C
166D
5056
306E
C000
```

If we assign the name PRICE to location 6C, TAX to 6D, and TOTAL to 6E, we can express the same routine as follows using the mnemonic technique:

```
LD R5,PRICE
LD R6,TAX
ADDI R0,R5 R6
ST R0,TOTAL
HLT
```

Most would agree that the second form, although still lacking, does a better job of representing the meaning of the routine than does the first. Note that the mnemonic ADDI is used to represent the op-code for adding integers, to distinguish it from the op-code for adding floating-point numbers, which might be represented by ADDF.

When these techniques were first introduced, programmers used such notation when designing a program on paper and later translated it into machine-language form. It was not long, however, before this translation process was recognized as a procedure that could be performed by the machine itself. Consequently, programs, called **assemblers,** were developed to translate other programs written in mnemonic form into machine-compatible form. These translation programs were called assemblers because their task was to assemble machine instructions out of the op-codes and operands obtained by translating mnemonics and identifiers. Mnemonic systems for representing programs were in turn recognized as programming languages called **assembly languages.**

At the time assembly languages were first developed, they appeared as a giant step forward in the search for better programming techniques. In fact, many considered them to represent a totally new generation of programming languages. In time, assembly languages came to be known as second-generation languages, the first generation being the machine languages themselves.

Although second-generation languages had many advantages over their machine-language counterparts, they still fell short of providing the ultimate programming environment. After all, the primitives used in an assembly language were essentially the same as those found in the corresponding machine language. The difference was simply in the syntax used to represent them. Thus a program written in an assembly language is inherently machine dependent—that is, the instructions within the program are expressed in terms of a particular machine's attributes. A program written in assembly language cannot be easily transported to another machine design because it must be rewritten to conform to the new machine's register configuration and instruction set.

Another disadvantage of an assembly language is that a programmer, although not required to code instructions in bit pattern form, is still forced to think in terms of the small, incremental steps of the machine's language. The

CROSS-PLATFORM SOFTWARE

A typical application program must rely on the operating system to perform many of its tasks. It may require the services of the window manager to communicate with the computer user or the file manager to retrieve data from mass storage. Unfortunately, different operating systems dictate that requests for these services be made in different ways. Thus, if programs are to be transferred and executed across networks and internets involving different machine designs and different operating systems, they must be operating-system independent as well as machine independent. The term **cross-platform** is used to reflect this additional level of independence. That is, cross-platform software is software that is independent of an operating system's design as well as the machine's hardware design and is therefore executable throughout a network.

situation is analogous to designing a house in terms of boards, nails, bricks, and so on. It is true that the actual construction of the house ultimately requires a description based on these elementary pieces, but the design process is easier if we think in terms of rooms, windows, doors, and so on.

In short, the elementary primitives in which a product must ultimately be constructed are not necessarily the primitives that should be used during the product's design. The design process is better suited to the use of high-level primitives, each representing a concept associated with a major feature of the product. Once the design is complete, these primitives can be translated to lower-level concepts relating to the details of implementation.

Following this philosophy, computer scientists began developing programming languages that were more conducive to software development than were the low-level assembly languages. The result was the emergence of a third generation of programming languages that differed from previous generations in that their primitives were both higher level and machine independent. The best-known early examples are FORTRAN (FORmula TRANslator), which was developed for scientific and engineering applications, and COBOL (COmmon Business-Oriented Language), which was developed for business applications by the U.S. Navy.

In general, the approach to third-generation programming languages was to identify a collection of high-level primitives (in essentially the same spirit with which we developed our pseudocode in Chapter 4) in which software could be developed. Each of these primitives was designed so that it could be implemented as a sequence of the low-level primitives available in machine languages. For example, the statement

assign Total **the value** Price + Tax

expresses a high-level activity without reference to how a particular machine should perform the task, yet it can be implemented by the sequence of machine instructions discussed earlier. Thus the structure

assign *identifier* **the value** *expression*

is a potential high-level primitive.

Once this collection of high-level primitives had been identified, a program, called a **translator,** was written that translated programs expressed in these high-level primitives into machine-language programs. Such a translator was similar to the second-generation assemblers, except that it often had to compile several machine instructions into short sequences to simulate the activity requested by a single high-level primitive. Thus these translation programs were often called **compilers.** The development of the first compiler is attributed to Grace Hopper, who was also instrumental in promoting the concept of third-generation programming languages. Indeed, the thought of writing programs in a form similar to a natural language was so revolutionary that many in managerial positions fought the notion at first.

A popular alternative to translators, called **interpreters,** emerged as another means of implementing third-generation languages. These programs were similar to translators except that they executed the instructions as they were translated instead of recording the translated version for future use. That is, rather than producing a machine-language copy of a program that would be executed later, an interpreter actually executed the instructions as they were translated.

Machine Independence and Beyond

With the development of third-generation languages, the goal of machine independence was largely achieved. Since the statements in a third-generation language did not refer to the attributes of any particular machine, they could be compiled as easily for one machine as for another. A program written in a third-generation language could theoretically be used on any machine simply by applying the appropriate compiler.

Reality, however, has not proven to be this simple. When a compiler is designed, certain restrictions imposed by the underlying machine are ultimately reflected as conditions on the language being translated. For example, the size of a machine's registers and memory cells affects the maximum size of integers that can be manipulated conveniently. Such conditions result in the fact that the "same" language tends to have different characteristics, or dialects, on different machines; consequently, it is often necessary to make at least minor modifications to a program to move it from one machine to another.

Compounding this problem of portability is the lack of agreement in some cases as to what constitutes the correct definition of a particular language. To aid in this regard, the American National Standards Institute and the International Organization for Standardization have adopted and published standards for many of the popular languages. In other cases, informal standards have evolved due to the popularity of a certain dialect of a language and the desire of other compiler writers to produce compatible products.

In the overall history of programming languages, the fact that third-generation languages fell short of true machine independence is actually of little significance for two reasons. First, they were close enough to being machine-independent that software could be transported from one machine to another with relative ease. Second, the goal of machine independence turned out to be only a seed for more demanding goals. By the time machine independence was within reach, its significance had been diluted in comparison to the loftier ambitions of the time. Indeed, the realization that machines could respond to such high-level statements as

assign Total **the value** Price + Tax

led computer scientists to dream of programming environments that would allow humans to communicate with machines in terms of abstract concepts rather than forcing them to translate these concepts into machine-compatible form. Moreover, computer scientists wanted machines that could perform much of the algorithm discovery process rather than just algorithm execution. The result has been an ever-expanding spectrum of programming languages that challenges a clear-cut classification in terms of generations.

Programming Paradigms

The generation approach to classifying programming languages insists on classifying programming languages on a linear scale (Figure 5.1), according to the degree to which the user of the language is freed from the world of computer gibberish and allowed to think in terms associated with the problem. In reality, the development of programming languages has not progressed in this manner but has developed along different paths as alternative approaches to the programming process (different paradigms) have surfaced and been pursued. Consequently, the historical development of programming languages is better represented by a multiple-track diagram as shown in Figure 5.2, in which different paths resulting from different paradigms are shown to emerge and progress independently. In particular, the figure presents four paths representing the functional, object-oriented, imperative, and declarative paradigms, with various languages associated with each paradigm positioned in a manner that indicates their births relative to other languages. It does not imply that one language necessarily evolved from a previous one.

The **imperative paradigm,** also known as the **procedural paradigm,** represents the traditional approach to the programming process. Indeed, the imperative paradigm is the one on which a CPU's fetch–decode–execute cycle

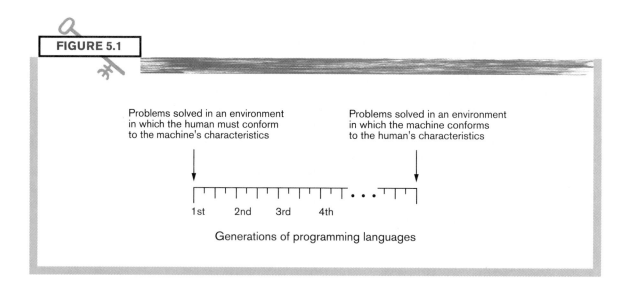

FIGURE 5.1

Problems solved in an environment in which the human must conform to the machine's characteristics

Problems solved in an environment in which the machine conforms to the human's characteristics

1st 2nd 3rd 4th

Generations of programming languages

FIGURE 5.2

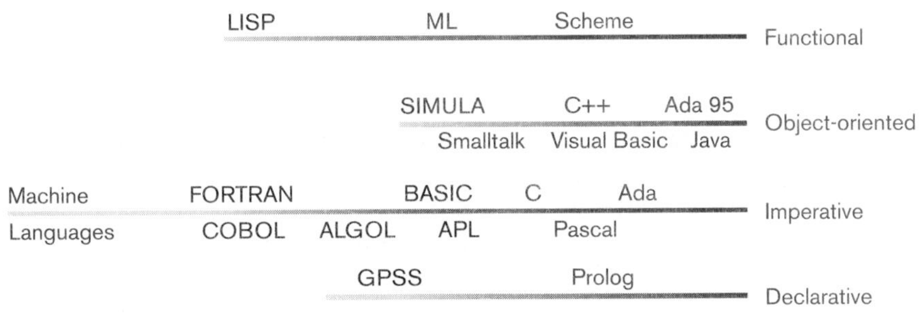

The evolution of programming paradigms

is based. As the name suggests, the imperative paradigm defines the programming process to be the development of a sequence of commands that when followed, manipulate data to produce the desired result. Thus the imperative paradigm tells us to approach a problem by trying to find an algorithm for solving it.

In contrast, consider the **declarative paradigm,** which emphasizes the question "What is the problem?" rather than "What algorithm is required to solve the problem?" The trick here is to discover and implement a general problem-solving algorithm. Once this is done, problems can be solved merely by stating them in a form that is compatible with this algorithm and then applying the algorithm. In this context the task of the programmer becomes that of developing a precise statement of the problem rather than of discovering an algorithm for solving the problem.

A major obstacle in developing a programming language based on the declarative paradigm is the discovery of the underlying problem-solving algorithm. For this reason early declarative languages tended to be special-purpose in nature, designed for use in particular applications. For example, the declarative approach has been used for many years to simulate a system (economic, physical, political, and so on) in order to test hypotheses. In these settings the underlying algorithm is essentially the process of simulating the passage of time by repeatedly recomputing values of parameters (gross domestic product, trade deficit, and so on) based on the previously computed ones. Implementing a declarative language for such simulations therefore requires that one implement an algorithm that performs this repetitive procedure. Following this, the only task required of a programmer is to describe the relationships among the parameters to be simulated. Then the simulation algorithm merely simulates the passage of time using these relationships to perform its calculations.

More recently, the declarative paradigm has been given a tremendous boost by the discovery that the subject of formal logic within mathematics provides a simple problem-solving algorithm suitable for use in a general-purpose declarative programming system. The result has been increased attention to the declarative paradigm and the emergence of logic programming, a subject discussed in Section 5.7.

The **functional paradigm** views the process of program development as the construction of "black boxes," each of which accepts inputs (at the top) and produces outputs (at the bottom). Mathematicians refer to such "boxes" as functions, which is the reason this approach is called the functional paradigm. The primitives of a functional programming language consist of elementary functions from which the programmer must construct the more elaborate functions required to solve the problem at hand. Thus a programmer using the functional paradigm approaches a problem by considering the input that is given, the output that is desired, and the transformation that is required to produce that output from the given input. The solution would probably be obtained by dividing this transformation into smaller transformations that produce intermediate outputs that serve as inputs to other small transformations. In short, the programming process under the functional paradigm is that of constructing functions as nested complexes of simpler functions.

As an example, Figure 5.3 shows how a function for computing the average of a list of numbers can be constructed from three simpler functions. One of these is called Sum. It accepts a list of values and produces the sum of those values. Another is called Count. It accepts a list of values and produces an output value equal to the number of entries in the input list. The third function is called Divide. It accepts two values and produces their quotient. This construction can be represented in the LISP programming language (a prominent functional programming language) by the expression

```
(Divide (Sum Numbers) (Count Numbers))
```

The nested structure of this expression reflects the fact that the inputs to the function Divide are the outputs of Sum and Count. As another example, suppose we had a function called Sort that sorts a list of numbers and another called First that retrieves the first entry from a list. Then the expression

```
(First (Sort List))
```

would retrieve the smallest entry in List. Here the nested structure indicates that the output of Sort is the input to First. That is, the list is sorted, and then the first entry is extracted from the sorted list.

FIGURE 5.3

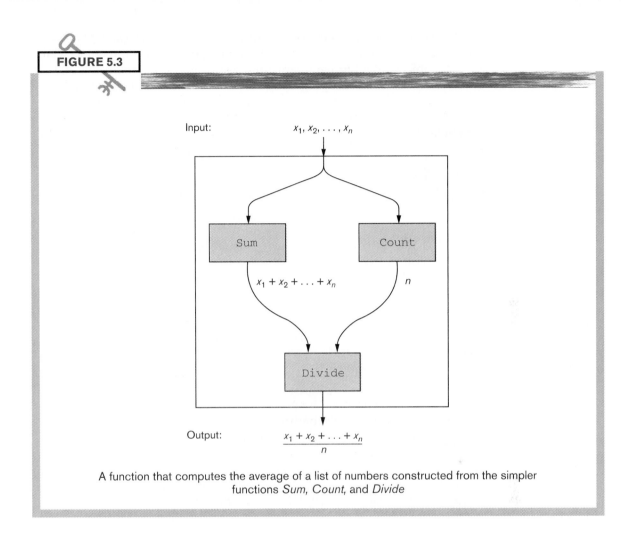

Input: $x_1, x_2, \ldots, x_n$

Sum

Count

$x_1 + x_2 + \ldots + x_n$

n

Divide

Output: $\dfrac{x_1 + x_2 + \ldots + x_n}{n}$

A function that computes the average of a list of numbers constructed from the simpler functions *Sum, Count,* and *Divide*

An advantage of the functional programming paradigm over the imperative model is that it encourages a modular approach to program construction. Indeed, the fact that programs are viewed as functions that must be constructed from other functions forces one to think in modular terms. For this reason, proponents of functional programming argue that their approach leads to well-organized programs more naturally than the imperative paradigm. Moreover, many argue that the functional paradigm is a natural environment for the "building block" approach to the construction of programs. This is the approach of constructing new programs from previously established pieces rather than from scratch, a technique generally accepted by computer scientists as a preferred approach to the development of large software packages. These arguments also support the object-oriented paradigm, as we are about to see.

The **object-oriented paradigm,** which leads to the programming process called **object-oriented programming (OOP)** is another approach to the software development process. In this approach, units of data are viewed as active "objects" rather than the passive units envisioned by the traditional imperative paradigm. To clarify, consider a list of names. In the traditional imperative paradigm, this list is considered merely a collection of data. Any program accessing this list must contain the algorithms for performing the required manipulations. Thus the list is passive in the sense that it is maintained by a controlling program rather than having the responsibility of maintaining itself. In the object-oriented approach, however, the list is considered an object consisting of the list together with a collection of procedures for manipulating the list. They may include procedures for entering a new entry in the list, detecting if the list is empty, and sorting the list. In turn, a program accessing the list does not need to contain algorithms for performing these tasks. Instead, it makes use of the procedures provided in the object. In a sense, rather than sorting the list as in the imperative paradigm, the program asks the list to sort itself.

As another example of the object-oriented approach, consider the task of developing a graphical user interface. Here the icons that appear on the screen are implemented as objects. Each of these objects encompasses a collection of procedures describing how that object is to respond to the occurrence of various events, such as being selected by a click of the mouse button or being dragged across the screen by the mouse. Thus, the entire system has the form of a collection of objects, each of which knows how to respond to certain events.

Many of the advantages of an object-oriented design are consequences of the modular structure that emerges as a natural by-product of the object-oriented philosophy. Each object is implemented as a separate, well-defined unit. Once the properties of an entity have been defined in this manner, that definition can be reused each time an occurrence of that entity is required. In turn,

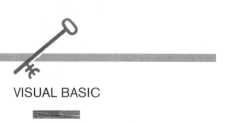

VISUAL BASIC

Visual Basic is an object-oriented programming language that was developed by Microsoft as a tool by which users of Microsoft's Windows operating system could develop their own GUI applications. Actually, Visual Basic is more than a language—it is an entire software development package that allows a programmer to construct a GUI from predefined components (such as buttons, check boxes, text boxes, scroll bars, etc.) and to customize these components by describing how they should react to various events. In the case of a button, for example, the programmer would describe what should happen when that button is clicked. In Chapter 6 we will learn that this strategy of constructing software from predefined components represents the current trend in software development techniques.

The popularity of the Windows operating system combined with the convenience of the Visual Basic development package has promoted Visual Basic to one of the most widely used programming languages today.

proponents of object-oriented programming argue that the object-oriented paradigm provides a natural environment for the "building block" approach to software development. They envision software libraries of object definitions from which new software systems can be constructed in the same way that many traditional products are constructed from off-the-shelf components.

Another advantage of the modular structure obtained via the object-oriented paradigm is that all communication between the modules is accomplished by passing messages—a technique that is fundamental to communication over computer networks. Thus, the concept of objects passing messages to each other is a natural way to approach the task of developing software systems that are to be distributed over a network. The implementation of such network-wide systems of objects is the goal of CORBA (Common Object Request Broker Architecture), which is an open system of specifications for implementing message passing between objects in a network. We have already met this phenomenon in the context of the client/server model (Section 3.3). Indeed, the client/server model is ideally suited to the object-oriented paradigm.

The object-oriented paradigm promises to be a major influence in the computing field, and therefore we will discuss it in more detail in Section 5.5. Moreover, we will repeatedly see the implications of this paradigm in future chapters. In particular, we will witness the influence of the object-oriented paradigm in the fields of software engineering (Chapter 6) and database design (Chapter 9), and in Chapter 7 we will see how the object-oriented approach to software construction has evolved as a natural extension of the study of data structures.

Finally, we should observe that although they are called *programming* paradigms, these alternative approaches have ramifications beyond the programming process. They represent fundamentally different approaches to building solutions to problems and therefore affect the entire software development process. In this sense, then, the term *programming paradigms* is a misnomer. A more realistic term would be *software development paradigms*.

QUESTIONS/EXERCISES

1. In what sense is a program in a third-generation language machine independent? In what sense is it still machine dependent?
2. What is the difference between an assembler and a compiler?
3. We can summarize the imperative programming paradigm by saying that it places emphasis on describing a process that leads to the solution of the problem at hand. Give a similar summary of the declarative, functional, and object-oriented paradigms.
4. In what sense are the third-generation programming languages at a higher level than the earlier generations?

5.2 Traditional Programming Concepts

In this section we consider some of the generic concepts found in imperative and object-oriented programming languages. For this purpose we will draw examples from the languages Ada, C, C++, FORTRAN, Java, and Pascal. FORTRAN, Pascal, and C are third-generation imperative languages. C++ is an object-oriented language that was developed as an extension of the language C. Java is an object-oriented language that was derived from C and C++. Ada was originally designed as a third-generation imperative language containing many object-oriented characteristics. Its newest version, however, more fully embraces the object-oriented paradigm.

Appendix D contains a brief introduction to each of these languages as well as an example of how the insertion sort algorithm could be implemented in each. You may wish to refer to this appendix as you read this section. Keep in mind, however, that our purpose here is to develop an understanding of the basic features found in programming languages. Our use of examples is merely to show how the features discussed actually appear in languages. Thus you should not allow yourself to become entangled in the details of any single example.

Statements in programming languages tend to fall into three categories: declarative statements, imperative statements, and comments. **Declarative statements** define customized terminology that is used later in the program, such as the names used to reference data items; **imperative statements** describe steps in the underlying algorithms; and **comments** enhance the readability of a program by explaining its esoteric features in a more human compatible form. In this section we begin with concepts associated with declarative statements, followed by those of imperative statements, and close with issues of documentation.

Variables, Constants, and Literals

In Section 5.1 we witnessed the advantage of identifying memory locations by means of descriptive names rather than by numeric addresses. Such identifiers are known as **variables,** in reference to the fact that by changing the value stored at the location, the value associated with the identifier changes as the program executes.

In contrast, in some cases a fixed, predetermined value is referenced in a program. For example, a program for controlling air traffic in the vicinity of a particular airport may contain numerous references to that airport's altitude above sea level. When writing such a program, one can include this value, say 645 feet, literally each time it is required. Such an explicit appearance of a value is called a **literal.** The use of literals leads to program statements such as

> **assign** EffectiveAlt **the value** Altimeter + 645

where EffectiveAlt and Altimeter are assumed to be variables and 645 is a literal.

Often, the use of literals is not good programming practice because literals can mask the meaning of the statements in which they appear. How, for instance, can a reader of the preceding statement know what the value 645 represents? Moreover, literals can complicate the task of modifying the program should it become necessary. If our air traffic program is moved to another airport, all references to the airport's altitude must be changed. If the literal 645 is used in each reference to that altitude, each such reference throughout the program must be located and changed. The problem is compounded if the literal 645 also occurs in reference to a quantity other than the airport's altitude. How do we know which occurrences of 645 to change and which to leave alone?

To solve these problems, programming languages allow descriptive names to be assigned to specific, non-changeable values. Such a name is called a **constant.** As an example, in Pascal, the declarative statement

```
const AirportAlt = 645;
```

associates the identifier `AirportAlt` with the fixed value 645. The similar concept in Java is expressed by

```
final int AirportAlt = 645;
```

Following such declarations, the descriptive name `AirportAlt` can be used in lieu of the literal 645. Using such a constant in our pseudocode, the statement

> **assign** EffectiveAlt **the value**
> Altimeter + 645

could be rewritten as

PROGRAMMING LANGUAGE CULTURES

As with natural languages, users of different programming languages tend to develop cultural differences and often debate the merits of their perspectives. Sometimes these differences are significant, as when different programming paradigms are involved. In other cases the distinctions are subtle. For example, whereas the text distinguishes between procedures and functions (Section 5.3), C programmers refer to both as functions. This is because a procedure in a C program is presented as a function that does not return a value. A similar example is that C++ programmers refer to procedures within objects as member functions, whereas the generic term is method. This discrepancy can be traced to the fact that C++ was developed as an extension of C. Another cultural difference is that programs in Pascal and Ada are normally typeset with reserved words in bold—a tradition that is not widely practiced by users of C, C++, FORTRAN, and Java.

The text attempts to be language neutral by using generic terminology. However, each specific example is presented in a form that is compatible with the style of the language involved. As you encounter these examples, you should keep in mind that they are presented as examples of how generic ideas appear in actual languages—not as a means of teaching the details of a particular language. Try to look at the forest rather than the trees.

> **assign** EffectiveAlt **the value** Altimeter + AirportAlt

which better represents the meaning of the statement. Moreover, if such constants are used in place of literals and the program is moved to another airport whose altitude is 267 feet, then changing the single declarative statement to read

```
const AirportAlt = 267;
```

or

```
final int AirportAlt = 267;
```

is all that is needed to convert all references to the airport's altitude to the new value.

Data Type

Declarative statements that assign descriptive names to data items often identify the type of that data as well. **Data type** refers to both the interpretation given data and the operations that can be performed on that data. Common types include integer, real, character, and Boolean. The type **integer** refers to numeric data consisting of whole numbers, probably stored using two's complement notation. Operations that can be performed on integer data include the traditional arithmetic operations and comparison of relative size, such as determining whether one value is greater than another. The type **real** refers to numeric data that may contain values other than whole numbers, probably stored in floating-point notation. Operations performed on data of type real are similar to those performed on data of type integer. Note, however, that the activity required for adding two items of type real differs from that for adding two items of type integer.

The type **character** refers to data consisting of symbols, probably stored using ASCII or Unicode. Operations performed on such data include comparison such as determining whether one symbol occurs before another in alphabetical order, testing to see whether one string of symbols appears inside another, and concatenating one string of symbols at the end of another to form one long string.

The type **Boolean** refers to data items that can take on only the values true or false. Examples occur as the result of comparisons such as Is Tax equal to withholding? Operations on data of type Boolean include inquiries as to whether the current value is true or false.

Other data types that have not yet become common primitives in general programming languages include audio and video. The Java programming environment contains tools for handling such types.

Most programming languages require that a declarative statement that introduces a variable also specify the type of data that will be referenced by that variable. Figure 5.4 gives examples of such variable declarations in Pascal, C, C++, Java, and FORTRAN. In each case the variables Length and Width are declared to be of type real, and Price, Tax, and Total are declared to be of type integer. Note that C, C++, and Java use the term *float* to refer to the type real, since data of this type are represented in floating-point notation.

In Section 5.5 we will see how a translator uses knowledge of data types when translating a program from a high-level language into machine language. For now, we note that such information can be used to identify errors. For

FIGURE 5.4

(a) Variable declarations in Pascal

```
var
    Length, Width:        real;
    Price, Tax, Total:    integer;
```

(b) Variable declarations in C, C++, and Java

```
float Length, Width;
int Price, Tax, Total;
```

(c) Variable declarations in FORTRAN

```
REAL Length, Width
INTEGER Price, Tax, Total
```

Variable declarations in Pascal, C, C++, Java, and FORTRAN

example, an attempt to add two values of type character or to perform an operation that combines data of different types should arouse suspicion.

Data Structure

Another concept associated with many declarative statements is **data structure,** which relates to the conceptual shape of data. For example, text is normally viewed as a long string of characters whereas sales records may be viewed as a rectangular block of numeric values, each representing the sales of a particular employee on a particular day.

One common data structure is the **homogeneous array,** which is a block of values of the same type such as a one-dimensional list, a two-dimensional table with rows and columns, or tables with higher dimensions. To declare such an array, most programming languages use a declaration statement in which the length of each dimension of the array is specified. For example, Figure 5.5 displays statements in C, Java, and Pascal that declare Scores to be a two-dimensional array of integers with two rows and nine columns.

FIGURE 5.5

```
int Scores [2][9]
```
(a) The declaration in C

```
int Scores [][] = new int[2][9];
```
(b) The declaration in Java

```
var
  Scores: array[1..2,1..9] of integer;
```
(c) The declaration in Pascal

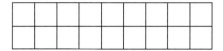

(d) The conceptual structure defined by the each declaration

Declaring a two-dimensional array named Scores

Once a homogeneous array has been declared, it can be referenced elsewhere in the program by its name, or an individual component can be referenced by means of indices that specify the row, column, and so on, desired. For example, in a Pascal program the entry in the second row and fourth column of the array Scores could be referenced as Scores[2,4]; in C, C++, and Java the same entry would be identified by Scores[1][3]. (Row and column numbers start at zero in these languages; for example, the entry in the first row and first column would be referenced by Scores[0][0].)

In contrast to a homogeneous array in which all data items are the same type, a **heterogeneous array** is a block of data in which different elements can have different types. For example, a block of data referring to an employee may consist of an entry called Name of type character, an entry called Age of type integer, and an entry called SkillRating of type real. Figure 5.6 shows how such an array would be declared in C and Pascal.

FIGURE 5.6

(a) The array declaration in Pascal

```
var
   Employee: record
                Name: packed array[1. . 8] of char;
                Age: integer;
                SkillRating: real
             end
```

(b) The array declaration in C

```
struct
{ char Name [8];
  int Age;
  float SkillRating;
  Employee;
}
```

(c) The conceptual organization of array

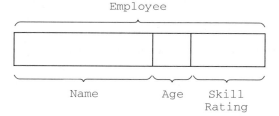

Declaration of heterogeneous arrays in Pascal and C

A component within a heterogeneous array is usually referenced by the name of the array, followed by a period and the component name. For example, the Age component in the array Employee in Figure 5.6 would be referenced by Employee.Age in C, C++, Java, and Pascal.

In Chapter 7 we will see how conceptual structures such as arrays are implemented in machines. In particular, we will learn that the data contained in an array may be scattered over a wide area of main memory or mass storage. This is why we refer to data structure as being the conceptual shape of data. Indeed, the actual "shape" within the machine's storage system may be quite different from its conceptual shape.

Assignment Statements

The most basic imperative statement is the **assignment statement,** which requests that a value be assigned to a variable. Such a statement normally takes the syntactic form of a variable, followed by a symbol representing the assignment operation and then by an expression indicating the value to be assigned. The semantics of such a statement is that the expression is to be evaluated and the result assigned as the value of the variable. For example, the statement

```
Total = Price + Tax;
```

in C, C++, and Java requests that the sum of `Price` and `Tax` be assigned to the variable `Total`. In Ada and Pascal the equivalent statement would appear as

```
Total := Price + Tax;
```

Note that these statements differ only in the syntax of the assignment operator, which in C, C++, and Java is merely an equal sign but in Ada and Pascal is a colon followed by an equal sign. Perhaps a better notation for the assignment operator is found in APL, a language that was designed by Kenneth E. Iverson in 1962. (APL stands for A Programming Language.) It uses an arrow to represent assignment. Thus, the preceding assignment would be expressed as

```
Total ← Price + Tax
```

in APL.

Much of the power of assignment statements comes from the scope of expressions that can appear on the right side of the statement. In general, any algebraic expression can be used, with the arithmetic operations of addition, subtraction, multiplication, and division typically represented by the symbols +, −, *, and /, respectively. Languages differ, however, in the manner in which these expressions are interpreted. For example, the expression 2 * 4 + 6 / 2 could produce the value 14 if it is evaluated from right to left, or 7 if evaluated from left to right. These ambiguities are normally resolved by rules of **operator precedence,** meaning that certain operations are given precedence over others. The traditional rules of algebra dictate that multiplication and division have precedence over addition and subtraction. That is, multiplications and divisions are performed before additions and subtractions. Following this convention, the preceding expression would produce the value 11. In most languages, parentheses can be used to override the language's operator precedence. Thus 2 * (4 + 6) / 2 would produce the value 10.

Expressions in assignment statements can also involve operations other than the traditional algebraic ones. For instance, if `First` and `Last` are variables associated with character strings, the FORTRAN statement

```
Both = First // Last
```

causes the variable `Both` to be assigned the string produced by concatenating the values of `First` and `Last`. Thus, if `First` and `Last` are associated with the strings *abra* and *cadabra*, respectively, then `Both` would be assigned the string *abracadabra*.

Many programming languages allow the use of one symbol to represent more than one type of operation. In these cases the meaning of the symbol is determined by the data type of the operands. For example, the symbol + traditionally indicates addition when its operands are numeric, but in some languages, such as Java, the symbol indicates concatenation when its operands are character strings. Such multiple use of a symbol is called **overloading.**

Control Statements

Control statements are imperative statements that alter the execution sequence of the program. Of all the programming statements, those from this group have probably received the most attention and generated the most controversy. The major villain is the simplest control statement of all, the goto statement. It provides a means of directing the execution sequence to another location that has been labeled for this purpose by a name or number. It is therefore nothing more than a direct application of the machine-level jump instruction. The problem with such a feature in a high-level programming language is that it allows programmers to write rat's nests like

```
     goto 40
20   Total = Price + 10
     goto 70
40   if Price < 50 then goto 60
     goto 20
60   Total = Price + 5
70   stop
```

when a two-statement program like this does the job:

```
if (Price < 50)
    then Total = Price + 5
    else Total = Price + 10
stop
```

To avoid such complexities, modern languages are designed with more elaborate control statements that allow a certain branching structure to be expressed within a single statement. Figure 5.7 presents some common branching structures and the control statements provided in various programming languages for representing those structures. Note that the first two structures are

FIGURE 5.7

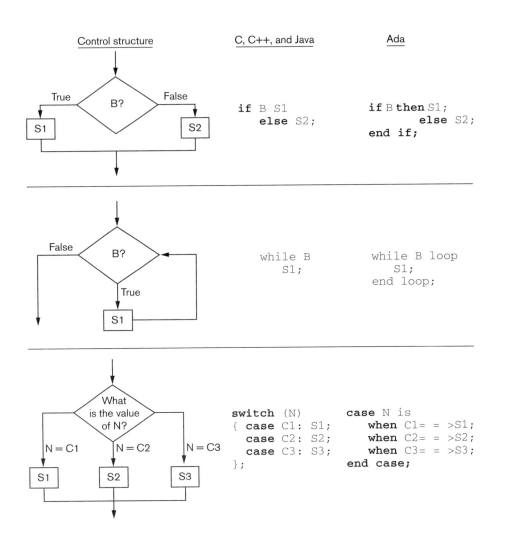

Control structures and their representations in C, C++, Java, and Ada

those that we have already encountered in Chapter 4. They are represented by the if-then-else and while statements in our pseudocode. The third structure, known as the case structure, can be viewed as an extension of the if-then-else structure. Whereas the if-then-else allows a choice between two options, the case allows a selection between many options.

Another common structure, often called the for structure, and its representation in various languages is shown in Figure 5.8. This is a looping structure similar to that of the while statement in our pseudocode. The difference is that all the initialization, modification, and termination of the loop structure is incorporated into a single statement. Such a statement is convenient when the body of the loop is to be performed once for each value within a specific range.

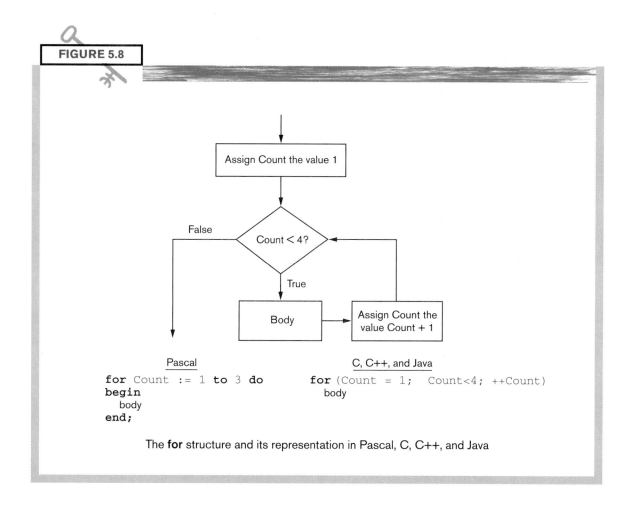

FIGURE 5.8

```
              Pascal                    C, C++, and Java
      for Count := 1 to 3 do        for (Count = 1;  Count<4; ++Count)
      begin                              body
         body
      end;
```

The **for** structure and its representation in Pascal, C, C++, and Java

In particular, the statements in Figure 5.8 direct that the loop body be performed repeatedly—first with the value of Count being 1, then with the value of Count being 2, and again with the value of Count being 3.

The purpose of these examples is to demonstrate that generic branching structures appear, with slight variations, throughout the gamut of imperative and object-oriented programming languages. A somewhat surprising result from theoretical computer science is that only a few of these structures are needed to ensure that a programming language provides a means of expressing a solution to any problem that has an algorithmic solution. We investigate this claim in Chapter 11. For now, we merely point out that learning a programming language is not an endless task of learning different control statements. Indeed, most of the control structures found in today's programming languages are essentially variations of those we have identified here.

The choice of which control structures to incorporate into a language is a design decision. The object is to provide a language that not only allows algorithms to be expressed in a readable form but also assists the programmer in obtaining such readability. This is done by restricting the use of those features that have historically led to sloppy programming while encouraging the use of better-designed features. The result is the often misunderstood practice known as **structured programming,** which encompasses an organized design methodology combined with the appropriate use of the language's control statements. The idea is to produce a program that can be readily comprehended and shown to meet its specifications.

Comments

Experience has shown that no matter how well a programming language is designed and how well the language's features are used, additional information is either helpful or mandatory when a human tries to understand a program of any significant size. For this reason, programming languages provide syntax for inserting explanatory statements, called **comments,** within a program. The documentation provided by these comments is called **internal documentation,** since it appears within the program itself rather than in a separate document.

Such internal documentation is ignored by a translator, and therefore its presence or absence does not affect the program from a machine's point of view. The machine-language version of the program produced by a translator will be the same with or without comments, but the information provided by these statements constitutes an important part of the program from a human's point of view. Without such documentation, large, complex programs can easily thwart the comprehensive powers of a human programmer.

There are two common ways of delimiting comments within a program from the rest of the program. One is to bracket the entire comment by special markers, one at the beginning of the comment and one at the end. The other is to mark the beginning of the comment and allow the comment to occupy the remainder of the line to the right of the marker. We find examples of both these techniques in C++ and Java. They allow comments to be bracketed by /* and */, but they also allow a comment to begin with // and extend through the remainder of the line. Thus in C++ and Java both

```
/* This is a comment. */
```

and

```
// This is a comment.
```

are valid comment statements.

A few words are in order about what constitutes a meaningful comment. Beginning programmers, when told to use comments for internal documentation, tend to follow a program statement such as

```
Total := Price + Tax;
```

with a comment such as "Calculate Total by adding Price and Tax." Such redundancy adds length rather than clarity to a program. Remember that the purpose of internal documentation is to explain the program, not to repeat it. A more appropriate comment associated with the preceding statement might be to explain why the total is being calculated if that is not obvious. For example, the comment, "Total is used later to compute GrandTotal and not needed after that" is more helpful than the previous one.

Additionally, a program in which comments are scattered among the program statements can be harder to comprehend than a program with no comments at all. A good approach is to collect comments that relate to a single program unit into one place, perhaps at the beginning of the unit. This provides a central place where the reader of the program unit can look for explanations. It also provides a location in which the purpose and general characteristics of the program unit can be described. If this format is adopted for all program units, the written program is given a degree of uniformity in which each unit consists of a block of explanatory statements followed by the formal presentation of the program unit. Such uniformities in a program enhance its readability.

QUESTIONS/EXERCISES

1. Why is the use of a constant considered better programming style than the use of a literal?
2. What is the difference between a declarative statement and an imperative statement?
3. List some common data types.
4. Identify some common control structures found in imperative and object-oriented programming languages.
5. What is the difference between a homogeneous array and a heterogeneous array?

5.3 Procedural Units

In previous chapters we have seen advantages to breaking large programs into manageable units. Programming languages are rich in methods for accomplishing this decomposition. Languages based on the functional paradigm naturally break programs into functions; languages based on the object-oriented paradigm lead to program units representing objects.

In this section we focus on methods for obtaining a modular representation of an algorithm. Here the approach is to group steps in the algorithm to form short, simple portions of the overall algorithm and to use these portions as abstract tools to express the final product. The result is the subprogram structure that we expressed in our pseudocode as a procedure.

Procedures

A **procedure,** in its generic sense, is a program unit written independently of other program units yet associated with them through a transfer/return process (Figure 5.9). Control is transferred to the procedure (by means of a machine language JUMP instruction) at the time its services are required and then returned to the original program unit after the procedure has finished. The

FIGURE 5.9

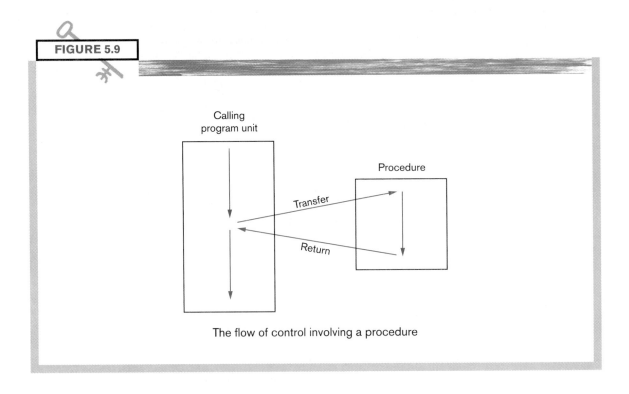

The flow of control involving a procedure

process of transferring control to a procedure is often referred to as calling or invoking the procedure. We will refer to a program unit that requests the execution of a procedure as the *calling unit*.

In our example programming languages, procedures are defined in much the same way as in our pseudocode in Chapter 4. The definition begins with a statement, known as the **procedure's header,** that identifies, among other things, the name of the procedure. Following this header are the statements that define the procedure's details. In many respects a procedure is a miniature program, consisting of declaration statements that describe such things as variables and constants used in the procedure as well as imperative statements that describe the steps to be performed when the procedure is executed.

As a general rule, variables declared within a procedure are **local variables,** meaning that they can be referenced only within that procedure. This rule eliminates any possible confusion that might occur if two procedures, written independently, happened to use variables of the same name. There are times, however, when an item of data should be shared by all units within a program. A variable representing such an item is called a **global variable.** Most languages provide a means of declaring both local and global variables.

The syntax used to request the execution of a procedure from another part of a program varies little from language to language. FORTRAN uses the term CALL to announce such a request. Ada, C, C++, Java, and Pascal merely state the procedure's name. Thus, if GetNames, SortNames, and WriteNames were procedures for acquiring, sorting, and printing a list of names (identified by a global variable), we could use them to obtain a program to get, sort, and print the list in FORTRAN by the statement sequence

```
CALL GetNames
CALL SortNames
CALL WriteNames
```

or in Ada, C, C++, Java, and Pascal by

```
GetNames;
SortNames;
WriteNames;
```

EVENT-DRIVEN SOFTWARE SYSTEMS

In the text we have considered cases in which procedures are activated as the result of statements elsewhere in the program that explicitly call the procedure. There are cases, however, in which procedures are activated implicitly by the occurrence of an event. Examples are found in GUIs where the procedure that describes what should happen when a button is clicked is not activated by a call from another program unit, but instead is activated as the result of the button being clicked. Software systems in which procedures are activated in this manner are called **event-driven** systems. In short, an event-driven software system consists of procedures that describe what should happen as the result of various events. When the system is executed, these procedures lie dormant until their respective event occurs—at which time they become active, perform their task, and return to dormancy.

Note that the result of this approach is a program consisting of three instructions, each of which requests the services of an abstract tool. The details of how each tool performs its task are isolated within the definition of the respective procedure.

Parameters

Sharing information by means of global variables is not normally a recommended practice since it makes it difficult to identify which parts of a program make use of the data. A better approach is to identify explicitly which data items are used by which program units. This is done by listing the data items to be shared with a procedure within the statement requesting the execution of the procedure. In turn, the procedure's header contains a list of variables it expects to be assigned values when the procedure is called, as in the case of our pseudocode in Chapter 4. The items in both lists are called **parameters.**

When the procedure is called, the parameters listed in the calling program unit are associated, entry by entry, with the parameters listed in the procedure's header—the first parameter in the calling unit is associated with the first parameter in the procedure's header, etc. Then, the values of the parameters in the calling unit are effectively transferred to their corresponding parameters in the procedure, and the procedure is executed. Thus, as in our pseudocode, the parameters listed in the procedure's header represent slots into which specific data will be plugged when the procedure's actions are requested. In turn, these parameters are often called **formal parameters,** whereas the parameters listed in the calling unit are called **actual parameters** since they represent the actual values to be used.

In some programming languages the transfer of data from actual parameters to formal parameters is accomplished by duplicating the data and allowing the procedure to manipulate only the copy. We often say that such parameters are passed **by value.** Passing parameters by value protects the data in the calling unit from being mistakenly altered by a poorly designed procedure. For example, if the calling unit passed an employee's Social Security Number to a procedure, it would not want that procedure to change that number.

Unfortunately, passing parameters by value is inefficient when the parameters represent large blocks of data. A more efficient way of passing parameters to a procedure is to give the procedure direct access to the actual parameters by telling it the addresses of the actual parameters. In this case, we say that the parameters are passed **by reference.** Note that passing parameters by reference allows the procedure to modify the data residing in the calling environment. Such an approach would be desirable in the case of a procedure for sorting a list. Indeed, the point of calling such a procedure would be to cause changes in the list.

As an example, let us suppose that the procedure Demo was defined as

procedure Demo (Formal)
    assign Formal **the value** Formal + 1;

Moreover, suppose that the variable Actual was assigned the value 5 and we called Demo with the statement

Demo (Actual)

(where we have used a syntax more common to programming languages than our pseudocode form "apply Demo to Actual"). Then, if parameters were passed by value, the change to Formal in the procedure would not be reflected in the variable Actual (Figure 5.10). But, if parameters were passed by reference, the value of Actual would be incremented by one (Figure 5.11).

FIGURE 5.10

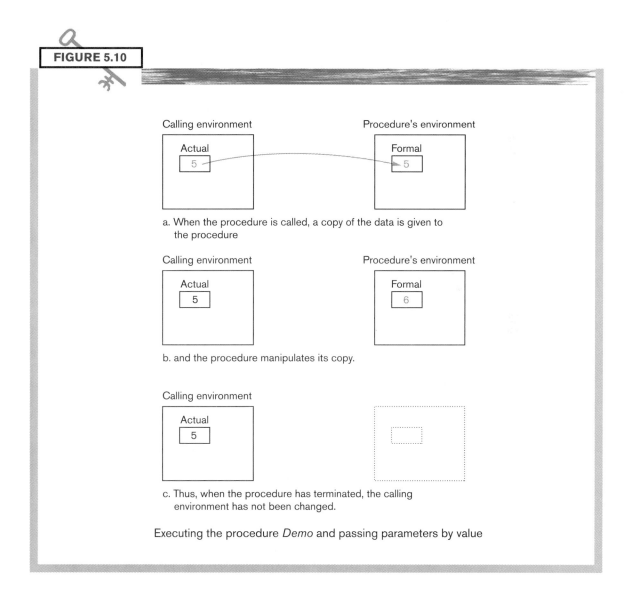

Calling environment   Procedure's environment

Actual   Formal
5   5

a. When the procedure is called, a copy of the data is given to the procedure

Calling environment   Procedure's environment

Actual   Formal
5   6

b. and the procedure manipulates its copy.

Calling environment

Actual
5

c. Thus, when the procedure has terminated, the calling environment has not been changed.

Executing the procedure *Demo* and passing parameters by value

FIGURE 5.11

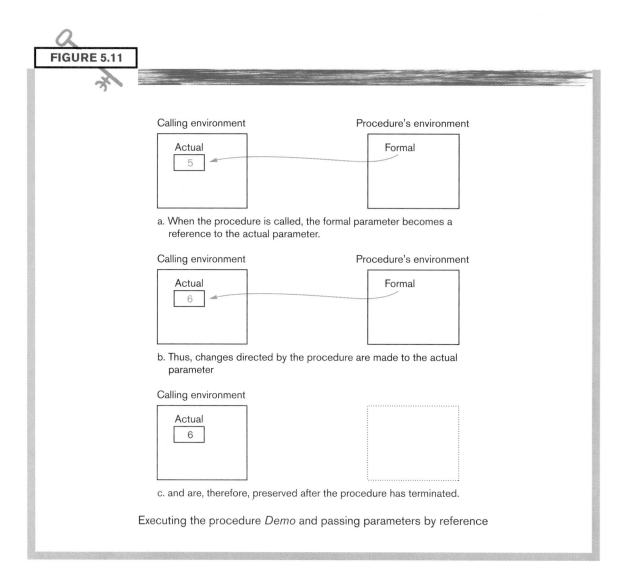

a. When the procedure is called, the formal parameter becomes a reference to the actual parameter.

b. Thus, changes directed by the procedure are made to the actual parameter

c. and are, therefore, preserved after the procedure has terminated.

Executing the procedure *Demo* and passing parameters by reference

Different programming languages provide different parameter-passing techniques, but in all cases the use of parameters allows a procedure to be written in a generic sense and applied to specific data at the appropriate time.

Functions

The purpose of a program unit is often to perform an action and/or to produce a value. When the emphasis is on producing a value, the program unit may be implemented as a function. Here the term **function** refers to a program unit similar to a procedure except that a value is transferred back to the calling program as "the value of the function" rather than via the parameter list. That is, the value is associated with the function's name in much the same way as a value is associated with a variable. The difference is in the effort required to obtain the value. In the case of a reference to a variable, the associated value is usually obtained from main memory; in the case of a function, the value is obtained by executing the instructions within the function.

As an example, if Total is a variable that has been assigned the total cost of an item (price plus purchase tax), then the cost of two such items could be computed by the expression

```
2 * Total
```

In contrast, if TotalCost is a function that computes the cost of an item based on the item's price and the sales tax rate, then the cost of two items could be computed by the expression

```
2 * TotalCost(Price, TaxRate)
```

In the first case, the value associated with Total would be retrieved from memory and multiplied by 2. In the second case, the function TotalCost would be executed with the input values Price and TaxRate, and the value produced would be multiplied by 2.

Input/Output Statements

Procedures and functions provide a means of expanding the features of a programming language. If the language does not provide a particular operation as a primitive, one can write a procedure or function to perform that task and then call upon that program unit when the operation is required. This is the manner in which most languages implement I/O operations except that the procedures and functions being called are ultimately routines within the machine's operating system.

As an example, to retrieve a value from the keyboard and assign it as the value of a variable named Value, a Pascal programmer writes

```
readln (Value);
```

and to write the value on the monitor,

```
writeln (Value);
```

Note that the syntax is that of calling a procedure with a parameter list.

In a similar manner, a C programmer could use the functions scanf and printf for performing input and output. These functions use parameters for communicating both the data to be transferred and the organization of that data in its printed form. The result is known as formatted input and output. For example, a C programmer writes

```
printf("%d %d\n", Value1, Value2);
```

to cause the values of the variables `Value1`, and `Value2` to be printed in decimal notation on a single line. The string in quotation marks indicates the data's format. Each `%d` indicates a position that is to be filled by a value in decimal notation. The values are supplied by the remaining parameters. The pattern `\n` indicates that a new line should be started after these values have been printed. Assuming the values of `Age1` and `Age2` are 16 and 25, respectively, the statement

```
printf("The ages are %d and %d.\n", Age1, Age2);
```

causes the message

The ages are 16 and 25.

to appear on the monitor.

Being object-oriented languages, C++ and Java approach I/O operations as transferring data to and from objects. In particular, C++ provides ready-made objects known as `cin` and `cout` to represent the standard input device (probably the keyboard) and output device (probably the monitor), respectively. Items to be retrieved from the keyboard or displayed on the monitor are transferred to and from these objects in the form of messages. For example, a value could be retrieved from the keyboard and assigned to the variable `Value` with the statement

```
cin >> Value;
```

and to have the value of the variable `Value` displayed on the monitor screen, we would send the value to the monitor with the statement

```
cout << Value;
```

QUESTIONS/EXERCISES

1. What is the difference between a global variable and a local variable?
2. What is the difference between a procedure and a function?
3. Why do many programming languages implement I/O operations as if they were calls to procedures?
4. What is the difference between a formal parameter and an actual parameter?

5.4 Language Implementation

In this section we investigate the process of converting a program written in a high-level language into a machine-executable form.

The Translation Process

The process of converting a program from one language to another is called **translation.** The program in its original form is the **source program;** the translated version is the **object program.** The translation process consists of three activities—lexical analysis, parsing, and code generation—that are performed by units in the translator known as the **lexical analyzer, parser,** and **code generator** (Figure 5.12).

Lexical analysis is the process of recognizing which strings of symbols from the source program represent a single entity. For example, the three symbols 153 should not be interpreted as a 1 followed by a 5 followed by a 3 but should be recognized as representing a single numeric value. Likewise, a word appearing in the program, although composed of individual symbols, should be interpreted as a single unit. Most humans perform lexical analysis with little conscious effort. When asked to read aloud, we pronounce words rather than individual characters.

FIGURE 5.12

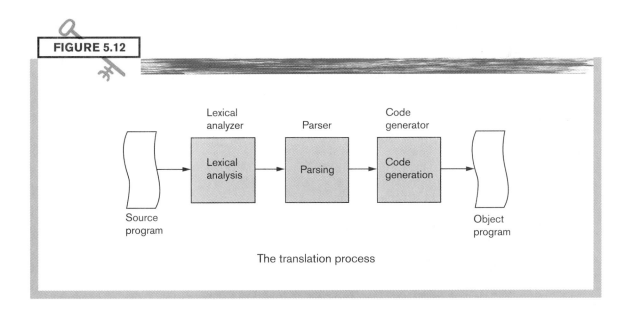

The translation process

Thus, the lexical analyzer reads the source program symbol by symbol, identifying which groups of symbols represent single units, classifying those units according to whether they are numeric values, words, arithmetic operators, and so on. As each unit is classified, the lexical analyzer generates a bit pattern known as a **token** to represent the unit and hands the token to the parser. During this process, the lexical analyzer skips over all comment statements.

Thus the parser views the program in terms of lexical units (tokens) rather than individual symbols. It is the parser's job to group these units into statements. Indeed, **parsing** is the process of identifying the grammatical structure of the program and recognizing the role of each component. It is the technicalities of parsing that cause one to hesitate when reading the sentence

The man the horse that lost the race threw was not hurt.

To simplify the parsing process, early programming languages insisted that each program statement be positioned in a particular manner on the printed page. Such languages were known as **fixed-format languages.** Today, most programming languages

IMPLEMENTATION OF JAVA

In the case of an animated Web page, the software that controls the animation is transferred across the Internet along with the page. If this software is supplied in source program form, additional delays will result when viewing the page because the software will have to be translated into the proper machine language. However, supplying the software in machine-language form would mean that a different version of the page would have to be available for each machine design.

Sun Microsystems has resolved this problem by designing a universal "machine language" called *bytecode* into which Java source programs can be translated. Although bytecode is not really a machine language, it can be executed quickly by any machine by means of an appropriate interpreter. Such interpreters are becoming a standard part of today's browser software. Thus, if the software for controlling a Web page is written in Java and translated into bytecode, then this bytecode version can be transmitted to the browsers viewing the Web page to provide efficient animation.

are **free-format languages,** meaning that the positioning of statements is not critical. Their advantage lies in a programmer's ability to organize the written program in a way that enhances readability from a human's point of view. In these cases it is common to use indentation to help a reader grasp the structure of a statement. Rather than writing

> **if** Cost < Cash on hand **then** pay with cash **else** use credit card

a programmer might write

> **if** Cost < Cash on hand
>   **then** pay with cash
>   **else** use credit card

For a machine to parse a program written in a free-format language, the syntax of the language must be designed so that the structure of a program can be identified regardless of the spacing used in the source program. To this end, most free-format languages use punctuation marks such as semicolons to mark the end of a statement, as well as **key words** such as if, then, and else to mark the beginning of individual phrases. These key words are often **reserved words,** meaning that they cannot be used by the programmer for other purposes within the program.

The parsing process is based on a set of syntax rules that define the syntax of the programming language. One way of expressing these rules is by means of **syntax diagrams,** which are pictorial representations of a program's grammatical structure. Figure 5.13 shows a syntax diagram of the if-then-else statement from our pseudocode in Chapter 4. This diagram indicates that an if-then-else structure begins with the word if, followed by a Boolean expression, followed by the word then, followed by a statement. This combination may or may not be followed by the word else and a statement. Notice that terms that actually appear in an if-then-else statement are enclosed in ovals, whereas terms that require further description, such as Boolean expression and Statement, are enclosed in rectangles. Terms that require further description (those in rectangles) are called **nonterminals;** terms that appear in ovals are called **terminals.** In a complete description of a language's syntax the nonterminals are described by additional diagrams.

As a more complete example, Figure 5.14 presents a set of syntax diagrams that describes the syntax of a structure called Expression, which is intended to be the structure of simple arithmetic expressions. The first diagram describes an Expression as consisting of a Term that may or may not be followed by a + or − symbol followed by another Expression. The second diagram describes a Term as consisting of a single x, y or z, or else a Term followed by a * or / symbol, followed by another Expression.

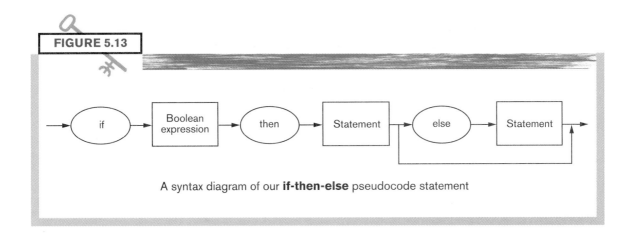

FIGURE 5.13

A syntax diagram of our **if-then-else** pseudocode statement

FIGURE 5.14

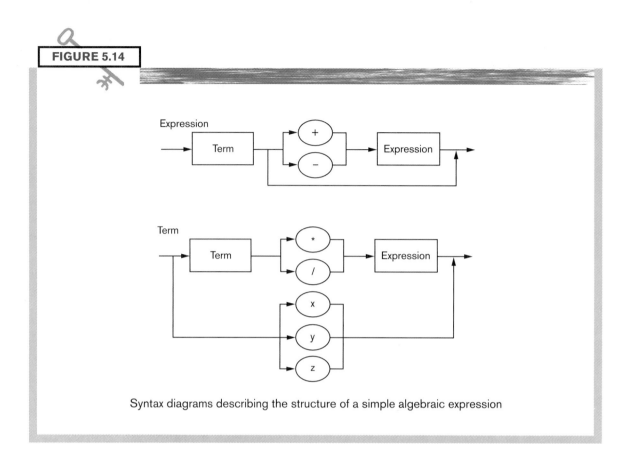

Syntax diagrams describing the structure of a simple algebraic expression

The manner in which a particular string conforms to a set of syntax diagrams can be represented in a pictorial form by a **parse tree,** as demonstrated in Figure 5.15 that presents a parse tree for the string

x + y * z

based on the set of diagrams in Figure 5.14. Note that the tree starts at the top with the nonterminal Expression and at each level shows how the nonterminals at that level are decomposed until the symbols in the string itself are obtained.

The process of parsing a program is essentially that of constructing a parse tree for the source program. Indeed, a parse tree represents the parser's understanding of the program's grammatical composition. For this reason the syntax rules describing a program's grammatical structure must not allow two distinct parse trees for one string, since this would lead to ambiguities within the parser. Such flaws can be quite subtle. Indeed, the rule in Figure 5.13 contains such a flaw. It allows both the parse trees in Figure 5.16 for the single statement

if B1 **then if** B2 **then** S1 **else** S2

FIGURE 5.15

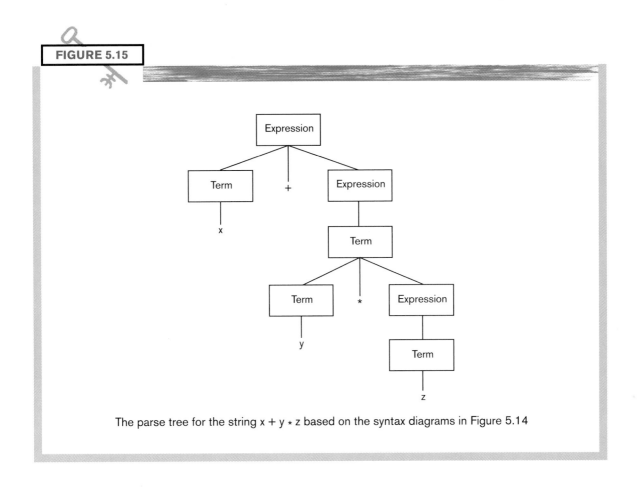

The parse tree for the string x + y * z based on the syntax diagrams in Figure 5.14

Note that these interpretations are significantly different. The first implies that statement S2 is to execute if B1 is false; the second implies that S2 is to execute only if B1 is true and B2 is false.

The syntax definitions of formal programming languages are designed to avoid such ambiguities. In our pseudocode we avoid such problems by using parentheses. In particular, we might write

if B1
   then (**if** B2 **then** S1)
   else S2

and

if B1
   then (**if** B2 **then** S1
         else S2)

to distinguish between the two possible interpretations.

FIGURE 5.16

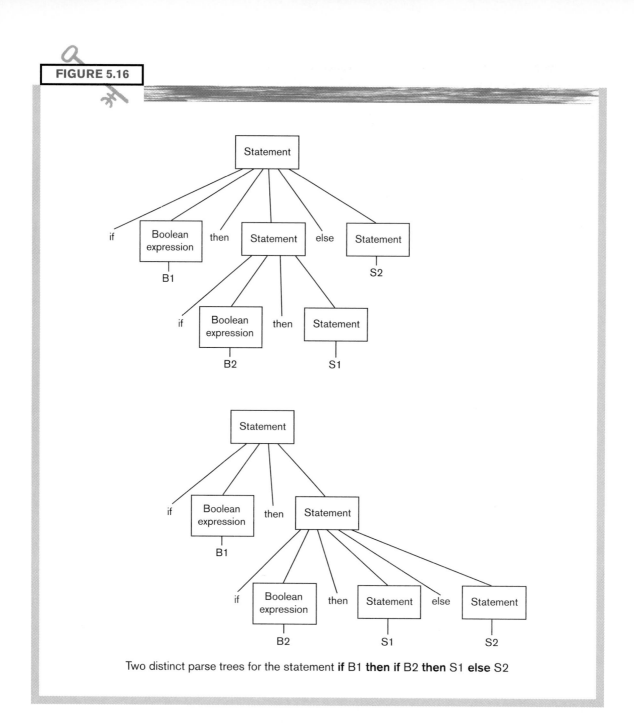

Two distinct parse trees for the statement **if** B1 **then if** B2 **then** S1 **else** S2

As a parser analyzes the declarative statements in a program, it records the information in these statements in a table called the **symbol table.** Thus the symbol table contains such information as which variables have been declared and what data types and data structures are associated with those variables. The parser then relies on this information when analyzing imperative statements such as

assign Total **the value** Price + Tax;

Indeed, to determine the meaning of the symbol +, the parser must know the data type associated with Price and Tax. If Price is of type real and Tax is of type character, then adding Price and Tax makes little sense and should be reported as an error. If Price and Tax are both of type integer, then the parser will request that the code generator build a machine-language instruction using the machine's integer addition op-code; if both are of type real, the parser will request that floating-point addition op-code be used.

The preceding program statement is also meaningful when the data types involved are not the same. For instance, if Price is integer and Tax is real, the concept of addition is still applicable. In this case the parser may choose to have the code generator build the instructions to convert one value to the other type and then perform the addition. Such implicit conversion between types is called **coercion.**

Coercion is frowned upon by many language designers. They argue that the need for coercion usually indicates a flaw in the program's design and therefore should not be accommodated by the parser. The result is that most modern languages are **strongly typed,** which means that all activities requested by a program must involve data of agreeable types without coercion. Parsers for these languages report all type conflicts as errors.

The final activity in the translation process is **code generation,** the process of constructing the machine-language instructions to simulate the statements recognized by the parser. This process involves numerous issues, one being that of producing efficient code. For example, consider the task of translating the two-statement sequence

assign x **the value** y + z;
assign w **the value** x + z;

These statements could be translated as individual statements. Such a single-statement approach, however, would not produce an efficient product. The code generator should recognize that once the first statement has been executed, the values of x and z will already be in the CPU's general-purpose registers and therefore should not be loaded from memory before executing the second statement. Implementing insights such as this is called **code optimization** and is an important task of the code generator.

The steps of lexical analysis, parsing, and code generation are not carried out in a strict sequential order. Instead, these activities are intertwined. The lexical analyzer begins by reading characters from the source program and identifying the first token. It hands this token to the parser. Each time the parser receives a token from the lexical analyzer, it analyzes the grammatical structure being read. At this point it may request another token from the lexical analyzer or, if the parser recognizes that a complete phrase or statement has been read, it calls on the code generator to produce the proper machine instructions. Each such request causes the code generator to build machine instructions that are added to the object program. In turn, the task of translating a program from one language to another conforms naturally to the object-oriented paradigm. The source program, lexical analyzer, parser, code generator, and object program are objects that interact by sending messages back and forth as each object goes about performing its task (Figure 5.17).

Linking and Loading

The object program produced by the translation process, although expressed in machine language, is rarely in a form that can be executed directly by the machine. One reason is that most programming environments allow the modules of a program to be developed and translated as individual units at different times (which supports the modular construction of software). Thus the object program produced from a single translation process is often only one of several pieces of a complete program, each piece of which requests services from the others in order to accomplish the task of the entire system. Even when a complete program is developed and translated as a single unit, its object program is rarely prepared to stand alone at execution time because it most likely contains

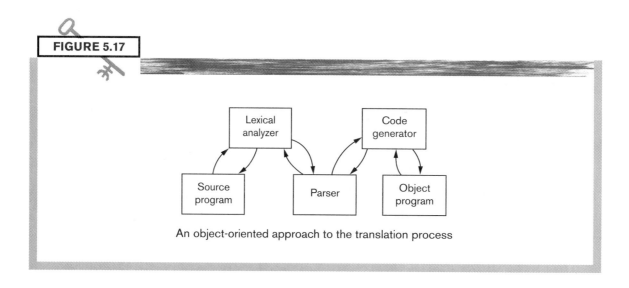

FIGURE 5.17

An object-oriented approach to the translation process

requests for services from utility software available through the operating system or from the operating system itself. Thus an object program is actually a machine-language program containing several loose ends that must be connected to other object programs before an executable program is obtained.

The task of making these connections is performed by a program called a **linker.** Its job is to link several object programs (the result of previous and separate translations), operating system routines, and other utility software to produce a complete, executable program (sometimes called a **load module**) that is in turn stored as a file in the machine's mass storage system.

Finally, to execute a translated program, the load module must be placed in memory by a program called a **loader,** which is usually part of the operating system's scheduler (Section 3.3). The significance of this step is most pronounced in multitasking systems. There, since a program must share memory with the other processes being executed and this process pool varies from one execution to the next, the exact memory area available to the program is not known until it is time to execute it. In this setting, the task of the loader is to place the program in the memory area identified by the operating system and make any last-minute (last-microsecond) adjustments that might be needed once the exact memory location of the program is known. (A jump instruction in the program must jump to the correct address within the program.) The desire to minimize these final adjustments by the loader has encouraged the development of techniques by which explicit references to memory addresses within a program can be avoided, resulting in program units (called relocatable modules) that, without modification, execute correctly regardless of where they are placed in memory.

In summary, the complete task of preparing a high-level-language program for execution consists of the three-step sequence of translate, link, and load, as represented in Figure 5.18. Once the translate and link steps have been completed, the program can be repeatedly loaded and executed without returning to the source version. If, however, a change is necessary to the program, it is

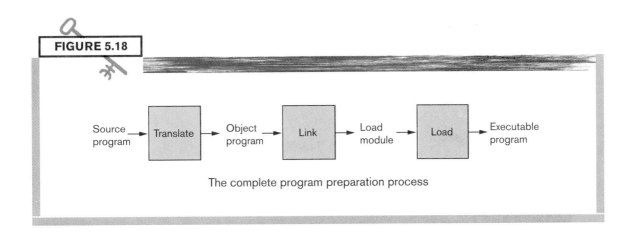

FIGURE 5.18

Source program → Translate → Object program → Link → Load module → Load → Executable program

The complete program preparation process

made to the source program, and then the modified source program is translated and linked to produce a new load module containing the change.

Software Development Packages

The current trend is to group a translator along with other software units used in the software development process into a package that functions as one integrated software system. Such a system would be classified as application software in the classification scheme of Section 3.2. By using this application package, a programmer gains ready access to an editor for writing programs, a translator for converting the programs into machine language, and a variety of debugging tools that allow the programmer to trace the execution of a malfunctioning program to discover where it goes astray.

The advantages of using such an integrated system are numerous. Perhaps the most obvious is that a programmer can move back and forth between the editor and debugging tools with ease, as changes to the program are made and tested. Moreover, many software development packages allow related program units that are under development to be linked in such a way that access to related units is simplified. Some packages maintain records regarding which program units within a group of related units have been altered since the last benchmark was made. Such capabilities are quite advantageous in the development of large software systems in which many interrelated units are developed by different programmers.

On a smaller scale, the editors in software development packages are often customized to the programming language being used. For example, an editor in a software development package will usually provide line indentation that is the de facto standard for the target language and in some cases may recognize and automatically complete key words after the programmer has typed only the first few characters.

Many software development packages use graphical interfaces to allow programmers to construct programs from prewritten blocks that are represented as icons on the screen. The selected blocks can then be customized by means of an editor. Such packages reflect the overall trend toward constructing programs from large, prefabricated blocks rather than writing them instruction by instruction.

QUESTIONS/EXERCISES

1. Describe the three major steps in the translation process.
2. What is a symbol table?
3. Draw the parse tree for the expression

   x * y + x + z

   based on the syntax diagrams in Figure 5.14.

4. Describe the strings that conform to the structure Chacha according to the following syntax diagrams.

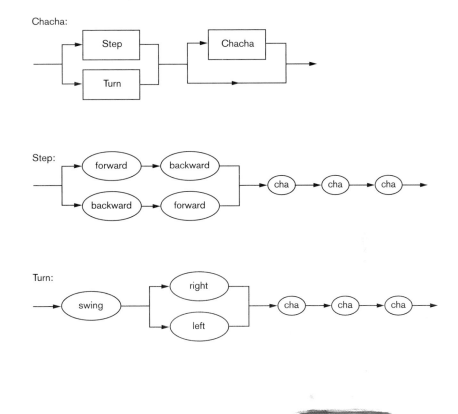

5.5 Object-Oriented Programming

In Section 5.1 we saw that the object-oriented paradigm entails the development of active program units called objects, each of which contains procedures describing how that object should respond to various stimuli. These internal procedures are called **methods** (or **member functions** in the C++ vernacular). The object-oriented approach to a problem is to identify the objects involved and describe them and their associated methods as self-contained units. In turn, object-oriented programming languages provide statements for expressing these ideas. We will introduce some of these in this section.

Let us approach this section in the context of developing a program that simulates the activities of small businesses, where a "small business" is considered to be an individually owned business with no more than 25 employees. Our goal might be to use the program to investigate the consequences that various economic changes might have on these businesses. Hence, we want a program that will simulate the existence of several of these businesses and monitor how they interact with each other and the rest of their environment. Using an object-oriented programming language, each business would be constructed as an object with internal methods that dictate how that business responds to interactions with its outside world.

In C++ and Java, we could use a statement of the form

```
SmallBusiness BusinessX;
```

to declare that the name `BusinessX` will be used to refer to an object of "type" `SmallBusiness`. Note that this is quite similar to the statement

```
int Cost;
```

which is used in the C programming language to declare that `Cost` is to be a variable of type integer. Although similar in many respects, these statements have several important distinctions. One is that the "type" of an object is called a class. That is, a **class** is the description of the structure of an object. In a sense, a class is a template that is used to construct objects. Another distinction between these statements is that the integer type is predefined within the programming language, but the class `SmallBusiness` is a "type" that must be described elsewhere in the program.

For the purpose of describing classes most object-oriented programming languages provide statements of the form

```
class SmallBusiness
    {
     .
     .
     .
    }
```

The first line of this statement indicates that the block of instructions within the braces defines the class referred to as `SmallBusiness`. It is within the braces that the various methods describing how an object of "type" `SmallBusiness` is to respond to various stimuli. These methods are described in a form reminiscent of procedures and functions.

In summary, in our simulation program we could use a class statement to define the class `SmallBusiness` and then use declaration statements similar to those above to declare `BusinessX`, `BusinessY`, and `BusinessZ` to be references to objects of "type" `SmallBusiness`.

Unfortunately, many of the small businesses involved in our simulation will have different properties. A mail-order business will need to respond to orders and replenish its stock, whereas a small consulting business will have to interact with its clients in a different manner. But, there are still many similarities among the businesses. For example, they all must deal with the same tax laws, process payroll, and replenish office supplies.

To simplify the description of objects with similar yet different characteristics, most object-oriented languages allow one class to encompass the properties of another through a system known as **inheritance.** As an example, suppose we were using Java to develop our simulation program. We could first use the class statement described above to define a class called `SmallBusiness` that encompassed those methods that are common to all the small businesses in the program. Then, we could use the statement

```
class MailOrderBusiness extends SmallBusiness
    {
        .
        .
        .
    }
```

to describe another class called `MailOrderBusiness`. Here the extends clause indicates that this class is to inherit the features of the class `SmallBusiness` as well as containing those features appearing within the braces. In a similar manner we could declare another class called `ConsultingBusiness` that inherited the properties of `SmallBusiness` but also contained those properties that are unique to the consulting business. Once these classes were defined, we could use the statement

```
MailOrderBusiness BusinessX;
```

to declare that `BusinessX` was to refer to a small mail-order business and the statement

```
ConsultingBusiness BusinessY;
```

to declare that `BusinessY` was to refer to a small consulting business.

The existence of a variety of objects with similar yet different characteristics leads to a phenomenon reminiscent of overloading, which we met in Section 5.2. (Recall that overloading referred to the use of a single symbol, such as +, for representing different operations depending on the type of its operands.) Suppose that an object-oriented graphics package consists of a variety of objects, each representing a shape (circle, rectangle, triangle, and so on). A particular image consists of a collection of these objects. Each object knows its size, location, and color as well as how to respond to messages telling it, for example, to move to a new location or to draw itself on the monitor screen. To draw an image, we merely send a "draw yourself" message to each object in the image. However, the routine used to draw an object varies according to the shape of the object—drawing a square is not the same process as drawing a circle. This customized interpretation of a message is known as **polymorphism;** the message is said to be polymorphic.

Another characteristic associated with object-oriented programming is **encapsulation,** which refers to restricting access to an object's internal properties. To say that certain features of an object are encapsulated means that only the object itself is able to access them. Features that are encapsulated are said to be private. Features that are accessible from outside the object are said to be public. For example, consider an object in our small business simulation program of "type" `MailOrderBusiness`. It would most likely contain a method describing how such an object should respond to the placement of an order. Other objects will need to initiate this method when they place an order. Thus access to this method should be public. However, the details of how the mail-order business fills the order should be accessible only within the object, which means that these details should be private. Most object-oriented programming languages allow a programmer to specify which parts of an object are to be public and which are to be private as a part of the class description. For example, a description of the class `MailOrderBusiness` written in Java might appear as

```
class MailOrderBusiness extends SmallBusiness
    {
    public ...
    private ...
    private ...
    public ...
    }
```

Here the key words public and private are used at the beginning of each component to indicate its accessibility.

QUESTIONS/EXERCISES

1. What is the difference between an object and a class?
2. Suppose the classes `PartTimeEmployee` and `FullTimeEmployee` inherited the properties of the class `Employee`. What are some features that you might expect to find in each class?
3. What is encapsulation?

5.6 Programming Concurrent Activities

Suppose we were asked to design a program to produce animation for an action computer game involving a stampeding herd of wildebeests, a cheering army of ants, or perhaps multiple attacking enemy spaceships. One approach would be to design a single program that would control the entire animation screen. Such a program would be charged with drawing each of the wildebeests, which (if the animation is to appear realistic) would mean that the program would have to keep up with the individual characteristics of 100 animals. An alternate approach would be to design a program to control the animation of a single wildebeest whose characteristics are determined by parameters assigned at the beginning of the program's execution. Then, the animation could be constructed by creating 100 activations of this program, each with its own set of parameters. By executing these activations simultaneously, we could obtain the illusion of 100 individual wildebeests stampeding across the screen at the same time. (Although conceptually accurate, executing as many as 100 activations of such a program would exceed the capabilities of today's desktop computer. However, five activations of attacking spaceships would pose no problem and, in fact, is done quite often.)

Such simultaneous execution of multiple activations is called **parallel processing** or **concurrent processing.** True parallel processing requires multiple CPUs, one to execute each activation. When only one CPU is available, the illusion of parallel processing is often obtained by allowing the activations to share the time of the single processor, as discussed in Chapter 3.

Programming languages for expressing programs involving parallel processing were originally designed for use in developing operating systems. However, as our introductory examples show, many modern computer applications are more easily solved in the context of parallel processing than in the more traditional context involving a single activation of a program. In turn, newer programming languages provide syntax for expressing the semantic structures involved in parallel computations. The design of such a language requires the identification of these semantic structures and the development of a syntax for representing them.

Each programming language tends to approach the parallel processing paradigm from its own point of view, resulting in different terminology. For example, what we have informally referred to as an activation is called a task in the Ada vernacular and a thread in Java. That is, in an Ada program, simultaneous actions are performed by creating multiple *tasks,* whereas in Java one creates multiple *threads.* In either case, the result is that multiple activities are generated and executed in much the same way as processes under the control of a multitasking operating system. Thus we will adopt the policy of referring to an activation, task, or thread as a process.

MOTION PICTURE ANIMATION

Although it would be incorrect to identify a single motion picture as the beginning of modern animation, many might consider *Star Wars* (produced by Lucasfilm 1977) as representing the beginning of the recent surge in motion picture computerized animation. Today, the multiple, hand-drawn frames that were required to produce Walt Disney's classics such as *Sleeping Beauty* and *Fantasia* have been replaced by computerized animation techniques that challenge the capabilities of modern multiprocessing computer architectures. Moviegoers will recognize that the examples introducing Section 5.6 (stampeding wildebeests and cheering armies of ants) are not fictitious. They are examples from actual motion pictures that drew heavily on the capabilities of computer technology (although not necessarily in the one-wildebeest-per-process format presented in the text since, unlike computer games, animation for motion pictures can be developed prior to performance). You might want to follow the links from the Web sites of motion picture producers such as http://www.lucasfilm.com http://www.disney.go.com, http://www.pixar.com and http://www.pdi.com. In particular, you might enjoy http://www.antz.com and http://www.dreamworksgames.com

Perhaps the most basic action that must be expressed in a program involving parallel processing is that of creating new processes. If we want 100 activations of the wildebeest program to be executed at the same time, we need a syntax for saying so. Such spawning of new processes is usually handled in a manner similar to that of requesting the execution of a traditional procedure. The difference is that, in the traditional setting, the program unit that requests the activation of a procedure does not progress any further until the requested procedure terminates, whereas in the parallel context the requesting program unit continues with its remaining statements while the requested procedure performs its task. Thus, to create 100 wildebeests running across the screen, we would write a main program that simply generates 100 activations of the wildebeest program, each provided with the parameters describing the distinguishing characteristics of that wildebeest.

A more complex issue associated with parallel processing involves handling communication between processes. For instance, in our wildebeest example, the processes representing the different wildebeests would need to communicate their locations among themselves in order to coordinate their activities. In the case of an action game, a process controlling a missile must communicate with the processes controlling the other objects on the screen to determine if any of those other objects should explode. In other cases one process may need to wait until another reaches a certain point in its computation, or one process may need to stop another one until the first has accomplished a particular task.

Such communication needs have long been a topic of study among computer scientists, and many of the newer programming languages reflect the various approaches to the interprocess communication problem. As an example, let us consider the communication problems encountered when two processes manipulate the same data. (This example is presented in more detail in the optional Section 3.4.) In particular, if each of two processes that are executing concurrently need to add the value three to a common item of data, a method is needed to ensure that one process is allowed to complete its transaction before the other is allowed to perform its task. Otherwise they could both start their individual computations with the same initial value, which would mean that the final result would be incremented by only three rather than six. Data that can be accessed by only one process at a time is said to have mutually exclusive access.

One approach to solving this problem is to write the programs describing the processes involved in such a way that a process accessing the shared data restricts other process from accessing the data until such access is safe. (This is the approach described in the optional Section 3.4, where we identified the portion of a process that accesses shared data as a **critical region.**) Experience has shown that this approach has the drawback of distributing the task of ensuring mutual exclusion throughout various parts of the program—a mistake in the description of any process accessing the shared data will corrupt the entire system. Thus many argue that a better solution is to embody the data item with the ability to control access to itself. Such a control mechanism is often called a

monitor. In short, instead of relying on the processes that access the data to guard against multiple access, the data item is assigned this responsibility. The result is that control of access is concentrated at a single point in the program rather than dispersed among many program segments.[1]

We see then that the design of programming languages for parallel processing involves developing ways to express such things as the creation of processes, the pausing and restarting of processes, the identification of critical regions, and the composition of monitors.

In closing, we should note that although animation provides an interesting setting in which to explore the issues of parallel computing, it is only one of many fields that benefit from parallel processing techniques. Other areas include weather forecasting, air traffic control, simulation of complex systems (from nuclear reactions to pedestrian traffic), computer networking, and database maintenance.

QUESTIONS/EXERCISES

1. What are some properties that would be found in a programming language for concurrent processing that would not be found in a more traditional language?
2. Describe two methods for insuring mutually exclusive access to data.

5.7 Declarative Programming

Earlier we claimed that formal logic provides a general problem-solving algorithm around which a declarative programming system can be constructed. In this section we investigate this claim by first introducing the rudiments of the algorithm and then taking a brief look at a declarative programming language based on it.

Logical Deduction

Suppose we know that either Kermit is on stage or Kermit is sick, and we are told that Kermit is not on stage. We could then conclude that Kermit must be sick. This is an example of a deductive-reasoning principle called **resolution.**

---

[1]This problem has a natural solution in object-oriented programming languages where the processes that access data are collected in the same object as the data. In particular, you may wish to explore the use of the synchronize command in Java.

To better understand this principle, let us first agree to represent simple statements by single letters and the negation of a statement by the symbol ¬. For instance, we might represent the statement "Kermit is a prince" by A and "Miss Piggy is an actress" by B. Then, the expression

A OR B

would mean "Kermit is a prince or Miss Piggy is an actress" and

B AND ¬ A

would mean "Miss Piggy is an actress and Kermit is not a prince." We will use an arrow to indicate "implies." For example, the expression

$A \rightarrow B$

means "If Kermit is a prince, then Miss Piggy is an actress."

In its general form, the resolution principle states that from two statements of the form

P OR Q

and

R OR ¬ Q

we can conclude the statement

P OR R

In this case, we say that the two original statements resolve to form the third statement, which we call the **resolvent.** It is important to observe that the resolvent is a logical consequence of the original statements. That is, if the original statements are true, the resolvent must also be true. (If Q is true, then R must be true; but if Q is false, then P must be true. Thus regardless of the truth or falseness of Q, either P or R must be true.)

We will represent the resolution of two statements pictorially as shown in Figure 5.19, where we write the original statements with lines projecting down to their resolvent. Note that resolution can be applied only to pairs of statements that appear in **clause form**—that is, statements whose elementary components are connected by the Boolean operation OR. Thus

P OR Q

is in clause form, whereas

$P \rightarrow Q$

is not. The fact that this potential problem poses no serious concern is a consequence of a theorem in mathematical logic that states that any statement expressed in the first-order predicate logic (a system for representing statements with extensive expressive powers) can be expressed in clause form. We will not

FIGURE 5.19

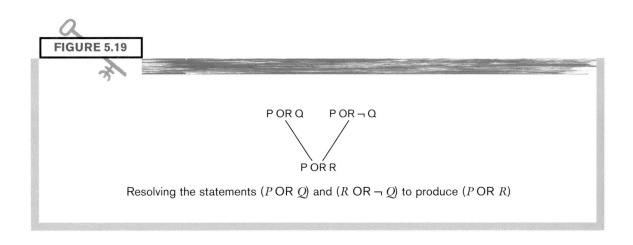

Resolving the statements (P OR Q) and (R OR $\neg Q$) to produce (P OR R)

pursue this important theorem here, but for future reference we observe that the statement

$$P \rightarrow Q$$

is equivalent to the clause form statement

$$Q \text{ OR } \neg P$$

A collection of statements is said to be **inconsistent** if it is impossible for all the statements to be true at the same time. In other words, an inconsistent collection of statements is a collection of statements that are self-contradictory. A simple example would be a statement of the form P combined with the statement $\neg P$. Logicians have shown that repeated resolution provides a systematic method of confirming the inconsistency of a set of self-contradictory clauses. The rule is that if repeated application of resolution produces the empty clause (the result of resolving a clause of the form P with a clause of the form $\neg P$), then the original collection of statements must be inconsistent. As an example, Figure 5.20 demonstrates that the collection of statements

$$P \text{ OR } Q \quad R \text{ OR } \neg Q \quad \neg R \quad \neg P$$

is inconsistent.

Suppose now that we want to confirm that a collection of statements implies the statement P. To imply the statement P is the same as contradicting the statement $\neg P$. Thus, to demonstrate that the original collection of statements implies P, all we need to do is apply resolution to the original statements and the statement $\neg P$ until an empty clause occurs. Upon obtaining an empty clause, we can conclude that statement $\neg P$ is inconsistent with the original statements, and thus the original statements must imply P.

FIGURE 5.20

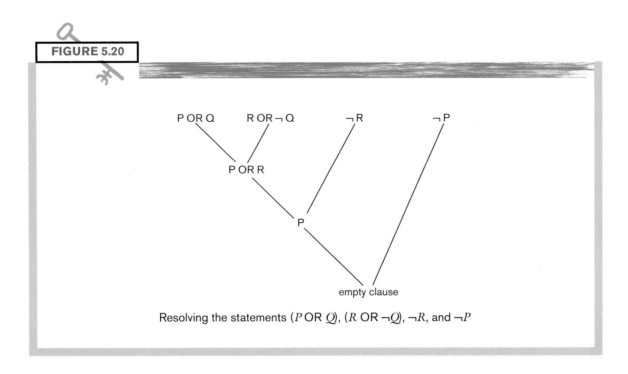

Resolving the statements (P OR Q), (R OR $\neg Q$), $\neg R$, and $\neg P$

One final point remains before we are ready to apply resolution in an actual programming environment. Suppose we have the two statements

(Mary is at X) $\rightarrow$ (Mary's lamb is at X)

where X represents any location and

Mary is at home

In clause form the two statements become

(Mary's lamb is at X) OR $\neg$(Mary is at X)

and

(Mary is at home)

which at first glance do not have components that can be resolved. On the other hand, the components (Mary is at home) and $\neg$(Mary is at X) are quite close to being opposites of each other. The problem is to recognize that Mary is at X, being a statement about locations in general, is a statement about home in particular. Thus a special case of the first statement is

(Mary's lamb is at home) OR $\neg$(Mary is at home)

which can be resolved with the statement

(Mary is at home)

to produce the statement

(Mary's lamb is at home)

The process of assigning values to variables (such as assigning the value *home* to X) so that resolution can be performed is called **unification.** It is this process that allows general statements to be applied to specific applications in a deduction system.

Prolog

The language Prolog (short for PROgramming in LOGic) is a declarative programming language whose underlying problem-solving algorithm is based on repeated resolution. A program in Prolog consists of a collection of initial statements upon which the underlying algorithm bases its deductive reasoning. The components from which these statements are constructed are called predicates. A predicate consists of a predicate identifier followed by a parenthetical statement listing the predicate's arguments. A single predicate represents a fact about its arguments, and its identifier is usually chosen to reflect this underlying semantics. Thus, if we want to express the fact that Bill is Mary's parent, we can use the predicate form

```
parent(bill, mary).
```

Note that the arguments in this predicate start with lowercase letters, even though they represent proper nouns. This is because Prolog distinguishes between constants and variables by insisting that constants begin with lowercase letters and variables begin with uppercase letters.

Statements in a Prolog program are either facts or rules, each of which is terminated by a period. A fact consists of a single predicate. For example, the fact that a turtle is faster than a snail could be represented by the Prolog statement

```
faster(turtle, snail).
```

and the fact that a rabbit is faster than a turtle could be represented by

```
faster(rabbit, turtle).
```

A Prolog rule is an "implies" statement. Instead of writing such a statement in the form X → Y, a Prolog programmer writes Y if X, except that the symbol :- is used in place of the word *if*. Thus the rule "X is faster than some Y and that Y is faster than Z implies that X is faster than Z" may be expressed by a logician as

```
(faster(X, Y) AND faster(Y, Z)) → faster(X, Z)
```

but would be expressed in Prolog as

```
faster(X, Z) :- faster(X, Y), faster(Y, Z).
```

The comma separating `faster(X, Y)` and `faster(Y, Z)` represents the conjunction AND. Such rules can be converted easily to clause form by the Prolog software.

Keep in mind that the Prolog system does not know the meaning of the predicates in a program; it simply manipulates the statements in a totally symbolic manner according to the resolution inference rule. Thus, it is up to the programmer to describe all the pertinent features of a predicate in terms of facts and rules. In this light, Prolog facts tend to be used to identify specific instances of a predicate, whereas rules are used to describe general principles. This is the approach followed by the preceding statements regarding the predicate `faster`. The two facts describe particular instances of "fasterness" while the rule describes a general property. Note that the fact that a rabbit is faster than a snail, though not explicitly stated, is a consequence of the two facts combined with the rule.

Most Prolog implementations are designed to be used interactively. In this context the task of a programmer is to develop the collection of facts and rules that constitute the set of initial statements to be used in the deductive system. Once this collection of statements is established, conjectures (called goals in Prolog terminology) can be proposed to the system by typing them at a computer's keyboard. When such a goal is presented to a Prolog system, the system applies resolution to try to confirm that the goal is a consequence of the initial statements. Based on our collection of statements describing the relationship `faster`, each of the goals

```
faster(turtle, snail).
faster(rabbit, turtle).
faster(rabbit, snail).
```

could be so confirmed because each is a logical consequence of the initial statements. The first two are identical to facts appearing in the initial statements, whereas the third requires a certain degree of deduction by the system.

More interesting examples are obtained if we provide goals whose arguments are variables rather than constants. In these cases Prolog tries to derive the goal from the initial statements while keeping track of the unifications required to do so. Then, if the goal is obtained, Prolog reports these unifications. For example, consider the goal

```
faster(W, snail).
```

In response to this, Prolog reports

```
faster(turtle, snail).
```

Indeed, this is a consequence of the initial statements and agrees with the goal via unification. Furthermore, if we asked Prolog to tell us more, it finds and reports the consequence

```
faster(rabbit, snail).
```

In contrast, we can ask Prolog to find instances of animals that are slower than a rabbit by proposing the goal

```
faster(rabbit, W).
```

In fact, if we started with the goal

```
faster(V, W).
```

Prolog ultimately reports all the `faster` relationships that can be derived from the initial statements. Thus a single Prolog program can be used to confirm that a particular animal is faster than another, to find those animals that are faster than a given animal, to find those animals that are slower than a given animal, or to find all faster relationships. This versatility is one of the features that has captured the imagination of computer scientists.

QUESTIONS/EXERCISES

1. Which of the statements R, S, T, U, and V are logical consequences of the collection of statements $(\neg R \text{ OR } T \text{ OR } S)$, $(\neg S \text{ OR } V)$, $(\neg V \text{ OR } R)$, $(U \text{ OR } \neg S)$, $(T \text{ OR } \neg U)$, and $(S \text{ OR } V)$?

2. Is the following collection of statements consistent? Explain your answer.

   $P \text{ OR } Q \text{ OR } R \qquad \neg R \text{ OR } Q \qquad R \text{ OR } \neg P \qquad \neg Q$

3. Suppose a Prolog program consisted of the statements

   ```
   thriftier(carol, john).
   thriftier(bill, sue).
   thriftier(sue, carol).
   thriftier(X,Z) :- thriftier(X,Y), thriftier(Y,Z).
   ```

   List the results that can be produced from each of the following goals:
   a. `thriftier(sue, V).`
   b. `thriftier(U, carol).`
   c. `thriftier(U,V).`

CHAPTER REVIEW PROBLEMS

(Asterisked problems are associated with optional sections.)

1. What does it mean to say that a programming language is machine independent?

2. Translate the following pseudocode program into the machine language described in Appendix C.

   assign x **the value** 0;
   while (x ≠ 3) **do**
     (**assign** x **the value** x + 1)

3. Translate the statement

   assign Halfway **the value** Length + Width

   into the machine language of Appendix C, assuming that Length, Width, and Halfway are all represented in floating-point notation.

4. Translate the high-level statement

   if (X equals 0)
     then assign Z **the value** Y + W
     else assign Z **the value** Y + X

   into the machine language of Appendix C, assuming that W, X, Y, and Z are all values represented in two's complement notation, each using one byte of memory.

5. Why was it necessary to identify the type of data associated with the variables in Problem 4 in order to translate the statements? Why do many high-level programming languages require the programmer to identify the type of each variable at the beginning of a program?

6. Name and describe four different programming paradigms.

7. Suppose the function f expects two numeric values as its parameters and returns the smaller of the two values as its output value. If w, x, y, and z represent numeric values, what is the result returned by f(f(w,x), f(y,z))?

8. Suppose f is a function that returns the result of reversing the string of symbols given as its input, and g is a function that returns the concatenation of the two strings given as its input. If x is the string *abcd*, what is returned by g(f(x),x)?

9. Suppose you are going to write an object-oriented program for maintaining your financial records. What data should be stored inside the object representing your checking account? To what messages should that object be able to respond? What are other objects that might be used in the program?

10. Summarize the distinction between a machine language and an assembly language.

11. Design an assembly language for the machine described in Appendix C.

12. John Programmer argues that the ability to declare constants within a program is not necessary because variables can be used instead. For example, our example of AirportAlt in Section 5.2 can be handled by declaring AirportAlt to be a variable and then assigning it the required variable at the beginning of the program. Why is this not as good as using a constant?

13. Summarize the distinction between declarative statements and imperative statements.

14. Explain the differences between a literal, a constant, and a variable.

15. What is operator precedence?

16. What is structured programming?

17. What is the difference between the meaning of the "equals" symbol in the statement

    ```
    if (X = 5) then ( ... )
    ```

    as opposed to the assignment statement

    ```
    X = 2 + Y
    ```

18. Draw a flowchart representing the structure expressed by the following C, C++, and Java statement.

```
for (x = 2; x < 8; ++x)
{ . . . }
```

19. Draw a flowchart representing the structure expressed by the following C, C++, and Java statement.

```
switch (suit)
  {case "clubs": bid(1);
   case "diamonds": bid(2);
   case "hearts": bid(3);
   case "spades": bid(4);
  }
```

20. If you are familiar with written music, analyze musical notation as a programming language. What are the control structures? What is the syntax for inserting comments? What music notation is similar to the for statements in Figure 5.8?

21. Rewrite the following program segment using a single case statement instead of nested if-then-else statements.

if (W = 5)
  then (**assign** Z **the value** 7)
  else (**if** (W = 6)
        then (**assign** Y **the value** 7)
        else (**if** (W = 7)
              then (**assign** X **the value** 7)
)
)

22. Summarize the following rat's-nest routine with a single if-then-else statement:

```
     if X > 5 then goto 80
     X = X + 1
     goto 90
  80 X = X + 2
  90 stop
```

23. Summarize the distinction between a translator and an interpreter.

24. Suppose the variable X in a program was declared to be of type integer. What error would occur when executing the program statement

assign X **the value** 2.5

25. What does it mean to say that a programming language is strongly typed?

26. Why would a large array probably not be passed to a procedure by value?

27. Suppose the procedure modify is defined by

procedure modify (Y)
assign Y **the value** 7;
print the value of Y.

If parameters are passed by value, what will be printed when the following program segment is executed? What if parameters are passed by reference?

assign X **the value** 5;
apply modify to X;
print the value of X;

28. Suppose the procedure modify is defined by

procedure modify (Y)
assign Y **the value** 9;
print the value of X;
print the value of Y.

Also suppose that X is a global variable. If parameters are passed by value, what will be printed when the following program segment is executed? What if parameters are passed by reference?

assign X **the value** 5;
apply modify to X;
print the value of X;

29. Sometimes an actual parameter is passed to a procedure by producing a duplicate for use by the procedure (as when the parameter is passed by value), but when the procedure is completed the value in the procedure's copy is transferred to the actual parameter before the calling procedure continues. In such cases the parameter is said to be passed by value-result. What would be printed by the program segment in Problem 28 if parameters were passed by value-result?

30. What ambiguity exists in the statement

assign X **the value** 3 + 2 * 5

31. Suppose a small company has five employees and is planning to increase the number to six. The following are excerpts from two equivalent programs used by the company that must be altered to reflect the change in the number of employees. Both programs are written in a Pascal-like language. Indicate what changes must be made to each program. What complications arise in the case of Program 1 that are avoided by the use of constants in Program 2?

Program 1

.

.

.

```
DailySalary := TotalSal/5;
AvgSalary := TotalSal/5;
DailySales := TotalSales/5;
AvgSales := TotalSales/5;
```

.

.

.

Program 2

.

.

.

```
const
  NumEmpl = 5;
  DaysWk = 5;
```

.

.

.

```
DailySalary := TotalSal/DaysWk;
AvgSalary := TotalSal/NumEmpl;
```

```
DailySales := TotalSales/DaysWk;
AvgSales := TotalSales/NumEmpl;
```

.

.

.

32. Draw a syntax diagram representing the structure of the while statement in the pseudocode of Chapter 4.

33. Design a set of syntax diagrams to describe the syntax of telephone numbers written in the form such as (444) 555–1234.

34. Design a set of syntax diagrams to describe simple English sentences.

35. Write a sentence describing the structure of a string as defined by the syntax diagram below. Then, draw the parse tree for the string *xxyxx*.

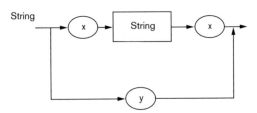

36. Add syntax diagrams to those in Question 4 of Section 5.4 to obtain a set of diagrams that defines the structure Dance to be either a Chacha or a Waltz, where a Waltz consists of one or more copies of the pattern

forward diagonal close

or

backward diagonal close

37. Draw a parse tree for the expression

x * y + y / x

based on the syntax diagrams in Figure 5.14.

38. What code optimization could be performed by a code generator when building the machine code representing the statement

    if (X = 5) then **(assign** Z **the value** X + 2)
        else **(assign** Z **the value** X + 4)

39. Simplify the following program segment

    assign Y **the value** 5;
    if (Y = 7)
        then **(assign** Z **the value** 8)
        else **(assign** Z **the value** 9)

40. Simplify the following program segment

    while (X not equal to 5) **do**
        (**assign** X **the value** 5)

*41. Draw a diagram (similar to Figure 5.20) representing the resolutions needed to show that the collection of statements (Q OR ¬R), (T OR R), ¬P, (P OR ¬T), and (P OR ¬Q) are inconsistent.

*42. Is the collection of statements ¬R, (T OR R), (P OR ¬Q), (Q OR ¬T), and (R OR ¬P) consistent? Explain your answer.

*43. What conclusions can Prolog find if faced with the goal

```
bigger(X, lassie).
```

and the initial statements

```
bigger(rex, lassie).
bigger(fido, rex).
bigger(spot, rex).
bigger(X,Z) :- bigger(X,Y),
               bigger (Y,Z).
```

*44. What conclusions can Prolog find if faced with the goal

```
eq(X,Y).
```

and the initial statements

```
grteq(a,b).
grteq(b,c).
grteq(c,a).
grteq(U,W) :- grteq(U,V),
              grteq(V,W).
eq(X,Y) :- grteq(X,Y),
           grteq(Y,X).
```

*45. What problem would be encountered if the following program segment was executed on a machine in which value are represented in the 8-bit floating-point format described in Section 1.7?

    assign X **the value** 0.01;
    while (X not equal to 1.00) **do**
        (print the value of X;
          assign X **the value** X + 0.01)

SOCIAL ISSUES

The following questions are provided to help you understand some of the ethical/social/legal issues associated with the field of computing as well as investigate your own beliefs and their foundations. The goal is not merely to answer these questions. You should also consider why you answered as you did and whether your justifications are consistent from one question to the next.

1. In general, copyright laws support ownership rights associated with the expression of an idea but not for the idea itself. As a result, a paragraph in a book is copyrightable but the ideas expressed in the paragraph are not. How should this right extend to source programs and the algorithms they express? To what extent should a person who knows the algorithms used in a commercial software package be allowed to write his or her own program expressing those same algorithms and market this version of the software?

2. Should a person who develops a new and useful programming language have a right to profit from the use of that language? If so, how can that right be protected? To what extent can a language be owned?

3. To what extent is a programmer who helps develop a violent computer game responsible for any consequences of that game? Should children's access to violent computer games be restricted? If so, how and by whom? What about other groups in society, such as convicted criminals?

4. To what extent should a computer professional be knowledgeable in the various programming paradigms? Some companies insist that all software developed in that company be written in the same, predetermined programming language. Does your answer to the original question change if the professional works for such a company?

5. With a deadline approaching, is it acceptable for a programmer to forgo documentation via comment statements to get a program running on time? (Beginning students are often surprised to learn how important documentation is considered among professional software developers.)

6. Much of the research in programming languages has been to develop languages that allow programmers to write programs that can be easily read and understood by humans. To what extent should a programmer be required to use such capabilities? That is, to what extent is it good enough for the program to perform correctly even though it is not well written from a human perspective?

7. Suppose an amateur programmer writes a program for his or her own use and in doing so is sloppy in the program's construction. The program does not use the programming language features that would make it more readable, it is not efficient, and it contains short cuts that take advantage of the particular situation in which the programmer intends to use the program. Over time the programmer gives copies of the program to friends who want to use it themselves, and these friends give it to their friends. To what extent is the programmer liable for problems that may occur?

ADDITIONAL READING

Aho, A. V., R. Sethi, and J. D. Ullman. *Compilers: Principles, Techniques, and Tools.* Reading, MA: Addison-Wesley, 1986.

Barnes, J. *Programming in Ada 95.* Reading, MA: Addison-Wesley, 1996.

Bergin, T. J., and R. G. Gibson. *History of Programming Languages.* New York: ACM Press, 1996.

Clocksin, W. F., and C. S. Mellish. *Programming in Prolog,* 3rd ed. New York: Springer-Verlag, 1987.

Fisher, C. N., and R. J. LeBlanc, Jr. *Crafting a Compiler with C.* Menlo Park, CA: Benjamin/Cummings, 1991.

Graham, P. *ANSI Common Lisp.* Englewood Cliffs, NJ: Prentice-Hall, 1996.

Jackson, J. R., and A. L. McClellan. *Java by Example.* Palo Alto, CA: Sun Microsystems, 1999.

Metcalf, M., and J. Reid. *Fortran 90 Explained.* Oxford, England: Oxford University Press, 1990.

Pohl, I., and A. Kelley. *A Book on C,* 2nd ed. Redwood City, CA: Benjamin/Cummings, 1990.

Pratt, T. W., and M. V. Zelkowitz. *Programming Languages, Design and Implementation,* 3rd ed. Englewood Cliffs, NJ: Prentice-Hall, 1996.

Savitch, W. *Problem Solving with C++.* Reading, MA: Addison-Wesley, 1996.

Sebesta, R. W. *Concepts of Programming Languages,* 4th ed. Reading, MA: Addison-Wesley, 1999.

c h a p t e r

SOFTWARE

ENGINEERING

s i x

6.1 The Software Engineering Discipline

6.2 The Software Life Cycle
The Cycle as a Whole
The Traditional Development Phase
Recent Trends

6.3 Modularity
Modular Implementation
Coupling
Cohesion

6.4 Design Methodologies
Top-Down Versus Bottom-Up
Tools of the Trade
Design Patterns

6.5 Testing

6.6 Documentation

6.7 Software Ownership and Liability

In this chapter we consider topics relating to the overall process of software development and maintenance. The topic is called *software engineering* because we consider software development to be an engineering process. However, we will see that software engineering has many characteristics that make it unique within the engineering discipline.

Our discussion concerns large software systems, the complete comprehension of which exceeds the short-term memory capabilities of the human mind. Examples include business inventory and accounting systems, distributed banking systems, environment/security control systems for office buildings, system software, and even computer games. The problems faced when developing such systems are more than enlarged versions of those problems faced when writing small programs. For instance, the development of such systems requires the effort of more than one person over an extended period of time during which the requirements of the proposed system may be altered and the personnel assigned to the project may change. Consequently, the subject of software engineering includes topics, such as personnel and project management, that are more readily associated with business management than computer science. In this chapter, however, we focus on topics readily related to computer science.

6.1 The Software Engineering Discipline

To appreciate the problems involved in software engineering, it is helpful to select any large complex device you want (an automobile, a multistory office building, or perhaps a cathedral) and imagine being asked to design it and then to supervise its construction. How can you estimate the cost in time, money, and other resources to complete the project? How can you divide the project into manageable pieces? How can you ensure that the pieces produced are compatible? How can those working on the various pieces communicate? How can you measure progress? How can you cope with the wide range of detail (the selection of the doorknobs, the design of the gargoyles, the availability of blue glass for the stained glass windows, the strength of the pillars, the design of the duct work for the heating system)? Questions of the same scope must be answered during the development of a large software system.

Since engineering is a well-established field, you might think that there is a wealth of previously developed engineering techniques that can be useful in answering such questions. This reasoning, however, overlooks the many distinctions between the properties of software and those of other fields of engineering.

One such distinction deals with the ability to construct systems from generic prefabricated components. Traditional fields of engineering have long benefited from the ability to use "off-the-shelf" components as building blocks when constructing complex devices. The designer of a new car does not have to design the engine, radio, air conditioner, and door locks. Instead, the designer uses previously designed versions of these components. In the context of software, however, previously designed components tend to be domain specific—that is, their internal design is dependent on a specific application. To reuse such a component would therefore require that it be redesigned. The result is that complex software systems have historically been built from scratch.

Another distinction between software engineering and traditional engineering deals with the role of tolerances. Traditional areas of engineering deal with the development of products that are acceptable as long as they perform their task within certain bounds. A washing machine that cycles through its wash–rinse–spin cycle within a 2 percent tolerance of the

ASSOCIATION FOR COMPUTING MACHINERY

The Association for Computing Machinery (ACM) was founded in 1947 as an international scientific and educational organization dedicated to advancing the arts, sciences, and applications of information technology. It is headquartered in New York and encompasses numerous special interest groups (SIGs) focusing on such topics as computer architecture, artificial intelligence, biomedical computing, computers and society, computer science education, computer graphics, hypertext/hypermedia, operating systems, programming languages, simulation and modeling, and software engineering. The ACM's Web site is at http://www.acm.org. Its Code of Ethics and Professional Conduct can be found at http://www.acm.org/constitution/code.html

desired time is acceptable. Software, in contrast, performs either correctly or incorrectly. An accounting system that is accurate only to within a 2 percent tolerance is not acceptable.

Still another distinction relates to the lack of quantitative systems, called **metrics,** for measuring the properties of software. The quality of a mechanical device is often measured in terms of the mean time between failures, which is a measurement of how well the device endures wear and tear. Software, in contrast, does not wear out, so this method of measuring quality does not carry over into software engineering.

The inability to measure software properties in a quantitative manner is one of the major reasons that software engineering has not yet found a rigorous footing in the same sense as mechanical and electrical engineering. Whereas these subjects are founded on the established science of physics, software engineering is still searching for its roots. Indeed, the state of software engineering today is similar to that of physics in the early seventeenth century before Isaac Newton and others discovered that properties such as mass, acceleration, and force could be measured and related to each other mathematically.

Thus research in software engineering is currently progressing on two levels: Some researchers, sometimes called practitioners, work toward developing techniques for immediate application, while others, called theoreticians, search for underlying principles and theories on which more stable techniques can someday be constructed. Being based on a subjective foundation, many methodologies developed and promoted by practitioners in the past have been replaced by other approaches that may themselves become obsolete with time. Meanwhile, progress by theoreticians continues to be evasive.

INSTITUTE OF ELECTRICAL AND ELECTRONICS ENGINEERS

The Institute of Electrical and Electronics Engineers (IEEE, pronounced "i-triple-e") was formed in 1963 as the result of merging the American Institute of Electrical Engineers (founded in 1884 by 25 electrical engineers, including Thomas Edison) and the Institute of Radio Engineers (founded in 1912). Headquartered in London, the IEEE is a worldwide organization of electrical, electronics, and manufacturing engineers. It encompasses 36 technical societies such as the Aerospace and Electronic Systems Society, the Lasers and Electro-Optics Society, the Robotics and Automation Society, the Vehicular Technology Society, and (most important for our study) the Computer Society. Among its activities, the IEEE is involved in the development of standards. In particular, it was IEEE's efforts that led to standardized floating-point formats.

You will find the IEEE's Web page at http://www.ieee.org, the IEEE Computer Society's Web page at http://www.computer.org, and the IEEE's Code of Ethics is http://www.ieee.org/about/whatis/code.html

The need for progress by both practitioners and theoreticians is enormous. Our society has become addicted to computer systems and their associated software. Our economy, health care, government, law enforcement, transportation, and defense depend on large software systems. Yet there continue to be major problems with the reliability of these systems. Software errors have caused such disasters and near disasters as the rising moon being interpreted as a nuclear attack, the loss of $5 million by the Bank of New York in only one day, the loss of the *Mariner 18* space probe, radiation overdoses that have killed and paralyzed, and the simultaneous disruption of telephone communications over large regions.

While science continues to search for methods of developing better-quality software, professional organizations have contributed their efforts indirectly by promoting high standards of ethics and professional conduct among their membership. For example, the Association of Computing Machinery (ACM) and the Institute of Electrical and Electronics Engineers (IEEE) have adopted codes of professional conduct and ethics that enhance the professionalism of software developers and counter nonchalant attitudes toward each individual's responsibilities.

In this chapter we introduce some of the results of software engineering research, including some of the basic principles of software engineering (the software life cycle, modularity, and design patterns) as well as some of the development tools and techniques that are used today.

QUESTIONS/EXERCISES

1. Why would the number of lines in a program not be a good measure of the complexity of the program?
2. What technique can be used to determine how many errors are in a piece of software?
3. Suggest a metric for measuring software quality. What weaknesses does your metric have?

6.2 The Software Life Cycle

The most fundamental concept in software engineering is the software life cycle.

The Cycle as a Whole

The software life cycle is shown in Figure 6.1. This figure represents the fact that once software is developed, it enters a cycle of being used and modified that continues for the rest of the software's life. Such a pattern is common for many manufactured products as well. The difference is that, in the case of other products, the modification phase is more accurately called a repair or mainte-

FIGURE 6.1

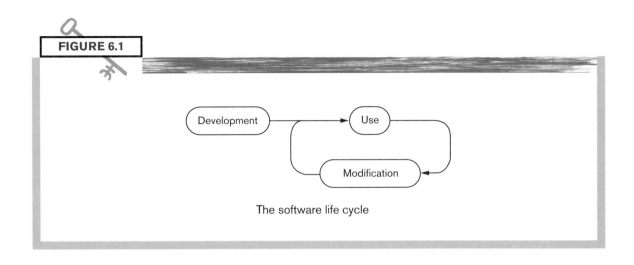

The software life cycle

nance phase because other products tend to move from being used to being modified as their parts become worn.

Software, on the other hand, does not wear out. Instead, software moves into the modification phase because errors are discovered, because changes in the software's application occur that require corresponding changes in the software, or because changes made during a previous modification are found to induce problems elsewhere in the software. For example, changes in tax laws may require modifications to payroll programs that calculate withholding taxes, and all too often these changes may have adverse effects in other areas of the program that may not be discovered until some time later.

Regardless of why software enters the modification phase, the process requires that a person (often not the original author) study the underlying program and its documentation until the program, or at least the pertinent part of the program, is understood. Otherwise, any modification could introduce more problems than it solves. Acquiring this understanding can be a difficult task even when the software is well-designed and documented. In fact, it is often within this phase that a piece of software is finally discarded under the pretense (too often true) that it is easier to develop a new system from scratch than to modify the existing package successfully.

Experience has shown that a little effort during the development of software can make a tremendous difference when modifications in the software are required. For example, in our discussion of data description statements in Chapter 5 we saw how the name AirportAlt might be used in lieu of the nondescriptive value 645 in a program and reasoned that if a change became necessary, it would be easier to change the value associated with the name instead of finding and changing numerous occurrences of the value 645. In turn, most of the research in software engineering focuses on the development stage of the software life cycle, with the goal being to take advantage of this effort-versus-benefit leverage.

The Traditional Development Phase

The stages within the development phase of the software life cycle are analysis, design, implementation, and testing (Figure 6.2).

Analysis   The development phase of the software life cycle begins with analysis—a major goal being to identify the needs of the user of the proposed system. If the system is to be a generic product sold in a competitive market, this analysis would involve a broad-based investigation to identify the needs of potential customers. If, however, the system is to be designed for a specific user, then the process would be a more narrow investigation.

As the needs of the potential user are identified, they are compiled to form a set of requirements that the new system must satisfy. These requirements are stated in terms of the application rather than in the technical terminology of the data processing community. One requirement might be that access to data must

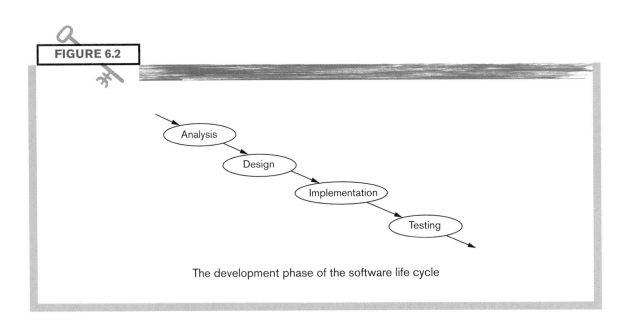

FIGURE 6.2

The development phase of the software life cycle

be restricted to authorized personnel. Another might be that the data must reflect the current state of the inventory as of the end of the last business day or that the arrangement of the data as displayed on the computer screen must adhere to the format of the paper forms currently in use.

After the system requirements are identified, they are converted into more technical system specifications. For example, the requirement that data be restricted to authorized personnel might become the specification that the system will not respond until an approved eight-digit password has been typed at the keyboard or that data will be displayed in encrypted form unless pre-processed by a routine known only to authorized personnel.

Design Whereas analysis concentrates on *what* the proposed system should do, design concentrates on *how* the system will accomplish those goals. It is here that the structure of the software system is established.

It is a well-established principle that the best structure for a large software system is a modular one. Indeed, it is by means of this modular decomposition that the implementation of large systems becomes a possibility. Without such a breakdown, the technical details required in the implementation of a large system would exceed a human's comprehensive powers. With a modular design, however, only the details pertaining to the module under consideration need be mastered. This same modular design is also conducive to future maintenance because it allows changes to be made on a modular basis. (If a change is to be made to the way each employee's health benefits are calculated, then only modules dealing with health benefits need be considered.)

There are, however, distinctions regarding the concept of a module. If one approaches the design task in terms of the traditional imperative paradigm, modules consist of procedures and the development of a modular design takes the form of identifying the various tasks that the proposed system must perform. In contrast, if one approaches the design task from the object-oriented perspective, modules are seen as objects and the design process becomes that of identifying the entities (objects) in the proposed system as well as how these entities should behave.

Implementation Implementation involves the actual writing of programs, creation of data files, and development of databases.

Testing Testing is closely associated with implementation, because each module of the system is normally tested as it is implemented. Indeed, each module in a well-designed system can be tested independently of the other modules by using simplified versions of the other modules, called stubs, to simulate the interaction between the target module and the rest of the system. Of course, this testing of components gives way to overall system testing as the various modules are completed and combined.

Unfortunately, the testing and debugging of a system is extremely difficult to perform successfully. Experience has shown that large software systems can contain numerous errors, even after significant testing. Many of these errors may go undetected for the life of the system, but others may cause major malfunctions. The elimination of such errors is one of the goals of software engineering. The fact that they are still prevalent means that a lot of research remains to be done.

Recent Trends

Early approaches to software engineering insisted on performing analysis, design, implementation, and testing in a strictly sequential manner. The feeling was that too much was at risk during the development of a large software system to allow for trial-and-error techniques. As a result, software engineers insisted that the entire analysis of the system be completed before beginning the design and, likewise, that the design be completed before beginning implementation. The result was a development process now referred to as the **waterfall model,** an analogy to the fact that the development process was allowed to flow in only one direction.

You will notice a similarity between the four problem-solving phases identified by Polya (Section 4.3) and the analysis, design, implementation, and testing phases of software development. After all, to develop a large software system is to solve a problem. On the other hand, the traditional waterfall approach to software development is in stark contrast to the "free-wheeling," trial-and-error process that is often vital to creative problem solving. Whereas the waterfall approach seeks to establish a highly structured environment in which development progresses in a sequential fashion, creative problem solving seeks a nonstructured environment in which one can drop previous plans of attack to pursue sparks of intuition without explaining why.

SOFTWARE ENGINEERING IN THE REAL WORLD

The following scenario is typical of the problems encountered by real-world software engineers. Company XYZ hires a software-engineering firm to develop and install a company-wide integrated software system to handle the company's data processing needs. As a part of this system, each employee is provided with a PC that is networked with the overall company system. These PCs provide access to the company-wide system, but they also serve as customizable tools with which each employee can increase his or her productivity. For example, one employee may develop a spreadsheet program that streamlines that employee's tasks. Unfortunately, such customized applications may not be well designed, and they often are not thoroughly tested and involve features that are not accurately understood by the employee. As the years go by, the use of these adhoc applications become integrated into the company's internal business procedures. The result is that what started out as a well-designed, coherent system can become dependent on a patchwork of poorly designed, undocumented, and error-prone applications.

In recent years, software engineering techniques have begun to reflect this underlying contradiction as illustrated by the emergence of the **incremental model** for software development. Following this model, the desired software system is constructed in increments—the first being a simplified version of the final product with limited functionality. Once this version has been tested and perhaps evaluated by the future user, more features are added and tested in an incremental manner until the system is complete. For example, if the system being developed is a student records system for a university registrar, the first increment may incorporate only the ability to view student records. Once that version is operational, additional features, such as the ability to add and update records, would be added in a stepwise manner.

The incremental model is evidence of the trend in software development toward **prototyping** in which incomplete versions of the proposed system, called **prototypes,** are built and evaluated. In the case of the incremental model these prototypes evolve into the complete, final system—a process known as evolutionary prototyping. In other cases, the prototypes may be discarded in favor of a fresh implementation of the final design. This approach is known as throwaway prototyping. An example that normally falls within this throwaway category is rapid prototyping in which a simple example of the proposed system is quickly constructed in the early stages of development. Such a prototype may consist of only a few screen images that give an indication of how the system will interact with the user and what capabilities it will have. The goal is not to produce a working version of the product but to obtain a demonstration tool that can be used to clarify communication between the parties involved. For example, rapid prototypes have proved advantageous in ironing out system requirements during the analysis stage or as aids during sales presentations to potential clients.

Another development in software engineering has been the application of computer technology to the software development process itself, resulting in what is called **computer-aided software engineering (CASE).** These computerized systems are known as CASE tools and include project planning tools (that assist in cost estimation, project scheduling, and personnel allocation), project management tools (that assist in monitoring the progress of the development project), documentation tools (that assist in writing and organizing documentation), prototyping and simulation tools (that assist in the development of prototypes), interface design tools (that assist in the development of GUIs), and programming tools (that assist in writing and debugging programs). Some of these tools are little more than the word processors, spreadsheet systems, and e-mail communication systems used in other applications. However, others are quite sophisticated packages designed primarily for the software engineering environment. For example, some CASE tools include code generators that, when given specifications for a part of a system, produce high-level language programs that implement that part of the system.

1. What is the difference between system requirements and system specifications?
2. Summarize each of the four stages (analysis, design, implementation, and testing) within the development phase of the software life cycle.
3. Summarize the distinction between the traditional waterfall model of software development and the newer prototyping paradigm.

6.3 Modularity

One of the key statements in Section 6.2 was that to modify software one must understand the program or at least the pertinent parts of the program. Such an understanding is often difficult enough to obtain in the case of small programs and would be close to impossible when dealing with large software systems if it were not for **modularity**–that is, the division of software into manageable units, each of which is designed to perform only a part of the overall task.

Modular Implementation

Modularity can be achieved in a variety of forms. In Chapters 4 and 5 we saw how modules can be formed in terms of procedures and used as building blocks in the construction of larger systems. In Chapter 5 we also met modularity in the context of the object-oriented paradigm. In this case modules take the form of objects, each with its own internal organization that is independent of the contents of other objects. In fact, it is this inherent modular structure that has led to the rise in popularity of the object-oriented approach to software development.

The **structure chart** is the traditional tool for representing a modular structure obtained by means of procedures. In such a chart, each module (procedure) is represented by a rectangle, and dependencies between modules are represented by arrows connecting the rectangles. The structure chart in Figure 6.3 represents such a modular structure for a simple fantasy role-playing game in which the player must move among the rooms of a medieval castle, solving a problem in each room before advancing to the next. The chart indicates that the module named CoordinateGame uses the modules InitializeGame, SimulateGreatHall, SimulateDungeon, and SimulateTurret as abstract tools to accomplish its task. More precisely, the procedure CoordinateGame calls the procedure InitializeGame to carry out the steps required to initialize a game (obtain the player's name, whether the game is to be at the beginner, intermediate, or advanced level, etc.) and then, each time the player moves to a new room,

FIGURE 6.3

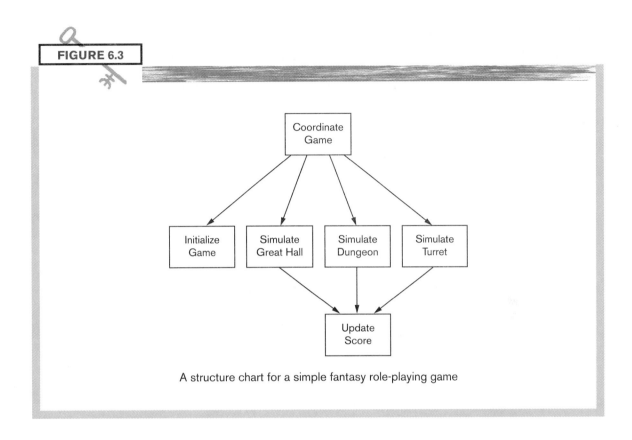

A structure chart for a simple fantasy role-playing game

CoordinateGame calls the procedure associated with that room to carry out the room's activities. Moreover, the chart indicates that each of these "room modules" uses the services of the procedure UpdateScore to record the player's performance in that particular room.

Whereas structure charts are used to represent the procedural organization of a software system, **class diagrams** are often used to represent an object-oriented system's structure in terms of the classes of objects within the system and the relationships between these classes. Figure 6.4 is a simple class diagram of our fantasy role-playing game example. It indicates that the system is composed of two types of objects, PlayerRecord and Room, that are related by the relationship called IsCurrentlyIn. The underlying idea is that an object of the type PlayerRecord contains the data and procedures regarding a particular player (name, level, and score) and an object of type Room contains the data and procedures regarding a particular room (the room's image for display purposes and the problem associated with the room). The relationship IsCurrentlyIn represents the association between rooms and players—that is, a player record is associated with the room in which the player currently resides. The numbers appearing at

FIGURE 6.4

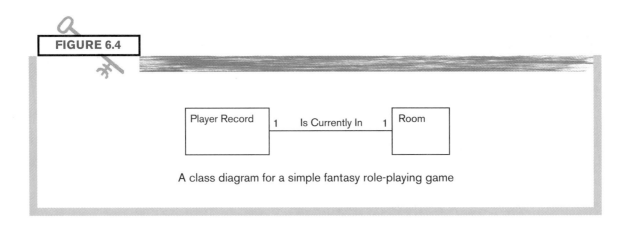

A class diagram for a simple fantasy role-playing game

the ends of the relationship line indicate that one player is associated with only one room at a time. Such a one-to-one relationship is different from a one-to-many relationship as exemplified by the "teaches" relationship that occurs when a single instructor teaches several courses during a semester.

In recent years, significant progress has been made toward establishing a standard notational system for representing object-oriented designs—the most prominent example being **UML (Unified Modeling Language),** which is a system for representing a variety of object-oriented concepts. The notation used in Figure 6.4 is based on UML conventions.

Coupling

We have introduced modularity as a way of obtaining manageable software. The idea is that a future modification will likely apply to only a few of the modules so that one's attention can be restricted to that portion of the system during the modification process. This, of course, depends on the assumption that changes in one module will not unknowingly affect other modules in the system. Consequently, a goal when designing a modular system should be to maximize independence between modules. Working against this objective is the fact that some connection between modules is necessary for them to form a coherent system. This connection is referred to as **coupling.** The goal of maximizing independence therefore corresponds to minimizing coupling.

Intermodule coupling actually occurs in several forms. One form is **control coupling,** which occurs when a module passes control to another, as in the transfer/return relationship associated with procedures. Another form is **data coupling,** which refers to the sharing of data between modules.

The structure chart in Figure 6.3 already represents the control coupling in a procedural approach to our fantasy role-playing game. Data coupling is traditionally represented in a structure chart with additional arrows, as represented in Figure 6.5. This chart indicates the data items that are passed to a module

FIGURE 6.5

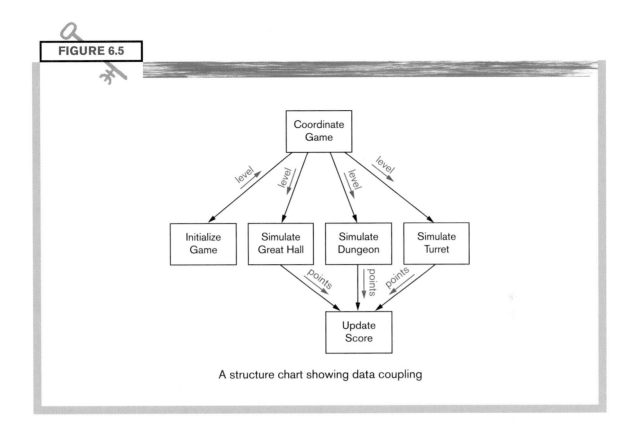

A structure chart showing data coupling

when its services are requested and those data items that are passed back to the original module when the requested task is completed. In particular, the chart indicates that the module CoordinateGame will pass the player's level to the procedure SimulateGreatHall when it requests the services of SimulateGreatHall. Note that CoordinateGame apparently receives this level information from the procedure InitializeGame. Moreover, the chart indicates that when a room module requests the services of UpdateScore, it will pass data in the form of points to UpdateScore.

The minimalization of data coupling is one of the main benefits of the object-oriented approach. Indeed, the motivating concept of an object is that of collecting the routines that manipulate a particular item of data into a single module. Thus, in an object-oriented system, most intermodule coupling takes the form of interobject communication, which is usually implemented as control coupling. That is, a request for an object to perform a task is essentially a request for the execution of a method (procedure) within the object. The request thus results in control being passed to the object in a manner similar to control being passed to a procedure in the imperative paradigm.

One way of representing interobject communication in an object-oriented design is to add the information to a class diagram to form a **collaboration diagram**—which is essentially a class diagram that also shows how the various objects in the system collaborate with each other. A simple collaboration diagram (using UML type notation) for our fantasy role-playing game is shown in Figure 6.6. It indicates that an object of type Room may send a message to a PlayerRecord object telling it to adjust its score and that an object of type PlayerRecord may send a message to a Room object telling it to pose its problem.

Regardless of the type of coupling involved, a programmer should strive to make that coupling apparent in the final written program. Coupling that is disguised is known as **implicit coupling** and is the cause of many software errors. A common form of implicit coupling is obtained by the use of **global data**—data elements that are automatically available to the modules throughout a system, as opposed to local data elements that are accessible only within a particular module unless explicitly passed to another. Most high-level languages provide methods for implementing both global and local data.

Cohesion

Just as important as minimizing the coupling between modules is maximizing the internal binding within each module. The term **cohesion** refers to this internal binding or, in other words, the degree of relatedness of a module's internal parts. To appreciate the importance of cohesion, we must look beyond the initial development of a system and consider the entire software life cycle. If it becomes necessary to make changes in a module, the existence of a variety of activities within it can confuse what would otherwise be a simple process. Thus,

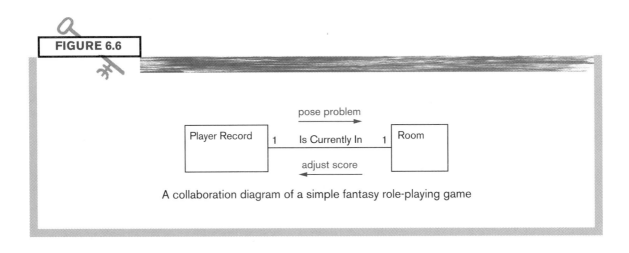

FIGURE 6.6

A collaboration diagram of a simple fantasy role-playing game in addition to seeking low intermodule coupling, software designers strive for high intramodule cohesion.

A weak form of cohesion is known as **logical cohesion.** This is the cohesion within a module induced by the fact that its internal elements perform activities logically similar in nature. For example, consider a module that performs all of a system's communication with the outside world. The "glue" that holds such a module together is that all the activities within the module deal with communication. However, the subjects of the communication can vary greatly. Some may deal with obtaining data, while others deal with reporting errors.

A stronger form of cohesion is known as **functional cohesion,** which means that all the parts of the module are geared toward the performance of a single activity. The module SimulateGreatHall in Figure 6.3 is not functionally cohesive if it contains the details of displaying an image of the hall on the computer screen, presenting the problem associated with the hall, and obtaining the player's response. However, if these details are isolated in other modules and used as abstract tools, each step in the SimulateGreatHall module can be presented in the overall context of overseeing the actions associated with the great hall, thus making SimulateGreatHall more functionally cohesive.

In object-oriented designs, entire objects are usually only logically cohesive since the methods within an object often perform loosely related activities—the only common bond being that they are activities performed by the same object. For example, in our fantasy role-playing game, each room object would probably contain a method for displaying an image of its room on the screen as well as methods for presenting the room's problem and obtaining the player's response. Such an object would therefore form a logically cohesive module. However, a software designer should strive to make each individual method within an object functionally cohesive. That is, even though the object in its entirety is only logically cohesive, each method within an object should perform only one functionally cohesive task (Figure 6.7).

QUESTIONS/EXERCISES

1. How does a novel differ from an encyclopedia in terms of the degree of coupling between its units such as chapters, sections, or entries? What about cohesion?
2. A hand of bridge is divided into two phases: the bidding and the actual playing of the cards. Analyze the coupling between these phases by identifying the information that is passed explicitly from the first phase to the second. What is passed implicitly?
3. Is the goal of maximizing cohesion compatible with minimizing coupling? That is, as cohesion increases, does coupling naturally tend to decrease?
4. Extend the collaboration diagram in Figure 6.6 to include other messages that should be passed between objects of type Room and PlayerRecord.

FIGURE 6.7

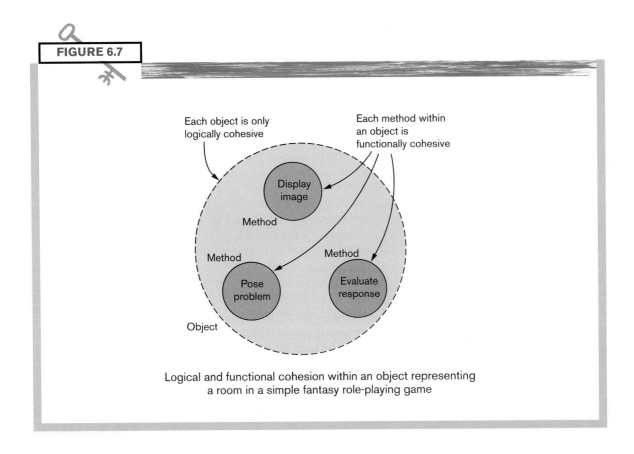

Logical and functional cohesion within an object representing
a room in a simple fantasy role-playing game

6.4 Design Methodologies

The development of methodologies for designing software systems is a major
quest within software engineering. In this section we discuss a variety of the
techniques that have been developed as well as directions of current research.

Top-Down Versus Bottom-Up

Perhaps the most well-known strategy associated with system design is the top-
down methodology. The point of this methodology is that one should not try
to solve a complex problem in a single step. Instead, one's first step should be
to break the problem into smaller, more manageable subproblems. Then, one
should proceed by breaking these subproblems into still smaller problems. In

this manner, a complex problem becomes a collection of simpler problems whose solutions collectively solve the original problem.

The result of top-down design tends to be a hierarchical system of refinements that often can be translated directly into a modular structure that is compatible with the imperative programming paradigm. The solutions to the smallest problems in the hierarchy become procedural modules that perform simple tasks and are used as abstract tools by more superior modules to solve the more complex problems in the system.

In contrast to the top-down design methodology is the bottom-up approach, in which one starts the design of a system by identifying individual tasks within the system and then considers how solutions to these tasks can be used as abstract tools in the solution to more complex problems. For many years, this approach was considered inferior to the top-down design paradigm. Today, however, the bottom-up methodology has gained support. One reason for this shift is that the top-down methodology seeks a solution in which a dominant module uses submodules, each of which relies on subsubmodules, and so on. However, the best design for many systems is not of a hierarchical nature. Indeed, a design consisting of two or more modules interacting as equals, as exemplified by the client-server model as well as general parallel processing applications, may be a better solution than a design consisting of a superior module that relies on subordinates to perform its task.

Another reason for increased interest in bottom-up design is that it is more consistent with the goal of building complex software systems from preconstructed, off-the-shelf components—an approach that is a current trend in software engineering. We will look more closely at this strategy later in this section.

Tools of the Trade

Software engineering has produced a variety of notational systems to aid in the system analysis and design process. Of these, we have already met structure charts, class diagrams, and collaboration diagrams. Another is the **dataflow diagram,** which is a pictorial representation of the data paths in a system. That is, a dataflow diagram identifies the origin, destination, and processing points of data in a system. The various symbols in such a diagram have specific meanings: Arrows represent data paths, bold lines represent data sources and sinks, circles (bubbles) represent locations of data manipulation, and heavy straight lines represent data storage. In each case, the symbol is labeled with the name of the object represented. A dataflow diagram for our simple fantasy role-playing game is shown in Figure 6.8.

The dataflow approach to software development originated in the context of the imperative programming paradigm. The idea was that by following the data paths through the proposed system, we discover where data units merge, split, or are otherwise altered. Because computational activity is needed at these

FIGURE 6.8

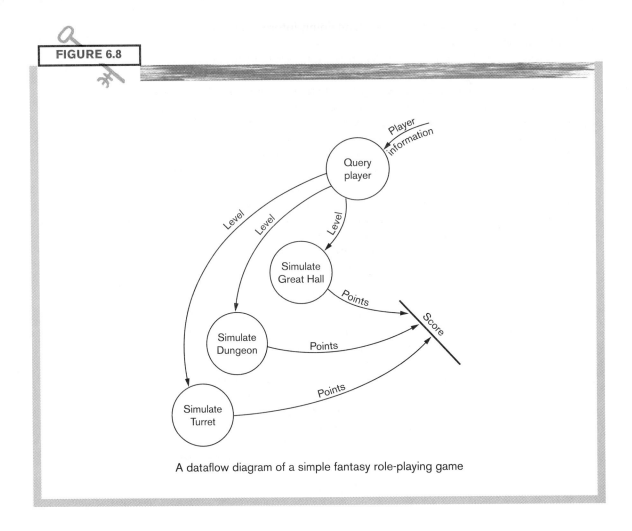

A dataflow diagram of a simple fantasy role-playing game

locations in the system, such activities, or groupings of activities, should form the procedural modules of the system. Consequently, concentrating on flow of data helps us discover a modular structure for a system.

Although developed with the imperative paradigm in mind, dataflow analysis has found some use in object-oriented environments as well. In particular, identifying the items of data in a system helps to identify objects, and identifying changes made to data helps to identify the actions these objects should perform.

Another tool used in the analysis and design of software systems is the **entity-relationship diagram,** which is a pictorial representation of the items of information (entities) within the system and the relationships between these pieces of information. As an example, let us consider part of an entity-relationship diagram for a software system for maintaining information about professors, students, and classes at a university.

We first identify the data entities involved. They include the entity Professor, which we think of as representing a single professor at the university; the entity Student, which represents a single student; and the entity Class, which represents a section of a given course. With each occurrence of the Professor entity is associated a name, address, employee identification number, salary, and so on; with each occurrence of the Student entity is associated a name, address, student identification number, grade point average, and so on; and with each occurrence of the Class entity is associated a course identification (History 101), semester and year, classroom, time of day, and so on.

Having identified the entities in our system, we now consider the relationships among the entities. We first note that each professor teaches classes and each student attends classes. We therefore identify the relationship between the entities Professor and Class as the relationship Teaches and that between the entities Student and Class as the relationship Attends. (Note that entities are referred to by nouns, whereas relationships are referenced by verbs.)

To represent these entities and relationships, we use the entity-relationship diagram in Figure 6.9. Here each entity is represented by a rectangle and each relationship is represented by a diamond. The diagram shows that professors are related to classes by means of the relationship Teaches and students are related to classes by means of the relationship Attends.

There is, however, a different structure associated with the two relationships in our example. The relationship between Professor and Class is a one-to-many relationship in that each professor teaches several classes but each class is taught by only one professor. In contrast, the relationship between Student and Class is a many-to-many relationship because each student attends several classes and each class is attended by several students. This additional information is represented in Figure 6.9 by the presence of pointers on the lines connecting relationships to entities. In particular, a single pointer toward an entity

FIGURE 6.9

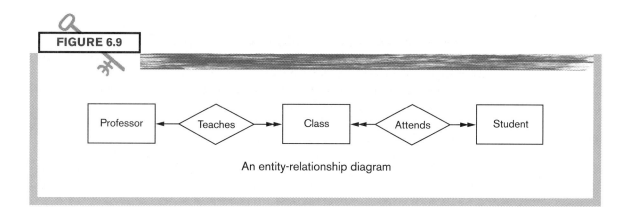

An entity-relationship diagram

indicates that only one occurrence of that entity is involved in each occurrence of the relationship, whereas a double pointer indicates that more than one occurrence of the entity may be involved. Thus the pointer toward the entity Professor in Figure 6.9 indicates that only one professor teaches a class, while the double pointer toward the entity Class in the Teaches relationship indicates that each professor may teach more than one class.

Among the various tools used by software engineers in the past, entity-relationship diagrams appear to be the most likely to survive the shift to object-oriented methodologies. This is because the identification of entities is essentially the identification of objects, and the classification of entity relationships is the first step toward identifying the relationships and communication paths required between objects. Indeed, the traditional entity-relationship diagram is readily recognizable as the predecessor of the UML class diagram (Figure 6.4) used in object-oriented design environments.

Still another tool in the development of a software system is the **data dictionary,** which is a central depository of information about the data items appearing throughout the system. This information includes the identifier used to reference each item; what constitutes valid entries in each item (Will the item always be numeric or perhaps always alphabetic? What will be the range of values that might be assigned to this item?); where the item is stored (Will the item be stored in a file or a database and, if so, which one?); and where the item is referenced in the software (Which modules will require the item's information?).

Several goals are associated with the development of a data dictionary. One is to enhance communication between the potential user of the system and the analyst charged with the task of converting the user's needs into requirements and specifications. It would be discouraging to find, after the system has been implemented, that part numbers are not really numeric or that the size of the inventory exceeds the maximum allowed by the system. The process of constructing a data dictionary helps avoid such misunderstandings.

Another goal associated with the data dictionary is to establish uniformity throughout the system. It is usually by means of constructing the dictionary that redundancies and contradictions surface. For example, the item referred to as PartNumber in the inventory records may be the same as the PartId in the sales records. Moreover, the personnel department may use the item Name to refer to an employee while inventory records may contain the item Name in reference to a part.

Finally, we should mention CRC (class-responsibility-collaboration) cards that are useful in the design of object-oriented systems. A CRC card is essentially a traditional index card on which the description of an object is written. The methodology of CRC cards is for the designer to produce a card for each object in the proposed system and then to use those cards to simulate the activities of the system—perhaps on a desktop or via a "theatrical" experiment in which each member of the design team plays the role of an object as described by the appropriate card. Such simulations are used to identify flaws in the design.

Design Patterns

In an effort to find ways by which software can be constructed from off-the-shelf components, software engineers have turned to the field of architecture for inspiration. Of particular interest is the book *A Pattern Language* by Christopher Alexander et al., which describes a set of patterns for designing communities. Each pattern consists of the statement of a problem followed by a proposed solution. The problems are intended to be universal, and the proposed solutions are generic in the sense that they address the universal nature of the problem rather than proposing a solution for a particular case.

For example, one pattern, called Quiet Backs, addresses the need to escape the commotion of a business center for short periods of refreshment. The proposed solution is to design "quiet backs" into business districts. In some cases, the district could be designed around a main street to which all buildings face—thus, providing for quiet side streets behind the buildings. In other cases, "quiet backs" can be obtained by means of parks, rivers, or cathedrals.

The important point for our discussion is that Alexander's work attempted to identify universal problems and provide templates for solving them. Today, many software engineers are attempting to apply this same approach to the design of large software systems. In particular, researchers are applying design patterns as a means of providing generic building blocks with which software systems can be constructed.

THE JAVA PROGRAMMING ENVIRONMENT

The Java programming language would be just another object-oriented programming language if it were not for such features as the collection of frameworks that have been developed to ease the Java programming process. These frameworks are collectively called the Application Programming Interface (API) and are available as part of the Java Development Kit (JDK) from Sun Microsystems. The frameworks in Java's API provide templates for such things as developing GUIs, manipulating audio and video data, transferring data across the Internet, and developing animated Web pages. Thus the Java programming environment provides a prime example of the move toward constructing software from prefabricated components.

An example of such a pattern is the publisher-subscriber pattern, consisting of a module (the publisher) that must send copies of its "publications" to other modules (the subscribers) (Figure 6.10). As a specific example, consider a collection of data that is being displayed on a computer screen in more than one format—perhaps as a pie graph as well as a bar graph—simultaneously. In this

FIGURE 6.10

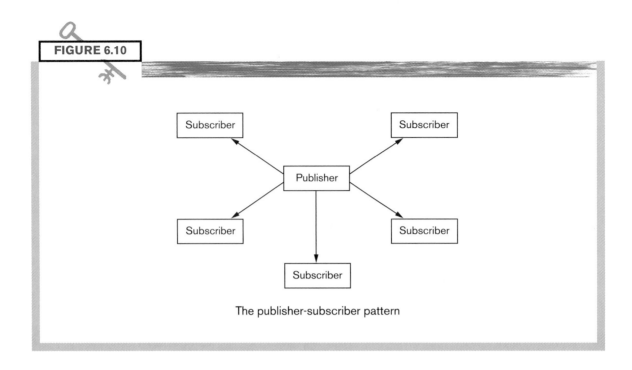

The publisher-subscriber pattern

setting, any change in the data should be reflected in both graphs. Thus the software modules in charge of drawing the graphs should be notified when changes in the data occur. In this case, then, the software module maintaining the data plays the role of the publisher that must send update messages to the subscribers, which are the modules charged with drawing the graphs.

Another example of a software design pattern is the container-component pattern. It captures the generic concept of a container that contains components that are themselves containers (Figure 6.11). Such a pattern is exemplified by the directories or folders used by an operating system's file manager. Each of these directories typically contains other directories, which may contain still other directories. In short, the container-component pattern is meant to capture the recursive concept of containers that contain containers.

Once a pattern such as publisher-subscriber or container-component has been identified, software engineers propose the development of skeletal program units, called **frameworks,** that implement the pertinent features of the pattern's solution while leaving features specific to particular applications as slots to be filled in later. To accompany frameworks, software engineers propose documentation that describes how the framework can be filled in to obtain a complete implementation of the underlying pattern in a particular setting. Such documentation is called a *recipe.* Collections of frameworks along with their recipes are fondly known as *cookbooks.*

FIGURE 6.11

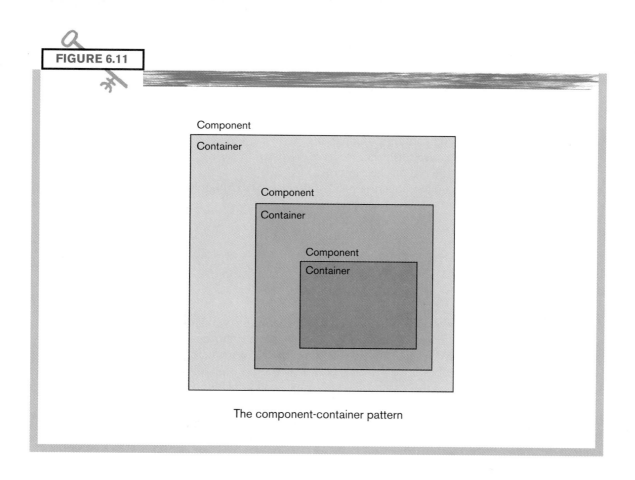

The component-container pattern

Researchers hope that by means of cookbooks, software engineers will finally be able to construct large, complex software systems from off-the-shelf components—the components being frameworks. Early results have indicated that such an approach can significantly reduce the amount of programming required in the development of a new system.

With all the excitement that has been generated in the software engineering community over design patterns, it is interesting to note that Alexander was not pleased with the results of his patterns in architecture. In short, he found that the systems designed from his patterns were lacking in character, and his work since the early 1980s has focused on ways to capture this evasive quality. However, software engineers argue that the goal in software development does not involve such qualities as beauty and character, but instead accuracy and efficiency. Thus, they continue, design patterns will prove to be more successful in the field of software engineering than in architecture.

QUESTIONS/EXERCISES

1. Suppose that a receptionist receives requests for appointments. The response to a request is either a schedule for a future appointment or an immediate appointment. Draw a dataflow diagram representing this part of the receptionist's job.

2. Draw an entity-relationship diagram representing airline companies, flights flown by each company, and the passengers on the various flights.

3. Identify some software structures that we have discussed in earlier chapters that could be considered design patterns.

4. What role in the software engineering process do researchers hope that frameworks will play?

6.5 Testing

In Section 4.6 we considered techniques for verifying the correctness of algorithms in a mathematically rigorous manner but concluded that most software today is "verified" by means of testing. Unfortunately, testing is an inexact science at best. We cannot declare that a piece of software is correct via testing unless we run enough tests to exhaust all possible scenarios. But, there are over 1,000 different paths that a simple loop structure containing a single if-then-else statement may traverse when the loop is cycled only ten times. Thus, testing all possible paths through a complex program is an impossible task.

On the other hand, software engineers have developed testing methodologies that improve the odds of revealing errors in software. One of these is based on the observation that errors in software tend to be clumped. (This observation is often referred to as the Pareto principle in honor of Vilfredo Pareto who observed that a small part of Italy's population controlled most of Italy's wealth.) That is, experience has shown that a small number of modules within a large software system tend to be more problematic than the rest. Thus, by identifying these modules and testing them more thoroughly, more of the system's errors can be discovered than if all modules were tested in a uniform, less-thorough manner. The problem, of course, is to identify the problematic modules.

Another software testing methodology, called basis path testing, is to develop a set of test data that insures that each instruction in the software is executed at least once. Techniques using an area of mathematics known as graph theory have been developed for identifying such sets of test data. Thus, although it is impossible to insure that every path through a software system is tested, it is possible to insure that every statement within the system is executed at least once during the testing process.

Techniques based on the Pareto principle and basis path testing rely on knowledge of the internal composition of the software being tested. They therefore fall within the category of **glass-box testing**—meaning that the software's interior is visible to the tester. In contrast is the category of **black-box testing,** which refers to tests that do not rely on knowledge of the software's interior composition. In short, black-box testing is performed from the user's point of view. In black-box testing, one is not concerned with how the software goes about its task but merely with whether the software performs correctly in terms of accuracy and timeliness.

One methodology that is often associated with black-box testing, called boundary value analysis, is to identify boundary points within the software's specification and test the software at these boundary points. For example, if the software is supposed to accept input values within a specified range, then the software would be tested at the lowest and highest values in that range, or if the software is supposed to coordinate multiple activities, then the software would be tested on a collection of the most demanding activities.

Another black-box testing methodology is to apply redundancy. Following this approach, two software systems for performing the same task are developed independently by different teams or even different companies. Then, the two systems are tested by applying them to the same data and comparing their results. Errors are indicted by discrepancies. Such redundancy techniques are often applied in space exploration systems.

Another methodology that falls within the black-box category that is being used increasingly by developers of "shrink-wrapped" software aimed at the PC market is to supply a segment of the intended audience with a preliminary version of the software, called a beta version. The main goal is to learn how the software performs in real-life situations before the final version of the product is solidified and released to the market.

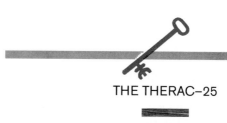

THE THERAC–25

The need for good design disciplines is exemplified by the problems encountered in the Therac–25, which was a computer-based electron-accelerator radiation-therapy system used by the medical community in the middle 1980s. Flaws in the machine's design contributed to six cases of radiation overdose—three of which resulted in death. Such flaws included a poor design for the machine's interface that allowed the operator to begin radiation before the machine had adjusted for the proper dosage and poor coordination between the design of the hardware and the software that resulted in the absence of certain safety features. You can learn more about such problems through the Risks Forum whose Web page is located at http://catless.ncl.as.uk/Risks

The advantages of such beta testing extend far beyond the traditional discovery of errors. General customer feedback (both positive and negative) is obtained that may assist in refining market strategies. Moreover, early distribution of beta software assists other software developers in designing compatible products. For example, in the case of a new operating system, the distribution of a beta version encourages the development of compatible utility software so that the final operating system ultimately appears on store shelves surrounded by companion products. Finally, the existence of beta software can generate a feeling of anticipation within the marketplace—an atmosphere that increases publicity and sales.

QUESTIONS/EXERCISES

1. When testing software, is a successful test one that does or does not find errors?
2. What techniques would you propose using to identify the modules within a system that should receive more thorough testing than others?
3. What would be a good test to perform on a software package that was designed to sort a list of no more than 100 entries?

6.6 Documentation

A software system is of little use unless people can learn to use and maintain it. Hence, documentation is an important part of a software package, and its development is, in turn, an important topic in software engineering.

Documentation of a software package is normally produced for two purposes. One is to explain the features of the software and describe how to use them. This is known as **user documentation** because it is designed to be read by the user of the software. Hence, user documentation tends to be nontechnical.

Today, user documentation is recognized as an important marketing tool. Good user documentation (combined with a well-designed user interface) makes a software package accessible and thus increases its sales. Recognizing this, many software developers hire technical writers to produce this part of their product, or they provide preliminary versions of their products to independent authors so that how-to books are available in book stores when the software itself is released to the public.

User documentation traditionally takes the form of a manual that presents an introduction to the most commonly used features of the software (often in the form of a tutorial), a section explaining how to install the software, and a reference section describing the details of each feature of the software. This manual is often available in book form, but in many cases the same information is included as part of the software itself. This allows a user to refer to the documentation while using the software. In this case the information may be broken into small units, sometimes called help packages, that may appear on the monitor screen automatically if the user dallies too long between commands.

The other purpose of documentation is to describe the software's internal composition so that the system can be maintained later in its life cycle.

Documentation of this type is known as **system documentation** and is inherently more technical than user documentation. A major component of system documentation is the source version of all the programs in the system. It is important that these programs be presented in a readable format, which is why software engineers support the use of well-designed, high-level programming languages, the use of comment statements for annotating a program, and a modular design that allows each module to be presented as a coherent unit. In fact, many companies that produce software products have adopted conventions for their employees to follow when writing programs. These include indentation conventions for organizing a program on the written page, naming conventions to establish a distinction between names of variables, constants, objects, classes, etc., and documentation conventions to ensure that all programs are sufficiently documented. Such conventions establish uniformity throughout a company's software, which ultimately simplifies the software maintenance process.

Another component of system documentation is a record of the design documents describing the system's specifications and how these specifications were obtained. Creating this documentation is an ongoing process that starts with the initial analysis. Being an ongoing process, the creation of this documentation leads to a conflict between the goals of software engineering and human nature. It is highly likely that the initial specifications and the initial software design will change during the development process. At issue is the temptation to make these changes without updating the earlier design documents. The result is a strong possibility that the documents will be incorrect and hence their use in the final documentation misleading.

Herein lies another argument in favor of CASE tools. They make such tasks as redrawing diagrams and updating data dictionaries much easier than with the older manual methods. Consequently, updates are more likely to be made and the final documentation is more likely to be accurate.

We close by emphasizing that the example of updating documents is only one of many instances in which software engineering must cope with the faults of human nature. Others include the inevitable personality conflicts, jealousies, and ego clashes that arise when people work together. Thus, as we have mentioned before, the subject of software engineering covers much more than those subjects directly associated with computer science.

QUESTIONS/EXERCISES

1. In what forms can software be documented?
2. At what phase (or phases) in the software life cycle is documentation prepared?
3. Which is more important, a program or its documentation?

6.7 Software Ownership and Liability

In general, a company or individual should be allowed to recoup, and profit from, the investment needed to develop quality software. Without a means of protecting this investment, few would be willing to undertake the task of producing the software our society desires. But questions of software ownership and ownership rights often fall between the cracks of well-established copyright and patent laws. These laws were developed to allow the developer of a "product" to release that product to the public while protecting his or her ownership rights, but the characteristics of software have repeatedly challenged the courts in their efforts to apply copyright and patent principles to issues of software ownership.

Copyright laws were originally established to protect an author's rights to literary works. In this case, the value of the product is in how ideas are expressed rather than in the ideas themselves. The value in a poem is in the rhythm, style, and format of the poem rather than the subject matter; the value of a novel is in the author's presentation of the story rather than the story itself. Thus a poet's or a novelist's investment can be protected by giving him or her ownership of that particular expression of the idea, but not the idea itself. Another person is free to express the same idea as long as that expression does not have "substantial similarity" to that of the original.

In contrast to a poem or novel, the value of software is usually not in the particular manner in which a program is expressed. Instead, it is in the algorithm (the idea) being communicated. Thus, a straightforward application of copyright laws tends not to protect a software developer's investment. Indeed, it allows an algorithm that the developer may have discovered as a result of major investments to be used by a competitor as long as that competitor's representation is not substantially similar to the original.

In short, copyright laws were developed to protect form rather than function, but the value of a program is often in its function rather than its form. As a result, copyright laws are better suited for protecting programs that implement well-known, unoriginal algorithms than they are at protecting investments that lead to new algorithms. If the algorithm is well known, the only value in the program is its expression; if, however, the algorithm expressed is new and creative, the major value of the program is the algorithm, which copyrights do not protect. This is somewhat paradoxical; the more that creative efforts are required to produce a program, the less likely it is that copyright laws will protect the investment of those efforts.

In an attempt to apply copyright laws to software, some have turned to the concept of the look and feel of a software system. Although the phrase *look and feel* was not used until 1985, the concept has its roots as early as the 1960s when IBM introduced its System/360 series of machines. This series consisted of a variety of machines ranging from designs for small-business applications to large machines for businesses with significant needs. All these machines were supplied with operating systems that communicated with their environments in essentially the same manner. That is, the entire series of machines had a standardized interface with the user. In turn, as a business grew, it could change to a larger machine in the 360 series without major reprogramming and retraining efforts. Indeed, the look (meaning the appearance projected by the system software) and the feel (meaning the manner in which the user interacted with the system software) were the same for all machines in the 360 series.

Today, the advantages of standardized interfaces are well recognized and sought after throughout the software spectrum. When the interface designed by one company becomes popular, it becomes advantageous for competing companies to design their systems to look and feel like the well-known one. This similarity makes it easier for users of the well-known system to convert to the competitor's system, even though the interior designs of the two systems may be quite different. Companies facing such competitive practices have sought protection under copyright laws by claiming ownership of the look and feel of the original system. After all, the look and feel of a software package has many of the characteristics of the properties protected by copyright laws.

An early test of the look and feel argument was in 1987, when Lotus Development Corporation sued Mosaic Software, claiming that the latter had copied the look and feel of the Lotus 1–2–3 spreadsheet system. The suit was successful. In more recent cases, however, look and feel arguments have met with mixed results.

Patents also suffer problems when used to protect software ownership rights. One obstacle is the longstanding principle that no one can own a natural phenomenon such as laws of physics, mathematical formulas, and thoughts. Courts have generally ruled that algorithms fall within this category. Thus, as in the case of copyright, patent laws tend not to protect the major item of value within a program—the algorithm. Moreover, obtaining a patent is an expensive and time-consuming process, often involving several years. During this time a software product could become obsolete, and until the patent is granted the applicant has only questionable authority to exclude others from appropriating the product. There have been cases, however, of patents being granted for algorithms, an example being the encryption algorithm known as RSA that is heavily used in many of today's public key encryption systems.

Copyright and patent laws are designed to allow, and even encourage, the dissemination of inventions and to encourage the free exchange of ideas for the betterment of society. The reasoning is that when ownership rights are protected, creators and inventors are more likely to make their achievements known to the public. In contrast, trade secret laws provide a means of restricting the distribution of ideas. Designed to maintain ethical conduct between competing businesses, these laws protect against improper disclosure or wrongful appropriation of a company's internal accomplishments. Companies often attempt to protect their trade secrets by means of written nondisclosure agreements in which personnel with access to company secrets agree not to disclose their knowledge to others. Courts have generally upheld such agreements.

To protect against liability, software developers often accompany their product with disclaimers, in which they state the limitations of their liability. Such statements as "In no event will Company X be liable for any damages arising out of the use of this software" are common. Courts, however, rarely consider a disclaimer if the plaintiff can show negligence on the part of the defendant. Thus liability cases tend to focus on whether the defendant used a level of care compatible with the product being produced. A level of care that might be deemed acceptable in the case of developing a word processing system may be considered negligent when developing software to control a nuclear reactor. Consequently, the best defense against liability claims in software development is a concerted approach to the software development process.

QUESTIONS/EXERCISES

1. What test can be applied to decide whether one program is substantially similar to another?
2. In what ways are copyright, patent, and trade secret laws designed to benefit society?
3. To what extent are disclaimers not recognized by the courts?

CHAPTER REVIEW PROBLEMS

1. Give an example of how efforts in the development of software can pay dividends later in software maintenance.

2. What is evolutionary prototyping?

3. Summarize how the use of CASE tools has changed the software development process.

4. Explain how the lack of metrics for measuring certain software properties affects the software engineering discipline.

5. How does software engineering differ from other, more traditional fields of engineering?

6. a. Identify a disadvantage of the traditional waterfall model for software development.

   b. Identify an advantage of the traditional waterfall model for software development.

7. How does the establishment of codes of ethics and professional conduct aid in the development of quality software?

8. Describe how the use of constants rather than literals can simplify software maintenance.

9. What is the difference between coupling and cohesion? Which should be minimized and which should be maximized? Why?

10. Which of the following statements is an argument for coupling, and which is an argument for cohesion:

a. For a student to learn, the subject should be presented in well-organized units with specific goals.

b. A student does not really understand a subject until the subject's overall scope and relationship with other subjects has been grasped.

11. In the text, we mentioned control coupling but did not pursue it. Contrast the coupling between two program units obtained by a simple goto statement with the coupling obtained by a procedure call.

12. Answer the following questions in relation to the accompanying structure chart:

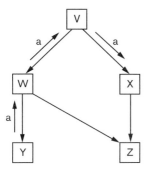

a. To which module does module Y return control?

b. To which module does module Z return control?

c. Are modules W and X linked via control coupling?

d. Are modules W and X linked via data coupling?

e. What data is shared by both module W and module Y?

f. In what way are modules Y and X related?

13. In relation to the structure chart in Problem 12, what stubs are necessary to test module V? What characteristics might these stubs have?

14. Answer the following questions in relation to the accompanying structure chart:

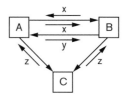

a. What is different between the way modules A and B use data items x and y?

b. If one of the modules was in charge of obtaining data item z from a user at a remote terminal, which module would that apparently be?

15. Draw a simple class diagram representing the relationship between magazine publishers, magazines, and subscribers.

16. Extend the class diagram you drew for Problem 15 to a collaboration diagram.

17. What is the difference between a class diagram and a collaboration diagram?

18. What is UML?

19. Using a structure chart, represent the procedural structure of an online inventory/customer records system for a mail-order business. What modules in your system must be modified because of changes in sales tax laws? What if the length of the postal system's ZIP code changes?

20. Design an object-oriented solution to Problem 19 and represent it by a class diagram.

21. Identify some design patterns in fields other than architecture and software engineering.

22. Summarize the role of design patterns in software engineering.

23. Draw a dataflow diagram depicting the registration process at a university.

24. Contrast the information represented in dataflow diagrams with that given in structure charts.

25. What is the difference between a one-to-many relationship and a many-to-many relationship?

26. Draw an entity-relationship diagram representing the relationships between the cooks, waitresses, customers, and cashiers in a restaurant.

27. Draw an entity-relationship diagram representing the relationships between magazines, publishers of magazines, and subscribers to magazines.

28. In each of the following cases, identify whether the activity relates to a structure chart, a dataflow diagram, an entity-relationship diagram, or a data dictionary.
    a. Identifying the data pertinent to the system to be developed.
    b. Identifying the relationship between the various items of data appearing in the system.
    c. Identifying the characteristics of each item of data in the system.

d. Identifying which items of data are shared among the various parts of the system.

29. What is the difference between a class diagram and an entity-relationship diagram?

30. Summarize the distinction between top-down and bottom-up design strategies.

31. What is the difference between black-box testing and glass-box testing?

32. Suppose that 100 errors were intentionally placed in a large software system before the system was subjected to final testing. Moreover, suppose that 200 errors were discovered and corrected during this final testing, of which 50 errors were from the group intentionally placed in the system. If the remaining 50 known errors are then corrected, how many unknown errors would you estimate are still in the system? Explain why.

33. In what way do traditional copyright laws fail to safeguard the investments of software developers?

34. In what way do traditional patent laws fail to safeguard the investments of software developers?

 SOCIAL ISSUES

The following questions are provided to help you understand some of the ethical/social/legal issues associated with the field of computing as well as investigate your own beliefs and their foundations. The goal is not merely to answer these questions. You should also consider why you answered as you did and whether your justifications are consistent from one question to the next.

1. a. Mary Analyst has been assigned the task of designing a system with which medical records will be stored on a machine that is connected to a large network. Her concerns regarding security have been overruled for financial reasons, and she has been told to proceed with the project using

a security system that she feels is inadequate. What should she do? Why?

b. Suppose that Mary Analyst developed the system as she was told, and now she is aware that the medical records are being observed by unauthorized personnel. What should she do? To what extent is she liable for the breach of security?

c. Suppose that instead of obeying her employer, Mary Analyst refuses to proceed with the system and blows the whistle by making the flawed design public, resulting in a financial hardship for the company and the loss of many innocent employees' jobs. Were Mary Analyst's actions correct? What if it turns out that, being only a part of the overall design team, Mary Analyst was unaware that sincere efforts were being made elsewhere within the company to develop a valid security system that would be applied to the system on which Mary was working. How does this change your judgment of Mary's actions? (Remember, Mary's view of the situation is the same as before.)

2. When large software systems are developed by many people, how should liabilities be assigned? Is there a hierarchy of responsibility? Are there degrees of liability?

3. We have seen that large, complex software systems are often developed by many individuals, few of which may have a complete picture of the entire project. Is it proper for an employee to contribute to a project without full knowledge of its function?

4. To what extent is someone responsible for how his or her accomplishments are ultimately applied by others?

5. In the relationship between a computer professional and a client, is it the professional's responsibility to implement the client's desires or rather to direct the client's desires? What if the professional foresees that a client's desires could lead to unethical consequences? For example, the client may wish to cut corners for the sake of efficiency, but the professional may foresee a potential source of erroneous data or misuse of the system if those shortcuts are taken. If the client insists, is the professional free of responsibility?

ADDITIONAL READING

Booch, G. *Object-Oriented Analysis and Design with Applications,* 2nd ed. Redwood City, CA: Benjamin/Cummings, 1994.

Fenton, N. E. and S. L. Pfleeger. *Software Metrics: A Rigorous and Practical Approach,* 2nd ed. Boston, MA: PWS, 1997.

Pooley, R. and P. Stevens. *Using UML: Software Engineering with Objects and Components.* Reading, MA: Addison-Wesley, 1999.

Pressman, R. S. *Software Engineering: A Practitioner's Approach,* 4th ed. New York: McGraw-Hill, 1997.

Schach, S. R. *Classical and Object-Oriented Software Engineering,* 4th ed. New York: McGraw-Hill, 1999.

Sommerville, I. *Software Engineering,* 5th ed. Reading, MA: Addison-Wesley, 1995.

part three

DATA ORGANIZATION

We have seen that information stored inside a machine is represented in coded form and organized in a manner that is compatible with the appropriate technology, such as individually addressable memory cells or as sectors on a disk. This organization is rarely the same as that envisioned by the data's user. For example, data representing the weekly sales of a company's sales force might be envisioned in tabular form, with a separate column for each day of the week and a separate row for each member of the sales force. Or, the names and positions of a company's employees might be pictured in the form of an organization chart. Moreover, a company may need to envision its inventory records organized by part number for one application and by cost for another.

In Part 3 we study how a machine can be programmed to present data as though it were stored in these conceptual and more useful forms and how this goal affects the way data items are actually stored within the machine. In Chapter 7 we concentrate on data stored in a machine's main memory; in Chapter 8 we consider data stored in mass storage; and in Chapter 9 we introduce the topic of database systems.

c h a p t e r

DATA STRUCTURES

s e v e n

A machine's main memory is organized as individual cells with consecutive addresses. However, it is often convenient to associate other data arrangements among these cells. For example, weekly sales records are more naturally viewed in a tabular form in which sales of different items on different days are arranged in rows and columns. In this chapter we consider how such abstract data organizations are simulated. The goal is to allow the data user to think in terms of abstract organizations rather than being concerned with the actual organization within a machine's main memory.

7.1 Arrays

7.2 Lists
Pointers
Contiguous Lists
Linked Lists
Supporting the Conceptual List

7.3 Stacks
Backtracking
Stack Implementation

7.4 Queues

7.5 Trees
Tree Implementation
A Binary Tree Package

*7.6 Customized Data Types
User-Defined Types
Abstract Data Types
Encapsulation
Classes

*7.7 Pointers in Machine Language

*Asterisks indicate suggestions for optional sections.

7.1 Arrays

In Chapter 5 we saw that many high-level languages allow a programmer to express algorithms as though the data being manipulated were stored in a rectangular arrangement called a homogeneous array, where the term *homogeneous* implied that all the entries in the array were of the same type. In this section we investigate how such arrays are actually implemented and how a translator converts the array references it finds in a source program into the terminology of memory cells and addresses.

Suppose an algorithm for manipulating a series of 24 hourly temperature readings is expressed in a high-level language. A programmer would probably find it convenient to think of these readings arranged as a one-dimensional array called `Readings` whose various entries are referenced in terms of their position in the list. This position is called an index. The first reading might be referenced by `Readings[1]`, the second by `Readings[2]`, and so on.

The conversion from this conceptual one-dimensional array organization to the actual arrangement within the machine's memory is straightforward since the data can be stored in a sequence of 24 memory cells with consecutive addresses in the same order envisioned by the programmer. Knowing the address of the first cell in this sequence, a translator can convert references such as `Readings[4]` into the proper memory terminology. It merely subtracts one from the index of the desired entry and then adds the result to the address of the memory cell containing the first temperature reading. If the first reading is at address x, the fourth reading is located at address $x + (4 - 1)$, as shown in Figure 7.1.

Now suppose a programmer wants to write a program dealing with the sales made by a company's sales force during a one-week period. We normally envision such data arranged in tabular form, with the names of the sales personnel listed down the left side and the days of the week listed across the top. Hence the programmer would probably like to write the program as though the data were arranged in a two-dimensional array, where the values across each row indicate the sales made by a particular employee, and the values down a column represent all the sales made during a particular day.

A machine's memory is not organized in this rectangular fashion but rather as individual cells with consecutive addresses. Thus the rectangular structure required by the array must be simulated. To do this, we first recognize that the size of the array does not vary as updates are made. We can therefore calculate the amount of storage area needed for the entire array and reserve a block of contiguous memory cells of that size. Next, we store the data in the array row by row. That is, starting at the first cell of the reserved block, we store the values from the first row of the array into consecutive memory locations; following this, we store the next row, then the next, and so on (Figure 7.2). Such a storage system is said to use **row major order** in contrast to **column major order,** in which the array is stored column by column.

FIGURE 7.1

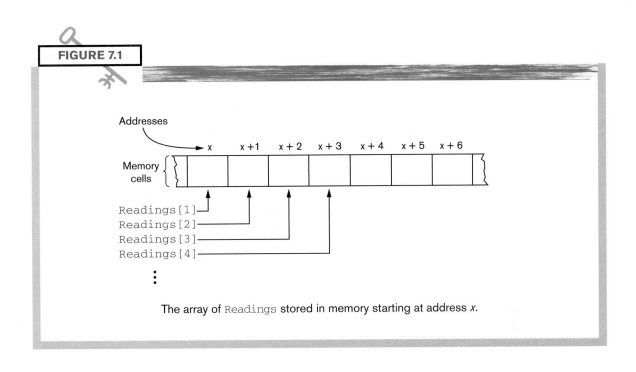

The array of `Readings` stored in memory starting at address *x*.

FIGURE 7.2

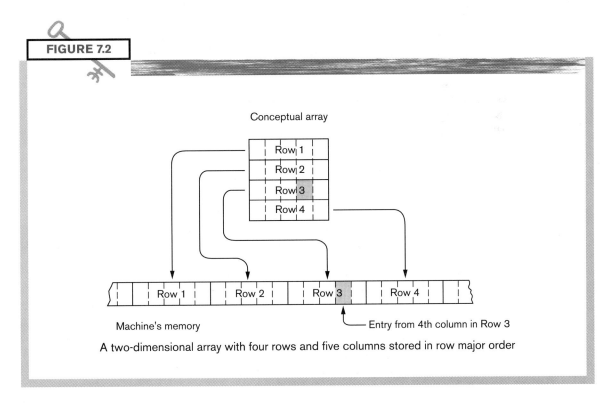

A two-dimensional array with four rows and five columns stored in row major order

With the data stored in this manner, let us consider how we would find the memory cell containing the value in the third row and fourth column of the array. We first envision ourselves as being at the first location in the reserved block of the machine's memory. From this location on, we find the data in the first row of the array followed by the second, then the third, and so on. To get to the data in the third row, we must move beyond both the first and second rows. Since each row contains five entries (one for each day from Monday through Friday), we must move beyond a total of ten entries to reach the first entry of the third row. From the beginning of the third row, we must move beyond another three entries to reach the entry in the fourth column of the array. Altogether, to reach the entry in the third row and fourth column, we must move beyond 13 entries from the beginning of the block.

The preceding calculation can be refined to obtain a general process that can be used by translators to convert references in terms of row and column positions into actual memory addresses. In particular, if we let c represent the number of columns in an array (which is the number of entries in each row), then the address of the entry in the ith row and jth column will be

$$x + (c \times (i - 1)) + (j - 1)$$

where x is the address of the cell containing the entry in the first row and first column. That is, we must move beyond $i - 1$ rows, each of which contains c entries, to reach the ith row and then $j - 1$ more entries to reach the jth entry in this row. In our prior example $c = 5$, $i = 3$, and $i = 4$ so if the array were stored starting at address x, then the entry in the third row, fourth column would be at address $x + (5 \times (3 - 1)) + (4 - 1) = x + 13$. (The expression $(c \times (i - 1)) + (j - 1)$ is sometimes called the **address polynomial.**)

With this information, software routines can be written to convert requests in terms of rows and columns into locations within the block of memory containing the array. A translator, for example, uses this technique to convert a reference such as `Sales[2,4]` into an actual memory address. A programmer can therefore enjoy the luxury of thinking of the data in tabular form (a conceptual structure) even though it is actually stored in a single row (the actual structure).

QUESTIONS/EXERCISES

1. Show how the array below would be arranged in main memory when stored in row major order.

5	3	7
4	2	8
1	9	6

2. Give a formula for finding the entry in the ith row and jth column of a two-dimensional array if it is stored in column major order rather than row major order.

3. If a two-dimensional array of 8 rows and 11 columns is stored in row major order beginning at memory address 25, what is the address of the entry in the third row, sixth column if each entry occupies two memory cells?

4. In the C, C++, and Java programming languages, indices of arrays start at 0 rather than at 1. Thus the entry in the first row, fourth column of an array named `Array` is referenced by `Array[0][3]`. In this case, what address polynomial is used by the translator to convert references of the form `Array[i][j]` into memory addresses?

7.2 Lists

An important property of arrays is that their size and shape are constant. Thus, simulating them in a machine's memory is essentially a process of converting the conceptual location of an entry into the actual location. A contrast is provided by dynamic structures that vary in size and shape, such as an organization's membership list, which grows as new members join and shrinks as old members leave. Simulating these conceptual structures requires accommodating variations in the structure itself.

In this section we will consider two ways of implementing the dynamic structure known as a list. But first, we should introduce the concept of a pointer, which is a basic tool used for implementing a variety of dynamic structures.

Pointers

Recall that the various storage locations in a machine's main memory are identified by numeric addresses. If we know the address of a piece of data, we can find that item. Being merely numeric values, these addresses themselves are easily stored in a machine's memory. Thus, having stored an item of data in one cell of memory, we could store the address of that data in another memory cell and later use this memory cell as a means of retrieving the data. That is, the value in this cell tells us where to find the data.

In a sense, then, a memory cell containing an address can be thought of as pointing to another memory cell. Such cells are called **pointers.** We have already encountered the concept of a pointer in our discussion of a machine's fetch–decode–execute cycle, in which a program counter is used to hold the address of the next instruction to be executed. In fact, another somewhat outdated name for a program counter is **instruction pointer.** The URLs used to link hypertext comments are also examples of the pointer concept, except that URLs are pointers to locations in the Internet rather than to locations in main memory.

Many programming languages today allow for the declaration, allocation, and manipulation of pointers, just as they allow for such operations for integers or character strings. Using such a language, a programmer can design elaborate networks of data items within a machine's memory. For example, suppose a library has its holdings represented in a machine's memory in alphabetical order by title. Although convenient in many applications, this arrangement makes it difficult to find all the books by a particular author, because the books are scattered throughout the list. To solve this problem, we can reserve an additional memory cell of type pointer within the block of cells representing each book. Then, in each of these pointer cells, we can place the address of another block representing a book by the same author so that the books with common authorship are linked in a loop (Figure 7.3). Once we find one book by a given author, we can then find all the others by following the pointers from one book to another.

Contiguous Lists

Let us now consider techniques for storing a list of names in a machine's main memory. One strategy is to store the entire list in a single block of memory cells with consecutive addresses. Assuming that each name is no longer than eight letters, we can divide this large block of cells into a collection of subblocks, each containing eight cells. Into each subblock we can store a name by recording its ASCII code using one cell per letter (Figure 7.4). If the name alone does not fill all the cells in the subblock allocated to it, we can merely fill the remaining cells with the ASCII code for a space. Using this system requires a block of 80 consecutive memory cells to store a list of 10 names.

Such an organization is referred to as a **contiguous list** and is typical of the storage system obtained when a programmer stores a list in an array. In particular, assuming that each name is no longer than eight characters, a programmer could store a list of 10 names in an array of characters with 10 rows and eight columns, producing the structure represented in Figure 7.4 (assuming that the array is stored in row-major order).

A contiguous list is convenient in its simplicity but has several disadvantages. Suppose we need to delete a name. If this name is currently toward the beginning of the list and we need to keep the list in the same (possibly alphabetical) order, we must move all the names occurring later in the list forward in memory to fill the hole left by the deleted entry. A more serious problem occurs if we need to add names, since we may have to move the entire list to obtain an available block of contiguous cells large enough for the expanded list.

FIGURE 7.3

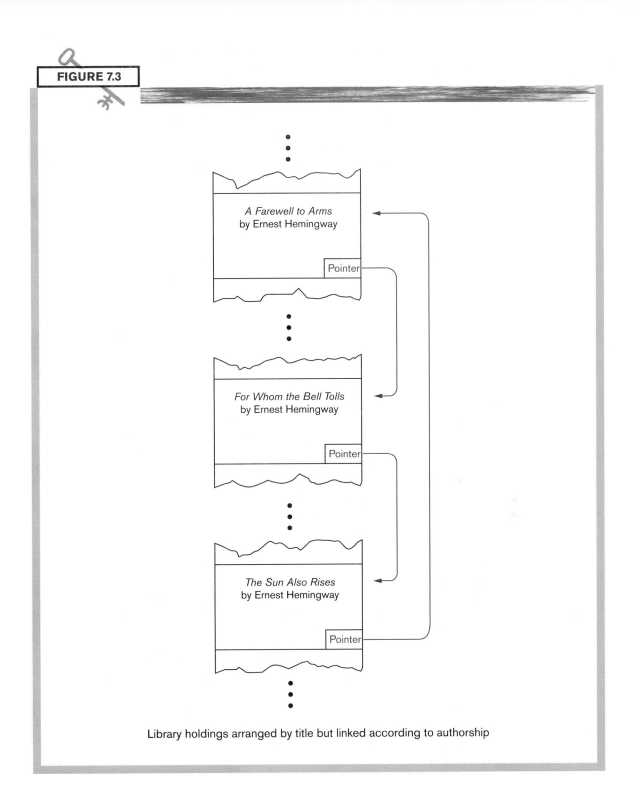

Library holdings arranged by title but linked according to authorship

FIGURE 7.4

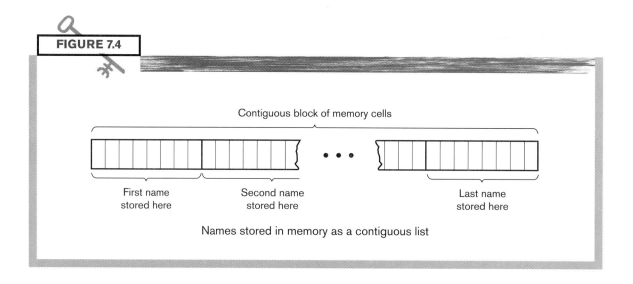

Names stored in memory as a contiguous list

Linked Lists

Such problems can be avoided if we allow the individual names in the list to be stored in different areas of memory rather than together in one large, contiguous block. To do this, we could store each name in a block of nine contiguous memory cells. The first eight of these cells are used to hold the name itself, and the last cell is used as a pointer to the next name in the list. Following this lead, the list can be scattered among several small nine-cell blocks linked together by pointers. Because of this linkage system, such an organization is called a **linked list.**

To keep track of the first entry in a linked list, we normally set aside a memory cell in which we save the address of that entry. Since this cell points to the beginning, or head, of the list, it is called a **head pointer.** To read the list, we start at the location indicated by this head pointer. There we find the first name in the list along with the pointer to the next entry. Following this pointer, we can find the second entry and so forth throughout the list. In this manner, we can traverse the entire list by hopping from one name to the next.

The end of a linked list is indicated by means of a **NIL pointer,** which is a special bit pattern appearing in the pointer cell of the last entry, indicating that no further entries appear in the list. For example, if we agree never to store a list entry at address 0, the value zero will never appear as a legitimate pointer value, and can therefore be used as the NIL pointer. In this case, traversing the list would involve following the pointer system from one entry to the next until reaching a pointer with the value zero.

The final linked list structure is represented by the diagram in Figure 7.5 in which we depict the scattered blocks of memory used for the list by individual rectangles. Each rectangle is labeled to indicate its composition. Each pointer is represented by an arrow that leads from the pointer itself to the pointer's addressee.

FIGURE 7.5

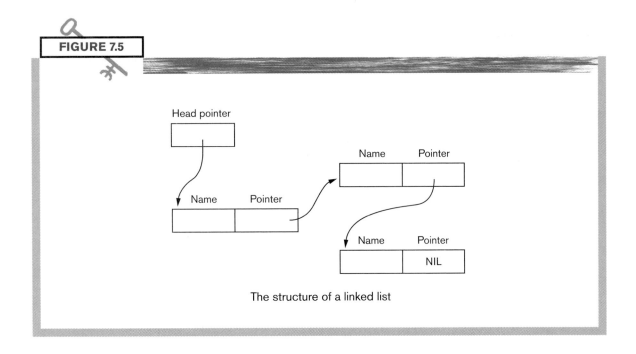

The structure of a linked list

Let us return now to the problem of deleting and inserting entries in the list. Our goal is to see how the use of pointers alleviates the movement of names encountered when storing the list in a single contiguous block. First we note that a name can be deleted by changing a single pointer. This is done by changing the pointer that formerly pointed to the name being deleted so that it points to the name following the deleted entry (Figure 7.6). From then on, when the list is traversed, the deleted name is passed by because it no longer is part of the chain.

Inserting a new name is only a little more involved. We first find an unused block of nine memory cells, store the new name in the first eight cells, and fill the ninth cell with the address of the name in the list that should follow the new name. Finally, we change the pointer associated with the name that should precede the new name so that it points to the new name (Figure 7.7). After this is done, the new entry will be found in the proper place each time the list is traversed.

Supporting the Conceptual List

When writing a program, a programmer must often decide whether to implement a list as a contiguous structure or a linked one. But once this decision is made and the list is established, the programmer should be able to set these

FIGURE 7.6

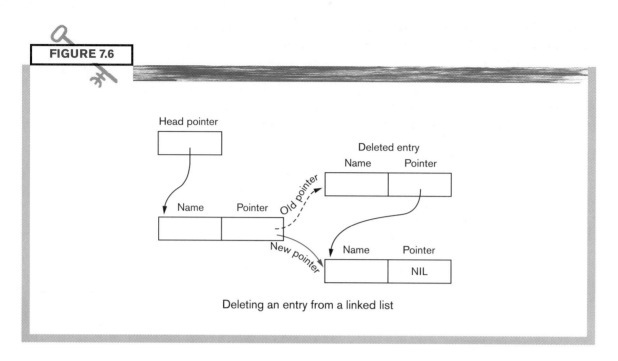

Deleting an entry from a linked list

FIGURE 7.7

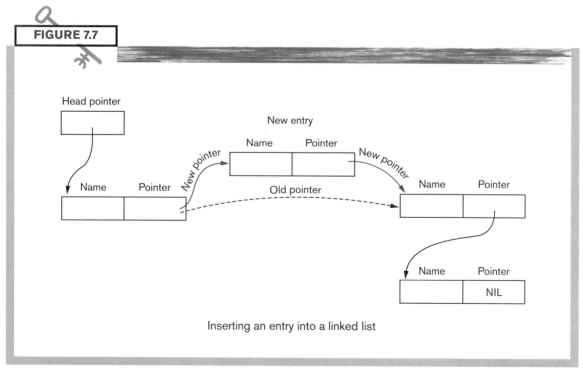

Inserting an entry into a linked list

issues aside and concentrate on other details. In short, the program should be constructed so that the list can be referenced by other portions of the program as an abstract tool.

For example, consider the task of developing a software package for maintaining the class enrollments for a university registrar. The programmer developing this package might approach the problem by establishing a separate list structure for each class, with each list containing an alphabetically ordered list of the students in that class. Once this is done, the programmer's attention should be allowed to shift to the more general concerns of the problem and not be repeatedly distracted by the details of how entries should be moved within a contiguous list or what shifting of pointers is required in a linked list.

To this end, the programmer could write a collection of procedures for performing such activities as inserting a new entry, deleting an old entry, searching for an entry, or printing a list and then use these procedures in the remaining software package to manipulate the lists in the registrar system. For example, to place J. W. Brown in the course Physics 208, the programmer could write a statement such as

A PROBLEM WITH POINTERS

Insert ("Brown, J.W.", "Physics 208")

and rely on the procedure Insert to carry out the details of the insertion. In this manner, the programmer can develop the other parts of the program without concern for the technicalities of how the list is actually implemented.

As an example of this approach, a procedure named PrintList for printing a linked list of names is shown in Figure 7.8. Recall that the first entry of the list is pointed to by a pointer called the head pointer, and each entry in the list consists of two pieces: a name and a pointer. Once this procedure has been developed, it can be used as an abstract tool to print the list without concern for how the list is actually stored. For example, to obtain a printed class list for Economics 301, a programmer need only write

PrintList ("Economics 301")

Just as the use of flowcharts led to tangled algorithm designs (Chapter 4) and the haphazard use of *goto* statements led to poorly designed programs (Chapter 5), undisciplined use of pointers has been found to produce needlessly complex and error-prone data structures. To bring order to this chaos, many programming languages restrict the flexibility of pointers. For example, Java does not allow pointers in their general form. Instead, it allows only a restricted form of pointers called references. One distinction is that a reference cannot be modified by an arithmetic operation. For example, if a Java programmer wanted to advance the reference *Next* to the next entry in a contiguous list, he or she would use a statement equivalent to

redirect Next to the next list entry

whereas a C programmer would use a statement equivalent to

assign Next the value Next + 1.

Note that the Java statement better reflects the underlying goal. Moreover, to execute the Java statement, there must be another list entry, but if *Next* already pointed to the last entry in the list, the C statement would result in Next pointing to something outside the list—a common error for beginning, and even seasoned, programmers.

FIGURE 7.8

procedure PrintList (List)

Assign CurrentPointer **the value** in the head pointer of List.
while (CurrentPointer is not NIL) **do**
  (Print the name in the entry pointed to by CurrentPointer;
  Observe the value in the pointer cell of the List entry
  pointed to by CurrentPointer, and reassign CurrentPointer
  to be that value.)

A procedure for printing a linked list

QUESTIONS/EXERCISES

1. If you know the address of the beginning of the first entry in a contiguous list, how can you find the address of the fifth entry? What about the case of a linked list?
2. What condition indicates that a linked list is empty?
3. Modify the procedure in Figure 7.8 so it stops printing once a particular name has been printed.
4. Design a procedure for finding a particular entry in a linked list and then deleting it.

7.3 Stacks

One of the properties of a list that makes a linked structure more inviting than a contiguous one is the need to insert and delete entries inside the list. Recall that it was such operations that had the potential of forcing the massive movement of names to fill or create holes in the case of a contiguous list. If we restrict such operations to the ends of the structure, we find that the use of a contiguous structure becomes a more convenient system. An example of this phenomenon is a **stack,** which is a list in which all insertions and deletions are performed at the same end of the structure. A consequence of this restriction is that the last entry entered will always be the first entry removed—an observation that leads to stacks being known as **last-in, first-out (LIFO)** structures.

The end of a stack at which entries are inserted and deleted is called the **top** of the stack. The other end is sometimes called the stack's base. To reflect the fact that access to a stack is restricted to the topmost entry, we use special terminology when referring to the insertion and deletion operations. The process of inserting an object on the stack is called a **push** operation, and the process of deleting an object is called a **pop** operation. Thus we speak of pushing an entry onto a stack and popping an entry off a stack.

Backtracking

A classic application of a stack involves the execution of a program involving procedures as found in our pseudocode. When the execution of a procedure is requested, the machine must transfer its attention to the procedure; yet later, when the procedure is completed, the machine must return to the original location before continuing. This means that, when the initial transfer is made, there must be a mechanism for remembering the location to which execution ultimately returns.

The situation is complicated by the fact that the procedure may itself request the execution of another procedure, which may request still another, and so on (Figure 7.9). Consequently, the return locations being remembered begin to pile up. Later, as each of these procedures is completed, execution must be returned to the proper place within the program unit that called the

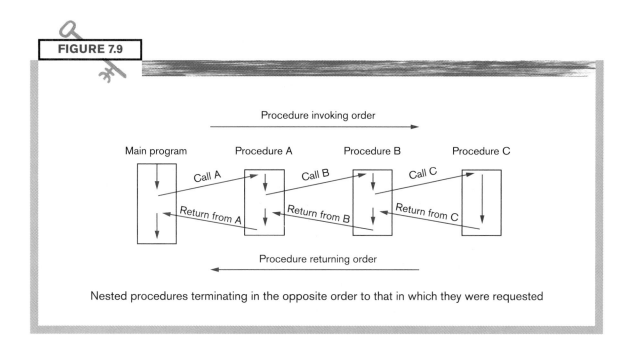

FIGURE 7.9

Nested procedures terminating in the opposite order to that in which they were requested completed procedure. A system is therefore needed to save the return locations and later retrieve them in the proper order.

A stack is an ideal structure for such a system. As each procedure is called, a pointer to the pertinent return location is pushed on a stack, and as each procedure is completed, the top entry from the stack is extracted with the assurance of obtaining a pointer to the proper return location. This example is representative of stack applications in general in that it demonstrates the relationship between stacks and the process of backtracking. Indeed, the concept of a stack is inherent in any process that entails backing out of a system in the opposite order from which it was entered.

As another example of backtracking, suppose we want to print the names in a linked list (as described in Section 7.2) in reverse order—that is, last name first. Our problem is that the only way we can access the names is by following the linked structure. Thus we need a way of holding each name retrieved until all of the names that follow have been retrieved and printed. Our solution is to traverse the list from its beginning to its end while pushing the names we find onto a stack. After reaching the end of the list, we print the names as we pop them off the stack (Figure 7.10). The procedure for this process is presented in Figure 7.11.

Stack Implementation

To implement a stack structure in a computer's memory, it is customary to reserve a block of contiguous memory cells large enough to accommodate the stack as it grows and shrinks. (Determining the size of this block can often be a critical decision. If too little room is reserved, the stack ultimately exceeds the allotted storage space; if too much room is reserved, memory space will be wasted.) One end of this block is designated as the stack's base. It is here that the first entry pushed on the stack is stored, with each additional entry being placed next to its predecessor as the stack grows toward the other end of the reserved block.

Thus, as entries are pushed and popped, the top of the stack moves back and forth within the reserved block of memory cells. A means is therefore needed to maintain a record of the location of the top entry. For this purpose, the address of the top entry is stored in an additional memory cell known as the **stack pointer.** That is, the stack pointer points to the top of the stack.

The complete system, as illustrated in Figure 7.12, works as follows: To push a new entry on the stack, we first adjust the stack pointer to point to the vacancy just beyond the top of the stack and then place the new entry at this location. To pop an entry from the stack, we read the data pointed to by the stack pointer and then adjust the pointer to point to the next entry down on the stack.

As we observed in the case of lists, a programmer would probably find it advantageous to write procedures that perform these push and pop operations

FIGURE 7.10

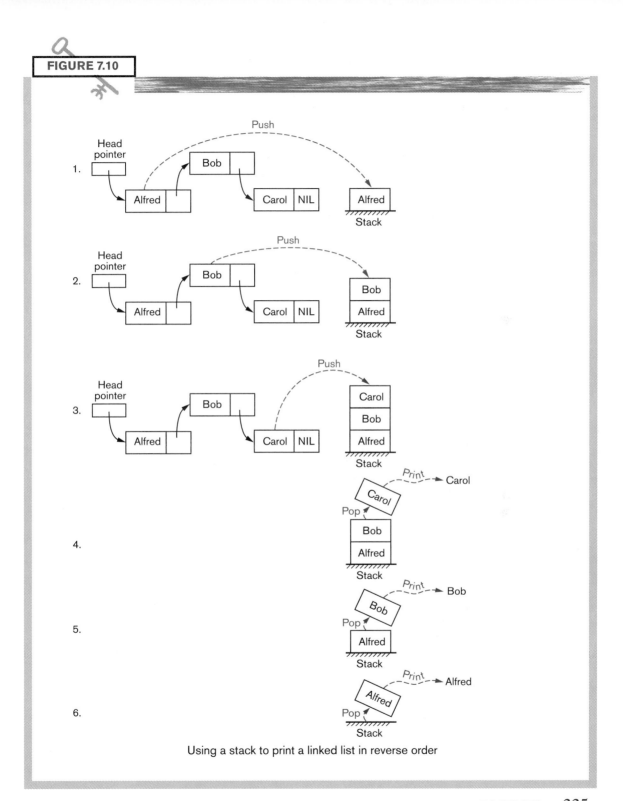

Using a stack to print a linked list in reverse order

FIGURE 7.11

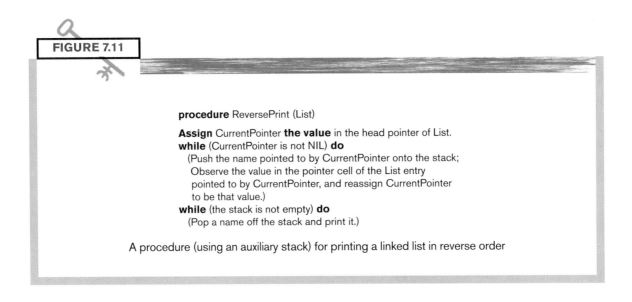

procedure ReversePrint (List)

Assign CurrentPointer **the value** in the head pointer of List.
while (CurrentPointer is not NIL) **do**
  (Push the name pointed to by CurrentPointer onto the stack;
  Observe the value in the pointer cell of the List entry
  pointed to by CurrentPointer, and reassign CurrentPointer
  to be that value.)
while (the stack is not empty) **do**
  (Pop a name off the stack and print it.)

A procedure (using an auxiliary stack) for printing a linked list in reverse order

FIGURE 7.12

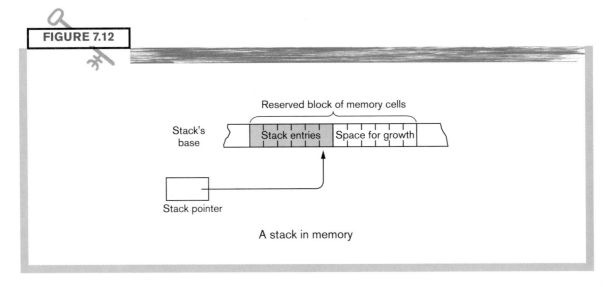

A stack in memory

so that the stack could be used as an abstract tool. Note that these procedures should handle such special cases as attempts to pop entries from an empty stack and to push entries onto a full stack. In particular, a complete stack system would probably contain procedures for pushing entries, popping entries, testing for an empty stack, and testing for a full stack.

A stack organized in a contiguous block of memory cells exhibits little difference between the conceptual structure and the actual structure in main memory. Suppose, however, that we cannot reserve a fixed block of memory and be assured that the stack will always fit. A solution is to implement the stack as a linked structure similar to that discussed in Section 7.2. This avoids the limitations of restricting the stack to a fixed-size block, since it allows the entries in the stack to be stuffed into small pieces of available space anywhere in memory. In such a situation, the conceptual stack structure will be quite different from the actual arrangement of the data in memory.

QUESTIONS/EXERCISES

1. List some additional occurrences of stacks in everyday life.
2. Suppose a main program calls procedure A, which in turn calls procedure B, and after B is completed, procedure A calls procedure C. Follow this scenario, maintaining the stack of return locations.
3. Based on the technique of this section for implementing a stack in a contiguous block of cells, what condition indicates that the stack is empty?
4. Design a procedure for popping an entry off a stack that is implemented with a stack pointer. Your procedure should print an error message if the stack is empty.
5. Describe how a stack can be implemented in a high-level language in terms of a one-dimensional array.

7.4 Queues

In contrast to a stack in which both insertions and deletions are performed at the same end, a **queue** is a list in which all insertions are performed at one end while all deletions are made at the other. We have already met this structure in relation to waiting lines in Chapter 3, where we recognized it as being a first-in, first-out (FIFO) storage system. Actually, the concept of a queue is inherent in any system in which objects are served in the same order in which they arrive. The ends of a queue get their names from this waiting-line relationship. The end at which entries are removed is called the **head** (or sometimes the front) of the queue just as we say that the next person to be served in a cafeteria is at the head (or front) of the line. Similarly, the end of the queue at which new entries are added is called the **tail** (or rear).

We can implement a queue in a computer's memory within a block of contiguous cells in a way similar to our storage of a stack. Since we need to perform operations at both ends of the structure, we set aside two memory cells to use as pointers instead of just one, as we did for a stack. One of these pointers, called the **head pointer,** keeps track of the head of the queue; the other, called the **tail pointer,** keeps track of the tail. When the queue is empty, both of these

FIGURE 7.13

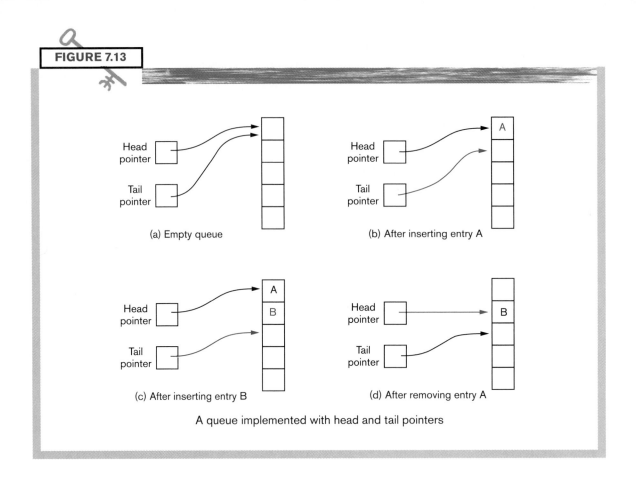

(a) Empty queue

(b) After inserting entry A

(c) After inserting entry B

(d) After removing entry A

A queue implemented with head and tail pointers

pointers point to the same location (Figure 7.13). Each time an entry is inserted, it is placed in the location pointed to by the tail pointer and then the tail pointer is adjusted to point toward the next unused location. In this manner, the tail pointer is always pointing to the first vacancy at the tail of the queue. Removing an entry from the queue involves extracting the entry pointed to by the head pointer and then adjusting the head pointer to point toward the entry that followed the removed entry.

A problem remains with the storage system as described thus far. If left unchecked, the queue crawls slowly through memory like a glacier, destroying any other data in its path (Figure 7.14). This movement is the result of the rather egocentric policy of inserting each new entry by merely placing it next to the previous one and repositioning the tail pointer accordingly. If we add enough entries, the tail of the queue ultimately extends all the way to the end of the machine's memory.

This consumption of memory is not the result of the queue's size but is a side effect of the queue's access procedure. (A small yet active queue can easily

FIGURE 7.14

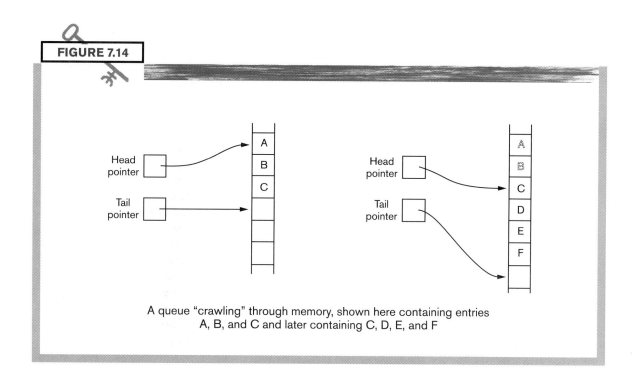

A queue "crawling" through memory, shown here containing entries
A, B, and C and later containing C, D, E, and F

require more of a machine's memory resources than a large, inactive one.) One solution to this memory space problem might be to move the entries in a queue forward as the leading ones are removed, in the same manner as people waiting to buy theater tickets step forward each time a person has been served. However, this mass movement of data would be very inefficient. What we need is a way of confining the queue to one area of memory without being forced to perform major rearrangements of data.

A common solution is to set aside a block of memory for the queue, start the queue at one end of the block, and let the queue migrate toward the other end of the block. Then, when the tail of the queue reaches the end of the block, we merely start inserting additional entries back at the original end of the block, which by this time is vacant. Likewise, when the last entry in the block finally becomes the head of the queue and is removed, the head pointer is adjusted back to the beginning of the block where other entries are, by this time, waiting. In this manner, the queue chases itself around within the block rather than wandering off through memory.

Such a technique results in an implementation that is called a **circular queue** because the effect is that of forming a loop out of the block of memory cells allotted to the queue (Figure 7.15). As far as the queue is concerned, the last cell in the block is adjacent to the first cell.

FIGURE 7.15

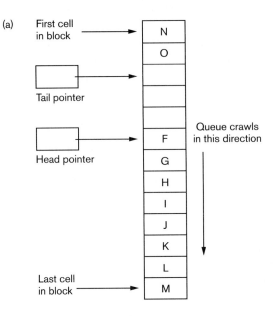

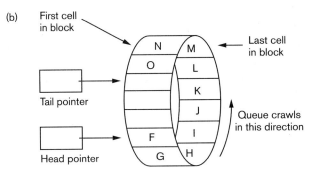

A circular queue (a) containing the letters F through O as actually stored in memory, and (b) in its conceptual form in which the last cell in the block is "adjacent" to the first cell

Once again, we should recognize the difference between the conceptual structure envisioned by the user of a queue and the actual cyclic structure implemented in the machine's memory. As in the case of the previous structures, these differences are normally bridged by software. That is, along with the collection of memory cells used for data storage, a queue implementation should include a collection of procedures that insert and remove entries from the queue as well as detect whether the queue is empty or full. Then, a programmer working on another software unit can request that entries be inserted or removed by means of these procedures without concern for the details of how the queue is actually implemented in memory.

QUESTIONS/EXERCISES

1. Using paper and pencil, keep a record of the circular queue structure described in this section during the following scenario. (Assume that the block reserved for the queue can contain only four entries.)

   Insert entry A.
   Insert entry B.
   Insert entry C.
   Remove an entry.
   Remove an entry.
   Insert entry D.
   Insert entry E.
   Remove an entry.
   Insert entry F.
   Remove an entry.

2. When a queue is implemented in a circular fashion as described in this section, what is the relationship between the head and tail pointers when the queue is empty? What about when the queue is full? How can one detect whether a queue is full or empty?

3. Design a procedure for inserting an entry in a circular queue.

7.5 Trees

The last data structure that we will consider is the **tree**, which is the structure reflected by an organization chart of a typical company (Figure 7.16). Here, the president is represented at the top, with lines branching down to the vice-presidents, who are followed by regional managers, and so on. To this intuitive definition of a tree structure we impose one additional constraint, which (in terms

FIGURE 7.16

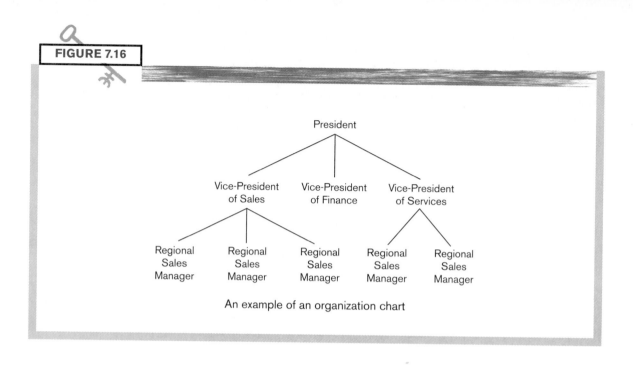

An example of an organization chart

of an organization chart) is that no individual in the company reports to two different people. That is, different branches of the organization do not merge at a lower level.

Each position in a tree is called a **node.** The node at the top is called the **root node** (since if we turned the drawing upside down, this node would represent the base or root of the tree). The nodes at the other extreme are called **terminal nodes** (or sometimes **leaf nodes**). If we select any node in a tree, we find that this node together with those nodes below it again have the structure of a tree. We call these smaller structures **subtrees.** At times we refer to tree structures as though each node gives birth to those nodes immediately below it. In this sense, we often speak of a node's ancestors or descendants. We refer to its immediate descendants as its **children** and its immediate ancestor as its **parent.** Moreover, we speak of nodes with the same parent as being **twins** or **siblings.** Finally, we often refer to the **depth** of a tree, which is the number of nodes in the longest path from the root to a leaf. In other words, the depth of a tree is the number of horizontal layers within it.

We encounter tree structures repeatedly in subsequent chapters, so we will not elaborate on applications now. Later in this section, as well as in our discussion of index organization in Chapter 8, we will find that information that must be searched quickly for data retrieval is often organized as a tree, and in Chapter 10, we will see how games can be analyzed in terms of trees.

Tree Implementation

For the purpose of discussing tree storage techniques, we restrict our attention to **binary trees,** which are trees in which each node has at most two children. Such trees normally are stored in memory using a linked structure similar to that of linked lists. However, rather than each entry consisting of two components (the data followed by a next-entry pointer), each entry (or node) of the binary tree contains three components: (1) the data, (2) a pointer to the node's first child, and (3) a pointer to the node's second child. Although there is no left or right inside a machine, it is helpful to refer to the first pointer as the **left child pointer** and the other pointer as the **right child pointer** in reference to the way we would draw the tree on paper. Thus each node of the tree is represented by a short, contiguous block of memory cells with the format shown in Figure 7.17.

Storing the tree in memory involves finding available blocks of memory cells to hold the nodes and linking these nodes according to the desired tree structure. That is, each pointer must be set to point to the left or right child of the pertinent node or assigned the NIL value if there are no more nodes in that direction of the tree. This means that a terminal node is characterized by having both of its pointers assigned NIL. Finally, we set aside a special memory location, called a **root pointer,** where we store the address of the root node. It is this root pointer that provides initial access to the tree.

An example of this linked storage system is presented in Figure 7.18, where a conceptual binary tree structure is exhibited along with a representation of how that tree might actually appear in a computer's memory. With this system we can always find the root node by means of the root pointer and then trace any path down the tree by following the appropriate pointers from node to node.

An alternative to a linked storage system for binary trees is the technique of setting aside a contiguous block of memory cells, storing the root node in the first of these cells (for simplicity, we assume that each node of the tree requires

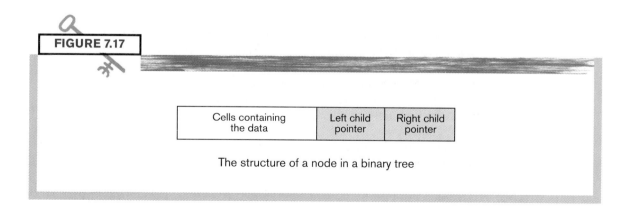

FIGURE 7.17

Cells containing the data	Left child pointer	Right child pointer

The structure of a node in a binary tree

FIGURE 7.18

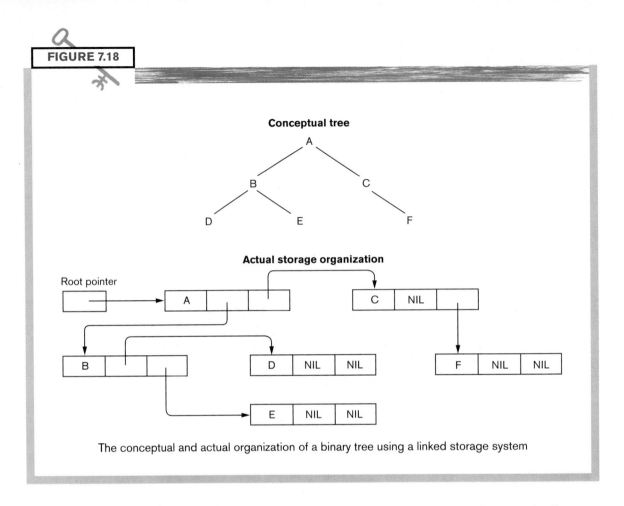

The conceptual and actual organization of a binary tree using a linked storage system

only one memory cell), storing the left child of the root in the second cell, storing the right child of the root in the third cell, and in general, storing the left and right children of the node found in cell n in the cells $2n$ and $2n + 1$, respectively. Cells within the block that represent locations not used by the current tree structure are marked with a unique bit pattern that indicates the absence of data. Following this technique, the conceptual tree shown in Figure 7.18 is stored as shown in Figure 7.19. Note that the system is essentially that of storing the nodes across successively lower levels of the tree as segments, one after the other. That is, the first entry in the block is the root node, followed by the root's children, followed by the root's grandchildren, and so on.

In contrast to the linked structure described earlier, this alternative storage system provides a convenient method for finding the parent or sibling of any node. (Of course, this can be done in the linked structure at the expense of additional pointers.) The location of a node's parent can be found by dividing the node's position in the block by 2 while discarding any remainder (the par-

FIGURE 7.19

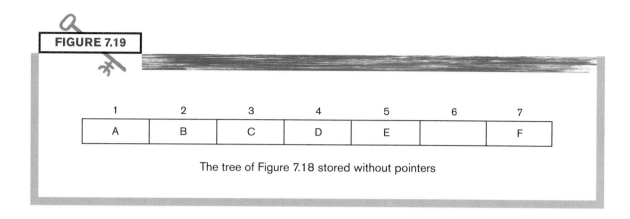

The tree of Figure 7.18 stored without pointers

ent of the node in position 7 would be the node in position 3). The location of a node's sibling can be found by adding 1 to the location of a node in an even-numbered position or subtracting 1 from the location of a node in an odd-numbered position (the sibling of the node in position 4 is the node in position 5, while the sibling of the node in position 3 is the node in position 2). Moreover, this storage system makes efficient use of space in the case of binary trees that are approximately balanced (in the sense that both subtrees below the root node have the same depth) and full (in the sense that they do not have long, thin branches). For trees without these characteristics, though, the system can become quite inefficient, as shown in Figure 7.20.

A Binary Tree Package

As in the case of the other structures we have studied, it is advantageous to isolate the technicalities of a tree's implementation from the other parts of a software system. Consequently, a programmer normally identifies the activities that will be performed on a tree, writes procedures to accomplish these activities, and then uses these procedures to access the tree from other parts of the program. Thus, these procedures together with the storage area form a package that is used as an abstract tool.

To demonstrate such a package, let us return to the problem of storing a list of names in alphabetical order. We assume that the operations to be performed on this list are the following:

> *search* for the presence of an entry,
> *print* the list in alphabetical order, and
> *insert* a new entry

Our goal is to develop a storage system along with a collection of procedures to perform these operations.

FIGURE 7.20

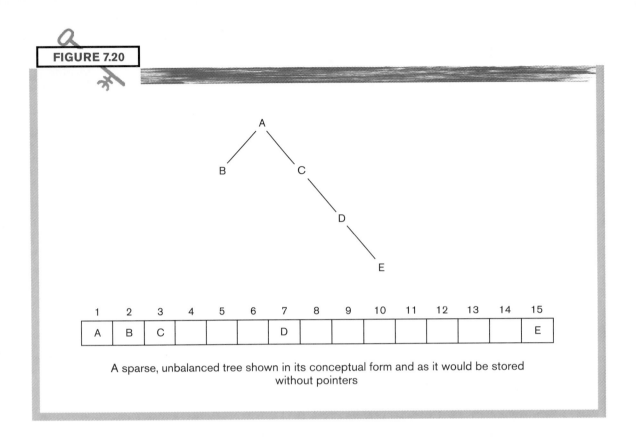

A sparse, unbalanced tree shown in its conceptual form and as it would be stored without pointers

We begin by considering options regarding the procedure for searching the list. If the list were stored according to the linked list model in Section 7.2, we would be forced to search the list in a sequential fashion, a process that, as we discussed in Chapter 4, could be very inefficient if the list should become long. We will therefore seek an implementation that allows us to use the binary search algorithm (Chapter 4) for our search procedure. To apply this algorithm, our storage system must allow us to find the middle entry of successively smaller portions of the list. Such an operation is possible when using a contiguous list, since we can compute the address of the middle entry in much the same manner as we can compute the locations of entries in an array. But using a contiguous list introduces problems when making insertions, as observed in Section 7.2.

Our problem can be solved by storing the list as a linked binary tree rather than using one of the traditional list storage systems. We make the middle list entry the root node, the middle of the remaining first half of the list the root's left child, and the middle of the remaining second half the root's right child. The middle entries of each remaining fourth of the list become the children of the root's children and so forth. For example, the tree in Figure 7.21 represents the list of letters A, B, C, D, E, F, G, H, I, J, K, L, and M. (We consider the

FIGURE 7.21

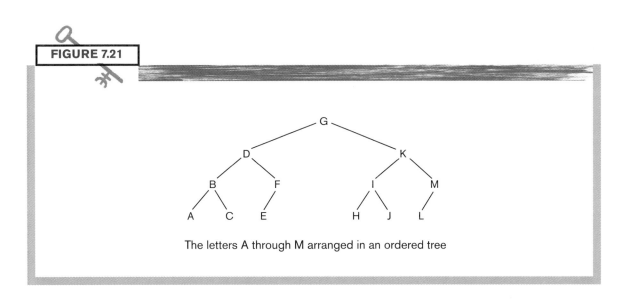

The letters A through M arranged in an ordered tree

larger of the middle two entries as the middle when the part of the list in question contains an even number of entries.)

To search the list stored in this manner, we compare the target value to the root node. If the two are equal, our search has succeeded. If they are not equal, we move to the left or right child of the root, depending on whether the target is less than or greater than the root, respectively. There we find the middle of the portion of the list necessary to continue the search. This process of comparing and moving to a child continues until we find the target (meaning that our search was successful) or we reach the bottom of the tree without finding the target (meaning that our search was a failure). Figure 7.22 shows how this search process can be expressed in the case of a linked tree structure. (Annotative comments are bracketed by asterisks.)

GARBAGE COLLECTION

As dynamic data structures such as linked lists and trees grow and shrink, storage space is used and released. The process of reclaiming unused storage space for future use is known as **garbage collection.** Garbage collection is required in numerous settings. The memory manager within an operating system must perform garbage collection as it allocates and retrieves memory space. The file manager performs garbage collection as files are stored on and deleted from the machine's mass storage. Moreover, any process running under the control of the dispatcher may need to perform garbage collection within its own allotted memory space.

Garbage collection involves some subtle problems. In the case of linked structures, each time a pointer to a data item is changed, the garbage collector must decide whether the storage space to which the pointer originally pointed is to be reclaimed. The problem becomes especially complex in intertwined data structures involving multiple paths of pointers. Inaccurate garbage collection routines can lead to loss of data or to inefficient use of storage space. In particular, if garbage collection fails to reclaim storage space, the available space will slowly dwindle away, a phenomenon known as a **memory leak.**

FIGURE 7.22

```
**  The variable CurrentPointer is used to hold a pointer  **
**  to the current position in the tree. The node at       **
**  this location is called the current node.              **

procedure BinarySearch (Tree, TargetValue)

assign CurrentPointer the value in the root pointer of Tree;
assign Found the value "false;"
while (Found is "false" and CurrentPointer is not NIL) do
    [Select the applicable case from those listed below and
     perform the associated activity:
    case 1, TargetValue = current node:
        (assign Found the value "true")
    case 2, TargetValue < current node:
        (assign CurrentPointer the value in the current
            node's left child pointer)
     case 3, TargetValue > current node:
        (assign CurrentPointer the value in the current
            node's right child pointer)
    ]
If (Found = "false") then (declare the search a failure)
                     else (declare the search a success)
```

The binary search applied to a linked binary tree

Having altered the natural sequential order of our stored list for the sake of search efficiency, you may think that the process of printing the list in alphabetical order would now be difficult. This hypothesis, however, proves to be false. To print the list in alphabetical order, we merely need to print the left subtree in alphabetical order, print the root node, and then print the right subtree in alphabetical order (Figure 7.23). After all, the left subtree contains those elements that are less than the root node, while the right subtree contains the elements larger than the root. A sketch of our resulting print routine looks like this:

```
if (tree not empty)
then (print the left subtree in alphabetical order;
     print the root node;
     print the right subtree in alphabetical order)
```

You may argue that this outline achieves little toward our goal of developing a complete print procedure, because it involves the tasks of printing the left subtree and the right subtree in alphabetical order, both of which are essentially the same as our original task. But printing subtrees is a smaller task than printing the entire tree. That is, solving the problem of printing a tree involves the

FIGURE 7.23

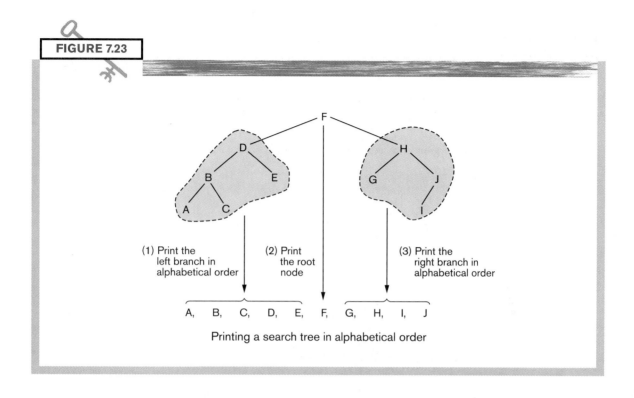

(1) Print the left branch in alphabetical order

(2) Print the root node

(3) Print the right branch in alphabetical order

A, B, C, D, E, F, G, H, I, J

Printing a search tree in alphabetical order

smaller task of printing subtrees, which suggests a recursive approach to our tree printing problem.

Following this lead, we can expand our outline into a complete pseudocode procedure for printing our tree as shown in Figure 7.24. We have assigned the routine the name PrintTree and then requested the services of PrintTree for printing the left and right subtrees. Note that the termination condition of the recursive process (reaching an empty subtree) is guaranteed to be reached, because each activation of the routine operates on a smaller tree than the one causing the activation.

The task of inserting a new entry in the tree is also easier than it may at first appear. You may guess that certain insertions would require cutting the tree open to allow room for the new entry, but actually the node being added can always be attached to the bottom of the tree as a leaf, regardless of the value involved. To find the proper place for a new entry, we move down the tree along the path that we would follow if we were searching for that entry. Since the entry is not in the tree, our search will lead to the bottom of the tree. At this point we will have found the proper location for the new node (Figure 7.25). Indeed, we have found the location to which a search for the new data would lead.

A procedure expressing this process in the case of a linked tree structure is shown in Figure 7.26. It first searches the tree for the value being inserted and

FIGURE 7.24

procedure PrintTree (Tree)

If (Tree is not empty)
   then (apply the procedure PrintTree to the tree that
              appears as the left branch in Tree;
          print the root node of Tree;
          apply the procedure PrintTree to the tree that
              appears as the right branch in Tree)

A procedure for printing a linked tree in alphabetical order

FIGURE 7.25

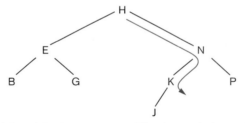

(a) Search for the new entry until its absence is detected

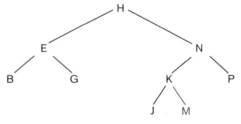

(b) This is the position in which the new entry should
be attached

Inserting the entry M into the list B, E, G, H, J, K, N, P stored as a tree

FIGURE 7.26

```
**    The variable CurrentPointer is used to hold a pointer    **
**    to the current position in the tree. The node at         **
**    this location is called the current node. Likewise,      **
**    PreviousPointer holds a pointer to the parent of the     **
**    current node, which is called the previous node.         **
```

procedure Insert (Tree, TargetValue)

```
**    First, find the location for the new node                **
```

assign CurrentPointer **the value** in the root pointer of Tree;
assign Found **the value** "false;"
while (Found is "false" and CurrentPointer is not NIL) **do**
  [Select the applicable case from those listed below and
  perform the associated activity:
  case 1, TargetValue = current node:
    (**assign** Found **the value** "true")
  case 2, TargetValue < current node:
    (**assign** PreviousPointer **the value** of CurrentPointer;
    assign CurrentPointer **the value** of the current
      node's left child pointer)
  case 3, TargetValue > current node:
    (**assign** PreviousPointer **the value** of CurrentPointer;
    assign CurrentPointer **the value** of the current
      node's right child pointer)
  ]

```
**    Now, insert the new node as a child of the current node.  **
**    Note that if CurrentPointer is still the same             **
**    as the root pointer, then the original Tree was           **
**    empty.                                                    **
```

If (Found = "false")
  then (Create a new node containing TargetValue;
      Select the applicable case from those listed below
        and perform the associated activity:
        case 1, CurrentPointer = root pointer:
          (connect the new node as the root node)
        case 2, TargetValue < previous node:
          (connect the new node as the left child
           of the previous node)
        case 3, TargetValue > previous node:
          (connect the new node as the right child
           of the previous node)
)

A procedure for inserting an entry in a linked ordered tree

then places the new node at the proper location. Note that a slightly special case occurs if the tree is empty in the first place. This case is detected by testing for the condition of CurrentPointer still being the same as the root pointer after the search process has been completed. Moreover, if the entry being inserted is actually found in the tree during the search, no insertion is made.

We conclude that a software package consisting of a linked tree structure together with our procedures for searching, printing, and inserting provides a complete package that could be used as an abstract tool by our hypothetical application.

QUESTIONS/EXERCISES

1. Identify the root and leaf nodes in the following tree. Identify the subtrees below node 9. Identify the groups of siblings within the tree.

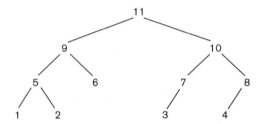

2. What condition indicates that a linked tree in a machine's memory is empty?
3. Draw a diagram representing how the tree below appears in memory when stored using the left and right child pointers, as described in this section. Then, draw another diagram showing how the tree would appear in contiguous storage using the alternative storage system described in this section.

4. Draw a binary tree that you could use to store the list R, S, T, U, V, W, X, Y, and Z for future searching.
5. Indicate the path traversed by the binary search algorithm in Figure 7.22 when applied to the tree in Figure 7.21 when searching for the entry J. What about the entry P?
6. Draw a diagram representing the status of activations of the recursive tree-printing algorithm in Figure 7.24 at the time node K is printed within the ordered tree in Figure 7.21.

7.6 Customized Data Types

In Chapter 5 we introduced the concept of a data type and discussed such elementary types as integer, real, character, and Boolean that most programming languages provide as primitives. In this section we consider ways in which a programmer can define his or her own data types that more closely fit the needs of a particular application.

User-Defined Types

The task of expressing an algorithm is often more convenient if types other than those provided as primitives in the programming language are available. For this reason, most modern programming languages allow programmers to define additional data types, using the primitive types and structures as building blocks. These "home-made" data types are known as **user-defined types.**

As an example, suppose we want to develop a program involving numerous variables, each with the same heterogeneous structure consisting of a name, age, and skill rating. One approach would be to restate the composition of the structure each time a reference to that structure is required. For example, to establish the variable Employee with such a heterogeneous structure, a C programmer would write

```
struct
{char    Name[8];
 int     Age;
 float   SkillRating;
} Employee;
```

as introduced in Figure 5.6 of Chapter 5.

A problem with this approach is that the program can become bulky and hard to read if this structure is repeated often. A better method is to describe the structure only once by assigning it a descriptive name and then using that name each time a reference to the structure is required. The C language allows a programmer to accomplish this with the statement

```
typedef struct
{char    Name[8];
 int     Age;
 float   SkillRating;
} EmployeeType;
```

This statement defines a new type, EmployeeType, that can be used to declare variables in the same way as a primitive type. For example, the variable Employee can be declared with the statement

```
EmployeeType Employee;
```

The benefits of such a user-defined type are more pronounced when multiple variables must be declared. Just as a C programmer can declare the variables Sleeve, Waist, and Neck to be of the primitive type real with the statement

```
float Sleeve, Waist, Neck;
```

the statement

```
EmployeeType DistManager, SalesRep1, SalesRep2;
```

declares the three variables DistManager, SalesRep1, and SalesRep2 to be of type EmployeeType.

It is important to distinguish between a user-defined type and an actual data item with that type. The latter is referred to as an **instance** of the type. A user-defined type is essentially a template that is used in constructing instances of the type. It describes the properties that all instances of that type have but does not itself constitute an actual occurrence of that type. In the preceding example the user-defined type EmployeeType was used to construct three instances of that type, known as DistManager, SalesRep1, and SalesRep2.

Abstract Data Types

Although the concept of a user-defined type is advantageous, it falls short of allowing the creation of new data types in the full sense. Recall that a data type consists of two parts: a predetermined storage system (such as a two's complement system in the case of the type integer and a floating-point system in the case of type real) and a collection of predefined operations (such as addition and subtraction). Traditional user-defined types, however, merely allow programmers to define new storage systems. They do not provide a means of defining operations to be performed on data with these structures.

An **abstract data type** is a more complete way of extending the types available in a programming language. As with a user-defined type, an abstract data type is a template that is distinct from instances of the type. But an abstract data type encompasses both the storage system and the associated operations. As such, an abstract data type consists of a description of a data storage system as well as a collection of procedures that define the operations that can be performed on an instance of the type.

Figure 7.27 shows how an abstract data type known as StackOfIntegers can be defined in the Ada programming language. Loosely translated, this figure defines a program unit (a package, in Ada terminology), StackPackage, that contains the description of a new type named StackOfIntegers and identifies two procedures, push and pop. StackOfIntegers is described as an array (called StackEntries) of 25 integers together with an additional integer, StackPointer, used to hold the position within the array of the stack's top (see Exercise 5 in Section 7.3). The details of the procedures push and pop must be described in another program unit called a package body. It is there that the

FIGURE 7.27

```
package StackPackage is
  type StackOfIntegers is
    record
       StackEntries: array(1...25) of integer;
       StackPointer: integer;
    end record;
  procedure push(Value: in integer; Stack: in out StackOfIntegers);
  procedure pop(Value: out integer; Stack: in out StackOfIntegers);
end StackPackage;
```

An abstract data type in Ada

instructions for actually pushing and popping entries (as well as initializing the StackPointer) would be described.

Using this package as a template, actual stacks of integers (instances of the type StackOfIntegers) can be declared by statements, such as

```
StackOne: StackOfIntegers;
```

and

```
StackTwo: StackOfIntegers;
```

that declare the variables StackOne and StackTwo to be of type StackOfIntegers. Later, the value 106 can be pushed onto StackOne using the statement

```
push(106, StackOne);
```

or the top entry from StackTwo can be retrieved in the variable OldValue using the statement

```
pop(OldValue, StackTwo);
```

Encapsulation

In this chapter we have repeatedly seen how a software package, consisting of a data structure (or structures) and a collection of procedures that manipulate that structure, can be used to represent an abstract structure such as a stack, queue, list, or tree. We have not, however, emphasized the importance of ensuring that all operations on the structure within the package be performed by the procedures provided. Such assurance is important since to allow direct access to the internal composition of the package often opens the door to unforeseen complications.

For example, suppose a programmer needs to reference the third entry on a stack of type StackOfIntegers (Figure 7.27). The programmer, who knows how the stack is actually implemented, might be tempted to violate the stack's integrity by referencing the array StackEntry directly, rather than going through the formal process of popping the first two entries. Such a tactic usually leads to complications later in the software's life cycle and is considered to be one of the worst evils by software engineers.

The problem is that future maintenance programmers could make changes that are not compatible with the "short-cut" reference hidden elsewhere in the program. For instance, to extend the maximum size of the stack, the internal structure of the type StackOfIntegers could be changed from an array to a linked structure, which would not be compatible with the "short-cut" reference that assumes the stack is implemented as an array.

To prevent such circumvention of abstract data types, newer programming languages provide techniques by which a software package can be **encapsulated,** meaning that the package is constructed in such a manner that its internal structure can be accessed only by means of the approved package procedures. If instances of the abstract data types occurring in a software system are encapsulated, the integrity of these data types is protected from poorly conceived modifications.

Figure 7.28 shows a modified version of the abstract data type StackOfIntegers, originally presented in Figure 7.27. The difference is that the new version takes advantage of Ada's encapsulation features. Note that we have moved the details of the stack's structure to the private part (the part following the key word private) of the package. Only the information in the public part (the part preceding the key word private) of the package is accessible outside the package. The information in the private part is local to the package. In our example, then, only the existence of a type called StackOfIntegers and the procedures push and pop are known outside the package; the fact that such a stack is implemented as an array called StackEntries is encapsulated within the package. In turn, statements such as

```
StackOne: StackOfIntegers;
StackTwo: StackOfIntegers;
push(106, StackOne);
```

and

```
pop(OldValue, StackTwo);
```

are still valid outside the package, but direct references to the array StackEntries or the integer StackPointer are not.

In closing, we observe that the use of abstract data types and encapsulation allows general-purpose programming languages to be customized to particular

FIGURE 7.28

```
package StackPackage is
  type StackOfIntegers is private;
  procedure push(Value: in integer; Stack: in out StackOfIntegers);
  procedure pop(Value: out integer; Stack: in out StackOfIntegers);
private
  type StackOfIntegers is
    record
      StackEntries: array(1...25) of integer;
      StackPointer: integer;
    end record;
end StackPackage;
```

An abstract data type in Ada using encapsulation

applications. A biologist studying the nervous system might develop and encapsulate a package whose internal data structures and routines simulate the pertinent characteristics of a single neuron. Once these abstract types have been defined, the biologist can use them as though they are primitives in the language. In a sense, the biologist will have extended the general-purpose programming language to a special-purpose language containing primitives particular to the task at hand.

Classes

The concepts of abstract data types and instances of those types are very near those of classes and objects found in object-oriented programming languages (Section 5.5). Both abstract data types and classes capture the idea of bundling data structures with the procedures that manipulate those structures to form packages that can be used as abstract tools elsewhere in a program. The major distinction is that a class is more flexible. It may contain only procedures, only data structures, both, or neither. Thus classes can be used to describe program components beyond the capabilities of abstract data types. Moreover, object-oriented programming languages provide ways in which classes can be defined in terms of other classes through inheritance (again, see Section 5.5).

THE STANDARD TEMPLATE LIBRARY

The data structures discussed in this chapter have become standard programming structures—so standard, in fact, that many programming environments treat them very much like primitives. One example is found in the C++ programming environment, which is often enhanced by the Standard Template Library (STL). The STL is merely a collection of pre-defined classes (much like the class StackOfIntegers in Figure 7.29) that describe popular data structures. Consequently, by incorporating the STL into a C++ program, the programmer is relieved from the task of describing these structures in detail. Instead, he or she needs merely declare identifiers to be of these types in the same manner that we declared StackOne and StackTwo to be of type StackOfIntegers in Section 7.6.

The template nature of classes combined with their flexible content and ability to inherit properties from other classes make them prime candidates for software engineers who are searching for ways to implement design patterns. Indeed, most of the frameworks being developed today are essentially class definitions. Thus it appears that the object-oriented paradigm might finally provide a means by which software engineers can construct large software systems from prefabricated components—those components being classes.

We close with Figure 7.29, which demonstrates how a stack of integers might be implemented in the object-oriented languages C++ and Java. Observe that StackOfIntegers is defined as a class, meaning that the code here merely defines the properties of a StackOfIntegers—actual instances are established elsewhere in the program as they are required. The procedure named StackOfIntegers, having the same name as the class itself, is known as a **constructor.** A constructor within a class is executed automatically each time a new instance of the class is established. In our examples, the constructor handles issues associated with establishing a new stack such as setting the stack pointer to indicate that the stack is empty.

Note that these examples incorporate encapsulation to protect the integrity of the interior characteristics of the class. Only those portions of the class that are designated public can be referenced from outside an instance of the class. Thus, in both examples, the array holding the stack within an object is accessible only from within that object. Any manipulation of that array must be performed by means of the methods that are declared public.

QUESTIONS/EXERCISES

1. In what way is a checking account at a bank encapsulated?
2. What is the difference between an abstract data type and an instance of that type?
3. In what ways are abstract data types and classes similar? In what ways are they different?
4. Describe two underlying structures that might be used to implement an object of type queue-of-integers.

FIGURE 7.29

(a) Stack of integers described in C++

```cpp
const int MaxStack = 25;

class StackOfIntegers
{int StackPointer;                    //Data structures are private.
 int StackEntries[MaxStack];

public:                               //Access to following methods is public.
   StackOfIntegers()                  //This is a constructor. It
    {StackPointer = 0;                //initializes the stack as empty.
    }

   void push(int Entry)
     {if (StackPointer < MaxStack)
       StackEntries[StackPointer++]= Entry;
     }

   int pop(void)
     {if (StackPointer > 0) return StackEntries[--StackPointer];
      else return 0;
     }
};
```

(b) Stack of integers described in Java

```java
class StackOfIntegers
{private final int MaxStack = 25;     //Data structures are private.
 private int StackPointer;
 private int[] StackEntries;

 public StackOfIntegers()             //This is a constructor. It
   {StackEntries = new int [MaxStack];  //establishes an array of integers
    StackPointer = 0;                 //to hold the stack.
   }

 public void push(int Entry)
   {if (StackPointer < MaxStack)
      StackEntries[StackPointer++] = Entry;
   }

 public int pop()
   {if (StackPinter > 0) return StackEntries[--StackPointer];
    else return 0;
   }
}
```

A stack of integers implemented (a) in C++ and (b) in Java

7.7 Pointers in Machine Language

In this chapter we have introduced pointers and have shown how they are used in constructing data structures. In this section we consider how pointers are handled in machine language.

Suppose that we want to write a program in the machine language described in Appendix C to pop an entry off the stack described in Figure 7.12 and place that entry in a general-purpose register. In other words, we want to load a register with the contents of a memory cell, that cell being the entry on top of the stack. Our machine language provides two instructions for loading registers—one with op-code 2, the other with op-code 1. Recall that in the case of op-code 2, the operand field contains the data to be loaded, and in the case of op-code 1, the operand field contains the address of the data to be loaded.

Since we do not know what the contents will be, we cannot use op-code 2 to obtain our goal. Moreover, we cannot use op-code 1, since we do not know what the address will be. After all, the address of the top of the stack will vary as the program is executed. What we do know is the address of the stack pointer. That is, we know the location of the address of the data we want to load. What we need, then, is a third op-code for loading a register, in which the operand contains the address of a pointer to the data to be loaded.

The designer of the machine in Appendix C might use op-code D to accomplish this goal. The language could be designed so that an instruction of the form DRXY would mean to load register R with the contents of the memory cell whose address is found at address XY. Thus, if the stack pointer is in the memory cell at address F0, then the instruction D4F0 would cause the data at the top of the stack to be loaded into register 4.

This instruction, however, does not complete the pop operation. We must also subtract one from the stack pointer so that it points to the new top of the stack. This means that following the load instruction, our machine language program would have to load the stack pointer into a register, subtract one from it, and store the result back in memory.

By using one of the registers as the stack pointer rather than a memory cell, we could reduce this movement of the stack pointer back and forth between registers and memory. But this would mean that we must redesign the load instruction so that it expects the pointer to be in a register rather than in main memory. Thus, instead of the earlier approach, the designer of the machine might define an instruction with op-code D to have the form DR0S, which would mean to load register R with the contents of the memory cell pointed to by register S.

Note that a similar instruction is needed to implement a push operation. The machine designer might therefore extend the language in Appendix C further by introducing the op-code E so that an instruction of the form ER0S would mean to store the contents of register R in the memory cell pointed to by register S.

With these extensions, the machine language described in Appendix C would exhibit three addressing techniques. In the first, the instruction contains the data involved as demonstrated by op-code 2. In the second, the instruction contains the address of the data involved as demonstrated by op-codes 1 and 3. In the third, the instruction contains the location of the address of the data involved as demonstrated by op-codes D and E. These techniques are known as **immediate addressing, direct addressing,** and **indirect addressing,** respectively. All three are common in today's machine languages.

QUESTIONS/EXERCISES

1. Suppose the machine language in Appendix C has been extended as described at the end of this section. Moreover, suppose register 8 contains the pattern DB, the memory cell at address DB contains the pattern CA, and the cell at address CA contains the pattern A5. What bit pattern will be in register 5 immediately after executing each of the following instructions?
   a. 25A5   b. 15CA   c. D508

2. Using the extensions described at the end of this section, write a complete machine language routine to perform a pop operation. Assume that the stack is implemented as shown in Figure 7.12, the stack pointer is in register F, and that the top of the stack is to be popped into register 5.

3. Using the extensions described at the end of this section, write a program to copy the contents of five contiguous memory cells starting at address A0 to the five cells starting at address B0. Assume your program starts at address 00.

CHAPTER REVIEW PROBLEMS

(Asterisked problems are associated with optional sections.)

1. Draw pictures showing how the array below appears in a machine's memory when stored in row major order and in column major order:

A	B	C	D
E	F	G	H
I	J	K	L

2. Suppose an array with 6 rows and 8 columns is stored in row major order starting at address 20 (base ten). If each entry in the array requires only one memory cell, what is the address of the entry in the third row and fourth column? What if each entry requires two memory cells?

3. Rework Problem 2 assuming column major order rather than row major order.

4. Suppose the list of letters A, B, C, E, F, and G is stored in a contiguous block of memory cells. What activities are required to insert the letter D in the list if the alphabetical order is to be maintained?

5. The table below represents the contents of some cells in a computer's main memory along with the address of each cell represented. Note that some of the cells contain letters of the alphabet, and each such cell is followed by an empty cell. Place addresses in these empty cells so that each cell containing a letter together with the following cell form an entry in a linked list in which the letters appear in alphabetical order. (Use zero for the NIL pointer.) What address should the head pointer contain?

Address	Contents
11	C
12	
13	G
14	
15	E
16	
17	B
18	
19	U
20	
21	F
22	

6. The following table represents a portion of a linked list in a computer's main memory. Each entry in the list consists of two cells: The first contains a letter of the alphabet; the second contains a pointer to the next list entry. Alter the pointers so that the letter N is no longer in the list. Then replace the letter N with the letter G and alter the pointers so that the new letter appears in the list in its proper place in alphabetical order.

Address	Contents
30	J
31	38
32	B
33	30
34	X
35	46
36	N
37	40
38	K
39	36
40	P
41	34

7. The table below represents a linked list using the same format as in the preceding problems. If the head pointer contains the value 44, what name is represented by the list? Change the pointers so that the list contains the name Jean.

Address	Contents
40	N
41	46
42	I
43	40
44	J
45	50
46	E
47	00
48	M
49	42
50	A
51	40

8. Which of the following routines correctly inserts NewEntry immediately after the entry called PreviousEntry in a linked list? What is wrong with the other routine?

Routine 1

1. Copy the value in the pointer field of PreviousEntry into the pointer field of NewEntry.

2. Change the value in the pointer field of PreviousEntry to the address of NewEntry.

Routine 2

1. Change the value in the pointer field of PreviousEntry to the address of NewEntry.

2. Copy the value in the pointer field of PreviousEntry into the pointer field of NewEntry.

9. Design a procedure for concatenating two linked lists (that is, placing one before the other to form a single list).

10. Design a procedure for combining two sorted contiguous lists into a single sorted contiguous list. What if the lists are linked?

11. Design a procedure for reversing the order of a linked list.

12. In Figure 7.11, we presented an algorithm for printing a linked list in reverse order using a stack as an auxiliary storage structure. Design a recursive procedure to perform this same task without making explicit use of a stack. In what form is a stack still involved in your recursive solution?

13. Sometimes a single linked list is given two different orders by attaching two pointers to each entry rather than one. Fill in the table below so that by following the first pointer after each letter one finds the name Carol, but by following the second pointer after each letter one finds the letters in alphabetical order. What values belong in the head pointer of each of the two lists represented?

Address	Contents
60	O
61	
62	
63	C
64	
65	
66	A
67	
68	
69	L
70	
71	
72	R
73	
74	

14. The table below represents a stack stored in a contiguous block of memory cells, as discussed in the text. If the base of the stack is at address 10 and the stack pointer contains the value 12, what value is retrieved by a pop instruction? What value is then in the stack pointer?

Address	Contents
10	F
11	C
12	A
13	B
14	E

15. Draw a table showing the final contents of the memory cells if the instruction in Problem 14 had been to push the letter D on the stack rather than to pop a letter. What would the value in the stack pointer be after the push instruction?

16. Design a procedure to remove the bottom entry from a stack.

17. Design a procedure to compare the contents of two stacks.

18. Suppose we want to create a stack of names that vary in length. Why is it advantageous to store the names in separate areas of memory and then build the stack out of pointers to these names

rather than allowing the stack to contain the names themselves?

19. Does a queue crawl through memory in the direction of its head or its tail?

20. Suppose the entries in a queue require one memory cell each, the head pointer contains the value 11, and the tail pointer contains the value 17. What are the values of these pointers after one entry is inserted and two are removed?

21. a. Suppose a queue implemented in a circular fashion is in the state shown in the diagram below. Draw a diagram showing the structure after the letters G and R are inserted, three letters are removed, and the letters D and P are inserted.

b. What error occurs in part (a) if the letters G, R, D, and P are inserted before any letters are removed?

22. Describe how an array could be used to implement a queue in a high-level language.

23. The table below represents a tree stored in a machine's memory. Each node of the tree consists of three cells. The first cell contains the data (a letter), the second contains a pointer to the node's left child, and the third contains a pointer to the node's right child. A value of 0 represents a NIL pointer. If the value of the root pointer is 55, draw a picture of the tree.

Address	Contents
40	G
41	0
42	0

43	X
44	0
45	0
46	J
47	49
48	0
49	M
50	0
51	0
52	F
53	43
54	40
55	W
56	46
57	52

24. The table below represents the contents of a block of cells in a computer's main memory. Note that some of the cells contain letters of the alphabet, and each such cell is followed by two blank cells. Fill in the blank cells so that the memory block represents the tree that follows. Use the first cell following a letter as the pointer to that node's left child and the next cell as the pointer to the right child. Use 0 for NIL pointers. What value should be in the root pointer?

Address	Contents
30	C
31	
32	
33	H
34	
35	
36	K
37	
38	
39	E
40	
41	
42	G
43	
44	

45
46
47   P

25. Design a nonrecursive algorithm to replace the recursive one represented in Figure 7.24. Use a stack to control any backtracking that may be necessary.

26. Apply the recursive tree-printing algorithm of Figure 7.24 to the tree represented in Problem 23. Draw a diagram representing the nested activations of the algorithm (and the current position in each) at the time node X is printed.

27. While keeping the root node the same and without changing the physical location of the data elements, change the pointers in the tree of Problem 23 so the tree-printing algorithm of Figure 7.24 prints the nodes alphabetically.

28. Draw a diagram showing how the binary tree below appears in memory when stored without pointers using a block of contiguous memory cells as described in Section 7.5.

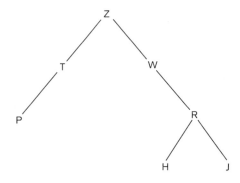

29. Suppose the contiguous cells representing a binary tree as described in Section 7.5 contained the values A, B, C, D, E, F, and F, respectively. Draw a picture of the tree.

30. Describe a data structure suitable for representing a board configuration during a chess game.

31. Identify the trees below whose nodes would be printed in alphabetical order by the algorithm in Figure 7.24.

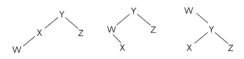

32. Modify the procedure in Figure 7.24 to print the "list" in reverse order.

33. Describe a tree structure that can be used to store the genealogical history of a family. What operations are performed on the tree? If the tree is implemented as a linked structure, what pointers should be associated with each node? Design procedures to perform the operations you identified above, assuming that the tree is implemented as a linked structure with the pointers you just described.

34. Design a procedure for finding and deleting a given value from a tree ordered in the fashion of Figure 7.21.

*35. What is the difference between a user-defined type and an abstract data type?

*36. What is the difference between an abstract data type and an instance of that type?

*37. Give a definition of encapsulation.

*38. What is the difference between the public and private parts of an abstract data type?

*39. Identify the data structures and procedures that might appear in an abstract data type representing an address book.

*40. Identify the data structures and procedures that might appear in an abstract data type representing a spacecraft in a video game.

*41. Using the extensions described at the end of Section 7.7, write a complete machine language routine to push an entry onto a stack implemented as shown in Figure 7.12. Assume that the stack pointer is in register F and that the data to be pushed is in register 5.

*42. Suppose each entry in a linked list consisted of one memory cell of data followed by a pointer to the next list entry. Moreover, suppose that a new entry located at memory address A0 is to be inserted between the entries at locations B5 and C4. Using the language described in Appendix C and the additional op-codes D and E as described at the end of Section 7.7, write a machine language routine to perform the insertion.

SOCIAL ISSUES

The following questions are provided to help you understand some of the ethical/social/legal issues associated with the field of computing as well as investigate your own beliefs and their foundations. The goal is not merely to answer these questions. You should also consider why you answered as you did and whether your justifications are consistent from one question to the next.

1. Suppose a software analyst, while working for a particular company, develops a data organization that allows for efficient manipulation of that data in a particular application. He or she is then hired by another company and assigned a similar project. Should the analyst be allowed to implement the same data organization for the second company? How can a company protect itself against its competitors regarding such developments?

2. To what extent is incorrect data worse than no data?

3. In many application programs, the size to which a stack can grow is determined by the amount of memory available. If the available space should ever be consumed, the software is designed to produce a message such as "stack overflow" and terminate. In most cases this error never occurs and the user is never aware of its existence. Who is liable if such an error occurs and sensitive data is lost? How could the software developer minimize his or her liability?

4. In a data structure based on a pointer system, the deletion of an item usually consists of changing a pointer rather than erasing memory cells. Thus, when an entry in a linked list is deleted, the deleted entry actually remains in memory until its memory space is required by

other data. What ethical and security issues result from this endurance of deleted data?

5. It is easy to transfer data and programs from one computer to another. Thus it is easy to transfer the knowledge held by one machine to many machines. In contrast, it sometimes takes a long time for a human to transfer knowledge to another human. For example, it takes time for a human to teach another human a new language. What implications could this contrast in knowledge transfer rate have if the capabilities of machines begin to challenge the capabilities of humans?

6. Should a designer have the right to copyright clever data structure designs? What about patent rights?

ADDITIONAL READING

Carrano, F. M., P. Helman, and R. Veroff. *Data Abstraction and Problem Solving with C++,* 2nd ed. Reading, MA: Addison-Wesley, 1997.

Kruse, R. L. and A. J. Ryba. *Data Structures and Program Design in C++.* Upper Saddle River, NJ: Prentice-Hall, 1999.

Weiss, M. A. *Data Structures and Problem Solving Using Java.* Reading, MA: Addison-Wesley, 1997.

8.1 The Role of the Operating System

8.2 Sequential Files
Sequential File Processing
Programming Concerns

8.3 Text Files
Composition of Text Files
Programming Concerns

8.4 Indexing
Index Fundamentals
Programming Concerns

8.5 Hashing
A Particular Hashing Technique
Distribution Problems
Programming Concerns

c h a p t e r

FILE STRUCTURES

e i g h t

In Chapter 7 we discussed ways of organizing data within a machine's main memory. In this chapter we concentrate on data storage techniques used in mass storage. A major theme is that the way information will be accessed plays an important role in determining the way it should be stored. As in our study of data structures, we see that the format ultimately presented to the user may not be the same as that in the actual storage system. Thus, as in Chapter 7, we find ourselves discussing and comparing both conceptual and real organizations.

8.1 The Role of the Operating System

As described at the end of Section 1.3, storing a file in mass storage dictates that the file be divided into blocks (physical records) that are compatible with the storage device involved. Files stored on disks, for example, must be manipulated in sector size units. Manipulating the file in terms of these blocks is handled by the operating system. If an application program needs to retrieve a portion of a file, it asks the operating system to perform the retrieval. The operating system normally responds by reading enough physical records to fulfill the request, placing the data obtained in an area of main memory called a buffer, and then making this buffer available to the application. Similarly, when storing information, an application program hands the data to the operating system. The operating system stores this data in a buffer until a complete physical record has been accumulated and then transfers the entire physical record to mass storage.

Application software is generally written in a third-generation programming language that provides primitives for making these requests of the operating system. In this chapter we will introduce many of these primitives. We will see that sometimes these statements manipulate data in units of entire logical records and in other cases they manipulate data in smaller units called **fields.** For example, a logical record containing information about an employee would consist of fields such as name, address, employee identification number, etc.

To fulfill its file access obligations, the operating system must maintain information about the file being manipulated. For example, it must know the device on which the file is stored, the name of the file, the location of the buffer being used to transfer data to the application software, and whether the file is to be saved after the application program has terminated. Such information is stored in a table called a **file descriptor,** or file control block. The process of creating a file descriptor in known as opening the file.

Before an application program can access a file via the operating system, it must ask the operating system to open the file. In the imperative paradigm, this is normally done by means of a high-level programming language statement equivalent to the pseudocode statement

Open the file document.txt as DocFile for input purposes

that requests the file document.txt be opened. The rest of the statement indicates that the file should already exist in mass storage ("input purposes" rather than "output purposes") and that this file will be referenced elsewhere in the program by the name DocFile. The reason that an alias (DocFile) is used in the program to refer to the file is that the actual file name (document.txt) used by the operating system may not be compatible with the syntax rules dictated by the design of the high-level programming language.

In an object-oriented programming language, files are treated as objects. Thus opening a file is done in the context of establishing the object that will play the role of the file. Thus, in an object-oriented environment, an instruction to establish a file descriptor would take a form such as

Create the object DocFile as the input file document.txt

that creates an object called DocFile through which we can access the file document.txt as an input file. Later in the program, data can be retrieved from the file by sending the appropriate message to the object DocFile. For example,

Send the message GetCharacter to DocFile to retrieve Symbol

Having been directed to construct a file descriptor, the operating system must also be told when the descriptor is no longer needed, a process known as closing the file. This is usually accomplished by a statement equivalent to

Close the file DocFile

Such a statement informs the operating system that access to the file DocFile is no longer required and thus the memory space used for the file descriptor can be used for something else; however, in some settings, the statement initiates more than this simple release of memory space. For instance, if there is a partially filled physical record containing data to be stored in the file, the operating system will fill in the record (perhaps with 0s) and transfer it to mass storage.

Closing a file in an object-oriented environment is done by sending the appropriate object a message instructing the object to close its file. For example,

Send the message Close to the object DocFile

sends the object called DocFile the message to close its file.

QUESTIONS/EXERCISES

1. Summarize the buffering system used to transfer data from a file to an application program.
2. What is a file descriptor?
3. What role would an operating system's file manager play when opening a file?

8.2 Sequential Files

A **sequential file** is a file that is accessed in a serial manner from its beginning to its end as though the information in the file were arranged in one long row. Examples include audio files, video files, files containing programs, and files containing text documents. In fact, most of the files created by a typical PC user are examples of sequential files.

Sequential File Processing

To investigate the technicalities of sequential file processing, let us consider a classic data processing example of a file containing information about a company's employees. Such a file consists of logical records, each of which contains information about a single employee. Each of these logical records is further divided into fields such as name, address, employee identification number, Social Security number, etc.

Suppose such an employee file is used for payroll processing, for which the entire file must be processed each pay period. As each employee record is retrieved, that employee's pay is calculated and the appropriate check produced. Since all records are processed, it makes little difference which records are handled first. The most straightforward technique therefore is to implement the file as a sequential file consisting of a long list of records and to process the records one at a time from the beginning of the list to the end.

The activity of processing such a sequential file is exemplified by the statement

while (the end of the file has not been
    reached) **do**
(retrieve the next record from the file and process it)

To support this sequential process, the file's records must be stored so that they have an order associated with them and so that they can be retrieved according to this order. If the mass storage system being used is a tape, this is a straightforward undertaking. Since the storage system itself is sequential, we need merely write the records on the tape one after the other. Then, processing the file is merely the task of reading the tape and processing the records in the order in which they are found.

In the case of disk storage, however, the file would be scattered over different sectors that could be retrieved in a variety of orders. To preserve the proper order, most operating systems maintain a list of the sectors on which

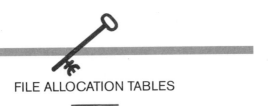

FILE ALLOCATION TABLES

The text indicates that, to retrieve files stored on magnetic disks, an operating system maintains a list of the sectors assigned to each file. In reality, disk space is usually allocated to a file in multisector blocks called *clusters*. A typical cluster in a PC consists of 4 to 16 sectors, and a high-capacity hard disk system contains thousands of clusters. To keep a record of which cluster is assigned to which file, an operating system maintains a table called a **file allocation table (FAT)** on each disk. This table contains an entry for each cluster on the disk. When a file is stored on the disk, the operating system records the number of the first cluster allocated to the file in the file's directory. Then, in the FAT entry representing that cluster, the operating system records the number of the next cluster allocated to the file, and in the entry representing that cluster, the operating system records the number of the next cluster. Thus, by starting with the file's directory and following this path through the FAT, the operating system is able to retrieve the file in the proper cluster-by-cluster order.

Early versions of Microsoft's Windows operating system used FATs with 16-bit entries, which meant that only 64K different cluster numbers could be represented. Since each cluster contained approximately 2 kilobytes, a single FAT could represent only 128 megabytes of disk space—a value that was reasonable when hard disk systems had capacities of only 10 to 40 megabytes. Today, 32-bit entries are used, which means that a FAT can be used to maintain file locations on disks with capacities measured in terabytes—the equivalent of 2^{40} bytes.

FIGURE 8.1

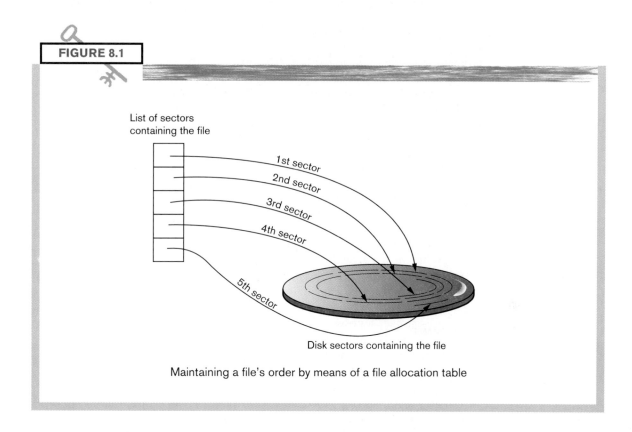

List of sectors
containing the file

1st sector
2nd sector
3rd sector
4th sector
5th sector

Disk sectors containing the file

Maintaining a file's order by means of a file allocation table

the file is stored (Figure 8.1). This list is recorded as part of the disk's directory system on the same disk as the file. By means of this list, the operating system can retrieve the sectors in the proper sequence, and therefore, the application software can be written as though the file were stored sequentially, even though the file is actually scattered over various portions of the disk.

Inherent in processing a sequential file is the need to detect when the end of the file is reached. Generically, we refer to the end of a sequential file as the **EOF (end-of-file).** There are a variety of ways of identifying the EOF. One is to place a special record, called a **sentinel,** at the end of the file. Of course, to avoid confusion, the fields in the sentinel must contain values that will never occur as data in the application. Using this technique, a program in a third-generation programming language would direct the processing of a sequential file by statements such as

retrieve the first record from the file;
while (the retrieved record is not the sentinel) **do**
   (process the record and
    retrieve the next record from the file)

Another approach is to leave the task of detecting the EOF to the operating system. For example, if the file is stored on a disk and the operating system is retrieving records by means of a sector list, then the operating system knows when the end of the file has been reached. Thus, it can report this to the application software by means of a variable called EOF, which is assigned the value true or false, depending on whether the end of file has been reached. Using this strategy, the application software would contain statements such as

while (not EOF) **do**
(retrieve a record from the file and process it)

In many cases maintaining the order of a sequential file is mandatory. An audio or video file would be worthless if the order of its records was scrambled. However, in other cases the order is a matter of convenience. A classic example occurs in our employee file example, in which individual records are identified by the value of a particular field, called the **key field.** For instance, in an employee file, this might be the field containing the employee's Social Security number or perhaps employee identification number.

Arranging such files according to a key field can greatly reduce processing time. For example, suppose that processing payroll requires that each employee record be updated to reflect the information on that employee's time sheet. If the file containing the time sheets is arranged according to the same key field as that of the employee records, then this updating process can be handled by accessing both files sequentially, using the time sheet retrieved from one file to update the corresponding record from the other file. If the files were not arranged by key field, the updating process would require retrieving records from one file while repeatedly searching for the corresponding record in the other file.

Thus updating classic sequential files is typically handled in multiple steps. First, the new information (such as the collection of time sheets) is recorded in a sequential file known as a transaction file, and this transaction file is sorted to match the order of the file to be updated, which is called the master file. Then, the records in the master file are updated by retrieving the records from both files sequentially.

Another classic example of sequential file processing is that of merging two files to form a new file containing the records from the original files. The records in the input files are assumed to be arranged in ascending order according to a common key field, and the output file is to possess this same property. The classic merge algorithm is summarized in Figure 8.2. The underlying theme is to build the output file as the two input files are scanned sequentially (Figure 8.3).

Programming Concerns

For the purpose of expressing algorithms involving sequential files, most high-level programming languages provide statements for placing records into a sequential file or retrieving records from a sequential file. If the language is

FIGURE 8.2

procedure MergeFiles (InputFileA, InputFileB, OutputFile)

if (both input files at EOF) **then** (Stop, with OutputFile empty)
if (InputFileA not at EOF) **then** (Declare its first record to be its current record)
if (InputFileB not at EOF) **then** (Declare its first record to be its current record)
while (neither input file at EOF) **do**
   (Put the current record with the "smaller" key field value in OutputFile;
    if (that current record is the last record in its corresponding input file)
      then (Declare that input file to be at EOF)
      else (Declare the next record in that input file to be the file's current record)
)
Starting with the current record in the input file that is not at EOF,
   copy the remaining records to OutputFile.

A procedure for merging two sequential files.

based on the imperative paradigm, these statements normally take the form of requests for the execution of preestablished procedures that perform the desired operations. For example, they may be equivalent to a pseudocode statement such as

Apply the procedure ReadFile to retrieve MailRecord from the file MailList

which retrieves the next logical record from the file MailList and assigns it to the variable MailRecord. As in this statement, some languages allow entire records to be transferred as heterogeneous arrays. In other cases records are transferred field by field in a manner similar to the pseudocode statement

Apply the procedure ReadFile to retrieve Name, Address, EmpNum from the file MailList

Programming languages that are based on the object-oriented paradigm treat files as objects. In turn, statements for transferring records to and from sequential files take the form of messages to the appropriate objects. For example, a programmer would write statements equivalent to

Send the ReadFile message to the object MailList to retrieve MailRecord

Most high-level programming languages treat peripheral devices as sequential files. For example, a computer's keyboard is typically treated as a sequential file from which data is retrieved, and the computer's monitor and printer are

FIGURE 8.3

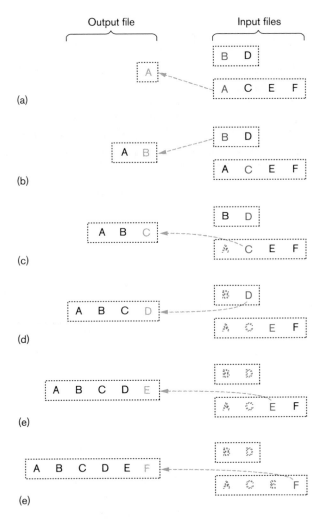

Applying the merge algorithm. (Letters are used to represent entire records. The particular letter indicates the value of the record's key field.)

treated as sequential files to which data is sent. Thus, to retrieve data typed at the keyboard, a programmer would use a statement equivalent to

Apply the procedure ReadFile to retrieve Name from the file KeyBoard

where Name is a variable of type character string.

QUESTIONS/EXERCISES

1. Follow the merge algorithm presented in Figure 8.2, assuming that one input file contains records with key field values equal to B and E while the other contains A, C, D, and F.
2. The merge algorithm is the heart of a popular sort algorithm called the merge sort. Can you discover this algorithm? (*Hint:* Any nonempty file can be considered to be a collection of one-entry files.)

8.3 Text Files

Sometimes the logical records in a sequential file are small. An example is a **text file,** which is a sequential file in which each logical record consists of a single "printable" character. We place *printable* in quotation marks because we are not only including alphabetic characters, numeric digits, and punctuation marks, but control codes such as carriage returns and line feeds as well. Loosely speaking, then, each logical record in a text file is a bit pattern representing a key on a traditional keyboard.

Composition of Text Files

For years text files have been constructed using ASCII, which means that the de facto standard for text files has become a one byte per symbol format in which each byte represents a printable character in ASCII. Indeed, the term *ASCII file* is often used as a synonym for *text file.* Whether the increasing popularity of Unicode will challenge this terminology is yet to be seen. It could be that terms that distinguish between the underlying code (such as Unicode file as opposed to ASCII file) will become common. For our purposes, however, the distinction will not be critical.

The term **binary file** is often used to refer to any file that is not a text file. The distinction is often important when transferring files from one system to another. For example, when dealing with text files, many systems (most PCs) use a line feed code to indicate the end of a line of text, whereas others (those using the UNIX operating system) require both a carriage return and a line feed, while still others (products from Apple Computer, Inc.) use only a carriage return. (Strictly speaking, a line feed is only a vertical shift and a carriage return is a horizontal shift.) Thus, transferring a text file between such systems requires conversions that are not necessary when transferring a general binary file.

We can draw a distinction between the basic utility programs called editors and the more elaborate application programs called word processors by comparing the composition of the "text files" they produce. Both are used to create and modify textual documents by presenting a document on the computer screen and allowing it to be altered via the keyboard and mouse. The distinction is that an editor creates and modifies strictly text files, whereas a word processor inserts nonprintable codes in the file in order to represent changes in fonts, alignment information, etc. Thus the documents manipulated by word processors could be considered "extended text files" but are not text files in the strict sense.

It is this distinction that dictates that files produced by word processors must be transferred via e-mail as attachments rather than as part of the message itself. Indeed, e-mail systems are designed to handle text files and are therefore not compatible with the extended features found in word processor documents.

Note that editors and word processors usually disguise the strict sequential nature of the file being manipulated. For example, they normally read a large portion of the file into main memory and allow the user to move back and forth within this block while making changes. In most cases, the entire file can be held in main memory at the same time. In the other

POSITIONING FILES ON DISKS

Suppose we wanted to store a sequential file, a text file, or perhaps an image on a magnetic disk. The significant point is that the data being stored will occupy more than one sector, which means that each time we retrieve the data, we will want to read several sectors sequentially. We might first observe that, if possible, we should record the entire file on the same track (or perhaps cylinder). Otherwise, retrieving the data would require repositioning the read/write heads during the retrieval process. Another point, however, is not as obvious—we should not store the data in consecutive sectors around a track. Instead, we should skip sectors after each sector we use.

The reason is that after reading one sector, there will be a slight delay before we are ready to read the next. If we had stored the next part of the file in the next sector on the track, that sector will have already passed the read/write heads by the time we are ready for it. Thus we would have to wait another revolution of the disk before that sector came by again. If, however, there are sectors between the last sector read and the next one desired, we will have time to get ready to read before the sector we want reaches the read/write heads. In the case of a track with 16 sectors, we could record a sequential file on sectors 5, 10, 15, 1, 6, 11, 16, 2, 7, etc. In this way we would use all the sectors on the track, and be able to retrieve the data from the entire track in only five revolutions of the disk.

cases, more of the file is retrieved from mass storage as the user moves farther down the text, while the earlier updated portions are transferred back to mass storage (Figure 8.4). In this way the editor or word processor provides random access to that portion of the file that is currently held in main memory. There

FIGURE 8.4

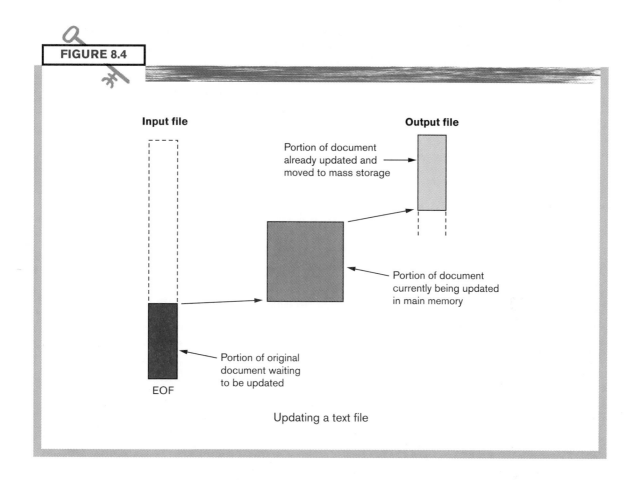

Input file

Output file

Portion of document
already updated and
moved to mass storage

Portion of document
currently being updated
in main memory

Portion of original
document waiting
to be updated

EOF

Updating a text file

are, however, complications in such designs when the user wants to return to early parts of the file that have already been transferred back to mass storage. This is why a simple editor or an inexpensive word processor may have trouble manipulating large documents.

Programming Concerns

Text files are among the most common file structures supported by high-level programming languages. Most of these languages provide statements for transferring data to or from a text file in a character-by-character manner. In addition, some languages support the transfer of data to or from a text file in a line-by-line manner, where a line consists of the characters appearing between "new line" markers. (Recall that the composition of "new line" markers varies from system to system.) Thus, a high-level programming language based on the imperative paradigm may contain statements equivalent to the pseuocode statement

Apply the procedure GetCharacter to retrieve Symbol from the file Text

where Symbol is a variable of type character, as well as statements equivalent to

Apply the procedure ReadLine to retrieve TextLine from the file Text

where TextLine is a variable of type string. In an object-oriented language these statements would be expressed as

Send the message GetCharacter to the object Text to retrieve Symbol

and

Send the message ReadLine to the object Text to retrieve TextLine

In many cases, the process of transferring data to or from a text file involves data conversion rather than merely data transfer. Consider, for example, the statement

Apply the procedure Write to place the value of Length in the file Text

where Length is a variable of type integer and Text is a text file based on ASCII. Then the value currently assigned to Length must be converted from two's complement notation into ASCII coded characters before it can be recorded in the file. More precisely, suppose that integers are represented in two's complement notation using 16 bits per value and the current value of Length is 134. Then, the bit pattern associated with Length will be

0000000010000110

(the two's complement representation for 134), but the bit pattern that should be recorded in the file is

001100010011001100110100

(the ASCII code for the symbol 1, followed by the ASCII code for the symbol 3, followed by the ASCII code for the symbol 4).

Conversely, consider the process required when we later retrieve the value of Length from the file using a statement such as

Apply the procedure ReadFile to retrieve the value of Length from the file Text.

This requires retrieving symbols from the file Text until all the digits representing the value have been obtained and then constructing the two's complement representation of the corresponding value before an assignment to Length can be made.

Such data conversion is quite common when transferring data to and from a machine's peripheral devices. As we mentioned at the end of the previous section, most high-level programming languages treat a computer's peripheral devices as sequential files. In fact, such files are often text files. A keyboard, for example, is normally considered to be a text file from which the machine receives data in a character-by-character format. Consider, then, the process required by a program statement such as

Apply the procedure ReadFile to retrieve Age from the file KeyBoard

where Age is a variable of type integer. If the value 34 is typed at the keyboard, the keyboard will produce a coded version of the symbol 3 followed by a coded version of the symbol 4. This text-oriented data must then be converted to the two's complement representation of 34 before an assignment to Age can be made.

QUESTIONS/EXERCISES

1. In what sense is a text file a special case of a sequential file?
2. Identify two applications in which the use of text files is appropriate.
3. What problems might be encountered when the word processor is required to backtrack a long distance within a document that is being updated?
4. In the closing example of this section, suppose the keys 2 and 4 were pressed one after the other at the keyboard. Furthermore, suppose the keyboard produces ASCII representations for symbols and the integer values are represented in two's complement notation using 16 bits per value. What bit patterns would be generated by the keyboard? What bit pattern would be assigned to the variable Age?

8.4 Indexing

The major disadvantage of sequential files is that they are not compatible with applications that require random access to records. To retrieve a single record from a sequential file requires a sequential search of the file—a process that we have seen to be time consuming (Section 4.6). One solution to the problem is to provide an index to the file, resulting in an **indexed file.** To find a record in such a file, one would first find the relevant entry in the file's index. There one would find the location of the desired record. A popular example is found on audio CDs where an index is used to allow access to individual pieces.

Index Fundamentals

An index for a file consists of a listing of entries, each of which contains an identifying property of a record (probably a key field value) followed by the location of that record. This index is usually stored on the mass storage device containing the file. To retrieve a record from the file, the index is first transferred to main memory where it is searched for the appropriate entry. Once this entry is found, the desired record can be retrieved from the storage device. Thus an index provides direct access to individual records in the file—that is, a particular record can be retrieved without interrogating other records in the file.

A classic example occurs in the problem of maintaining employee records. Here an index can be used to avoid lengthy sequential searches when retrieving individual records. In particular, if the file of employee records is indexed by employee identification numbers, then an employee's record can be retrieved quickly if that employee's identification number is known.

This is also an example of a case when a multiple index system is convenient. For instance, it may also be necessary to retrieve employee records by means of Social Security numbers. This can be accomplished by maintaining an additional index based on Social Security numbers rather than employee identification numbers (Figure 8.5). Then, regardless of whether one starts with an employee number or a Social Security number, the desired record can be accessed quickly by interrogating the appropriate index. (You sometimes hear

FIGURE 8.5

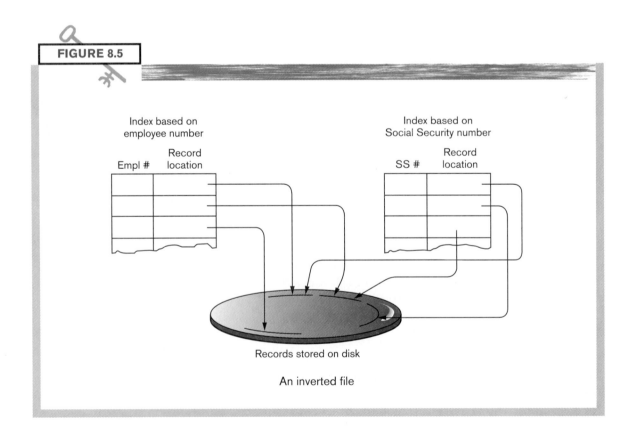

Index based on
employee number

Empl #	Record location

Index based on
Social Security number

SS #	Record location

Records stored on disk

An inverted file

such a file referred to as an **inverted file,** with one key field designated as the **primary key** and the other as the **secondary key.**)

Sometimes it is convenient to construct an index that provides only an approximate, rather than the precise, location of the desired record. This can be accomplished by storing an otherwise sorted sequential file as several multi-record segments. Each segment is then represented in the index by a single entry, which is normally the last key field value in the segment. The result is a partial index containing only a portion of the key field values appearing in the file.

The partial-index structure is summarized in Figure 8.6, in which we have indicated only the key field entry in each record and have assumed that these entries are single, alphabetic letters. The retrieval of a record from such a file consists of finding the first entry in the index that is equal to or greater than the desired entry and then searching the corresponding sequential segment for the target record. For example, to find the record with key field entry E in the file

FIGURE 8.6

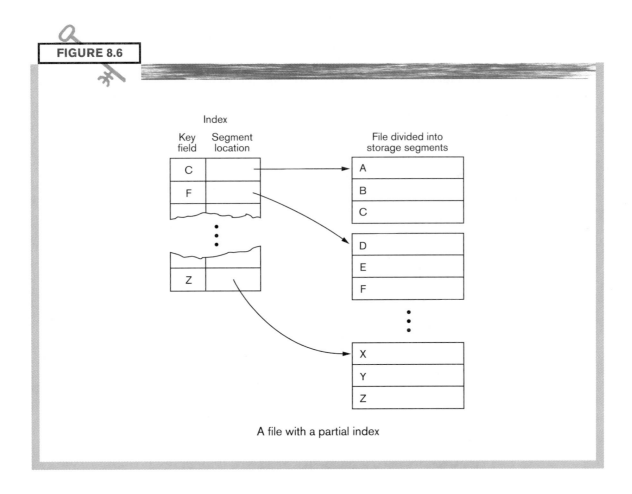

A file with a partial index

in Figure 8.6, we follow the pointer associated with the index entry F and then search that segment to find the desired record.

Another approach to indexing files is to construct the index in a hierarchical manner in which the overall index takes on a layered or tree structure. A prominent example of such an index structure is the hierarchical directory system used by most operating systems for maintaining files. In such a case, the directories, or folders, play the role of indexes, each containing links to its subindexes. From this perspective, the entire file system is merely one large indexed file.

Programming Concerns

Several application programs for PCs (including spreadsheet and database systems) create indexed files in the performance of their duties. For the purpose of developing these applications, many third-generation programming languages offer the building blocks required to construct and manipulate indexed files. In these closing paragraphs we explore the features found in C.

In a C program, the functions fgetpos (file get position) and fsetpos (file set position) are ideal for constructing and using an index. In particular, the function fgetpos can be used to obtain the current position in a file. For example, the statement

```
fgetpos(Personnel, &Position);
```

assigns the current position in the file Personnel to the variable Position. (Exactly how this position is coded varies from system to system.) This "current position" is the position at which the next read or write operation with respect to the file will be performed. Thus, this position can be used in an index to preserve the location at which a record was stored. That is, if we obtain and save the current position in the file prior to writing each record, we will be left with an index containing the locations of the records.

The function fsetpos is used to establish a new position in a file. In particular, the statement

```
fsetpos(Personnel, &Position);
```

requests that the current position in the file Personnel be established at the location identified by the value of the variable Position. If we followed this statement with

```
fscanf(Personnel, "%s", Name);
```

the variable Name would be assigned the data retrieved from that position in the file. Thus, fsetpos provides the tool needed to retrieve a particular record by means of the information stored in the index.

1. What activities would an operating system perform when asked to retrieve a record from an indexed file?
2. What might be added to your answer to Exercise 1 if the operating system is also controlling a time-sharing system?

8.5 Hashing

Although indexing provides direct access to records within a file, it does so at the expense of maintaining the index. **Hashing** is a technique that provides direct access to records without such overhead. The process can be summarized as follows: The file storage space is divided into several sections, each called a **bucket.** The records are dispersed among the buckets according to an algorithm (called the **hash algorithm**) that converts key field values into bucket numbers. Each record is stored in the bucket identified by this process. Therefore, a record can be retrieved by applying the hash algorithm to its key field value and then retrieving the records in the appropriate bucket. A file constructed in this manner is called a **hashed file.**

A Particular Hashing System

Let us apply the hashing concept to the classic employee file. First, we establish several empty sequential files that will play the role of buckets. (The approach of using separate files for the buckets has undesirable consequences that we address in a later subsection on programming concerns. How many buckets we use is a design decision that we also will return to later.) For now, let us assume that we have created 40 buckets, which we refer to as bucket number 0, bucket number 1, through bucket number 39. Next, we establish the employee identification number as the key field.

Our next task is to develop the hash algorithm to convert any key field value into a bucket number. To this end, we recall that the employee identification numbers are stored as bit patterns, each of which can be interpreted as a numeric value represented in binary notation. Thus, although the identification "numbers" may have the form 25X3Z or J2-X35, we can still interpret the bit patterns as numbers. Using this numeric interpretation, we can divide any key field value stored in memory by the number of buckets, which in our case is 40. Note that the result of this division is an integer value, called the quotient, and another integer value known as the remainder. The important point is that this remainder is always in the range from 0 to 39. That is, if we consider only the remainder from the division, we always find one of the 40 possible values 0, 1, 2, 3,... 39.

HASHING AS A GENERAL TECHNIQUE

Although we have introduced hashing techniques in their traditional file context, hashing is not restricted to this environment. Today hashing is often used to distribute and later to find data within main memory. For example, the symbol table in a translator is often implemented as a collection of linked lists, where hashing is used to identify the list containing a particular identifier. Hashing is also used as a means of authenticating messages transferred over the Internet. The underlying theme is to hash the message (in a secret way) and encrypt the value obtained. This value is then transferred with the message. To authenticate the message, the receiver hashes the message received and confirms that the value produced agrees with the original value.

Thus we can relate exactly one of the 40 buckets to each of these possible remainders (Figure 8.7).

With this system we can convert any key field value into an integer (the remainder of the division) that identifies one of the buckets, and we can use this system to determine the bucket in which to store the corresponding record. That is, we can consider each record individually, convert its key field value to an integer, apply our hash algorithm to identify a bucket, and then store the record in that bucket as summarized in Figure 8.8. Later, if we need to retrieve a record with a certain key field value, we can simply transform this value to a bucket number as before and then search that bucket for the record in question.

FIGURE 8.7

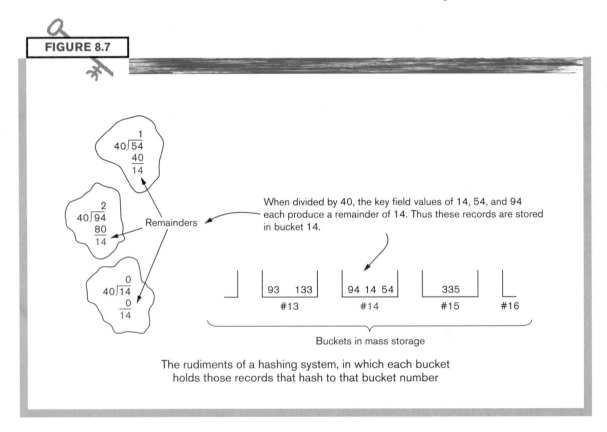

The rudiments of a hashing system, in which each bucket holds those records that hash to that bucket number

FIGURE 8.8

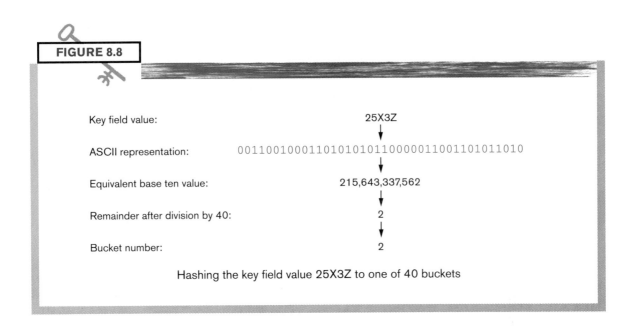

Key field value:	25X3Z
ASCII representation:	001100100011010101011000001100110101 1010
Equivalent base ten value:	215,643,337,562
Remainder after division by 40:	2
Bucket number:	2

Hashing the key field value 25X3Z to one of 40 buckets

Distribution Problems

Our simple hashing system has a few problems, at the root of which is the fact that once we have chosen the hash algorithm, we have no more control over the distribution of the records among the buckets. For instance, if we use the divide-by-40 algorithm previously presented, and if the numeric interpretation of the key field values tends to be multiples of 40, a disproportionate number of the records are placed in the bucket assigned to the remainder zero. The result is that searching through that bucket approximates a search through the entire file, resulting in little advantage over a sequential file structure.

It is therefore to our advantage to select a hash algorithm that evenly distributes the records among the buckets provided in mass storage. However, the selection process is complicated by the fact that we normally do not know in advance exactly what the key field values will be because of employee turnover; the employee identification numbers used today will not be those used tomorrow. For this reason, the choice of a hash algorithm must be based on a combination of one's artistic abilities, statistical analysis, and rules of thumb.

One such rule of thumb concerns our decision to use 40 buckets, which is generally not a good choice. To see why, recall that if a dividend and a divisor both have a common factor, this factor is present in the remainder. In turn, the remainders produced by the division process tend to be multiples of this common factor, while other values are ignored. We saw a specific case of this effect when we conjectured the possibility of the key fields being multiples of 40, which produced remainders of zero. A similar problem exists if the key fields are multiples of 5. Since 40 is also a multiple of 5, the factor of 5 appears in the remainder of our division process, and the records in the file cluster in those buckets associated with the remainders 0, 5, 10, 15, 20, 25, 30, and 35.

Similar situations occur in the case of key field values that are multiples of 2, 4, 8, 10, and 20, because they are all also factors of 40. Of course, the observation of this fact suggests a partial solution. That is, the chance of clustering due to this phenomenon can be minimized by selecting the number of buckets to have as few factors as possible. Thus one usually selects the number of buckets to be a prime number. For instance, the chance of clustering in the employee file example can be greatly reduced by dividing mass storage into 41 buckets rather than 40, because the only factors of 41 are 1 and 41.

Sometimes clustering can be reduced by selecting a hash algorithm based on principles other than division. One suggested technique, called the *mid-square method,* is to multiply the key field value by itself and select the middle digits from the product to represent the bucket number. Still another, called the *extraction method,* is to select the digits appearing in certain positions within the key field and to construct the bucket number by combining these selected digits using some predetermined process. In any case, one often tests the performance of several hash algorithms on sample records before settling on a final choice.

Unfortunately, regardless of the hash algorithm we ultimately use, clustering of records will most likely occur as a file is modified over a period of time. We can gain an understanding of how quickly this might occur by considering what happens as we initially insert records into the modified 41-bucket employee file.

Assume that we have found a hash algorithm that arbitrarily distributes records among the buckets, that our file is empty, and that we are going to insert records one at a time. When we insert the first record, that record must go into an empty bucket. However, when we insert the next record, only 40 of the 41 buckets are empty and so the probability that the second record will be placed in an empty bucket is only 40/41. Assuming that the second record is placed in an empty bucket, the third finds only 39 empty buckets, and the probability of its being placed in one of them is 39/41. Continuing this process, we find that if the first seven records are placed in empty buckets, the eighth record then has a 34/41 probability of being placed in one of the remaining empty buckets.

This analysis allows us to compute the probability of the first eight records being placed in empty buckets, because it is the product of the probabilities of each record being placed in an empty bucket, assuming that the preceding records were so placed. This probability is therefore

$$(41/41)(40/41)(39/41)(38/41) \ldots (34/41) = .482$$

The point is that the result is less than one-half. That is, it is more likely than not that at least two of the first eight records will hash to the same bucket, a phenomenon called a *collision*. Thus clustering probably begins with only eight records stored among 41 buckets.

The high probability of collisions indicates that a hashing system should never be implemented under the assumption that clustering will not occur. In our employee records example, each bucket, being an individual file, can expand indefinitely. Thus the only consequence of uncontrolled clustering is that retrieval times could become long. In other cases, however, hashing may be applied in a context in which bucket sizes are fixed. As a result, buckets may fill up as records are added and data could be lost.

A classic technique for handling this problem is to reserve an additional storage area to hold overflow records. Then, if a bucket fills up, records that would normally be added to it are placed in the overflow area and linked to the appropriate bucket through an organization analogous to a linked list. With such a system, a file stored in five buckets might have the structure shown in Figure 8.9, in which the storage area occupied by records is indicated by shading. (Note that buckets 1 and 4 have spilled into the overflow area, whereas one additional record in bucket 2 will cause bucket 2 to do the same.)

When trying to retrieve a record from such a file, we would first identify the proper bucket using the hash algorithm and then search through that bucket. If the desired record was not found there, we would search the overflow records linked to that bucket. Note that if a lot of overflowing takes place, the efficiency

FIGURE 8.9

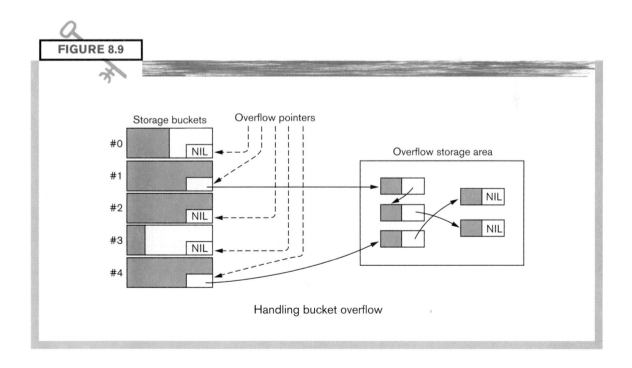

Handling bucket overflow

of searching the file can drop significantly. The design of a hashed file therefore requires a careful analysis involving the choice of the hash algorithm, the number and size of the buckets, and the size and structure of the overflow area.

Programming Concerns

Let us now suppose that we are writing an application program using a third-generation programming language and need to implement a hashing system for a file. Our first observation is that the separated file per bucket strategy that we presented earlier in this section might not be compatible with the underlying operating system. The reason is that there may be a limit to the number of files that an application program can have open at any time, and the number of buckets needed to obtain efficient record retrieval would most likely exceed that limit.

The more practical approach is to reserve a large space in mass storage by establishing a single large empty file. We could then use portions of this file as the buckets in our system. Several programming languages support this approach. For example, COBOL allows a programmer to establish a large empty file that can be accessed in a manner similar to an array. That is, the locations in the file can be identified by indices. A programmer can, therefore, create such a file and use various segments of it as the buckets in a hashed file (Figure 8.10). For instance, locations 1 through 20 could be used as the first bucket, locations 21 through 40 as the second, etc. In this manner the individual bucket contents can be referenced directly as they are needed.

A similar system can be implemented in a C program using the functions `fgetpos` and `fsetpos` introduced in the previous section to access different portions of the file as required.

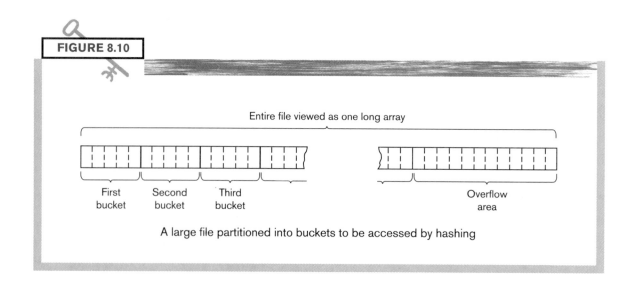

FIGURE 8.10

Entire file viewed as one long array

First bucket   Second bucket   Third bucket   Overflow area

A large file partitioned into buckets to be accessed by hashing

QUESTIONS/EXERCISES

1. Suppose an employee record system is implemented as a hashed file using 1000 buckets of mass storage with the Social Security number field as the key field. Observe that one possible hash algorithm is to select the first three digits from the Social Security number, because this would always result in a value between 0 and 999, inclusive. Why is this not a good choice?

2. Explain how a poorly chosen hash algorithm can result in a hashed file system becoming little more than a sequential file.

3. Suppose a hashed file is constructed using the division hash algorithm as presented in the text but with six storage buckets. For each of the following key field values, identify the bucket in which the record with that key field value is placed. What goes wrong and why?
   - a. 24
   - b. 30
   - c. 3
   - d. 18
   - e. 15
   - f. 21
   - g. 9
   - h. 39
   - i. 27
   - j. 0

4. How many people must be gathered together before the odds are that two members of the group will have birthdays on the same day of the year?

CHAPTER REVIEW PROBLEMS

1. Suppose a sequential file contains 50,000 records and 5 milliseconds is required to interrogate an entry. How long should we expect to wait when retrieving a record from the middle of the file?

2. What conversions might be necessary when transferring a text file across the Internet that would not be required if the file was a JPEG image?

3. List the steps that are executed in the merge algorithm in Figure 8.2 if one of the input files is empty at the start.

4. Modify the algorithm in Figure 8.2 to handle the case in which both input files contain a record with the same key field value. Assume that these records are identical and that only one should appear in the output file.

5. Design a system by which a file stored on a disk can be processed as a sequential file with either of two different orderings.

6. Why is a company-assigned employer identification number a better choice for a key field than the last name of each employee?

7. In what sense is the advantage of an index lost if, to keep the index small, the segments used for a partial-index system are made extremely large?

8. The following table represents the contents of a partial index. Indicate which segment should be retrieved when searching for the record with each of the following key field values:
   - a. 24X17
   - b. 12N67
   - c. 32E75
   - d. 26X28

Key field	Segment number
13C08	1
23G19	2
26X28	3
36Z05	4

9. Based on the index in Problem 8, what is the largest key field value in the file? What do you know about the smallest?

10. What is the difference between a file produced by an editor and a file produced by a word processor?

11. What is a file allocation table?

12. What advantages does an indexed file have over a hashed file? What advantages does a hashed file have over an indexed file?

13. The chapter drew parallels between a traditional file index and the file directory system maintained by an operating system. In what ways does an operating system's file directory differ from a traditional index?

14. What file structure do you recommend for a file containing descriptions of a library's holdings, assuming that books must be referenced by author's name, book title, and subject? Support your recommendation.

15. If the only way to extract information from a hashed file is by actually hashing the key of each record, what information is required to obtain a complete listing of all the records?

16. If a hashed file is partitioned into 10 buckets, what is the probability of at least two of three arbitrary records hashing to the same section? (Assume the hash algo-

rithm gives no bucket priority over the others.) How many records must be stored in the file until it is more likely for collisions to occur than not?

17. Solve the previous problem, assuming that the file is partitioned into 100 buckets instead of 10.

18. If we are using the division technique discussed in this chapter as a hash algorithm and the file storage area is divided into 23 buckets, which section should we search to find the record whose key field value, when interpreted as a binary value, reduces to the integer 124?

19. Compare the implementation of a hashed file to that of a homogeneous array. How are the roles of the hash function and the address polynomial similar?

20. Design a hashed file of words that could be used as a spell checker. What would you use as a hash function? Would your choice of a hash function depend on the language from which the words are chosen? Why should such a file not be stored as a sequential file?

21. Estimate the size of the file in the previous problem, assuming that it contains 50,000 words. Would such a file fit in an 8MB block of main memory? If so, why would it be advantageous to move the whole file to main memory and use it from there?

22. Design an indexed file of words that could be used as a spell checker. Why should such a file not be stored as a sequential file?

23. If the division hash algorithm as presented in the text is being used, why is clustering more likely to occur when the

file storage space is divided into 60 sections rather than 61?

24. Why is it advantageous to keep the list of overflow records (from a bucket in a hashed file) sorted according to key field values?

25. If we divided the storage area for a hashed file into 41 buckets that can each hold exactly one record, we expect at least one section to overflow after only eight records are stored. On the other hand, if we combine the same storage area into one bucket that can hold 41 records, we can always store 41 records before overflow occurs. What keeps us from deciding to implement hashed files using this latter configuration?

26. Suppose a record's key field value is XY. Using the division technique for hashing discussed in the text, convert this value into the section number that should contain the record in a hashed file consisting of 41 buckets. (Assume characters are coded using ASCII, one byte per character.)

27. Suppose a hashed file is to be constructed containing information about the residents of a local community in the United States. If the key field of this file is to consist of seven-digit telephone numbers, why would it not be a good idea to base the hashing algorithm on the first three digits in the key field?

28. A hashed file using the division hash algorithm discussed in the text is to be constructed with 50, 51, 52, or 53 buckets. Which of these choices is best? Why?

29. Suppose a hashed file was constructed using the division technique discussed in this chapter as the hash algorithm. Moreover, suppose that a record from bucket 3 is found to have a key field value that, when interpreted as a binary value, reduces to the integer 26. Into how many buckets was the mass storage area for this file divided?

30. Give an advantage that
    a. a sequential file has over an indexed file.
    b. a sequential file has over a hashed file.
    c. an indexed file has over a sequential file.
    d. an indexed file has over a hashed file.
    e. a hashed file has over a sequential file.
    f. a hashed file has over an indexed file.

31. In each of the following cases, indicate which file structure (sequential, text, indexed, or hashed) you recommend. Support your recommendations.
    a. A rough draft of a speech
    b. A file of a dentist's patient records
    c. A mailing list
    d. A reference file of 50,000 words and their definitions

32. Suppose that a magnetic disk is divided into 512 byte sectors. Approximately how many sectors would be required to hold a 20-page text document stored in ASCII? What if the document were stored in Unicode?

33. In what way is a sequential file similar to a linked list?

34. Identify two techniques that might be used for identifying the end of a text file.

35. Explain how a sequential file of employee records can be implemented using a programming language's primitives for manipulating text files.

36. Define each of the following:
    a. Text file
    b. Indexed file
    c. Hashed file

37. Why would a programmer need to write a program using an internal identifier to refer to a file rather than the file's actual external name?

38. Identify three items of information that might be found in a file descriptor.

39. What is the purpose of opening a file? What is the purpose of closing a file?

40. How does the implementation of a sequential file differ if it is stored on tape rather than disk?

41. Suppose a sequential file contains 2000 records. If, over an extended period, various records are retrieved from the file, what do you expect to be the average number of records interrogated per retrieval? Explain your answer.

42. Estimate the amount of mass storage space required to store a term paper consisting of 40 pages represented as a text file.

SOCIAL ISSUES

The following questions are provided to help you understand some of the ethical/social/legal issues associated with the field of computing as well as investigate your own beliefs and their foundations. The goal is not merely to answer these questions. You should also consider why you answered as you did and whether your justifications are consistent from one question to the next.

1. To what extent should organizations be allowed to combine files to obtain information that would not otherwise be available? For example, should income tax records be combined with welfare records? Should medical records be combined with insurance records?

2. Due to a heavy workload, a social worker copies some of the files regarding current cases onto floppy disks and takes them home to work during the evenings. Is this acceptable behavior? Would your answer change if the materials taken home were printed records rather than magnetic records? Would your answer change if the worker were a university employee and the records were student records? Would your answer change if the employee merely accessed the records via telephone lines while working at home?

3. As a joke, suppose a programmer added an additional field to each record of a personnel file and programmed the associated software to place facetious comments in this field. If only the programmer knows how to access the additional information, is any harm done?

4. When a file is deleted from a disk, it is usually not erased but merely marked as deleted. The information in the file may be on the disk for some time before that portion of the disk is finally reused for another file. Is it ethical to reconstruct deleted files from disks that were previously used by others?

5. What ethical issues would be raised if a major software developer designed software so that it secretly labeled each file created with information about the originator of the file? For example, a developer of software for personal computers could design its software so that the name of the personal computer owner would be secretly attached to all the files created by that machine, and this information would travel with the file if sent over the Internet.

ADDITIONAL READING

Folk, M. J., B. Zoellick, and G. Riccardi. *File Structures—An Object-Oriented Approach in C++*, 3rd ed. Reading, MA: Addison-Wesley, 1998.

Kay, D. C. and J. R. Levine. *Graphic File Formats*, 2nd ed. New York: McGraw-Hill, 1995.

McFedries, P. *Windows 98 Unleashed*. Indianapolis, IN: Sams, 1998.

Miller, N. E. and C. G. Petersen. *File Structures with Ada*. Redwood City, CA: Benjamin/Cummings, 1990.

Shaffer, C. A. *A Practical Introduction to Data Structures and Algorithm Analysis*. Upper Saddle River, NJ: Prentice-Hall, 1998.

9.1 General Issues

9.2 The Layered Approach
to Database mplementation

9.3 The Relational Model
Relational Design
Relational Operations
SQL

*9.4 Object-Oriented
Databases

*9.5 Maintaining Database
Integrity
**The Commit/Rollback
Protocol**
Locking

9.6 Social Impact of
Database Technology

*Asterisks indicate suggestions for
optional sections.

chapter
DATABASE
STRUCTURES
nine

The subject of databases represents a synthesis of data
structures and file structures. A modern database applies
techniques from both fields to obtain a single mass storage
data system that can appear to have a multitude of organizations for serving a variety of applications. Such structures
eliminate the duplication found in the file-oriented approach,
providing separate data systems for each application. In
this chapter we investigate the composition of database
systems and the direction of current research.

9.1 General Issues

The term **flat file** is sometimes used to refer to a traditional file system as opposed to a database. More generally, a flat file is considered to be a one-dimensional storage system in that it presents its information from a single point of view. In contrast, the term **database** refers to a collection of data that is multidimensional in that it contains internal links between its entries so that its information is accessible from a variety of perspectives. Whereas a flat file containing information about composers and their compositions might provide only a list of compositions arranged by composer, a database would allow one to find all the works by a single composer, all the composers who wrote a particular type of music, or perhaps the composers who wrote variations of another composer's work.

Historically, databases have evolved as a means of integrating data storage systems. As computing machinery found wider and wider uses in information management, each application tended to be implemented as a separate system with its own collection of data. Typically, the need to process payroll gave rise to a sequential file, and later the need for interactive data retrieval produced an entirely different system using an indexed file. Although each of these systems represented an improvement over the corresponding manual techniques previously used, taken as a whole the collection of individual automated systems still constituted a limited and inefficient use of resources when compared with the possibilities of a integrated database system. For example, different departments were not able to share the data they all needed, so much of the information required by an organization was duplicated in storage. The result was that when an employee moved, visits were required to numerous departments throughout the organization where address change cards were filed. Typographical errors, misplaced cards, and employee apathy could soon result in erroneous and conflicting data within the various data systems. After a move, an employee's newsletter might begin to arrive at the new address but with the wrong name, while the payroll records could continue to reflect the old address. In this setting, database systems emerged as a means of integrating the information stored and maintained by a particular organization (Figure 9.1). With such a system, both payroll and the mailing of newsletters could be processed from a single integrated data system.

Another advantage of an integrated data system is the control achieved by an organization when the information it owns is placed in one common pot. As long as each department has its own independent data, those data tend to be used for the good of the department rather than for the good of the organization. In contrast, when an integrated database is implemented in a large organization, the control of information is normally concentrated in the administrative position known as the **database administrator (DBA),** which may or may not be held by a single individual. This central administrator (or administrative position) is cognizant of both the data available within the organization and the needs of the various departments. It is thus within this structure that decisions regarding data organization and access can be made with the entire organization in mind.

FIGURE 9.1

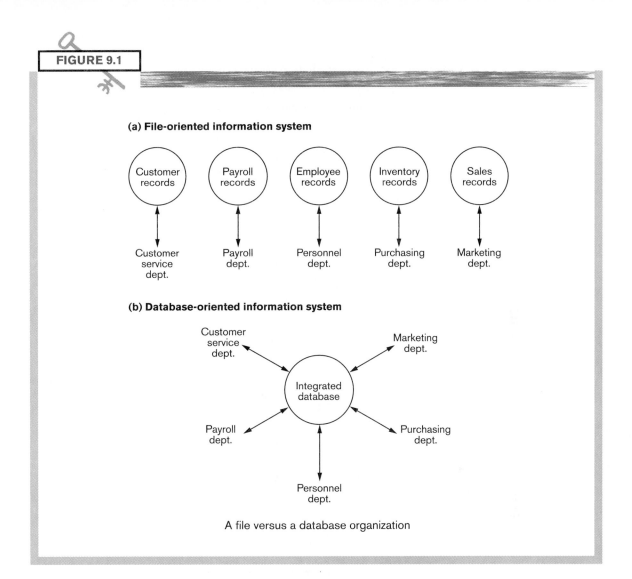

(a) File-oriented information system

(b) Database-oriented information system

A file versus a database organization

Along with the benefits of data integration come disadvantages. One concern is the control of access to sensitive data. For example, someone working on the organization's newsletter might need access to employee names and addresses but should not have access to payroll data; similarly, an employee processing payroll should not have access to the other financial records of the corporation. Thus the ability to control access to the information in the database is often as important as the ability to share it.

To provide for this distinction of access privileges, database systems often rely on schemas and subschemas. A **schema** is a description of the entire database structure that is used by the database software to maintain the database. A

subschema is a description of only that portion of the database pertinent to a particular user's needs. For example, consider a schema for a university database that indicates that each student record contains such items as the current address and phone number of that student in addition to that student's academic record. Moreover, it indicates that each student record is linked to the record of that student's faculty adviser. In turn, the record for each faculty member contains that person's address, employment history, and so on. Based on this schema, a pointer system is maintained that ultimately links the information about a student to the employment history of a faculty member.

To keep the university's registrar from using this linkage to obtain privileged information about the faculty, the registrar's access to the database must be restricted to a subschema whose description of the faculty records does not include employment history. Under this subschema a user can find out which faculty member is a particular student's adviser but cannot obtain access to additional information about that faculty member. In contrast, the subschema for the payroll department provides the employment history of each faculty member but does not include the linkage between students and advisers. Thus the payroll department can modify a faculty member's salary but cannot obtain the names of the students advised by that person.

There are other disadvantages connected to the evolution of database technology in addition to those directly associated with security. The size and scope of databases have increased rapidly. Today, extremely large collections of data can be assembled and interrogated with little effort over wide geographic areas, and with this increase in magnitude comes an increase in misinformation and misapplications of information. Incidents abound of injustices due to inaccurate credit reports, faulty criminal records, and discrimination resulting from unauthorized or unethical access to personal information.

In other cases, the underlying problem deals with the right to collect and hold information in the first place. What kind of information does an insurance company have a right to collect regarding its clients? Does a government have the right to maintain accounts of an individual citizen's voting record? Does a credit card company have the right to sell records of its customers' purchasing patterns to marketing firms? These questions represent some of the issues with which society must deal as a result of the influx of database technology.

QUESTIONS/EXERCISES

1. Identify two departments in a manufacturing plant that would have different uses for the same or similar inventory information.
2. Identify a variety of data collections found in a university environment that might be collected into one integrated database.
3. Describe how the subschema for the two departments in Question 1 might differ.

9.2 The Layered Approach to Database Implementation

To hide the complexities of a database's implementation, a database system is constructed from layers of abstraction (Figure 9.2). The image of the data given to the person using the database is produced by the application software that communicates with the user in an interactive manner and in the application's terminology. In a large company this software might be written by the programming staff within the business; in the personal computing environment it is usually purchased in the form of a fourth-generation software package that can be customized to fit the individual's needs. It is in the design of this software that the overall system is given its personality. It may, for example, communicate with the user through such means as a question-and-answer dialogue or a fill-in-the-blanks scenario. Regardless of the user interface ultimately adopted, the application software communicates with the user to learn what information is required and later, having obtained the requested information, presents it to the user in a meaningful format.

Note that we did not say that the application software manipulates the information in the database. The actual manipulation of the database is accomplished by another software layer called the **database management system (DBMS).** This dichotomy has several benefits. One is that the

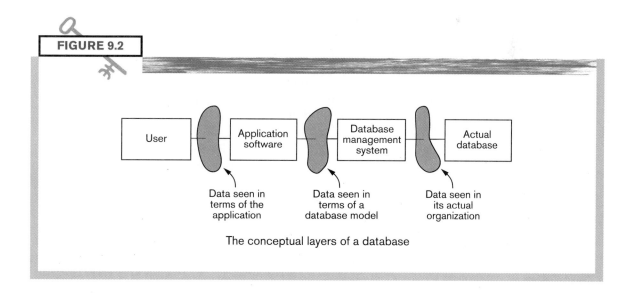

FIGURE 9.2

The conceptual layers of a database

division of duties simplifies the design process. Just as the user's task would be complicated by the requirement to consider computer concepts along with the task of solving a problem in the application world, the application programmer's task would be more complex if the actual data manipulation were a part of the application software. This is particularly true in the context of a **distributed database** (a database spread over several machines in a network). Without the services of a database management system, the application program must contain routines for keeping up with the actual location of the various portions of the database. With a well-designed database management system, the application software can be written as though the database were stored on a single machine.

A second advantage of separating the application software from the database management system is that such an organization provides a means for controlling access to the database. By dictating that all access to the database be performed by a single database management system, that system is placed in a position to enforce the restrictions imposed by the various subschemas. In particular, the database management system can use the entire database schema for its internal needs but require that each user remain within the bounds described by that user's subschema.

Still another reason for separating the user interface and actual data manipulation into two different software units is to achieve **data independence**—the ability to change the organization of the database itself without changing the application software. For example, the personnel department might need to add an additional field to each employee's record to indicate whether the corresponding employee chose to participate in the company's new health insurance program. If the application software dealt directly with the database, such a change in the data's format would require modifications to all application programs dealing with the same database. As a result, the change insti-

DISTRIBUTED DATABASES

As implied in the text, databases were originally constructed as a means of consolidating or centralizing information. The more modern perspective, however, is to view databases as a means of integrating information that may be stored on different machines throughout a network or an internet. For instance, an international corporation may store and maintain local employee records at local sites yet link those records via a network to create a *distributed database*—a single large integrated database that consists of data residing on different machines.

A distributed database may contain fragmented and/or replicated data. The first case is exemplified by the previous employee-records example in which different fragments of the database are stored in different locations. In the second case, duplicates of the same database component are stored at different locations. Such replication may occur as a means of reducing information retrieval time. Both cases pose problems not present in more traditional centralized systems—such as how to disguise the distributed nature of the database so that it functions as a coherent system or how to ensure that replicated portions of a database remain duplicates of each other as updates occur. In turn, the study of distributed databases is a current area of research.

gated by the personnel department would cause changes to the payroll program as well as to the program for printing mailing labels for the company's newsletter.

The distinction between application software and the database management system removes the need for such reprogramming. To implement a change required by a single user, one needs to change only the overall schema and the subschemas of those users involved in the change. All other subschemas remain the same, so the corresponding application software executes as though no changes were made.

One final advantage of the separation of application software and the database management system is that it allows the application software to be written in terms of a simplified, conceptual view of the database rather than the actual, complex structure involving disk tracks, pointers, and overflow areas. Recall that in our discussion of data structures, we saw that software routines could be used to translate requests (such as push and pop) in terms of a conceptual structure (a stack) into the proper activities in the actual storage organization. In a similar manner a database management system contains routines that can be used as abstract tools in the application software to convert commands in terms of a conceptual view of the database, called the **database model,** into terms of the actual database storage.

More precisely, application software is often written in general-purpose programming languages, such as those discussed in Chapter 5. These languages provide the basic ingredients for algorithm expression but lack the operations that make manipulation of the database convenient. The routines provided by the database management system in effect extend the capabilities of the language being used (as we shall see in the following sections) in a manner that supports the conceptual image of the database model. This concept of the general-purpose language being the foundation to which the capabilities of the database management system are added results in the original language being referred to as the **host language.** (Many commercial database management system packages today are actually combinations of the traditional database system and a host language. This tends to disguise the two as one, although the distinction still exists within.)

To develop application software for a database installation, a programmer must understand the abstract tools provided by the database management system being used. This is the subject of the next section where we look through the eyes of the application programmer at the relational database model. This is the model provided by most of today's database management systems. It allows the application software to be written as though the data in the database were stored in tables with rows and columns.

The search for better database models is an ongoing process. The goal is to find models that allow complex data systems to be conceptualized easily, lead to concise ways of expressing requests for information, and produce efficient database management systems.

1. Does the use of a common indexed file for both payroll processing and interactive data retrieval provide data independence?
2. In a form similar to Figure 9.2, draw a diagram representing the machine language, high-level language, and programmer views of a computer.
3. Summarize the roles of the application software, the database management system, and the actual data-manipulating routines in retrieving information from a database.

9.3 The Relational Model

In this section we introduce the **relational database model,** which is the most popular model today. Its popularity stems from the simplicity of its structure. It portrays data as being stored in rectangular tables, called **relations,** that are similar to the format in which information is displayed by spreadsheet programs. As an example, the relational model allows information regarding the employees of a firm to be represented by a relation such as that in Figure 9.3.

A row in a relation is called a **tuple.** In the relation of Figure 9.3 tuples consist of the information about a particular employee. Columns in a relation are

FIGURE 9.3

EmplId	Name	Address	SSNum
25X15	Joe E. Baker	33 Nowhere St.	111223333
34Y70	Cheryl H. Clark	563 Downtown Ave.	999009999
23Y34	G. Jerry Smith	1555 Circle Dr.	111005555
⋮	⋮	⋮	⋮

A relation containing employee information

referred to as **attributes** because each entry in a column describes some characteristic, or attribute, of the entity represented by the corresponding tuple.

Relational Design

The design of a database in terms of the relational model centers on the design of the relations making up the database. Although this may appear to be a simple task, many subtleties are waiting to trap the unwary designer.

Suppose that in addition to the information contained in the relation of Figure 9.3 we want to include information about the jobs held by the employees. Associated with each employee, we may want to include a job history, consisting of such attributes as job title (secretary, office manager, floor supervisor), a job identification code (unique to each job), the skill code associated with each job, the department in which the job exists, and the period during which the employee held the job in terms of a starting date and termination date. (We use an asterisk as the termination date if the job represents the employee's current position.)

One approach to this problem is to extend the relation in Figure 9.3 to include these attributes as additional columns in the table, as shown in Figure 9.4. However, close examination of the result reveals several problems. One is a lack of efficiency. Indeed, the relation no longer contains one tuple for each employee but rather one tuple for each assignment of an employee to a job. If an employee has advanced in the company through a sequence of several jobs, several tuples in the new relation are dedicated to that single employee. The problem is that the information contained in the original relation (each employee's name, address, identification number, and Social Security number) must be repeated. (For example, the personal information about Baker and Smith is repeated because they have held more than one job.) Moreover, if a particular job has been held by numerous employees, the department associated with that job along with the appropriate skill code must be identified in each tuple representing an assignment of the job. (For example, the description of the floor manager job is duplicated because it has been held by more than one person.)

Another, perhaps more serious problem with our extended relation surfaces when we consider deleting information from the database. Suppose, for example, that Joe E. Baker is the only employee to hold the job identified as D7. If he were to leave the company and be deleted from the database represented in Figure 9.4, we would lose the information about job D7. Indeed, the only tuple containing the fact that job D7 requires a skill level of D2 is the tuple relating to Joe Baker. If we were then to delete all references to Joe Baker and later return to the database to retrieve information about the job D7, we would not find the needed data.

FIGURE 9.4

EmplId	Name	Address	SSN	JobId	JobTitle	SkillCode	Dept	StartDate	TermDate
25X15	Joe E. Baker	33 Nowhere St.	111223333	F5	Floor manager	FM3	Sales	9-1-1998	9-30-1999
25X15	Joe E. Baker	33 Nowhere St.	111223333	D7	Dept. head	D2	Sales	10-1-1999	*
34Y70	Cheryl H. Clark	563 Downtown Ave.	999009999	F5	Floor manager	FM3	Sales	10-1-1998	*
23Y34	G. Jerry Smith	1555 Circle Dr.	111005555	S25X	Secretary	T5	Personnel	3-1-1996	4-30-1998
23Y34	G. Jerry Smith	1555 Circle Dr.	111005555	S25Z	Secretary	T6	Accounting	5-1-1998	*
⋮	⋮	⋮	⋮	⋮	⋮	⋮	⋮	⋮	⋮

A relation containing redundancy

You might argue that the ability to erase only a portion of a tuple could solve the problem, but this would in turn introduce other complications. (Should the information relating to job F5 also be retained in a partial tuple, or does this information reside elsewhere in the relation?) Moreover, the temptation to use partial tuples is a strong indication that the design of the relation is not compatible with the application.

The source of these problems is that we have combined more than one concept into a single relation. As it is proposed, the extended relation contains information dealing directly with employees (name, identification number, address, Social Security number), information about the jobs available in the company (job identification, job title, department, skill code), and information regarding the relationship between employees and jobs (start date, termination date). Based on this observation, we can solve our problems by redesigning the system using three relations—one for each of the preceding topics. We can keep the original relation (which we now call the EMPLOYEE relation) as it is and insert the additional information in the form of the two new relations called JOB and ASSIGNMENT, which produces the database in Figure 9.5.

FIGURE 9.5

EMPLOYEE relation

EmplId	Name	Address	SSNum
25X15	Joe E. Baker	33 Nowhere St.	111223333
34Y70	Cheryl H. Clark	563 Downtown Ave.	999009999
23Y34	G. Jerry Smith	1555 Circle Dr.	111005555
•	•	•	•
•	•	•	•
•	•	•	•

JOB relation

JobId	JobTitle	SkillCode	Dept
S25X	Secretary	T5	Personnel
S26Z	Secretary	T6	Accounting
F5	Floor manager	FM3	Sales
•	•	•	•
•	•	•	•
•	•	•	•

ASSIGNMENT relation

EmplId	JobId	StartDate	TermDate
23Y34	S25X	3-1-1996	4-30-1998
34Y70	F5	10-1-1998	*
23Y34	S25Z	5-1-1998	*
•	•	•	•
•	•	•	•
•	•	•	•

An employee database consisting of three relations

FIGURE 9.6

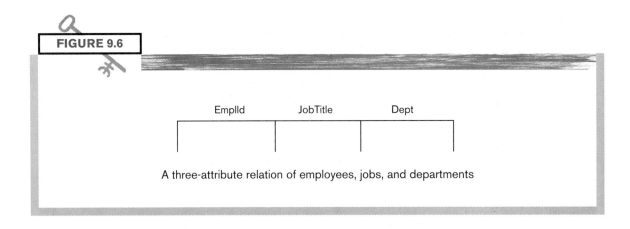

A three-attribute relation of employees, jobs, and departments

A database consisting of these three relations contains the pertinent information about employees in the EMPLOYEE relation, about available jobs in the JOB relation, and about job history in the ASSIGNMENT relation. Additional information is implicitly available by combining the information from different relations. For instance, we can find the departments in which a given employee has worked by first finding all the jobs that employee has held using the ASSIGNMENT relation and then finding the departments associated with those jobs by means of the JOB relation. Through processes such as these, any information that could be obtained from the single large relation can be obtained from the three smaller relations without the problems previously cited.

Unfortunately, dividing information into various relations is not always as trouble-free as in the preceding example. For instance, compare the relation in Figure 9.6, having attributes EmplId, JobTitle, and Dept, to its decomposition into two relations in Figure 9.7.

At first glance, the two-relation system may appear to contain the same information as the single-relation system, but in fact it does not. Consider, for

FIGURE 9.7

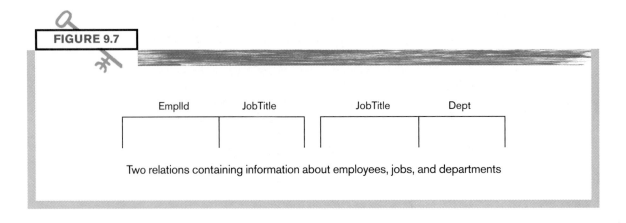

Two relations containing information about employees, jobs, and departments

example, the problem of finding the department in which a given employee works. This is easily done in the single-relation system by interrogating the tuple containing the employee identification number of the target employee and extracting the corresponding department. However, in the two-relation system, the desired information is not necessarily available. We can find the job title of the target employee and a department having such a job but this does not necessarily mean that the target employee works in that particular department, because several departments may have jobs with the same title.

In some cases a relation can be decomposed into smaller relations without losing information (called a **nonloss decomposition**), and in other cases information is lost. The study of such relational characteristics has been, and still is, a topic in computer science. Indeed, research has revealed a hierarchy of relation classes called first normal form, second normal form, third normal form, and so on, with the relations in each class being more conducive to use in a database than those in the preceding class.

Relational Operations

Now that you have a basic understanding of the structure involved in the relational model, it is time to see how such an organization can be used from a programmer's point of view. We begin with a look at some operations that we may want to perform on relations.

At times we need to select certain tuples from a relation. To retrieve the information about an employee, we must select the tuple with the appropriate identification attribute value from the EMPLOYEE relation, or to obtain a list of the job titles in a certain department, we must select the tuples from the JOB relation having that department as their department attribute. The result of this selection is another relation (another table) consisting of the tuples selected from the parent relation. The outcome of selecting information about a particular employee results in a relation containing only one tuple from the EMPLOYEE relation. The outcome of selecting the tuples associated with a certain department probably results in several tuples from the JOB relation.

Consequently, one operation we may want to perform on a relation is to select tuples possessing certain characteristics and to place these selected tuples in a new relation. To express this operation, we adopt the syntax

NEW ← SELECT from EMPLOYEE where EmplId = "34Y70"

The semantics of this statement is to create a new relation called NEW containing those tuples (there should be only one in this case) from the relation EMPLOYEE whose EmplId attribute equals 34Y70 (Figure 9.8).

In contrast to the SELECT operation, which extracts rows from a relation, the PROJECT operation extracts columns. Suppose, for example, that in searching for the job titles in a certain department, we had already SELECTed the tuples from the JOB relation that pertained to the target department and

FIGURE 9.8

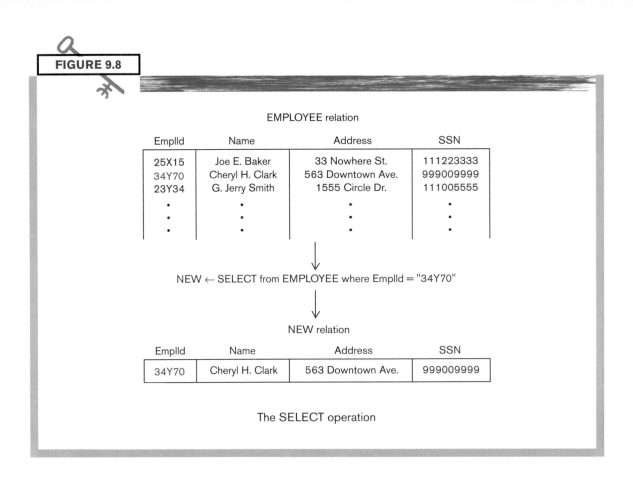

EMPLOYEE relation

EmplId	Name	Address	SSN
25X15	Joe E. Baker	33 Nowhere St.	111223333
34Y70	Cheryl H. Clark	563 Downtown Ave.	999009999
23Y34	G. Jerry Smith	1555 Circle Dr.	111005555

NEW ← SELECT from EMPLOYEE where EmplId = "34Y70"

NEW relation

EmplId	Name	Address	SSN
34Y70	Cheryl H. Clark	563 Downtown Ave.	999009999

The SELECT operation

placed these tuples in a new relation called NEW1. The list we are seeking is the JobTitle column within this new relation. The PROJECT operation allows us to extract this column (or columns if required) and place the result in a new relation. We express such an operation as

NEW2 ← PROJECT JobTitle from NEW1

The result is the creation of another new relation (called NEW2) that contains the single column of values from the JobTitle column of relation NEW1.

As another example of the PROJECT operation, the statement

MAIL ← PROJECT Name, Address from EMPLOYEE

can be used to obtain a listing of the names and addresses of all employees. This list is in the newly created (two-column) relation called MAIL (Figure 9.9).

The third operation we introduce is the JOIN operation. It is used to combine different relations into one. The JOIN of two relations produces a new relation whose attributes consist of the attributes from the original relations

FIGURE 9.9

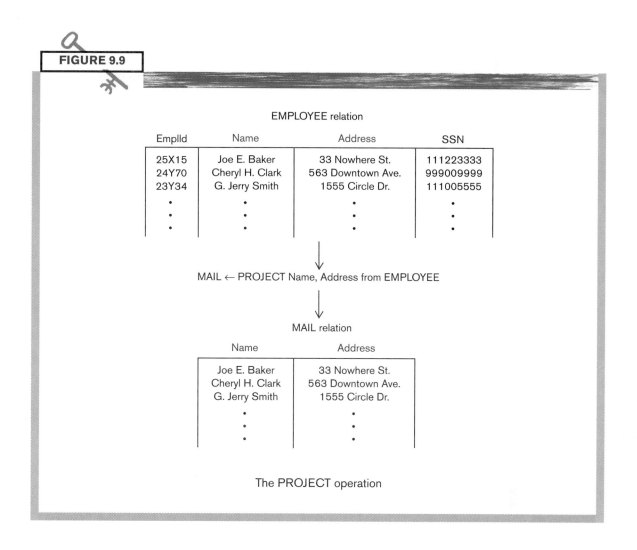

EMPLOYEE relation

Emplld	Name	Address	SSN
25X15	Joe E. Baker	33 Nowhere St.	111223333
24Y70	Cheryl H. Clark	563 Downtown Ave.	999009999
23Y34	G. Jerry Smith	1555 Circle Dr.	111005555
.	.	.	.
.	.	.	.
.	.	.	.

MAIL ← PROJECT Name, Address from EMPLOYEE

MAIL relation

Name	Address
Joe E. Baker	33 Nowhere St.
Cheryl H. Clark	563 Downtown Ave.
G. Jerry Smith	1555 Circle Dr.
.	.
.	.
.	.

The PROJECT operation

(Figure 9.10). The names of these attributes are the same as those in the original relations except that each is prefixed by the relation of its origin. (If relation A containing attributes V and W is JOINed with relation B containing attributes X, Y, and Z, then the result has five attributes named A.V, A.W, B.X, B.Y, and B.Z.) This naming convention ensures that the attributes in the new relation have unique names, even though the original relations may have attribute names in common.

The tuples (rows) of the new relation are produced by concatenating tuples from the two original relations (see again Figure 9.10). Which tuples are actually joined to form tuples in the new relation is determined by the condition under which the JOIN is constructed. One such condition is that designated

FIGURE 9.10

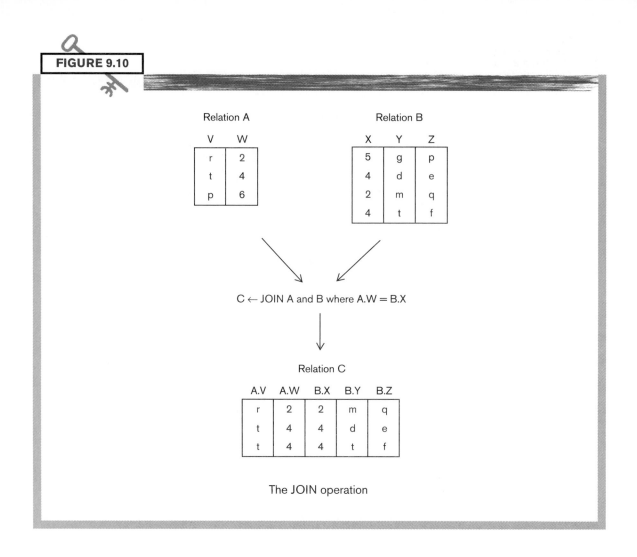

Relation A

V	W
r	2
t	4
p	6

Relation B

X	Y	Z
5	g	p
4	d	e
2	m	q
4	t	f

C ← JOIN A and B where A.W = B.X

Relation C

A.V	A.W	B.X	B.Y	B.Z
r	2	2	m	q
t	4	4	d	e
t	4	4	t	f

The JOIN operation

attributes have the same value. This in fact is the case represented in Figure 9.10, where we demonstrate the result of executing the statement

C ← JOIN A and B where A.W = B.X

In this example, a tuple from relation A should be concatenated with a tuple from relation B if and only if the attributes W and X in the two tuples are equal. Thus the concatenation of the tuple (r, 2) from relation A with the tuple (2, m, q) from relation B appears in the result because the value of attribute W in the first equals the value of attribute X in the second. On the other hand, the result of concatenating the tuple (r, 2) from relation A with the tuple (5, g, p) from

FIGURE 9.11

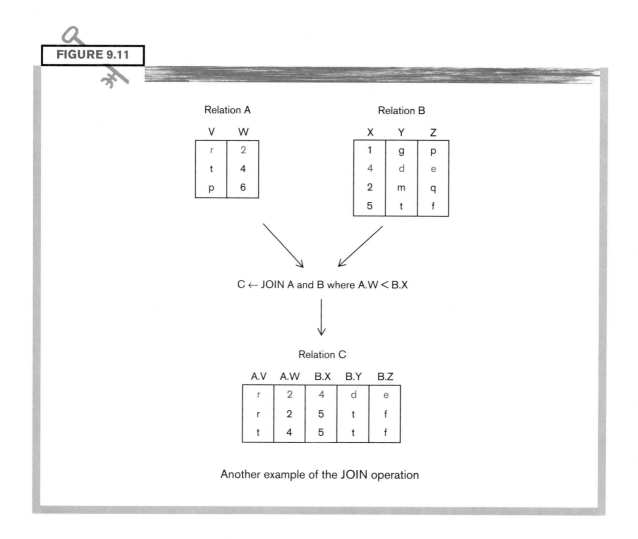

Another example of the JOIN operation

relation B does not appear in the final relation because these tuples do not share common values in attributes W and X.

As another example, Figure 9.11 represents the result of executing the statement

C ← JOIN A and B where A.W < B.X

Note that the tuples in the result are exactly those in which attribute W in relation A is less than attribute X in relation B.

Let us now see how the JOIN operation can be used with the database of Figure 9.5 to obtain a listing of all employee identification numbers along with the department in which each employee works. Our first observation is that the data required are distributed over more than one relation, and thus the process of retrieving the information must entail more than SELECTions and PROJECTions. In fact, the weapon we need is the statement

NEW1 ← JOIN ASSIGNMENT and JOB
where ASSIGNMENT.JobId = JOB.JobId

that produces the relation NEW1, as shown in Figure 9.12. From this relation, our problem can be solved by first SELECTing those tuples in which ASSIGNMENT.TermDate equals "*" and then PROJECTing the attributes ASSIGNMENT.EmplId and JOB.Dept. In short, the information we need can be obtained from the database in Figure 9.5 by executing the statements

NEW1 ← JOIN ASSIGNMENT and JOB
where ASSIGNMENT.JobId = JOB.JobId
NEW2 ← SELECT from NEW1 where ASSIGNMENT.TermDate = "*"
LIST ← PROJECT ASSIGNMENT.EmplId, JOB.Dept from NEW2

FIGURE 9.12

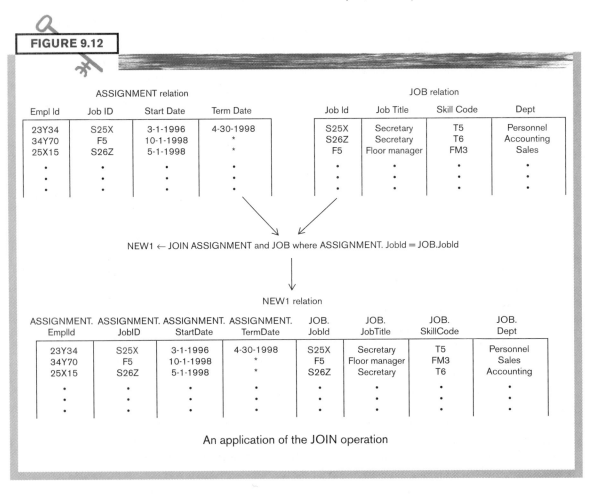

An application of the JOIN operation

Now that we have introduced the basic relational operations, let us reconsider the overall structure of a database system. Remember that the data in a database are actually stored in terms of a mass storage system. To relieve the application programmer from these concerns, a database management system is provided that allows the application software to be written in terms of a database model, such as the relational system we have been discussing. It is the duty of the database management system to accept commands in terms of the relational model and convert them into actions relative to the actual storage structure. This is done by providing a collection of routines that can be used by the application software as abstract tools. Thus a database management system based on the relational model would include routines to perform the SELECT, PROJECT, and JOIN operations, which could then be called from the application software using a syntactic structure compatible with the host language. In this manner, the application software can be written as though the data were actually stored in the simple tabular form of the relational model.

It is instructive to consider how a database management system might store the data in a database and how that storage would affect its operations. For example, the simplest way for a database management system to implement a relation is to store it as a sequential file in which each tuple is a logical record. However, following this strategy would mean that executing a SELECT operation would require a sequential search through the file—a process that would be time consuming in the case of a large relation. Thus it is likely that the database management system would instead store the relation as an indexed file. For example, if the EMPLOYEE relation in Figure 9.5 was indexed by employee identification number, then information about a particular employee could be SELECTed quickly.

Finally we should note that today's database management systems do not necessarily present the SELECT, PROJECT, and JOIN operations in their raw form. Rather, they provide operations that may be combinations of these basic steps. An example is the language SQL.

DATABASE SYSTEMS FOR PCs

Personal computers are used in a variety of applications, ranging from elementary to sophisticated. In elementary "database" applications, such as storing Christmas card lists or maintaining bowling league records, spreadsheet systems are often used in lieu of database software since the application calls for little more than the ability to store, print, and sort data. There are, however, quite sophisticated database systems available for the PC market, one of which is Microsoft's Access. This is a complete relational database system with all the features discussed in Section 9.3 as well as chart and report generation software. The major difference from a user's point of view is that Access uses a graphical user interface that allows queries to be posed in a graphical manner rather than in the SQL syntax presented in the text. In addition, newer versions of Access provide Internet capabilities that, for example, allow an entry in a tuple to consist of a URL, which means that the associated Web site is readily accessible via the database.

SQL

The language called SQL (Structured Query Language) is used extensively in the data processing community for manipulating databases that are viewed in terms of the relational model. One reason for its popularity is that it has been standardized by the American National Standards Institute. Another is that it was originally developed and marketed by IBM and has thus benefited from a high level of exposure. In this section we explain how relational database queries are expressed in SQL.

Our first observation is that a query involving a sequence of SELECT, PROJECT, and JOIN operations can be expressed as a single SQL statement. More important, however, is that SQL statements do not specify a particular sequence of operations. Although a query stated in SQL is expressed in an imperative-sounding form, the reality is that it is essentially a declarative statement. The significance of this is that SQL relieves database users from the burden of developing a sequence of steps needed to obtain the information desired. They need merely to describe that information. For example, our last query in which we developed a three-step process for obtaining all employee identification numbers along with their corresponding departments could be stated in SQL by the single statement

```
select EmplId, Dept
from ASSIGNMENT, JOB
where ASSIGNMENT.JobId = JOB.JobId
  and ASSIGNMENT.TermDate = '*'
```

As indicated by this example, each SQL query statement can contain three clauses—a `select` clause, a `from` clause, and a `where` clause. Roughly speaking, such a statement is a request for the result of forming the JOIN of all the relations listed in the `from` clause, SELECTing those tuples that satisfy the conditions in the `where` clause, and then PROJECTing those tuples listed in the `select` clause. (Note that the terminology is somewhat reversed, in that the `select` clause in an SQL statement identifies the attributes used in the PROJECT operation.) Let us consider some simple examples.

The statement

```
select Name, Address
from EMPLOYEE
```

produces a listing of all employee names and addresses contained in the relation EMPLOYEE. Note that this is merely a PROJECT operation.

The statement

```
select EmplId, Name, Address, SSNum
from EMPLOYEE
where Name = 'Cheryl H. Clark'
```

produces all the information from the tuple associated with Cheryl H. Clark in the EMPLOYEE relation. This is essentially a SELECT operation.

The statement

```
select Name, Address
from EMPLOYEE
where Name = 'Cheryl H. Clark"
```

produces the name and address of Cheryl H. Clark as contained in the EMPLOYEE relation. This is a combination of SELECT and PROJECT operations.

The statement

```
select EMPLOYEE.Name, ASSIGNMENT.StartDate
from EMPLOYEE, ASSIGNMENT
where EMPLOYEE.EmplId = ASSIGNMENT.EmplId
```

produces a listing of all employee names and their dates of initial employment. Note that this is the result of JOINing the relations EMPLOYEE and ASSIGNMENT and then SELECTing and PROJECTing the appropriate tuples and attributes as identified in the `where` and `select` clauses.

We close by noting that SQL encompasses statements for defining the structure of relations, creating relations, and modifying the contents of relations as well as performing queries. For example, the following are examples of the `insert into`, `delete from`, and `update` statements.

The statement

```
insert into EMPLOYEE
values ('42Z12', 'Sue A. Burt', '33 Fair St.', '444661111')
```

adds a tuple to the EMPLOYEE relation containing the values given;

```
delete from EMPLOYEE
where Name = 'G. Jerry Smith'
```

removes the tuple relating to G. Jerry Smith from the EMPLOYEE relation; and

```
update EMPLOYEE
set Address = '1812 Napoleon Ave.'
where Name = 'Joe E. Baker'
```

changes the address in the tuple associated with Joe E. Baker in the EMPLOYEE relation.

QUESTIONS/EXERCISES

1. Answer the following questions based on the partial information given in the EMPLOYEE, JOB, and ASSIGNMENT relations in Figure 9.5:
   a. Who is the secretary in the accounting department with experience in the personnel department?
   b. Who is the floor manager in the sales department?
   c. What job does G. Jerry Smith currently hold?

2. Based on the EMPLOYEE, JOB, and ASSIGNMENT relations presented in Figure 9.5 write a sequence of relational operations to obtain a list of all job titles within the personnel department.

3. Based on the EMPLOYEE, JOB, and ASSIGNMENT relations presented in Figure 9.5, write a sequence of relational operations to obtain a list of employee names along with the employees' departments.

4. Convert your answers to Questions 2 and 3 into SQL.

5. How does the relational model provide for data independence?

6. How are the different relations in a relational database tied together?

9.4 Object-Oriented Databases

One of the newer areas in database research involves applying the object-oriented paradigm to the construction of a database. The result is an **object-oriented database** consisting of objects that are linked to each other to reflect their relationships. For example, an object-oriented implementation of the employee database from the previous section would consist of three classes (types of objects): EMPLOYEE, JOB, and ASSIGNMENT. An object from the EMPLOYEE class would contain such entries as EmplId, Name, Address, and SSNum; an object from the class JOB would contain such entries as JobId, JobTitle, SkillCode, and Dept; and each object from the class ASSIGNMENT would contain entries such as StartDate and TermDate.

Each of these objects would also contain methods describing how the object should respond to messages regarding its contents and relationships. For example, each object from the class EMPLOYEE would contain methods for reporting and updating the information in the object as well as a method for reporting that employee's job history and probably a method for changing that employee's job assignment. Likewise, each object from the JOB class would have a method for reporting the specifics of the job and perhaps a method for reporting those employees who have held that particular job. Thus to retrieve an employee's job history we would not need to write an external procedure describing how the information is to be obtained. Instead, we could merely ask the appropriate employee object to report its job history.

A conceptual representation of such a database is shown in Figure 9.13 where the relationships between the various objects are represented by lines connecting related objects. If we focus on an object of type EMPLOYEE, we find it linked to a collection of objects of type ASSIGNMENT, representing the various assignments that that particular employee has had. In turn, each of these objects of type ASSIGNMENT is linked to an object of type JOB representing the job associated with that assignment. Thus, all the assignments of an employee

FIGURE 9.13

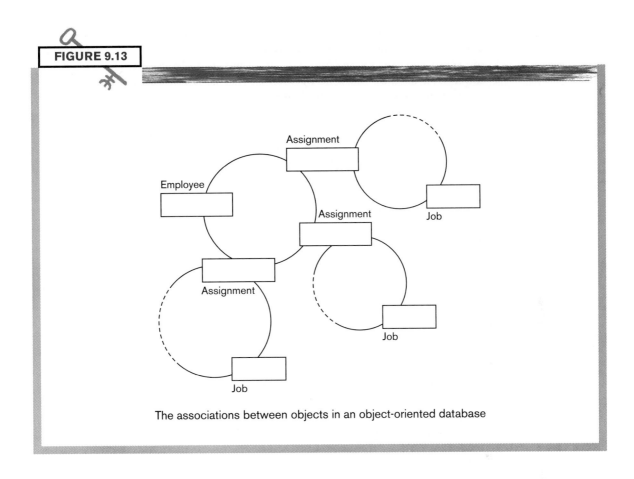

The associations between objects in an object-oriented database

can be found by following the links from the object representing that employee. Similarly, all the employees who have held a particular job can be found by following the links from the object representing that job.

The links between objects in an object-oriented database are normally maintained by the DBMS, and thus, the details of how these links are implemented are not a concern of the programmer writing application software. Instead, when a new object is added to the database, the application software need merely specify the other objects to which it should be linked. The DBMS then creates any pointer system that may be required to record these associations. In particular, a DBMS may link the objects representing the assignments of a given employee in a manner similar to a linked list.

Another task of an object-oriented DBMS is to provide permanent storage for the objects entrusted to it—a requirement that may seem obvious but is inherently distinct from the manner in which objects are normally treated.

Normally, when an object-oriented program is executed, the objects created during the program's execution are discarded when the program terminates. In this sense, the objects are considered transient. But objects that are created and added to a database must be persistent—that is, they must be saved after the program that created them terminates. Hence, providing permanent storage for objects is a significant departure from the norm.

An important benefit of object-oriented databases is that they allow the entire software system to be designed in the same paradigm. That is, the application software that accesses the database and the database itself can be designed in the object-oriented paradigm. This is in contrast to the common practice of using an imperative programming language to develop application software for interrogating a relational database. Inherent in such a task is the clash between imperative and relational paradigms—a distinction that has proved to be the source of many software errors over the years. In turn, the ability to remove this distinction in paradigms is a major benefit sighted by proponents of object-oriented databases.

To appreciate another advantage that object-oriented databases have over their relational counterparts, consider the problem of storing employee names in a relational database. If an entire name is stored as a single attribute, then inquiries regarding only last names are awkward. However, if the name is stored as three separate attributes—allowing for a first name, middle name, and last name—then it becomes awkward to deal with people whose names do not conform to the first-name, middle-name, family-name template. In an object-oriented database these issues can be hidden within the object that holds the employee's name. An employee's name can be stored as an intelligent object that is capable of reporting the related employee's name in a variety of formats. Thus, from outside these objects, it would be just as easy to deal with last names only as with entire names, maiden names, or nicknames. The details involved with each perspective would be encapsulated within the objects.

This ability to encapsulate the technicalities of different data formats is advantageous in other cases as well. In a relational database, the attributes in a relation are part of the overall design of the database, and thus the types associated with these attributes permeate the entire database management system. Such a design is reasonable when dealing with data consisting of character strings and numeric values. But extending a relational database by adding a new relation containing attributes of type audio and video can be problematic. Indeed, a variety of procedures throughout the database design might need to be expanded to incorporate these new data types. In an object-oriented design, however, the same procedures used to retrieve an object representing an employee's name can be used to retrieve an object representing a motion picture because the distinctions in type can be hidden within the objects involved. Thus the object-oriented approach appears to be more compatible with the construction of multimedia databases—a feature that is already proving to be a great advantage.

1. What methods would be contained in an instance of an object from the ASSIGNMENT class in the employee database discussed in this section?
2. Identify some classes, as well as some of their internal characteristics, that can be used in an object-oriented database dealing with a warehouse inventory.
3. Identify an advantage that an object-oriented database can have over a relational database.

9.5 Maintaining Database Integrity

Inexpensive database management systems for personal use are relatively simple systems. They tend to have a single objective—to shield the user from the technical details of the database implementation. The databases maintained by these systems are relatively small and generally contain information whose loss or corruption would be inconvenient rather than disastrous. When a problem does arise, the user can usually correct the erroneous items directly or reload the database from a backup copy and manually make the modifications required to bring that copy up to date. This process may be inconvenient, but the cost of avoiding the inconvenience tends to be greater than the inconvenience itself. In any case, the inconvenience is restricted to only a few people, and any financial loss is generally limited.

In the case of large, multiuser, commercial database systems, however, the stakes are much higher. The cost of incorrect or lost data can be enormous and can have devastating consequences. In these environments, a major role of the database management system is to maintain the database's integrity by guarding against problems such as operations that for some reason are only partially completed or different operations that may interact inadvertently to cause inaccurate information in the database. It is this role of a database management system that we address in this section.

The Commit/Rollback Protocol

A single transaction, such as the transfer of funds from one bank account to another, the cancellation of an airline reservation, and the registration of a student in a university course, may involve multiple steps at the database level. For example, a transfer of funds between bank accounts requires that the balance in one account be decremented and the balance in the other be incremented. Between such steps the information in the database may be inconsistent.

Indeed, funds are missing during the brief period after the first account has been decremented but before the other has been incremented. Likewise, when reassigning a passenger's seat on a flight, there may be an instant when the passenger has no seat or an instant when the passenger list appears to be one passenger greater than it actually is.

In the case of large databases that are subject to heavy transaction loads, it is highly likely that a random snapshot will find the database in the middle of some transaction. A request for the execution of a transaction or an equipment malfunction will therefore likely occur at a time when the database is in an inconsistent state.

Let us first consider the problem of a malfunction. The goal of the database management system is to ensure that such a problem will not freeze the database in an inconsistent state. This is often accomplished by maintaining a log containing a record of each transaction's activities in a nonvolatile storage system, such as a disk. Before a transaction is allowed to alter the database, the alteration to be performed is first recorded in the log. Thus, the log contains a permanent record of each transaction's actions.

The point at which all the steps in a transaction have been recorded in the log is called the **commit point.** It is at this point that the database management system has the information it needs to reconstruct the transaction on its own if that should become necessary. At this point the database management system becomes committed to the transaction in the sense that it accepts the responsibility of guaranteeing that the transaction's activities will be reflected in the database. In the case of an equipment malfunction, the database management system can use the information in its log to reconstruct the transactions that have been completed (committed) since the last backup was made.

If problems should arise before a transaction has reached its commit point, the database management system may find itself with a partially executed transaction that cannot be

TEMPORAL DATABASES

Traditional databases are designed to maintain current records. A traditional inventory database, for example, is used to record current inventory for the purpose of maintaining appropriate stock levels. In such cases, records of past inventories are often available only through archival copies of the database or by explicitly recording dates as a part of the data. There are many applications, however, where more convenient access to past records as well as the ability to store future entries is advantageous. Such is the case of a university registrar who must schedule course offerings, maintain class roles, track room assignments, record teaching assignments, etc., not only for the current semester but for past and future semesters as well. Temporal databases are databases designed for such applications. When new entries are made to a temporal database, old information is not deleted. Instead, the new entries merely become the latest entries in a historical record, any part of which is readily available.

Temporal databases represent an active area of current research. The goal is to find efficient ways to store and maintain past, present, and future information, to develop techniques to search such records for requested information, and to develop languages for expressing requests for temporal information.

completed. In this case the log can be used to **roll back** (undo) the activities actually performed by the transaction. In the case of a malfunction, for instance, the database management system could recover by rolling back those transactions that were incomplete (noncommitted) at the time of the malfunction.

Rollbacks of transactions are not restricted, however, to the process of recovering from equipment malfunctions. They are often a part of a database management system's normal operation. For example, a transaction may be terminated before it has completed all its steps due to an attempt to access privileged information, or it may be involved in a deadlock in which competing transactions find themselves waiting for data being used by the other. In these cases, the database management system can use the log to roll back a transaction and thus avoid an erroneous database due to incomplete transactions.

To emphasize the delicate nature of database management system design, we should note that there are subtle problems lurking within the rollback process. The rolling back of one transaction may affect database entries that have been used by other transactions. For example, the transaction being rolled back may have updated an account balance, and another transaction may have already based its activities on this updated value. This may mean that these additional transactions must also be rolled back, which may adversely affect still other transactions. The result is the problem known as **cascading rollback.**

Locking

We now consider the problem of a transaction being executed while the database is in a state of flux from another transaction, a situation that can lead to inadvertent interaction between the transactions and produce erroneous results. For instance, the problem known as the **incorrect summary problem** can arise if one transaction is in the middle of transferring funds from one account to another when another transaction tries to compute the total deposits in the bank. This could result in a total that is either too large or too small depending on the order in which the transfer steps are performed. Another possibility is known as the **lost update problem,** which is exemplified by two transactions, each of which makes a deduction from the same account. If one transaction reads the account's current balance at the point when the other has just read the balance but has not yet calculated the new balance, then both transactions will base their deductions on the same initial balance. In turn, the effect of one of the deductions will not be reflected in the database.

To solve such problems, a database management system could force transactions to execute in their entirety on a one-at-a-time basis by holding each new transaction in a queue until those preceding it have completed. But a transaction often spends a lot of time waiting for disk operations to be performed. By interweaving the execution of transactions, the time during which one transaction is waiting can be used by another transaction to process data it has already retrieved. Most large database management systems therefore contain a scheduler to coordinate time-sharing among transactions in much the same way that a time-sharing operating system coordinates interweaving of processes.

To guard against such anomalies as the incorrect summary problem and the lost update problem, such schedulers incorporate a **locking protocol** in which the items within a database that are currently being used by some transaction are marked as such. These marks are called locks; marked items are said to be locked. Two types of locks are common—**shared locks** and **exclusive locks.** They correspond to the two types of access a transaction may require to a data item—shared access and exclusive access. If a transaction is not going to alter the data item, then it requires shared access, meaning that other transactions are also allowed to view the data item. However, if the transaction is going to alter the item, it must have exclusive access, meaning that it must be the only transaction with access to the item.

In a locking protocol, each time a transaction requests access to a data item it must also tell the database management system the type of access it requires. If a transaction requests shared access to a data item that is either unlocked or locked with a shared lock, that access is granted and the item is marked with a shared lock. If, however, the requested item is already marked with an exclusive lock, the additional access is denied. If a transaction requests exclusive access to a data item, that request is granted only if the item has no lock associated with it. In this manner, a transaction that is going to alter a data item protects that item from other transactions by obtaining exclusive access. At the same time, several transactions can share access to a data item if none of them are going to change it. Of course, once a transaction is finished with an item, it notifies the database management system and the associated lock is removed.

Various algorithms are used to handle the case when a transaction's access request is rejected. One is that the transaction is merely forced to wait until the requested item becomes available. This approach, however, can lead to deadlock, since two transactions that require exclusive access to the same two data items could block each other's progress if each obtains exclusive access to one of the items and then insists on waiting for the other. To avoid such deadlocks, some database management systems give priority to older transactions. That is, if an older transaction requires access to a data item that is locked by a younger transaction, the younger transaction is forced to release all of its data items, and its activities are rolled back (based on the log). Then, the older transaction is given access to the data item it required, and the younger transaction is forced to start again. If a younger transaction is repeatedly preempted, it will grow older in the process and ultimately become one of the older transactions. This protocol, known as the **wound-wait protocol** (old transactions wound young transactions, young transactions wait for old ones), ensures that every transaction will ultimately be allowed to complete its task.

1. What is the difference between a transaction that has reached its commit point and one that has not?
2. How could a database management system guard against extensive cascading rollback?
3. Show how the uncontrolled interweaving of two transactions, one deducting $100 from an account and the other deducting $200 from the same account, could produce final balances of $100, $200, and $300, assuming that the initial balance is $400.
4. a. Summarize the possible results of a transaction requesting shared access to an item in a database.
   b. Summarize the possible results of a transaction requesting exclusive access to an item in a database.
5. Describe a sequence of events that would lead to deadlock among transactions performing operations on a database system.
6. Describe how the deadlock in your answer to Question 5 could be broken. Would your solution require use of the database management system's log? Explain your answer.

9.6 Social Impact of Database Technology

In the past, collections of data were seen as dormant, passive entities. Each was designed and used for a specific purpose. A local library maintained a physical list consisting of the names and addresses of its patrons. Each book contained a removable card containing the name of the book. When the book was checked out, the card was removed, the name of the person taking the book was recorded on this card, and the card was filed in the library. When the book was returned, the card was placed back in the book; if the book was not returned on time, the library staff could contact the person holding the book by means of its patron list.

With this manual system, one could conceivably obtain a list of all the books checked out by a single individual. But this required searching through all the books in the library to see which cards contained the individual's name, and the cost of this search made such an undertaking impractical. Thus, although the library's records contained subtle information about its patrons that could be used for purposes other than the direct needs of the library, the library's patrons could be sure that such alternative uses would not be made. Today, however, most library records are automated, and profiles of an individual's reading habits are within easy reach. It is now feasible for libraries to provide such information to marketing firms, law enforcement agencies, political parties, employers, and private individuals. The ramifications are enormous.

This library example is representative of the potentials that permeate the entire spectrum of database applications. Technology has made it easy to collect data and to merge or compare different data collections to obtain relationships that would otherwise remain buried in the heap.

Data collection is now conducted on a massive scale. In some cases the process is readily apparent; in others it is more subtle. Examples of the former occur when one is explicitly asked to provide information. This may be in a voluntary context, such as surveys or contest registration forms, or it may be in an involuntary context, such as those imposed by government regulations. Sometimes whether releasing information is voluntary or involuntary depends on one's point of view. Is providing personal information when applying for a loan voluntary or involuntary? The distinction is in the degree to which you need the loan. To use a credit card at some retailers now requires that you allow your signature to be recorded in a digitized format. Whether such a requirement constitutes a demand or a request depends on the necessity of the purchase involved.

More subtle cases of data collection avoid direct communication with the subject. Examples include a credit company that records the purchasing practices of the holders of its credit cards, sites on the World Wide Web that record the identities of those who visit the site, and advocates who record the license numbers on the cars parked next to a targeted institution. In these cases the subject of the data may not be aware that information is being collected and even less likely to be aware of the existence of the databases holding information related to the individual. Sometimes the underlying activities are self-evident if one merely stops to think. For example, a grocery store may offer discounts to its regular customers who register in advance with the store. The registration process may involve the issuance of identification cards that must be presented at the time of purchase to obtain the discount. The result is that the store is able to compile a record of the customer's purchases—a record whose value far exceeds the value of the discounts awarded.

Of course, the force driving this boom in data collection is the value of the data, which is mainly the result of advances in database technology that allow data to be linked in ways that reveal information that would otherwise remain obscure. The result is combined collections of data that contain information that exceeds the sum of its parts. For example, the purchasing habits of credit card holders can be classified and cross-listed to obtain customer profiles of immense marketing value. Subscription forms for bodybuilding magazines can be mailed to those who have recently purchased exercise equipment, whereas similar forms for dog obedience magazines can be targeted toward those who have recently purchased dog food. Alternative ways of combining information are sometimes very imaginative. Welfare records have been compared to criminal records to find and apprehend parole violators, and in 1984 the Selective Service in the United States used the birthday registration list from a popular ice cream retailer to identify citizens who had failed to register for the draft.

In this latter case the list was returned to the retailer when the retailer claimed that the sale of the list was made in error, but by then the information had been used. Unfortunately, such erroneous use of data is a recurring event. Examples continue to surface involving company or government employees who misuse the information in their employers' databases.

The sale of the birthday list also raises questions regarding ownership of information. Does someone who collects information automatically own that information? To what extent do you own personal information about yourself? To what extent can someone else own personal information about you?

There are several approaches that can be taken to protect society from abusive use of databases. One is to apply legal remedies. Unfortunately, passing a law against an action does not stop the action from occurring but merely makes the action illegal. A prime example in the United States is the Privacy Act of 1974 whose purpose was to protect citizens from abusive use of government databases. One provision of this act was to require government agencies to publish the existence of their databases in the Federal Register—the purpose being to allow citizens to access and correct information relating to themselves. However, government agencies have been slow to comply with this provision. This does not necessarily imply malicious intent. In many cases the problem has been one of bureaucracy. But, the fact that a bureaucracy may be constructing personnel databases that it is unable to identify is not a reassuring situation.

Another, and perhaps more powerful, approach to controlling database abuse is public opinion. Databases will not be abused if the penalties outweigh the benefits, and one penalty many businesses fear the most is adverse public opinion—it goes right to the bottom line. In the early 1990s it was public opinion that ultimately stopped major credit bureaus from selling mailing lists for marketing purposes. More recently, America Online (a major Internet access provider) buckled under public pressure against its policy of selling customer-related information to telemarketers. Even government agencies have bowed to public opinion. In 1997 the Social Security Administration in the United States modified its plan to make social security records available via the Internet when public opinion questioned the security of the information. In these cases results were obtained in days—a stark contrast to the extended time periods associated with legal processes.

Of course, in many cases database applications are beneficial to both the holder and subject of the data, but in all cases there is a loss of privacy that should not be taken lightly. Such privacy issues are serious when the information is accurate, but they become enormous when the information is erroneous. Imagine the feeling of hopelessness you would feel if you realized that your credit rating was adversely affected by erroneous information. Imagine how your problems would be amplified in an environment in which this misinformation was readily shared with other institutions.

Privacy problems are, and will be, a major side effect of advancing technology in general and database techniques in particular. The solutions to these problems will require an educated, alert, and active citizenry.

QUESTIONS/EXERCISES

1. Should law enforcement agencies be given access to databases for the purpose of identifying individuals with criminal tendencies, even though the individuals may not have committed a crime?

2. Should insurance companies be given access to databases for the purpose of identifying individuals with potential medical problems, even though the individuals have not shown any symptoms?

3. Suppose you were financially comfortable. What benefits could you derive if this information were shared among a variety of institutions? What penalties could you suffer from the distribution of this same information? What if you were financially uncomfortable?

4. What role does a free press have in controlling database abuse? (For example, to what extent does the press affect public opinion?)

CHAPTER REVIEW PROBLEMS
(Asterisks indicate an optional section.)

1. Summarize the distinction between a flat file and a database.

2. What is meant by data independence?

3. What is the role of a database management system in the layered approach to a database implementation?

4. What is the difference between a schema and a subschema?

5. Identify two benefits of separating application software from the database management system.

6. Identify the level within a database system (user, programmer of application software, designer of the database management system software) at which each of the following concerns or activities occur:
   a. How should data be stored on a disk to maximize efficiency?
   b. Is there a vacancy on flight 243?
   c. Could a relation be stored as a sequential file?
   d. How many times should a user be allowed to mistype a password before the conversation is terminated?
   e. How can the PROJECT operation be implemented?

7. Describe how the following information about airlines, flights (for a particular day), and passengers would be represented in a relational database.

   Airlines: Clear Sky, Long Hop, and Tree Top

   Flights for Clear Sky: CS205, CS37, and CS102

   Flights for Long Hop: LH67 and LH89

   Flights for Tree Top: TT331 and TT809

   Smith has reservations on CS205 (seat 12B), CS37 (seat 18C), and LH 89 (seat 14A).

   Baker has reservations on CS37 (seat 18B) and LH89 (seat 14B).

Clark has reservations on LH67 (seat 5A) and TT331 (seat 4B).

8. In terms of the relations shown below, what is the appearance of the relation RESULT after executing each of these instructions:

X relation

U	V	W
A	Z	5
B	D	3
C	Q	5

Y relation

R	S
3	J
4	K

a. RESULT ← PROJECT W from X
b. RESULT ← SELECT from X
     where W = 5
c. RESULT ← PROJECT S from Y
d. RESULT ← JOIN X and Y
     where X.W ≥ Y.R

9. Using the commands SELECT, PROJECT, and JOIN, write a sequence of instructions to answer each of the following questions about parts and their manufacturers in terms of the following database:

PART relation

PartName	Weight
Bolt 2X	1
Bolt 2Z	1.5
Nut V5	0.5

MANUFACTURER relation

CompanyName	PartName	Cost
Company X	Bolt 2Z	.03
Company X	Nut V5	.01
Company Y	Bolt 2X	.02
Company Y	Nut V5	.01
Company Y	Bolt 2Z	.04
Company Z	Nut V5	.01

a. Which companies make Bolt 2Z?

b. Obtain a list of the parts made by Company X along with each part's cost.
c. Which companies make a part with weight 1?

10. Answer Problem 9 using SQL.

11. What redundancy is introduced if the information in the PART and MANUFACTURER relations in Problem 9 are combined into one single relation?

12. Using commands such as SELECT, PROJECT, and JOIN, write sequences to answer the following questions about the information in the EMPLOYEE, JOB, and ASSIGNMENT relations in Figure 9.5:
    a. Obtain a list of the names and addresses of the company's employees.
    b. Obtain a list of the names and addresses of those who have worked or are working in the personnel department.
    c. Obtain a list of the names and addresses of those who are working in the personnel department.

13. Answer Problem 12 using SQL.

14. Design a relational database containing information about music composers, their lives, and their compositions.

15. Design a relational database containing information about music performers, their recordings, and the composers of the music they recorded.

16. Design a relational database containing information about manufacturers of computing equipment and their products.

17. Design a relational database containing information about publishers, magazines, and subscribers, in which the relationships between these entities are represented by the following entity-relationship diagram.

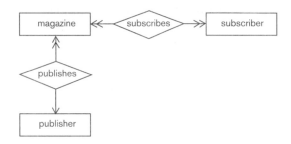

18. Design a relational database containing information about parts, suppliers, and customers. Each part may be supplied by several suppliers and ordered by many customers. Each supplier may supply many parts and have many customers. Each customer may order many parts from many suppliers; in fact, the same part may be ordered from more than one supplier.

19. What changes are required in the design of the relational database shown in Figure 9.5 to allow one to obtain a list of all employees with the last name Smith using only the SELECT operation?

20. What inconvenience may arise because of our decision to combine the month, day, and year into a single attribute in the relational database in Figure 9.5?

21. Write a sequence of instructions (using the operations SELECT, PROJECT, and JOIN) to retrieve the JobId, StartDate, and TermDate for each job in the accounting department from the relational database described in Figure 9.6.

22. Answer Problem 21 using SQL.

23. Write a sequence of instructions (using the operations SELECT, PROJECT, and JOIN) to retrieve the Name, Address, JobTitle, and Dept of every current employee from the relational database described in Figure 9.5.

24. Answer Problem 23 using SQL.

25. Write a sequence of instructions (using the operations SELECT, PROJECT, and JOIN) to retrieve the Name and JobTitle of each current employee from the relational database described in Figure 9.5.

26. Answer Problem 25 using SQL.

27. What is the difference in the information supplied by the single relation

Name	Department	TelephoneNumber
Jones	Sales	111-2222
Smith	Sales	111-3333
Baker	Personnel	111-4444

and the two relations

Name	Department
Jones	Sales
Smith	Sales
Baker	Personnel

Department	TelephoneNumber
Sales	111-2222
Sales	111-3333
Personnel	111-4444

28. Design a relational database containing information about automobile parts and their subparts. Be sure to allow for the fact that one part may contain smaller parts and at the same time be contained in still larger parts.

29. Based on the database represented in Figure 9.5, state the question that is answered by the following program segment:

```
TEMP ← SELECT from ASSIGNMENT
          where TermDate = "*"
RESULT ← PROJECT JobId, StartDate
          from TEMP
```

30. Translate the query in Problem 29 into SQL.

31. Based on the database represented in Figure 9.5, state the question that is answered by the following program segment:

```
TEMP1 ← JOIN EMPLOYEE
          and ASSIGNMENT
          where EMPLOYEE.EmplId =
          ASSIGNMENT.EmplId
TEMP2 ← SELECT from TEMP1
          where TermDate = "*"
RESULT ← PROJECT name, StartDate
          from TEMP2
```

32. Translate the query in Problem 31 into SQL.

33. Based on the database represented in Figure 9.5, state the question that is answered by the following program segment:

```
TEMP1 ← JOIN EMPLOYEE and JOB
          where EMPLOYEE.EmplId =
          JOB.EmplId
TEMP2 ← SELECT from TEMP1
          where Dept = "SALES"
RESULT ← PROJECT Name from TEMP2
```

34. Translate the query in Problem 32 into SQL.

35. Translate the SQL statement

```
select JOB.JobTitle
from ASSIGNMENT, JOB
where ASSIGNMENT.JobId = JOB.JobId
    and ASSIGNMENT.EmplId = "34Y70"
```

into a sequence of SELECT, PROJECT, and JOIN operations.

36. Translate the SQL statement

```
select ASSIGNMENT.StartDate
from ASSIGNMENT, EMPLOYEE
where ASSIGNMENT.EmplId =
        EMPLOYEE.EmplId
        and EMPLOYEE.Name =
        "Joe E. Baker"
```

into a sequence of SELECT, PROJECT, and JOIN operations.

37. Describe the effect that the following SQL statement would have on the database in Problem 9.

```
insert into MANUFACTURER
values ('Company Z',
        'Bolt 2X', .03)
```

38. Describe the effect that the following SQL statement would have on the database in Problem 9.

```
update MANUFACTURER
set Cost = .03
where CompanyName = 'Company Y'
        and PartName = 'Bolt 2X'
```

39. Why would it be advantageous to store a relation as an indexed file rather than a simple sequential file?

*40. Identify some of the objects that you would expect to find in an object-oriented database used to maintain a grocery store's inventory. What methods would you expect to find within each of these objects?

*41. Identify some of the objects that you would expect to find in an object-oriented database used to maintain records of a library's holdings. What methods would you expect to find within each of these objects?

*42. Compare the relationship between a class and an object (in an object-oriented environment) to that between a database schema and an actual database.

*43. What incorrect information is generated by the following schedule of transactions T1 and T2?

T1 is designed to compute the sum of accounts A and B; T2 is designed to transfer $100 from account A to account B. T1 begins by retrieving the balance of account A; then, T2 performs its transfer; and finally, T1 retrieves the balance of account B and reports the sum of the values it has retrieved.

*44. Explain how the locking protocol described in the text would resolve the error produced in Problem 43.

*45. What effect would the wound-wait protocol have on the sequence of events in Problem 43 if T1 was the younger

transaction? If T2 was the younger transaction?

*46. Suppose one transaction tries to add $100 to an account whose balance is $200 while another tries to withdraw $100 from the same account. Describe an interweaving of these transactions that would lead to a final balance of $100. Describe an interweaving of these transactions that would lead to a final balance of $300.

SOCIAL ISSUES

The following questions are provided to help you understand some of the ethical/social/legal issues associated with the field of computing as well as investigate your own beliefs and their foundations. The goal is not merely to answer these questions. You should also consider why you answered as you did and whether your justifications are consistent from one question to the next.

1. In the United States, DNA records of all federal prisoners are now stored in a database for use in criminal investigations. Would it be ethical to release this information for other purposes—for example, for genetic research? If so, for what purposes? If not, why not? What are the pros and cons in each case?

2. To what extent should a university be allowed to release information about its students? What about their names and addresses? What about grade distributions without identifying the students? Is your answer consistent with your answer to Question 1?

3. What restrictions are appropriate regarding the construction of databases about

individuals? What information does a government have a right to hold regarding its citizens? What information does an insurance company have a right to hold regarding its clients? What information does a company have a right to hold regarding its employees? Should controls in these settings be implemented and, if so, how?

4. Is it proper for a credit card company to sell the purchasing patterns of its clients to marketing firms? Is it acceptable for a sports car mail order business to sell its mailing list to a sports car magazine? Is it acceptable for the Internal Revenue Service to sell the names and addresses of those taxpayers with significant capital gains to stockbrokers?

5. To what extent is the designer of a database responsible for how the information in that database is used?

6. Suppose a database mistakenly allows unapproved access to information in the database. If that information is obtained and used adversely, to what degree do the database designers share responsibility for the misuse of the information? Does your answer depend on the amount of effort required by the perpetrator to discover the flaw in the database design and obtain the unauthorized information?

ADDITIONAL READING

Date, C. J. *An Introduction to Database Systems,* 6th ed. Reading, MA: Addison-Wesley, 1995.

Elmasri, R., and S. B. Navathe. *Fundamentals of Database Systems,* 2nd ed. Redwood City, CA: Benjamin/Cummings, 1994.

Özsu, M. T., and P. Valduriez. *Principles of Distributed Database Systems.* Upper Saddle River, NJ: Prentice Hall, 1999.

Ramakrishnan, R. *Database Management Systems.* New York: McGraw-Hill, 1998.

part four

THE POTENTIAL OF ALGORITHMIC MACHINES

In Part 4 we consider the potential of algorithmic machines. We begin by investigating the subject of artificial intelligence in Chapter 10. There we find that major advances are being made in the production of machines that mimic the activities of humans and thus project the image of intelligent behavior. This technology raises the question as to what, if any, the limitations of machines are.

We address this question in Chapter 11, where we study the theory of computation. There we learn that there are in fact bounds on the tasks that machines can accomplish. Moreover, we find that issues of practicality limit these tasks even further. That is, we find that there are tasks that, although within the theoretical powers of computers, would require so much time that they are not feasible in reality, even with advances in technology.

c h a p t e r

ARTIFICIAL INTELLIGENCE

t   e   n

10.1 Intelligence and Machines

10.2 Understanding Images

10.3 Reasoning
Production Systems
Search Trees
Heuristics

10.4 Artificial Neural Networks
Basic Properties
A Specific Application

10.5 Genetic Algorithms

10.6 Applications of Artificial Intelligence
Language Processing
Robotics
Database Systems
Expert Systems

10.7 Considering the Consequences

A major goal among computer scientists is to develop machines that communicate with their environments through traditionally human sensory means and proceed intelligently without human intervention. Such a goal often requires that the machine "understand," or perceive, the input received and be able to draw conclusions through some form of a reasoning process.

Both perception and reasoning fall within the category of common sense activities that, although natural for the human mind, are apparently quite difficult for machines. The result is that the area of research associated with this pursuit, known as artificial intelligence, is still in its infancy when compared with its goals and expectations.

10.1 Intelligence and Machines

Although the computer is often personified, an important distinction exists between its properties and the properties of the human mind. Today's machines are capable of performing precisely defined tasks with speed and accuracy. However, these machines are not gifted with common sense. When faced with a situation not foreseen by the programmer, a machine's performance is likely to deteriorate rapidly. In contrast, the human mind often flounders on complex computations but is capable of understanding and reasoning. Consequently, whereas a machine might outperform a human in computing solutions to problems in nuclear physics, the human is more likely to understand the results and determine what the next computation should be.

If we are to build machines that are able to continue without human intervention when faced with unforeseen situations, the machines must become more humanlike in the sense that they must possess (or at least simulate) the ability to reason. Recognizing this requirement, computer scientists have turned to psychologists and their models of the human mind in hopes of finding principles that can be applied to the construction of more flexible machines and programs. The result is that it is often difficult to distinguish between the research of a psychologist and that of a computer scientist. The distinction is not in what they do but rather in their goals. The psychologist is trying to learn more about the human mind and its thought processes; the computer scientist is trying to build more useful machines. Similar comparisons exist between the work of computer scientists and researchers in still other fields. A linguist, for example, is interested in learning how humans process language, a computer scientist is interested in developing machines that can process language. Thus research in artificial intelligence encompasses a multitude of disciplines.

One consequence of this breadth in the field is that research in artificial intelligence tends to follow two different paradigms. To clarify, suppose that a computer scientist and a psychologist each embark independently on projects to develop a poker-playing program. The computer scientist would tend to design a program based on the foundations of probability and statistics. The

THE ORIGINS OF ARTIFICIAL INTELLIGENCE

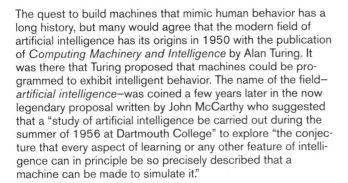

The quest to build machines that mimic human behavior has a long history, but many would agree that the modern field of artificial intelligence has its origins in 1950 with the publication of *Computing Machinery and Intelligence* by Alan Turing. It was there that Turing proposed that machines could be programmed to exhibit intelligent behavior. The name of the field—*artificial intelligence*—was coined a few years later in the now legendary proposal written by John McCarthy who suggested that a "study of artificial intelligence be carried out during the summer of 1956 at Dartmouth College" to explore "the conjecture that every aspect of learning or any other feature of intelligence can in principle be so precisely described that a machine can be made to simulate it."

result would be a program that would play the odds, bluff at random, show no emotion, and consequently maximize its chances of winning. The psychologist, on the other hand, might develop a program based on theories of human thought and behavior. The project could even result in the production of several different programs; one might play aggressively while another might be easily intimidated. In contrast to the computer scientist's program, the psychologist's program might become "emotionally involved" in the game and lose everything it owned.

Reconsidering, the computer scientist's main concern while developing the program would probably be the program's final performance. Such an approach is said to be **performance oriented.** In contrast, the psychologist would be more interested in understanding the processes of natural intelligence and so would approach the project as an opportunity to test theories by building computer models based on those theories. From this point of view, the development of the "intelligent" program is actually a side effect of another pursuit—progress in understanding human thought and behavior. This approach is said to be **simulation oriented.**

Both approaches are sound and make significant contributions to the field of artificial intelligence. However, they also raise elusive philosophical questions within the discipline. Consider, for example, the discussion that might ensue if a group were asked to decide whether the programs developed by the computer scientist and the psychologist actually possess intelligence and if so, which program is more intelligent. Is intelligence measured by the ability to win or the ability to be humanlike?

The latter option was adopted by Alan Turing in 1950 in his proposed test (now known as the **Turing test**) for evaluating the intelligent behavior of a machine. Turing's proposal was to allow a human, whom we call the interrogator, to communicate with a test subject by means of a typewriter system, without being told whether the test subject was a human or a machine. In this environment, a machine would be declared to behave intelligently in the event that the interrogator was not able to distinguish it from a human. Thus the Turing test measured the ability of a machine to be human-like. Turing proposed that by the year 2000 machines would have a 30 percent chance of passing a five-minute Turing test—a conjecture that has turned out to be surprisingly accurate.

A well-known example of a Turing test scenario arose as a result of the program DOCTOR (a version of the more general system called ELIZA) developed by Joseph Weizenbaum in the mid–1960s. This interactive program was designed to project the image of a Rogerian analyst conducting a psychological interview; the computer played the role of analyst while the user played the patient. Internally, all that DOCTOR did was restructure the statements made by the patient according to some well-defined rules and direct them back to the terminal screen. For example, in response to a statement such as "I am tired today," DOCTOR might have replied with "Why do you think you're tired today?" If DOCTOR was unable to recognize the sentence structure, it merely responded with something like "Go on" or "That's very interesting."

Weizenbaum's purpose in developing DOCTOR dealt with the study of natural language communication. From this point of view, the subject of psychotherapy played the secondary role of providing an environment (or a domain of discourse) in which the program could function. To Weizenbaum's dismay, however, several psychologists proposed using the program for actual psychotherapy. (The Rogerian thesis is that the patient, not the analyst, should lead the discussion during the therapeutic session, and thus, they argued, a computer could possibly conduct a discussion as well as a therapist could.) Moreover, DOCTOR projected the image of comprehension so strongly that many who "communicated" with it found themselves relating intimate thoughts and feelings and, in many cases, actually becoming subservient to the machine's question-and-answer dialogue. In a sense, DOCTOR passed the Turing test. The result was that ethical, as well as technical, issues were raised.

Even if a machine passes the Turing test, would it possess intelligence? Ultimately, a major difficulty in determining whether or not a machine possesses intelligence is rooted in the difficulty of distinguishing between the mere appearance of intelligence and its actual existence. Intelligence is an interior characteristic whose existence is detected from the outside only indirectly in the context of a stimulus/reaction dialogue. But do intelligent reactions imply the actual existence of intelligence?

With such philosophical questions residing at the very foundation of artificial intelligence, it is not surprising that the subject is associated with an aura of mystery often exploited by both the news media and fiction writers. Fortunately, our present task is not to resolve these issues but instead to investigate how machines can be programmed to *appear* to be intelligent. We approach this task by considering the design of a machine having elementary intelligence characteristics.

Our machine takes the form of a metal box equipped with a gripper, a video camera, and a finger with a rubber end so that it does not slip when pushing something (Figure 10.1). Imagine such a machine on a table on which an eight-puzzle is placed. This is a puzzle consisting of eight square tiles labeled 1 through 8 mounted in a frame capable of holding a total of nine such tiles in three rows and three columns. Among the tiles in the frame there is a vacancy into which any of the adjacent tiles can be pushed. The tiles are currently arranged as shown in Figure 10.2.

We begin by picking up the puzzle and rearranging it by repeatedly pushing arbitrarily chosen tiles into the vacancy. We then turn on the machine, and the gripper begins to open and close as if asking for the puzzle. We place the puzzle in the gripper, and the gripper closes on the puzzle. After a short time the machine's finger lowers and begins pushing the tiles around in the frame (in an orderly fashion) until they are back in their original order. At this point the machine releases the puzzle and turns itself off. Because such a machine involves elementary perception as well as reasoning abilities, its design provides a basis for presenting the topics of the following two sections.

FIGURE 10.1

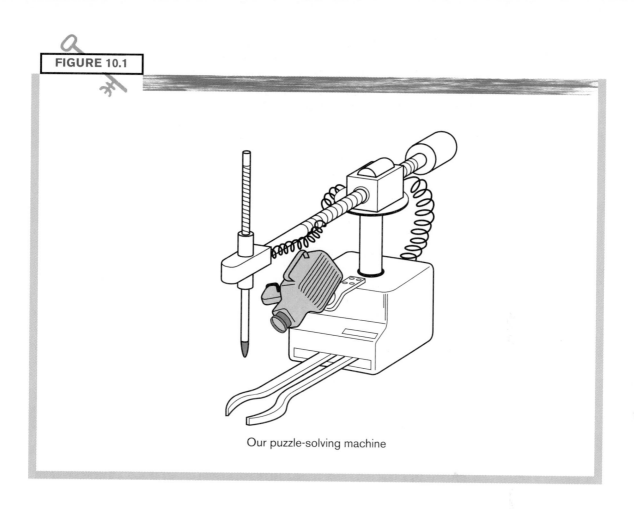

Our puzzle-solving machine

FIGURE 10.2

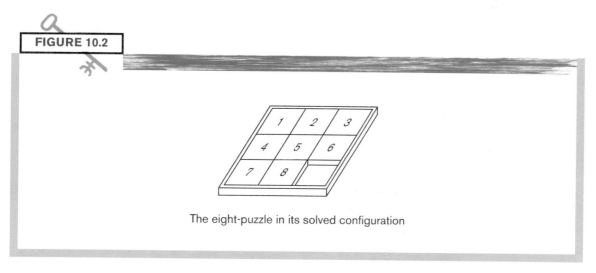

The eight-puzzle in its solved configuration

QUESTIONS/EXERCISES

1. A plant placed in a dark room with a single light source grows toward the light. Is this an intelligent response? Does the plant possess intelligence?
2. Suppose a vending machine is designed to dispense various products depending on which button is pressed. Would you say that such a machine is "aware" of which button is pressed?
3. If a machine passed the Turing test, would you agree that it was intelligent? If not, would you agree that it appeared to be intelligent?

10.2 Understanding Images

The opening and closing of the gripper on our machine presents no serious problem, and the ability to detect the presence of the puzzle in the gripper during this process is straightforward because our application requires very little precision. (Automatic garage door openers are able to detect and react to the presence of an obstacle in the doorway when closing.) Even the problem of focusing the camera on the puzzle can be handled simply by designing the gripper to position the puzzle at a particular predetermined position for viewing. Consequently, the first intelligent behavior required by our puzzle-solving machine is the extraction of information through a visual medium.

It is important to realize that the problem faced by our machine when looking at the puzzle is not that of merely producing and storing an image. Technology has been able to do this for years as in the case of traditional photography and television systems. Rather, the problem is to understand the image in order to extract the current status of the puzzle (and later to monitor the movement of the tiles). This is a significant distinction from the activity of a television receiver that simply transforms the image from one medium to another with no conceptual understanding of the image. In short, our machine must demonstrate the ability to perceive.

In the case of our puzzle-solving machine, the options as to what the images might be are relatively limited. We can assume that what appears is always an image of the puzzle containing the digits 1 through 8 in a well-organized pattern. The problem is merely to extract the arrangement of these digits. For this, we imagine that the picture of the puzzle has been coded in terms of bits in the computer's memory, with each bit representing the brightness level of a particular part of the picture called a pixel. Assuming a uniform size of the image (the machine holds the puzzle at a predetermined location in front of the camera), our machine can detect which tile is in which position by comparing the different sections of the picture to prerecorded templates consisting of the bit patterns produced by the individual digits used in the puzzle. As matches are found, the condition of the puzzle is revealed.

This technique of recognizing images is one method used in optical character readers. It has the drawback, however, of requiring a certain degree of uniformity among the style, size, and orientation of the symbols being read. In particular, the bit pattern produced by a physically large character does not match the template for a smaller version of the same symbol, even though the shapes are the same. Moreover, you can imagine how such problems increase when trying to process handwritten material.

Another approach to the problem of character recognition is based on matching the geometric characteristics rather than the exact appearance of the symbols. In such cases the digit 1 might be characterized as a single vertical line, 2 might be an opened curved line joined with a horizontal straight line across the bottom, and so on. This method of recognizing symbols involves two steps—the first is to extract the features from the image being processed, the second is to compare the features to those of known symbols. As with the template matching approach, this technique for recognizing characters is not foolproof. For instance minor errors in the image can produce a set of entirely different geometric features, as in the case of distinguishing between an O and a C or, in the case of the eight-puzzle, a 3 and an 8.

We are fortunate in our puzzle application that we do not need to understand images of general three-dimensional scenes. Consider, for example, the advantage we have by being assured that the shapes to be recognized (the digits 1 through 8) are isolated in different parts of the picture rather than appearing as overlapping images, as is common in more general settings. In a general photograph, for instance, one is faced not only with the problem of recognizing an object from different angles but also with the fact that some portions of the object may be hidden from view.

The task of understanding general images is usually approached as a two-step process: (1) **image processing** which refers to identifying characteristics of the image, and (2) **image analysis** which refers to the process of understanding what these characteristics mean. We have already observed this dichotomy in the context of recognizing symbols by means of their geometric features. There we found image processing represented by the process of identifying the geometric features found in the image and image analysis represented by the process of identifying the meaning of those features.

The process of image processing entails numerous subjects. One is edge enhancement, which is the process of applying mathematical techniques to clarify the boundaries between components of an image. In a sense, edge enhancement is an attempt to convert a photograph into a line drawing. Another activity in image analysis is known as region finding. This is the process of identifying those areas in an image that have common properties such as brightness, color, or texture. Such a region probably represents a section of the image that belongs to a single object. It is the ability to recognize regions that allows computers to add color to cartoons or to old fashioned black and white motion pictures. Still another activity within the scope of image processing is smoothing, which is the process of removing flaws in the image. Smoothing keeps errors in the image from confusing the other image-processing steps, but too much smoothing can cause the loss of important information as well.

Smoothing, edge enhancement, and region finding are all steps toward identifying the various components in an image. Image analysis is the process of finding what these components represent and ultimately what the image means. Here one faces such problems as recognizing partially obstructed objects from different perspectives. One approach to image analysis is to start with an assumption about what the image might be and then try to associate the components in the image with the objects whose presence is conjectured. This appears to be an approach applied by humans. For instance, we sometimes find it hard to identify an unexpected object in a setting in which our vision is blurred, but once we have a clue as to what the object might be, we can easily recognize it.

The problems associated with general image analysis are enormous, and much research in the area remains to be done. Tasks that are performed quickly and apparently easily by the human mind continue to lie beyond the capabilities of machines. On the other hand, there are indications that alternative machine architectures may someday overcome the problems that elude us today (see Section 10.4).

QUESTIONS/EXERCISES

1. How do the requirements of a video system on a robot differ if the pictures are used by the robot itself to control its activities as opposed to being relayed to a human who controls the robot remotely?

2. What tells you that the following drawing is nonsense? How can this insight be programmed into a machine?

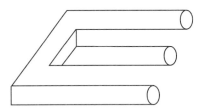

3. How many blocks are in the stack represented below? How could a machine be programmed to answer such questions accurately?

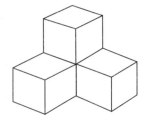

10.3 Reasoning

Once our puzzle-solving machine has deciphered the positions of the tiles from the visual image, its task becomes that of figuring out what moves are required to solve the puzzle. An approach to this problem that might come to mind is to preprogram the machine with solutions to all possible arrangements of the tiles. Then, the machine's task would merely be to select and execute the proper program. However, the eight-puzzle has 181,440 different configurations, so the idea of providing an explicit solution for each is certainly not inviting and probably not even possible when time and storage constraints are considered.

We are thus forced to program the machine so that it can construct solutions to the eight-puzzle on its own. That is, the machine must be programmed to make decisions, draw conclusions, and in short, perform elementary reasoning activities.

Production Systems

The development of reasoning abilities within a machine has been a topic of research for many years. One of the results of this research is the recognition that a large class of reasoning problems have common characteristics. These common characteristics are isolated in a system known as a **production system,** which consists of three main components:

1. *A collection of states.* Each **state** is a situation that might occur in the application environment. The beginning state is called the **start** (or initial) **state;** the desired state (or states) is called the **goal state.** (In our case, a state is a configuration of the eight-puzzle; the start state is the configuration of the puzzle when handed to the machine; the goal state is the configuration of the solved puzzle, as shown in Figure 10.2.)
2. *A collection of productions (rules or moves).* A **production** is an operation that can be performed in the application environment to move from one state to another. Each production may be associated with preconditions; that is, conditions may exist that must be present in the environment before a production can be applied. (Productions in our case are the movements of tiles. Each movement of a tile has the precondition that the vacancy must be next to the tile in question.)
3. *A control system.* The **control system** consists of the logic that solves the problem of moving from the start state to the goal state. At each step in the process the control system must decide which of those productions whose preconditions are satisfied should be applied next. (Given a particular state in our eight-puzzle example, there would be several tiles next to the vacancy and therefore several applicable productions. The control system must decide which tile to move.)

We see, then, that the control system is a program within the machine. This program inspects the current state of the target system, identifies a sequence of productions that leads to the goal state, and executes this sequence.

An important concept in the development of a control system is that of a **state graph,** which is a convenient way of representing, or at least conceptualizing, all the states, productions, and preconditions in a production system. Here we use the term **graph** in its mathematical sense, meaning a collection of locations called **nodes** connected by arrows, or **arcs.** A state graph consists of a collection of nodes representing the states in the system connected by arcs representing the productions that shift the system from one state to another. Two nodes are connected by an arc in the state graph if and only if there is a production in the production system that transforms the system from the state at the origin of the arc to the state at the destination of the arc. Preconditions are implicitly represented by the absence of arcs between certain nodes.

We might emphasize here that just as the number of possible states prevented us from explicitly providing predesigned solutions to the eight-puzzle, the problem of magnitude prevents us from explicitly representing the entire state graph. A state graph is then a way of conceptualizing the problem at hand but not something that we would consider expressing in its entirety. Nonetheless, you may find it helpful to consider (and possibly extend) the portion of the state graph for the eight-puzzle displayed in Figure 10.3.

When viewed in terms of the state graph, the problem faced by the control system becomes that of finding a sequence of arcs that leads from the start state to the goal state. Indeed, this sequence of arcs represents a sequence of productions that solves the original problem. Thus, regardless of the application, the task of the control system can be viewed as that of finding a path through a state graph. This universal view of control systems is the prize that we obtain by analyzing problems requiring reasoning in terms of production systems. To emphasize this point, let us consider how other tasks can be framed in terms of production systems and thus as control systems finding paths through state graphs.

One of the classic problems in artificial intelligence is the playing of games such as chess. These games involve moderate complexity in a well-defined context and hence provide an ideal environment for testing theories. In chess the states of the underlying production system are the possible board configurations, the productions are the moves of the pieces, and the control system is embodied in the players (human or otherwise). The start node of the state graph represents the board with the pieces in their initial positions. Branching from this node are arcs leading to those board configurations that can be reached after the first move in a game; branching from each of these nodes one finds those configurations reachable by the next move; and so on. With this formulation we can imagine a game of chess as consisting of two players, each trying to find a path through a large state graph to a goal node of his or her own choosing.

FIGURE 10.3

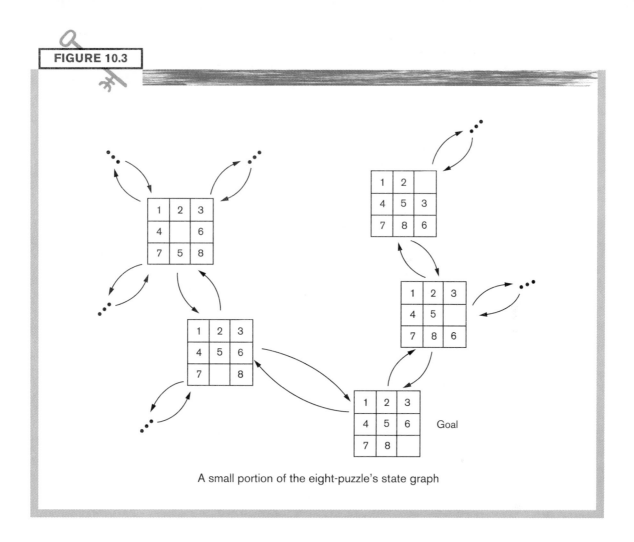

A small portion of the eight-puzzle's state graph

Perhaps a less obvious example of a production system is the problem of drawing logical conclusions from given facts. The productions in this context are the rules of logic that allow new statements to be formed from old ones. For example, the statements "All students work hard" and "John is a student" can be combined to produce "John works hard." Similarly, "Mary and George are smart" can be reworded as "Neither Mary nor George is not smart." States in such a system consist of collections of statements known to be true at particular points in the deduction process: The start state is the collection of basic statements (often called axioms) from which conclusions are to be drawn, and a goal state is any collection of statements that contain the proposed conclusion.

FIGURE 10.4

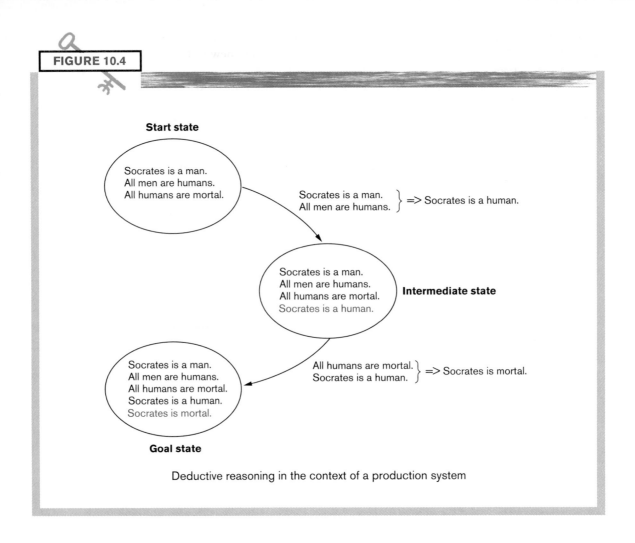

Start state

Socrates is a man.
All men are humans.
All humans are mortal.

Socrates is a man.
All men are humans. } => Socrates is a human.

Socrates is a man.
All men are humans.
All humans are mortal.
Socrates is a human.

Intermediate state

Socrates is a man.
All men are humans.
All humans are mortal.
Socrates is a human.
Socrates is mortal.

All humans are mortal. } => Socrates is mortal.
Socrates is a human.

Goal state

Deductive reasoning in the context of a production system

As an example, Figure 10.4 shows the portion of a state graph that might be traversed when the conclusion "Socrates is mortal" is drawn from the collection of statements "Socrates is a man," "All men are humans," and "All humans are mortal." There we see the body of knowledge shifting from one state to another as the reasoning process applies appropriate productions to generate additional statements.

Search Trees

We have seen that the control system's job involves searching the state graph to find a path from the start node to the goal. A simple method of performing this search is to traverse each of the arcs leading from the start state and in each case record the destination state, then traverse the arcs leaving these new states and again record the results, and so on. Our search for the goal spreads out from the start state like a drop of dye in water. This process continues until one of the new states is the goal, at which point a solution has been found, and the control system needs merely to apply the productions along the discovered path from the start state to the goal.

The effect of this strategy is to build a tree, called a **search tree,** that consists of the part of the state graph that has been investigated by the control system. The root node of the search tree is the start state, and the children of each node are those states reachable from the parent by applying one production. Each arc between nodes in a search tree represents the application of a single production, and each path from the root to a leaf represents a path between the corresponding states in the state graph.

The search tree that would be produced when solving the eight-puzzle from the configuration shown in Figure 10.5 is shown in Figure 10.6. The leftmost branch of this tree represents an attempt to solve the problem by first moving the 6 tile up, the center branch represents the approach of moving the 2 tile to the right, and the rightmost branch represents moving the 5 tile down. Furthermore, the search tree shows that if we do begin by moving the 6 tile up, the only production allowable next is to move the 8 tile to the right. (Actually, at that point we could also move the 6 tile down but that would return us to the state represented by the root node and thus be an extraneous move.)

The goal state occurs in the last level of the search tree of Figure 10.6. Since this represents the completion of the search, the control system can terminate its search procedure and begin constructing the instruction sequence that will be used to solve the puzzle in the external environment. This turns out to be the simple process of walking up the search tree from the location of the goal

FIGURE 10.5

An unsolved eight-puzzle

FIGURE 10.6

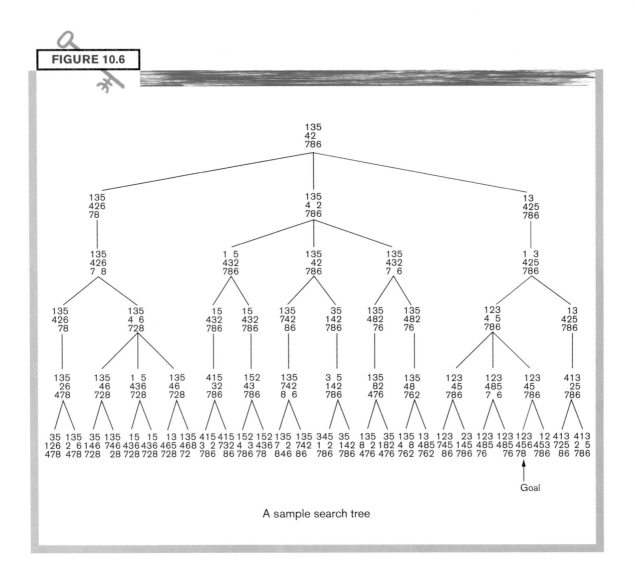

A sample search tree

node while pushing the productions represented by the tree arcs on a stack as they are encountered. Applying this technique to the search tree in Figure 10.6 produces the stack of productions in Figure 10.7. Note that the control system can now solve the puzzle in the outside world by executing the instructions as they are popped from this stack.

One point remains. Recall that the trees we discussed in Chapter 7 use a pointer system that points down the tree, thereby allowing us to move from a parent node to its children. In the case of a search tree, however, the control system must be able to move from a child to its parent as it moves up the tree

FIGURE 10.7

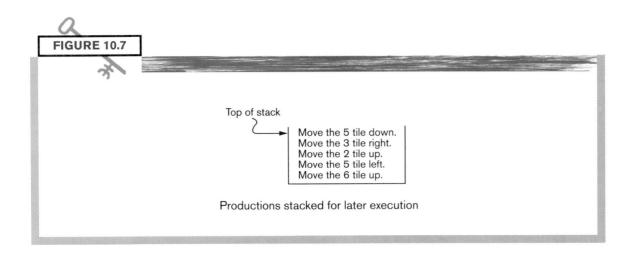

Top of stack

Move the 5 tile down.
Move the 3 tile right.
Move the 2 tile up.
Move the 5 tile left.
Move the 6 tile up.

Productions stacked for later execution

from the goal state to the start state. Such trees are constructed with their pointer systems pointing up rather than down (or in some cases, with two sets of pointers that allow movement in the tree in both directions).

Heuristics

For our example in Figure 10.6, we chose a starting configuration that produces a manageable search tree. In contrast, the search tree generated in an attempt to solve a more complex problem could grow much larger. For example, in a game of chess there are 20 possible first moves so the root node of the search tree in such a case would have 20 children rather than the 3 in the case of the eight-puzzle. Moreover, a game of chess can easily consist of 30 to 35 pairs of moves rather than the 5 straightforward ones in our example. Even in the eight-puzzle example, the search tree can become quite large if the goal is not quickly reached. As a result, developing a full search tree can be as impractical as representing the entire state graph in terms of both time and memory space. These cases require more economical methods of manipulating the search tree.

One strategy is to change the order in which the search tree is constructed. Rather than building it in a **breadth-first** manner (meaning that the tree is constructed layer by layer), we can pursue the more promising paths to greater depths and consider the other options only if these original choices turn out to be false leads. This results in a **depth-first** construction of the search tree, meaning that the tree is constructed by building vertical paths rather than horizontal layers.

The depth-first approach is more like the strategy that we as humans would proceed when faced with the eight-puzzle. We would rarely pursue several options at the same time, as modeled by the breadth-first approach. When faced with a choice, we probably would select the option that appeared most promising and follow it. Note that we said *appeared* most promising. We usually do not know for sure which option is best at a particular point but follow our intuition, which may, of course, lead us into a trap. Nonetheless, the use of such intuitive information seems to give humans an advantage over the brute-force methods in which each option was given equal attention.

The first step toward applying this approach to automated control systems is to identify those characteristics that we as humans use when deciding which option to pursue. In general, humans tend to keep the goal state in mind and pick the option that appears to lead toward that state. In the case of the eight-puzzle this means that a human, when given a choice, tends to select the option that moves a tile in the direction of its final position.

Our strategy, then, is to develop a **heuristic**—a quantitative measure by which a program can determine which of several states is considered closest to the goal. A simple heuristic in the case of the eight-puzzle would be to associate with each state the value equal to the number of tiles out of position and consider the state with the smallest value to be closest to the goal. However, this value does not take into account how far out of position the tiles are. A slightly more complicated measure that accounts for this distance is to measure the distance each tile is from its destination and add these values to obtain a single quantity. The distance in this case can be taken as the minimum number of moves a tile must make to reach its goal position, disregarding any complexities introduced by the location of the other tiles. Thus a tile immediately adjacent to its final destination is associated with a distance of one, whereas a tile whose corner touches the square of its final destination is associated with a distance of two (because it must move at least one position vertically and another position horizontally).

The quantity associated with each state using this heuristic is actually an approximation of the number of moves required to reach the goal from that state, which we refer to as the projected cost. For instance, the total projected cost associated with the configuration in Figure 10.8 is seven (because tiles 2, 5, and 8 are each a distance of one from their final destinations while tiles 3 and 6 are each a distance of two from home). In fact, it actually takes seven moves to return this puzzle configuration to the solved configuration.

The projected cost has two important characteristics. First, as just noted, it constitutes a reasonable estimate of the amount of work remaining in the solution if that state were reached. This means that it should be helpful in decision making. Second, it can be calculated easily. This means that its use has a chance of benefiting the search process rather than of becoming a burden. (In contrast, although the actual number of moves required to reach the goal from the given state is an excellent piece of information to have when making decisions, computing this information involves finding the actual solution first.)

Now that we have a heuristic for the eight-puzzle, the next step is to incorporate it into our decision-making process. Recall that a human faced with a

FIGURE 10.8

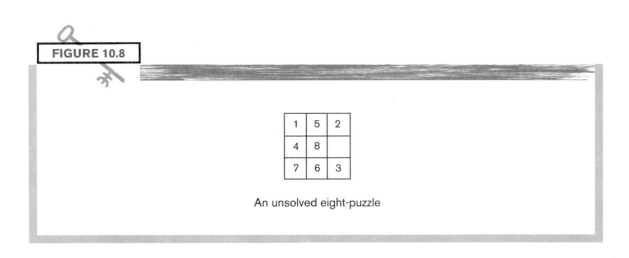

An unsolved eight-puzzle

decision tends to select the option that appears closest to the goal. Thus our search procedure should consider the projected cost of each leaf node in the tree and pursue the search from a leaf node associated with the smallest such cost. This is the strategy adopted in Figure 10.9, which presents an algorithm for developing a search tree and executing the solution obtained.

FIGURE 10.9

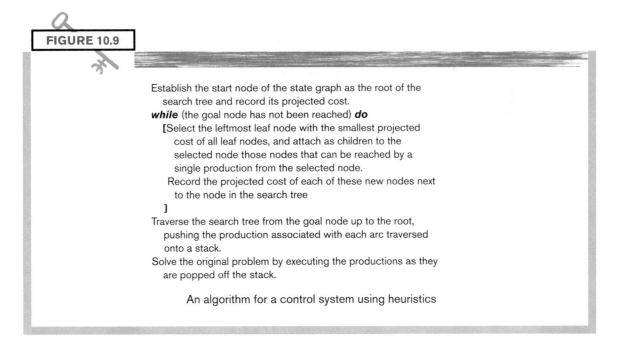

Establish the start node of the state graph as the root of the
    search tree and record its projected cost.
while (the goal node has not been reached) **do**
    [Select the leftmost leaf node with the smallest projected
        cost of all leaf nodes, and attach as children to the
        selected node those nodes that can be reached by a
        single production from the selected node.
    Record the projected cost of each of these new nodes next
        to the node in the search tree
    ]
Traverse the search tree from the goal node up to the root,
    pushing the production associated with each arc traversed
    onto a stack.
Solve the original problem by executing the productions as they
    are popped off the stack.

An algorithm for a control system using heuristics

Let us apply this algorithm to the eight-puzzle, starting from the initial configuration in Figure 10.5. First, we establish this initial state as the root node and record its projected cost, which is five. Then, the first pass through the body of the while structure instructs the addition of the three nodes, as in Figure 10.10. Note that we have recorded in parentheses the projected cost of each leaf node beneath it.

The goal node has not been reached, so we again pass through the body of the while structure, this time extending our search from the leftmost node ("the leftmost leaf node with the smallest projected cost"). After this, the search tree has taken the form displayed in Figure 10.11.

Note that the projected cost of the leftmost leaf node is now five, indicating that this is perhaps not a good choice to pursue after all. The algorithm picks up on this and in the next pass through the loop instructs us to expand the tree from the rightmost node (which now is the "leftmost leaf node with the smallest projected cost"). Having been expanded in this fashion, the search tree appears as in Figure 10.12.

FIGURE 10.10

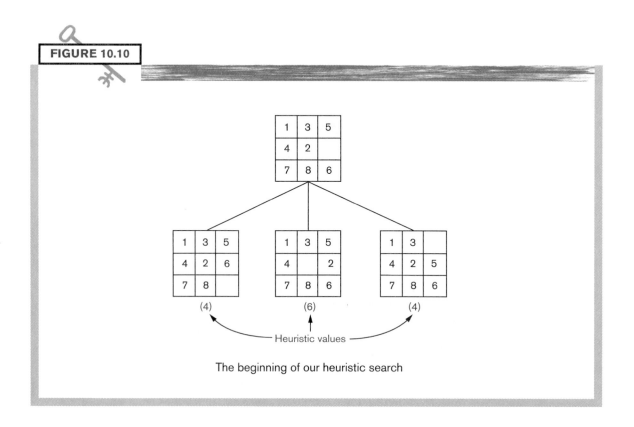

The beginning of our heuristic search

FIGURE 10.11

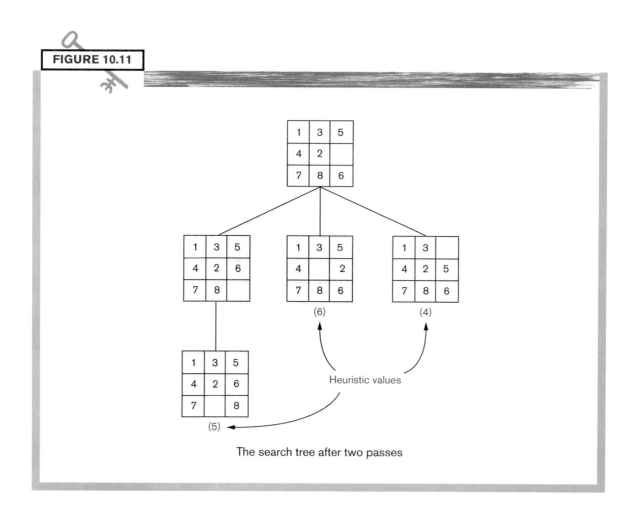

The search tree after two passes

At this point the algorithm seems to be on the right track. Because the projected cost of this last node is only three, the while structure instructs us to continue pursuing this path, and the search finally arrives at the goal, with the search tree appearing as in Figure 10.13. Comparing this with the tree in Figure 10.6 shows that, even with the temporary wrong turn taken early on by the new algorithm, the use of heuristic information has greatly decreased the size of the search tree and produced a much more efficient process.

After reaching the goal state, the while structure terminates, and we move on to traverse the tree from the goal node up to the root, pushing the

FIGURE 10.12

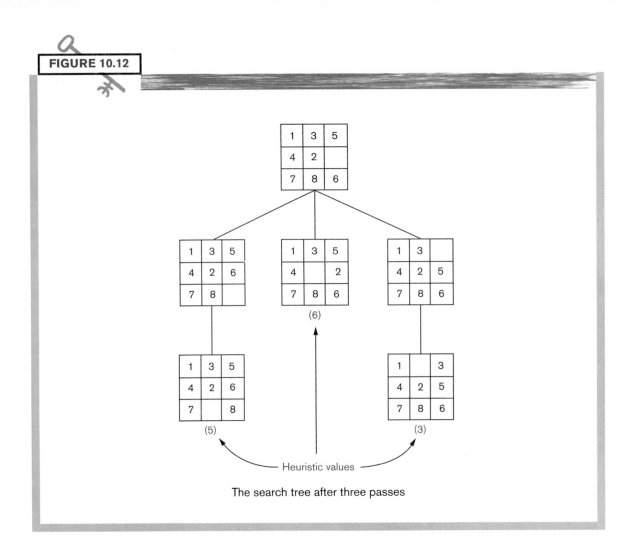

(6)

Heuristic values

The search tree after three passes

productions encountered onto a stack as we go. The resultant stack appears as depicted earlier, in Figure 10.7.

Finally, we are instructed to execute these productions as they are popped from the stack. At this point, we would observe the puzzle-solving machine lower its finger and begin to move the tiles.

FIGURE 10.13

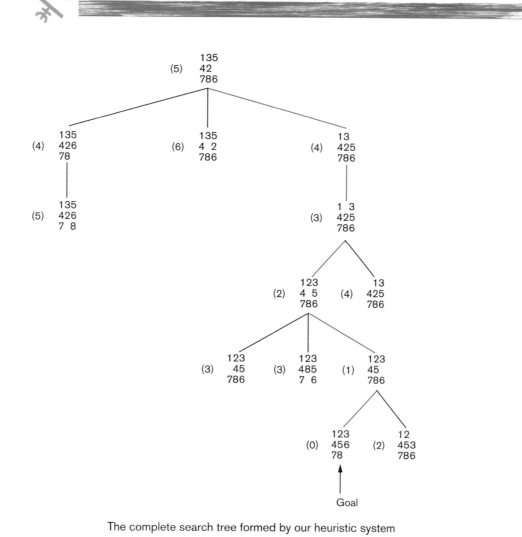

The complete search tree formed by our heuristic system

QUESTIONS/EXERCISES

1. What is the significance of production systems in artificial intelligence?
2. Draw a portion of the state graph for the eight-puzzle surrounding the node representing the following state:

4	1	3
	2	6
7	5	8

3. Using a breadth-first approach, draw the search tree that is constructed by a control system when solving the eight-puzzle from the following start state:

1	2	3
4	8	5
7	6	

4. Use pencil, paper, and the breadth-first approach to try to construct the search tree that is produced when solving the eight-puzzle from the following start state. (You do not have to finish.) What problems do you encounter?

4	3	
2	1	8
7	6	5

5. What analogy can be drawn between our heuristic system for solving the eight-puzzle and a mountain climber who attempts to reach the peak by considering only the local terrain and always proceeding in the direction of steepest ascent?
6. Using the heuristic presented in this section, apply the control-system algorithm of Figure 10.9 to the problem of solving the following eight-puzzle.

1	2	3
4		8
7	6	5

7. Refine our method of computing the projected cost for a state so that the search algorithm of Figure 10.9 does not make the wrong choice, as it did in the example in this section. Can you find an example in which your system still causes the search to go astray?

10.4 Artificial Neural Networks

With all the progress that has been made in artificial intelligence, many problems in the field continue to tax the abilities of today's traditional computers. Central processing units that execute single sequences of instructions do not seem capable of perceiving and reasoning at levels comparable to those of the multiprocessor human mind. For this reason, many researchers are turning to machines with multiprocessing architectures. One of these is the artificial neural network.

Basic Properties

As introduced in Chapter 2, artificial neural networks are constructed from many individual processors, which we will call processing units (or just units for short), in a manner that models networks of neurons in living biological systems. A biological neuron is a single cell with input tentacles called dendrites and an output tentacle called the axon (Figure 10.14). The signals transmitted via a cell's axon reflect whether the cell is in an inhibited or excited state. This state is determined by the combination of signals received by the cell's dendrites. These dendrites pick up signals from the axons of other cells across small gaps known as synapses. Research suggests that the conductivity across a single synapse is controlled by the chemical composition of the synapse. That is, whether the particular input signal will have an exciting or inhibiting effect on the neuron is determined by the chemical composition of the synapse. Thus it is believed that a biological neural network learns by adjusting these chemical connections between neurons.

A processing unit in an artificial neural network is a simple device that mimics this basic understanding of the biological neuron. It produces an output of 1 or 0, depending on whether its effective input exceeds a given threshold value. This effective input is a weighted sum of the actual inputs, as represented in Figure 10.15. In this figure, the outputs of three processing units (denoted by v_1, v_2, and v_3) are used as inputs to another unit. The inputs to this fourth unit are associated with values called weights (denoted by w_1, w_2, and w_3). The receiving unit multiplies each of its input values by the weight associated with that particular input position and then adds these products to form the effective

FIGURE 10.14

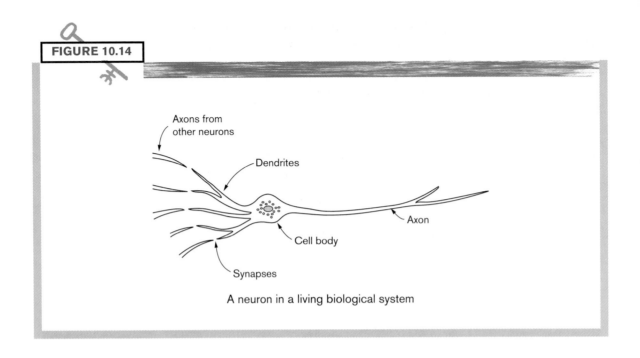

A neuron in a living biological system

FIGURE 10.15

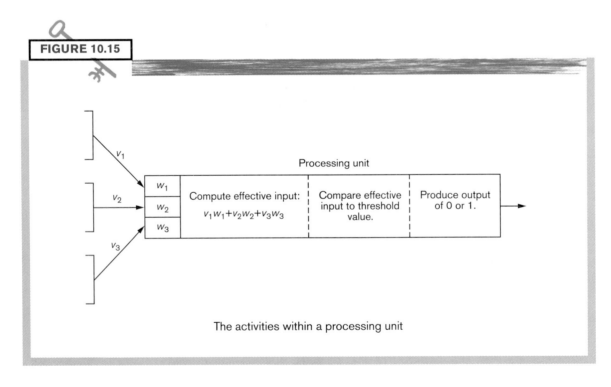

The activities within a processing unit

input $(v_1w_1 + v_2w_2 + v_3w_3)$. If this sum exceeds the processing unit's threshold value, the unit produces an output of 1; otherwise the unit produces a 0 as its output.

Following the lead of Figure 10.15, we adopt the convention of representing processing units as rectangles. At the input end of the unit, we place a smaller rectangle for each input, and in this rectangle we write the weight associated with that input. Finally, we write the unit's threshold value in the middle of the large rectangle. As an example, Figure 10.16 represents a processing unit with three inputs and a threshold value of 1.5. The first input is weighted by the value -2, the second is weighted by 3, and the third is weighted by -1. Therefore, if the unit receives the inputs 1, 1, and 0, its effective input is $(1)(-2) + (1)(3) + (0)(-1) = 1$, and thus its output is 0. But, if the unit receives 0, 1, and 1, its effective input is $(0)(-2) + (1)(3) + (1)(-1) = 2$, which exceeds the threshold value. The unit's output will thus be 1.

The fact that a weight can be positive or negative means that the corresponding input can have either an inhibiting or exciting effect on the receiving unit. (If the weight is negative, then a 1 at that input position reduces the weighted sum and thus tends to hold the effective input below the threshold value. In contrast, a positive weight causes the associated input to have an increasing effect on the weighted sum and thus increase the chances of that sum exceeding the threshold value.) Moreover, the actual size of the weight controls the degree to which the corresponding input is allowed to inhibit or excite the receiving unit. Consequently, by adjusting the values of the weights throughout an artificial neural network, we can program the network to respond to different inputs in a predetermined manner.

As an example, the simple network presented in Figure 10.17(a) is programmed to produce an output of 1 if its two inputs differ and an output of 0 otherwise. If, however, we change the weights to those shown in Figure

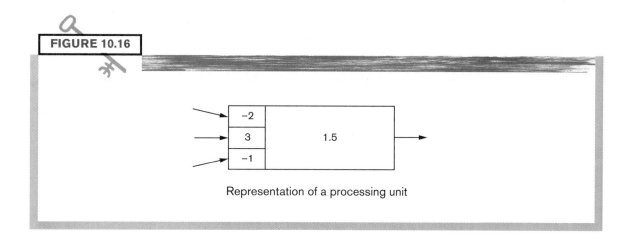

FIGURE 10.16

Representation of a processing unit

FIGURE 10.17

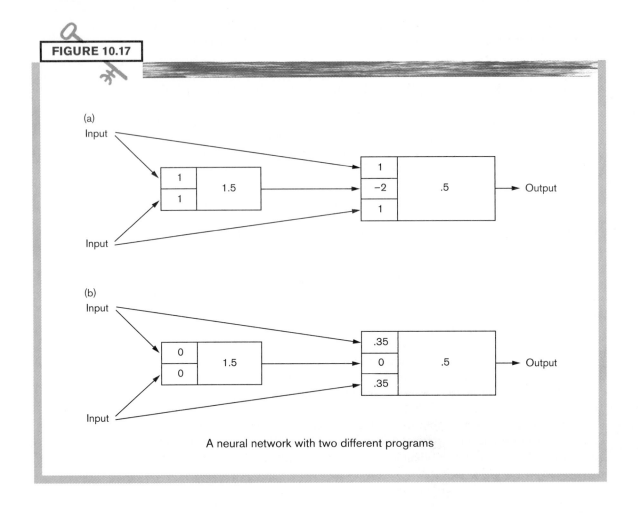

A neural network with two different programs

10.17(b), we obtain a network that responds with a 1 if both of its inputs are 1s and with a 0 otherwise.

We should note that the network in Figure 10.17 is far more simplistic than an actual biological network. A human brain contains approximately 10^{11} neurons with about 10^4 synapses per neuron. Indeed, the dendrites of a biological neuron are so numerous that they appear more like a fibrous mesh than the individual tentacles represented in our figures.

A Specific Application

To appreciate the potential of artificial neural networks, let us consider the particular character recognition problem of distinguishing between the uppercase

FIGURE 10.18

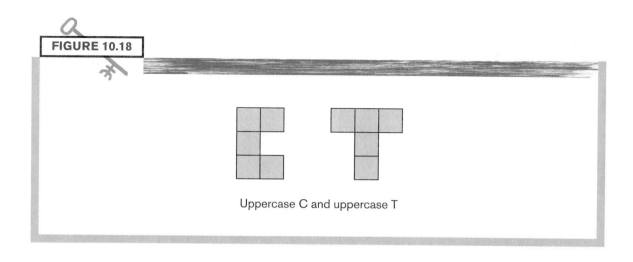

Uppercase C and uppercase T

letters C and T, as represented in Figure 10.18. The problem is to identify either letter when it is placed in the field of vision, regardless of its orientation. All of the patterns in Figure 10.19(a) should be identified as Cs, and all of those in part (b) should be recognized as Ts.

We begin by assuming that the field of view consists of square pixels, each of which is the size of the squares from which the letters are constructed. Each of these pixels is attached to a sensor that produces a 1 if that pixel is covered by the letter being viewed and produces a 0 otherwise. We then use the outputs from these sensors as the inputs to our artificial neural network.

The network contains two levels of processing units. The first level consists of many units—one for each three-by-three block of pixels in the field of view (see Figure 10.20). Each of these units has nine inputs, to which the sensors associated with that unit's three-by-three block are attached. (Note that the three-by-three blocks associated with the first-level processing units overlap. Thus each sensor provides input to nine of the processing units at the first level.)

The second level of our network consists of a single processing unit, with a separate input for each of the units in the first level. The processing unit at the second level has a threshold value of .5, and each of its inputs is associated with a weight of 1. Thus this unit produces an output of 1 if and only if at least one of its inputs is 1.

Each processing unit at the first level has the threshold value of .5. Each input is given a weight of −1, except for the input associated with the center pixel of that unit's three-by-three block, which is given a weight of 2. Each of these units can therefore produce an output of 1 only if it receives a 1 from the sensor associated with the pixel in the center of the unit's three-by-three block.

Now, if the letter C is placed in the field of view (Figure 10.21), all the first level processing units will produce an output of 0. This is because the only units

FIGURE 10.19

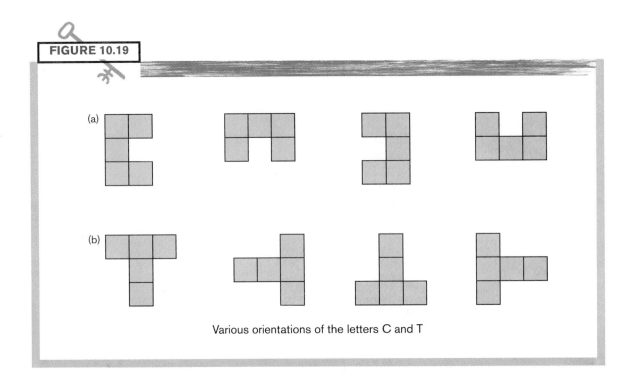

(a)

(b)

Various orientations of the letters C and T

whose center pixel is covered by the letter will also have at least two other pixels in their three-by-three blocks covered and the signals received from these sensors will negate the effect of the center pixel. Consequently, if the letter in the field of view is C, all of the inputs to the second level processing unit will be 0, which means that the output of the entire network will be 0.

In contrast, suppose that the letter in the field of view is T. Consider the three-by-three block whose center is the square covered by the bottom of the T's stem (Figure 10.22). The processing unit assigned to this square receives an effective input of 1 (2 from the center pixel and –1 from the other pixel covered by the stem). This exceeds the unit's threshold, so the unit sends an output of 1 to the upper-level unit. This, then, causes the upper-level unit to produce an output of 1.

In summary, we have an artificial neural network that distinguishes between the letters C and T, regardless of the letter's orientation in the field of view. If the letter is a C, the network produces a 0 as its output; if the letter is a T, the network produces a 1.

Of course, the ability to distinguish between just two letters is a far cry from the image-processing capabilities of the human mind. But the elegance of solutions such as these indicates that further research in the area is justified.

FIGURE 10.20

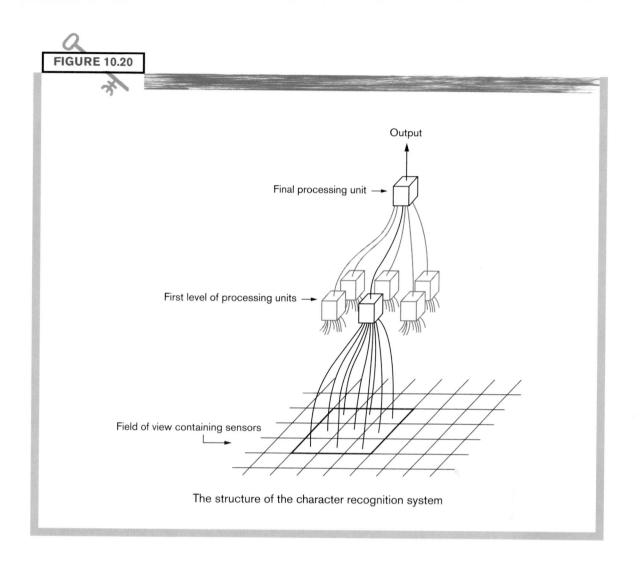

The structure of the character recognition system

The result is that the field of artificial neural networks is an active area of research. The major obstacles are associated with designing and programming such networks. Typical goals relating to network design include determining how many processing units and how many levels of units are required to solve certain problems and what patterns of connections between these units are most productive.

As for the subject of network programming, we have already seen that the task of programming an artificial neural network is that of assigning the proper weights to the various processing unit inputs throughout the system. The most popular way of doing this at the present is to perform a repetitive training

FIGURE 10.21

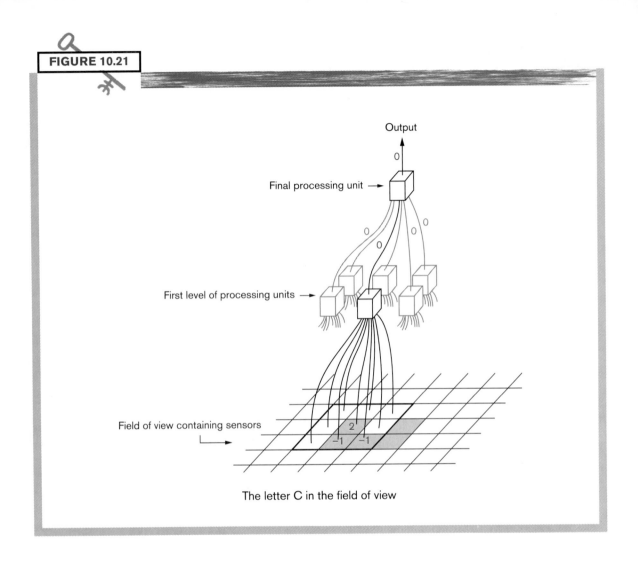

Output

Final processing unit →

First level of processing units →

Field of view containing sensors

The letter C in the field of view

process, in which sample inputs are applied to the network and then the weights are adjusted by small increments so that the actual output of the network approaches the desired output. As this process is repeated among the sample inputs, one hopes that the weights require less and less adjusting until the network begins to perform correctly over the entire range of sample data. What is needed is a strategy for adjusting these weights so that each new adjustment leads toward the overall goal rather than destroying the progress made on the previous samples.

FIGURE 10.22

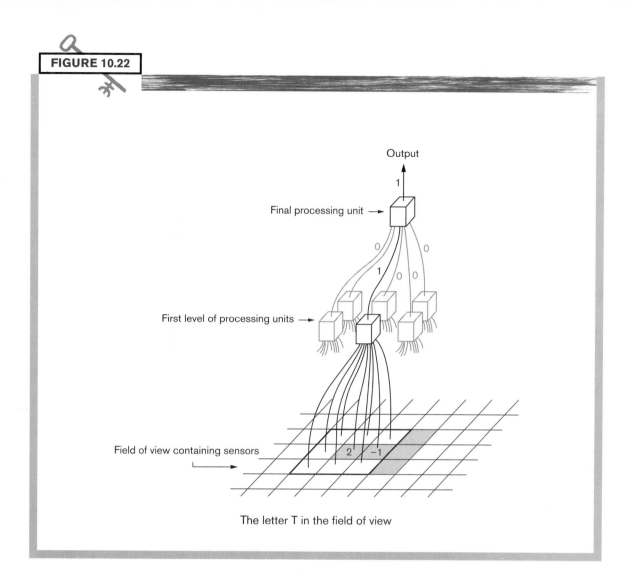

The letter T in the field of view

QUESTIONS/EXERCISES

1. What is the output of the following processing unit when both its inputs are 1s? What about the input patterns 0, 0; 0, 1; and 1, 0?

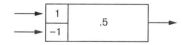

2. Adjust the weights and threshold value of the following processing unit so that its output is 1 if and only if at least two of its inputs are 1s.

3. Design an artificial neural network that can detect which of the following two patterns is in its field of view.

4. Design an artificial neural network that can detect which of the following two patterns is in its field of view.

10.5 Genetic Algorithms

The field of **genetic algorithms** is the research area that seeks to apply our knowledge of natural evolution to the problem-solving task. The approach is to intermix the best performers within a collection of proposed solutions to obtain another generation of proposed solutions that represent improvements over the original collection. By repeating this process over and over, one hopes to simulate the evolutionary process and ultimately obtain feasible solutions to the problem at hand.

As an example, let us assume that you play poker with the same group of friends every Wednesday evening and you want to develop a strategy that will maximize your winnings. An evolutionary approach to this problem would begin by identifying the various situations that may occur in a poker game and the potential responses to each. This, of course, would be a major undertaking since there would be many situations to be considered. Once this analysis was done, however, we could construct a poker-playing strategy by assigning a response to each situation. In turn, we could represent each strategy as a list of the form $S_1R_1, S_2R_2, \ldots, S_nR_n$, where each S is one of the potential situations and the following R is the response to be used in that situation. The representations for different strategies would contain the same situations, but these situations would be followed by different responses. To apply a given strategy, you would merely find the appropriate situation in the list and then perform the response that follows it.

The next step in our poker problem would be to select an initial collection of strategies and apply them during an evening of poker playing, recording the earnings obtained under each strategy. Based on this analysis we would then select the best of the initial strategies and group these selected strategies into pairs. From each such pair we would produce two new strategies by first cutting the lists representing the two strategies in the pair and then attaching the head from each to the tail from the other (Figure 10.23). All of these new strategies would form the collection of strategies to be tested the following week. Each week we would again select the best performing strategies and use them to produce yet another generation of strategies to be tested the following week. Thus, as the weeks go by, our process would simulate nature's evolutionary process in

FIGURE 10.23

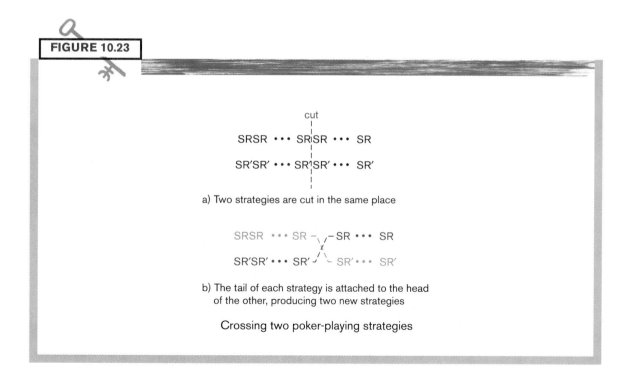

cut

SRSR ••• SR|SR ••• SR

SR'SR' ••• SR'|SR' ••• SR'

a) Two strategies are cut in the same place

SRSR ••• SR –\ /–SR ••• SR

SR'SR' ••• SR' ⌐ ⌐ SR' ••• SR'

b) The tail of each strategy is attached to the head
of the other, producing two new strategies

Crossing two poker-playing strategies

which the survivors of each generation reproduce to generate the next generation. In fact, we could even simulate mutations by arbitrarily changing a single response within a strategy at times.

Unfortunately, our poker example is somewhat unrealistic since it would not be possible to test a large generation of strategies in a single evening of poker. But if the process of playing test games could be automated, as is the case in many applications, the evolutionary approach would be quite feasible. This is the process proposed by research in genetic algorithms. First one finds a way to represent potential solutions as strings of symbols. Then, a collection of potential solutions is generated and tested. The better examples from this collection are then crossed to form a new generation of potential solutions that are tested and used to form yet another generation. At times random mutations may be inserted during the crossing process.

The evolutionary approach has been applied in numerous settings with promising results. One has been in designing configurations for artificial neural networks. Suppose, for example, we want to solve a problem by means of an artificial neural network that consists of a predetermined number of processing units. Before we begin training the network, we need to decide how the units should be connected. To this end, we agree to code artificial neural network configurations as strings of 0s and 1s in the following manner (Figure 10.24). Assuming that the number of processing units to be used in the network is n, we first label the processing units with the integers from 1 to n. We then build a square table with n rows and n columns. We place a 1 in the ith row and the jth column if the network being coded has a connection from the output of the ith processing unit to the input of the jth unit. All other table entries are assigned the value 0. We then rewrite this table as a single string by writing the rows in the table one after the other.

Now, to find a good configuration for our particular problem, we select a variety of potential configurations and start the training process for each.

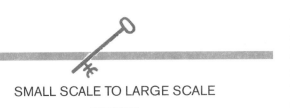

SMALL SCALE TO LARGE SCALE

A recurring phenomenon in the development and testing of theories is the transition from small-scale experimentation to large-scale applications. Initial experimentation of a new theory often involves small, simple cases. If success is achieved, then the experimental environment is extended to more realistic, larger-scale systems. Some theories are able to survive this transition; others are not. Sometimes success on the small scale is strong enough to encourage proponents of the theory to persist well after failures on the large scale have discouraged other researchers. In some cases, such persistence ultimately pays off; in others it represents wasted effort.

Such scenarios are readily observable in the field of artificial intelligence. One example is in the area of natural language processing, where early successes in limited settings led many to believe that general natural language understanding was just over the horizon. Unfortunately, extending success to the large scale has proved much more difficult, and victory is being achieved slowly as the result of significant effort. Another example is the subject of artificial neural networks, a topic that came on the scene with significant fanfare, faded for several years when its large-scale capabilities came under question, and has now returned in a more subdued atmosphere. As indicated in the text, the subject of generic algorithms is currently undergoing this transition test. Whether the evolutionary approach will prove to be a valid tool of the future is an open question.

FIGURE 10.24

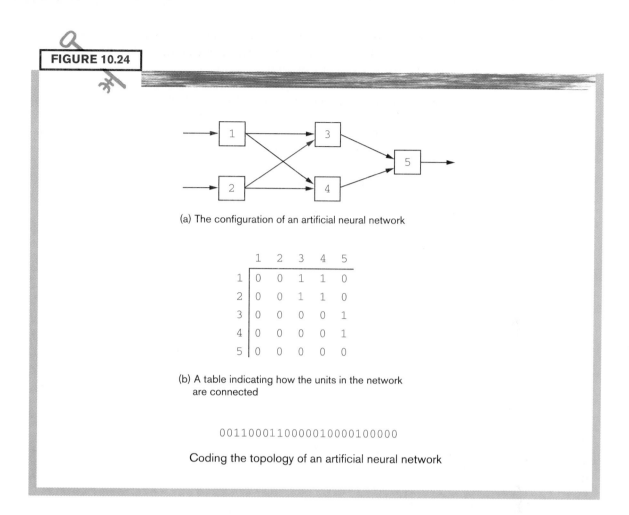

(a) The configuration of an artificial neural network

	1	2	3	4	5
1	0	0	1	1	0
2	0	0	1	1	0
3	0	0	0	0	1
4	0	0	0	0	1
5	0	0	0	0	0

(b) A table indicating how the units in the network
   are connected

0011000110000010000100000

Coding the topology of an artificial neural network

After a short training period, we select those configurations that seem to be making the best progress, represent those configurations as strings of 0s and 1s, and cross these strings to obtain a new generation of potential configurations. In turn, this new generation would be partially trained and the best performers would be selected to produce still another generation. Such an approach has been successful in designing simple artificial neural networks.

Genetic algorithm techniques have also been applied to the task of program development, leading to a field known as **evolutionary programming.** The goal is to develop programs by allowing them to evolve rather than by explicitly writing them. An important step in this setting is to find ways in which parts of programs can be interchanged to produce meaningful new programs. The functional programming paradigm has proved useful in this context. Indeed, a program written in the functional paradigm consists of nested functions in which the output of one function is used as the input to another. Thus it is feasible that a function from one program could be exchanged with a function in another program without destroying the program's structure.

Following such reasoning, researchers have applied evolutionary programming techniques to the program development process using functional programming languages. The approach has been to start with a collection of programs that contain a rich variety of functions. After all, the functions in this starting collection form the "gene pool" from which future generations of programs will be constructed. One then allows the evolutionary process to run for many generations, hoping that by producing each generation from the best performers in the previous generation, a solution to the target problem will ultimately evolve.

The field of evolutionary programming is still in its infancy. As yet, success has been obtained in simple cases. For example, evolutionary techniques have been used to obtain programs that compute properties of simple geometric shapes, such as the area of a square or the circumference of a circle. A major problem is to identify the "best performers" out of a group of programs of which none seem to be anywhere close to the desired product. As is the case in other areas of genetic algorithms, whether the techniques being developed will be successfully up-scaled to solve significant, meaningful problems is still an open question. In any case, the field of genetic algorithms is representative of the creativity and imagination being applied in today's computer science research.

QUESTIONS/EXERCISES

1. Code the configuration of the artificial neural network below using the system described in this section.

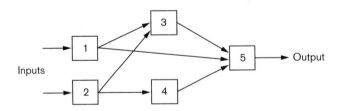

2. Select a problem that you feel would be suitable for the evolutionary approach and describe how potential solutions could be coded as strings. Then, describe how these strings could be crossed to form future generations.
3. Give an argument to the effect that the functional programming paradigm is more compatible with evolutionary programming than the object-oriented paradigm.

10.6 Applications of Artificial Intelligence

Having considered some of the techniques used in artificial intelligence, we now turn to the areas in which these techniques have found or are finding applications.

Language Processing

We begin by considering the task of translating statements from one language to another. Here, we find both traditional and artificial intelligence systems being used, depending on the languages involved. The distinction centers on whether the semantics of a statement must be considered to produce the translation. For instance, traditional programming languages are designed so that they can be translated through the rather straightforward process of essentially finding the original statement (or statement part) in a table in which its translated equivalent is stored. The machine is therefore never called upon to understand the statements being translated; it merely recognizes their syntax, looks them up in the table, and extracts the translation. Such applications therefore fall within the scope of traditional computer applications.

In contrast, the problem of translating natural languages such as English, German, and Latin, often requires an understanding of a sentence's semantics before a correct translation can be made. For example, the task of translating the sentences

Norman Rockwell painted people.

and

Cinderella had a ball.

cannot be accomplished by merely translating each word. Instead, to translate these sentences requires the ability to understand them.

Developing computers that can understand natural language has become a major research area in artificial intelligence. It is also an area that demonstrates how challenging research in artificial intelligence can become.

One problem in natural language processing is that people do not always conform to rules when they speak. In some cases they do not even say what they mean. For example,

Do you know what time it is?

often means "Please tell me what time it is," or if the speaker has been waiting for a long time, it may mean "You are very late."

To unravel the meaning of a statement in a natural language therefore requires several levels of analysis. The first of these is **syntactic analysis** whose major component is parsing. It is here that the subject of the sentence

Mary gave John a birthday card.

is recognized as *Mary* while the subject of

John got a birthday card from Mary.

is found to be *John*.

Another level of analysis is called **semantic analysis.** In contrast to the parsing process, which merely identifies the grammatical role of each word, semantic analysis is charged with the task of identifying the semantic role of each word in the statement. Semantic analysis seeks to identify such things as the action described, the agent of that action (which may or may not be the subject of the sentence), and the object of the action. It is through semantic analysis that the sentences "Mary gave John a birthday card" and "John got a birthday card from Mary" would be recognized as saying the same thing.

A third level of analysis is **contextual analysis.** It is at this level that the context of the sentence is brought into the understanding process. For example, it is easy to identify the grammatical role of each word in the sentence

The bat slipped from his hand.

We can even perform semantic analysis by identifying the action involved as *slipping,* the agent as *bat,* and so on. But it is not until we consider the context of the statement that its meaning becomes clear. Indeed, it has a different meaning in the context of a baseball game than it does in the context of exploring a cave. Moreover, it is at the contextual level that the true meaning of the question "Do you know what time it is?" would finally be revealed.

We should note that the various levels of analysis—syntactic, semantic, and contextual—are not necessarily independent. The subject of the sentence

Stampeding cattle can be dangerous.

is the noun *cattle* (modified by the adjective *stampeding*) if we envision the cattle stampeding on their own. But, the subject is the gerund *stampeding* (with object *cattle*) in the context of a troublemaker whose entertainment consists of starting stampedes.

In addition to the problem of translation, a major direction of research in natural language understanding involves the problems of **information retrieval** and **information extraction.** Information retrieval refers to the task of identifying documents that relate to the topic at hand. An example is the problem faced by attorneys when trying to find all the case histories that relate to current litigation. We will return to this example shortly in the context of database retrieval.

Information extraction refers to the task of extracting information from documents so that it takes a form that is useful in other applications. This may mean identifying the answer to a specific question or recording the information in a form from which questions can be answered at a later date. One such form is known as a template. It is essentially a questionnaire in which specifics are recorded. For example, consider a system for reading a newspaper. The system may make use of a variety of templates, one for each type of article that may appear in a newspaper. If the system identifies an article as reporting on a burglary, it would proceed by trying to fill in the slots in the burglary template. This template would probably request such items as the address of the burglary, the time and date of the burglary, the items taken, and so on. In contrast, if the system identifies an article as reporting on a natural disaster, it would fill in the natural disaster template, which would lead the system toward identifying the type of disaster, amount of damage, and so on.

Another form in which information extractors record information is known as a **semantic net.** This is essentially a large linked data structure in which pointers are used to indicate associations among the data items. Figure 10.25 shows part of a semantic net in which the information obtained from the sentence

> Mary hit John.

has been circled.

RECURSION IN NATURAL LANGUAGE

Recursive structures involving sentences within sentences are common in English (as well as other languages), where the embedded sentence is called a clause. In fact, techniques for handling such structures were an early focus of research in computerized natural language processing systems. Sometimes these structures involve several layers of recursion, which blur the meaning of the sentence even though the overall structure is grammatically correct. For example, consider the sentence

> The man the horse that lost the race threw was not hurt.

This sentence involves three sentence structures—one within another. The outer sentence is

> The man was not hurt.

The next inner structure identifies the man as the one the horse threw. Within this structure is another sentence structure that identifies the horse as being the one that lost the race. The following sentences involve slightly different recursive structures:

> The picture the man the woman who lives next door hired hung fell down.

> The new cook the chef who yells a lot hired but who could not sauté was fired.

Robotics

Another application of artificial intelligence is found in the area of robotics or, from a less flamboyant perspective, machinery control. In this area, traditional techniques are applicable when the machine performs its task in a controlled

FIGURE 10.25

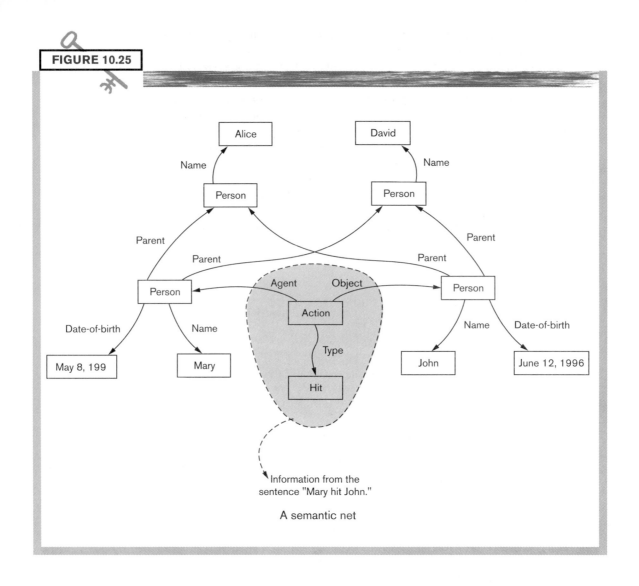

Information from the
sentence "Mary hit John."

A semantic net

environment. For example, consider the use of computer-controlled systems in factory assembly lines. In this setting a machine is often asked to repeat a task over and over in an identical way. If the task is to pick up assemblies and place them in boxes, the assemblies arrive on a conveyer belt at regular intervals, and full boxes are consistently replaced by empty ones in the same location. In this context, the machine does not really pick up an assembly but merely closes its gripper at a particular time at a particular location and moves its arm to another location where, rather than placing the assembly in a box, it merely opens its gripper. Most would agree, then, that intelligence is not embedded in such an application.

A major difference arises, however, when machines must perform their tasks in uncontrolled environments. Prominent examples occur in uninhabitable and unknown environments, as found in such exotic pursuits as space exploration, or even in our factory assembly lines. Indeed, slight modifications of the task of picking up assemblies previously cited can result in the machine's being required to exhibit significant intelligent characteristics. For example, suppose the assemblies are delivered in a box containing an assortment of other parts rather than being isolated on a conveyer belt. Then the machine's task would include recognizing the correct assemblies, moving other parts out of the way, and picking up the correct objects. Assuming that the objects were placed in the box in an arbitrary manner, the retrieval of each assembly would require a unique sequence of steps that must be developed within the machine itself. Moreover, the machine would have to monitor and comprehend the situation constantly because parts in the box might shift. Resolving such problems is an ongoing pursuit within artificial intelligence research.

Database Systems

We next consider data storage and retrieval systems, a major application of natural language processing systems. The goal is to be able to request information from these systems by means of a natural language rather than requiring the human using the system to conform to a special and somewhat technical query language.

We would also like systems that give intelligent answers to the questions posed. Traditional data storage and retrieval systems can merely retrieve facts that are explicitly requested. In contrast, a goal of artificial intelligence is to develop systems that retrieve information that is related although not directly requested. A need for such capabilities occurs in legal searches. A lawyer might need to retrieve information about all previous cases relating to the present litigation; however, whether a case relates to the current one is a concept requiring judgment. Thus, the lawyer would like a retrieval system with the intelligence to identify related material rather than merely retrieving what was explicitly requested. More precisely, a traditional approach to this problem is to require the lawyer to identify key words and phrases that should appear in any relevant case. The system then searches through all the case histories and retrieves those cases containing these words and phrases. Such a system is really merely a sieve that reduces the number of cases that must be reviewed by the lawyer and may even overlook the most important case because it deals with "infants" rather than with "minors." A truly intelligent system, however, would produce a more reliable selection.

As another example, suppose we have a database consisting of the courses taught by the professors at a university along with the grades they awarded the students. Consider the following sequence of events: We ask the database for the number of A grades awarded by Professor Johnson last semester. The database replies, "none." We conclude that Professor Johnson was a rather demanding instructor and ask for the number of F grades awarded by Professor Johnson last semester. Again, the database replies, "none." We decide that Professor Johnson considers all students to be average except in extreme cases, so we ask for the number of C grades awarded by Professor Johnson last semester. The database again replies, "none." At this point we begin to get suspicious and ask whether Professor Johnson taught a course last semester. The database replies, "no." If only it had said so in the first place!

Another problem with traditional data storage and retrieval systems is that they can respond only with information that was explicitly stored, whereas we would like systems with the ability to draw conclusions and provide information that is merely implied by the data actually residing in the database. Consider, for example, a database consisting of information about the presidents of the United States. When asked if there has ever been a president who was 10 feet tall, a traditional retrieval system would not be able to reply with the answer unless the height of each president was actually stored in the database. On the other hand, an intelligent system could reply correctly without knowing each president's height. The line of reasoning might go like this: If there had been a president who was 10 feet tall, that would have been significant and would be stored in the database. Therefore, since no president is recorded as being 10 feet tall, there have been no such presidents.

The conclusion that there have not been presidents who were 10 feet tall involves an important concept in database design—the distinction between closed-world databases and open-world databases. Loosely speaking, a **closed-world database** is one that is assumed to contain all true facts about the topic involved, whereas an open-world database does not encompass this assumption. The ability to reject the hypothesis of a 10-foot president in the previous example was based on the closed-world assumption that if the fact is not recorded then it must be false.

Although the closed-world assumption appears innocent enough on the surface, its application can lead to subtle complications. Consider a database consisting of the single statement

Item A is overstocked, or item B is overstocked.

From this statement alone we cannot conclude that item A is in fact overstocked. Thus the closed-world assumption forces us to conclude that

Item A is not overstocked.

In a similar manner, the closed-world assumption forces us to conclude that

Item B is not overstocked.

We see, then, that the closed-world assumption has led us to the contradictory conclusion that although item A or item B is overstocked, neither of them is overstocked. Understanding the limitations of such innocent-looking reasoning techniques is a goal of current research in artificial intelligence.

Still another goal of artificial intelligence research within the database environment deals with the problem of figuring out what the user of the system really wants to know or should be told instead of literally answering the question posed.

Expert Systems

An important extension of the intelligent database concept is the development of **expert systems**—software packages designed to assist humans in situations in which an expert in a specific area is required. These systems are designed to simulate the cause-and-effect reasoning that experts would accomplish if confronted with the same situations. Thus a medical expert system should propose the same procedure as a medical expert who knows that a biopsy should be performed if an abnormality is noticed and an X ray shows the presence of mass in that location.

It follows that a major task in constructing an expert system is to obtain the required knowledge from an expert. How this can be done has become an important area of research. The problem is actually twofold. One task is to procure and maintain the expert's cooperation—an undertaking that may not be easy because the questioning involved is likely to be long and frustrating, and the expert may not wish to relinquish knowledge to a system that might ultimately take the expert's place. The other complicating factor is that most experts have never considered what reasoning process they use in reaching their conclusions. When asked, "How did you know to do that?" they often reply, "I don't know."

Once these acquisition problems are overcome, the knowledge gained from the expert must be organized into a format compatible with a software system. This organization is often done by expressing the knowledge as a collection of rules in the form of if-then statements. For instance, the rule that an abnormality, confirmed by X-rays, leads to the performance of a biopsy can be expressed as

(abnormality noticed and X ray shows presence of mass)
   (implies perform biopsy)

(Those who read the optional section on declarative programming in Chapter 5 will recognize the similarity between the structure of an expert system and that of a Prolog program. This similarity is a major reason for the popularity of Prolog in the field of artificial intelligence. Indeed, Prolog is an excellent language in which to develop an expert system.)

Notice the similarity between the rules of an expert system and the productions of a production system. The first portion of the rule essentially states the preconditions for performing or concluding the statement found in the second portion. Indeed, many expert systems are essentially production systems, with the rules obtained from the human expert being the productions and the underlying reasoning based on these rules being simulated by the control system. In this context the collection of productions is often called the system's knowledge base, and the control system is sometimes referred to as an inference engine.

Do not be misled, however, into thinking that an expert system is merely a large version of the puzzle-solving system discussed earlier. Some expert systems are organized as collections of production systems that combine their efforts to solve problems. Examples include expert systems that are based on the blackboard model in which several problem-solving systems, called knowledge sources, share a common storage area called the blackboard. This blackboard contains the current state of the problem being solved and, since it is shared by all the knowledge sources, provides a medium through which the knowledge sources can contribute to the problem's solution. To coordinate the activities of the knowledge sources, a control module is provided that is given the task of activating the appropriate knowledge source at the appropriate time. In the terminology of the blackboard model, this control module is said to determine the "focus of attention" of the system.

Another distinction between an expert system and a simple production system is that an expert system is not necessarily charged with reaching a predetermined goal but is more likely to be charged with deriving well-founded advice. For example, suppose that an expert system is charged with the problem of diagnosing diseases. Ideally, one would like the systems to conclude with a definitive statement of the form "The disease is X," where in place of X the statement gives the name of the disease present. Unfortunately, such precision may not be possible. Instead, the best answer might be "The disease is most likely X" or perhaps "The disease is either X or Y. Please perform the following test to determine which is more likely." Because of this ambiguity, the control system within an expert system may choose to follow several paths through the system's state graph and report on the results of each. Indeed, if the production applied at some state is

(rheumatoid factor present and patient has pain in joints)
    (implies 80% chance of rheumatoid arthritis)

then any further reasoning based on the fact that the disease is rheumatoid arthritis has the potential of being invalid.

As in other research areas, early applications of expert systems were limited to a few areas. Today, however, the number of areas in which expert systems find applications is extensive. One catalyst for this expansion was the realization that an expert system can be separated into its reasoning component and its knowledge component. By removing the knowledge base from an existing expert system, one is left with a system of reasoning routines that is likely to be applicable in other settings as well. New expert systems in other areas can therefore be constructed merely by attaching a new knowledge base to this already existing reasoning system. This is essentially the observation that the control system we developed for solving the eight-puzzle can be applied to other problems merely by replacing the eight-puzzle productions with the productions representing those other problems.

1. Identify the ambiguities involved when translating the sentence "They are racing horses."
2. Compare the results of parsing the following two sentences. Then, explain how the sentences differ semantically.

    The farmer built the fence in the field.
    The farmer built the fence in the winter.
3. Based on the semantic net in Figure 10.25, what is the family relationship between Mary and John?
4. A database about magazine subscribers typically contains a list of subscribers to each magazine but does not contain a list of those who do not subscribe. How, then, does such a database determine that a person does not subscribe to a particular magazine?
5. What is the difference between a traditional database and a knowledge base for an expert system?

10.7 Considering the Consequences

Without a doubt, advances being made in artificial intelligence have the potential of benefiting humankind, and it is easy to become caught up in the enthusiasm generated by these potential benefits. But there are also potential perils lurking in the future whose ramifications could be as devastating as their counterparts are beneficial. The distinction is often merely one's point of view or perhaps one's position in society—one person's benefit may be another's peril. It is fitting then that we take a moment to look at advancing technology from alternative perspectives.

Some view the advancement of technology as a gift to humanity—a means of freeing humans from boring, remedial tasks and opening the door to more enjoyable lifestyles. But others see this same phenomenon as a curse that robs citizens of employment and channels wealth toward those with power. This, in fact, was a common message of the devoted humanitarian Mahatma Gandhi who was a major influence in India's struggle to free itself from the British. He repeatedly argued that India would be better served by replacing large textile mills with spinning wheels placed in the homes of the peasants. In this way, he claimed, centralized mass production that employed only a few would be replaced by a distributed mass production system that would benefit multitudes.

History is full of revolutions whose roots are found in the disproportionate distribution of wealth and privilege. If today's advancing technology is allowed to entrench such discrepancies, it could lead to catastrophic consequences.

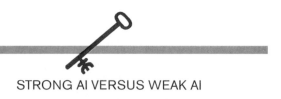

STRONG AI VERSUS WEAK AI

The conjecture that machines can be programmed to exhibit intelligent behavior is known as **weak AI** and is accepted, to varying degrees, by a wide audience today. However, the conjecture that machines can be programmed to possess intelligence and, in fact, consciousness, which is known as **strong AI,** is widely debated. Opponents of strong AI argue that a machine is inherently different from a human and thus can never feel love, tell right from wrong, and think about itself in the same way that a human does. However, proponents of strong AI argue that the human mind is constructed from small components that individually are not human and are not conscious but, when combined, are. Why, they argue, would the same phenomenon not be possible with machines?

The problem in resolving the strong AI debate is that, as observed in the text, such things as intelligence and consciousness are internal characteristics that cannot be identified directly. As Alan Turing pointed out, we credit other humans with intelligence because they behave intelligently—even though we cannot observe their internal mental states. Are we, then, prepared to grant the same latitude to a machine if it exhibits the external characteristics of consciousness? Why or why not?

But the consequences of building more and more intelligent machines is more subtle—more fundamental—than those dealing with power struggles between different segments of society. The issues strike at the very heart of humanity's self-image. In the nineteenth century, society was appalled by Charles Darwin's theory of evolution and the thought that humans may have evolved from lesser life forms. How then will society react if faced with the onslaught of machines whose mental capabilities challenge those of humans?

In the past, technology has developed slowly, allowing time for our self-image to be preserved by readjusting our concept of intelligence. In a sense we have learned to define intelligence as "that which machines cannot do." Our ancient ancestors would have interpreted the mechanical devices of the nineteenth century as having supernatural intelligence, but today we do not credit these machines with any intelligence at all. But how will humanity react if machines truly challenge the intelligence of humans or, more likely, if the capabilities of machines begin to advance faster than our ability to adapt?

You may argue that such questions border on science fiction rather than computer science. It was not too long ago, however, that many dismissed the question "How will humanity react if computers take over society?" with the same it-will-never-happen attitude. But in many respects, that day has already arrived. If a computerized database erroneously reports that you have a bad credit rating, a criminal record, or an overdrawn checking account, is it the computer's statement or your claim of innocence that will prevail? If a malfunctioning navigational system indicates that a fog-covered runway is in the wrong place, where will the aircraft land? If a machine is used to predict the public's reaction to various political decisions, which decision does a politician make? Who (or what), then, is in charge? Have we not already subordinated society to machines? Would our comfort level with today's situation change depending on whether we interpret the machines that affect our lives as making conscious decisions based on intelligence or as merely producing preprogrammed responses—even though the decisions remained the same?

We might get a clue to humanity's potential reaction to machines that challenge our intellect by considering society's response to IQ tests in the middle of the twentieth century. These tests were considered to identify a child's level of intelligence. Children in the United States were often classified by their performances on these tests and channeled into educational programs accordingly. In turn, educational opportunities were opened to those children who performed well on these tests, whereas children who performed poorly were directed toward more remedial programs of study. In short, when given a scale on which to measure an individual's intelligence, society tended to disregard the capabilities of those who found themselves on the lower end of the scale. What then would society do if the "intellectual" capabilities of machines became compatible, or even appeared to be compatible, with those of humans? Would society discard those whose abilities were seen as "inferior" to those of machines? If so, what would be the consequences for those members of society? Should a person's dignity be subject to how he or she compares to a machine?

We have already begun to see the intellectual powers of humans challenged by machines in specific fields. Machines are now capable of beating experts in chess, computerized expert systems are capable of giving medical advice, and portfolios managed by simple programs often outperform those managed by investment professionals. How do such systems affect the self-image of the individuals involved? How will an individual's self-esteem be affected as that individual is outperformed by machines in more and more areas?

Many argue that intelligence possessed by machines will always be inherently different than that of humans since humans are biological and machines are not. Thus, they argue, machines will never reproduce a human's decision making process. Machines may reach the same decisions as humans but those decisions would not be made on the same basis as those made by humans. To what extent, then, are there different kinds of intelligence, and would it be ethical for society to follow paths proposed by nonhuman intelligence?

We close with the following quotation from Joseph Weizenbaum's book, *Computer Power and Human Reason*, in which he argues against the unchecked application of computing technology.

> Computers can make judicial decisions, computers can make psychiatric judgements. They can flip coins in much more sophisticated ways than can the most patient human being. The point is that they *ought* not be given such tasks. They may even be able to arrive at "correct" decisions in some cases—but always and necessarily on bases no human being should be willing to accept.
>
> There have been many debates on "Computers and Mind." What I conclude here is that the relevant issues are neither technological nor even mathematical; they are ethical. They cannot be settled by asking

questions beginning with "can." The limits of the applicability of computers are ultimately statable only in terms of oughts. What emerges as the most elementary insight is that, since we do not now have any ways of making computers wise, we ought not now to give computers tasks that demand wisdom.

QUESTIONS/EXERCISES

1. How much of today's population would survive if the machines developed over the last 100 years were removed? What about the last 50 years? What about 20 years? Where would the survivors be located?
2. To what extent is your life controlled by machines? Who controls the machines that affect your life?
3. Where do you get the information on which you base your daily decisions? What about your major decisions? What confidence do you have in the accuracy of that information? Why?

CHAPTER REVIEW PROBLEMS

1. Sometimes the ability to answer a question depends as much on knowing the limits of knowledge as it does on the facts themselves. For example, suppose databases A and B both contain a complete list of employees who belong to the company's health insurance program, but only database A is aware that the list is complete. What could database A conclude about a member who was not on its list that database B could not?

2. In the text we briefly discussed the problems of understanding natural languages as opposed to formal programming languages. As an example of the complexities involved in the case of natural languages, identify situations in which the question "Do you know what time it is?" has different meanings.

3. As demonstrated by Problem 2, humans may use a question for a purpose other than asking. Another example is "Do you know that your tire is flat?" which is used to inform rather than to ask. Give examples of questions used to reassure, to warn, and to criticize.

4. Compare the roles of the prepositional phrases in the following two sentences (that differ by only one word):

    The pigpen was built by the barn.

    The pigpen was built by the farmer.

5. If a researcher uses computer models for studying the memorization capabilities and processes of the human mind, do the programs developed for the machine necessarily memorize to the best of the machine's abilities? Explain.

6. Which of the following activities do you expect to be performance oriented and which are simulation oriented?
    a. The design of a flight simulator
    b. The design of an automatic pilot system

c. The design of a database dealing with library materials

d. The design of a model of a nation's economy for testing theories

e. The design of a program for monitoring a patient's vital signs

7. Identify a small set of geometric properties that can be used to distinguish between the symbols O, G, C, and Q.

8. Describe the similarities between the technique of identifying characteristics by comparing them to templates and the error-correcting codes discussed in Chapter 1.

9. Describe two interpretations of the following line drawing based on whether the "corner" marked A is convex or concave:

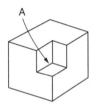

10. In the context of a production system, what is the difference between a state graph and a search tree?

11. Characterize the task of solving the Rubik's cube as a production system. (What are the states, the productions, and so on?)

12. In the text, we mentioned that a production system is often used as a technique for drawing conclusions from known facts. The states of the system are the facts known to be true at each stage of the reasoning process, and the productions are the rules of logic for manipulating the known facts. Identify some rules of logic that allow the conclusion "John is tall" to be obtained from the facts that "John is a basketball player," "Basketball

players are not short," and "John is either short or tall."

13. The tree below represents possible moves in a competitive game, showing that player X currently has a choice between move A and move B. Following the move of player X, player Y is allowed to select a move, and then player X is allowed to select the last move of the game. The leaf nodes of the tree are labeled W, L, or T, depending on whether that ending represents a win, loss, or tie for player X. Should player X select move A or move B? Why? How does selecting a "production" in a competitive atmosphere differ from a one-person game such as the eight-puzzle?

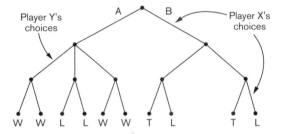

14. By considering the manipulation rules of algebra as productions, problems involving the simplification of algebraic expression can be solved in the context of a production system. Identify a set of algebraic productions that allow the equation $3/(2x + 1) = 2/(2x - 2)$ to be reduced to the form $x = 4$. What are some rules of thumb (that is, heuristic rules) used when performing such algebraic simplifications?

15. Draw the search tree that is generated by a breadth-first search in an attempt to solve the eight-puzzle from the following start state without using the assistance of any heuristic information.

	1	3
4	2	5
7	8	6

16. Draw the search tree that is generated by the algorithm of Figure 10.9 in an attempt to solve the eight-puzzle from the start state in Problem 15 if the number of tiles out of place is used as a heuristic.

17. Draw the search tree that is generated by the algorithm of Figure 10.9 in an attempt to solve the eight-puzzle from the following start state, assuming the heuristic used is the same as that developed in Section 10.3.

1	2	3
5	7	6
4		8

18. When solving the eight-puzzle, why would the number of tiles out of place not be as good a heuristic as the one used in Section 10.3?

19. What is the distinction between the technique of deciding which half of the list to consider when performing a binary search (Section 4.5) and deciding which branch to pursue when performing a heuristic search?

20. Note that if a state in the state graph of a production system has an extremely low heuristic value in comparison to the other states and if there is a production from that state to itself, the algorithm in Figure 10.9 can get caught in the loop of considering that state over and over again. Show that if the cost of executing any production in the system is at least

one, then by computing the projected cost to be the sum of the heuristic value plus the cost of reaching the state along the path being traversed, this endless looping process will be avoided.

21. What heuristic do you use when searching for a route between two cities on a large road map?

22. List two properties that a heuristic should have if it is to be useful in a production system.

23. Suppose you have two buckets. One has a capacity of exactly 3 liters; the other has a capacity of 5 liters. You can pour water from one bucket to another, empty a bucket, or fill a bucket at any time. Your problem is to place exactly 4 liters of water in the 5-liter bucket. Describe how this problem could be framed as a production system.

24. Suppose your job is to supervise the loading of two trucks, each of which can carry at most 14 tons. The cargo is a variety of crates whose total weight is 28 tons but whose individual weights vary from crate to crate. The weight of each crate is marked on its side. What heuristic would you use for dividing the crates between the two trucks?

25. Design an artificial neural network that can tell which of the following two patterns is in its field of view.

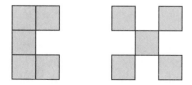

26. Design an artificial neural network that can tell which of the following two patterns is in its field of view.

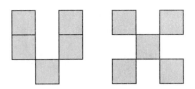

27. Design an artificial neural network that can tell which of the following four patterns is in its field of view.

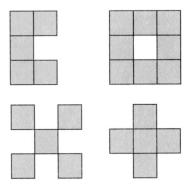

28. How do the results of parsing the following two sentences differ? How do the results of semantic analysis differ?

    Theodore rode the zebra.

    The zebra was ridden by Theodore.

29. How do the results of parsing the following two sentences differ? How do the results of semantic analysis differ?

    If X = 5 then add 1 to X else subtract 1 from X.

    If X ≠ 5 then subtract 1 from X else add 1 to X.

30. Give an example in which the closed-world assumption leads to a contradiction.

31. Give two examples where the closed-world assumption is commonly used.

32. Adjust the weights and threshold values in the artificial neural network in Figure 10.17 so that its output is 1 when both inputs are the same (both 0 or both 1) and 0 when the inputs are different (one being 0 while the other is 1).

33. Draw a diagram similar to Figure 10.4 representing the process of simplifying the algebraic expression $7x + 3 = 3x - 5$ to the expression $x = -2$.

34. Expand your answer to the previous problem to show other paths that a control system might pursue when attempting to solve the problem.

35. Draw a diagram similar to Figure 10.4 representing the reasoning process involved when concluding that "Polly can fly" from the initial facts "Polly is a parrot," "A parrot is a bird," and "All birds can fly."

36. In contrast to the statement in the preceding problem, some birds, such as an ostrich or a robin with a broken wing, cannot fly. Indeed, it would not seem reasonable to construct a deductive reasoning system in which all the exceptions to the statement "All birds can fly" are explicitly listed. How then do we as humans decide whether a particular bird can or cannot fly?

37. Explain how the semantics of the sentence "I met the fat lady's husband" depend on the context.

38. Describe how the problem of traveling from one city to another could be framed as a production system. What are the states? What are the productions?

39. Suppose you must perform three tasks, A, B, and C, that can be performed in any order (but not simultaneously). Describe how this problem can be framed as a production system and draw its state graph.

40. How does the state graph in the previous problem change if task C must be performed before task A?

41. Describe how a strategy for playing tic-tac-toe (naughts-and-crosses) could be

developed using the genetic algorithm approach.

42. The method of crossing strategies described in Section 10.5 is known as single-point crossover. An alternative is two-point crossover in which the "middle" segments of two strategies are interchanged. Show that any strategy that can be constructed using one-point crossover can also be constructed using two-point crossover, and vice versa.

43. a. If the notation (i, j), where i and j are positive integers, is used to mean "if the entry in the ith position in the list is greater than the entry in the jth position, interchange the two entries," which of the following two sequences does a better job of sorting a list of length three?

$(1, 3) (3, 2)$
$(1, 2) (2, 3) (1, 2)$

b. Use this notational system to develop a genetic algorithm for developing a program that sorts lists of length ten.

44. Changes in the context of a sentence can change the significance of the sentence as well as its meaning. In the context of Figure 10.25, how would the significance of the sentence "Mary hit John." change if the birth dates were in the 1960s rather than the 1990s? What if one were in the 1960s and the other in the 1990s?

45. Draw a semantic net representing the information in the following paragraph.

Donna threw the ball to Jack, who hit it into center field. The center fielder tried to catch it, but it bounced off the wall instead.

SOCIAL ISSUES

The following questions are provided to help you understand some of the ethical/social/legal issues associated with the field of computing as well as investigate your own beliefs and their foundations. The goal is not merely to answer these questions. You should also consider why you answered as you did and whether your justifications are consistent from one question to the next.

1. To what extent should researchers in nuclear power, genetic engineering, and artificial intelligence be held responsible for the way the results of their work are used?

2. How would you distinguish between intelligence and simulated intelligence? Do you believe there is a difference?

3. Suppose a computerized medical expert system gains a reputation within the medical community for giving sound advice. To what extent should a physician allow that system to alter his or her decisions regarding the treatment of patients? (If the physician gives a treatment contrary to that proposed by the expert system and the system turns out to be right, is the physician guilty of malpractice?) In general, if an expert system becomes well known within a field, to what degree could it hamper, rather than enhance, the ability of human experts when making their own judgments?

4. Many would argue that a computer's actions are merely consequences of how it was programmed, and thus a computer cannot possess free will. In turn, a computer should not be held responsible for its actions. Is a human's mind a computer? Are humans preprogrammed at birth? Are humans programmed by their environments? Are humans responsible for their actions?

5. Are there avenues that science should not pursue even though it may be capable of doing so? For instance, if it becomes possible to construct a machine with perception and reasoning skills comparable to those of humans, would the construction of such a machine be appropriate? What issues could the existence of such a machine raise? What are some of the issues being raised today by advancements in other scientific fields?

6. History abounds with instances in which the work of scientists and artists was affected by the political, religious, or other social influences of their times. In what ways are such issues affecting current scientific efforts? What about computer science in particular?

7. Many cultures today take at least some responsibility toward helping to retrain those whose jobs have been made redundant by advancing technology. What should/can society do as technology makes more and more of our capabilities redundant?

8. Suppose you receive a bill for $0.00. What should you do? Suppose you do nothing and 30 days later you receive a second notice of $0.00 due in your account. What should you do? Suppose you do nothing and 30 days later you receive another notice of $0.00 due in your account along with a note stating that, unless the bill is paid promptly, legal action will be taken. Who is in charge?

ADDITIONAL READING

Allen, J. *Natural Language Understanding*, 2nd ed. Reading, MA: Addison-Wesley, 1995.

Banzhaf, W., P. Nordin, R. E. Deller, and F. D. Francone. *Genetic Programming: An Introduction*. San Francisco, CA: Morgan Kaufmann, 1998.

Mitchell, M. *An Introduction to Genetic Algorithms*. Cambridge, MA: MIT Press, 1998.

Mitchell, T. M. *Machine Learning*. New York: McGraw-Hill, 1997.

Nilsson, N. *Artificial Intelligence: A New Synthesis*. San Francisco, CA: Morgan Kaufmann, 1998.

Rumelhart, D. E., and J. L. McClelland. *Parallel Distributed Processing*. Cambridge, MA: MIT Press, 1986.

Russell, S., and P. Norvig. *Artificial Intelligence: A Modern Approach*. Englewood Cliffs, NJ: Prentice-Hall, 1995.

Tanimoto, S. L. *The Elements of Artificial Intelligence Using Common Lisp*, 2nd ed. New York: Computer Science Press, 1995.

Weizenbaum, J. *Computer Power and Human Reason*. New York: W. H. Freeman, 1979.

Zurada, J. M. *Introduction to Artificial Neural Systems*. St. Paul, MN: West, 1992.

11.1 A Bare Bones Programming Language
Data Description Statements
Imperative Statements
The Scope of Bare Bones

11.2 Turing Machines
Turing Machine Fundamentals
A Specific Example

11.3 Computable Functions
Functions and Their Computation
The Church–Turing Thesis
The Universality of Bare Bones

11.4 A Noncomputable Function
Some Preliminaries
The Halting Problem

11.5 Complexity of Problems
Measuring a Problem's Complexity
Polynomial Versus Nonpolynomial Problems
NP Problems

11.6 Public Key Cryptography
Encryption via Knapsack Problems
Modular Arithmetic
Back to Encryption

c h a p t e r

THEORY OF COMPUTATION

eleven

In this chapter we discuss some theoretical ideas founded on the question of what machines can and cannot do. We start by introducing a very simple programming language. Next, we see that any problem that can be solved on a modern computer has a solution that can be expressed in that language. Thus if a programming language encompasses the features of this simple language, it is guaranteed to provide a means of expressing a solution to any problem that the machine is capable of solving. Using this language, we then discover that there are problems that today's machines cannot solve and that apparently no future algorithmic machine will be able to solve. Finally, we find that even among the machine-solvable problems, there are problems whose solutions are so complex that they are apparently unsolvable from any practical point of view.

11.1 A Bare Bones Programming Language

Let us assume that we have been asked to design a new imperative programming language that can serve as a general-purpose programming language well into the future. Our task is complicated by the fact that we cannot foresee the particular applications that the future will bring. How, then, can we guarantee that our language will contain those features required to express solutions to any problems future programmers may encounter?

Our answer is to design our language to encompass the power of algorithmic processes themselves. That is, we want to ensure that if a problem can be solved algorithmically, then an algorithm for solving that problem can be expressed in our language. Hence, if a future programmer finds that a problem cannot be solved using our language, then the reason will not be a fault of our language. Instead, it will be that there is not an algorithm for solving the problem. A programming language with this property is called a **universal programming language.**

Let us also assume that considerations of expense dictate that we not provide an abundance of features that merely enhance convenience. Our task is to design a powerful yet concise programming language.

In this section we describe an imperative programming language that fulfills these requirements. Because our language has few of the conveniences found in other languages, it is fitting that we refer to it as Bare Bones. Indeed, our language isolates the minimum requirements of a general-purpose programming language.

Data Description Statements

As we have seen, the data description statements found in high-level programming languages allow programmers the luxury of thinking in terms of arrays of numeric values and strings of alphabetic characters, even though the machine itself does not associate interpretations to the bit patterns representing these objects. The machine merely manipulates the patterns as directed by the instructions being executed. Before being presented to a machine for execution, a high-level instruction directing that two characters in a string be interchanged must be translated into machine-level instructions to interchange two bit patterns.

In turn, the design of a programming language can be simplified by forcing the programmer to express all operations in terms of bit patterns in the first place. Such a language would have a single data type and data structure, so it would not need data description statements.

For simplicity sake, our Bare Bones language adopts this approach. All variables are considered to be of type "bit pattern of any length." Thus in a Bare Bones program we do not need declarative statements by which variable names and their associated properties are described; we can simply begin using a new variable name when it is needed, with the understanding that it refers to a bit pattern of any length.

Of course, a translator for our Bare Bones language must be able to distinguish variable names from the other terms. This is done by designing the syntax of Bare Bones so that the role of any term can be identified by its context. For this purpose, we specify that variable names consist only of letters from the traditional alphabet. Thus the strings XYZ, Bill, and abcdefghi can be used as variable names, whereas 2G5, %o, or x.y cannot. Furthermore, we adopt the policy of terminating each statement with a semicolon so that a translator can easily separate statements.

Imperative Statements

Bare Bones contains only three assignment statements, each of which takes the form of modifying the contents of the variable identified in the statement. The first allows us to associate a string of zeros with a variable. Its syntax is

clear *name;*

where *name* can be any legal variable name.

The other assignment statements are essentially opposites of each other:

incr *name;*

and

decr *name;*

Again, *name* represents any legal variable name. The first of these statements causes the value associated with the identified variable to be incremented. Here the term *increment* refers to the interpretation of bit patterns as representing numeric values in base two notation and means to change the pattern to represent the next larger integer. To illustrate, if the pattern 101 is associated with the variable Y before the statement

incr Y;

is executed, the pattern 110 is associated with Y afterward. That is, 1 is added to the value assigned to Y.

In contrast, the decr statement is used to decrement the value associated with the identified variable or, in other words, to decrease the represented value by one. An exception is when the identified variable is already associated with zero, in which case this statement leaves the value unaltered. Therefore, if the value associated with Y is 101 before the statement

decr Y;

is executed, the pattern 100 is associated with Y afterward. However, if the value of Y had been zero before executing the statement, the value would remain zero after execution.

Bare Bones contains only one control structure represented by a while-end statement pair. The statement sequence

```
while name not 0 do;
  .
  .
  .
end;
```

(where *name* represents any legal variable name) causes any statement or statement sequence positioned between the while and end statements to be repeated as long as the value of the variable *name* is not zero. To be more precise, when a while-end structure is encountered during program execution, the value of the identified variable is first compared to zero. If it is zero, the structure is skipped and execution continues with the statement following the end statement. If, however, the variable's value is not zero, the statement sequence within the while-end structure is executed and control is returned to the while statement, whereupon the comparison is conducted again. Note that the burden of loop control is partially placed on the programmer, who must explicitly request that the variable's value be altered within the loop body to avoid an infinite loop. For instance, the sequence

```
incr X;
while X not 0 do;
  incr Z;
end;
```

results in an infinite process because the value associated with X can never be zero, whereas the sequence

```
clear Z;
while X not 0 do;
  incr Z;
  decr X;
end;
```

ultimately terminates with the effect of transferring the value initially associated with X to the variable Z.

Observe that while and end statements must appear in pairs with the while statement appearing first. However, a while-end statement pair may appear within the instructions being repeated by another while-end pair. In such a case the pairing of while and end statements is accomplished by scanning the program in its written form from beginning to end while associating each end statement with the nearest preceding while statement not yet paired. Although not syntactically necessary, we often use indentation to enhance the readability of such structures.

As a closing example, the instruction sequence in Figure 11.1 results in the product of the values associated with X and Y being associated with Z, although it has the side effect of destroying any nonzero value that may have been associ-

FIGURE 11.1

```
clear Z;
while X not 0 do;
  clear W;
  while Y not 0 do;
    incr Z;
    incr W;
    decr Y;
  end;
  while W not 0 do;
    incr Y;
    decr W;
  end;
  decr X;
end;
```

A Bare Bones program for computing $X \times Y$

ated with X. (The while-end structure controlled by the variable W has the effect of restoring the original value of Y.)

Finally, we note that a Bare Bones program terminates when the end of the list of instructions is reached.

The Scope of Bare Bones

Keep in mind that although we set the stage for this section with a proposal for a usable programming language, our goal is actually to investigate what is possible, not what is practical. Bare Bones would probably prove to be awkward if used in an applied setting. On the other hand, in Sections 11.2 and 11.3 we argue that this simple language fulfills our goal of providing a no-frills universal programming language.

Although not practical in an application programming environment, languages such as Bare Bones find use within theoretical computer science. For example, in Appendix E we use Bare Bones as a tool to settle the question regarding the equivalence of iterative and recursive structures raised in Chapter 4. There we find that our suspicion of equivalence was, in fact, justified.

For now, we support our claims regarding the power of Bare Bones by demonstrating how it can be used to express some elementary operations. We first note that with a combination of the assignment statements, any value (any bit pattern) can be associated with a given variable. For example, the following sequence assigns the bit pattern 11 (the binary representation for 3) to the variable X by first clearing any previous association and then incrementing its value three times:

```
clear X;
incr X;
incr X;
incr X;
```

Another common activity in programs is to move data from one location to another. In terms of Bare Bones, this means that we need to be able to assign to one variable a bit pattern previously assigned to another. This can be accomplished by first clearing the destination and then incrementing it an appropriate number of times. In fact, we have already observed that the sequence

```
clear Z;
while X not 0 do;
  incr Z;
  decr X;
end;
```

transfers the value associated with X to Z. On the other hand, this sequence has the side effect of destroying the original value of X. To correct for this, we can introduce an auxiliary variable to which we first transfer the subject value from its initial location. We then use this auxiliary variable as the data source from which we restore the original variable while placing the subject value in the desired destination. In this manner, the movement of Tax to Extra can be accomplished by the sequence shown in Figure 11.2.

We adopt the syntax

```
move name1 to name2;
```

(where *name1* and *name2* represent variable names) as a shorthand notation for a statement structure of the form in Figure 11.2. Thus, although Bare Bones itself does not have an explicit move instruction, we often write programs as though it did, with the understanding that to convert such informal programs into real Bare Bones programs, we must replace the move statements with their equivalent while-end structures using an auxiliary variable whose name does not clash with a name already used elsewhere in the program.

QUESTIONS/EXERCISES

1. Show that the statement invert X; (whose action is to convert the value of X to zero if its initial value is nonzero and to 1 if its initial value is zero) can be simulated by a Bare Bones program segment.
2. Show that even our simple Bare Bones language contains more statements than necessary by showing that the clear statement can be replaced with combinations of other statements in the language.

FIGURE 11.2

```
clear Aux;
clear Extra;
while Tax not 0 do;
    incr Aux;
    decr Tax;
end;
while Aux not 0 do;
    incr Tax;
    incr Extra;
    decr Aux;
end;
```

A Bare Bones implementation of the instruction "move Tax to Extra"

3. Show that the if-then-else structure can be simulated using Bare Bones. That is, write a program sequence in Bare Bones that simulates the action of the statement

    if X not 0 then S1 else S2;

    where S1 and S2 represent arbitrary statement sequences.
4. Show that each of the Bare Bones statements can be expressed in terms of the machine language of Appendix C. (Thus, Bare Bones can be used as a programming language for such a machine.)
5. How can negative numbers be dealt with in Bare Bones?

11.2 Turing Machines

In Section 11.1 we claimed that Bare Bones is a universal programming language, meaning that with Bare Bones we can express a solution for any problem that machines are capable of solving. We discuss this claim in more detail in Section 11.3, but first we must develop a better understanding of the capabilities of machines themselves.

Turing Machine Fundamentals

We now consider the class of computing machines known as **Turing machines.** These machines were introduced by Alan M. Turing in 1936 as a tool for studying the power of algorithmic processes and are still used for that purpose today. Keep in mind that Turing "invented" these machines before technology could produce them. Thus a Turing machine is a conceptual device rather than an actual machine.

A Turing machine consists of a control unit that can read and write symbols on a tape by means of a read/write head (Figure 11.3). The tape extends indefinitely at both ends and is divided into cells, each of which can contain any one of a finite set of symbols. This set is called the machine's alphabet.

At any time during a Turing machine's computation, the machine must be in one of a finite number of conditions, called states. A Turing machine's computation begins in a special state called the start state and ceases when the machine reaches another special state known as the halt state.

A Turing machine's computation consists of a sequence of steps that are executed by the machine's control unit. Each step consists of observing the symbol in the current tape cell (the one viewed by the read-write head), writing a symbol in that cell, possibly moving the read-write head one cell to the left or right, and then shifting states. The exact action to be performed is determined by a program that tells the control unit what to do based on the

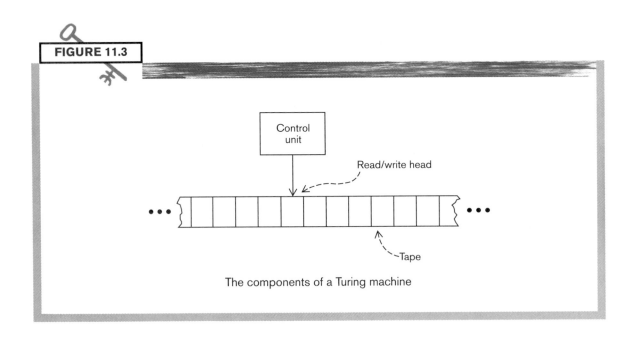

FIGURE 11.3

The components of a Turing machine

machine's state and the contents of the current tape cell.

Being conceptual in nature, a Turing machine can be implemented in a variety of forms. In fact, today's general-purpose computers are essentially Turing machines (except that their memories are finite, whereas an abstract Turing machine has an unlimited supply of tape). The CPU is the control unit, whose states are the various bit pattern configurations that can be assigned to the registers; the machine's memory takes the place of the traditional tape storage system; and the alphabet consists of the symbols 0 and 1.

This similarity between Turing machines and the machines of today is not completely coincidental. It was Turing's objective to design an abstract machine that captured the essence of computational processes. It is fitting, then, for the machines of today to incorporate the basic features identified by Turing.

THE ORIGINS OF TURING MACHINES

Alan Turing developed the concept of a Turing machine in the 1930s, well before technology was capable of providing the machines we know today. In fact, Turing's motivation was the concept of a human performing computations with pencil and paper. Turing's goal was to provide a model by which the limits of "computational processes" could be studied. The time was shortly after the publication in 1931 of Gödel's famous paper exposing the limitations of computational systems, and a major research effort was being directed toward understanding these limitations. In the same year that Turing presented his model (1936), Emil Post presented another model (now known as Post production systems) that has been shown to have the same capabilities as Turing's. As a testimony to the insights of these early researchers, their models of computational systems still serve as valuable tools in computer science research.

The significance of Turing machines in theoretical computer science lies in the conjecture that (according to the Church–Turing thesis, which we will discuss later) the computational power of Turing machines is as great as any algorithmic system. That is, if a problem cannot be solved by a Turing machine, then it cannot be solved by any algorithmic system. Thus Turing machines are simple in design yet represent a theoretical bound on the capabilities of actual machines. In turn, Turing machines are useful as tools for investigating the limitations of machines and of algorithmic processes themselves.

A Specific Example

Let us consider an example of a specific Turing machine. For this purpose, we represent the machine's tape as a horizontal strip divided into cells in which we can record symbols from the machine's alphabet. We indicate the machine's current position on the tape by placing a pointer under the current cell. The alphabet for our example consists of the symbols 0, 1, and *. The tape of our machine might appear as follows:

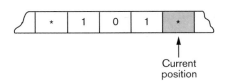

Current
position

By interpreting a string of symbols on the tape as representing binary numbers separated by asterisks, we recognize that this particular tape contains the value 5. Our Turing machine is designed to increment such a value on the tape by 1. More precisely, it assumes that the starting position is at an asterisk marking the right end of a string of 0s and 1s, and it proceeds to alter the bit pattern to the left so that it represents the next larger integer.

The states for our machine are START, ADD, CARRY, NO CARRY, OVERFLOW, RETURN, and HALT. The actions corresponding to each of these states and the content of the current cell are described in the table in Figure 11.4. We assume that the machine always begins in the START state.

Let us apply this machine to the tape pictured earlier that contains the value 5. Observe that when in the START state with the current cell containing * (as is our case), we are instructed by the table to rewrite the *, move our position one

FIGURE 11.4

Current state	Current cell content	Value to write	Direction to move	New state to enter
START	*	*	Left	ADD
ADD	0	1	Left	NO CARRY
ADD	1	0	Left	CARRY
ADD	*	*	Right	HALT
CARRY	0	1	Left	NO CARRY
CARRY	1	0	Left	CARRY
CARRY	*	1	Left	OVERFLOW
NO CARRY	0	0	Left	NO CARRY
NO CARRY	1	1	Left	NO CARRY
NO CARRY	*	*	Right	RETURN
OVERFLOW	(ignored)	*	Right	RETURN
RETURN	0	0	Right	RETURN
RETURN	1	1	Right	RETURN
RETURN	*	*	No move	HALT

A Turing machine for incrementing a value

cell to the left, and enter the ADD state. Having done this, our situation can be described as follows:

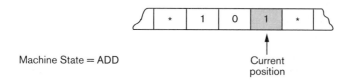

Machine State = ADD

Current position

To proceed, we look at the table to see what to do when in the ADD state with the current cell containing 1. The table tells us to replace the 1 in the current cell with 0, move one cell to the left, and enter the CARRY state. Our situation can then be described by the following:

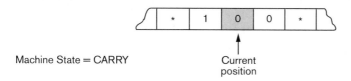

Machine State = CARRY

Current position

We again refer to the table to see what to do next and find that when in the CARRY state with the current cell containing 0, we should replace the 0 with 1, move one cell to the left, and enter the NO CARRY state. After doing this our situation is as follows:

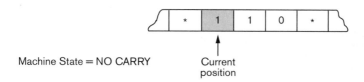

Machine State = NO CARRY

Current position

From this situation, the table instructs us to proceed by replacing the 1 in the current cell with another 1, move one cell to the left, and remain in the NO CARRY state. Consequently, we find our machine in the following condition:

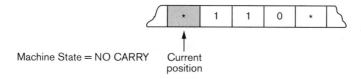

Machine State = NO CARRY

Current position

Now the table tells us to rewrite the asterisk in the current cell, move one position to the right, and enter the RETURN state. Continuing in this fashion, we remain in the RETURN state as we move back to the right cell by cell until we finally arrive at the condition as follows:

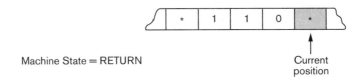

Machine State = RETURN

Current position

At this point, we see that the table instructs us to rewrite the asterisk in the current cell and HALT. The machine thus stops in the following configuration (the symbols on the tape now represent the value 6 as desired):

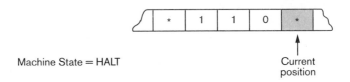

Machine State = HALT

Current position

In closing, we note that this example has shown how a Turing machine can perform the action described by the statement

incr X;

in the Bare Bones language of Section 11.1.

QUESTIONS/EXERCISES

1. Apply the Turing machine described in this section, starting with the following initial status:

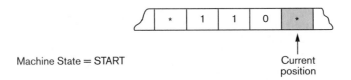

Machine State = START

Current position

2. Describe a Turing machine that replaces a string of zeros and ones with a single zero.
3. Describe a Turing machine that decrements the value on the tape if it is greater than zero or leaves the value unaltered if it is zero.
4. Identify an everyday situation in which calculating takes place. How is that situation analogous to a Turing machine?

11.3 Computable Functions

Our goal is to use Turing machines to investigate the power of our Bare Bones programming language. But first we need a method of measuring computing power. The concept of computable functions leads to such a method.

Functions and Their Computation

Let us consider the actions of a computer at a very fundamental level. If we were to take snapshots of the machine's storage facilities before and after executing a program, we would find one collection of bit values before the execution and another collection afterward. Thus a program actually does only one thing: direct the conversion of some initial collection of bits, which we will call the input, into another collection, which we will call the output. This association between inputs and outputs is called a **function.** Many functions are so common that they have been given names, such as addition, which with each input pair associates an output value equal to the sum of the inputs; multiplication, which again accepts an input pair but produces an output equal to the product of the inputs; and the successor function, which with each input value associates an output that is one greater than the input.

The process of determining an output of a function from its input values is called *computing the function.* In turn, the action of a computer when executing a program can be considered that of computing a function. This insight provides a means of measuring the computational power of a machine or, in fact, any computational system. We need merely identify the functions that the system is capable of computing and use this set as the measure. If one machine or algorithmic system is capable of computing more functions than another, the former is considered to be more powerful.

Consider, for example, a system in which function outputs are predetermined and recorded in a table along with their associated inputs. Each time the output of a function is required we merely look for the given input in the table and find the required output. Thus the computation of the function is reduced to the process of searching the table. Such systems are convenient but limited because many functions cannot be represented in tabular form. An example is shown in Figure 11.5 where we have attempted to display the successor function. Since there is no limit to the list of possible input/output pairs, the table is destined to be incomplete. The addition function suffers the same fate—no table can display all the possible inputs and outputs for addition.

Another approach for determining a function's output values would be to describe how to compute the output rather than trying to display all possible input/output combinations in a table. We could, for example, use algebraic formulas to describe the input/output associations of many functions. To describe

FIGURE 11.5

Input	Output
0	1
1	10
10	11
11	100
100	101
101	110
110	111
111	1000
1000	1001
.	.
.	.
.	.

The successor function

the function whose output is the value of an original investment of P that has earned an annually compounded interest rate of r for n years, we could write

$$V = P(1 + r)n$$

which describes how the computation is done rather than presenting the results in tabular form. In a similar manner, the successor function could be described by

$$Output = Input + 1$$

But the expressive power of algebraic formulas has its limitations as well. There are functions whose input/output relationships are too complex to be described by algebraic manipulations of the function's input values. Examples include the trigonometric functions such as sine and cosine. If pressed to calculate the sine of 38 degrees, you might draw the appropriate triangle, measure its side, and calculate the desired ratio—a process that cannot be expressed in terms of algebraic manipulations of the value 38. Your pocket calculator also struggles with the task of computing the sine of 38 degrees. In reality, it is forced to apply rather sophisticated mathematical techniques to obtain a very good approximation to the sine of 38 degrees, which it reports to you as being the exact answer.

We see, then, that as we consider functions whose input/output relationships are more and more complex, we are forced to apply more complex algorithms for computing the relationships, and thus we are forced to find more powerful techniques for describing these algorithms.

A striking result from mathematics is that there are functions whose input/output relationships are so complex that there is no well-defined, step-by-step process for determining the function's output based on its input value. That is, there are functions whose input/output relationships cannot be determined by any algorithmic means. These functions are said to be noncomputable, whereas the functions whose output values can be determined algorithmically from their input values are said to be **computable.**

Since there is no algorithmic method of finding the output values of the non-computable functions, these functions lie beyond the powers of today's, as well as tomorrow's, computers. Remember that to have a machine perform a task, we must first find an algorithm for performing that task. Thus understanding the boundary between the computable and noncomputable functions is equivalent to understanding the limitations of computers in general. The Church–Turing thesis represents an important step toward identifying this boundary.

The Church–Turing Thesis

We have already seen that finite tables and algebraic formulas are insufficient for describing the input/output relationships of all computable functions. For example, we claimed that the trigonometric functions cannot be described by either method. Alan Turing developed the concept of a Turing machine in an attempt to establish a single context in which all the computable functions could be described.

Consider again the Turing machine example of Section 11.2. This machine can be used to find the output values for the successor function by placing the input value in its binary form on the tape, running the machine until it halts, and reading the output value from the tape. In other words, the Turing machine described in Section 11.2 calculates the successor function outputs for us. A function that can be computed in this manner by a Turing machine is said to be **Turing computable.**

Turing's conjecture was that the Turing computable functions were the same as the computable functions. In other words, he conjectured that the computational power of Turing machines encompasses that of any algorithmic system or, equivalently, that (in contrast to such approaches as tables and algebraic formulas) the Turing machine concept provides a context in which all the computable functions can be described. Today, this conjecture is often referred to as the **Church–Turing thesis,** in reference to the contributions made by both Alan Turing and Alonzo Church. Since Turing's initial work, much evidence has been collected to support this thesis, and today the Church–Turing thesis is widely accepted. That is, the computable functions and the Turing-computable functions are considered one and the same.

The significance of this conjecture is that it gives insight to the capabilities and limitations of computing machinery. More precisely, it establishes the set of Turing-computable functions as a test set to which the computational powers of various computational systems can be compared. If a computational system is capable of computing all the Turing-computable functions, it is considered to be a universal system.

The Universality of Bare Bones

As an example of the significance of the Church–Turing thesis, let us apply it to confirm our claim that Bare Bones is a universal programming language. First, we observe that any program written in Bare Bones can be thought of as directing the computation of a function. The function's input consists of the values given to certain variables prior to executing the program, and the function's output consists of the values of certain variables when the program terminates. To compute the function, we merely execute the program, starting with the input variables containing the proper values, and observe the output variables when the program terminates.

Under these conditions the program

```
incr X;
```

directs the computation of the same function (the successor function) that is computed by the Turing machine example of Section 11.2. Indeed, it increases the value associated with X by one. Likewise, if we consider the variables X and Y as inputs and the variable Z as the output, the program

```
move Y to Z;
while X not 0 do;
  incr Z;
  decr X;
end;
```

directs the computation of the addition function.

Thus we see that the Bare Bones programming language can be used to describe the input/output relationships of functions. In fact, researchers have shown that the Bare Bones programming language can be used to describe exactly the same input/output relationships that can be computed by Turing machines.

This equivalence is what we need to complete our solution to the problem posed in Section 11.1 of developing a simple yet powerful programming language. Since any Turing-computable function can be computed by a program written in Bare Bones, then (by the Church–Turing thesis) any computable function can be computed by a program written in Bare Bones. That is, Bare Bones is a universal programming language in the sense that if an algorithm exists for solving a problem, then that problem can be solved by some Bare

Bones program. In turn, Bare Bones could theoretically serve as a general-purpose programming language.

We say *theoretically* because such a language is certainly not as convenient as the high-level languages introduced in Chapter 5. However, each of those languages essentially contains the features of Bare Bones as its core. It is, in fact, this core that ensures the universality of each of those languages; all the other features in the various languages are included for convenience.

QUESTIONS/EXERCISES

1. Identify other functions whose output can be described as an algebraic expression involving its input.
2. Identify a function that cannot be described in terms of an algebraic formula. Is your function nonetheless computable?
3. Describe the function computed by the following Bare Bones program, assuming the function's input is represented by X and its output by Z:

```
clear Z;
while X not 0 do;
  incr Z;
  incr Z;
  decr X;
end;
```

4. Describe a Turing machine that ultimately halts for some inputs but never halts for others.

11.4 A Noncomputable Function

We now identify a function that is not Turing computable and so, by the Church–Turing thesis, is widely believed to be noncomputable in the general sense.

Some Preliminaries

Our presentation of a noncomputable function requires the understanding of two additional concepts. The first is Gödel numbering, which refers to a technique initially used by Kurt Gödel for assigning a unique nonnegative integer to each object in a collection. The objects in Gödel's case were such things as formulas and proofs. In our case, they are programs written in Bare Bones. Gödel's system was built around the properties of prime numbers and consisted of a more complex process than we need here. For our purpose, the process summarized in Figure 11.6 suffices. We first consider any program written in Bare

FIGURE 11.6

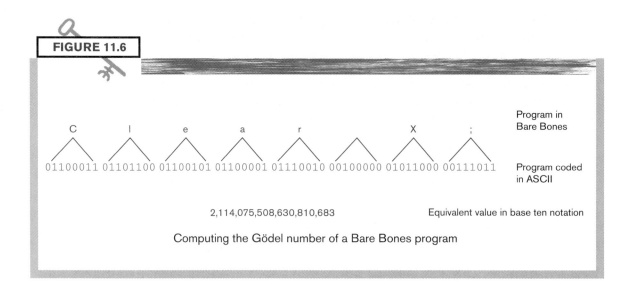

C	l	e	a	r		X	;	Program in Bare Bones
01100011	01101100	01100101	01100001	01110010	00100000	01011000	00111011	Program coded in ASCII

2,114,075,508,630,810,683   Equivalent value in base ten notation

Computing the Gödel number of a Bare Bones program

Bones as one single long string of characters (in which the instructions are separated by semicolons). We then code each character of this string into a bit pattern using the ASCII code. After this, any program appears as a long string of 0s and 1s that can be interpreted as representing a (rather large) number in binary notation. In this manner we can associate any program written in Bare Bones with a unique positive integer.

It is not important in our case whether the positive integers associated with the programs in Bare Bones are obtained by the process just described or by Gödel's original technique. The important point is that such an association is possible. Having established this possibility, we continue by assuming such an association has been carried out. Moreover, we call the number associated with a given program that program's **Gödel number.**

The second concept we need is that of a self-terminating program. To introduce this idea, let us first consider the Bare Bones program

```
while X not 0 do;
  incr X;
end;
```

If we execute this program with the initial value of X being 0, the loop will not be executed and the program will quickly terminate. However, if we execute the program with any other initial value of X, the loop will be executed forever and the program will never terminate.

Now observe that any program written in Bare Bones must contain at least one variable name, and since each such variable consists of a string of letters, the variable names in a given program can be placed in alphabetical order. In terms of this order, we can speak of the first variable of a program. We say that a program is **self-terminating** if the program ultimately terminates after being started with its first variable initialized to the program's own Gödel number and its other variables being set to 0. (Note that this use of the program probably has no relation to the purpose for which the program was originally written.) Any program written in Bare Bones either is self-terminating or it is not.

As an example, the previous program is not self-terminating. More precisely, we know that the Gödel number of the program is not zero. Thus, if we set the variable X equal to the program's Gödel number and executed the program, the process would never terminate.

Essentially, a program is self-terminating if and only if it ultimately terminates if started with itself as its input. Thus the concept of a self-terminating program involves self-reference—the idea of an object referring to itself. This ploy has repeatedly led to amazing results in mathematics from such informal curiosities as the statement "This statement is false" to the more serious paradox represented by the question "Does the set of all sets contain itself?" What we have done, then, in defining the concept of a self-terminating program, is to set the stage for a line of reasoning similar to "If it does, then it doesn't; but, if it doesn't, then it does," as we see shortly.

The Halting Problem

We are now in position to define a function that is not computable. It associates with each Gödel number of a program in Bare Bones (the function's input) a 1 or a 0 (the function's output) depending on whether the program in question is self-terminating. More precisely we define the function so that Gödel numbers of self-terminating programs produce the output value 1 and Gödel numbers of non–self-terminating programs produce the output value 0. The problem of computing this function is actually the problem of calculating whether programs ultimately terminate, or halt, after being started from a particular initial state. It is therefore commonly referred to as the **halting problem.**

Our task is to show that the preceding function is not computable. To this end, we show that the assumption that it is computable leads to an impossible situation. Consequently, we are forced to conclude that the function is not computable.

Referring to Figure 11.7, we proceed with the assumption that the function is computable. This means that there must be a program in Bare Bones that computes the function. In other words, there is a program that halts with its output equal to 1 if its input variable is the Gödel number of a self-terminating program and halts with its output equal to 0 otherwise. We can assume that the variables in this program are named so that the input variable is the first in alphabetical order; otherwise we could simply rename them to have this property. Likewise, we may assume that the program's output variable is named X.

We could then modify the program by attaching the statements

```
while X not 0 do;
end;
```

FIGURE 11.7

FIRST: Propose the existence of a program that,

given the Gödel number of a program

↓

Proposed program

↓

will halt with variable X equal to 1 if the input represents a self-terminating program, or 0 otherwise.

THEN: If such a program exists, we could modify it by

adding a while-end structure

Proposed program

while X not 0 do; end;

to produce a new program with Gödel number g,

HOWEVER: If this new program were not self-terminating and

we started it with input g,

↓

execution would reach this point with X equal to 0,

Proposed program

while X not 0 do; end;

↓

so this loop would be skipped

and execution would halt;

i.e., if the new program is not self-terminating, then it is self-terminating

Proving the unsolvability of the halting program

FIGURE 11.7

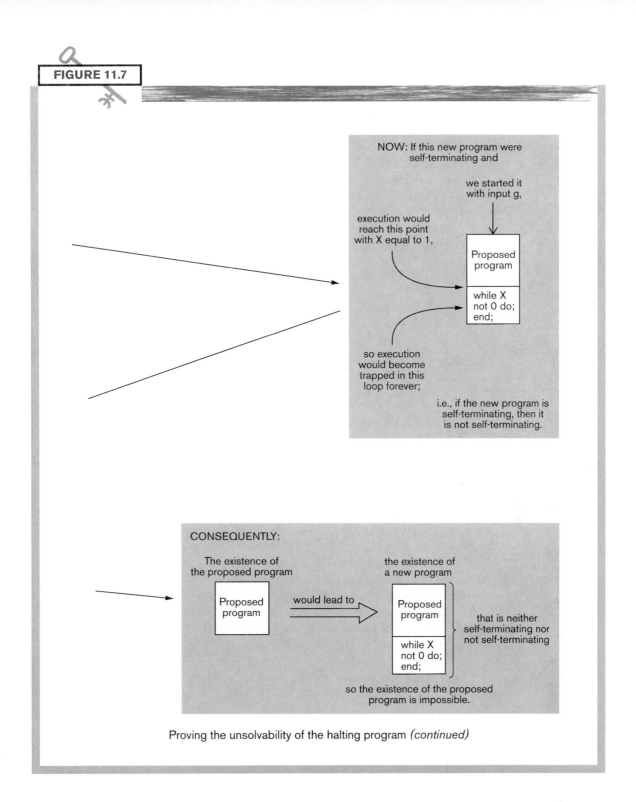

NOW: If this new program were self-terminating and

we started it with input g,

execution would reach this point with X equal to 1,

Proposed program

while X not 0 do; end;

so execution would become trapped in this loop forever;

i.e., if the new program is self-terminating, then it is not self-terminating.

CONSEQUENTLY:

The existence of the proposed program

Proposed program

would lead to

the existence of a new program

Proposed program

while X not 0 do; end;

that is neither self-terminating nor not self-terminating

so the existence of the proposed program is impossible.

Proving the unsolvability of the halting program *(continued)*

at its end, producing a new program. This new program must be either self-terminating or not. However, we are about to see that it can be neither. In particular, if this new program were self-terminating and we ran it with its input being equal to its own Gödel number, then when its execution reached the while statement that we added, the variable X would contain a 1. (To this point the new program is identical to the original program that produced a 1 if its input was the Gödel number of a self-terminating program.) At this point, the program's execution would be caught forever in the while-end structure because we made no provisions for X to be decremented within the loop. But this contradicts our assumption that the new program is self-terminating. Therefore we must conclude that the new program is not self-terminating.

If, however, this new program were not self-terminating and we executed it with its input being its own Gödel number, it would reach the added while statement with X being assigned the value 0. (This occurs because the statements preceding the while statement constitute the original program that produces an output of 0 when its input represents a program that is not self-terminating.) In this case, the loop in the while-end structure would be avoided and the program would halt. But this is the property of a self-terminating program, so we are forced to conclude that the new program is self-terminating, just as we were forced to conclude earlier that it is not self-terminating.

In summary, we see that we have the impossible situation of a program that on the one hand must be either self-terminating or not and on the other hand can be neither. Consequently, the assumption that led to this dilemma must be false. In other words, the function in question is not computable.

With this conclusion, we have found an example of a function that is not Turing computable and hence, by the Church–Turing thesis, accepted as being noncomputable in the general context. We can conclude that the halting problem is an example of an **unsolvable problem,** meaning that its solution requires finding the output of a noncomputable function and therefore lies beyond the capabilities of computing machinery.

In closing, we should relate what we have just discussed to the ideas in Chapter 10. There, a major underlying question was whether the powers of computing machines include those required for intelligence itself. We have now seen that there are limits to the abilities of machines that technology cannot overcome. They can solve only problems with algorithmic solutions. The question, then, is whether natural intelligence embodies more than the execution of algorithmic processes. Needless to say, this is a highly debatable and sometimes emotional issue.

QUESTIONS/EXERCISES

1. What value would our Gödel numbering technique associate with the following simple Bare Bones program?

   decr X;

2. Is the program "incr X; decr Y;" self-terminating?

3. What is wrong with the following scenario?

> In a certain community, everyone owns his or her own house. The house painter of the community claims to paint all those and only those houses that are not painted by their owners.

(*Hint:* Who paints the house painter's house?)

11.5 Complexity of Problems

In Section 11.4 we investigated problems in terms of their solvability. In this section we are interested in the question of whether a solvable problem has a practical solution. We will find that some problems that are theoretically solvable are so complex that they are essentially unsolvable from a practical point of view.

Measuring a Problem's Complexity

We begin by returning to our study of algorithm efficiency that we started in Section 4.6. There we used big theta notation to classified algorithms according to the time required to execute them. We found that the insertion sort algorithm is in the class $\Theta(n^2)$, the sequential search algorithm is in $\Theta(n)$, and the binary search algorithm is in $\Theta(\lg n)$. We now use this classification system to help us identify the complexity of problems. Our goal is to develop a classification system that tells us which problems are more complex than others and ultimately which problems are so complex that their solutions lie beyond practicality.

The reason that our present study is based on our knowledge of algorithm efficiency is that we wish to measure the complexity of a problem in terms of the complexity of its solutions. We consider a simple problem to be one that has a simple solution; a complex problem is one that does not have a simple solution. Note that the fact that a problem has a difficult solution does not necessarily mean that the problem is necessarily complex. After all, a single problem will typically have many solutions. Thus to conclude that such a problem is complex would require that we show that none of these solutions are simple.

In computer science, the problems of interest are those that are solvable by machines. The solutions to these problems are formulated as algorithms. Thus the complexity of a problem is determined by the properties of the algorithms that solve that problem. More precisely, the complexity of the simplest algorithm for solving a problem is considered to be the complexity of the problem itself.

But how do we measure the complexity of an algorithm? Unfortunately, the term *complexity* has different interpretations. One deals with the amount of decision making and branching involved in the algorithm. In this light, a complex algorithm would be one that involves a twisted, entwined set of directions. This interpretation might be compatible with the point of view of a software engineer who is interested in issues relating to algorithm discovery and representation, but it does not capture the concept of complexity from a machine's point of view. A machine does not really make decisions when selecting the next instruction for execution but merely follows its machine cycle over and over, each time executing the instruction that is indicated by the program counter. Consequently, a machine can execute a set of tangled instructions as easily as it can execute a list of instructions in a simple sequential order. This interpretation of complexity, therefore, tends to measure the difficulty encountered during an algorithm's development rather than the complexity of the algorithm itself.

An interpretation that more accurately reflects the complexity of an algorithm is obtained by considering algorithms from a machine's point of view. In this context, we measure an algorithm's complexity in terms of the time required for its execution, which is proportional to the number of steps that must be performed. Note that this is not the same as the number of instructions appearing in the written program. A loop whose body consists of a single print statement but whose control requests the body's execution 100 times is equivalent to 100 print statements when executed. Such a routine is, therefore, considered more complex than a list of 50 individually written print statements, even though the latter appears longer in written form. The point is that this meaning of *complexity* is ultimately concerned with the time it takes a machine to execute a solution and not with the size of the program representing the solution. A problem is considered complex if all its solutions require a lot of time, and this concept of complexity is often referred to as **time complexity.**

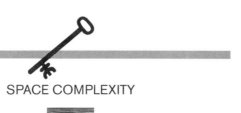

SPACE COMPLEXITY

An alternative to measuring complexity in terms of time is to measure storage space requirements instead—resulting in a measure known as **space complexity.** That is, the space complexity of a problem is determined by the amount of storage space required to solve the problem. In the text we have seen that the time complexity of sorting a list with n entries is $O(n \lg n)$. The space complexity of the same problem is no more than $O(n + 1) = O(n)$. Indeed, sorting a list with n entries using the insertion sort requires space for the list itself plus space to store a single entry on a temporary basis. Thus, if we were asked to sort longer and longer lists, we would find that the time required for each task would increase more rapidly than the space required. This is in fact a common phenomenon. Since it takes time to use space, a problem's space complexity never grows more rapidly than its time complexity.

There are often tradeoffs made between time and space complexity. In some applications it may be advantageous to perform certain computations in advance and store the results in a table from which they can be retrieved quickly when needed. Such a "table lookup" technique decreases the time required by the final system at the expense of the additional space required by the table. On the other hand, data compression is often used to reduce storage requirements at the expense of the additional time required to compress and decompress the data.

This, then, is where our previous study of algorithm efficiency is significant. The study of an algorithm's efficiency is the study of the algorithm's time complexity—the two are merely inverses of each other. Whereas an algorithm in $\Theta(\lg n)$ is more efficient than an algorithm in $\Theta(n)$, the algorithm in $\Theta(n)$ is more complex than the algorithm in $\Theta(\lg n)$. Thus, in terms of time complexity, the sequential search algorithm is a more complex solution to the problem of searching a list than is the binary search algorithm, even though students often consider the binary search to be harder to understand.

Let us now consider the classification of problems according to their time complexities. We define the (time) complexity of a problem to be $\Theta(f(n))$, where $f(n)$ is some mathematical expression in n, if there is an algorithm for solving the problem whose time complexity is in $\Theta(f(n))$ and no other algorithm for solving the problem has a better time complexity. That is, the (time) complexity of a problem is defined to be the (time) complexity of its best solution. Unfortunately, finding the best solution to a problem and knowing that it is the best is often a difficult problem in itself. In such situations, big O notation (a variation of big theta notation) is used to represent what is known about a problem's complexity. More precisely, if $f(n)$ is a mathematical expression in n and if a problem can be solved by an algorithm in $\Theta(f(n))$, then we say that the problem is in $O(f(n))$, which is read "big oh of $f(n)$." Thus, to say that a problem belongs to $O(f(n))$ means that it has a solution whose complexity is in $\Theta(f(n))$ but it could possibly have a better solution.

Our investigation of searching and sorting tells us that the problem of searching within a list of length n (when all we know is that the list has previously been sorted) is in $O(\lg n)$ since the binary search algorithm solves the problem. Moreover, researchers have shown that the searching problem is actually in $\Theta(\lg n)$ so the binary search represents an optimal solution for that problem. In contrast, we know that the problem of sorting a list of length n (when we know nothing about the distribution of the values in it) is in $O(n^2)$ since the insertion sort algorithm solves the problem. The problem of sorting, however, is known to be in $\Theta(n \lg n)$, which tells us that the insertion sort algorithm is not an optimal solution (in the context of time complexity).

An example of a better solution to the sorting problem is the merge sort algorithm. Its approach is to merge small sorted portions of the list repeatedly, each time obtaining larger sorted portions, until the entire list is in the correct order. Each merging process applies the merge algorithm that we encountered when discussing sequential files (Figure 8.2). For convenience, we present it again in Figure 11.8, this time in the context of merging two lists. The complete (recursive) merge sort algorithm is presented as the procedure called MergeSort in Figure 11.9. When asked to sort a list, this procedure first checks to see if the list is shorter than two entries. If so, the procedure's task is complete. If not, the procedure divides the list into two pieces, asks other copies of the procedure MergeSort to sort these pieces, and then merges these sorted pieces together to obtain the final sorted version of the list.

FIGURE 11.8

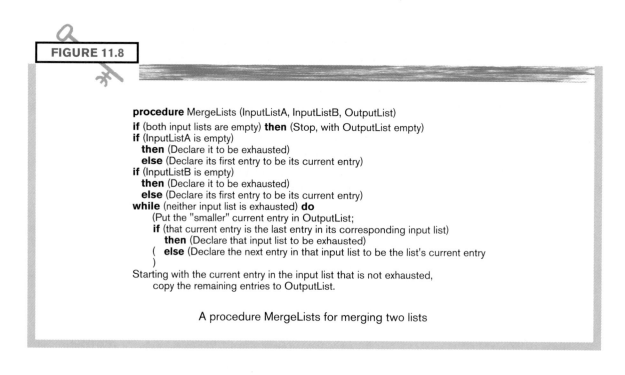

```
procedure MergeLists (InputListA, InputListB, OutputList)
if (both input lists are empty) then (Stop, with OutputList empty)
if (InputListA is empty)
   then (Declare it to be exhausted)
   else (Declare its first entry to be its current entry)
if (InputListB is empty)
   then (Declare it to be exhausted)
   else (Declare its first entry to be its current entry)
while (neither input list is exhausted) do
      (Put the "smaller" current entry in OutputList;
      if (that current entry is the last entry in its corresponding input list)
         then (Declare that input list to be exhausted)
   (   else (Declare the next entry in that input list to be the list's current entry
      )
Starting with the current entry in the input list that is not exhausted,
      copy the remaining entries to OutputList.
```

A procedure MergeLists for merging two lists

To analyze the complexity of this algorithm, we first consider the number of comparisons between list entries that must be made when merging a list of length r with a list of length s. The merge process proceeds by repeatedly comparing an entry from one list with an entry from the other and placing the smaller of the two entries in the output list. Thus each time a comparison is made, the number of entries still to be considered is reduced by one. Since there are only $r + s$ entries to begin with, we can conclude that the process of merging the two lists will involve no more than $r + s$ comparisons.

FIGURE 11.9

```
procedure MergeSort (List)
if (List has more than one entry)
   then(Apply the procedure MergeSort to sort the first half of List;
         Apply the procedure MergeSort to sort the second half of List;
         Apply the procedure MergeLists to merge the first and second
            halves of List to produce a sorted version of List
         )
```

The merge sort algorithm implemented as a procedure MergeSort

We now consider the entire merge sort algorithm. It attacks the task of sorting a list of length n in such a way that the initial sorting problem is reduced to two smaller problems, each of which is asked to sort a list of length approximately $n/2$. These two problems are in turn reduced to a total of four problems of sorting lists of length approximately $n/4$. This division process can be summarized by the tree structure in Figure 11.10, where each node of the tree represents a single problem in the recursive process and the branches below a node represent the smaller problems derived from the parent. Hence, we can find the total number of comparisons that occur in the entire sorting process by adding together the number of comparisons that occur at the nodes in the tree.

Let us first determine the number of comparisons made across each level of the tree. Observe that each node appearing across any level of the tree has the task of sorting a unique segment of the original list. This is accomplished by the merge process and therefore requires no more comparisons than there are entries in the list segment, as we have already argued. Hence, each level of the tree requires no more comparisons than the total number of entries in the list segments, and since the segments across a given level of the tree represent disjoint portions of the original list, this total is no greater than the length of the original list. Consequently, each level of the tree involves no more than n com-

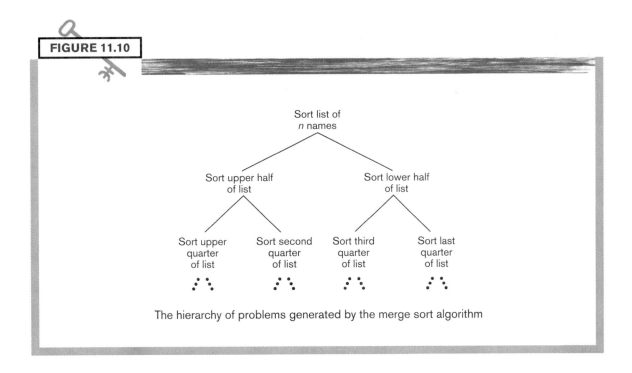

FIGURE 11.10

The hierarchy of problems generated by the merge sort algorithm

parisons. (Of course the lowest level involves sorting lists of length one or less, which involves no comparisons at all.)

Now we determine the number of levels in the tree. For this, observe that the process of dividing problems into smaller problems continues until lists of length less than two are obtained. Thus the number of levels in the tree is determined by the number of times that, starting with the value n, we can repeatedly divide by two until the result is no larger than one, which is lg n. More precisely, there are no more than $\lceil \lg n \rceil$ levels of the tree that involve comparisons, where the notation $\lceil \lg n \rceil$ represents the value of lg n rounded up to the next integer.

Finally, the total number of comparisons made by the merge sort algorithm when sorting a list of length n is obtained by multiplying the number of comparisons made at each level of the tree by the number of levels in which comparisons are made. We conclude that this is no larger than $n \lceil \lg n \rceil$. Since the graph of $n \lceil \lg n \rceil$ has the same general shape as the graph of n lg n, we conclude that the merge sort algorithm belongs to O(n lg n). Combining this with the fact that researchers tell us that the sorting problem has complexity $\Theta(n \lg n)$ implies that the merge sort algorithm represents an optimal solution to the sorting problem.

Polynomial Versus Nonpolynomial Problems

Suppose $f(n)$ and $g(n)$ are mathematical expressions. To say that $g(n)$ is bound by $f(n)$ means that as we apply these expressions to larger and larger values of n, the value of $f(n)$ will ultimately become greater than that of $g(n)$ and remain greater than $g(n)$ for all larger values of n. In other words, $g(n)$ is bound by $f(n)$ means that the graph of $f(n)$ will be above the graph of $g(n)$ for "large" values of n. For instance, the expression lg n is bound by the expression n (Figure 11.11a), and n lg n is bound by n^2 (Figure 11.11b). We say that a problem is a **polynomial problem** if the problem is in O($f(n)$), where the expression $f(n)$ is either a polynomial itself or bound by a polynomial. The collection of all polynomial problems is traditionally represented by **P**. Note that our previous investigations tell us that the problems of searching a list and of sorting a list belong to P.

To say that a problem is a polynomial problem is a statement about the time required to solve the problem. We often say that a problem in P can be solved in polynomial time or that the problem has a polynomial time solution.

Identifying the problems that belong to P is of major importance in computer science because it is closely related to the questions regarding whether problems have practical solutions. Indeed, problems that are outside the class P are characterized as having extremely long execution times, even for inputs of moderate size. Consider, for example, a problem whose solution requires 2^n steps. The exponential expression 2^n is not bound by any polynomial—if $f(n)$ is a polynomial, then as we increase the value of n, we will find that the values of 2^n will ultimately be larger than those of $f(n)$. This means that an algorithm with complexity $\Theta(2^n)$ will generally be less efficient, and thus require more

FIGURE 11.11

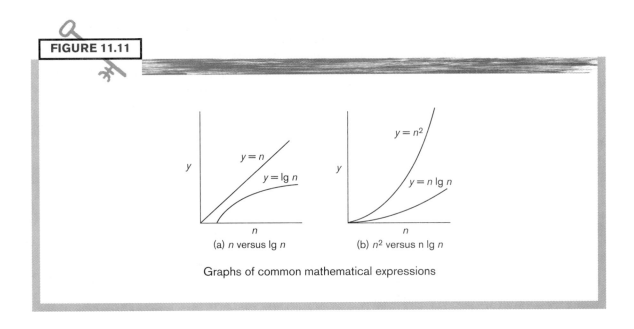

(a) *n* versus lg *n*   (b) *n*^{2} versus n lg *n*

Graphs of common mathematical expressions

time, than an algorithm with complexity $\Theta(f(n))$. An algorithm whose complexity is identified by an exponential expression is said to require exponential time.

As a particular example, consider the problem of listing all possible subcommittees that can be formed from a group of *n* people. Since there are $2^n - 1$ such subcommittees (we allow a subcommittee to consist of the entire group but do not consider the empty set to be a subcommittee), any algorithm that solves this problem must have at least $2^n - 1$ steps and thus a complexity at least that large. But, the expression $2^n - 1$, being an exponential expression, is not bound by any polynomial. Hence any solution to this problem becomes enormously time-consuming as the size of the group from which the committees are selected increases.

In contrast to our subcommittee problem, whose complexity is large merely because of the size of its output, problems exist whose complexities are large even though their ultimate output is merely a simple yes or no answer. An example involves the ability to answer questions about the truth of statements involving the addition of real numbers. For instance, we can easily recognize that the answer to the question "Is it true that there is a real number that when added to itself produces the value 6?" is yes, whereas the answer to "Is it true that there is a nonzero real number which when added to itself is 0?" is no. However, as such questions become more involved, our ability to answer them begins to fade. If we found ourselves faced with many such questions, we might be tempted to turn to a computer program for assistance. Unfortunately, the ability to answer these questions has been shown to require exponential time, so even a computer ultimately fails to produce answers in a timely manner as the questions become more involved.

The fact that the theoretically solvable problems that are not in P have such enormous time complexities leads us to conclude that these problems are essentially unsolvable from a practical point of view. In turn, the problems that have practical solutions are contained in P. Thus, an understanding of the boundaries of the class P has become an important pursuit of computer scientists.

NP Problems

Let us now consider the **traveling salesman problem,** which involves a traveling salesman who must visit each of his clients in different cities without exceeding his travel budget. His problem, then, is to find a path (starting from his home, connecting the cities involved, and returning to his home) whose total length does not exceed his allowed mileage.

The traditional solution to this problem is to consider the potential paths in a systematic manner, comparing the length of each path to the mileage limit until either an acceptable path is found or all possibilities have been considered. This approach, however, does not produce a polynomial time solution. As the number of cities increases, the number of paths that may require testing grows more rapidly than any polynomial. In turn, solving the traveling salesman problem in this manner is impractical for cases involving large numbers of cities.

We conclude that to solve this problem in a reasonable amount of time, we must find a faster algorithm. Our appetite is whetted by the observation that if a satisfactory path exists and we happen to select it first, our present algorithm terminates quite quickly. In particular, the following list of instructions can be executed quickly and has the potential of solving the problem:

> Pick one of the possible paths, and compute its total distance.
> **If** this distance is not greater than the allowable mileage,
>   **then** declare a success
>   **else** declare nothing.

However, this set of instructions is not an algorithm in the technical sense. Its first instruction is ambiguous in that it does not specify which path is to be selected. The result of executing the instruction is therefore not predetermined at the moment prior to its execution. We say that such instructions are nondeterministic, and we call an "algorithm" containing such statements a **nondeterministic algorithm.**

Note that as the number of cities increases, the time required to execute the preceding nondeterministic algorithm grows relatively slowly. The process of selecting a path is merely that of producing a list of the cities, which can be done in a time proportional to the number of cities. Moreover, the time required to compute the total distance along the chosen path is also proportional to the number of cities to be visited, and the time required to compare this total to the mileage limit is independent of the number of cities. In turn, the time required to execute the nondeterministic algorithm is bound by a polynomial. Thus it is possible to solve the traveling salesman problem by a nondeterministic algorithm in polynomial time.

Of course, our nondeterministic solution is not totally satisfactory. It relies on a lucky guess. But its existence is enough to suggest that perhaps there is a deterministic solution to the traveling salesman problem that runs in polynomial time. Whether or not this is true remains an open question. In fact, the traveling salesman problem is only one of many problems that are known to have nondeterministic solutions that execute in polynomial time but for which no deterministic polynomial time solution has yet been found. The tantalizing efficiency of the nondeterministic solutions to these problems causes some to hope that efficient deterministic solutions will be found someday, yet most believe that these problems are just complex enough to escape the capabilities of efficient deterministic algorithms.

A problem that can be solved in polynomial time by a nondeterministic algorithm is called a **nondeterministic polynomial problem,** or an **NP problem** for short. It is customary to denote the class of NP problems by **NP.** Note that all the problems in P are also in NP, since any (deterministic) algorithm can have a nondeterministic instruction added to it without affecting its performance.

Whether all of the NP problems are also in P, however, is an open question, as we have already observed in our discussion of the traveling salesman problem. In fact, this is perhaps the most widely known unsolved problem in computer science today. Its solution could have significant consequences. For example, in the next section we will learn that encryption systems have been designed whose integrity relies on the enormous time required to solve problems similar to the traveling salesman problem. If it turns out that efficient solutions to such problems exist, these encryption systems will be compromised.

Efforts to resolve the question of whether the class NP is, in fact, the same as the class P have led to the discovery of a class of problems within the class NP known as the **NP-complete problems.** These problems have the property that a polynomial time solution for any of them would provide a polynomial time solution for all the other problems in NP as well. That is, if a (deterministic) algorithm can be found that solves one of the NP-complete problems in polynomial time, then that algorithm can be extended to solve any other problem in NP in polynomial time. In turn, the class NP would be the same as the class P. The traveling salesman problem is an example of an NP-complete problem.

In summary, we have found that problems can be classified as either solvable (having an algorithmic solution) or unsolvable (not having an algorithmic

FIGURE 11.12

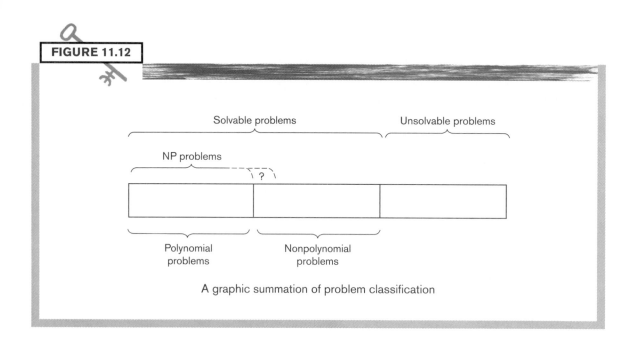

A graphic summation of problem classification

solution), as depicted in Figure 11.12. Moreover, within the class of solvable problems are two subclasses. One is the collection of polynomial problems that contains those problems with practical solutions. The second is the collection of nonpolynomial problems whose solutions are practical for only relatively small or carefully selected inputs. Finally, there are the mysterious NP problems that thus far have evaded precise classification.

QUESTIONS/EXERCISES

1. Suppose a problem can be solved by an algorithm in $\Theta(2^n)$. What can we conclude about the complexity of the problem?
2. Suppose a problem can be solved by an algorithm in $\Theta(n^2)$ as well as another algorithm in $\Theta(2^n)$. Will one algorithm always outperform the other?
3. List all of the subcommittees that can be formed from a committee consisting of the two members Alice and Bill. List all the subcommittees that can be formed from the committee consisting of Alice, Bill, and Carol. What about the subcommittees from Alice, Bill, Carol, and David?
4. Give an example of a polynomial problem. Give an example of a nonpolynomial problem. Give an example of an NP problem that as yet has not been shown to be a polynomial problem.

11.6 Public Key Cryptography

The fact that no efficient solution to an NP-complete problem is known leads to many interesting applications, one of which deals with encrypting sensitive information. In this section we investigate such an encryption technique. It involves values known as keys that are used to encrypt data and to decode encrypted data. However, the keys used for data encryption are not the same as those used to decode the encrypted information. To decode a message requires knowledge of the decoding keys. Thus the encryption keys can be widely distributed without violating the security of the system. People who know the encryption keys can encrypt messages, but they cannot decode messages that have been encrypted by others, even though the others used the same encryption keys. With such an encryption system, many different people can send secure messages to the same addressee—that common addressee being the only person to hold the decoding keys. Such encryption techniques compose a field of study known as **public key cryptography,** a term that reflects the fact that the keys used to encrypt messages can be public knowledge.

Encryption via Knapsack Problems

To describe a specific public key encryption system, we begin with the NP-complete problem known as the **knapsack problem.** This is the problem of selecting numbers from a collection so that the sum of the selected numbers is a particular value. It is called the knapsack problem because it is analogous to the problem of selecting a collection of items that exactly fill a knapsack. An example of a knapsack problem is the problem of selecting a collection of values from the list

191   691   573   337   365   730   651   493   177   354

whose sum is 2063.

The best known method for solving knapsack problems in general is to try all possible combinations systematically until a solution is found. But, if there are n values from which to select, there are 2^n different combinations to test. Thus, unless we are lucky, the time required to find the solution will be quite large. To appreciate this phenomenon for yourself, try solving the knapsack problem given above. You will find that it can be rather time-consuming, even though there are only ten values from which to choose. Imagine your frustration if there were 20 values from which to select and therefore more than a million combinations to test.

We can use knapsack problems based on the list above to encrypt messages as follows: We first represent a message as a string of bits, perhaps using ASCII or Unicode. Then, we break this string into segments of ten bits each and represent each segment by a single number. This number is obtained by adding the

POPULAR ENCRYPTION SYSTEMS

One of the most popular encryption systems used by individuals for secure Internet communication is PGP (Pretty Good Privacy), which was developed by Philip Zimmermann in 1991. PGP is a general-purpose, easy-to-use public key encryption system that is available from a variety of Internet sources at no cost for noncommercial use. The algorithm on which PGP's public key encryption is based is RSA, named in honor of its developers—Ron Rivest, Adi Shamir, and Leonard Adleman. Whereas the encryption system discussed in the text is based on the difficulty of solving large knapsack problems, RSA is based on the difficulty of finding the factors of large integers. RSA is owned by RSA Data Security, a subsidiary of Security Dynamics Technologies, and thus commercial use of RSA requires a license from RSA Data Security. You may wish to search the Web to learn about the roles that patent rights and the U.S. government's goal of limiting the export of technology have played in controlling the distribution of PGP and RSA. A good way to start would be to search for sites dealing with PGP or RSA.

values that occupy the positions in the list that are occupied by 1s in the ten-bit segment. For instance, the pattern 1001100001 would be represented by 1247. This is because the 1s in the pattern are found in the first, fourth, fifth, and tenth positions, and the sum of the corresponding values in the list (191, 337, 365, and 354) is 1247 (Figure 11.13). Likewise the pattern 0010011010 would be represented by 2131 (which is 573 + 730 + 651 + 177). In turn, the message 10011000010010011010 would be encrypted as 1247 followed by 2131.

Suppose someone intercepted this encrypted message and suppose that person even knew the list of values that was used to encrypt it. That person would still have to solve two knapsack problems to decode the message, which would be a time-consuming process. Moreover, if the size of the list used to encrypt messages were significantly larger than ten, the task of decoding intercepted messages would be completely intractable—which means that the contents of the message would be secure.

The problem with this simple system is that no one would be able to decode the message quickly—not even the addressee. What we need is a trick that would allow the addressee to solve the knapsack problems quickly, while everyone else is faced with an unbearably time-consuming task.

To obtain such a trick, we first observe that some knapsack problems are easy to solve. Suppose the values from which we are asked to select are

1 4 6 12 24 51 105 210 421 850

Each number in this list is larger than the sum of the preceding numbers. So, if we needed to select a collection of values whose sum is 995, we would know immediately that 850 must be one of the required values because the sum of all the other values would be too small. Having made this selection, our problem would be reduced to selecting numbers whose sum is 995 – 850, or 145. But this means that we must select 105 because the sum of the other possible values would be smaller than 145. Continuing in this fashion, we could quickly conclude that the values to be selected are 850, 105, 24, 12, and 4.

FIGURE 11.13

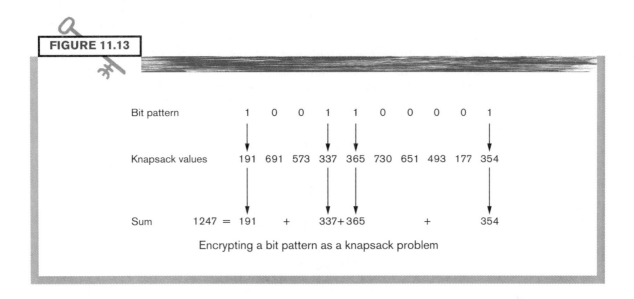

Bit pattern	1	0	0	1	1	0	0	0	0	1

Knapsack values   191 691 573 337 365 730 651 493 177 354

Sum   1247 = 191   +   337+365   +   354

Encrypting a bit pattern as a knapsack problem

And now for the punch line—there is a way of converting such easy knapsack problems into hard knapsack problems and back again. For now we will consider this conversion process in terms of three "magic" numbers. Later we will consider the origin of these magic numbers and how you can build your own encryption system. The magic numbers we will use are 642, 2311, and 18.

Our first step is to convert the list

1 4 6 12 25 51 105 210 421 850

with which easy knapsack problems are constructed into another list in terms of which knapsack problems are more difficult. This we do by multiplying each entry in the list by 642 (the first magic number), dividing these products by 2311 (the second magic number), and recording the remainders from these division problems. This produces the list

642 57 1541 771 2184 388 391 782 2206 304

In particular, the value 4 in the original list is replaced by 57 in the new list, because $4 \times 642 = 2568$ and $2568 \div 2311$ produces a remainder of 57.

Observe that a knapsack problem posed in terms of this new list would be difficult since our translation process has destroyed the relationship that existed among the values in the original list. But by knowing the magic numbers, we can solve such problems quickly. Our approach is to multiply the target sum by 18 (the third magic number), divide the product by 2311 (the second magic number), and record the remainder from this division. We then use this remainder as the target sum in a knapsack problem posed in terms of the original easy knapsack system. Once this easy problem is solved, the values in the original list that solve the original knapsack problem are those in the positions that correspond to the solution to the easy knapsack problem.

For example, suppose the problem was to select the values from the list

642 57 1541 771 2184 388 391 782 2206 304

whose sum is 4895. We first compute $4895 \times 18 = 88110$, which produces the remainder 292 when divided by 2311. We then determine that the values 6, 25, 51, and 210 are the values in the list

1 4 6 12 25 51 105 210 421 850

whose sum is 292. Since these are the third, fifth, sixth, and eighth values in their respective list, we conclude that the third, fifth, sixth, and eighth entries in the list

642 57 1541 771 2184 388 391 782 2206 304

are the ones whose sum is 4895. Indeed, $1541 + 2184 + 388 + 782 = 4895$, as desired.

The entire public key encryption system works as follows: We openly distribute the list

642 57 1541 771 2184 388 391 782 2206 304

and allow people to encrypt messages in terms of knapsack problems based on this list. But, we keep the original list as well as the three secret numbers to ourselves. As we receive encrypted messages, we decode them quickly by converting them into easy knapsack problems, but no one else can do so. Thus the messages sent to us are secure (Figure 11.14).

Modular Arithmetic

The public key encryption system just described is based on a mathematical concept known as modular arithmetic. A modular arithmetic system is merely a system obtained by substituting each integer in the traditional arithmetic system with the remainder that is obtained by dividing the integer by a predetermined value. This predetermined value is called the *modulus*. For example, if we pick 7 to be the modulus, then the integer values

0 1 2 3 4 5 6 7 8 9 10 11 12 13 14 15 ...

would be translated into the values

0 1 2 3 4 5 6 0 1 2 3 5 6 0 1 ...

It is customary to use the notation $x \pmod{m}$, which is read "x modulo m" or sometimes just "x mod m," to represent the remainder obtained when the value x is divided by m. Thus, $9 \pmod 7$ is 2 because $9 \div 7$ produces a remain-

FIGURE 11.14

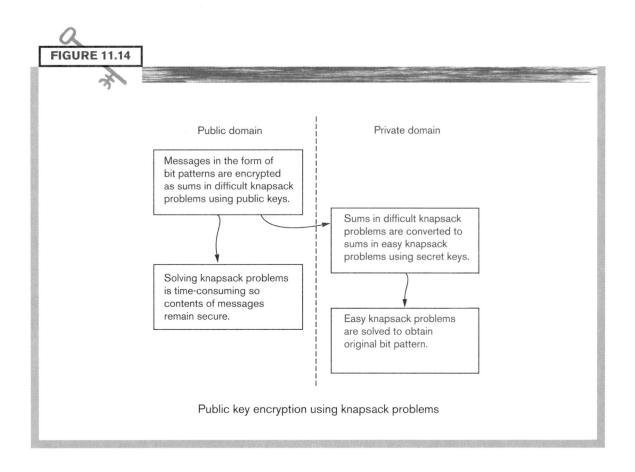

Public domain   Private domain

Messages in the form of
bit patterns are encrypted
as sums in difficult knapsack
problems using public keys.

Sums in difficult knapsack
problems are converted to
sums in easy knapsack
problems using secret keys.

Solving knapsack problems
is time-consuming so
contents of messages
remain secure.

Easy knapsack problems
are solved to obtain
original bit pattern.

Public key encryption using knapsack problems

der of 2. Similarly, 24 (mod 7) is 3 because 24 ÷ 7 produces a remainder of 3, and 5 (mod 7) is 5 because 5 ÷ 7 produces a remainder of 5.

Two integers that produce the same remainder when divided by m are said to be equivalent modulo m. Thus, 16 and 23 are equivalent modulo 7 because 16 (mod 7) is the same as 23 (mod 7). Indeed, both values produce the remainder 2 when divided by 7. It is customary to use the notation $x \equiv y \pmod{m}$, read "x is equivalent to y mod m," to mean that x is equivalent to y when using the modulus m.

After translating the traditional integer values into a modular system using m as the modulus, we are left with only the values $0, 1, 2, 3, \ldots, m - 1$. We can perform arithmetic within this restricted set of values by first performing an operation as in traditional arithmetic and then translating the answer, say x, back into the restricted range by replacing it with the value $x \pmod{m}$. Thus, in a modular system based on the modulus 7, we would be restricted to the values $0, 1, 2, 3, 4, 5,$ and 6. The sum $2 + 6$ would be the value 1 since $2 + 6 = 8$, which produces the remainder 1 when divided by 7. Moreover, the product

2×6 would be the value 5 since $2 \times 6 = 12$, which produces the remainder 5 when divided by 7.

Arithmetic within a modular system is therefore a distorted reflection of arithmetic in the traditional system. It is a reflection in the sense that if $x \equiv a$ (mod m) and $y \equiv b$ (mod m), then $x + y \equiv a + b$ (mod m). But it is also a distortion in the sense that sums and products are not the same in the two systems. In particular, the product of two distinct values can be 1 in a modular system, a phenomenon that does not occur in the traditional system of integers. For example, in the modular system based on the modulus 7, we have $3 \times 5 = 1$ (since $3 \times 5 = 15$ and $15 \div 7$ produces a remainder of 1). But this means that if x is any value in our modular system, then $3 \times 5 \times x$ must be x itself since $3 \times 5 \times x = 1 \times x = x$.

Two numbers that produce the product 1 are called multiplicative inverses of each other. Within the traditional system of integers the value 3 does not have a multiplicative inverse. Instead, the traditional multiplicative inverse of 3, which is $1/3$, lies outside the system of integer values. But in the system of integers modulo 7 we have seen that the value 3 does have a multiplicative inverse, which is 5. Mathematics tells us that if x and m are two positive integers such that $x < m$ and the only common divisor (in the traditional system of integers) among x and m is 1, then the value x will have a multiplicative inverse in the modular system based on the modulus m.

Back to Encryption

Note that if the value x is nonnegative and less than the modulus m, then x (mod m) is x itself. This means that as long as we perform arithmetic operations whose results fall within the range from 0 to $m - 1$, the results obtained in the modular system will agree with those in the traditional arithmetic system. Thus, if we pick an extremely large modulus, we could perform our daily arithmetic computations without ever knowing whether we were in the traditional arithmetic system or a modular system. In particular, since the sum of all the values in the list

1 4 6 12 25 51 105 210 421 850

is 1685, the additions performed when trying to solve a knapsack problem based on this list will never produce results larger than 1685. When solving these problems, we thus do not need to be concerned with whether we are working within the traditional arithmetic system or a modular system whose modulus is greater than 1685.

On the other hand, if we pretend that our easy knapsack problem is posed in such a large modular system, we can obtain a method of converting it into a more difficult problem and back again. To explain, let us suppose that we have a list of values

a_1 a_2 a_3 a_4 a_5 a_6 a_7 a_8 a_9 a_{10}

such that each entry in the list is larger than the sum of its predecessors. That is, it is a list in terms of which knapsack problems are easily solved. Let us pick a modulus m that is larger than the sum of all the values in this list and pick two other values x and y that are multiplicative inverses in the modular system based on the modulus m. If we multiply each entry in our original list by x, we obtain the list

$$a_1x \; a_2x \; a_3x \; a_4x \; a_5x \; a_6x \; a_7x \; a_8x \; a_9x \; a_{10}x$$

in terms of which knapsack problems are again easily solved. In particular, any sum of values from this list would have to be the sum of the corresponding entries from the first list multiplied by x. For example, $a_1x + a_3x + a_5x = (a_1 + a_3 + a_5)x$. Thus we could solve knapsack problems posed in terms of the second list by dividing the target sum by x, finding the entries in the original list whose sum is the quotient, and then selecting the corresponding entries from the second list.

In fact, knapsack problems posed in terms of the second list would also be solvable without dividing by x since, as in the original list, each entry in this second list will be larger than the sum of its predecessors. All we have done is increase the size of the numbers being used.

But let us now exchange each entry in our new list with a value that is equivalent to it modulo m. In particular, in place of a_1x we will put the value a_1x (mod m), in place of a_2x we will put the value a_2x (mod m), and so on. This will produce another list

$$b_1 \; b_2 \; b_3 \; b_4 \; b_5 \; b_6 \; b_7 \; b_8 \; b_9 \; b_{10}$$

where each entry is equivalent modulo m to the corresponding entry in the list

$$a_1x \; a_2x \; a_3x \; a_4x \; a_5x \; a_6x \; a_7x \; a_8x \; a_9x \; a_{10}x$$

In turn, any sum of values from this new list must be equivalent modulo m to the sum of the corresponding values in the list

$$a_1x \; a_2x \; a_3x \; a_4x \; a_5x \; a_6x \; a_7x \; a_8x \; a_9x \; a_{10}x$$

Suppose, then, that we are given a sum such as $b_1 + b_3 + b_5$ and asked to select the entries from the list

$$b_1 \; b_2 \; b_3 \; b_4 \; b_5 \; b_6 \; b_7 \; b_8 \; b_9 \; b_{10}$$

that produce that sum. Since

$$b_1 + b_3 + b_5 \equiv a_1x + a_3x + a_5x \; (\text{mod} \; m)$$

and y is the multiplicative inverse of x, we know that

$$(b_1 + b_3 + b_5)y \equiv (a_1x + a_3x + a_5x)y \; (\text{mod} \; m)$$
$$\equiv (a_1 + a_3 + a_5)xy \; (\text{mod} \; m)$$
$$\equiv (a_1 + a_3 + a_5) \; (\text{mod} \; m)$$

This means that if we multiply a sum of values selected from the list

$$b_1 \; b_2 \; b_3 \; b_4 \, b_5 \; b_6 \; b_7 \; b_8 \; b_9 \; b_{10}$$

by y, divide the product by m, and record the remainder, then that remainder will be the sum of the corresponding entries in the original list

$$a_1 \; a_2 \; a_3 \; a_4 \, a_5 \; a_6 \, a_7 \; a_8 \, a_9 \; a_{10}$$

But, since knapsack problems are easily solved in terms of this list, we can quickly discover what these entries are. In turn, we can solve the original knapsack problem by selecting the corresponding entries from the list

$$b_1 \; b_2 \; b_3 \; b_4 \, b_5 \; b_6 \; b_7 \; b_8 \; b_9 \; b_{10}$$

In short to select the values from the list

$$b_1 \; b_2 \; b_3 \; b_4 \, b_5 \; b_6 \; b_7 \; b_8 \; b_9 \; b_{10}$$

that were used to form a given sum, s, we need merely compute the value $s \times y$ (mod m), find the entries in the list

$$a_1 \; a_2 \; a_3 \; a_4 \, a_5 \; a_6 \, a_7 \; a_8 \, a_9 \; a_{10}$$

whose sum is this value, and then select the corresponding values from the list

$$b_1 \; b_2 \; b_3 \; b_4 \, b_5 \; b_6 \; b_7 \; b_8 \; b_9 \; b_{10}$$

As an example, let us start with the list

1 4 6 12 25 51 105 210 421 850

in terms of which knapsack problems are easily solved. Since the sum of all the values in this list is 1685, the value 2311 is sufficiently large to play the role of m. Moreover, 642 and 18 are multiplicative inverses in the modular system using modulus 2311, so let us use 642 for the value x and 18 for the value y. Our first step is to multiply each entry in the list above by 642 and record the remainder obtained by dividing this product by 2311. This produces the list

642 57 1541 771 2184 388 391 782 2206 304

Suppose we were now given the problem of selecting the values in this list whose sum is 4507. We would multiply 4507 by 18 to obtain 81126, divide this value by 2311 and record the remainder, which would be 241. Then, we would find that the values 6, 25, and 210 are the numbers in the original list whose sum is 241, and from this conclude that the third, fifth, and eighth entries in the list

54 162 324 594 1242 443 1048 2096 1935 1991

are those whose sum is 4507. Indeed, the values 1541, 2184, and 782 solve the original knapsack problem.

In summary, we can build a public key encryption system as shown in Figure 11.15. We first write down a list of values from which easy knapsack problems are constructed. Next, we pick values m, x, and y such that m is larger than the sum of all the values in the list and x is the multiplicative inverse of y in the modular system modulo m. We then multiply the values in the original list

FIGURE 11.15

1. Select values for which knapsack problems are easily solved.

   Example: 2 5 8 17

2. Select three numbers m, x, and y such that m is larger than the sum of the knapsack values and x is the multiplicative inverse of y in the modular system with modulus m.

   Example: $m = 37$, $x = 25$, $y = 3$

3. Replace each value a_i in the original list with $xa \pmod m$.

   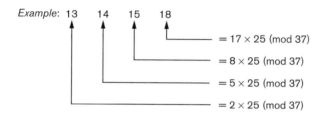

   Example: 13   14   15   18

   $= 17 \times 25 \pmod{37}$
   $= 8 \times 25 \pmod{37}$
   $= 5 \times 25 \pmod{37}$
   $= 2 \times 25 \pmod{37}$

4. Publish this list of values as the public key with which messages are to be encrypted.

Constructing a public key encryption system

by x, divide these products by m, and record the remainders. The list of these remainders is the public encryption key. Anyone can encrypt a message as a sequence of knapsack problems based on this list, and we will be the only ones who can decode such messages easily. We need merely multiply each sum we are given by y, divide these products by m, and record the remainders. Then, we can quickly solve each of the knapsack problems in terms of our original list and from these solutions reconstruct the bit patterns that formed the message.

We should make one final comment. An adversary could try to break our encryption system by guessing the values m, x, and y rather than solving the difficult knapsack problems. This is why the numbers used in an actual encryption system should be much larger than the values we have used in our examples. Indeed, by selecting large values, the time required to guess the private keys can be made greater than that required to solve the difficult knapsack problems.

QUESTIONS/EXERCISES

1. Find the values in the list below that produce the sum 2200.

    191 691 573 337 365 730 651 493 177 354

    (Don't waste too much time on this one. The point is that it can be time-consuming.)

2. Find the values in the list below that produce the sum of 3023.

    642 57 1541 771 2184 388 391 782 2206 304

    In contrast to the previous question, this should not take you very long. Why?

3. Find the multiplicative inverse of 5 in the modular system whose modulus is 23.

4. Design a public key encryption system based on the list

    2 3 6 12 24

    and the fact that 30 and 38 are multiplicative inverses in a modular system with modulus 67.

CHAPTER REVIEW PROBLEMS

1. Show how a structure of the form

    while X equals 0 do;

    .
    .
    .

    end;

    can be simulated with Bare Bones.

2. Write a Bare Bones program that places a 1 in the variable Z if the variable X is less than or equal to the variable Y and places a 0 in the variable Z otherwise.

3. Write a Bare Bones program that places the Xth power of 2 in the variable Z.

4. In each of the following cases write a program sequence in Bare Bones that performs the indicated activity:
    a. Assign 0 to Z if the value of X is even; otherwise assign 1 to Z.
    b. Calculate the sum of the integers from 0 to X.

5. Write a Bare Bones routine that divides the value of X by the value of Y.

Disregard any remainder; that is, 1 divided by 2 produces 0, and 5 divided by 3 produces 1.

6. The example given in the text of a Turing machine that never halts used the fact that the tape was infinitely long. Design a Turing machine that never halts but uses no more than a single cell on its tape.

7. Design a Turing machine that places 0s in all the cells to the left of the current cell until it reaches a cell containing an asterisk.

8. Suppose a pattern of 0s and 1s on the tape of a Turing machine is delimited by asterisks at either end. Design a Turing machine that rotates this pattern one cell to the left, assuming that the machine starts with the current cell being the asterisk at the right end of the pattern.

9. Design a Turing machine that reverses the pattern of 0s and 1s that it finds between

the current cell (which contains an asterisk) and the first asterisk to the left.

10. Summarize the Church–Turing thesis.

11. What value does our Gödel numbering technique associate with the program incr A;?

12. What Bare Bones program is represented by the number

    28,258,975,461,955,643

    when using our Gödel numbering system described in this chapter?

13. Is the following Bare Bones program self-terminating?

    ```
    while X not 0 do;
    end;
    ```

14. Analyze the validity of the following two statements:

    The next statement is true.
    The previous statement is false.

15. Analyze the validity of the statement "The cook on a ship cooks for all those and only those who do not cook for themselves."

16. Summarize the significance of Turing machines in the field of theoretical computer science.

17. Summarize the significance of the halting problem in the field of theoretical computer science.

18. Is the problem of searching through a list for a particular entry a polynomial problem? Justify your answer.

19. Design an algorithm for deciding whether a given positive integer is prime. Is your solution efficient? Is your solution a polynomial or nonpolynomial one?

20. Is a polynomial solution to a problem always better than an exponential solution? Explain.

21. Does the fact that a problem has a polynomial solution mean that it can always be solved in a practical amount of time? Explain.

22. Charlie Programmer is given the problem of dividing a group (of an even number of people) into two disjoint subgroups of equal size so that the difference between the total ages of each subgroup is as large as possible. He proposes the solution of forming all possible subgroup pairs, computing the difference between the age totals of each pair, and selecting the pair with the largest difference. Mary Programmer, on the other hand, proposes that the original group first be sorted by age and then divided into two subgroups by forming one subgroup from the younger half of the sorted group and the other from the older half. What is the complexity of each of these solutions? Is the problem itself of polynomial, NP, or nonpolynomial complexity?

23. Is the following algorithm deterministic? Explain your answer.

    ```
    procedure mystery (Number)
    if (Number >5)
      then (answer "yes")
      else (pick a value less than 5 and
            give this number as the answer)
    ```

24. Is the following algorithm deterministic? Explain your answer.

    ```
    Drive straight ahead.
    At the third intersection, ask the person
      standing on the corner if you should turn
      right or left.
    Turn according to that person's directions.
    Drive two more blocks and stop there.
    ```

25. Identify the points of nondeterminism in the following algorithm:

    ```
    Select three numbers between 1 and 100.
    if (the sum of the selected numbers is greater
        than 150)
      then (answer "yes")
      else (select one of the chosen numbers and
            give that number as the answer)
    ```

26. Does the following algorithm have a polynomial or nonpolynomial time complexity? Explain your answer.

procedure mystery (ListOfNumbers)
Pick a collection of numbers from
   ListOfNumbers.
if (the numbers in that collection add to 125)
   then (answer "yes")
   else (do not give an answer)

27. Which of the following problems are in the class P?
   a. A problem with complexity n^2
   b. A problem with complexity $3n$
   c. A problem with complexity $n^2 + 2n$
   d. A problem with complexity $n!$

28. Summarize the distinction between stating that a problem is a polynomial problem and stating that it is a nondeterministic polynomial problem.

29. Give an example of a problem that is in both the class P and the class NP.

30. Suppose you are given two algorithms for solving the same problem. One algorithm has time complexity n^4 and the other has time complexity 4^n. For what size inputs is the former more efficient than the latter?

31. Suppose we were faced with solving the Traveling Salesman Problem in a context involving 15 cities in which any two cities were connected by a unique road. How many different paths through the cities would there be? How long would it take to compute the length of each of these paths assuming that the length of a path can be computed in one microsecond?

32. How many comparisons between names are made if the merge sort algorithm (Figures 11.9 and 11.8) is applied to the list Alice, Bob, Carol, and David? How many are required if the list was Alice, Bob, Carol, David, and Elaine?

33. Give an example of a problem in each of the categories represented in Figure 11.12.

34. Design an algorithm for finding integer solutions for equations of the form $x^2 + y^2 = n$, where n is some given positive integer. Determine the time complexity of your algorithm.

35. Design an algorithm for determining whether a given positive integer (the input value) is prime. How does the time required by your algorithm depend on the input value?

36. The following algorithm for sorting a list is called the bubble sort. How many comparisons between list entries does the bubble sort require when applied to a list of n entries?

procedure BubbleSort (List)
assign Counter the value 1;
while (Counter < number of entries in List) do
   [assign N the number of entries in List;
    while (N > 1) do
      (if (the Nth List entry is less than the
            entry preceding it)
        then (interchange the Nth entry
               with the preceding entry)
       Subtract 1 from N
)
   ]

37. How long would it take to test all possible combinations when solving a knapsack problem involving 40 values if a microsecond was required to test each combination?

38. Why would it be easier to solve knapsack problems based on the values

1 2 4 8 16 32 64 128 256 512 1028

than knapsack problems based on the values

191 691 573 337 365 730 651 493 177 354

39. Find the values in the list below that produce the sum of 3012.

642 57 1541 771 2184 388 391 782 2206 304

(Note that these are the values used in the public key encryption system developed in Section 11.6.)

40. Find the multiplicative inverse of 5 in a modular system with modulus 8. Find the multiplicative inverse of 3 in a modular system with modulus 8.

41. Design a public key encryption system based on the list

1 3 5 10 20

and the fact that 30 and 38 are multiplicative inverses in a modular system with modulus 67.

SOCIAL ISSUES

The following questions are provided to help you understand some of the ethical/social/legal issues associated with the field of computing as well as investigate your own beliefs and their foundations. The goal is not merely to answer these questions. You should also consider why you answered as you did and whether your justifications are consistent from one question to the next.

1. Suppose the best algorithm for solving a problem would require 100 years to execute. Would you consider the problem to be solvable or unsolvable? Why?

2. Should citizens have the right to encrypt messages in such a manner that precludes monitoring from government agencies? Does your answer provide for "proper" law enforcement? Who should decide what "proper" law enforcement is?

3. If the human mind is an algorithmic device, what consequences does Turing's thesis have in regard to humanity? To what extent do you believe that Turing machines encompass the computational abilities of the human mind?

4. Today there are Web sites that provide roadmaps of most cities. These sites assist in finding particular addresses and provide zooming capabilities for viewing the layout of small neighborhoods. Starting with this reality, consider the following fictitious sequence. Suppose these map sites were enhanced with satellite photographs with similar zooming capabilities. Suppose these zooming capabilities were increased to give a more detailed image of individual buildings and surrounding landscape. Suppose these images were enhanced to include real-time video. Suppose these video images were enhanced with infrared technology. At this point others could watch you inside your own home 24 hours a day. At what point in this progression were your privacy rights first violated? At what point in this progression do you think we moved beyond the capabilities of current spy-satellite technology? To what degree is this scenario fictitious?

5. Suppose a company develops and patents an encryption system. Should the company's national government have the right to use the system as it sees fit in the name of national security? Should the company's national government have the right to restrict the company's commercial use of the system in the name of national security?

ADDITIONAL READING

Garey, M. R., and D. S. Johnson. *Computers and Intractability.* New York: W. H. Freeman, 1979.

Hofstadter, D. R. *Gödel, Escher, Bach: An Eternal Golden Braid.* St. Paul, MN: Vintage, 1980.

Kozen, D. C. *Automata and Computability.* New York: Springer-Verlag, 1997.

Lewis, H. R., and C. H. Papadimitriou. *Elements of the Theory of Computation.* Englewood Cliffs, NJ: Prentice-Hall, 1981.

Sipser, M. *Introduction to the Theory of Computation.* Boston: PWS, 1996.

A p p e n d i x e s

A ASCII
B Circuits to Manipulate Two's Complement Representations
C A Typical Machine Language
D Program Examples
E The Equivalence of Iterative and Recursive Structures
F Answers to Questions/Exercises

appendix

ASCII

A

The following is a partial listing of ASCII code, in which each bit pattern has been extended with a 0 on its left to produce the eight-bit pattern commonly used today.

Symbol	ASCII	Symbol	ASCII	Symbol	ASCII
(space)	00100000	?	00111111	^	01011110
!	00100001	@	01000000	—	01011111
"	00100010	A	01000001	a	01100001
#	00100011	B	01000010	b	01100010
$	00100100	C	01000011	c	01100011
%	00100101	D	01000100	d	01100100
&	00100110	E	01000101	e	01100101
'	00100111	F	01000110	f	01100110
(	00101000	G	01000111	g	01100111
)	00101001	H	01001000	h	01101000
*	00101010	I	01001001	i	01101001
+	00101011	J	01001010	j	01101010
,	00101100	K	01001011	k	01101011
-	00101101	L	01001100	l	01101100
.	00101110	M	01001101	m	01101101
/	00101111	N	01001110	n	01101110
0	00110000	O	01001111	o	01101111
1	00110001	P	01010000	p	01110000
2	00110010	Q	01010001	q	01110001
3	00110011	R	01010010	r	01110010
4	00110100	S	01010011	s	01110011
5	00110101	T	01010100	t	01110100
6	00110110	U	01010101	u	01110101
7	00110111	V	01010110	v	01110110
8	00111000	W	01010111	w	01110111
9	00111001	X	01011000	x	01111000
:	00111010	Y	01011001	y	01111001
;	00111011	Z	01011010	z	01111010
<	00111100	[	01011011	{	01111011
=	00111101	\	01011100	}	01111101
>	00111110	]	01011101		

appendix

CIRCUITS TO MANIPULATE TWO'S COMPLEMENT REPRESENTATIONS

B

This appendix presents circuits for negating and adding values represented in two's complement notation. We begin with the circuit in Figure B.1 that converts a four-bit two's complement representation to the representation for the negative of that value. For example, given the two's complement representation of 3, the circuit produces the representation for -3. It does this by following the same algorithm as presented in the text. That is, it copies the pattern from right to left until a 1 has been copied and then complements each remaining bit as it is moved from the input to the output. Since one input of the rightmost XOR gate is fixed at 0, this gate will merely pass its other input to the output. However, this output is also passed to the left as one of the inputs to the next XOR gate. If this output is 1, the next XOR gate will complement its input bit as it passes to the output. Moreover, this 1 will also be passed to the left through the OR gate to affect the next gate as well. In this manner, the first 1 that is copied to the output will also be passed to the left, where it will cause all the remaining bits to be complemented as they are moved to the output.

Next, let us consider the process of adding two values represented in two's complement notation. In particular, when solving the problem

```
  0110
+ 1011
```

we proceed from right to left in a column-by-column manner, executing the same algorithm for each column. Thus once we obtain a circuit for adding one column of such a problem, we can construct a circuit for adding many columns merely by repeating the single-column circuit.

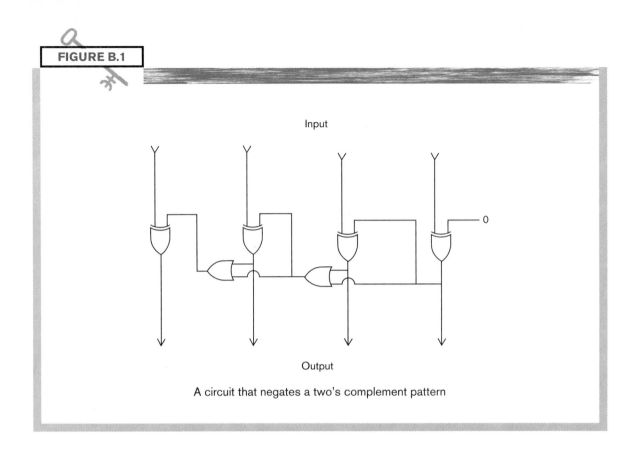

Input

Output

A circuit that negates a two's complement pattern

The algorithm for adding a single column in a multiple-column addition problem is to add the two values in the current column, add that sum to any carry from the previous column, write the least significant bit of this sum in the answer, and transfer any carry to the next column. The circuit in Figure B.2 follows this same algorithm. The upper XOR gate determines the sum of the two input bits. The lower XOR gate adds this sum to the value carried from the previous column. The two AND gates together with the OR gate pass any carry to the left. In particular, a carry of 1 will be produced if the original two input bits in this column were 1 or if the sum of these bits and the carry were both 1.

Figure B.3 shows how copies of this single-column circuit can be used to produce a circuit that computes the sum of two values represented in a four-bit two's complement system. Each rectangle represents a copy of the single-column addition circuit. Note that the carry value given to the rightmost rectangle is always 0 because there is no carry from a previous column. In a similar manner, the carry produced from the leftmost rectangle is ignored.

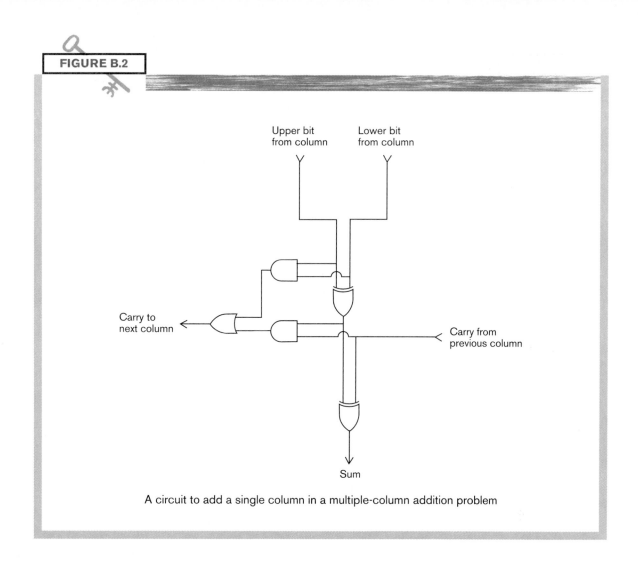

A circuit to add a single column in a multiple-column addition problem

The circuit in Figure B.3 is known as a ripple adder because the carry information must propagate, or ripple, from the rightmost to the leftmost column. Although simple in composition, such circuits are slower to perform their functions than more clever versions, such as the lookahead carry adder, which minimize this column-to-column propagation. Thus the circuit in Figure B.3, although sufficient for our purposes, is not the circuit that is used in today's machines.

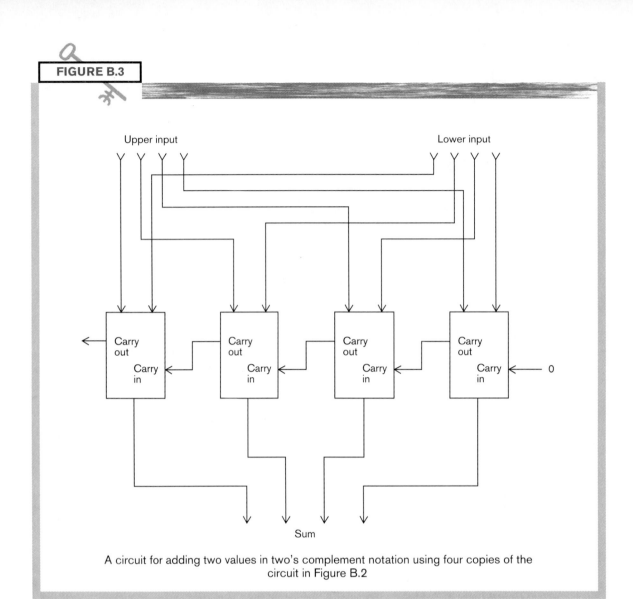

A circuit for adding two values in two's complement notation using four copies of the circuit in Figure B.2

appendix

A TYPICAL MACHINE LANGUAGE

C

Machine Architecture

The machine has 16 general-purpose registers numbered 0 through F (in hexadecimal). Each register is one byte (eight bits) long. For identifying registers within instructions, each register is assigned the unique four-bit pattern that represents its register number. Thus register 0 is identified by 0000 (hexadecimal 0), and register 4 is identified by 0100 (hexadecimal 4).

Since there are 256 cells in memory, each cell is assigned a unique address consisting of an integer in the range of 0 to 255. An address can therefore be represented by a pattern of eight bits ranging from 00000000 to 11111111 (or a hexadecimal value in the range of 00 to FF).

Floating-point values are assumed to be stored in the following format:

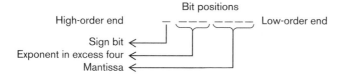

Machine Language

Each machine instruction is two bytes long. The first four bits consist of the opcode; the last 12 bits make up the operand field. The table that follows lists the instructions in hexadecimal notation together with a short description of each. The letters R, S, and T are used in place of hexadecimal digits in those fields representing a register identifier that varies depending on the particular application of the instruction. The letters X and Y are used in lieu of hexadecimal digits in variable fields not representing a register.

Op-code	Operand	Description
1	RXY	LOAD the register R with the bit pattern found in the memory cell whose address is XY. *Example:* 14A3 would cause the contents of the memory cell located at address A3 to be placed in register 4.
2	RXY	LOAD the register R with the bit pattern XY. *Example:* 20A3 would cause the value A3 to be placed in register 0.
3	RXY	STORE the bit pattern found in register R in the memory cell whose address is XY. *Example:* 35B1 would cause the contents of register 5 to be placed in the memory cell whose address is B1.
4	0RS	MOVE the bit pattern found in register R to register S. *Example:* 40A4 would cause the contents of register A to be copied into register 4.
5	RST	ADD the bit patterns in registers S and T as though they were two's complement representations and leave the result in register R. *Example:* 5726 would cause the binary values in registers 2 and 6 to be added and the sum placed in register 7.
6	RST	ADD the bit patterns in registers S and T as though they represented values in floating-point notation and leave the floating-point result in register R. *Example:* 634E would cause the values in registers 4 and E to be added as floating-point values and the result to be placed in register 3.
7	RST	OR the bit patterns in registers S and T and place the result in register R. *Example:* 7CB4 would cause the result of ORing the contents of registers B and 4 to be placed in register C.
8	RST	AND the bit patterns in register S and T and place the result in register R. *Example:* 8045 would cause the result of ANDing the contents of registers 4 and 5 to be placed in register 0.
9	RST	EXCLUSIVE OR the bit patterns in registers S and T and place the result in register R. *Example:* 95F3 would cause the result of EXCLUSIVE ORing the contents of registers F and 3 to be placed in register 5.
A	R0X	ROTATE the bit pattern in register R one bit to the right X times. Each time place the bit that started at the low-order end at the high-order end. *Example:* A403 would cause the contents of register 4 to be rotated 3 bits to the right in a circular fashion.
B	RXY	JUMP to the instruction located in the memory cell at address XY if the bit pattern in register R is equal to the bit pattern in register number 0. Otherwise, continue with the normal sequence of execution. *Example:* B43C would first compare the contents of register 4 with the contents of register 0. If the two were equal, the execution sequence would be altered so that the next instruction executed would be the one located at memory address 3C. Otherwise, program execution would continue in its normal sequence.
C	000	HALT execution. *Example:* C000 would cause program execution to stop.

appendix

PROGRAM EXAMPLES

D

This appendix presents sample programs in the languages Ada, C, C++, FORTRAN, Java, and Pascal. Each program receives a list of names typed at the keyboard, sorts the list using the insertion sort algorithm, and prints the sorted list on the monitor screen.

Ada

The language Ada, named after Augusta Ada Byron (1815–1851), who was an assistant of Charles Babbage and the daughter of poet Lord Byron, was developed at the initiative of the U.S. Department of Defense in an attempt to obtain a single, general-purpose language for all its software development needs. A major emphasis during Ada's design was to incorporate features for programming real-time computer systems used as a part of larger machines, such as missile guidance systems, environmental control systems within buildings, and control systems in automobiles and small home appliances. Ada thus contains features for expressing activities in parallel processing environments as well as convenient techniques for handling special cases (called exceptions) that might arise in the application environment. The newest version of Ada, known as Ada 95, embraces the object-oriented paradigm.

Figure D.1 presents a sample Ada program.

```
--Program to manipulate a list
with TEXT_IO;
use TEXT_IO;
procedure MAIN is
    subtype NAME_TYPE is STRING (1..8);
    LIST_LENGTH: constant:= 10;
    NAMES: array (1..LIST_LENGTH) of NAME_TYPE;
    PIVOT: NAME_TYPE;
    HOLE: INTEGER;
begin
--First, get the names from the terminal.
    for K in 1 .. LIST_LENGTH loop
      GET(NAMES(K));
    end loop;
--Sort the list (HOLE contains the location of the
--             hole in the list from the time the
--             pivot is removed until it is
--             reinserted.)
    for N in 2 .. LIST_LENGTH loop
      PIVOT := NAMES(N);
      HOLE := N;
      for M in reverse 1 .. N - 1 loop
        if NAMES(M) > PIVOT
            then NAMES(M + 1) := NAMES(M);
            else exit;
        end if;
          HOLE := M;
      end loop;
        NAMES(HOLE) := PIVOT;
    end loop;
--Now, print the sorted list.
    for K in 1 .. LIST_LENGTH loop
      NEW_LINE;
      PUT(NAMES(K));
    end loop;
end MAIN;
```

A sample Ada program

C

The language C was developed by Dennis Ritchie at Bell Laboratories in the early 1970s. Although originally designed as a language for developing operating systems and compilers, C has achieved popularity throughout the programming community and is enjoying the benefits of standardization through the efforts of the American National Standards Institute.

C was originally envisioned as merely a step up from machine language. Consequently, its syntax is terse compared with other high-level languages that use complete English words to express some primitives that are represented by special symbols in C. This terseness is one of the reasons for C's popularity, because it allows for efficient representations of complex algorithms. (Often a concise representation is more readable than a lengthy one.)

Figure D.2 presents a sample program in C.

C++

The language C++ was developed by Bjarne Stroustrup at Bell Laboratories as an enhanced version of the language C. The goal was to produce a language compatible with the object-oriented paradigm.

Figure D.3 presents an implementation of the insertion sort algorithm in C++. The last four statements in this program request that an object named `namelist` be established having "type" `list` and that this new object perform the operations `getnames`, `sortnames`, and `printnames` on itself. The preceding portion of the program defines the properties that any object of "type" `list` is to possess. In particular, any such object is to contain an internal array of characters called `names` and three operations called `getnames`, `sortlist`, and `printnames`. Note that the definitions of these operations are the same as portions of the C language program in Figure D.2. The difference is that in the C++ program these operations are considered to be a part of an object's properties, whereas in the C program they are considered as units within the procedural part of the program.

FORTRAN

FORTRAN is an acronym for FORmula TRANslator. This language was one of the first high-level languages developed (announced in 1957) and the first to gain wide acceptance within the computing community. Over the years its official description has undergone numerous extensions, so you may hear computer scientists mention FORTRAN IV or FORTRAN 77. The latest in the series is FORTRAN 90, which extended FORTRAN 77 to include such features as

```
/* Program to manipulate a list */

#include <stdio.h>
#include <string.h>

main ()
{
  char names[10][9],pivot[9];
  int i,j;

/* get the names */
  for (i = 0; i < 10; ++i)
    scanf("%s",names[i]);

/*sort the list */
  for (i = 1; i < 10; ++i)
  {
    strcpy(pivot,names[i]);
    j = i - 1;
    while ((j >= 0)&&(strcmp(pivot,names[j]) < 0))
      {strcpy(names[j+1],names[j]);--j;};
    strcpy(names[j+1], pivot);
  }
/*print the sorted list */
  for (i = 0; i < 10; ++i)
    printf ("%s\n",names[i]);
}
```

A sample C program

recursion and user-defined data types. Although criticized by many, FORTRAN continues to be a popular language within the scientific community. In particular, many numerical analysis and statistical packages are, and will probably continue to be, written in FORTRAN. Figure D.4 presents a sample program in FORTRAN.

Java

Java is an object-oriented language developed by Sun Microsystems in the early 1990s. Its designers borrowed heavily from C and C++. Being a new language, Java has not had the benefits of standardization. Indeed, the language is still in

```
// Program to manipulate a list

#include <iostream.h>
#include <string.h>
const int ListLength = 10;

// All list objects contain a list of names and three public
// methods called getnames, sortlist, and printnames.

class list
(private:
  char names[ListLength][9]:

public:

void getnames()
(int i;
 for (i = 0; i < ListLength; ++i)
   cin >> names[i]:
}
void sortlist()
{int i,j:
  char pivot[9];
  for (i = 1; i < ListLength; ++1)
   {strcpy(pivot, names[i]);
    j = i - 1;
    while ((j >= 0) && (strcmp(pivot, names [j]) < 0))
      {strcpy(names[j+1], names[j]);
        --j;
      }
    strcpy(names[j+1], pivot);
   }
 }

 void printnames()
 {int i;
  cout << endl;
  for (i = 0; i < ListLength; ++i)
    cout << names[i] << endl;
};}

// Establish an object called namelist and ask it to
// collect some names, sort them, and print the list.

void main()
{list namelist;
 namelist.getnames();
 namelist.sortlist();
 namelist.printnames();
}
```

A sample C++ program

```
!     Program to manipulate a list
      INTEGER J,K
      CHARACTER(LEN=8) Pivot
      CHARACTER(LEN=8) DIMENSION(10) Names
!     First, get the names.
      READ(UNIT=5, FMT=100) (Names(K), K=1,10)
100   FORMAT(A8)
!        Now, sort the list.
OuterLoop: DO J=2,10
          Pivot = Names(J)
 InnerLoop: DO K=J-1, 1,-1
            IF (Names(K) .GT. Pivot) THEN
                   Names(K+1) = Names(K)
               ELSE
                   EXIT InnerLoop
            ENDIF
            END DO InnerLoop
            Names (K+1) = Pivot
            END DO OuterLoop
!     Now, print the sorted list.
      WRITE(UNIT=6,FMT=400) (Names(K),K=1,10)
400   FORMAT ('',A8)
      END
```

A sample FORTRAN program

its evolutionary stage. Part of the excitement over Java stems from its promise of becoming a standard by which programs, known as Java applets, can be transported over the Internet in an executable form and run on any host machine. With this capability, hypertext documents, which are static in nature, can be replaced by dynamic programs with which the user can interact.

Figure D.5 presents a sample program in Java. Note the resemblance between Java and C++.

```
// Program to manipulate a list

import java.io.*;

// All list objects contain a list of names and three public
// methods called getnames, sortlist, and printnames.

class list {
  final int ListLength = 10;
  private String[] names;
  public list() {
    names = new String[ListLength]}
  }
  public void getnames() {
    int i;
    DataInput data = new DataInputStream(System.in);
    for (i=0; i < ListLength; i++)
      try {names[i] = data.readLine();}
        }
      catch(IOException e) {};
  }
  public void sortnames() {
    int i,j;
    String pivot;
    for (i=1; i < ListLength; i++) {
      pivot = names[i];
      j = i - 1;
      while ((j >= 0) && (pivot.compareTo(names[j]) < 0)) {
        names [j+1] = names[j];
        j--;
      }
      names[j+1] = pivot;
    }
  }
  public void printnames() {
    int i;
    for (i=0; i < ListLength; i++)
      System.out.println(names[i]);
  }
}
// Establish an object called namelist and ask it to
// collect some names, sort them, and print the results.
class sort {
  public static void main(String args[]){
    list namelist = new list();
    namelist.getnames();
    namelist.sortnames();
    namelist.printnames();
  }
```

A sample Java program

Pascal

Pascal is named after the French mathematician and inventor Blaise Pascal (1623–1662). Announced by Niklaus Wirth in 1971, it incorporates many of the later design features such as an emphasis on data type in addition to structure, a free-format syntax, and numerous control structures. Today, Pascal is used mainly in computer science education because its design reinforces an organized approach to program development. Figure D.6 presents a sample program in Pascal.

```
      {Program to manipulate a list}
   program InsertSort(input, Output);
   const Blanks = '        ';
        ListLength = 10;

   type NameType = packed array [1 .. 8] of char;
   var Names: Array[1 .. ListLength] of Nametype;
        Pivot: NameType;
        LocationFound: Boolean;
        J,M,N: Integer;
   {GetName is a procedure for reading an entire name.}
   procedure GetName(var Name: NameType);
   var J: Integer;
   begin J := 1;
        repeat read(Name[J]); J := j + 1; until (J > 8) or eoln;
        readln
   end;
   begin
   {First, get the names from the terminal.}
        for J := 1 to ListLength do
            begin Names[J] := Blanks; GetName(Names[J])end;
   {Sort the list.}
        N := 2;
        repeat
            Pivot := Name[N];
            M := N - 1;
            LocationFound := false;
            while (not LocationFound)do
                if Names[M] > Pivot
                    then begin Names[M+1] := Names[M];
                                M := M - 1;
                                if M = 0 then LocationFound := true
                          end
                    else LocationFound := true;
                Names[M+1] := Pivot;
                N := N + 1
        until N > ListLength;
   {Now print the sorted list.}
        for J := 1 to ListLength do writeln (Names[J])
   end.
```

A sample Pascal program

THE EQUIVALENCE OF ITERATIVE AND RECURSIVE STRUCTURES

E

In this appendix, we use our Bare Bones language of Chapter 11 as a tool to answer the question posed in Chapter 4 regarding the relative power of iterative and recursive structures. Recall that Bare Bones contains only three assignment statements (clear, incr, and decr) and one control structure (constructed from a while-end statement pair). Moreover, this simple language has the same computing power as a Turing machine; thus, if we accept the Church–Turing thesis, we may conclude that any problem with an algorithmic solution has a solution expressible in Bare Bones.

The first step in the comparison of iterative and recursive structures is to replace the iterative structure of Bare Bones with a recursive structure. We do this by removing the while and end statements from the language and in their place providing the ability to divide a Bare Bones program into units along with the ability to call one of these units from another location in the program. More precisely, we propose that each program in the modified language consist of a number of syntactically disjoint program units. We suppose that each program must contain exactly one unit called MAIN having the syntactic structure of

```
MAIN: begin;
        .
        .
        .
      end;
```

(where the dots represent other Bare Bones statements) and perhaps other units (semantically subordinate to MAIN) that have the structure

```
unit: begin;
        .
        .
        .
      return;
```

(where *unit* represents the unit's name that has the same syntax as variable names). The semantics of this unit system is that the program always begins execution at the beginning of the unit MAIN and halts when that unit's end statement is reached. Other program units can be called as procedures by means of the conditional statement

    if *name* not 0 perform *unit;*

(where *name* represents any variable name and *unit* represents any of the program unit names other than MAIN). Moreover, we allow the units other than MAIN to call themselves recursively.

With these added features, we can simulate the old while-end structure. For example, a Bare Bones program of the form

    while X not 0 do;
      S;
    end;

(where S represents any sequence of Bare Bones statements) can be replaced by the unit structure

    MAIN: begin;
            if X not 0 perform unitA;
            end;
    unitA: begin;
            S;
            if X not 0 perform unitA;
            return;

Consequently, we may conclude that the modified language has all the capabilities of the original Bare Bones.

It can also be shown that any problem that can be solved using the modified language can be solved using Bare Bones. One method of doing this is to show how any algorithm expressed in the modified language could be written in the original Bare Bones. However, this involves an explicit description of how recursive structures can be simulated with the while-end structure of Bare Bones.

For our purpose, it is simpler to rely on the Church–Turing thesis as presented in Chapter 11. In particular, the Church–Turing thesis, combined with the fact that Bare Bones has the same power as Turing machines, dictates that no language can be more powerful than our original Bare Bones. We can therefore conclude that any problem solvable in our modified language can also be solved using Bare Bones.

We can conclude that the power of the modified language is the same as that of the original Bare Bones. The only distinction between the two languages is that one provides an iterative control structure and the other provides recursion. We must therefore conclude that the two control structures are in fact equivalent in terms of computing power.

appendix

ANSWERS TO QUESTIONS/EXERCISES

F

Part 1

Chapter 1

Section 1.1

1. One and only one of the upper two inputs must be 1, and the lowest input must be 1.
2. The 1 on the lower input is negated to 0 by the NOT gate, causing the output of the AND gate to become 0. Thus both inputs to the OR gate are 0 (remember that the upper input to the flip-flop is held at 0) so the output of the OR gate becomes 0. This means that the output of the AND gate will remain 0 after the lower input to the flip-flop returns to 0.
3. The output of the upper OR gate will become 1, causing the upper NOT gate to produce an output of 0. This will cause the lower OR gate to produce a 0, causing the lower NOT gate to produce a 1. This 1 is seen as the output of the flip-flop as well as being fed back to the upper OR gate, where it holds the output of that gate at 1, even after the flip-flop's input has returned to 0.
4. The flip-flop will be shielded from the circuit's input values when the clock is 0. The flip-flop will respond to the circuit's input values when the clock is 1.
5. a. 6AF2 b. E85517 c. 48
6. a. 0101111111101100010111
   b. 0110000100001010
   c. 1010101111001101
   d. 0000000100000000

Section 1.2

1. In the first case, memory cell number 6 ends up containing the value 5. In the second case, it ends up with the value 8.

2. Step 1 erases the original value in cell number 3 when the new value is written there. Consequently, Step 2 does not place the original value from cell number 3 in cell number 2. The result is that both cells end up with the value that was originally in cell number 2. A correct procedure is the following:

   Step 1. Move the contents of cell number 2 to cell number 1.
   Step 2. Move the contents of cell number 3 to cell number 2.
   Step 3. Move the contents of cell number 1 to cell number 3.

3. 32768 bits.

Section 1.3

1. Faster retrieval of data and higher transfer rates.

2. The point to remember here is that the slowness of mechanical motion compared with the speed of the internal functioning of the computer dictates that we minimize the number of times we must move the read/write heads. If we fill a complete surface before starting the next, we must move the read/write head each time we finish with a track. The number of moves therefore is approximately the same as the total number of tracks on the two surfaces. If, however, we alternate between surfaces by electronically switching between the read/write heads, we must move the read/write heads only after each cylinder has been filled.

3. In this application, a constant expansion and shrinking takes place within the data. If the information were stored on tape, this would result in an endless rewriting process to accommodate the upheaval taking place within the data. (One envisions the last block of the data yo-yoing back and forth as reservations earlier on the tape are made, dropped, or become outdated.) When using disk storage, however, each change affects only the portion of the data stored on the sector involved. Consequently, much less rewriting of data is required when updates are made.

4. Spreading logical records across different sectors means that more than one sector must be retrieved from the disk to obtain a complete logical record. The time required to retrieve these additional sectors could easily outweigh the benefits of saving storage space.

Section 1.4

1. Computer science.

2. The two patterns are the same, except that the sixth bit from the low-order end is always 0 for uppercase and 1 for lowercase.

3. a. 01010111   01101000   01100101   01110010
     01100101   00100000   01100001   01110010
     01100101   00100000   01111001   01101111
     01110101   00111111

   b. 00100010   01001000   01101111   01110111
     00111111   00100010   00100000   01000011
     01101000   01100101   01110010   01111001
     01101100   00100000   01100001   01110011
     01101011   01100101   01100100   00101110

   c. 00110010   00101011   00110011   00111101
     00110101   00101110

4.

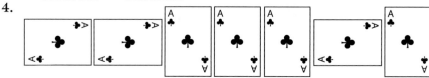

5. a. 5   b. 9   c. 11   d. 6   e. 16   f. 18

6. a. 110   b. 1101   c. 1011   d. 10010
   e. 11011   f. 100

7. In 24 bits, we can store three symbols using ASCII. Thus we can store values as large as 999. However, if we use the bits as binary digits, we can store values up to 16,777,215.

8. a. 15.15   b. 51.0.128   c. 10.160

Section 1.5

1. a. 42   b. 33   c. 23   d. 6   e. 31

2. a. 100000   b. 1000000   c. 1100000   d. 1111   e. 11011

3. a. $3\frac{1}{4}$ b. $5\frac{7}{8}$ c. $2\frac{1}{2}$ d. $6\frac{3}{8}$ e. $\frac{5}{8}$

4. a. 100.1   b. 10.11   c. 1.001   d. 0.0101   e. 101.101

5. a. 100111   b. 1011.110   c. 100000   d. 1000.00

Section 1.6

1. a. 3   b. 15   c. −4   d. −6   e. 0   f. −16

2. a. 00000110   b. 11111010   c. 11101111
   d. 00001101   e. 11111111   f. 00000000

3. a. 11111111   b. 10101011   c. 00000100
   d. 00000010   e. 00000000   f. 10000001

4. a. With 4 bits the largest value is 7 and the smallest is −8.
   b. With 6 bits the largest value is 31 and the smallest is −32.
   c. With 8 bits the largest value is 127 and the smallest is −128.

5. a. 0111 (5 + 2 = 7)   b. 0100 (3 + 1 = 4)   c. 1111 (5 + (−6) = −1)
   d. 0001 (−2 + 3 = 1)   e. 1000 (−6 + (−2) = −8)

6. a. 0111   **b.** 1011 (overflow)   **c.** 0100 (overflow)
     d. 0001   **e.** 1000 (overflow)

7.

a.	**b.**	**c.**	**d.**	**e.**
0110	0011	0100	0010	0001
+ 0001	+ 1110	+ 1010	+ 0100	+ 1011
0111	0001	1110	0110	1100

8. No. Overflow occurs when an attempt is made to store a number that is too large for the system being used. When adding a positive value to a negative value, the result must be between the values being added. Thus, if the original values are small enough to be stored, the result is also.

9. a. 6 since $1110 \rightarrow 14 - 8$

     b. -1 since $0111 \rightarrow 7 - 8$

     c. 0 since $1000 \rightarrow 8 - 8$

     d. -6 since $0010 \rightarrow 2 - 8$

     e. -8 since $0000 \rightarrow 0 - 8$

     f. 1 since $1001 \rightarrow 9 - 8$

10. a. 1101 since $5 + 8 = 13 \rightarrow 1101$

     b. 0011 since $-5 + 8 = 3 \rightarrow 0011$

     c. 1011 since $3 + 8 = 11 \rightarrow 1011$

     d. 1000 since $0 + 8 = 8 \rightarrow 1000$

     e. 1111 since $7 + 8 = 15 \rightarrow 1111$

     f. 0000 since $-8 + 8 = 0 \rightarrow 0000$

11. No. The largest value that can be stored in excess eight notation is 7, represented by 1111. To represent a larger value, at least excess 16 (which uses patterns of 5 bits) must be used. Similarly, 6 cannot be represented in excess four notation. (The largest value that can be represented in excess four notation is 3.)

Section 1.7

1. a. ⅝   **b.** 3¼   **c.** ⁹⁄₃₂   **d.** $-1\frac{1}{2}$ **e.** $-^{11}\!/_{64}$

2. a. 01101011   **b.** 01111010 (round-off error)
     c. 01001100   **d.** 11101110
     e. 11111000 (round-off error)

3. 01001001 (⁹⁄₁₆) is larger than 00111101 ($^{13}\!/_{32}$). The following is a simple way of determining which of two patterns represents the larger value:

Case 1. If the sign bits are different, the larger is the one with 0 sign bit.

Case 2. If the sign bits are both 0, scan the remaining portions of the patterns from left to right until a bit position is found where the two patterns differ. The pattern containing the 1 in this position represents the larger value.

Case 3. If the sign bits are both 1, scan the remaining portions of the patterns from left to right until a bit position is found where the two patterns differ. The pattern containing the 0 in this position represents the larger value.

The simplicity of this comparison process is one of the reasons for representing the exponent in floating-point systems with an excess notation rather than with two's complement.

4. The largest value would be $7\frac{1}{2}$ which is represented by the pattern 01111111. As for the smallest positive value, you could argue that there are two "correct" answers. First, if you stick to the coding process described in the text, which requires the most significant bit of the mantissa to be 1 (called normalized form), the answer is $\frac{1}{32}$, which is represented by the pattern 00001000. However, most machines do not impose this restriction for values close to 0. For such a machine, the correct answer is $\frac{1}{256}$ represented by 00000001.

Section 1.8

1. In hexadecimal notation the message is B5E95EFA56.
2. Answers will vary. One possibility is ββαββΒααβα (5, 5, β) (10, 7, α).
3. Color cartoons consist of blocks of solid color with sharp edges. Moreover, the number of colors involved is limited.
4. There would be 1,049,576 pixels, each requiring one byte to represent the pixel's color. Thus, 1 MB would represent the maximum size of the GIF image. The additional compression techniques involved in GIF encoding reduce this significantly, although their efficiency depends on the complexity of the image. Typically, simple images require no more than a few KB of storage when encoded using GIF. If JPEG's baseline standard were used, each two-by-two pixel block would require only six components. Assuming one byte per component, the 1024 by 1024 pixel image would require a maximum of 1.5 MB, but the additional compression techniques typically reduce such an image to under 100 KB.
5. JPEG's baseline standard takes advantage of the fact that the human eye is not as sensitive to changes in color as it is to changes in brightness. Thus it reduces the number of bits used to represent color information without noticeable loss in image quality.

Section 1.9

1. b, c, and e.
2. Yes. If an even number of errors occurs in one byte, the parity technique does not detect them.
3. In this case, errors occur in bytes a and d of Question 1. The answer to Question 2 remains the same.

4. a. 001010111 001101000 101100101
101110010 101100101 100100000
001100001 101110010 101100101
000100000 001111001 101101111
001110101 100111111

b. 100100010 101001000 101101111
101110111 100111111 100100010
000100000 001000011 001101000
101100101 101110010 001111001
101101100 000100000 001100001
001110011 001101011 101100101
001100100 100101110

c. 000110010 100101011 100110011
000111101 100110101 100101110

5. a. BED **b.** CAB **c.** HEAD

6. One solution is the following:

```
A   0 0 0 0 0
B   1 1 1 0 0
C   0 1 1 1 1
D   1 0 0 1 1
```

Chapter 2

Section 2.1

1. On small machines this is often a two-step process consisting of first reading the contents from the first cell into a register and then writing it into the destination cell. On most large machines, this activity appears as one event.

2. The value to be written, the address of the cell in which to write, and the command to write.

3. The term *move* often carries the connotation of removing from one location and placing in another, thus leaving a hole behind. In most cases within a machine, this removal does not take place. Rather, the object being moved is most often copied (or cloned) into the new location.

4. A common technique, called relative addressing, is to state how far rather than where to jump. For example, an instruction might be to jump forward three instructions or jump backward two instructions. You should note, however, that such statements must be altered if additional instructions are later inserted between the origin and the destination of the jump.

5. This could be argued either way. The instruction is stated in the form of a conditional jump. However, because the condition that 0 be equal to 0 is always satisfied, the jump will always be made as if there were no condition

stated at all. You will often find machines with such instructions in their repertoires because they provide an efficient design. For example, if a machine is designed to execute an instruction with a structure such as "If... jump to..." this instruction form can be used to express both conditional and unconditional jumps.

Section 2.2

1. 156C = 0001010101101100
   166D = 0001011001101101
   5056 = 0101000001010110
   306E = 0011000001101110
   C000 = 1100000000000000
2. a. STORE the contents of register 6 in memory cell number 8A.
   b. JUMP to location DE if the contents of register A equals that of register 0.
   c. AND the contents of registers 3 and C, leaving the result in register 0.
   d. MOVE the contents of register F to register 4.
3. The instruction 15AB requires that the CPU query the memory circuitry for the contents of the memory cell at address AB. This value, when obtained from memory, is then placed in register 5. The instruction 25AB does not require such a request of memory. Rather, the value AB is placed in register 5.
4. a. 2356   b. A503   c. B7F3   d. 80A5

Section 2.3

1. Hexadecimal 34
2. a. 0F   b. C3
3. a. 00   b. 01   c. four times
4. It halts. This is an example of what is often called self-modifying code. That is, the program modifies itself. Note that the first two instructions place hexadecimal C0 at memory location F8, and the next two instructions place 00 at location F9. Thus, by the time the machine reaches the instruction at F8, the halt instruction (C000) has been placed there.

Section 2.4

1. a. 00001011   b. 10000000   c. 00101101
   d. 11101011   e. 11101111   f. 11111111
   g. 11100000   h. 01101111   i. 11010010
2. 0011100 with the AND operation
3. 0011100 with the XOR operation
4. a. The final result is 0 if the string contained an even number of 1s. Otherwise it is 1.
   b. The result is the value of the parity bit for even parity.

5. The logical XOR operation mirrors addition except for the case where both operands are 1, in which case the XOR produces a 0, whereas the sum is 10. (Thus the XOR operation can be considered an addition operation with no carry.)

6. Use AND with the mask 01011111 to change lowercase to uppercase. Use OR with 00100000 to change uppercase to lowercase.

7. a. 01001101   b. 11100001   c. 11101111

8. a. 57   b. B8   c. 6F   d. 6A

9. 5

10. 00110110 in two's complement; 01011110 in floating-point. The point here is that the procedure used to add the values is different depending on the interpretation given the bit patterns.

11. One solution is as follows:

   12A7 (LOAD register 2 with the contents of memory cell A7.)
   2380 (LOAD register 3 with the value 80.)
   7023 (OR registers 2 and 3 leaving the result in register 0.)
   30A7 (STORE contents of register 0 in memory cell A7.)
   C000 (HALT.)

12. One solution is as follows:

   15E0 (LOAD register 5 with the contents of memory cell E0.)
   A502 (ROTATE 2 bits to the right the contents of register 5.)
   260F (LOAD register 6 with the value 0F.)
   8056 (AND registers 5 and 6, leaving the result in register 0.)
   30E1 (STORE the contents of register 0 in memory cell E1.)
   C000 (HALT.)

Section 2.5

1. a. 37B5
   b. One million times
   c. No. A typical page of text contains less than 4000 characters. Thus the ability to print five pages in a minute indicates a printing rate of no more than 20,000 characters per minute, which is much less than one million characters per second. (The point is that a computer can send characters to a printer much faster than the printer can print them; thus the printer needs a way of telling the computer to wait.)

2. The disk will make 50 revolutions in one second, meaning that 800 sectors will pass under the read/write head in a second. Since each sector contains 1024 bytes, bits will pass under the read/write head at approximately 6.5 Mbps. Thus communication between the controller and the disk drive will have to be at least this fast if the controller is going to keep up with the data being read from the disk.

3. A 300-page novel represented in ASCII consists of about one MB or 8,000,000 bits. Thus approximately 139 seconds (or $2\frac{1}{3}$ minutes) would be required to transfer the entire novel at 57600 bps.

Section 2.6

1. One set of registers is used for fetching, decoding, and executing microinstructions, while the other set is used for fetching, decoding, and executing the machine-language instructions as directed by the microprogram.
2. The pipe would contain the instructions B1B0 (being executed), 5002, and perhaps even B0AA. If the value in register 0 is equal to the value in register 1, the jump to location B0 is executed, and the effort already expended on the instructions in the pipe is wasted. On the other hand, no time is wasted because the effort expended on these instructions did not require extra time.
3. If no precautions are taken, the information at memory locations F8 and F9 is fetched as an instruction before the previous part of the program has had a chance to modify these cells.
4. a. The CPU that is trying to add 1 to the cell can first read the value in the cell. Following this the other CPU reads the cell's value. (Note that at this point both CPUs have retrieved the same value.) If the first CPU now finishes its addition and writes its result back in the cell before the second finishes its subtraction and writes its result, the final value in the cell reflects only the activity of the second CPU.
   b. The CPUs might read the data from the cell as before, but this time the second CPU might write its result before the first. Thus, only the activity of the first CPU is reflected in the cell's final value.

Part Two

Chapter 3

Section 3.1

1. A traditional example is the line of people waiting to buy tickets to an event. In this case there may be someone who tries to "break in line," which would violate the FIFO structure.
2. Options (b) and (c).
3. Real-time processing refers to coordinating the execution of a program with activities in the machine's environment. Interactive processing refers to a person's interaction with a program as it executes. Good real-time characteristics are needed for successful interactive processing.
4. Time-sharing is the technique by which multitasking is accomplished on a single-processor machine.

Section 3.2

1. *Shell:* Communicates with the machine's environment.

File manager: Coordinates the use of the machine's mass storage.

Device drivers: Handles communication with the machine's peripheral devices.

Memory manager: Coordinates the use of the machine's main memory.

Scheduler: Coordinates the processes in the system.

Dispatcher: Controls the assignment of processes to CPU time.

2. The line is vague, and the distinction is often in the eye of the beholder. Roughly speaking, utility software performs basic, universal tasks, whereas application software performs tasks unique to the machine's application.
3. Virtual memory is the imaginary memory space whose apparent presence is created by the process of swapping data and programs back and forth between main memory and mass storage.
4. When the machine is turned on, the CPU begins executing the bootstrap, which resides in ROM. This bootstrap directs the CPU through the process of transferring the operating system from mass storage into the volatile area of main memory. When this transfer is complete, the bootstrap directs the CPU to jump to the operating system.

Section 3.3

1. A program is a set of directions. A process is the action of following those directions.
2. The CPU completes its current machine cycle, saves the state of the current process, and sets its program counter to a predetermined value (which is the location of the interrupt handler). Thus the next instruction executed will be the first instruction within the interrupt handler.
3. They could be given higher priorities so that they would be given preference by the dispatcher. Another option would be to give the higher-priority processes longer time slices.
4. The machine would provide a complete quantum to 18 processes in one second.
5. A total of $^{10}\!/_{11}$ of the machine's time would be spent actually performing processes. When a process requests an I/O activity, its time slice is terminated while the controller performs the request. Thus, if each process made such a request after only 5 milliseconds of its quantum, the efficiency of the machine would drop to $^1\!/_2$. That is, the machine would spend as much time making context switches as it would executing processes.
6. How about a mail order business and its clients, a stock broker and his or her clients, or a pharmacist and his or her customers?

Section 3.4

1. This system guarantees that the resource is not used by more than one process at a time; however, it dictates that the resource be allocated in a strictly alternating fashion. Once a process has used and relinquished the resource, it must wait for the other process to use the resource before the original process can access it again. This is true even if the first process needs the resource right away and the other process won't need it for some time.

2. If two cars enter opposite ends of the tunnel at the same time, they will not be aware of the other's presence. The process of entering and turning on the lights is another example of a critical region, or in this case we might call it a critical process. In this terminology, we could summarize the flaw by saying that cars at opposite ends of the tunnel could execute the critical process at the same time.

3. a. This guarantees that the nonshareable resource is not required and allocated on a partial basis; that is, a car is given the whole bridge or nothing at all.
   b. This means that the nonshareable resource can be forcibly retrieved.
   c. This makes the nonshareable resource shareable, which removes the competition.

4. A sequence of arrows that forms a closed loop in the directed graph. It is on this observation that techniques have been developed, allowing some operating systems to recognize the existence of deadlock and consequently to take appropriate corrective action.

Section 3.5

1. An open network is one whose specifications and protocols are public, allowing different vendors to produce compatible products.

2. A router is a machine connecting two networks. More technically, a router is a machine connecting two networks that use the same internet protocols. The term *gateway* is used to refer to a machine connecting two networks that use different protocols for handling internet activities.

3. The complete Internet address of a host consists of the network identifier and the host address.

4. A URL is essentially the address of a document in the World Wide Web. A browser is a program that assists a user in accessing hypertext.

5. Any break in the ring would disrupt communication. If messages could be transferred in either direction, one break in the ring would not disrupt communication.

Section 3.6

1. The link layer receives the message and hands it to the network layer. The network layer notes that the message is for another host, attaches another

intermediate destination address to the message, and gives the message back to the link layer.

2. Unlike TCP, UDP is a connectionless protocol that does not confirm that the message was received at the destination.

3. Each message is assigned a hop count that determines the maximum number of times the message will be relayed.

4. Nothing really. A programmer at any host could modify the software at that host to keep such records. This is why sensitive data should be encrypted.

Section 3.7

1. The use of passwords protects data (and therefore information as well). The use of encryption protects information.

2. In the context of our study, the ECPA defines privacy rights involving electronic communication.

3. If compliance with a law is technically infeasible, then that law will not (cannot) be obeyed. The requirements of the CALEA are technically, as well as financially, demanding—meaning that compliance with the law is problematic.

Chapter 4

Section 4.1

1. A process is the activity of executing an algorithm. A program is a representation of an algorithm.

2. In the introductory chapter we cited algorithms for playing music, operating washing machines, constructing models, performing magic tricks, and the Euclidean algorithm. Many of the "algorithms" you meet in everyday life fail to be algorithms according to our formal definition. The example of the long-division algorithm was cited in the text. Another is the algorithm executed by a clock that continues to advance its hands and ring its chimes day after day.

3. The informal definition fails to require that the steps be ordered and unambiguous. It merely hints at the requirements that the steps be executable and lead to an end.

4. There are two points here. The first is that the instructions define a non-terminating process. In reality, however, the process will ultimately reach the state in which there are no coins in your pocket. In fact, this may be the starting state. At this point the problem is that of ambiguity. The algorithm, as represented, does not tell us what to do in this situation.

Section 4.2

1. One example is found in the composition of matter. At one level, the primitives are considered molecules, yet these particles are actually composites made up of atoms, which in turn are composed of electrons, protons, and neutrons. Today, we know that even these "primitives" are composites.

2. Once a procedure is correctly constructed, it can be used as a building block for larger program structures without reconsidering the procedure's internal composition.

3. **assign** X the value of the larger input;
   assign Y the value of the smaller input;
   while (Y not zero) **do**
     (**assign** Remainder the value of the
        remainder after dividing X by Y;
      assign X the value of Y;
      assign Y the value of Remainder)
   assign GCD the value of X

4. All other colors of light can be produced by combining red, blue, and green. Thus a television picture tube is designed to produce these three basic colors.

Section 4.3

1. a. **if** $(n = 1$ or $n = 2)$
         then (the answer is the list containing the single value n)
         else (Divide n by 3, obtaining a quotient q and a remainder r.)
             if $(r = 0)$
             then (the answer is the list containing q 3s)
             if $r = 1$
             then (the answer is the list containing $q - 1$ 3s and two 2s;)
             if $r = 2$
             then (the answer is the list containing q 3s and one 2)
)

   b. The result would be the list containing 667 threes.

   c. You probably experimented with small input values until you began to see a pattern.

2. a. Yes. *Hint:* Place the first tile in the center so that it avoids the quadrant containing the hole while covering one square from each of the other quadrants. Each quadrant then represents a smaller version of the original problem.

   b. The board with a single hole contains $2^{2^n} - 1$ squares, and each tile covers exactly three squares.

c. Parts (a) and (b) of this question provide an excellent example of how knowing a solution to one problem helps solve another. See Polya's fourth phase.

3. It says, "This is the correct answer."

Section 4.4

1. Change the test in the while statement to read "target value not equal to current entry and there remain entries to be considered."

2. **assign** Z the value 0;
   assign X the value 1;
   repeat (**assign** Z the value Z + X;
       assign X the value X + 1)
   until (X = 6)

3.
Cheryl	Alice	Alice
George	Cheryl	Bob
Alice	George	Cheryl
Bob	Bob	George

4. It is a waste of time to insist on placing the pivot above an identical entry in the list. For instance, make the proposed change and then try the new program on a list in which all entries are the same.

5. **procedure** sort (List)
   assign N the value 1;
   while (N is less than the length of List) **do**
    (**assign** J the value N + 1;
    while (J is not greater than length of List) **do**
     (**if** (the entry in position J is less than the entry in position N)
      then (interchange the two entries)
     assign J the value J + 1)
    assign N the value N + 1)

6. The following is an inefficient solution. Can you make it more efficient?

   procedure sort (List)
   assign N the value of the length of List;
   while (N is greater than 1) **do**
    (**assign** J the value of the length of List;
    while (J is greater than 1) **do**
     (**if** (the entry in position J is less than the entry in position J − 1)
      then (interchange the two entries)
     assign J the value J − 1)
    assign N the value N − 1)

Section 4.5

1. The first sublist consists of the names following Henry—that is, Irene, Joe, Karl, Larry, Mary, Nancy, and Oliver. Next are the names from this list preceding Larry—that is, Irene, Joe, and Karl. At this point, the search process would find the target Joe at the center of the sublist in question.

2. 8, 17

3.
Alice	Alice
Carol	Bob
Bob	Carol
Larry	Larry
John	John

   A total of four activations of the procedure will be constructed.

4. The resulting process will sort the list, but it will waste time as the first activation of the procedure removes the first entry in the list and then puts it back where it was.

5. Multiple activations of the procedure will be created, each of which will merely remove its pivot entry and then put it back in the same place.

Section 4.6

1. If the machine can sort 100 names in one second, it can perform $\frac{1}{4}(10{,}000 - 100)$ comparisons in one second. This means that each comparison takes approximately 0.0004 second. Consequently, sorting 1000 names [which requires an average of $\frac{1}{4}(1{,}000{,}000 - 1000)$ comparisons] requires roughly 100 seconds or $1\frac{2}{3}$ minutes.

2. The binary search belongs to $\Theta(\lg n)$, the sequential search belongs to $\Theta(n)$, and the insertion sort belongs to $\Theta(n^2)$.

3. The class $\Theta(\lg n)$ is most efficient, followed by $\Theta(n)$, $\Theta(n^2)$, and $\Theta(n^3)$.

4. No. The answer is not correct, although it may sound right. The truth is that two of the three cards are the same on both sides. Thus the probability of picking such a card is two-thirds.

5. No. If the dividend is less than the divisor, such as in $\frac{3}{7}$, the answer given is 1, although it should be 0.

6. No. If the value of X is zero and the value of Y is nonzero, the answer given will not be correct.

7. Each time the test for termination is conducted, the statement "Sum = $1 + 2 + \ldots + I$ and I less than or equal to N" is true. Combining this with the termination condition "I greater than or equal to N" produces the desired conclusion "Sum = $1 + 2 + \ldots + N$." Since I is initialized at zero and incremented by one each time through the loop, its value must ultimately reach that of N.

8. Unfortunately, no. Problems beyond the control of hardware and software design, such as mechanical malfunctions and electrical problems, can affect computations.

Chapter 5

Section 5.1

1. A program in a third-generation language is machine independent in the sense that its steps are not stated in terms of the machine's attributes such as registers and memory cell addresses. On the other hand, it is machine dependent in the sense that arithmetic overflow and round-off errors will still occur.
2. The major distinction is that an assembler translates each instruction in the source program into a single machine instruction, whereas a compiler often produces many machine-language instructions to obtain the equivalent of a single source program instruction.
3. The declarative paradigm is based on developing a description of the problem to be solved. The functional paradigm forces the programmer to describe the problem's solution in terms of solutions to smaller problems. The object-oriented paradigm places emphasis on describing the components in the problem's environment.
4. The third-generation languages allow the program to be expressed more in terms of the problem's environment and less in terms of computer gibberish than do the earlier-generation languages.

Section 5.2

1. Using a descriptive constant can improve the accessibility of the program.
2. A declarative statement describes terminology; an imperative statement describes steps in an algorithm.
3. Integer, real, character, and Boolean.
4. The if-then-else and while loop structures are very common.
5. All components of a homogeneous array have the same type.

Section 5.3

1. A local variable is accessible only within a program unit such as a procedure; a global variable is accessible program wide.
2. A function is a procedure that returns a value associated with the function's name.
3. Because that is what they are. I/O operations are actually calls to routines within the machine's operating system.
4. A formal parameter is an identifier within a procedure. It serves as a placeholder for the value, the actual parameter, that is passed to the procedure when the procedure is called.

Section 5.4

1. *Lexical analysis:* the process of identifying tokens.

   Parsing: recognizing the grammatical structure of the program.

   Code generation: producing the instructions in the object program.

2. A symbol table is the record of information the parser has obtained from the program's declarative statements.

3. Actually, the grammar is ambiguous. Here is one answer. Can you find another? (Hint: Start by considering an Expression as a single Term.)

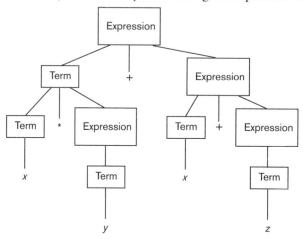

4. They are one or more instances of the substrings
   forward backward cha cha cha
   backward forward cha cha cha
   swing right cha cha cha
   swing left cha cha cha

Section 5.5

1. A class is the description of an object.

2. The Employee class might contain features relating to an employee's name, address, years in service, etc. The FullTimeEmployee class might contain features relating to retirement benefits. The PartTimeEmployee class might contain features relating to hours worked per week, hourly wage, etc.

3. Encapsulation is restriction of access. To encapsulate features of an object is to restrict access to them to the object itself.

Section 5.6

1. The list would include techniques for initiating the execution of concurrent processes and techniques for implementing interprocess communication.

2. One is to place the burden on the processes, another is to place the burden on the data. The latter has the advantage of concentrating the task at a single point in the program.

Section 5.7

1. R, T, and V. For instance, we can show that R is a consequence by adding its negation to the collection and showing that resolution can lead to the empty statement, as shown here:

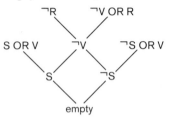

2. No. The collection is inconsistent, since resolution can lead to the empty statement, as shown here:

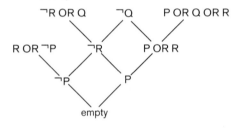

3. a. thriftier(sue, carol)
      thriftier(sue, john)
   b. thriftier(sue, carol)
      thriftier(bill, carol)
   c. thriftier(carol, john)
      thriftier(bill, sue)
      thriftier(sue, carol)
      thriftier(bill, sue)
      thriftier(sue, john)

Chapter 6

Section 6.1

1. A long sequence of assignment statements is not as complex in the context of program design as a few nested if statements.

2. One approach is to intentionally place some errors in the software when it is designed. Then, after the software has supposedly been debugged, check to see how many of the original errors are still present. If 5 of the 7 original errors have been removed, then conclude that only $\frac{5}{7}$ of the total errors in the software have been removed.

3. How about the number of errors found after a fixed period of use? One problem here is that this value cannot be measured in advance.

Section 6.2

1. System requirements are stated in terms of the application environment, whereas the specifications are stated in technical terms and identify how the requirements will be met.

2. The analysis phase concentrates on what the proposed system must accomplish. The design phase concentrates on how the system accomplishes its goals. The implementation phase concentrates on the actual construction of the system. The testing phase concentrates on making sure that the system does what it is intended to do.

3. The traditional waterfall approach dictates that the analysis, design, implementation, and testing phases be performed in a linear manner. The prototyping model allows for a more relaxed trial-and-error approach.

Section 6.3

1. The chapters of a novel build on one another, whereas the sections in an encyclopedia are largely independent. Hence a novel has more coupling between its chapters than an encyclopedia has between its sections. However, the sections within an encyclopedia probably have a higher level of cohesion than the chapters in a novel.

2. Explicit coupling includes the identification of the trump suit, which hand is dummy, who will lead, and so on. Insights gained from the bidding process, such as who holds which cards, can be considered implicit coupling.

3. This is a tough one. From one point of view, we could start by placing everything in a single module. This would result in little cohesion and no coupling at all. If we then begin to divide this single module into smaller ones, the result would be an increase in coupling. We might therefore conclude that increasing cohesion tends to increase coupling.

   On the other hand, suppose the problem at hand naturally divides into three very cohesive modules, which we will call A, B, and C. If our original design did not observe this natural division (for example, half of task A might be placed with half of task B, and so on), we would expect the cohesion to be low and the coupling high. In this case, redesigning the system by isolating tasks A, B, and C into separate modules would most likely decrease intermodule coupling as intramodule cohesion increases.

4. To add a personal touch, an object of type Room could use the player's name in its communication with the player. For this, the Room object would need to send a request to a PlayerRecord object to obtain the name of the player. Another extension would be that a PlayerRecord object will need to send the player's level to the Room objects.

Section 6.4

1.

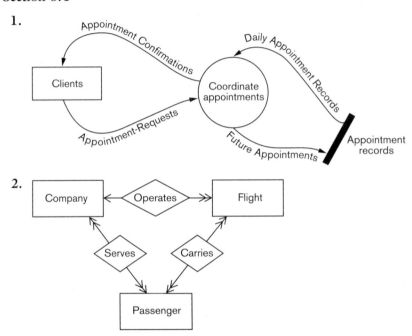

3. In a sense, the loop structure represented by the while statement in our pseudocode could be considered a design pattern. Another good answer would be the client-server model.

4. Researchers hope that frameworks will serve as prefabricated building blocks from which large software systems can be constructed in a manner similar to the way in which complex devices are constructed from off-the-shelf components in other engineering disciplines.

Section 6.5

1. The purpose of testing software is to find errors. Therefore, software engineers generally consider a test that does not reveal an error as a failure.

2. One would be to consider the amount of branching in the modules. For instance, a procedural module containing numerous loops and if-then-else statements would probably be more prone to errors than a module with a simple logical structure.
3. Boundary value analysis would suggest that you test the software on a list with 100 entries as well as a list with no entries. You might also perform a test with a list that is already in the correct order.

Section 6.6

1. In accompanying manuals, within the source program in the form of comments and well-written code, through interactive messages that the program itself writes at a terminal, through data dictionaries, and in the form of design documents such as structure charts, class diagrams, dataflow diagrams, and entity-relationship diagrams.
2. In both the development and modification phases. The point is that modifications must be documented as thoroughly as the original program. (It's also true that software is documented while in its use phase. For example, a user of the system might discover problems, which are then reported in the system user's manual. Moreover, books written on the use and design of popular software systems are common. These are sometimes written by people other than the original designers and after the software has been in use for some time and has gained popularity.)
3. Different people will have different opinions on this one. Some will argue that the program is the point of the whole project and thus is naturally the more important. Others will argue that a program is worth nothing if it is not documented, because if you can't understand a program, you can't use it or modify it. Moreover, with good documentation, the task of creating the program can be "easily" re-created.

Section 6.7

1. This is a problem the courts must resolve. It would certainly involve more than just the format of the program and choice of variable names.
2. Copyright and patent laws benefit society because they encourage creators of new products to make them available to the public. Trade secret laws benefit society because they allow a company to protect the steps in a product's development from competitors. Without such protection, companies would hesitate to make major investments in new products.
3. A disclaimer does not protect a company against negligence.

Part 3

Chapter 7

Section 7.1

1. 5 3 7 4 2 8 1 9 6
2. If R is the number of rows in the matrix, the formula is $R(J-1)+(I-1)$.
3. From the beginning address of 25, we must skip over $11(3-1) + (6-1) = 27$ entries in the matrix, each of which occupies two memory cells. Thus we must skip over 54 memory cells. The final address can therefore be found by adding 54 to the address of the first entry, resulting in the address of 79.
4. $(C-I)+J$

Section 7.2

1. As an example, to find the fifth entry in a dense list, multiply the number of cells in each entry by 4 and add the result to the address of the first entry. The situation is quite different in the case of the linked list because the address of the fifth entry is in no way related to the address of the first. Thus, to find the fifth entry, one must actually traverse each preceding entry.
2. The head pointer contains the NIL value.
3. **assign** Last the value of the last name to be printed
   assign Finished the value false
   assign Current Pointer the value in the head pointer;
   while (Current Pointer not NIL and Finished = false) **do**
      (print the entry pointed to by Current Pointer,
         if (the name just printed = Last)
            then (assign Finished the value true)
         assign Current Pointer the value in the pointer
            cell in the entry pointed to by Current Pointer)
4. **procedure** delete (Target)
   assign Current the value in the head pointer
   assign Previous the value NIL
   assign Found the value false
   while (Current not NIL and Found is false) **do**
      (**if** (the entry pointed to by Current is Target)
            then (assign Found the value true)
            else (assign Previous the value of Current;
         assign Current the value in the pointer
            cell of the entry pointed to by Current))
   if (Found is true)
      then (if (Previous = NIL)

then (assign head pointer the value in the
pointer cell of the entry pointed to by Current)
else (assign the pointer cell in the entry
pointed to by Previous the value in
the pointer cell in the entry pointed to
by Current))

Section 7.3

1. One traditional example is the stack of trays in a cafeteria. Many of these set-ups are spring-loaded to keep the top tray at a convenient level. In this case, the term *push* is truly representative of the process of adding more entries to the stack.

2.

Activity	Stack immediately following activity
Main program calls subprogram A.	Position in main
Subprogram A calls subprogram B.	Position in A Position in main
Subprogram B completes.	Position in main
Subprogram A calls subprogram C.	Position in A Position in main
Subprogram C completes.	Position in main
Subprogram A completes.	Stack empty

3. The stack pointer points to the cell immediately below the base of the stack.

4. **procedure** pop ()
   if (the stack pointer points below the stack base)
      then (exit with error message)
   Extract the stack entry pointed to by the stack pointer;
   Adjust the stack pointer to point to the next lower stack entry

5. Represent the stack as a one-dimensional array and the stack pointer as a variable of integer type. Then use this stack pointer to maintain a record of the position of the stack's top within the array rather than of the exact memory address.

Section 7.4

1.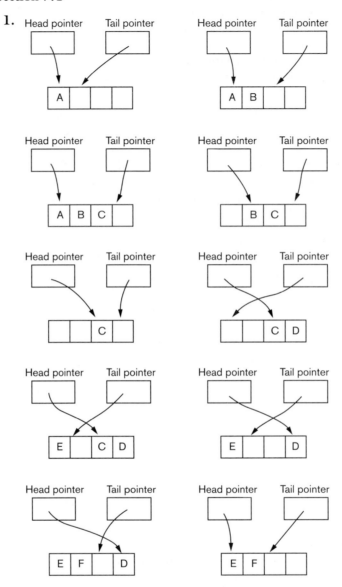

2. Both empty and full conditions are indicated by the equal head and tail pointers. Thus additional information is required to distinguish between the two conditions.

3. **procedure** insert (NewEntry)
   if (Full is true) **then** (exit with error message)
   Store NewEntry in the location pointed to by the tall pointer;
   Advance the tail pointer;
   if (the tail pointer points beyond the reserved block)
      then (alter the tail pointer to point to the first cell of the reserved block)
   if (head pointer = tail pointer)
      then (assign Full the value true)

Section 7.5

1. The root is 11, the leaf nodes are 1, 2, 6, 3, and 4. There are four (non-empty) subtrees below the node 9, with roots 5, 1, 2, and 6. The nodes 9 and 10 are siblings, as are 5 and 6, 1 and 2, and 7 and 8.
2. The root pointer is NIL.
3. Root pointer

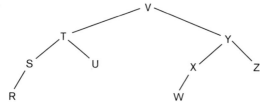

4.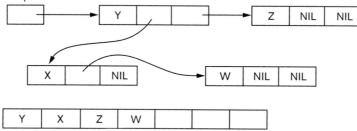

5. When searching for J:

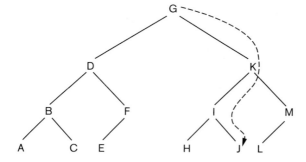

When searching for P:

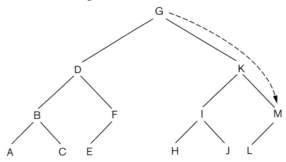

6.

procedure PrintTree(Tree)	procedure PrintTree(Tree)
if (root pointer of Tree is not NIL)	**if** (root pointer of Tree is not NIL)
then (Apply the procedure PrintTree to the Tree that appears as the left branch in Tree;	**then** (Apply the procedure PrintTree to the Tree that appears as the left branch in Tree;
Print root node of Tree;	Print root node of Tree;
Apply the procedure PrintTree to the tree that appears as the right branch in Tree.)	Apply the procedure PrintTree to the tree that appears as the right branch in Tree.)

Here, when K
is printed

Section 7.6

1. Deposits and withdrawals to and from a checking account can be executed only through specific procedures that are supported by laws.
2. An abstract data type is a concept; an instance of that data type is an actual object of that type. For example, dog is a type of animal, whereas Lassie and Rex are instances of that type.
3. Both abstract data types and classes are templates and represent the concept of bundling data with the procedures that manipulate the data. But classes are more general in that a class may not encompass a data structure.
4. A queue of integers might be implemented using either a contiguous or linked list as the underlying structure; or, perhaps as a circular queue restricted to a specific block of memory cells or a roaming block of cells, although this latter implementation would prove dangerous to the other data structures residing in memory.

Section 7.7

1. a. A5   b. A5   c. A5
2. D50F, 2EFE, 5FFE
3. 2EA0, 2FB0, 2101, 20B4, D50E, E50F, 5EE1, 5FF1, DF14, B008, C000

Chapter 8

Section 8.1

1. Physical records are read from mass storage into a buffer area from where the application program accesses the data in terms of logical records.
2. A file descriptor is a table holding the information needed by the operating system to manipulate a file.
3. It is the file manager that constructs the file descriptor.

Section 8.2

1. You should be led through these stages:

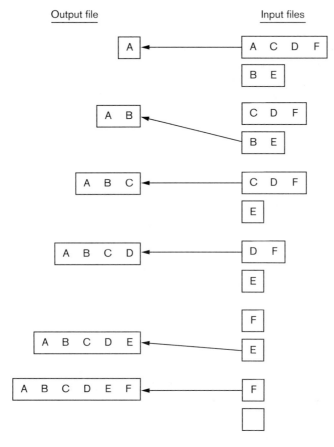

2. The idea is to first divide the file to be stored into many separate files containing one record each. Next, group the one-record files into pairs, and apply the merge algorithm to each pair. This results in half as many files, each with two records. Furthermore, each of these two-record files is

sorted. We can group them into pairs and again apply the merge algorithm to the pairs. Again we find ourselves with fewer but larger files, each of which is sorted. Continuing in this fashion, we are ultimately left with only one file that consists of all the original records but in sorted order. (If an odd number of files occurs at any stage of this process, we need merely to set the odd one aside and pair it with one of the larger files in the next stage.)

Section 8.3

1. A text file is essentially a sequential file in which each record is a single symbol.
2. Documents processed by word processors (letters, manuscripts, memoranda, brochures) are normally stored as text files. Mail transferred via e-mail is also normally handled as text files.
3. Normally a large part of the document is held in main memory, allowing random access to that portion of the document. However, as the latter portion of the document is processed, the earlier portion may be placed in mass storage. If one then wanted to back up this earlier portion, and that portion had been stored as a text file, then the processor would have to read from the beginning of the document to find the part to be updated.
4. The keyboard would produce the patterns 00110010 and 00110100, representing the characters 2 and 4. The variable Age would be assigned the bit pattern 0000000000011000, which is the two's complement representation for 24.

Section 8.4

1. The operating system first searches the index to find which segment should be interrogated. Having established the desired segment number, the operating system might then check to see whether that segment is already in main memory. (It may be the same segment that was previously accessed.) If it is already in main memory, the operating system searches it and relays the correct record to the program. Otherwise, the segment must be retrieved from mass storage and then searched.
2. The operating system in a time-sharing environment does its best to use all time efficiently. If the required storage segment is not already in main memory, the operating system asks the controller of the disk drive to retrieve the correct segment; but rather than wait for the data to arrive, the operating system terminates the original process's time slice and starts another process. After the controller has placed the requested segment in main memory, the operating system returns to the original process, gives it the record needed, and allows it to continue execution in the normal sequence of time slices.

Section 8.5

1. This is a good example of the kinds of things that must be considered when selecting a hash algorithm. In this case, using the first three digits of the Social Security numbers is a poor choice because these digits represent the area of the country in which the number was assigned. Consequently, citizens in one area of the country tend to have the same starting digits in their Social Security numbers, and this would result in more clustering than normal in the hashed file.

2. A poorly chosen hash algorithm results in more clustering than normal and thus in more overflow. Since the overflow from each section of mass storage is organized as a linked list, searching through the overflow records is essentially searching a sequential file.

3. The section assignments are as follows:

   a. 0   b. 0   c. 3   d. 0   e. 3
   f. 3   g. 3   h. 3   i. 3   j. 0

   Thus all the records hash into buckets 0 and 3, leaving buckets 1, 2, 4, and 5 empty. The problem here is that the number of buckets being used (6) and the key field values have the common factor of 3. (You might try rehashing these key field values using 7 buckets and see what improvement you find.)

4. The point here is that we are essentially applying a hash algorithm to place the people in the group into one of 365 categories. The hash algorithm, of course, is the calculation of one's birthday. The amazing thing is that only 23 people are required before the probability is in favor of at least two of the birthdays being the same. In terms of a hashed file, this indicates that when hashing records into 365 available buckets of mass storage, clustering is likely to be present after only 23 records have been entered.

Chapter 9

Section 9.1

1. The purchasing department would be interested in inventory records to place orders for more raw goods, whereas the accounting department would need the information to balance the books.

2. Employee, student, alumni, finance, registration, equipment/supplies, and so on.

3. The subschema for the purchasing department would probably include the addresses of the various manufacturers who supply the parts in inventory and perhaps the name of the sales representative for each of these companies. The subschema for the accounting department would probably not include this information.

Section 9.2

1. No. The use of file systems invariably dictates that the application program be expressed in terms of the actual organization of records in the file. Thus a change in the record structure would require changes in all programs accessing that file.

2.

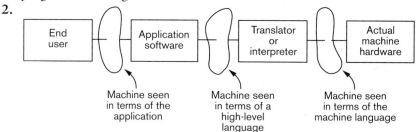

3. The application software translates the user's requests from the terminology of the application into terminology compatible with the database management system. The database management system in turn converts the requests into a form understood by the routines that actually manipulate the data in mass storage. These last routines perform the retrieval of data.

Section 9.3

1. a. G. Jerry Smith
    b. Cheryl H. Clark
    c. S26Z
2. One solution is

   TEMP ← SELECT from JOB
           where Dept = "PERSONNEL"
   LIST ← PROJECT JobTitle from TEMP

   In some systems this results in a list with a job title repeated, depending on how many times it occurred in the personnel department. That is, our list may contain numerous occurrences of the title secretary. It is more common, however, to design the PROJECT operation so that it removes duplicate tuples from the resulting relation.
3. One solution is

   TEMP1 ← JOIN JOB and ASSIGNMENT
           where JOB.JobId = ASSIGNMENT.JobId
   TEMP2 ← SELECT from TEMP1
           where TermDate = "*"
   TEMP3 ← JOIN EMPLOYEE and TEMP2
           where EMPLOYEE.EmplId = TEMP2.EmplId
   RESULT ← PROJECT Name, Dept from TEMP3

4. select JobTitle
    from JOB
    where Dept = "PERSONNEL"

    select EMPLOYEE.Name, JOB.Dept
      from JOB, ASSIGNMENT, and EMPLOYEE
      where (Job.Job = ASSIGNMENT.JobId) and
        (ASSIGNMENT.EmpId = EMPLOYEE.EmpIID)
        and (ASSIGNMENT.TermDate = "*")

5. The model itself does not provide data independence. This is a property of the data management system. Data independence is achieved by providing the data management system the ability to present a consistent relational organization to the application software even though the actual organization may change.

6. Through common attributes. For instance, the EMPLOYEE relation in this section is tied to the ASSIGNMENT relation via the attribute EmpId, and the ASSIGNMENT relation is tied to the JOB relation by the attribute JobId. Attributes used to connect relations like this are sometimes called connection attributes.

Section 9.4

1. There may be methods for assigning and retrieving the StartDate as well as the TermDate. Another method may be provided for reporting the total time in service.

2. One approach is to establish an object for each type of product in inventory. Each of these objects could maintain the total inventory of its product, the cost of the product, and links to the outstanding orders for the product.

3. As indicated at the beginning of this section, object-oriented databases appear to handle composite data types more easily than relational databases. Moreover, the fact that objects can contain methods that take an active role in answering questions promises to give object-oriented databases an advantage over relational databases whose relations merely hold the data.

Section 9.5

1. Once a transaction has reached its commit point, the database management system accepts the responsibility of seeing that the complete transaction is performed on the database. A transaction that has not reached its commit point does not have such assurance. If problems arise, it may have to be resubmitted.

2. One approach would be to stop interweaving transactions for an instant so that all current transactions can be completed in full. This would establish a point at which a future cascading rollback would terminate.

3. A balance of $100 would result if the transactions were executed one at a time. A balance of $200 would result if the first transaction were executed after the second transaction retrieved the original balance and before that second transaction stored its new balance. A balance of $300 would result if the second transaction were executed after the first retrieved the original balance and before the first transaction stored its new balance.
4. a. If no other transaction has exclusive access, the shared access will be granted.
   b. If another transaction already has some form of access, the database management system will normally make the new transaction wait, or it could rollback the other transactions and give access to the new transaction.
5. Deadlock would occur if each of two transactions acquired exclusive access to different items and then required access to the other.
6. The deadlock above could be removed by rolling back one of the transactions (using the log) and giving the other transaction access to the data item previously held by the first.

Section 9.6

1. The point here is to compare your answer to this question with that of the next. The two raise essentially the same question but in different contexts.
2. See previous problem.
3. You might receive announcements or advertisements for opportunities that you would not have otherwise received, but you might also become the subject of solicitation or the target of crime.
4. The point here is that a free press can alert the public to abuses or potential abuses and thus bring public opinion into play. In most of the cases cited in the text, it was a free press that initiated corrective action by alerting the public.

Part 4

Chapter 10

Section 10.1

1. Our purpose here is not to give a decisive answer to this issue but to use it to show how delicate the argument over the existence of intelligence really is.

2. Although most of us would probably say no, we would probably claim that if a human dispensed the same products in a similar atmosphere, awareness would be present even though we might not be able to explain the distinction.

3. There is not a right or wrong answer. Most would agree that the machine at least appeared to be intelligent.

Section 10.2

1. In the remote control case, the system needs only to relay the picture, whereas to use the picture for maneuvering, the robot must be able to "understand" the meaning of the picture.

2. The possible interpretations for one section of the drawing do not match any of those of another section. To embed this insight into a program, you might isolate the interpretations allowable for various line junctions and then write a program that tries to find a set of compatible interpretations (one for each junction). In fact, if you stop and think about it, this is probably what your own senses did in trying to evaluate the drawing. Did you detect your eyes scanning back and forth between the two ends of the drawing as your senses tried to piece possible interpretations together? (If this subject interests you, you'll want to read about the work of people such as D. A. Huffman, M. B. Clowes, and D. Waltz.)

3. There are four blocks in the stack but only three are visible. The point is that understanding this apparently simple concept requires a significant amount of "intelligence."

Section 10.3

1. Production systems provide a uniform approach to a variety of problems. That is, although apparently different in their original form, all problems reformulated into terms of production systems become the problem of finding a path through a state graph.

2.

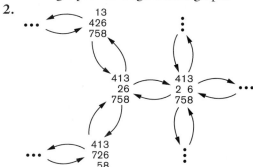

3. The tree is four moves deep. The upper portion appears as follows:

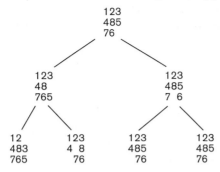

4. The task requires too much paper as well as too much time.

5. Our heuristic system for solving the eight-puzzle is based on an analysis of the immediate situation, just as that of the mountain climber. This short-sightedness is what allowed our algorithm to proceed initially along the wrong path in the example of this section just as a mountain climber can be led into trouble by always plotting a course based only on the local terrain. (This analogy often causes heuristic systems based on local or immediate information to be called hill-climbing systems.)

6. The system rotates the 5, 6, and 8 tiles either clockwise or counterclockwise until the goal state is reached.

7. The problem here is that our heuristic scheme ignores the value of keeping the hole adjacent to the tiles that are out of place. If the hole is surrounded by tiles in their correct position, some of these tiles must be moved before those tiles still seeking their correct place can be moved. Thus it is incorrect to consider all those tiles surrounding the hole as actually being correct. To fix this flaw, we might first observe that a tile in its correct position but blocking the hole from incorrectly positioned tiles must be moved away from its correct position and later moved back. Thus each correctly positioned tile on a path between the hole and the nearest incorrectly positioned tile accounts for at least two moves in the remaining solution. We can therefore modify our projected cost calculation as follows:

> First, calculate the projected cost as before. However, if the hole is totally isolated from the incorrectly positioned tiles, find a shortest path between the hole and an incorrectly positioned tile, multiply the number of tiles on this path by two, and add the resulting value to the previous projected cost.

With this system, the leaf nodes in Figure 10.10 have projected costs of 6, 6, and 4 (from left to right), and thus the correct branch is pursued initially.

Our new system is not foolproof. For example, consider the following configuration. The solution is to slide the 5 tile down, rotate the top two rows clockwise until those tiles are correct, move the 5 tile back up, and finally move the 8 tile to its correct position. However, our new heuristic system wants us to start by moving the 8 tile, because the state obtained by this initial move has a projected cost of only 6 compared with the other options that have costs of 8.

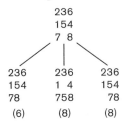

Section 10.4

1. All patterns produce an output of 0 except for the pattern 1, 0, which produces an output of 1.

2. Assign a weight of 1 to each input, and assign the unit a threshold value of 1.5.

3. Design a two-level network as described in the text. The lower-level units should assign each of their inputs the weight 1 and have a threshold of $7\frac{1}{2}$. Thus one of these units produces a 1 if the pattern in the field of view is the circle; otherwise, all the lower-level units produce an output of 0. In turn, if the upper-level unit assigns each of its inputs the weight 1 and has a threshold of $\frac{1}{2}$, then the entire network produces a 1 when the pattern is a circle and a 0 when the pattern is an X.

4. Design a two-level network as described in the text. Each lower-level unit should have a threshold of $2\frac{1}{2}$, assign the weight of 0 to the corner squares in its field of view, and assign the weight of 1 to the other squares. The only way one of these units can produce a 1 as its output is to have the C pattern in its field of view. In fact, if this is the pattern, two lower-level units produce an output of 1. Thus, if the upper-level unit assigns each of its inputs the weight 1 and has a threshold of 1, then it produces an output of 1 when the pattern in the field of view is the C and an output of 0 when the pattern is the V.

Section 10.5

1. 00101001100000100001000100000

2. How about the problem of developing a strategy for investing in the stock market?

3. The structure of a program based on the functional paradigm is that of functions within functions. That is, the structure is homogeneous at all levels. However, a program based on the object-oriented paradigm consists of objects that may contain methods as well as other objects. Thus

the structure is not as homogeneous as that of a functional program. In turn, it is harder to mix the components of object-oriented programs to form new programs.

Section 10.6

1. Is the sentence describing what kind of horses they are, or is it telling what some people are doing?
2. The parsing process produces identical structures, but the semantic analysis recognizes that the prepositional phrase in the first sentence tells where the fence was built, whereas the phrase in the second sentence tells when the fence was built.
3. They are brother and sister.
4. It uses the closed-world assumption.
5. In many ways, the two are the same. However, traditional databases tend to contain only facts such as an employee's name, address, and so on, whereas knowledge bases tend to include rules such as "if raining, check rain gauge" that can be used to direct the reasoning process.

Section 10.7

1. There is no right or wrong answer.
2. There is no right or wrong answer.
3. There is no right or wrong answer.

Chapter 11

Section 11.1

1.
```
clear AUX;
incr AUX;
while X not 0 do;
  clear X;
  clear AUX;
end;
while AUX not 0 do;
  incr X;
  clear AUX;
end;
```

2.
```
while X not 0 do;
  decr X;
end;
```

3. move X to AUX;
   while AUX not 0 do;
    S1
    clear AUX;
   end;
   move X to AUX;
   invert AUX;
   while AUX not 0 do;
    S2
    clear AUX;
   end;
   while X not 0 do;
    clear AUX;
    clear X;
   end;

4. If we assume that X refers to the memory cell at address 40 and that each program segment starts at location 00, we have the following conversion table:

	Address	Contents
clear X;	00	20
	01	00
	02	30
	03	40

	Address	Contents
incr X;	00	11
	01	40
	02	20
	03	01
	04	50
	05	01
	06	30
	07	40

	Address	Contents
decr X;	00	20
	01	00
	02	23
	03	00
	04	11
	05	40
	06	22
	07	01
	08	B1
	09	10
	0A	40
	0B	03
	0C	50
	0D	02
	0E	B1
	0F	06
	10	33
	11	40

	Address	Contents
while X not	00	20
0 do;	01	00
.	02	11
.	03	40
.	04	B1
end;	05	WZ
	.	.
	.	.
	.	.
	WX	B0
	WY	00

5. Just as in a real machine, negative numbers could be dealt with via a coding system. For example, the rightmost bit in each string can be used as a sign but with the remaining bits used to represent the magnitude of the value.

Section 11.2

1. The result is the following diagram:

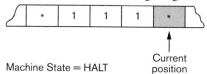

Machine State = HALT

Current position

2.

Current state	Cell content	Value to write	Direction to move	New state to enter
START	*	*	left	STATE 1
STATE 1	0	0	left	STATE 2
STATE 1	1	0	left	STATE 2
STATE 1	*	0	left	STATE 2
STATE 2	0	*	right	STATE 3
STATE 2	1	*	right	STATE 3
STATE 2	*	*	right	STATE 3
STATE 3	0	0	right	HALT
STATE 3	1	0	right	HALT

3.

Current state	Current cell content	Value to write	Direction to move	New state to enter
START	*	*	left	SUBTRACT
SUBTRACT	0	1	left	BORROW
SUBTRACT	1	0	left	NO BORROW
BORROW	0	1	left	BORROW
BORROW	1	0	left	NO BORROW
BORROW	*	*	right	ZERO
NO BORROW	0	0	left	NO BORROW

Current state	Current cell content	Value to write	Direction to move	New state to enter
NO BORROW	1	1	left	NO BORROW
NO BORROW	*	*	right	RETURN
ZERO	0	0	right	ZERO
ZERO	1	0	right	ZERO
ZERO	*	*	no move	HALT
RETURN	0	0	right	RETURN
RETURN	1	1	right	RETURN
RETURN	*	*	no move	HALT

4. The point here is that the concept of a Turing machine is supposed to capture the meaning of "to compute." That is, any time a situation occurs in which computing is taking place, the components and activities of a Turing machine should be present. For example, a person figuring income tax is doing a certain degree of computing. The computing machine is the person and the tape is represented by the paper on which values are recorded.

Section 11.3

1. The computation of a loan payment, the area of a circle, or a car's mileage.
2. Mathematicians call such functions transcendental functions. Examples include the logarithmic and trigonometric functions. These particular examples can still be computed but not by algebraic means. For example, the trigonometric functions can be calculated by actually drawing the triangle involved, measuring its sides, and only then turning to the algebraic operation of dividing.
3. The function is multiplication by 2.
4. The machine described by the following table halts if started with an even input but never halts if started with an odd input:

Current state	Cell content	Value to write	Direction to move	New state to enter
START	*	*	left	STATE 1
STATE 1	0	0	right	HALT
STATE 1	1	1	no move	STATE 1
STATE 1	*	*	no move	STATE 1

Section 11.4

1.

decr X;   (program)

↓

0110010001100101011000110111001000010000001011000001111011   (ASCII code)

↓

28,258,975,461,955,643   (Gödel number in base ten)

2. Yes. In fact, this program halts for any input value. Thus it must halt if its input is its own Gödel number.

3. The point here is that the logic is the same as in our argument that the halting problem does not have an algorithmic solution. If the house painter paints his or her own house, then he or she does not and vice versa.

Section 11.5

1. We could conclude only that the problem has complexity $\Theta(2^n)$. If we could show that the "best algorithm" for solving the problem belongs to $\Theta(2^n)$, we could conclude that the problem belongs to $\Theta(2^n)$.

2. No. As a general rule, the algorithm in $\Theta(n^2)$ will outperform the one in $\Theta(2^n)$, but for small input values an exponential algorithm often outperforms a polynomial algorithm. In fact, it is true that exponential algorithms are sometimes preferred as opposed to polynomial ones when the application involves only small inputs.

3. The point is that the number of subcommittees is growing exponentially, and from this point on, the job of listing all the possibilities becomes a laborious task.

4. Within the class of polynomial problems is the sorting problem, which can be solved by polynomial algorithms such as the insertion sort.

   Within the class of nonpolynomial problems is the task of listing all the subcommittees that could be formed from a given parent committee.

   Any polynomial problem is an NP problem. The Traveling Salesman problem is an example of an NP problem that has not been shown to be a polynomial problem.

Section 11.6

1. $691 + 365 + 651 + 493 = 2200$

2. $57 + 2184 + 782 = 3023$. This is the encryption system that is developed in this section. Solve the problem by converting it into a problem based on the list

   1 4 6 12 25 51 105 210 421 850

3. Multiply each entry in the list by 30, divide each product by 67, and record the remainders. This produces the list 60, 23, 46, 55, 50 which serves as the public encryption key.

4. You must find a multiple of 5 that is one greater than a multiple of 23. Note that $5 \times 14 = 70$ and $3 \times 23 = 69$. Therefore the multiplicative inverse of 5 is 14 in the modular system whose modulus is 23.

INDEX

Abacus 6
Abstract data type 354
Abstraction 11
Abstract tools 12, 21, 331, 336, 345
Access (Microsoft database system) 415
Access time 31
Actual parameter 250
Ada 236, 237, 242, 244, 249, 269, 354, 547
Adaptive dictionary encoding 61
Address 26
Address polynomial 324
Adleman, Leonard 524
Adobe Systems 43
Aiken, Howard 7
Alexander, Christopher 305
Algebraic coding theory 69
Algorithm 2, 169
discovery of 178
complexity/efficiency of 207, 513
representation of 170
Alta Vista 147
America Online 427
American National Standards Institute (ANSI) 36, 229
American Standard Code for Information Interchange (ASCII) 36, 377, 380, 439
Analog 58

AND 18
APL 242
Apple Computer, Inc. 9, 43, 80, 105
Applet (Java) 553
Application layer (Internet) 152
Application software 125
Arc 446
Argument (of a predicate)
Arithmetic/logic unit 80
Arithmetic shift 98
Array
heterogeneous 240
homogeneous 239, 322
Artificial intelligence 437
performance-oriented approach 439
simulation-oriented approach 439
Artificial neural network 107, 459
ASCII. See American Standard Code for Information Interchange
Assembler 227
Assembly language 227
Assertions 214
Assignment statements 175, 242
Association for Computing Machinery (ACM) 286, 288
Atanasoff, John 7

AT&T 145, 216
Attribute 405
Axiom 214
Axon 459

Babbage, Charles 6, 7, 547
Backtracking 334
Balanced tree 345
Bare Bones language 492, 557
   Universality of 506
Base case 205
Base Two. *See* Binary system
Basis path testing 308
Batch processing 120
Bell Laboratories 7
Benchmarking 91
Beta version 309
Berry, Clifford 7
Big O notation 515
Big theta notation 211
Binary file 377
Binary notation (*See also* Binary system) 38
Binary search algorithm 196
complexity of 207
Binary system 44
Binary tree 343
Bi-quinary representation 40
Bit 18
Bit map 42, 96
Bits per second (bps) 102
Blackboard model 480
Black-box testing 309
Body (of a loop) 187
Boole, George 19
Boolean data type 238
Boolean operations 19
Booting 129
Bootstrap 130
Borne shell 126
Bottom-up methodology 301
Boundary value analysis 309
Bps. *See* Bits per second
Breadth-first search 451
Browser 147
Bubble sort algorithm 195, 196
Bucket (hashing) 385
Buffer 35, 370
Bus 81
   ISA (Industrial Standard Architecture) 103

   EISA (Extended Industrial Standard Architecture) 103
   PCI (Peripheral Component Interconnect) 103
Bus network configuration 142
Byron, Augusta Ada 7, 547
Byte 26
Bytecode 256

C 236, 237, 238, 239, 240, 241, 242, 244, 245, 247, 249, 253, 331, 353, 384, 390, 549
C++ 236, 237, 238, 239, 240, 241, 242, 244, 245, 247, 249, 254, 265, 266, 358, 549
Cache memory 81
Capacitor 23
Carnegie-Mellon University 159
Carrier Sense, Multiple Access with Collision Detection (CSMA/CD) 150, 155
Cascading rollback 423
CASE. *See* Computer-aided software engineering
Case control structure 245
CASE tools 293
CD. *See* Compact disk
CD-DA. *See* Compact disk-digital audio
CD-ROM. *See* Compact disk-read only memory
CD-WORM. See Compact disk-write once, read many
Cell (memory) 26
Central processing unit (CPU) 80
Character data type 238
Children (in a tree) 342
Chip 24
Church, Alonzo 506
Church–Turing thesis 499, 506, 507, 557, 558
Circular queue 339
CISC. *See* Complex instruction set computer
Class 266, 357
Class diagram 295
Class-responsibility-collaboration (CRC) cards 304
Clause form 272
Client 134
Client/Server model 134
Clock 25, 90, 91
Closed network 142
Closed-world database 478
Close statement 371
Clowes, M. B. 591
Cluster 372
COBOL 228, 390
Code generation 261
Code generator 255

Code optimization 261
Coercion 261
Cohesion (intramodule) 298
Collision (hashing) 389
COLOSSUS 7
Column major order 322
Comments 236, 246
Commit point 422
Commit/Rollback protocol 421
Communication Assistance for Law Enforcement At
    (CALEA) 160
Compact disk 31
Compact disk-digital audio (CD-DA) 32, 69
Compact disk-read-only memory (CD-ROM) 32, 69
Compact disk-write once-read many (CD-WORM) 32
Compiler 228
Complement 49
Complex instruction set computer (CISC) 80, 104
Complexity/Efficiency
of binary search 207
of insertion sort 208
of merge sort 516
of sequential search 207
Computable function 505
Computer-aided design (CAD) 43
Computer-aided software engineering (CASE) 293
Computer Emergency Response Team (CERT) 159
Computer Science 1
Concatenation 243
Concurrent processing 269
Conditional jump 83
Connectionless protocol 157
Constant 237
Constructor 358
Contextual analysis 474
Contiguous list. See List
Control coupling 296
Controller 100
Control of repetitive structures
iteration (looping) 187
recursion 204
Control statements 243
Control unit 80
Cookbooks 306
Copyright law 312
CORBA (Comman Object Request Broker
    Architecture) 136, 235
Core 23
Core wars 111

Coupling (intermodule) 296
CPU. See Central processing unit
CRC cards. See Class-responsibility-collaboration cards
Critical region 138, 270
Cross-platform software 227
C shell 126
CSMA/CD. See Carrier Sense, Multiple Access with
    Collision Detection
Cylinder 29

Dartmouth College 438
Darwin, Charles 482
Database 398
Database administrator (DBA) 398
Database management system (DBMS) 402
Database model 403
Data compression 60
Data coupling 296
Data dictionary 304
Dataflow diagram 301
Data independence 402
Data structure 239
Data type 238
    Audio 238
    Boolean 238
    Character 238
    Integer 238
    Real 238
    Video 238
Deadlock 138
Debugging 226
Declarative programming. See Programming para-
    digms
Declarative statements 236
Defense Advanced Research Projects Agency
    (DARPA) 142, 159
Defense Information Systems Agency Network
    Information Center (DISANIC) 145
Degenerative case 205
Dendrite 459
Depth (of a tree) 342
Depth-first search 451
Design patterns 305
Device driver 128
Digital versatile disk 32
Direct addressing 361
Directed graph 141
Direct memory access (DMA) 10
Directory 128

Disclaimers 314
Diskette 30
Disk storage
Dispatcher 129
Distributed database 402
DMA. *See* Direct memory access
DOCTOR (ELIZA) program 439
Documentation 310
Domain 142
Domain name 145
Dotted decimal notation 44, 144
DVD. *See* Digital versatile disk

Eckert, J. Presper 7
Edison, Thomas 287
Editor 264, 378
Effective 169
Effective input (of a processing unit) 459
Eight-puzzle 440
Electronic Communication Privacy Act (ECPA) 160
E-mail 145
Encapsulation 267, 355
End-of-file (EOF) 373
ENIAC 7, 40
Entity-relationship diagram 302
ELIZA 439
EOF. *See* End-of-file
Error-correcting code 67
Ethernet 149
Euclid 2
Euclidean algorithm 2, 4
Euclidean geometry 214
Even parity 66
Event-driven software 249
Evolutionary programming 470
Excess notation 52
Exclusive lock 424
Exclusive or (XOR) 18
Expert systems 479
Exponent field 55
Extraction hashing 388

Factorial 220
FAT. *See* File allocation table
Federal Communications Commission (FCC) 160
Fibonacci sequence 219
Field 370
FIFO. *See* First in, first out
File 34

File allocation table (FAT) 372
File control block 370
File descriptor 128, 370
File manager 128
File transfer protocol (FTP) 152, 154
Flip-flop 20
First-generation language 227
First in, first out (FIFO) 120, 337
First-order predicate logic 272
Fixed-format language 256
Floating-point notation 42, 55, 214
 normalized form 57
Floppy disk 30
Flowchart 174, 189
Folder 128
Formal parameter 250
Formatted I/O 254
Formatting (a disk) 30
For statement 245
FORTRAN 228, 236, 237, 238, 239, 243, 249, 549
Frameworks 306
Free-format language 256
Frequency-dependent encoding 60
Full tree 345
Function 176, 251
 abstract 503
 computation of 503
 program unit 251
Functional cohesion 299
Functional programming. *See* Programming paradigms

Gandhi, Mahatma 481
Garbage collection 347
Gate 19
Gateway 142, 569
GB. *See* Gigabyte
General Atomics 145
General Motors 114
General-purpose register 80
Genetic algorithms 468
GIF 43, 63
Gigabyte 26
Glass-box testing 309
Global data 298
Global variable 249
Gödel, Kurt 6, 507
Gödel number 508
Gödel's incompleteness theorem 6, 10, 499
Goto statement 243

Graph 446
Graphical user interface (GUI) 126, 234, 249, 293
Greatest common divisor 2
GUI. *See* Graphical user interface

Halting problem 509
Hamming, R. W. 67
Hamming distance 67
Hard disk 31
Hardware 2
Harvard University 7, 214
Hash algorithm 385
Hashed file 385
Head (of a queue) 337
Head crash 31
Head pointer 328, 338
Help packages 310
Hertz (Hz) 91
Heuristic 452
Hexadecimal notation 24
High-order end 28
Hill climbing 592
Hollerith, Herman 7
Home page 147
Hop count 158
Hopper, Grace 228
Host 144
Host address 144
Host language 403
HTML. *See* Hypertext Markup Language
Huffman code 60
Huffman, David A. 60, 591
Hypermedia 147
Hypertext 146
Hypertext Markup Language (HTML) 148

IBM 7, 9, 80, 105
Identifiers 226
If statement 174, 257
Image analysis 443
Image processing 443
Immediate addressing 361
Imperative statements 236
Implicit coupling 298
Inconsistent 273
Incorrect summary problem 423
Incremental model 293
Incubation period 181
Indexed file 381

Indirect addressing 361
Inference engine 480
Information extraction 474
Information retrieval 474
Infoseek 147
Inheritance 267
Input/output (I/O) 83
Input/output instructions (machine level) 83, 101
Input/output program statements 251
Insertion sort 193
complexity of 208
Instance (of a data type) 354
Institute of Electrical and Electronics Engineering (IEEE) 287, 288
Instruction pointer 325
Instruction register 89
Integer data type 238
Intel 80
Interactive processing 121
Internal documentation 246
International Organization for Standardization (ISO) 37, 156, 229
Internet 2, 123, 145
Internet access provider 146
Internet Network Information Center (InterNIC) 143, 145, 146
Internet Protocol (IP) 156, 158
InterNIC. *See* Internet Network Information Center
Interprocess communication 132
Interrupt 133
Interrupt handler 133
Inverted file 383
I/O. *See* Input/output
I/O bound 162
Iomega Corporation 31
Iowa State College (University) 7
IP. *See* Internet Protocol
IQ test 483
Irregular network configuration 142
ISO. *See* International Organization for Standardization
Iterative structures 184
Iverson, Kenneth E. 242

Jacquard, Joseph 7
Jacquard loom 7, 8
Java 236, 237, 238, 240, 241, 242, 244, 245, 247, 249, 254, 256, 266, 267, 268, 269, 305, 331, 358, 550

Java applets 552
Java Development Kit (JDK) 305
JCL (job control language)
Job 120
Job queue 120
Jobes, Steve 8
JOIN (database operation) 410
JPEG 43, 63

KB. *See* Kilobyte
Kernel 128
Key field 374
Key words 257
Kill (a process) 139
Kilobyte 26
Knapsack problem 523
Knowledge base 480
Knuth, Donald E. 196
Korn shell 126

LAN. *See* Local area network
Language processing 473
Last in, first out (LIFO) 332
Latency time 31
Leaf node 342
Least significant bit 28
Left child pointer 343
Lempel, Abraham 60
Lempel–Ziv encoding 60
Lexical analysis 255
Lexical analyzer 255
Liebniz, Gottfried Wilhelm 6
LIFO. *See* Last in, first out
Linker 263
Link layer (Internet) 155
Linux 127
LISP 232
List
contiguous 326
linked 328
Literal 236
Load balancing 107, 124
Loader 263
Load module 263
Local area network (LAN) 141
Local variables 249
Locking protocol 424
Logical cohesion 299
Logical deduction 271

Logical record 34
Logical shift 98
Long division algorithm 2
Lookahead carry adder 543
Look and feel 312
Loop invariant 215
Loop structures (*See also* Iterative structure) 187
Lost update problem 423
Lotus Development Corporation 313
Low-order end 28
Lucasfilm 269
LZ77 61

Machine cycle 89
Machine independence 229
Machine instructions 82
ADD 87
AND 83, 96
BRANCH 83
I/O 83
JUMP 83, 88, 90, 248
LOAD 83, 88
OR 83, 96, 97
ROTATE 83, 98
SHIFT 83, 98
STORE 83
Test-and-set 138
XOR (exclusive or) 83, 96, 97
Machine language 85
Magnetic disk 29
Magnetic tape 33
Main memory 26
Mantissa field 55
Many-to-many relationship 303
Mariner 18 space probe 288
Mark I 7, 214
Mask 96
Masking 96
Mass storage 29
Master file 374
Mauchly, John 7
MB. *See* Megabyte
McCarthy, John 438
Megabyte 26
Member function 265
Memory leak 347
Memory manager 128
Memory mapped I/O 101
Merge algorithm 374

Merge sort algorithm 196, 515
Complexity of 514
Method 265
Metric 287
Micromemory 105
Microprogram 105
Microsecond 72
Microsoft Corporation 9, 43, 123, 126, 127, 234
Mid-square hashing 388
Miller, George A. 174
Millisecond 31
MIMD 107
Modem 103
Modular arithmetic 526
Modularity 294
Module 176
Modulus 526
Mondrian, Piet 204
Monitor 271
Moore School of Engineering 7
Mosaic Software 313
Most significant bit 28
Motorola 80, 105
Mouse 126
MP3 64
MPEG 64, 65
MS-DOS 126
Multiplicative inverse 528
Multitasking 122
Mutual exclusion 138

Name server 124, 145
Nanosecond 105
National Science Foundation (NSF) 145
Network 123
Network configurations 142
Network identifier 143
Network layer (Internet) 155
Network security 158
Network Solutions 145
Neuron 107, 459
Newton, Isaac 287
NIL pointer 328
Node 342, 446
Nondeterministic algorithm 521
Nondeterministic polynomial (NP) problems 521
Nondisclosure agreement 313
Nonloss decomposition 409
Nonterminal 257

Normal forms (relational database) 409
Normalized form 57
NOT 19
NP problems (*See also* Nondeterministic polynomial problems) 520
NP-complete problem 521
Numerical analysis 58

Object 234, 265
Object-oriented database 418
Object-oriented programming (*See also* Programming paradigms)
Object program 255
Odd parity 66
Off-line 29
One-to-many relationship 296, 303
One-to-one relationship 296
On-line 29
OOP. *See* Object-oriented programming
Op-code 85, 86
Open network 142
Open statement 370
Open System Interconnect (OSI) 156
Operand 85, 87
Operating system 119, 125
Operator precedence 242
OR 18
OSI. *See* Open System Interconnect
OSI reference model 156
Overflow error 51
Overloading 243

P (*See also* Polynomial problems) 518
Packet 154
Page (memory) 129
Parallel algorithm 168
Parallel communication 103
Parallel processing 106, 269
Parameter 250
passed by reference 250
passed by value 250
Parent node 342
Pareto principle 308
Pareto, Vilfredo 308
Parity bit 66
Parse tree 258
Parser 255
Parsing 256
Partial index 383

Pascal 236, 237, 238, 239, 240, 241, 242, 244, 245, 249, 252, 554
Pascal, Blaise 6, 554
Patent law 313
Path (directory) 128
PC. *See* Personal computer
Pentium 80, 91, 105, 214
Personal computer 9
PGP. *See* Pretty Good Privacy
Phillips, E. W. 40
Physical record 34
Pipelining 106
Pixel 42
Planned obsolescence 114
Poincare, H. 180
Pointer 325
Polya, G. 178
Polymorphism 267
Polynomial problems 518
Pop (stack operation) 333
Port 101
Post, Emil 499
PostScript 43
PowerPC 80, 91, 105
Precedence (of operators) 242
Preconditions (proof of correctness) 214
Predicate 275
Pretty Good Privacy (PGP) 524
Primary key 383
Prime number388
Primitive 171
Privacy Act of 1974 427
Problem solving 178
Procedural programming. *See* Programming paradigms
Procedure 176,248
Procedure's header 249
Process 131, 168
Processing unit 459
Process state 131
Process switch 132
Process table 132
Production system 445
control system 445
goal state 445
production 445
start state 445
Program 168
Program counter 89

Programming language 171
Programming paradigms 230
declarative 231, 271
functional 232, 472
imperative 230
object-oriented 234, 265
procedural 230
PROJECT (database operation) 409
Prolog 275
Proof of correctness 213
Proprietar network 142
Protocol 149
Prototype 293
Prototyping 293
Pseudocode 171, 174
Public-key encryption 159, 523
Push (stack operation) 333

Quantum 132
Queue 120, 337
Quick sort algorithm 196

Radix point 46
RAM. *See* Random access memory
Random access memory (RAM) 27
Ravel, Maurice 146
Read-only memory (ROM) 129
Read operation 27
Ready (process) 132
Real data type 238
Real-time processing 122
Recursion 204, 475, 557
Recursive structures 196, 475, 557
Reduced instruction set computer (RISC) 80, 104
Reference 331
Register 80
Relation 404
Relational database model 404
Relative addressing 564
Relative encoding 60
Relocatable module 263
Repeat control structure 189
Requirements (of software) 290
Reserved words 257
Resolution 271
Resolvent 272
Right-child pointer 343
Ring network 142

Ripple adder 543
RISC. *See* Reduced instruction set computer
Ritchie, Dennis 549
Rivest, Ron 524
Robotics 475
Rogerian thesis 440
Roll back 423
ROM. *See* Read-only memory
Root node 342
Root pointer 343
Rotation delay 31
Round-off error 57
Router 142
Row major order 322
RSA 313, 524
RSA Data Security 524
Rubik's cube 485
Run-length encoding 60

Scalable fonts 43
Scaling 124
Scheduler 129
Schema 400
Search engine 147
Search tree 449
Secondary key 383
Second-generation language 227
Sectors 29, 378
Security Dynamics Technologies 524
Seek time 31
SELECT (database operation) 409
Selection sort algorithm 195, 196
Selective Service 426
Self-reference 509
Self-terminating program 508
Semantic analysis 474
Semantic net 475
Semantics 171
Semaphore 138
Sentinel 373
Sequential file 371
Sequential search 186
complexity of 207
Serial communication 103
Server 134
Set theory 214
Shamir, Adi 524
Shared lock 424

Shell 126
Siblings (in a tree) 342
Sign bit 48, 55
SIMD 107
SISD 107
Sloan, Alfred 114
Social Security Administration 427
Software 2
Software engineering 285
Software life cycle 288
Software verification 211
Source program 255
Space complexity 514
Special-purpose register 80
Specifications (of software) 291
Spider 147
Spooling 140
SQL. *See* Structured Query Language
Stack 332
Stack pointer 334, 360
Standard Template Library (STL) 358
Star network configuration 142
Starvation 164
State
of process 131
of production system 445
of Turing machine 498
State graph 446
Status word 102
Stepwise refinement 182
Stibitz, George 7
Stored program concept 85
Streaming tape unit 33
Strong AI 482
Strongly typed 261
Stroustrup, Bjarne 549
Structure chart 294
Structured programming 246
Structured Query Language (SQL) 415, 416
Stub 192
Subprogram 176
Subroutine 176
Subschema 400
Subtree 342
Successor function 503, 505
Sun Microsystems 305, 550
Symbol table 261
Synapse 107, 459

Syntactic analysis 474
Syntax 171
Syntax diagram 257
System documentation 311
System requirements 290
System software 125
System specifications 291
System/360 (IBM) 312

Tail (of a queue) 337
Tail pointer 337
Task 269
TCP. *See* Transmission Control Protocol
TCP/IP 141, 156
Telnet 153, 154
Temporal database 422
Therac-25 309
Terminal (in a syntax diagram) 257
Terminal node 342
Termination condition 188
Test-and-set instruction 138
Testing (software) 308
Text file 377
Third-generation language 228
Thoreau, henry David 115
Thread (Java) 269
Throughput 106
Throwaway prototyping 293
Time complexity 514
Time-sharing 122, 132
Time slice 132
Token (in a network) 149
Token (in a translator) 256
Top-down methodology 300
Top of stack 332
Torvalds, Linus 127
Tower of Hanoi 220, 221
Track 29, 32
Trade secret law 313
Transaction file 374
Transcendental functions 597
Transfer rate 31
Translation 255
Translator 228
Transmission Control Protocol (TCP) 156
Transport layer (Internet) 154
Trapdoor 159
Traveling salesman problem 520
Tree 341

TrueType 43
Truncation error 57
Tuple (in a relation) 404
Turing, Alan M. 438, 439, 482, 498, 499, 505, 506
Turing computable 505
Turing machine 498, 499, 505
Turing test 439
Twins (in a tree) 342
Two's complement notation 41, 47
Type. *See* Data type

UDP. *See* User Datagram Protocol
UML. *See* Unified Modeling Language
Unconditional jump 83
Unicode 37
Unification 275
Unified Modeling Language (UML) 296
Uniform resource locator (URL) 147
Universal programming language 492
University of Helsinki 127
University of Pennsylvania 7
UNIX 126
Unsolvable problem 512
URL. *See* Uniform resource locator
US Department of Defense 547
User Datagram Protocol (UDP) 157
User-defined type 353
User documentation 310
Utility software 126

Variable 236
Vector (image) 42
Virtual memory 129
Virus 161
Visual Basic 234
von Helmholtz, H. 180
von Neumann bottleneck 10
von Neumann, John 85

WAN, *See* Wide area network
Waiting (process) 132
Waltz, D. 591
Waterfall model 292
Weak AI 482
Webcrawler 147
Weight (in a processing unit) 459
Weighted sum 459
Weizenbaum, Joseph 439, 483
While control structure 175, 187, 215

Wide area network (WAN) 141
Window manager 127
Windows 127, 372
Wirth, Niklaus 554
World Wide Web 146
Worm 161
Wound-wait protocol 424
Wozniak, Stephen 8

Write operation 27

XOR. *See* Exclusive

Zimmermann, Philip 524
Zip disk 31
Zip/unzip (data compression) 61
Ziv, Jacob 60